RXpert SERIES
Student's Companion

Pharmacology - III

RXpert SERIES
Student's Companion

Pharmacology - III

Dr. K. Ravi Shankar
M.Pharm, Ph.D.
Professor, Department of Pharmacology, Faculty of Pharmacy,
Aditya University, Surampalem.

G.V.N. Kiranmayi
M.Pharm, Ph.D.
Professor, Department of Pharmacology, Faculty of Pharmacy,
Dr. M.G.R Educational and Research Institute, Chennai.

PharmaMed Press
An imprint of BSP Books Pvt. Ltd
4-4-309/316, Giriraj Lane,
Sultan Bazar, Hyderabad - 500 095.

Pharmacology - III

by Dr. K. Ravishankar and Dr. G.V.N Kiranmayi

Disclaimer: The authors and the publishers have taken due care to provide the authentic, reliable and up to date information related to the subject. However, neither the authors nor the publisher shall be responsible for any liability for any damage caused as a result of use of this book. The respective user must check the accuracy from other sources too.

Published by:

PharmaMed Press

An imprint of BSP Books Pvt. Ltd.

4-4-309/316, Giriraj Lane, Sultan Bazar, Hyderabad - 500 095.

Phone: 040-23445688; Fax: 91+40-23445611

e-mail: info@pharmamedpress.com

www.pharmamedpress.com/pharmamedpress.net

ISBN: 978-93-48734-15-0 (Hardback)

Dedication to,

To our mentors, who inspired the journey of discovery, championed the passions and exposed the frontiers. To our colleagues, who enriched the path, multiplying the dimensions beyond imagination. To our institutions, which nurtured the nascent trajectory and fostered the ultimate destination. To our families, who shared the ideals and enabled this extraordinary journey to progress every day.

Dr. K. Ravishankar

Dr. G. V. N. Kiranmayi

Preface

Pharmacology is a very dynamic branch of medicine marked by continual development and marketing of new drugs and simultaneous withdrawal of older products.

The major difficulty in teaching pharmacology and therapeutics is that the subject matter stretches from fundamental studies to details of clinical management. The main objective kept in view while preparing this text book is to provide sound pharmacological basis and detailed information to the reader for rational drug use in therapeutics.

This text book is divided in 35 chapters and each chapter indicates all important and detailed information. The text is supported by background, neat diagrams, tables knowledge of physiology, chemistry and medicine related to drug action is provided. We have rendered our level best to make the text book readable and interesting.

This book Pharmacology is oriented to reflect the contemporary advancements. All the chapters have been updated and special emphasis is given. This book provides valuable substantial information and can be considered as a book of choice for under graduate students of pharmacy, medical and dental students.

Dr. K. Ravishankar

Dr .G. V. N. Kiranmayi

Acknowledgements

We owe to express our utmost gratefulness to the Almighty for bestowing upon us the patience, courage and abundant blessings to complete the book. Indeed, without his help and will, nothing is accomplished.

At the outsight we express our sincere pranams to our esteemed Professor and Pharmacologist **Late Prof. Dr. D.Visweswaram, University College of Pharmaceutical Sciences, Andhra University, Viskhapatnam** and **Retd. Prof. Dr. M.C. Prabhakara, Pharmacologist, Kakatiya University** for giving us valuable education and what we are today is because of them.

We would like to extend our heartiest gratitude to **Mrs. M. Sridevi,** Associate Professor for extending her help in preparing this text book. We are also thankful to **Mrs. K. Vedavathi**, Office Incharge for her efforts and help in preparing tables and figures.

We would like to express our special gratitude and thanks to our beloved Chairman **Dr. N. Sesha Reddy Garu** and Vice Chairman **Dr. N. Satish Reddy Garu**, Aditya Group of Institutions, Surampalem for their encouragement.
The authors also express their special thanks to **Dr. M.G.R. Deemed University Management** for their support and encouragement.

We would like to convey our special thanks to our publisher **PharmaMed Press** for accepting and publishing our book and extending their whole hearted cooperation, and also thanks to **Dr.Mohammed Mazzuddin**, for editorial input.

Our sincere thanks to all our well wishers who supported us.

Dr. K. Ravishankar
Dr. G. V. N. Kiranmayi

Contents

Chapter - 4
Respiratory Stimulants

PART - II
DRUGS AFFECTING GASTROINTESTINAL TRACT

Chapter - 5
Drugs Used to Treat Peptic, Ulcer Disease

Chapter - 6
Drugs Used in Constipation

Chapter - 7
Emetics and Antiemetic Drugs

Chapter - 8
Drugs Used in Diarrhoea

Chapter - 9
Digestants and GERD

Chapter - 10
Appetite Stimulants and Suppressants

Chapter - 11
Carminatives

PART - III
CHEMOTHERAPEUTIC DRUGS

Chapter - 12
General Principles of Chemotherapy

Chapter - 13
Sulfonamides, Trimethoprim and Cotrimoxazole

Chapter - 14
Cell Wall Inhibitors

Chapter - 15
Protein Synthesis Inhibitors

Chapter - 16
Quinolones and Urinary Antiseptics

Chapter - 17
Antimycobacterials

Chapter - 18
Antifungal Drugs

Chapter - 22
Anticancer Drugs

Chapter - 23

Chemotherapy of Sexually Transmitted Diseases

PART - IV
IMMUNOPHARMACOLOGY

Chapter - 24

Immunosuppressants and Immunostimulants

Chapter - 25

Protein Drugs, Monoclonal Antibodies and Biosimilars

PART - V
PRINCIPLES OF TOXICOLOGY

Chapter - 26

General Toxicity Testing

Chapter - 27

Genotoxicity

Chapter - 28

Carcinogenicity

Chapter – 29

Drug Therapy in Pregnancy

Chapter - 30

Mutagencity

Chapter - 31

Introduction to Toxicology

Chapter - 32

Heavy Metal Intoxication and Chelators

Chapter - 33

Management of Barbiturates, Morphine, Organophosphosphorus Compound Poisoning

Chapter - 34

Management of the Poisoned Patient

Chapter - 35

Chronopharmacology

Abbreviations

AAC : Antimicrobial associated colitis
Ach : Acetylcholine
AECB : Acute exacerbation of chronic bronchitis
AIA : Aspirin induced asthma
ATG : Antithymocyte globulins
ATN : Acute tubular necrosis
ATP : Adenosine triphosphate
BB : Midborderline
BBB : Blood brain barrier
BCG : Bacillus calmette guérin
BDZ : Benzodiazepines
BL : Borderline Lepromatous
BPH : Benign prostatic hyperplasia
BT : Borderline tuberculoid
BUN : Blood urea nitrogen
CAD : Coronary artery disease
CaM : Calmodulin
cAMP : Cyclic adenosine monophosphate
CBC : Complete blood count
CF : Cystic fibrosis
CHF : Congestive heart failure
CMV : Cytomegalovirus
CN : Cranial nerve
COX : Cyclooxygenase
CSF : Cerebrospinal fluid
CSF : Colony-stimulating factors
CTZ : Chemoreceptor Trigger Zone
CYP : Cytochrome P450
DHF : Dihydrofolic acid
DHFR : Dihydrofolatereductase
DNA : Deoxyribonucleic acid
DR : Drug receptor complex
dTMP : Deoxythymidine monophosphate
dUMP : Deoxyuridine monophosphate
EC : Emetic centre
ECL : Enterochromaffin-like
EIA : Exercise-induced asthma
EIB : Exercise induced bronchospasm
EP : Epinephrine
ET : Estrogen therapy
FDA : Food and drug administration
G-6-PD : Glucose-6 phosphate dehydrogenase
G-CSF : Granulocyte colony stimulating Factor
GERD : Gastroesophageal reflux disease
GIT : Gastro intestinal tract
GnRH : Gonadotropin-releasing hormone
GSH : Glutathione
HCTZ : Hydrochlorothiazide
HSV : Herpes simplex virus
IBD : Inflammatory bowel disease
IBS : Irritable bowel syndrome
IFN : Interferon
IL : Interleukin
IOP : Intraocular pressure
LH : Luteinizing hormone
LL : Lepromatous
LMIT : Lymphocyte migration inhibition test
M : Muscarinic receptors
MAB : Monoclonal antibodies
MAO : Monoamine oxidase
MAOIs : Monoamine oxidase inhibitors
MDR : Multi drug resistance
MIC : Minimal inhibitory concentrations
MOA : Mechanism of Action
MT : Urinary metallothionein
MTT : N-methylthiotetrazole
NAD : Nicotinamide adenine dinucleotide
NADPH : Nicotinamide adenine dinucleotide phosphate

NADPH	:	Nicotinamide-adenine dinucleotide phosphate
NMS	:	Neuroleptic malignant syndrome
NRTIs	:	Nucleoside reverse transcriptase Inhibitors
NSAIDs	:	Non steroidal Anti inflammatory drugs
NTM	:	Nontuberculous mycobacteria
OCD	:	Obsessive compulsive disorder
ORT	:	Oral rehydration therapy
PCP	:	Pneumocystis carinii pneumonia
PD	:	Parkinson's disease
PEG	:	Polyethylene glycol
PGs	:	Prostaglandins
PKA	:	Protein kinase
PRL	:	Prolactin
PSNS	:	Parasympathetic nervous system
PZA	:	Pyrazinamide
RA	:	Rheumatoid arthritis
SNS	:	Sympathetic nervous system
TACT	:	Trial to assess chelation therapy
THC	:	Tetrahydrocannabinol
THF	:	Tetrahydrofolic acid
TNF	:	Tumor necrosis factor
TT	:	Tuberculoid
VC	:	Vomiting centre
Vd	:	Volume of distribution
VZV	:	Varicella zoseter virus
WBI	:	Whole bowel irrigation
XRF	:	X-ray fluorescence
ZES	:	Zollinger–ellison syndrome

Part - I

Pharmacology of Drugs Acting on Respiratory System

CHAPTER

1 Drugs Used to Treat Asthma

Introduction

Asthma is physiologically characterized by increased responsiveness of trachea and bronchi to various stimuli and by widespread narrowing of the airways. Most common chronic condition in children. Death rate up 50% from 1980 to 2000. Death rate up 80% in people under 19. Morbidity and mortality highly correlated with poverty, urban air quality, indoor allergens, lack of patient education and inadequate medical care. Usually associated with airflow obstruction of variable severity. Airflow obstruction is usually reversible, either spontaneously, or with treatment. The inflammation associated with asthma causes an increase in the baseline bronchial hyper responsiveness to a variety of stimuli.

Asthma Triggers

1. Allergens
   (a) Dust mites, mold spores, animal dander, cockroaches, pollen, indoor and outdoor pollutants, irritants (smoke, perfumes, cleaning agents)
2. Pharmacological agents (β-blockers)
3. Physical triggers (exercise, cold air)
4. Physiologic factors
   (a) Stress, GERD, viral and bacterial URI, rhinitis

Diagnostic Testing

Peak Expiratory Flow (PEF)

- o Inexpensive
- o Patients can use at home
  - May be helpful for patients with severe disease to monitor their change from baseline every day
  - Not recommended for all patients with mild or moderate disease to use every day at home
  - Effort and technique dependent
- o Should not be used to make diagnosis of asthma

Spirometry

Recommended to do Spirometry pre and post use of an albuterol MDI to establish reversibility of airflow obstruction. > 12% reversibility or an increase in *forced expiratory volume* (FEV1) of 200cc is considered significant.

Obstructive pattern: Reduced FEV1/FVC ratio

Restrictive pattern: Reduced FVC with a normal FEV1/FVC ratio

Can be used to identify reversible airway obstruction due to triggers.

Can diagnose Exercise-induced asthma (EIA) or Exercise induced bronchospasm (EIB) by measuring FEV1/FVC before exercise and immediately following exercise, then for 5-10 minute intervals over the next 20-30 minutes looking for post-exercise bronchoconstriction.

Methacholine Challenge

Most common bronchoprovocative test in US. Patients breathe in increasing amounts of methacholine and perform Spirometry after each dose. Increased airway hyper responsiveness is established with a 20% or more decrease in FEV1 from baseline at a concentration < 8 mg/dl. Diagnostic trial of anti inflammatory medication (preferably corticosteroids) or an inhaled bronchodilator. It is especially helpful in very young children unable to cooperate with other diagnostic testing. There is no one single test or measure that can definitively be used to diagnose asthma in every patient.

Classification of Antiasthmatics.

1. Brochodilators:
   (a) β_2 adenergic receptor agonists.
       Ex : Salbutamol, Fenuterol, Bitolterol Salmetaol and formoterol.
   (b) Phosphodiesterase Inhibitors
       Ex : Theophylline
   (c) Anti cholinergics: Ipratropiumbromide
2. Anti - Inflammatory drugs :
   (a) Glucocorticoids
   (b) Leukotriene (LT) modifiers :
       Lt Syntesis inhibitors : Zileuton
       Lt Antagonists : Monteleukast, Zajirleukast
   (c) Mast cell stabilizers :
       Sodium cromoglycae, Nedocromil
   (d) PAF Antagonists : Ketotifen.

Pharmacotherapy

Asthma therapies are divided into two categories: Short-term relievers and long-term controllers.

Short-Term Relievers: β-adrenoceptor stimulants, theophylline, antimuscarinic agents, leukotriene antagonists.

Long-Term Controllers: Anti-inflammatory agents, inhibitor of mast cell degranulation.

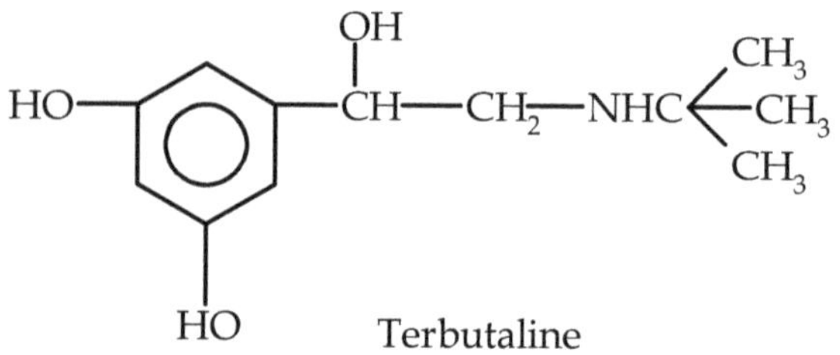

Terbutaline

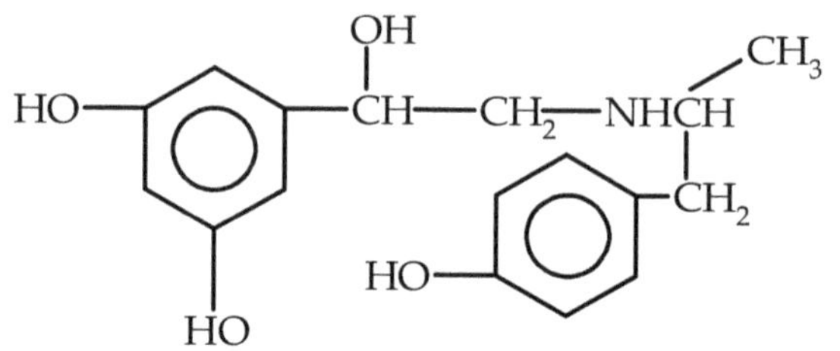

Fenoterol

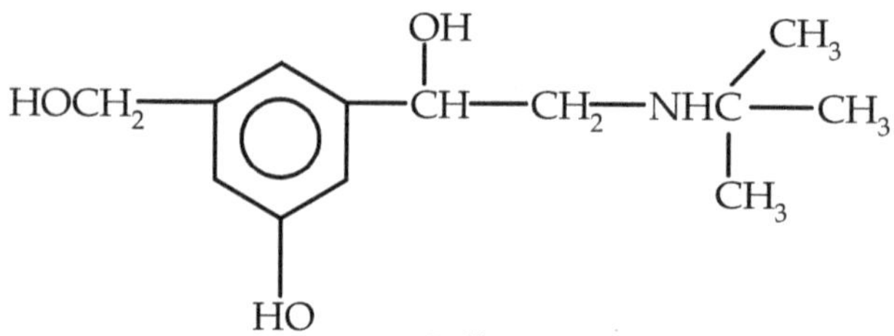

Salbutamol

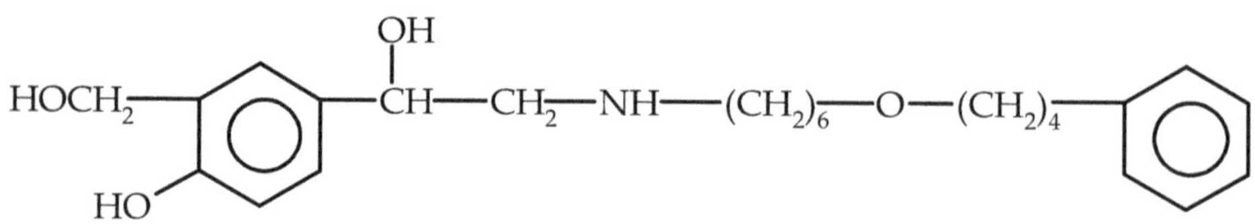

Salmeterol

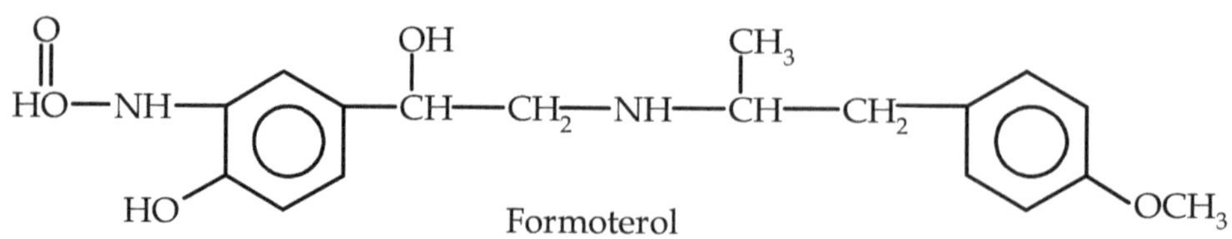

Formoterol

Fig 1-1: Beta adrenoceptor agonists.

Adrenoceptor Agonists

β_2 agonists (Fig 1-1) are bronchodilators that act on the bronchial smooth muscle by combining with β_2-adrenergic receptors to cause bronchial muscle relaxation and, thus, bronchodilation. Bronchodilation occurs regardless of the mechanism for the bronchial constriction and β_2 agonists also provide protection against bronchial constriction; however, they do not significantly alter the progression of the inflammatory process. In other words, they dilate the bronchial muscle even though the inflammation is occurring. Bronchial smooth muscle contains β_2-adrenergic receptors, whereas the heart contains both, β_1 receptors and β_2 receptors. Consequently, no therapeutic rationale exists for using nonselective β_2 agonists (i.e., agents that are not selective for β_2 receptors relative to β_1 receptors); such agents (e.g., isoproterenol, metaproterenol, epinephrine) have an increased incidence of sympathetic stimulatory effects, including increased heart rate and force of contraction. Since these cardiac effects could improve exercise performance, nonselective β agonists are not allowed in Olympic competition, and only selected β_2 agonists (albuterol, terbutaline, salmeterol) by inhalation are allowed upon written notification before competition. The β-agonist components of over the counter oral and inhalation asthma products are nonselective and, thus, a poor choice to treat asthma. Inhaled β_2 agonists are the only agents providing an immediate response for acute asthma attacks (rescue therapy).

They are also the most effective medication to prevent an anticipated attack, such as immediately before exercise, without the onset of significant cardiac or other systemic effects. After inhalation of short-acting β_2 agonists, onset of action is usually within 5 minutes and maximal bronchodilation occurs within about 15 minutes. Duration of action is 4 to 8 hours, depending upon the agent, although a shorter period of protection (2 to 4 hours) is experienced during exercise. When given at equipotent doses, all of the β_2 agonists will produce the same intensity of bronchodilation; their main difference is the duration of action. Some agents are effective orally, but the oral route delays onset of action and is less selective for bronchial muscle, thus increasing the incidence of side effects.

Salmeterol

Is a long acting β_2 agonist available by inhalation, but its slower onset of action (up to 20 minutes) and time for maximal effect (1 to 4 hours) preclude its use as rescue therapy for treatment of acute attacks. Users of salmeterol must clearly understand that it is not effective for treatment of acute bronchospasms and that the dose should not exceed 2 puffs every 12 hours. Depending upon the duration of the athletic activity, some athletes may benefit from salmeterol, which has a longer duration of action (12 hours) as compared with albuterol (4 hours). Patients who suffer from nocturnal asthma may also benefit from the longer acting β_2 agonist. Regularly scheduled, daily use of a short acting β_2 agonist is generally not recommended, since there is no apparent advantage over use on an as needed basis. If the frequency of β_2- agonist use increases or if use exceeds 1 canister of β_2 agonist (e.g., 200 dosage of the drug puffs of albuterol) per month to control exacerbations, asthma control is poor, and reevaluation of the anti-inflammatory therapy is necessary. Regular use of short acting β_2 agonists has not demonstrated a clinically significant tolerance to the pulmonary effects, although daily use of salmeterol has resulted in a shorter duration of protection from exercise induced bronchoconstriction (EIB). Regular use of a long acting β_2 agonist is recommended for some patients with moderate to severe asthma, especially to control night time symptoms, in conjunction with corticosteroid therapy. The most frequent side effects from inhalation of β_2 agonists are tachycardia and muscle tremor, although these are more pronounced with the nonselective agents and with oral use. During an acute asthma attack, the dose of the short-acting β_2 agonists can be increased several fold to counter the bronchoconstriction without toxicity. However, if an athlete has escalating symptoms of asthma that are no longer being alleviated by the normal regimen of β_2 agonist, adjustment of the anti-inflammatory therapy may be required.

Albuterol

Like many drugs, including all currently available selective β_2 agonists, it is an equal mixture of R and S isomers. These isomers are mirror images of each other and interact differently at receptor sites. The R isomer, originally thought to be the only bioactive form, produces virtually all of the bronchodilation; the S isomer appears to dosage of the drug contribute to some adverse effects (e.g., nervousness and tremor) and has a longer duration because it is metabolized more slowly. Levalbuterol (Xopenex, Sepracor Inc, Marlborough, MA) is (R)-albuterol and is available for use with a nebulizer. Since levalbuterol contains only the active isomer, it provides comparable or better FEV1 values than albuterol, with a lower incidence of side effects and at a smaller dose. R isomers of other β_2 agonists are also being investigated.

Anticholinergics

Another group of bronchodilators is the anticholinergic agents (Fig 1-2). Rather than activating adrenergic receptors, these drugs inhibit the cholinergic receptors of the parasympathetic system, which, through the vagus nerve, maintain normal bronchial smooth muscle tone. The use of these agents has diminished over the years as the inhaled β_2 agonists have become available and because these agents cause significant anticholinergic side effects (e.g., urinary retention, blurred vision, nasal congestion) and sedation through their central nervous system actions. Part of the bronchoconstriction caused by some asthma-inducing stimuli is mediated through the parasympathetic system, but the extent of this involvement varies significantly among patients. Anticholinergics are only effective in reducing bronchoconstriction mediated through this system.

Ipratropium bromide is a newer anti-cholinergic agent without sedative properties due to poor distribution into the central nervous system. It is available by inhalation for a more selective response. Onset of action is slower than that for the β_2 agonists, and peak broncho-dilation dosage occurs in 1 to 2 hours. The effectiveness of ipratropium varies considerably among asthmatic patients, although it does provide additional bronchodilation when combined with a short acting β_2 agonist. It has limited effectiveness in preventing EIB.

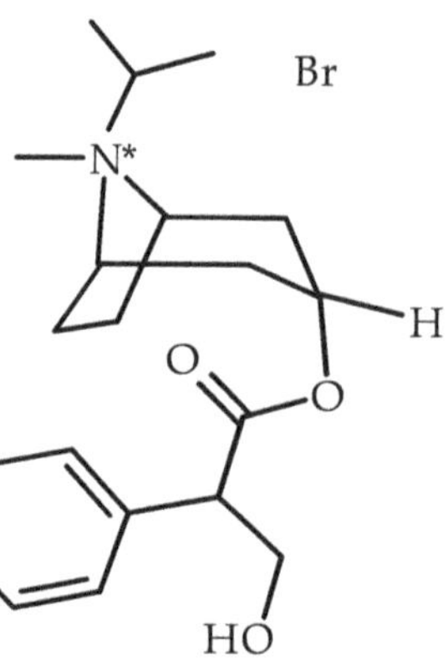

Fig 1-2: Ipratropium bromide

Methylxanthines

Theophylline is a methylxanthine broncho-dilator (Fig 1- 3). Caffeine and theobromine are also members of this chemical group, but they are not used therapeutically to treat asthma since

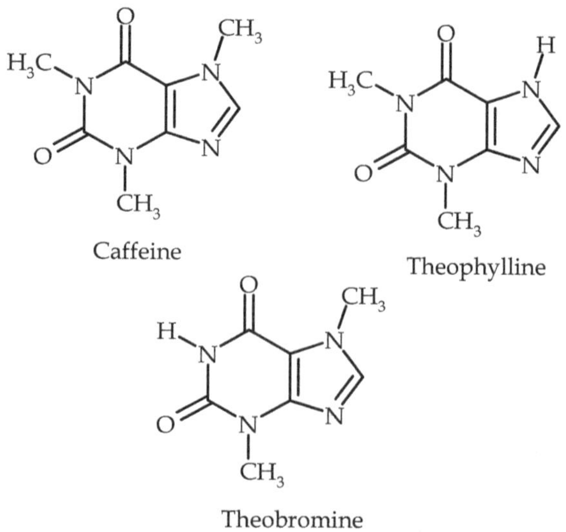

Fig 1-3: Methylxanthines

they have only a mild bronchodilating effect. The mechanism by which theophylline relaxes bronchial smooth muscle is not clearly understood, for all the drugs the dosage should provide but the inhibition of phospho-diesterase and subsequent increase in intracellular cyclic adenosine monphosphate may be a contributor.

Theophylline is used orally since it is not effective by inhalation and it is available in immediate and sustained release formulations. A major disadvantage of theophylline is that it has a narrow therapeutic window; that is, the blood level between too little and too much is narrow. Consequently, routine monitoring of theophylline blood levels is a standard procedure to prevent toxicity during long term use. Potential side effects at the upper end of the normal therapeutic blood level include anorexia, nausea, vomiting, headache and anxiety. As blood levels increase, seizures, arrhythmias and death can occur. Complicating the problem is patient variability in the rate of excretion by the kidney and the potential for several other drugs (e.g., erythromycin, cimetidine, zileuton) to alter the metabolism rate of theophylline by the liver, thus intensifying the need for blood-level monitoring. For most patients, theophylline is less effective than other bronchodilators. Nonetheless, long-term use at appropriate steady state blood levels will maintain significant bronchodilation and it is recommended as a second or third line of treatment for moderate to severe asthma in adults and children and to treat nocturnal asthma. For patients who do not respond to β_2-agonist therapy for prevention of EIB, theophylline offers an alternative. Long term therapy is effective in preventing EIB, and, for some patients, protection from EIB is obtained from a single dose of theophylline before exercise.

Anti Inflammatory Agents

Since asthma is a chronic inflammatory disease, long term use of anti-inflammatory agents is an important part of therapy to control inflammation (Fig 1-4) and to prevent exacerbations. The cellular mechanism for airway inflammation includes the activation of phospholipase, an enzyme that releases arachidonic acid from membrane bound phospholipid in the mast cell. Arachidonic acid is the precursor to prostaglandins and leukotrienes, which are mediators released by several cell types, including T lymphocytes, macrophages and mast cells of the lung. These mediators contribute to bronchoconstriction, edema and mucous production. These cells also release an array of other compounds (e.g., histamine, platelet activating factor, cytokines) that contribute to the inflammatory process, which includes increased vascular permeability, increased mucus secretion and structural changes in the airways. The anti-inflammatory drugs affect 1 or more of the steps in the inflammatory process, thereby diminishing the destructive effects of chronic inflammation. Use of corticosteroids early in the disease can preserve lung function for a longer time compared with delayed use of these drugs.

Anti-inflammatory agents can be grouped in the following categories: Corticosteroids, mast cell-stabilizing agents and antileukotrienes. Specific agents in all 3 groups are used as long term therapy to prevent the onset of recurring asthma symptoms and to reduce the frequency of acute exacerbations, thus also reducing β_2-agonist usage for quick relief. Poor asthma outcomes are often a result of underuse of these agents for long term therapy.

Phospholipase A_2 catalyzes the release of membrane-bound arachidonic acid, which can be converted to prostaglandins, prostacyclin, or thromboxanes by the action of cyclooxygenase (COX) or converted to cysteinyl leukotrienes (LTC_4, LTD_4, LTE_4) by the action of 5-lipoxygenase. The leukotrienes and COX products are released in the lung by mast cells, as well as other cell types, and contribute to symptoms of asthma. The sites of action of NSAIDs and antiasthma drugs (corticosteroids, antileukotrienes, and mast cell-stabilizing agents) are shown in Fig 1-4.

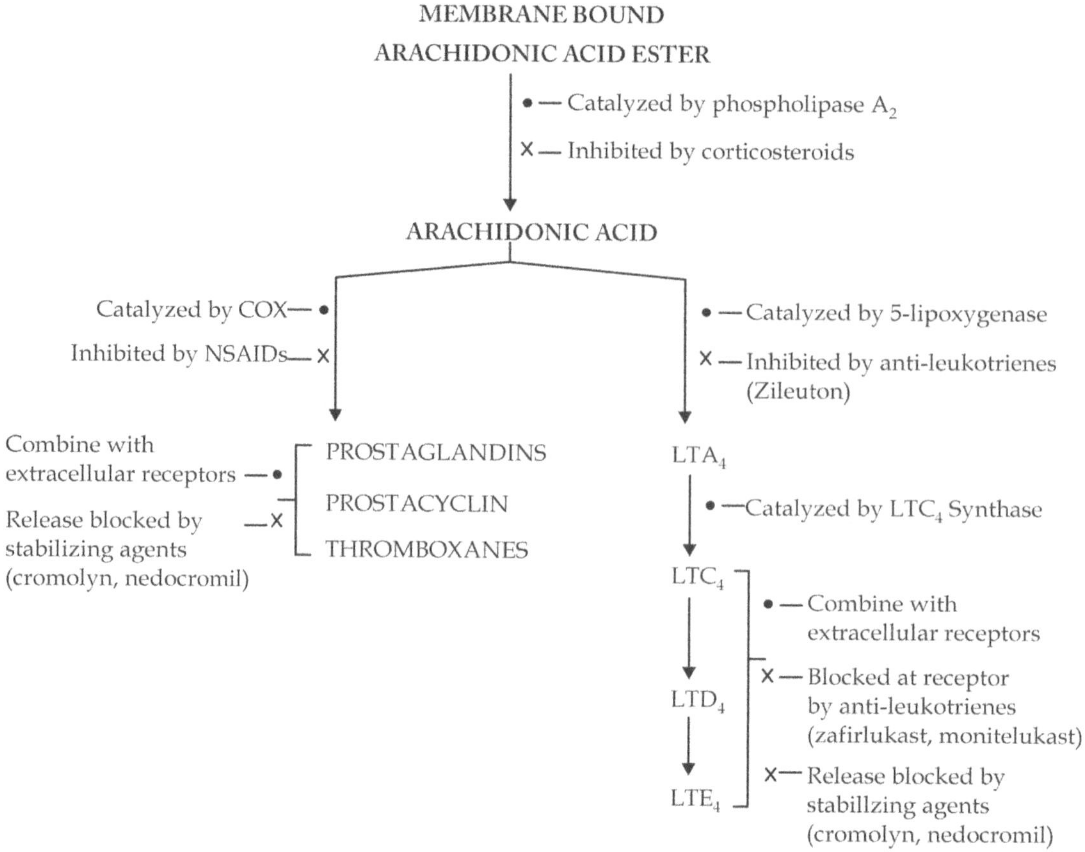

Fig 1-4: The sites of action of anti-inflammatory agents

Corticosteroids

The corticosteroids (Fig 1-5) have multiple mechanisms of action that contribute to their use in asthma. For example, they inhibit the production of prostaglandins and leukotrienes by inhibiting the action of phospholipase; inhibit cytokine gene transcription; and increase gene transcription of β receptors, which increases the responsiveness to β agonists. These drugs are effective in suppressing inflammation when used on a regular dosing schedule as long term therapy. Inhaled corticosteroids are recommended as the first line agents to control mild, moderate and severe asthma, with dosage adjustment according to the severity of the disease. Benefit from inhalation corticosteroid therapy occurs over several weeks and may require 3 months for maximal effect. Consequently, inhalation corticosteroids are not beneficial on an as-needed basis to prevent EIB or to treat acute attacks (rescue therapy). As the cornerstone of long term anti inflammatory therapy, however, inhaled corticosteroids have been shown to reduce both symptoms and the number of acute exacerbations of chronic asthma, thus also reducing the reliance on β_2 agonists. In addition, long-term use of inhaled corticosteroids is effective in managing nocturnal asthma and in providing protection against EIB symptoms. The potential for systemic side effects is minimized with long-term use of inhaled compared with oral corticosteroids and even more so with lower doses of inhaled corticosteroids. There is some concern that inhaled corticosteroids may reduce linear growth or delay growth in children, but generally the benefits of low-dose inhaled corticosteroids outweigh the risks. The most frequent side effects of inhaled corticosteroids

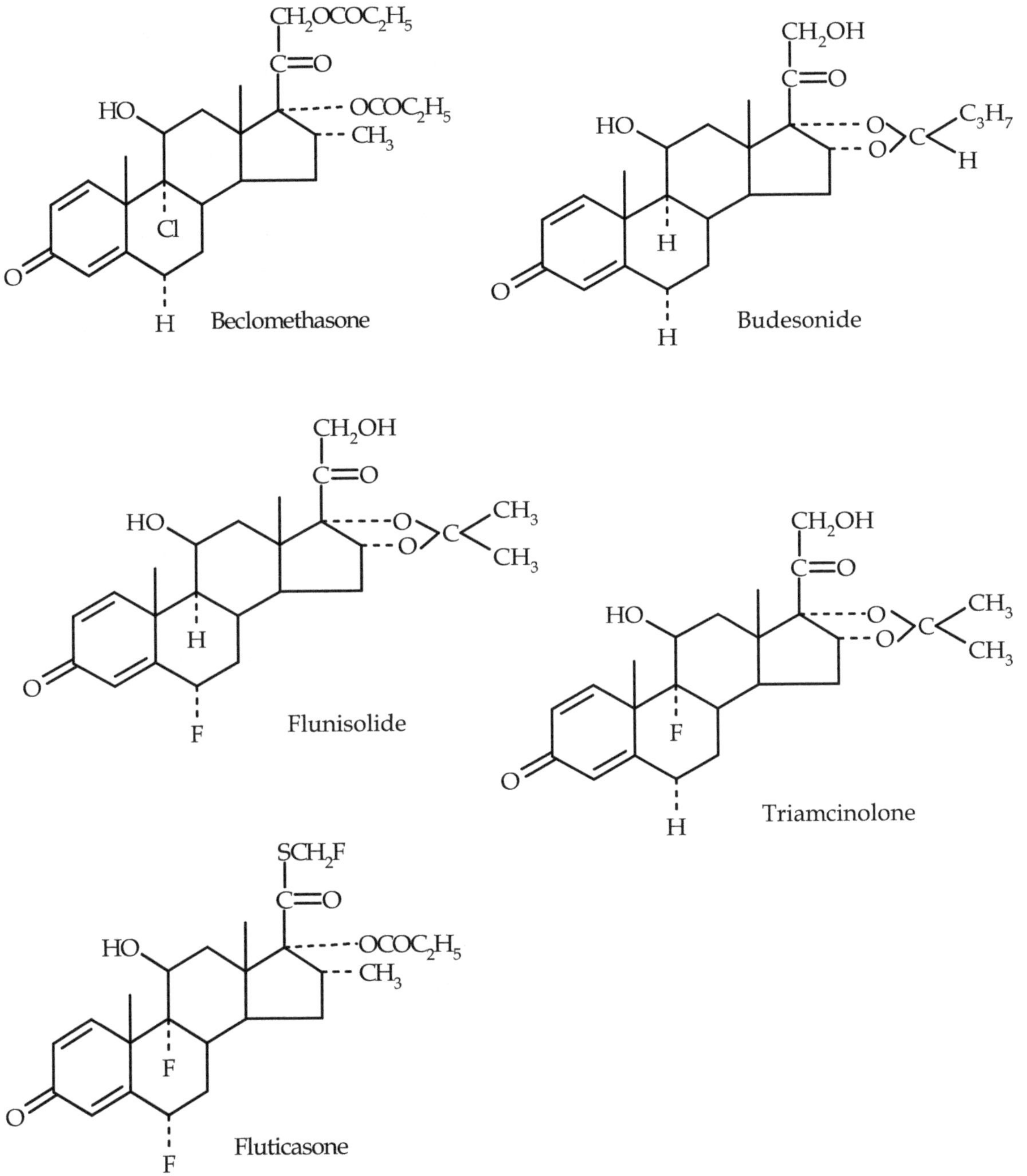

Fig 1-5: Corticosteroids

are dysphonia (hoarseness), cough and the potential for the development of oral fungal (candidiasis) infection. The incidence of these effects depends upon the total daily dose of corticosteroid in the oropharynx. Consequently, the incidence can be significantly reduced by the use of a spacer and by rinsing the mouth with water and spitting after every use; these procedures also reduce the amount of corticosteroid swallowed, which may otherwise contribute to systemic effects. The cough may be due to throat irritation from additives in the MDI and is less frequent with DPI. For some asthmatic patients, once per day, low dose inhalation of corticosteroids may provide appropriate management of stable, mild to moderate asthma and may further diminish side effects. At equipotent doses, generally no corticosteroid appears to be significantly more efficacious than another. However, the 2 newest inhaled corticosteroids, budesonide and fluticasone, are potent and consequently require fewer puffs per day, thus providing an advantage for compliance in patients who require higher doses of inhaled corticosteroids. Budesonide and fluticasone also have the advantage of rapid metabolism by the liver compared with other inhaled corticosteroids, which reduces the potential for systemic side effects, especially in patients who require higher dosages. Additionally, fluticasone is poorly absorbed orally, thus further diminishing the potential for systemic side effects from drug swallowed after inhalation. Long term use of oral corticosteroids is not recommended except for the control of severe asthma. Long-term oral use for treatment of severe persistent asthma presents the potential for an array of systemic side effects, such as fluid and electrolyte abnormalities, hyperglycemia, behavioral disturbances, osteoporosis, fat redistribution, cataracts, glaucoma and growth suppression. Short term use of oral or parenteral corticosteroids, however, is useful as a beneficial adjunct to β_2 agonists for the treatment of acute exacerbations. The duration of systemic therapy for treatment of acute exacerbations depends upon the patient's response, but 3 to 10 days of therapy can reduce the effects of acute episodes. These short bursts of systemic corticosteroid therapy do not produce serious toxicities, although mood disturbances and loss of glucose control in diabetic patients may occur. Any adrenal suppression (i.e., decrease in physiological production of steroids) is readily reversible in a few days after therapy. Tapering of corticosteroid therapy is unnecessary in acute asthma therapy. Because systemic corticosteroids have an array of metabolic effects, some of which could provide an advantage in competitive sports, their use is carefully monitored. However, inhalation corticosteroids (e.g., Beclomethasone, Budesonide, Flunisolide, Fluticasone, Triamcinolone) are permissible in Olympic competition upon written notification before competition.

Mast Cell-Stabilizing Agents

Two mast cell-stabilizing agents (Fig 1-6) (also referred to as khellin derivatives) are currently available: Cromolyn and Nedocromil. These drugs are only effective by inhalation and are used primarily to prevent allergen-induced bronchospasm and EIB. They are most effective in maintaining protection when used 2 to 4 times daily and although initial improvement is observed in 1 to 2 weeks, about 4 weeks of therapy are necessary to obtain maximal benefit. Since they do not produce bronchodilation, mast cell stabilizing agents are not effective in

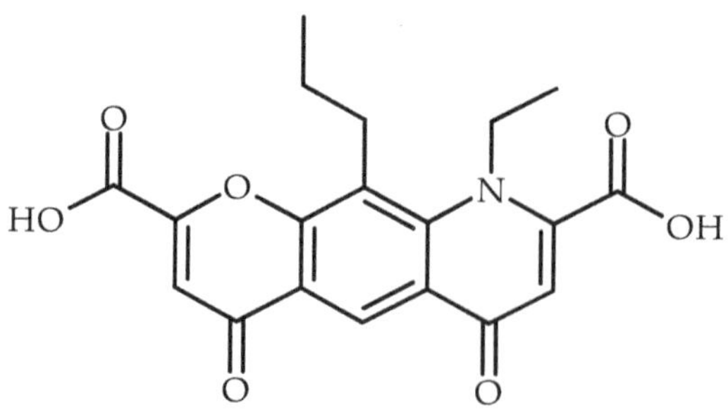

Nedocromil

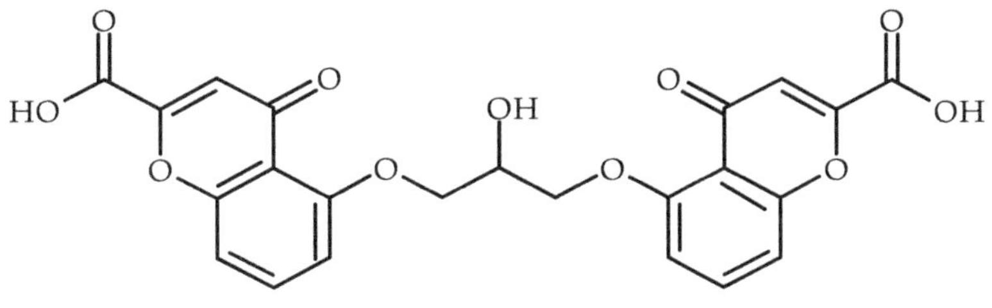

Cromolyn

Fig 1-6: Mast cell-stabilizing agents

alleviating acute asthmatic attacks. Although the exact mechanism of action of the mast cell stabilizing agents is unknown, they appear to stabilize the membrane to prevent the release of inflammatory mediators (e.g.,leukotrienes, prostaglandins, cytokines) from the cell. These mediators play an important role in the hyperreactivity response, especially as a result of exposure to allergens and exercise. At equipotent doses, cromolyn and nedocromil are equally effective. They are not as effective as inhaled corticosteroids for the prevention of asthma symptoms, but they have fewer potential side effects and virtually no systemic toxicity. These drugs are recommended for prevention of EIB and are frequently added if inhaled β_2 agonist alone before exercise is insufficient to block the bronchospasms. They are also used for the treatment of mild persistent asthma, especially in children, since they lack the potential to delay growth. Reduced effectiveness with daily use has not been demonstrated. Some patients experience minor mouth and throat irritation, which can be alleviated by drinking water immediately after use. Additionally, some patients complain that nedocromil has such a bad taste that they discontinue the therapy.

Antileukotrienes

The antileukotrienes (also known as leukotriene modifiers) (Fig 1-7) are the newest group of antiasthma drugs available. These drugs either

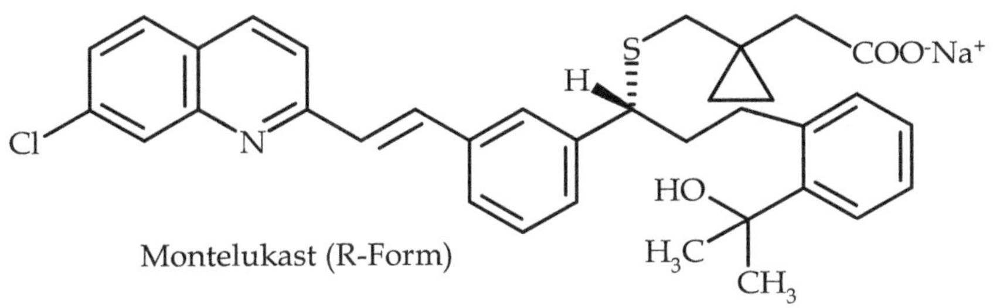

Montelukast (R-Form)

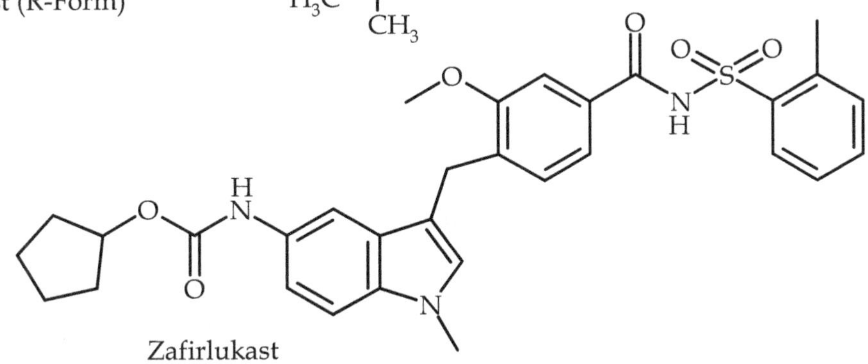

Zafirlukast

Fig 1-7: Antileukotrienes

decrease the synthesis of cysteinyl leukotrienes by inhibiting 5-lipoxygenase (e.g., zileuton) or by inhibiting the binding of leukotrienes at the receptor (e.g., montelukast, zafirlukast). In either case, these agents diminish the effect of leukotrienes, which contribute to broncho-constriction, edema and mucous production. Antileukotrienes are effective for long term control of mild to moderate asthma, especially in asthma induced by allergens, exercise and aspirin. These drugs are only available for oral use and are not effective to treat acute asthma attacks.

All 3 of the antileukotrienes are well tolerated orally. The most frequent side effects have been headaches and gastrointestinal disturbances. A potential problem associated with zileuton is an increase in blood alanine aminotransferase, an indicator of potential liver toxicity. Consequently, alanine aminotransferase should be checked monthly for the first 3 months and then every other month for the first year to monitor for hepatic toxicity. In addition, Churg Strauss syndrome has been associated with the use of leukotriene receptor antagonists in a few patients. This syndrome is a vasculitis that primarily affects the respiratory tract during the early stages and can develop into a life-threatening systemic vasculitis. Most, but not all, of these reports have been in patients being withdrawn from corticosteroid therapy after being maintained on a leukotriene receptor antagonist. Therefore, there is some question as to whether undiagnosed Churg-Strauss syndrome existed before antileukotriene therapy and the symptoms, which include asthma, were masked by the corticosteroid therapy.

In addition to side effects, other differences exist among the antileukotrienes. The oral absorption of zafirlukast, the first of the leukotriene receptor antagonists approved for asthma therapy, is reduced significantly by food, and, thus, the medication should be taken either 1 hour before or 2 hours after meals. It has been approved for use in children as young as 7 years old. Zafirlukast acts as an inhibitor of CYCYP450 enzymes; these enzymes are important for the metabolism (inactivation) of many drugs. Consequently, the potential exists for zafirlukast to increase the blood level of other drugs as a result of the inhibitory action on the CYP450 enzymes. Warfarin is a drug that is metabolized by these same CYP450 enzymes, and, as a result, drug-dosing modifications may be necessary when patients are taking zafirlukast concurrently with warfarin or other drugs metabolized by selected CYP450 enzymes.

Zileuton, the inhibitor of 5-lipoxygenase, is similar to zafirlukast in that it inhibits the ability of CYP450 enzymes to metabolize many drugs, such as warfarin, but also theophylline. Zileuton should not be used in children less than 12 years old. The absorption of zileuton from the gastrointestinal tract is not affected by food. Montelukast, like zafirlukast, inhibits the binding of leukotrienes to the receptor. Montelukast can be taken without regard to food, can be used to treat children at least 6 years old, and is available as a chewable tablet. Unlike zileuton and zafirlukast, montelukast does not inhibit the CYP450 enzymes and, thus, does not have the same potential for drug interactions. Since antileukotrienes are relatively new agents for the treatment of asthma, their usefulness has not been clearly identified. Some patients respond well to therapy with these agents, whereas others do not. The reason for this difference is not certain, but the agents causing the asthma symptoms in some patients may not significantly affect the leukotriene pathway; other asthmatic patients may have a genetic disposition determining their response to these drugs. For example, asthma patients with diminished expression of the 5-lipoxygenase gene may not respond adequately to drug therapy targeting that pathway alone. Alternatively, some patients with aspirin induced asthma (AIA) may have an enhanced expression of 5(S)-hydroxy-6(R)-S-glutathionyl-7,9- trans-11, 14-cis-eicosatetraenoic acid (LTC4) synthase and, therefore, respond well to leukotriene receptor antagonists.

Exercise Induced Bronchoconstriction (EIB)

Since most asthmatic patients (70% to 90%) experience some degree of EIB, the treatment of athletes for EIB is of obvious importance to the athletic trainer. Of additional importance is that many athletes have no other history of asthma and are thus unaware that they have EIB. Symptoms of airway obstruction typically occur as a result of 5 to 8 minutes of strenuous exertion, but the time period of exercise free symptoms can be extended somewhat with a warm-up period of 15 to 30 minutes of submaximal exercise. Maximal airway obstruction occurs 5 to 15 minutes after exercise cessation. Symptoms include coughing, wheezing, prolonged recovery times after exercise and chest tightness. Airflow returns to baseline levels during the following 20 to 60 minutes. Some athletes experience a subsequent refractory period of 2 to 4 hours, in which exercise results in diminished bronchoconstriction, possibly due to depletion of mast cell mediators. A late asthmatic response 3 to 9 hours after exercise causes additional bronchoconstriction in some athletes, but is typically less severe. In athletes with EIB, inhalation of a β_2 agonist 5 to 15 minutes before exercise offers protection. If symptoms develop during exercise, puffs can be repeated. Increased use of a β_2 agonist by an athlete could indicate a need for additional anti inflammatory therapy. Use of salmeterol, a long-acting inhaled β_2 agonist, provides protection against EIB for as long as 12 hours, although long term daily use has been shown to diminish the duration of effect. Nonetheless, a long acting inhaled β_2 agonist may be specifically advantageous for the athlete who is active for longer periods. The mast cell-stabilizing agents, cromolyn and nedocromil, have also demonstrated good effectiveness in protecting against EIB when administered before exercise. The duration of protection is dose dependent but similar to that of short acting β_2 agonists (about 2 to 4 hours), and the low incidence of side effects make them appealing. In addition, cromolyn and nedocromil can alleviate the late asthmatic response and can be used in combination with a β_2 agonist for enhanced protection if 1 agent alone is not sufficient. The antileukotrienes have also demonstrated protective effects against EIB; they have the convenience of oral use and no tolerance to the protective effects with long-term use. Inhaled corticosteroid given immediately before exercise is of no benefit, but daily, long term use may reduce the severity of EIB. Factors that reduce the effectiveness of all drugs used to treat EIB are increased intensity and duration of the exercise and exercise in cooler, drier air. Inhaled corticosteroids and albuterol, terbutaline and salmeterol by inhalation are allowed in Olympic competition upon advance written notification. Cromolyn, nedocromil, ipratropium, theophylline and all the antileukotrienes are allowed by the US Olympic Committee without prior notification.

References

Asthma in America: A Landmark Survey, Executive Summary. Washington, DC: Asthma in America, 1998.

Cull MA (1998). Leukotriene modifiers for asthma treatment. *World Drug Information* **9:** 1-4.

Dahlen B, Margolskee DJ, Zetterstrom O and Dahlen S (1993). Effect of the leukotriene receptor antagonist MK-0679 on baseline pulmonary function in aspirin sensitive asthmatic subjects. *Thorax.* **48:** 1205-1210.

D'Cruz DP, Barnes NC and Lockwood CM (1999). Difficult asthma or Churg-Strauss syndrome? *Brit Med J.* **318:** 475-476.

Drazen JM, Yandava CN, Dube L, *et al.*, (1999). Pharmacogenetic association between ALOX5 promoter genotype and the response to anti-asthma treatment. *Nat Genet* **22:** 168-170.

Green RL and Vayonis AG (1999). Churg-Strauss syndrome after zafirlukast in two patients not receiving systemic steroid treatment. *Lancet.* **353:** 725-726.

Katz RS, Papernick M (1998). Zafirlukast and Churg-Strauss syndrome [letter].*JAMA* **279:** 1949.

Kinoshita M, Shiraishi T, Koga T, Ayabe M, Rikimaru T, Oizumi K (1999). Churg-Strauss syndrome after corticosteroid withdrawal in an asthmatic patient treated with pranlukast. *J Allergy Clin Immunol.* **103(3Pt1):**534-535.

Knorr B, Matz J, Bernstein JA, *et al.*, (1998). Montelukast for chronic asthma in 6 to 14 year old children: a randomized, double-blind trial. Pediatric Montelukast Study Group. *JAMA* **279:** 1181-1186.

Montelukast for persistent asthma (1998). *The Medical Letter* **40:** 71-73.

Stempel DA (1998). Leukotriene modifiers in the treatment of asthma. *Respir Care.* **43:** 481-489.

CHAPTER

Drugs Used to Treat Allergic Rhinitis

2

Definition

Allergic rhinitis is an IgE-antigen and mast cell mediated inflammation of the membranes lining the nose. The disease is characterized by sneezing, congestion, clear rhinorrhea and nasal or palatal itching. The disease may also coexist with allergic conjunctivitis (chara-cterized by itchy, watery eyes that may also be red or swollen). Allergic rhinitis may be seasonal, perennial, or may occur sporadically after specific exposures.

Diagnosis

The diagnosis is listed in Table 2-1, 2-2.

Adults, General People

Assessment of a patient who presents with symptoms of allergic rhinitis begins with a detailed history regarding the pattern, frequency, duration, severity and seasonality of symptoms (or lack thereof), response to medications, presence of coexisting conditions (especially atopic conditions), occupational exposure, environmental history and identification of precipitating factors. Family history of atopic disease is often positive in patients with allergic rhinitis. An integral part of the assessment is an evaluation of the degree to which symptoms affect the patient's quality of life, physical and social functioning, mental health, energy level and general health perception. Physical examination should be made of the external nose, nasal mucosa, secretions, turbinates, and septum. In the allergic patient (especially the inferior turbinates), the nasal mucosa typically appears pale pink, swollen and may have a bluish gray tinge. Secretions in acute allergies may be thin and clear, but with chronic allergies may be thick and clear/white. There may be polypoid changes along the anterior end of the middle turbinate.

Paediatrics

Symptoms exhibited by children and adolescents with allergic rhinitis are indistinguishable from those of adults with the exceptions that paediatric patients have a greater frequency of the allergic salute and eye rubbing. These are linked to chronic nasal obstruction, which may lead to "the allergic facies", a complex of infraorbital darkening, facial maldevelopment, including overbite, crossbite, narrow arched palate and molar flattening.

Testing

Testing is not indicated in many allergic rhinitis cases. For other allergic symptoms skin tests and RAST (radioallergosorbent test) identify the presence of IgE antibody to a particular allergen. Testing is helpful to

(a) Differentiate allergic from nonallergic rhinitis symptoms,

(b) To identify specific allergens that may cause symptoms, and

(c) Identify allergens for immunotherapy.

Skin tests are more sensitive, faster and more cost effective than RAST testing. Antihistamines should be stopped 7-10 days (7 days to be safe) before skin testing, but do not need to be stopped prior to RAST serum tests. Intranasal corticosteroids, leukotriene inhibitors, decongestants, oral corticosteroids do not need to be stopped for skin testing.

Table 2-1: Symptoms and signs suggestive of allergic rhinitis

Symptoms	Seasonal, perennial or episodic (associated with exposure, e.g., cat) itching of eyes, ears, nose, palate; sneezing, nasal congestion, chronic sniffling, clear rhinorrhea, post nasal drip, pressure of nose or over paranasal sinus', morning cough. Red, watery eyes or ropy discharge.
Family or personal history	Atopic dermatitis, asthma, food allergy.
Physical findings	Ocular-allergic shiners, Dennie's lines, sclera injection with corkscrewing of vessels, conjunctival erythema with possible cobblestoning. Nasal-transverse nasal crease (salute), congestion, pale pink or bluish mucosa, clear or thick mucoid discharge, presence of nasal polyps, pharyngeal cobblestoning.

Table 2-2: Alternative diagnosis with typical characteristics

Alternative Diagnosis	Typical Characteristics
Acute rhinosinusitis	Facial pressure or pain, purulent nasal discharge; maxillary toothache; failure to respond to decongestants; fever or cough may be present; typically follows an allergy flare-up or a viral Upper respiratory tract infections (URI)
Chronic rhinosinusitis	Facial pressure or pain, purulent discharge; fever often absent; may be present in addition to allergic rhinitis; symptoms may wax and wane over time; chronic hyposmia.
Viral URI	Self-limited course with symptoms (clear rhinorrhea, cough, ache, low grade fever) usually resolving within 3-7 days.
Structural abnormalities	Include nasal septal deviation, nasal polyps, enlarged tubinates, adenoidal hypertrophy. Obstruction may be unilateral or bilateral and may or may not be seen on routine nasal examination.
Rhinitis medicamentosa	Also called "rebound rhinitis'; caused by overuse of topical decongestants; diagnosis is easily made by history; may mask another underlying condition such as septal deviation or allergic rhinitis.
Vasomotor rhinitis	Clear rhinorrhea, nasal obstruction, often depends on position (e.g., supine), may be episodic. Pregnancy may exacerbate symptoms
Atrophic rhinitis	Also called "ozena", caused by over-resection of nasal turbinate tissue or poor mucus production, resulting in nasal dryness and crusting. Foul odor may be present.
Gastroesophageal reflux	Under-recognized cause of post-nasal drip, cough, and globus sensation, hoarseness or frequent throat clearing may also be present.

Patients who cannot stop their antihistamines because of symptoms should keep their appointment with the allergist. Skin testing should be performed by a physician trained in allergy testing and interpretation. Effective testing requires a well controlled process with consistent application technique and proper precautions for patients who react to skin testing (approximately 1-10% of patients). Proper technique is vital to producing accurate and reproducible results. Interpreting skin or *in-vitro* tests for a specific IgE requires knowledge of locally present aeroallergens, their clinical importance and their cross-reactivity with botanically related species. The number of skin tests needed may vary with the patient's age, potential allergen exposures, and geographic region. Nasal smears, although rarely performed, identify the presence of neutrophils and eosinophils, the latter of which suggests an allergic disease.

Treatment

Treatment of Rhintis by avoidance or environmental control of causing factors. Avoidance of inciting factors (e.g., allergens, irritants, medications) is fundamental to the management of allergic rhinitis. Food allergies may cause rhinorrhea in young children but this is rarely the overriding symptom.

Triggers for allergic rhinitis may be grouped into five major categories: pollens, molds, house dust mites, animals and insect allergens (e.g., cockroaches, bee venom). The effectiveness of control measures instituted is assessed primarily by patient symptoms and the necessity of medications.

Pollens

Pollen triggering allergic rhinitis is principally derived from wind-pollinated trees, grasses and weeds. In Michigan, the predominant sources of pollen vary with the season:

- April – May = Tree pollen
- May – June – early summer = Grass pollen
- August – September = Weed pollen
- September – October = Seasonal mold

Reducing pollen exposure is important to the effective management of allergic rhinitis; this can be accomplished by closing doors and windows, using air conditioning on an indoor cycle, minimizing the use of window or attic fans, and limiting outdoor activity. Showering or bathing after outdoor activity removes pollen from the hair and skin and helps avoid contamination of bedding. In highly sensitive patients, effective allergen avoidance may require severely curtailing the patient's outdoor activity.

Molds

Molds proliferate in both indoor and outdoor environments. Most mold allergens are encountered through inhalation of mold spores.

Patients can avoid outdoor molds by remaining indoors and using air conditioning on an indoor cycle; however, it is important to note that air conditioning units themselves may be heavily contaminated with mold. Indoor mold is influenced by the age and construction of the building, presence of basement or crawl space, type of heating system and use of humidifiers and air conditioning. Indoor mold can be controlled somewhat *via* chemical and physical measures such as fungicides, careful cleaning of humidifiers and vaporizers and placement of a plastic vapor barrier over exposed soil in crawl spaces. Dehumidifiers in basements and other damp areas may help reduce mold levels. The overall effectiveness of these measures, however, is dependent upon reducing relative humidity and condensation levels.

House Dust Mites

Fecal residue from dust mites is the primary allergen in household dust. The dust mites' principle food source is exfoliated human skin; as such, mite concentrations are highest in bedding, fabric covered furniture, soft toys and carpeting. Physical barriers may include allergen proof encasings for mattresses, pillows, box springs, and bedding, using plastic, wood, or leather furniture in lieu of upholstered furniture, and replacing carpeting with wood or vinyl flooring. Chemical barriers include using 3% tannic acid solution to denature dust mites in upholstered furniture and treating carpeting with Acarosan®, a compound containing benzyl benzoate. The effectiveness of chemical barriers depends upon their repeated application. Finally, while it is possible that air conditioning reduces mite numbers by lowering indoor humidity, evidence regarding the effect of air purifiers on alleviating dust mite allergy symptoms is either nonexistent (for electrostatic purifiers) or conflicting (for High-efficiency particulate air (HEPA) air purifiers). Similarly, cleaning heating ducts is of no demonstrated value.

Animal Allergens

All warm-blooded animals, including birds, are capable of sensitizing a susceptible allergenic patient. While exposures to mice, rats, guinea pigs, and farm animals constitute occupational hazards for some, the most common manifestations of animal allergy are to cats and dogs. Cat and dog allergens are notable for the ease and extent of their dissemination, particularly through passive means (i.e., transport on clothing). Removing the offending animal from the household is preferred. While significant cleaning measures are required to reduce cat and dog allergen levels to those found in environments not inhabited by cats or dogs, if the animal is still present, the effectiveness of cleaning is limited.

Cleaning may include washing the animal itself on a weekly basis. Evidence in support of this practice is mixed, but washing should never be attempted by the allergic patient. If the allergenic animal is not to be removed from the home, confining it to an un carpeted room with an electrostatic or HEPA air purifier may markedly reduce airborne allergens in the rest of the home.

Insect Allergens

Sources of insect allergens include cockroaches, flies, midges and moths. Debris from these insects is associated with allergic rhinoconjun-ctivitis and asthma. The most common of these, the cockroach allergen, is found on the insect's body and in its feces. While careful sanitation practices are often effective in reducing or eliminating cockroaches, heavy infestation may require application of pesticides by a professional exterminator.

Pharmacological Therapy

Several classes of drugs comprise the mainstay of treatment of allergic rhinitis; of these, the primary ones are intranasal corticosteroids and oral antihistamines.

Intranasal Corticosteroids

A number of studies have shown these drugs to be the most effective treatment of the itching, sneezing, rhinorrhea and stuffiness associated with allergic rhinitis. Their effect is not immediate, however; onset of relief is seen on day 2 to 3 with effects reaching their peak at 2 to 3 weeks. Regular, consistent use is required to maintain a maximum effect. Patient education for the correct use of intranasal pump sprays is essential. Intranasal corticosteroids do not treat ocular symptoms. Intranasal corticosteroids (Table 2-3) are well tolerated and have a relatively good safety profile. Newer, more potent formulations offer the advantages of once daily dosing, minimal to no systemic absorption, and demonstrated tolerability in pediatric patients. The incidence of adverse effects is between 5-10%; local effects most commonly reported include sneezing, stinging and burning or irritation. However, these effects are generally mild and do not preclude the use of intranasal preparations. Aqueous formulations are preferred because they are less irritating to the nasal mucosa.

Oral Antihistamines

Antihistamines (Fig 2-1) are effective in reducing symptoms of itching, sneezing and rhinorrhea and should be tried with most patients as first line therapy for allergic rhinitis. Antihistamines also reduce symptoms of allergic conjunctivitis, which are often associated with allergic rhinitis. While they tend to be less efficacious overall compared to the intranasal steroids, antihistamines appear to be equally effective in blocking histamine mediated responses to allergens .

All antihistamines appear to be equally effective; however, first generation agents adversely affect cognition and performance. It is therefore recommended that therapy be initiated with generic loratadine. Some patients may get better symptom relief with cetirizine; however, it is more sedating than loratadine and requires a prescription. For patients that cannot afford

OTC loratadine, generic, OTC, chlorphenir-amine is inexpensive and effective. It is the least sedating of the 1st generation antihistamines; however, it must still be used with caution in patients requiring mental alertness in the workplace and in driving.

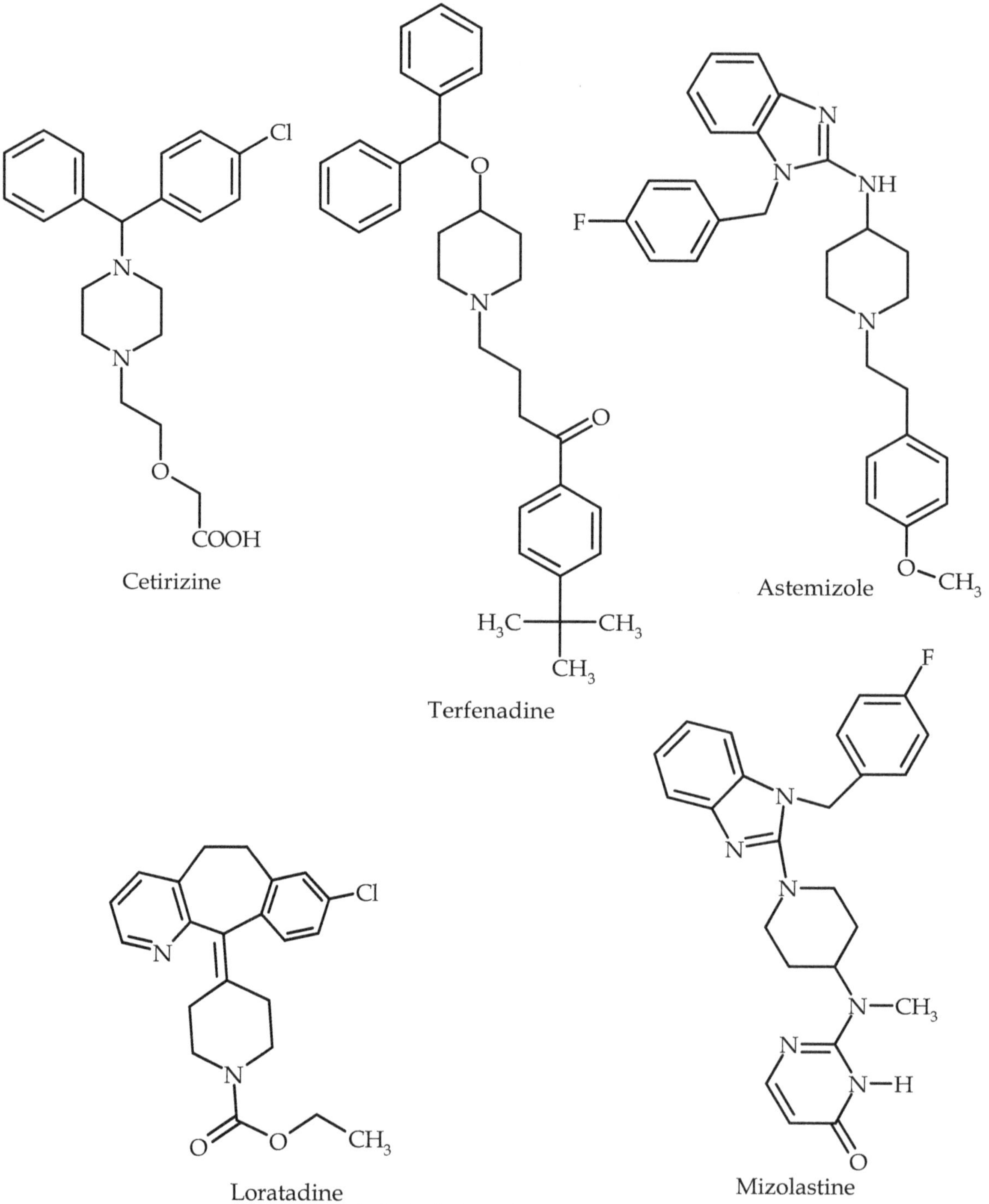

Fig 2-1: Oral antihistamines

Decongestants

Decongestants act on adrenergic receptors to produce vasoconstriction and decrease swelling of the nasal mucosa which, in turn, alleviates nasal congestion. Oral decongestants may be used until symptoms resolve. Although they have not been found to affect blood pressure significantly in patients with stable hypertension, oral decongestants (including combination products containing a decongestant) should be used with caution in patients with unstable hypertension, ischemic heart disease, glaucoma, prostatic hypertrophy, or diabetes mellitus. Urinary retention in elderly males is a common side effect. Oral decongestants are contraindicated in patients using monoamine oxidase inhibitors (MAOIs) or having uncontrolled hypertension or severe coronary artery disease. In addition, geriatric patients may be more sensitive to the side effects of oral decongestants. Topical decongestants do not exhibit significant systemic absorption in usual doses, but due to the risk of rebound vasodilation (rhinitis medicamentosa) or atrophic rhinitis with chronic use, these agents have no role in the maintenance treatment of allergic rhinitis. They may be used short term (3-5 days) for the severely congested patient to improve initial drug delivery with intranasal corticosteroids.

Combination antihistamine/decongestant. Patients for whom an antihistamine or decongestant alone fails to provide complete relief may benefit from an antihistamine/ decongestant combination; studies have show improved allergy symptom control when a decongestant has been added to antihistamine therapy. Decongestant containing products are approved only for patients 12 years of age and older; however, pseudoephedrine can be added as a separate agent in children as young as 2 years of age. The cautions enumerated above for decongestant use also apply to combination products.

Leukotriene Inhibitors

Leukotriene inhibitors (Fig 2-2) are the newest class of medications used for allergic rhinitis. They reduce allergy symptoms through inhibition of inflammation and also have proven efficacy for control of asthma. Several large studies have evaluated montelukast and have shown a reduction in itching, sneezing, rhinorrhea, and congestion. Efficacy appears comparable to oral antihistamines but studies demonstrate that inhaled corticosteroids have superior improvement in nasal obstructive symptoms compared to leukotriene inhibitors. Combination therapy of leukotriene inhibitors and antihistamines improved intranasal symptom compared to monotherapy, but were again less effective when compared to inhaled nasal steroids alone . Leukotriene inhibitors may have a role as first line therapy in patients with comorbid persistent asthma to control both diseases and reduce medication costs. Nasal cromolyn, although less effective than intranasal corticosteroids, cromolyn is a good alternative for patients who are not candidates for corticosteroids. It is most effective when used regularly prior to the onset of allergic symptoms. The four times daily dosing can cause compliance problems. Adverse effects are minimal and include nasal irritation, sneezing, and unpleasant taste.

Anticholinergics

Ipratropium bromide (Atrovent) is an effective anticholinergic spray for patients with severe vasomotor symptoms or atrophic rhinitis (profuse thin rhinorrhea). Anticholinergics decrease the production of mucus and diminish

Montelukast
$C_{35}H_{35}ClNNaO_3S$

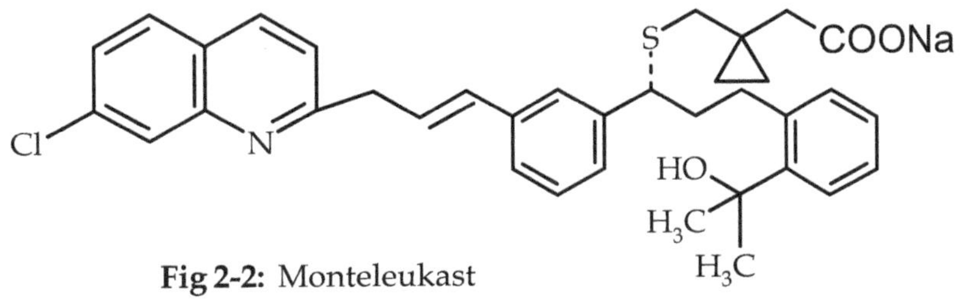

Fig 2-2: Monteleukast

rhinorrhea. Both topical medications and oral preparations (usually first generation antihistamines) have been shown to be effective. One therapeutic effect of the first generation antihistamines is related to their anticholinergic properties. Therefore newer, less sedating antihistamines are less likely to produce this benefit.

Table 2-3: Dosages of drugs used to treat allergic rhinitis

Drug	Adult dosage	Pediatric dosage
Corticosteroid nasal sprays		
Beclomethasone dipropionate – *Beconase AQ* (GlaxoSmithKline)	1-2 sprays each nostril bid	6-12 yr: 1-2 sprays each nostril bid
Budesonide – *Rhinocort Aqua* (AstraZeneca)	1-4 sprays each nostril once/d	6-12 yr: 1-4 sprays each nostril once/d
Fluisolide – *Nasarel* (IVAX)	2 sprays each notril bid or tid	6-14 yr: 1 spray each nostril tid or 2 sprays each nostril bid
Fluticasone propionate – *Flonase* (GlaxoSmithKline)	2 sprays each nostril once/d or 1 spray each nostril bid	≥ 4 yr: 1-2 sprays each nostril once/d
Mometasone furoate – *Nasonex* (Schering-Plough)	2 sprays each nostril once/d	2-12 yr: 1 spray each nostril once/d
Triamcinolone acetonide – *Nasacort AQ* (Aventis)	1-2 sprays each nostril once/d	6-12 yr: 1-2 sprays each nostril once/d
Oral h1-antihistamines		
Cetirizine – *Zyrtec* (Pfizer)	5-10 mg PO once/d	6-12 month: 2.5 mg PO once/d 12-24 month: 2.5 mg PO once/d or bid 2-6 yr: 2.5-5 mg PO once/d > 6 yr: 5-10 mg PO once/d
Desloratadine – *Clarines* (Schering-Plough)	5 mg PO once/d	6-11 month: 1 mg PO once/d 1-5 yr: 1.25 mg PO once/d 6-11 yr: 2.5 mg PO once/d
Fexofenadine – generic *Allegra* (Aventis)	60 mg PO bid or 180 mg PO once/d	6-11 yr: 30 mg PO bid
Loratadine – generic *Claritin* (Schering-Plough) *Alavert* (Wyeth)	10 mg PO once/d	2-5 yr: 5 mg PO once/d > 6 yr: 10 mg PO once/d
Leukotriene antagonist		
Montelukast – *Singulair* (Merck)	10 mg PO once/d	6-23 month: 4 mg PO once/d 2-5 yr: 4 mg PO once/d 6-14 yr: 5 mg PO once/d

Cost for 30 days' treatment at the lowest initial dosage for adults, based on most recent data available (September 30, 2005) from NDC Health, a healthcare information services company. For conticosteroid nasal sprays, cost is for the smallest multidose container available.
Available formulations include: tablets (Alavert, Allegra, Clarinex, Claritin, Zyrtec.) chewable tablets (Zyrtec.) dissolvable tablets (Alavert, Clarinex Reditabs, Claritin Reditabs), syrups (Alavert, Clarinex, Claritin, Zyrtec), and tablets in combination with pseudoephedrine (Allegra-D, Clarinex-D, Claritin-D, Zyetec-D).
Available without a prescription.
Available as tablets, chewable tablets and oral granules.

Nasal Antihistamines

Intranasal antihistamines are effective in treating the nasal symptoms associated with seasonal and perennial rhinitis and nonallergic vasomotor rhinitis. When administered intranasally, the primary adverse effects are nasal burning and altered taste (i.e., bitter or metallic taste). While effective in the symptomatic treatment of seasonal allergic rhinitis, intranasal antihistamines offer no therapeutic benefit over conventional treatment.

Ocular Medications

Ocular medications for allergic conjunctivitis are available as topical solutions or suspensions. They contain antihistamines or mast cell stabilizers. Side effects of ocular medications are generally mild and include a brief stinging, burning sensation. Ocular antihistamines can be used as needed for acute symptomatic relief and prophylaxis of allergic symptoms with minimal systemic side effects. Sodium cromolyn has been shown to be effective for the treatment of seasonal allergic conjunctivitis and should be administered on a regular basis. Lodoxamide has been shown to be as effective as or more effective than sodium cromolyn in vernal conjunctivitis. Soft contact lens users and patients with sensitivities to certain preservatives should consult their eye care provider or refer to specific product information regarding the use of these products.

Nasal Saline

Saline sprays theoretically moisten the nasal cavity and promote mucociliary clearance. Saline solutions also contain magnesium, which possibly reduces inflammation in the nasal mucosa. One small comparative study showed that intranasal hypertonic saline spray improved symptoms of allergic rhinitis, but saline was not as effective as intranasal corticosteroids. Therefore, saline solution can be an effective adjunctive medication for mild to moderate allergic rhinitis.

Immunotherapy

Allergen immunotherapy is the repeated administration of specific allergens to patients with IgE mediated conditions for the purpose of desensitizing them to the offending allergens. It is the only disease remitting agent available. Well controlled clinical trials have demonstrated its effectiveness for seasonal and perennial allergic rhinitis, seasonal asthma and ocular allergy. It may prevent polysensitization to other allergens in children and prevent the development of asthma.

Table 2-4: Order of medication based on presenting symptoms.

Addition sequence	Nasal obstructive symptoms	Rhinorrhea without obstruction	Comorbid persistent asthma
First	Intranasal corticosteroid	Antithistamine +/- decongestant	Intranasal corticosteroid
Second	Antihistamine +/- decongestant	Intranasal corticosteroid	Leukotriene inhibitors OR Antihistamine +/- decongestant
Third	Leukotriene inhibitors	Leukotriene inhibitors	If intranasal corticosteroid use above, ADD antihistamine +/- decongestant If antihistamine +/- decongestant, ASS intranasal corticosteroid
Fourth	Intranasal antihistamine	Intranasal antihistamine	Intranasal antihistamine
Fifth	Intranasal mast cell stabilizer	Intranasal mast cell stabilizer	Intranasal mast cell stabilizer
Sixth	Intranasal anticholinergics	Intranasal anticholinergics	Intranasal anticholinergics

Omalizumab (Xolair)

A recombinant DNA derived IgG1 monoclonal antibody that selectively binds to circulating IgE and limits the amount of IgE available to bind to FCR1 receptors on mast cells. This limits the release of mediators and modifies the allergic response. It decreases the number of FCR1 receptors on basophils. Studies in patients with allergic rhinitis have shown a decrease in mediators released, decrease in symptoms and need for rescue medication, and improved quality of life scores. Long term effects are not known. The drug is expensive and is currently not approved for use in clinical practice.

Table 2-5: Possible side effects associated with medical therapy for allergic rhinitis

Oral antihistamines (1st generation)	**Intranasal corticosteroids**	**Leukotriene inhibitors**
Anticholinergic effects • blurred vision • dry mouth • urinary retention Central nervous system • drowsiness (increased accidents) • cognitive impairment (any age) Gastrointestinal • constipation • GI upset • Nausea Sensory • taste: bitter taste, loss of taste	Nasopharyngeal • nasal irritation • epistaxis • pharyngitis, coughing • septal perforation Sensory • smell: reduced sense of smell • taste: unpleasant taste, loss of taste	General • headache • rash (uncommon) • dream abnormalities • gastritis, dyspepsia • dental pain • respiratory tract infections
Oral antihistamines (2nd generation)	**Oral decongestants**	**Intranasal mast cell stabilizers**
General rare • GI upset • headache • drowsiness (1-3%) • myalgias	General • dizzinesss • headache • nervousness • tachycardia • drowsiness • insomnia • palpitations • weakness	Nasopharyngeal • epistaxis, sneezing • nasal irritation: burning, stinging Sensory • taste: unpleasant taste
Ocular Preparation		
• headache • ophthalmic irritation: burning, dryness, pruritus, stingning • possible contact lens irritation (consult with eye care provider)		

Surgical Therapy

For patients who have persistent nasal obstruction after adequate trial of medical therapy (including or not including immunotherapy), referral to a surgical specialist should be considered for possible surgical reduction of the inferior turbinates, which has been demonstrated to lead to objective and subjective improvements in airflow symptoms.

References

Baker JR (1997). Primer on Allergic and Immunologic Diseases (4th Edition). *JAMA* **278(22):** 1799-2034.

Dykewicz MS, Fineman S, Nicklas R, *et al.*, (1998). Diagnosis and Management of Rhinitis: Parameter Documents of the Joint Task Force on Practice Parameters in Allergy, Asthma, & Immunology. *Annals of Allergy, Asthma and Immunology* **81(Part II):** 463-468.

Stroebel R, Graft D, Takahashi M, *et al.*, (2003). Health Care Guideline: Rhinitis. Bloomington, MN: Institute for Clinical Systems Improvement (ICSI).

CHAPTER

Drugs Used to Treat Cough, COPD and Cystic Fibrosis

3

Cough

Introduction

Cough can be a symptom of upper or lower respiratory tract infection or may be a consequence of a non infectious condition such as asthma, exposure to cigarette smoke, or aspiration of a foreign body. The distinction between cough due to an upper respiratory infection and cough due to bronchitis is not important since both conditions in children are self limited viral infections and do not require antibiotic treatment. The distinction between wet and dry coughs or productive and non productive coughs is of little therapeutic value, especially in children who usually swallow their sputum. Occasionally, the characteristics of a cough can give information about the likely cause of the illness for example, prolonged coughing followed by a whoop is found in established pertussis infection and a barking cough is typical of croup.

Most children suffering with a common cold or bronchitis cough. Coughing is a protective reflex, particularly when secretions are copious. Children with cough and fast breathing or chest indrawing may have pneumonia and should receive antibiotic treatment. Children with cough should therefore be assessed for any clinical signs that suggest pneumonia (fast breathing, chest indrawing) or danger signs of very severe disease (such as meningitis). In some children with asthma, cough (especially nocturnal cough) may be the predominant symptom and may be relieved by bronchodilator therapy.

Since non-productive cough is unusual in infants and young children, few of them require cough suppression. Parents and health workers should be discouraged from trying to eliminate this symptom. The cough reflex, which is a physiological response to airway irritation, functions to clear secretions from the respiratory tract and may therefore, be beneficial. Retention of these secretions may lead to potentially harmful airway obstruction. Cough should therefore not be eliminated by drug therapy but can be relieved by a safe, soothing remedy. Practical observation suggests that a nocturnal cough associated with an upper respiratory infection is more commonly distressing to the parent than the child, and more frequently interferes with the sleep pattern of the adult. Rarely, a child may become exhausted or have insomnia or repeated vomiting due to cough. In these circumstances the use of a safe and effective cough suppressant would be helpful.

Cough is a useful physiological mechanism that serves to clear the respiratory passages of foreign material and excess secretions.

- There are, however, many situations in which cough does not serve any useful purpose but may, instead only annoy the patient or prevent rest and sleep.
- Chronic cough can contribute to fatigue, especially in elderly patients, in such situations the physicians should use a drug that will reduce the frequency or intensity of the coughing.
- Cough reflex is complex, involving the central and peripheral nervous systems as well as the smooth muscle of the bronchial tree.

- It has been suggested that irritation of the bronchial mucosa causes broncho-constriction, which in turn, stimulates cough receptors (which probably represent a specialized type of stretch receptor) located in the tracheobronchial passages.
- Afferent conduction from these receptors is *via* fibers in the vagus nerve; central components of the reflex probably involve several mechanisms or centres that are distinct from the mechanisms involved in the regulation of respiration.
- The drugs that directly or indirectly can affect this complex mechanism are diverse. For example, cough may be the first or only symptom in bronchial asthma or allergy and in such cases bronchodilators (e.g., β_2 - adrenergic receptor agonists have been shown to reduce cough without having any significant central effects, other drugs act primarily on the central or the peripheral nervous system components of the cough reflex).
- Forceful release of air from lungs Sudden, often involuntary (protective) reflex and major defensive mechanism.

Causes of Cough

- Expulsion of respiratory secretion or foreign particles or irritant or excessive mucus from air passages.
- Symptom of an underlying respiratory and/or cardiovascular pathology.

Mechanism of Cough

Stimulation of mechano- or chemoreceptor's
(throat, respiratory passages or stretch receptors in lungs)

↓

Afferent impulses to cough centre (medulla)

↓

Efferent impulses *via* parasympathetic and motor nerves to
diaphragm, intercostal muscles and lung

↓

Increased contraction of diaghramatic, abdominal and
intercostal (ribs) muscle ⇒ noisy expiration (cough)

Types of Cough

A. Acute cough = lasting < 3 weeks

B. Chronic cough = lasing > 8 weeks

Cough may be

(i) Unproductive (dry) cough or

(ii) Productive cough (sputum)

Most Common Causes of Cough

- Common cold
- Upper/lower respiratory tract infection
- Allergic rhinitis
- Smoking
- Chronic bronchitis
- Pulmonary tuberculosis
- Asthma
- Gastroesophageal reflux
- Pneumonia
- Congestive heart failure
- Bronchiectasis
- Use of drugs (e.g., Angiotensin converting enzyme inhibitors)

Treatment of Cough

1. Antitussives (cental cough suppressants)
2. Expectorants
3. Mucolytics
4. Antihistamines
5. Bronchodilators
6. Pharyngeal Demulcents

Antitussives (Central Cough Suppressants)

Codeine and other Opiate Derivatives

(e.g., Noscapine, Hydrocodone, Pholcodine)

Morphine is well recognized to be an antitussive but only at doses which cause marked sedation. Codeine an opium derivative made by methylation of morphine. It is classified as a CNS, narcotic agent, analgesic and antitussive. The dose required to suppress cough is lower than the doses required for analgesia. Codeine, an Opioid chemically related to morphine, acts on the cough centre of the medulla to depress the cough reflex, perhaps by increasing the cough threshold. Like other opioids, codeine has analgesic and sedative properties, but its action as an antitussive is achieved at lower doses than its analgesic and sedative effects.

Codeine, which has a half-life in the plasma of 2-4 hours, is metabolized by the liver and excreted in the urine, mostly in inactive forms. However, about 10% is demethylated to form morphine, which may be the active form of the drug. Young infants are more susceptible to codeine intoxication due to their immature hepatic glucuronidation system. Codeine is available in the sulfate and phosphate forms. it is sold alone in the form of syrup and capsules or tablets, or in combination with other medicines.

Indications: For suppression of cough induced by chemical or mechanical respiratory tract irritation. Also for relief of mild to moderate pain since it is a narcotic analgesic.

Contraindications: Hypersensitivity to the drug, acute asthma, acute alcoholism, premature infants or during labor when delivery of a premature infant is anticipated.

Recommended dosage

Adult: 10-20 mg PO q 4-6 hr; max 120 mg/24 hr.

Child (6-12 y): 5-10 mg q 4-6 hr; max 60 mg/24 hr.

Child (2-6 y): 2.5-5 mg q 4-6 hr; max 30mg/24 hr.

Adverse effects: In usual oral antitussive doses, codeine has mild side effect. Nausea, vomiting, sedation, dizziness, constipation are most common. Other effects may include: CNS depression, respiratory depression, biliary tract spasms, tachycardia, palpitation, faintness, orthostatic hypotension, urinary retention, antidiuretic effect, hallucination, disorientation, light headedness, euphoria, weakness, convulsions, as well as allergic reactions have been reported. Warn patients against performing tasks that require full alertness and coordination (i.e. , driving or operating machines) until the full effect of the medication is known. Instruct patients to make position changes slowly, particularly from recumbent to upright posture, and to lie down immediately if light-headedness/dizziness occur, especially in elderly patients, to avoid falling down.

Drug Interactions

Table 3-1: Overview of codeine drug-drug interaction

Drug	Interaction
CNS depressants, and alcohol	Including other opiates, general anaesthetics, phenothiazines, tricyclic anti depressants, tranquilizers; all have additive effects when given concomitantly with codeine. Avoid, or use extreme caution.

Dextromethorphan HBr

Dextromethorphan is a non narcotic derivative of levorphanol classified as an antitussive. Chemically related to morphine but without the capacity to cause tolerance or addiction. It controls cough spasms by depressing the cough center in the medulla. It does not depress respiration or inhibit cilliary action. Antitussive activity comparable to that of codeine, but it is less likely to cause constipation drowsiness, or GI disturbances.

Pharmacokinetics: Dextromethorphan is rapidly absorbed from the gastrointestinal tract. Its antitus-sive effect persists for up to 6 hours. Like codeine, it is metabolized in the liver and excreted in the urine, both unchanged and with demethylated metabolites.

Indications: Temporary relief of cough spasms in nonproductive coughs due to colds, pertussis (whooping cough) and influenza.

Recommended dosage:

Adult: 10-20 mg PO q 4 hr or 30 mg q 68 hr; max 120 mg/24 hr. Child (6 - 12 y): 5-10 mg q 4 hr or 15 mg q 6-8 hr; max 60 mg/24 hr. Child (2 - 6 y): 2.5 mg q 4 hr, 7.5 mg q 68 hr; max 30 mg/24hr.

Adverse effects: Side effects are rare, but may include; dizziness, drowsiness, CNS depression, GI upset, constipation and abdominal discomfort.

Drug Interactions

Table 3-2: Overview of dextromethorphan drug-drug interaction

Drug	Interaction
MAO inhibitors	Dextromethorphan should not be given to patients taking MAOI. Patient may develop hypotension, nausea, myoclonic leg jerks or coma following co-administration.

Clearing Thick Sputum

In theory, the two approaches for clearing thick sputum are by the use of:

- Expectorants, which aim to stimulate bronchial mucus production, thereby making the secretions easier to remove by cough or by ciliary transport.
- Mucolytics, which are designed to alter the viscosity of bronchial secretions, thereby making them easier to clear by cough or ciliary transport.

Expectorants

Expectorants are often prescribed to patients with a dry cough who complain that they cannot cough up mucus from their lungs. They may act indirectly by stimulating efferent vagal nerve fibres to bronchial glands, resulting in increased volume of bronchial secretions. Because vagal stimulation also irritates the gastric mucosa, large doses of expectorants such as guaifensin, ipecac, terpin hydrate and ammonium chloride will cause nausea and vomiting. Expectorants such as guaifensin and potassium iodide act directly on bronchial glands to stimulate mucus production. Potassium iodide may also act as a mucolytic agent by breaking down mucoproteins and stimulating ciliary activity.

Expectorants are generally sold in combination with decongestants, antihi-stamines, bronchodilators and antitussives. Although expectorants are popular with patients and some physicians, many doctors remain sceptical of their efficacy and these agents have shown little benefit in controlled studies. According to a recent critical review, expectorants—in order to be considered useful—should not only ease the removal of bronchial secretions, but also improve the patient's condi-tion for the duration of treatment.

Side Effects

The physiological response to an expectorant is affected by the person's general condition, state of hydration, condition of the respiratory tract, and by other drugs ingested with the expectorant. Large doses of expectorants irritate the gastric mucosa and may produce nausea and vomiting. Iodides can cause iodine reactions (skin eruptions, hypersensitivity reactions with angioedema, pulmonary edema) in sensitive persons. Since iodides are taken up by the salivary and lachrymal glands as well as mucus cells, expectoration may be associated with rhinorrhoea, salivation and lacrimation. Ammonium chloride is converted to urea in the liver, causing a metabolic acidosis and a mild diuresis (in larger doses it is used to treat metabolic alkalosis). Terpin hydrate elixir preparations have a high alcohol content and therefore a potential for intoxication and abuse.

Some agents used as expectorants are potentially dangerous and should not be given to children. Chloroform was once widely used as an ingredient in cough syrups and other pharmaceutical products, but has been banned in over a dozen countries because of concerns about hepatotoxicity and carcinogenicity.

1. Ammonium Chloride

Ammonium chloride is primarily used as an acidifying agent. Allegedly, it increases the removal of respiratory tract secretions by reflex stimulation of bronchial mucous glands that result from irritation of the gastric mucosa, which makes it a common ingredient in cough mixtures. But it has questionable efficacy. In the presence of renal, hepatic or chronic heart diseases, ammonium Cl doses of 5 gm have caused severe poisoning. Symptoms of toxicity including nausea, vomiting, thirst, rash, headache, bradycardia, mental confusion, hyperventilation and electroencephalogram abnormalities. A relative contraindication for use in patients with hepatic, renal or pulmonary insufficiency exists. Use in diabetics should also be avoided. Doses larger than those recommended may predispose the patient to hyperammonemia and metabolic acidosis. Since ammonium Cl acidifies the urine, it may also affect the excretion of other drugs when given in large doses; (i.e. amphetamines, methadone, ephedrine, pseudoephedrine, sulfonylureas and salicylates). The expectorant safe dosing recommendations to be used are;

Adults: 300 mg q 2-4 hr.

Child (6-12 y): 150 mg q 2-4 hr.

Child (2 to < 6 y): 75 mg q 2-4 hr.

Most companies include ammonium Cl in their cough products and list it as a nonactive ingredient. Used with caution in susceptible patients.

2. Guaifenesin

Guaifenesin (glyceryl guaiacolate) is claimed to enhance the output of respiratory tract fluid by reducing adhesiveness and surface tension facilitating the removal of viscous mucus. As a result nonproductive cough becomes more productive and less frequent. There is a lack of convincing studies to document efficacy just like any other expectorant.

Indications: For the symptomatic relief of respiratory conditions characterized by dry, nonproductive cough and in the presence of mucus in the respiratory tract.

Contraindications: Hypersensitivity to the product, no other absolute contraindications to its use.

Recommended dosage

Adults and children (> 12 y): 200-400 mg PO q 4 hr.

Do not exceed 2400 mg/24 hr.

Child (6-12 y): 100-200 mg q 4 hr. Do not exceed 1200 mg/24 hr.

Child (2-5 y): 50-100 mg q 4 hr. Do not exceed 600 mg/24 hr.

Adverse Effects: These are uncommon, but may include nausea, vomiting, headache, and rash.

Interactions: Guaifenesin may increase risk of hemorrhage in patients receiving heparin therapy.

Mucolytic Drugs

These include drugs such as N-acetylcysteine, which work by breaking sulfhydryl bonds and directly thinning the sputum. Mucolytic agents are often administered by mouth or by inhalation to persons with chronic respiratory conditions characterized by excess mucus production, such as cystic fibrosis and chronic bronchitis. Although mucolytics alter sputum viscosity and may lead to subjective improvement in these patients, their use has not resulted in any consistent improvement in pulmonary function.

Side Effects

Adverse effects reported following oral administration of acetylcysteine include bronchospasm, gastrointestinal disturbances and fever. Some antibiotics, including ampicillin, erythromycin and some tetracyclines are physically incompatible with or may be inactivated by acetylcysteine.

Antihistamines

"Classical" antihistamines, now referred to as H_1-receptor inhibitors, resemble histamine in structure and competitively inhibit the physiological effects of histamine stimulation at receptor sites. In addition to their use as anti-allergy drugs, H-receptor antagonists often have anti emetic, sedative and anticholinergic properties. Antihistamines are added to many cough and cold remedies as both antitussives and to treat rhinorrhoea and nasal congestion.

Although some antihistamines may have an antitussive action, their clinical efficacy has not been well documented. Antihistamines do not appear to have any direct antitussive effect, but it has been proposed that they may act indirectly by reducing postnasal drip.

Because histamine is similar in structure to biogenic amines such as acetylcholine, adrenaline and serotonin, it is not surprising that antihistamines may block the receptors of these other amines. As there are few data about the pharmacokinetic properties of many widely used antihistamines and considerable variation in response among the population, particularly to its sedative effects, it may be difficult to determine the ideal dosage range.

Side Effects of Antihistamine Drugs

Side effects of antihistamines include central nervous system stimulation, extrapyramidal symptoms, antimuscarinic effects and gastrointestinal disturbances. The anticholinergic (atropine like) action of antihistamines frequently causes a drying sensation in the throat and nasal passages and may result in thickening of bronchial secretions, antihistamines also cause drowsiness and diphenhydramine, the most sedating of the antihistamines, is used in non-prescription sleeping medications.

Therapeutic Uses

Antihistamines exhibit other actions apart from their abilities to inhibit the activity of histamine. They can both stimulate and depress the central nervous system. Central nervous system effects are the most common clinically important adverse effects of antihistamines. Paradoxical central nervous system stimulation has been found particularly in children, with irritability, insomnia, tremors, arid occasionally convulsions. Paradoxical stimulation is occasionally seen with therapeutic doses, particularly in children, but occurs more often in drug overdose. Promethazine, a phenothiazine used as an antihistamine, may enhance sleep apnea in infants and may contribute to sudden infant death syndrome.

Antihistamines are chemical agents that exert their effect in the body primarily by competitively blocking the action of histamine at H-receptor sites. They do not prevent histamine release. These have no therapeutic effect on the common cold.

Their continued popularity stems from their drying effect.

1. Chlorpheniramine

Chlorpheniramine maleate will be used as the prototype of commonly used antihistamines. It is a H_1 receptor antagonist, that generally produces less drowsiness than other antihistamines, but side effects involving CNS stimulation may be more common. It also has some antitussive, anticholinergic and local anesthetic action, but no antiemetic properties.

Indications: Symptomatic relief of various allergic conditions, hay fever, urticaria, insect stings, conjunctivitis, angioedema, as well as adjunct in the emergency treatment of anaphylactic shock and severe angioedema.

Contraindications: Hypersensitivity to antihistamines, premature or newborn infants, nursing mothers, narrow angle glaucoma, obstructive prostatic hypertrophy or other bladder neck obstruction, GI obstruction/ stenosis, asthmatic attack and during or within 14 days of MAO inhibitor therapy.

Recommended dosage: Adult: 2-4 mg PO t.i.d. or q.i.d., or 8-12 mg b.i.d or t.i.d.; max 24 mg/ 24 hr. [For anaphylaxis: can be given by slow s.c or i.m injection over 1 min, 10-20 mg repeated if required (max 40 mg/24hr)]. Child (6-12 y): 2 mg q 4-6 hr, max 12 mg/d (2-6 y): 1 mg q 4-6 hr, max 6 mg/d.

Adverse effects: Chlorpheniramine has a low incidence of side effects. Possible side effects include: Drowsiness, headache, tinnitus, disturbed coordination, nervousness, restlessness, mild hypotension, tachycardia, dryness of mouth, nose and throat, blurred vision, diplopia, epigastric distress, nausea, constipation or diarrhoea, or urinary retention.

Interactions:

Table 3-3: Overview of chlorpheniramine drug interactions

Drug	Interaction
Alcohol and other CNS depressants	These potentiate the side effects of the medication.
MAO inhibitors	Intensify and prolong the anticholinergic effects of the antihistamines. May cause severe hypotension and extrapyramidal reactions. Avoid use of antihistamines within 14 days of MAO inhibitor therapy.

2. Astemizole

Astemizole is a long acting selective histamine H_1 receptor antagonist. It binds preferentially to peripheral rather than central H_1- receptors. It does not block histamine release, antibody production or antigen antibody interactions. Has little or no anticholinergic and sedative effects compared with diphenhydramine. Astemizole has a slow onset of action and is more appropriate for use on a regular basis than when symptoms occur. Good choice for people who cannot tolerate the sedative or anticholinergic effects of other antihistamines that are indicated for rhinitis, as well as having the benefit of once a day dose. The downside to its use, is the high cost, potential rare but possible adverse cardiac events including death, as well as the serious side effects that can result from drug-drug interactions.

Indications: Relief of symptoms associated with seasonal allergic rhinitis and chronic idiopathic urticaria.

Contraindications: Same as chlorphineramine. Also in patients with significant hepatic dysfunction, concomitant erythromycin, ketoconazole or itraconazole therapy, patients with hypokalemia and other electrolyte imbalances.

Recommended dosage

Adult and child > 12 yr: 10 mg PO q.d.

Child 6-12 yr: 5 mg daily. Child < 6 yr: Not prefered

Adverse effects: These may include; headaches, dizziness, appetite increase, weight gain, nervousness, depression, nausea, diarrhoea, abdominal pain, angioedema, arrhythmias, photosensitivity, or rash.

Interactions:

Table 3-4: Overview of astemizole drug interaction

Drug	Interaction
Anti-arrhythmic	Do not prescribe at the same time. Medication use increases the risk of ventricular arrhythmias if astemizole is added.
Azole antifungals (Fluconazole, itraconazole, Ketoconazole and miconazole)	Use is contraindicated. These increase astemizole (and terfenadine) plasma levels, which may lead to serious cardiovascular effects.
Fluvoxamine	Use is contraindicated. Increased concentration of the Astemizole/ terfenadine increasing its cardiotoxicity.
Macrolide antibiotics	Use is contraindicated. Erythromycin coadministration increases risk of cardiac toxicity. Other macrolides may have the same risk. Loratidine antihistamine may be a safe alternative.
Tricyclic antidepressants	Increased antimuscarinic and ventricular arrhythmia risks.

Orally Administered Anti Histamine Drugs
Antihistamines are the mainstay of therapy for allergic rhinitis and the resemblance between cold symptoms and symptoms of allergic rhinitis led to the use of antihistamines for the common cold. However, since histamine is not present in increased concentrations in persons with upper respiratory infections, the rationale for their use in the common cold has been questioned.

Side effects: Promethazine, a phenothiazine antihistamine widely used for its anti-emetic and sedative properties, has been reported to cause agitation, hallucinations, seizures, dystonic reactions, sudden infant death syndrome and apnea. These adverse reactions are generally more severe and significant in infants, leading manufacturers to warn against administration in children under 2 years of age. However, the efficacy of promethazine as a sedative could lead to its misuse by parents who may have to cope with a screaming child. Second generation antihistamines have fewer anticholinergic side effects and are considered not to sedate children in therapeutic doses.

Intransal Antihistamines

Nasal patency tended to improve after treatment with diphenhydramine, but the effect was of short duration and not statistically significant. The intranasally administered diphenhydramine in the dosage used (2 mg four times a day for 5 days) was ineffective compared with placebo in improving either the subjective or objective signs of experimental rhinovirus colds. However, the small sample size means that a clinically important effect cannot be excluded.

Bronchodilators

Anticholinergic Drugs

Anticholinergic agents decrease the production of saliva, as well as bronchial, nasal, gastric and intestinal secretions, and act as a bronchodilator. They include the tertiary ammonium compounds such as atropine sulfate and quaternary ammonium compounds such as ipratropium. There is considerable variation between individuals in susceptibility to atropine sulfate, severely limiting its therapeutic margin. Most remedies contain atrophic in very low concentrations, for which efficacy has not been demonstrated.

The effect was most marked in the first 3 days and lasted 3-4 hours after administration. The reduced nasal discharge and sneezing did not, however, contribute greatly to the overall symptom score in many patients except when nasal discharge was prominent and troublesome.

Side effects of orally administered anticholinergics: Side effects include dryness in the mouth and gastrointestinal mucosa, mydriasis, cycloplegia (paralysis of the ciliary muscle of the eye), tachycardia and cardiac arrhythmias, diz-ziness, urinary urgency and constipation. Children may be more susceptible to adverse effects. Atropine may provoke hyperpyrexia when the ambient temperature is high or when the child has fever.

Ipratropium nasal spray is reported to cause blood tinged secretions in 10-15% of cases and nasal dryness, which can lead to irritation sufficient to result in stopping treatment in some adults.

Relief of Nasal Congestion and Other Cold Symptoms

Sympathomimetic Drugs

Most decongestants contain sympathomimetics in oral or topical form (drops and sprays) to reduce the swelling of the nasal mucosa and promote easier breathing. The decrease in blood flow and edema presumably decreases nasal discharge as well.

Topical Sympathomimetic Drugs

Sympathomimetic agents imitate the actions produced by stimulation of postganglionic sympathetic or adrenergic nerves. These include stimulation of the heart and central nervous system, constriction of blood vessels supplying the skin and mucus membranes and dilation of the bronchi. Sympathetic agents may act directly on adrenergic receptors, or indirectly by releasing stored norepinephrine from nerve endings. Some drugs such as ephedrine are both direct and indirect in their actions.

Topical sympathomimetic agents cause constriction of nasal blood vessels, there by reducing mucosal swelling. Ephedrine, oxymetazoline, phenylephrine and phenylpropanolamine are used in local preparations for this purpose.

Side effects: Topical agents when used for more than 2 or 3 days can cause rhinitis, a rebound congestion of the nasal mucosa. Nasal congestion may be as severe as, or worse than, the original symptoms, which is of particular concern in young infants who are obligate nose breathers. Therefore, topical decongestants should never be used in infants.

It is difficult to control the dose of topical agents and young children risk toxicity from systemic absorption of nasal decongestants. Phenylephrine may cause local irritation when given topically. Therapeutic doses of oxymetazoline nose drops in infants and young children have reportedly caused central nervous system effects ranging from sedation to excitement and convulsive attacks resembling seizures.

Orally Administered Sympathomimetic Drugs

Oral sympathomimetics, including phenylephrine, pseudoephedrine, oxymetazoline and phenylpropanolamine cause systemic vasoconstriction, reducing the volume of blood circulated to the nasal mucosa. Pseudoephedrine is a stereoisomer of ephedrine. It is similar to ephedrine in its action, but appears to have a less marked effect on blood pressure and fewer central nervous system effects. Phenylephrine produces little central nervous stimulation, but increases the blood pressure and is sometimes used as a pressor during anaesthesia. Phenylpropanolamine has an indirect action as a sympathomimetic. In addition to its use as a decongestant, it is an ingredient used in diet pills. It is structurally similar to amphetamine, a potent central nervous system stimulant.

Side effects: The adverse effects of sympathomimetics are essentially those of adrenergic stimulation. Psychic disturbances reported among children following phenylpropanolamine administration include irritability, sleep disturbances, hallucinations, aggressiveness and seizures. Severe hypertensive episodes have been reported following phenylpropanolamine ingestion. Pseudoephedrine may have a higher margin of safety than other sympathoinimetic agents.

Pharyngeal Demulcents

- Soothe the throat (directly and also by promoting salivation)
- Decrease afferent impulses from inflamed/ irritated pharyngeal mucosa
- Provide symptomatic relief in dry cough arising from throat

E.g., lozenges, cough drops, glycerine, liquorice, honey.

Soothing Remedies (syrups) for Cough

A demulcent is a liquid which coats the throat and soothes irritated mucous membranes. These preparations may help reduce coughing associated with a dry throat and are soothing to many patients.

Demulcents consist primarily of sugar. They may act by increasing saliva production and swallowing, thereby interfering with the cough reflex, or by coating the peripheral sensory receptors that trigger the cough. Soothing substances such as hot tea with honey and lemon, a syrup, or glycerol are, harmless and inexpen-sive.

Side effects of syrups: Some cough syrups contain as much as 40% alcohol, similar to the alcohol concentration of whisky. Alcohol may suppress the cough reflex by sedating the child. Some cough syrups also may contain a high level of sugar. If given in excess, they can cause osmotic diarrhoea. Syrups should not be given to exclusively breastfed infants, as the sugar they contain may suppress an infant's appetite for breast milk.

Oral Hydration and Mist Therapy

Water and water vapour can promote expectoration of sputum, but opinions differ about its effect on the tissues of the respiratory tract. Some authors claim that water vapour acts as a mucolytic and has a soothing action on the respiratory mucosa. Others, however, state that water is not readily incorporated into mucus when it is administered by inhalation and that it may promote expectoration by an irritant action on the respiratory mucosa.

The value of steam and cold mist therapy as a mucolytic or expectorant has been questioned by some authors. A double blind randomized study in which a group of adults and children breathed either steam (hot humidified air) or ambi-ent air showed no beneficial effects on common cold symptoms. The group breathing steam demonstrated increased airway resistance and a fourfold increase in sideeffects, leading the authors to conclude that hot humidified air might actually damage the nasal mucosa of patients with the common cold.

Side effects: Cases of water intoxication after mist therapy with electronic nebulizers have been reported. Preparation of steam carries the risk of burns, both from fire and from failure to cool the steam. Finally, mist can induce bronchospasm in asthmatic patients.

Saline Nose Drops

It has been reported that saline nose drops may be effective in softening dry or thick nasal mucus and clearing a blocked nose, although they do not appear to bring any overall improvement in the condition of children with colds. An easy way to administer them is by moistening a wick in clean, salted water and using it to drip a few drops onto the nasal mucus.

Side-effects: If too large a volume of drops is administered by dropper, infants may choke due to aspiration. There is one report of increased rates of bacteraemia in rabbits treated with saline nose drops. No data are available to suggest a comparable risk in humans.

Hot Fluids

Studies reported that in addition to having a soothing effect, hot fluids may increase the flow of nasal mucus. Another report suggested that hot beverages such as chicken soup may stimulate mucus production and loosen respiratory secretions, enhancing expectoration.

Specific Treatment Approach to Cough

Etiology of cough	Treatment
1. Upper/lower respiratory tract infections	Appropriate antibiotics
2. Smoking/ chronic bronchitis	Cessation of smoking
3. Pulmonary tuberculosis	Antibiotics
4. Asthmatic cough	Inhaled β2
	Agonists/ Ipratropium/ corticosteroid
5. Postnasal drip (sinusitis)	Antibiotics, nasal decongestants, antihistamines

Traditional Cough and Cold Remedies

Most families prepare home remedies such as tea with honey or a mixture of one part lemon juice and one part honey. Several other ingredients are also common: tamarind, ginger and eucalyptus. Recipes vary widely. Traditional medicines derived from plants have been and will continue to be used for respiratory infections in many parts of the world. There have been few efficacy studies of traditional medicines as therapy flir the common cold. There is no reason to believe that a safe, soothing home made remedy is less effective than a safe commercial remedy. Home remedies are usually inexpensive and promote self-reliance. Unlike commercial preparations, which may contain potentially harmful ingredients, most home remedies are harmless. Ingredients such as menthol and camphor may be used in topical preparations to be rubbed on the chest. However, these products may be toxic and should not be used in teas and oral preparations. The use of safe, soothing home-made remedies for sore throat, such as lemon tea, should be encouraged.

Recommendations for Management of a Simple Cough or Cold or Sore Throat

The health worker should advise the mother about safe remedies which can soothe the child's throat or relieve cough or nasal congestion. National ART, IMCI (Integrated Management of Childhood Illness) or child health programmes should decide whether to provide or prescribe a cough or cold medicine in the clinic, or advise the mother to prepare one at home. Other aspects of essential home care advice, such as continued feeding, increasing oral fluid intake, and being alert for signs of pneumonia or other more serious illness, should be given due attention by the health worker when communicating with the child's parents.

Health workers can safely recommend:

- Oral hydration (e.g., teas, hot soups).
- Relief of nasal congestion when it interferes with feeding: saline nose drops can be tried.
- Use of paracetamol for reduction of high fever when this distresses the child and for relief of pain.
- Safe, soothing remedies (e.g., simple linctus) are useful for both a cough and sore throat. Remedies can be commercially prepared, mixed at the health facility, or made at home.

These measures can be taken by the mother of any child with a cough or cold. Children with signs suggesting pneumonia should immediately be taken to a health worker for assessment.

It is important to educate mothers and health workers that a child's cough performs a useful function in clearing secretions from the anyway and is not an illness in itself, which must be treated.

Although they have a role in symptomatic relief of recurrent allergic rhinitis, anti-histamines are not indicated for relief of nasal congestion due to the common cold. Doctors often prescribe them for their sedative properties. However, cough or cold remedies containing atropine, codeine, alcohol or high doses of antihistamines may sedate the child sufficiently to interfere with feeding and the child's ability to clear secretions from the lungs.

Cough and cold remedies other than saline nose drops should not be given to young infants (less than 2 months old), or to exclusively breastfed infants (aged up to 4-6 months).

In addition to these statements about the use of cough and cold medicines for symptomatic relief of the symptoms of cough and cold, it should be noted that there is no evidence that antibiotic or other medical therapy prevents pneumonia; antihistamines and sympathomimetics do not reduce the incidence of otitis media following a cold; and controlled clinical trials have shown no benefit from antihistamine or decongestant drug therapy in the prevention or treatment of otitis media or otitis media with effusion, or in the prevention of eustachian tube dysfunction.

COPD (Chronic Obstructive Pulmonary Disease)

Chronic obstructive pulmonary disease (COPD) is a progressive disease characterized by airflow limitation that is not fully reversible. It is caused by exposure to noxious particles or gases, most commonly cigarette smoke. It is a major cause of morbidity and mortality and a leading cause of disability in the United States. COPD includes chronic bronchitis and emphysema. Chronic bronchitis is defined clinically as a chronic productive cough for at least 3 months in each of two consecutive years in a patient in whom other causes have been excluded. Emphysema is defined pathologically as the presence of permanent enlargement of the airspaces distal to the terminal bronchioles, accompanied by destruction of their walls without obvious fibrosis. The major risk factor for both conditions is cigarette smoking and many patients share characteristics of each condition. Therefore, new consensus guidelines have moved away from using these subsets and instead focus on chronic airflow limitation. The Global Initiative for Chronic Obstructive Lung Disease (GOLD) is an expert panel of health professionals who have developed a consensus document with recommendations for the diagnosis and care of patients with COPD.

Pathophysiology

The pathophysiology of COPD is shown in Fig. 3-1.

COPD is characterized by pathologic changes in the central airways, peripheral airways, lung parenchyma and pulmonary vasculature. Chronic inflammation in the lung from repeated exposure to noxious particles and gases is primarily responsible for these changes. An imbalance between proteinases and antiproteinases in the lung and oxidative stress are also thought to be important in the pathogenesis of COPD. These processes may be a result of ongoing inflammation or may arise from environmental (e.g., oxidants in cigarette smoke) or genetic [e.g., alpha-1-Antitrypsin (AAT) deficiency] factors. In addition to these destructive processes, chronic inflammation and exposure to noxious particles and gases disrupts or impairs the normal protective and repair mechanisms. Inflammation is present in the lungs of all smokers. It is unclear why only 15% to 20% of smokers develop COPD, but susceptible individuals appear to have an exaggerated inflammatory response. The inflammation of COPD differs from that seen in asthma, so the use of anti inflammatory medications and the response to those medications are different. The inflammation of asthma is mainly mediated through eosinophils and mast cells. In COPD the primary inflammatory cells include neutrophils, macrophages and CD8+ T lymphocytes. Eosinophils may be increased in some patients, particularly during exacerbations. Activated inflammatory cells release a variety of mediators, most notably leukotriene B4, interleukin 8 and tumor necrosis factor-α (TNF-α). Various proteinases, such as elastase, cathepsin G and proteinase-3, are secreted by activated neutrophils. These mediators and proteinases are capable of sustaining inflammation and damaging lung structures. Proteinases and antiproteinases are part of the normal protective and repair mechanisms in the lungs. The imbalance of proteinase antiproteinase activity in COPD is a result of either increased production or activity of destructive proteinases or inactivation or reduced production of protective antiproteinases. AAT (an antiproteinase) inhibits trypsin, elastase and several other proteolytic enzymes. Deficiency of AAT results in unopposed proteinase activity, which promotes destruction of alveolar walls and lung parenchyma, leading to emphysema. Markers of oxidative stress (e.g., hydrogen peroxide nitric oxide and isoprostane F2α-III) have been found in the epithelial fluid, breath and urine of cigarette smokers and patients with COPD. Increased oxidative stress contributes to COPD in a variety of ways. Oxidants (e.g., reactive oxygen species, superoxide and nitric oxide) can react with and damage a variety of molecules leading to cell dysfunction and damage to the lung extracellular matrix. Oxidative stress promotes inflammation and contributes to the proteinases-antiproteinase imbalance by reducing antiproteinase activity. In addition, oxidants constrict airway smooth muscle, contributing to reversible airway narrowing. In the central airways (the trachea, bronchi and bronchioles greater than 2 to 4 mm in internal diameter), inflammatory cells and mediators stimulate mucus secreting gland hyperplasia and mucus hypersecretion. Mucus hypersecretion and ciliary dysfunction lead to chronic cough and sputum production. The major site of airflow obstruction is the peripheral airways (small bronchi and bronchioles with an internal diameter less than 2 mm). Three mechanisms are postulated to be involved in the narrowing of these small airways. Airways may be blocked by inflammatory exudates and mucus hypersecretion. Loss of elasticity and destruction of alveolar attachments leads to loss of support and closure of small airways during expiration. Infiltration of inflammatory cells, increased smooth muscle tissue and fibrosis cause thickening of airway walls. Of these mechanisms, the structural changes in the airway walls are the most important cause of fixed airflow obstruction. As airflow obstruction worsens, the rate of lung emptying is slowed and the interval between inspirations does not allow expiration to the relaxation volume of the lungs. This leads to pulmonary hyperinflation, which initially only occurs during exercise, but later is also seen at rest. Hyperinflation contributes to the discomfort associated with airflow obstruction by flattening the diaphragm and placing it at a mechanical disadvantage. In advanced COPD, airflow obstruction, damaged bronchioles and alveoli and pulmonary vascular abnormalities lead to impaired gas exchange. This results in hypoxemia and eventually hypercapnia. Hypoxemia is initially present only during exercise but occurs at rest as the disease progresses. Inequality in the ventilation/perfusion ratio (VAQ) is the major mechanism behind hypoxemia in COPD. Pulmonary hypertension develops late in the course of COPD, usually after the development of severe hypoxemia. It is the most common cardiovascular complication of COPD and can result in cor pulmonale, or right sided heart failure. Hypoxemia plays the primary role in the development of pulmonary hypertension by causing vasoconstriction of the pulmonary arteries and by promoting vessel wall remodeling. Destruction of the pulmonary capillary bed by emphysema further contributes by increasing the pressure required to perfuse the pulmonary vascular bed. Cor pulmonale is associated with venous stasis and thrombosis that may result in pulmonary embolism. Another important systemic effect is the progressive loss of skeletal muscle mass, which contributes to exercise limitations and declining health status.

Definition

- COPD is a group of lung diseases that reduce the ability of the lungs to oxygenate the blood.
- Emphysema and chronic bronchitis are the main diseases that make up COPD.

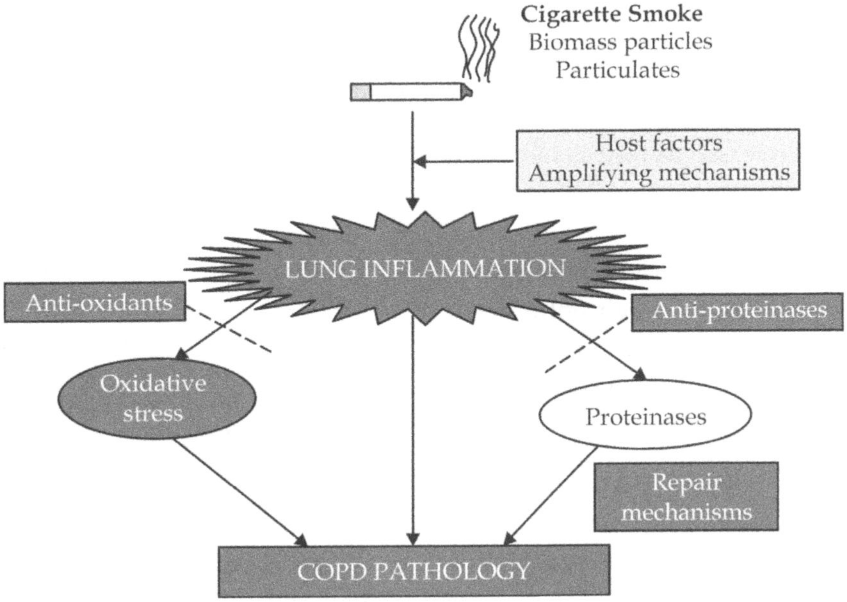

Fig 3-1: Pathophysiology of COPD

Chronic Bronchitis

Chronic bronchitis (Fig 3-2) is inflammation and irritation of the airways of the bronchial tubes, which is characterized by thickening of the muscular wall of the large airways and an increase in size and activity of mucous glands.

This leads to airway narrowing and blockage by thick, tenacious secretions result in productive cough that is present for a period of 3 months in each of 2 consecutive years.

Symptoms

- Chronic cough
- Mucus production (sputum)
- Shortness of breath
- Fever (due to infection)
- Mild wheezing
- Chest pain

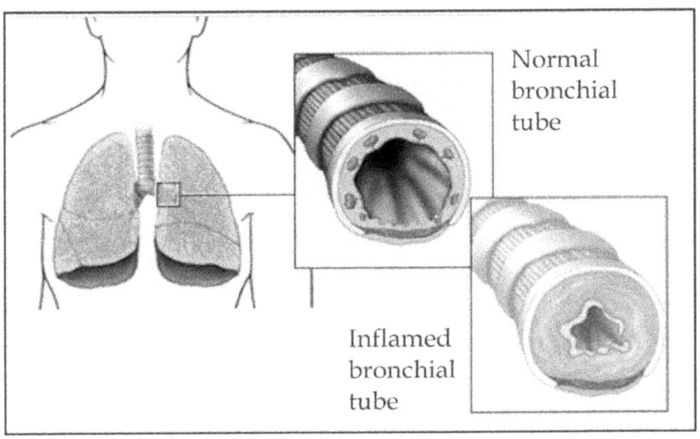

Fig 3-2: Normal and inflamed bronchiole

Pathogenesis of Bronchitis

1. Susceptible individual exposed to trigger (e.g., cigarette smoke) initiate an inflammatory processes and several mediators are released as well as increased mucus secretion.
2. Risk of infection increase.
3. In severe cases, mucus plug the lung → difficulty in expiration air entrapment elasticity of alveoli decrease (+ infection) destruction of alveoli walls emphysema

Emphysema

- Emphysema develops over many years.
- It is an inflammation (edema) which is usually induced by cigarette smoke.
- The tiny air sacs within the lungs (alveoli) are gradually destroyed.
- As a result, the alveoli are not able to pick up enough oxygen (more and more short of breath).

Pathogenesis of Emphysema

- The exposure of a susceptible individual to noxious particles and gases (Cigarette smoke as well as other gases and particles) an inflammatory process.
- The predominant inflammatory cell is the neutrophil, macrophages and T-lymphocytes are increased in the various parts of the lungs and several mediators are released, including leukotriene B4, interleukin 8, and TNFα leading to sever inflammatory process and edema.
- Altered protease/antiprotease balance, at least in individuals with severe deficiency of alpha-1-antitrypsin (AAT), has been shown to predispose to emphysema. Individuals with severe deficiency of alpha1-antitrypsin may develop emphysema at an early age (fourth decade), in contrast to the "usual" emphysema, which typically begins in the sixth decade.

Symptoms

Initial symptoms include:

- Chronic coughing, which may be worse upon awakening.
- Increased production of mucus (which is actually a symptom of chronic bronchitis).
- Shortness of breath.
- Fatigue easily even with little physical exercise (stair climbing, walking).
- As the disease progresses: Shortness of breath may be present at rest.
- Some people with emphysema develop body changes; their chest begins to take on a "barrel-like" appearance as the lungs compensate for the loss of functioning tissue by expanding.
- Others develop a bluish color of the lips and nail beds, resulting from chronically low levels of oxygen in the blood.
- Some people with emphysema will develop heart failure that may lead to swelling in the lower extremities and increased fluid in the lungs.

Etiology of COPD

1. The most important cause is tobacco smoke.
2. It can also develop after exposure to chemicals or air pollution.
3. Deficiency of alpha-1-antitrypsin has been shown to predispose to emphysema.
4. Bronchitis is also can be caused by infection with a virus (less commonly with a bacteria or fungus).

Diagnosis of COPD

- Detailed medical history including family history of lung disease
- Physical exam
- Breathing tests and X-rays
- Special blood tests used for diagnosis of inherited emphysema. The test measures the concentration of alpha-1 antitrypsin in the blood.

Treatment of Chronic Obstructive Pulmonary Disease

Nonpharmacological Therapy

- Smoking cessation is the most effective strategy to reduce the risk of developing COPD and the only intervention proven to affect the long term decline in FEV1 and slow the progression of COPD.
- Pulmonary rehabilitation programs include exercise training along with smoking cessation, breathing exercises, optimal medical treatment, psychosocial support, and health education. Supplemental oxygen, nutritional support and psycho educational care (e.g., relaxation) are important adjuncts in a pulmonary rehabilitation program.
- One dose of the polyvalent pneumococcal vaccine is indicated for patients at any age with COPD; revaccination is recommended for patients older than 65 years if the first vaccination was more than 5 years earlier and the patient was younger than 65 years.

Pharmacological Therapy

Bronchodilators are the mainstay of treatment for symptomatic COPD. They reduce symptoms and improve exercise tolerance and quality of life. They can be used for relieving symptoms or on a scheduled basis to prevent or reduce symptoms. Bronchodilator drugs commonly used in COPD include beta 2-agonists, anticholinergics and theophylline. The choice depends on availability, individual response and preferences. The inhaled route is preferred, but attention must be paid to proper inhaler technique training. Long-acting inhaled bronchodilators are more effective and convenient but more expensive than short acting inhaled bronchodilators. Combination therapy improves efficacy and is preferred over increasing the dose of a single agent, especially since the dose response relationship using FEV1 as the outcome is relatively flat for single-agent therapy.

Sympathomimetics

Mechanism of action:

- β_2-Selective sympathomimetics cause relaxation of bronchial smooth muscle and bronchodilation by stimulating the enzyme adenylcyclase to increase the formation of cyclic adenosine monophosphate. They may also improve mucociliary clearance.
- Administration *via* metered dose inhaler (MDI) or dry powder inhaler is at least as effective as nebulisation therapy and is usually favoured for reasons of cost and convenience.
- Albuterol, Levalbuterol, Bitolterol, Pirbuterol, and Terbutaline are the preferred short acting agents because they have greater β_2 selectivity and longer durations of action than other short acting agents (Isoproterenol, Metaproterenol and Isoetharine). The inhalation route is preferred to the oral and parenteral routes in terms of both efficacy and adverse effects. Short-acting agents can be used for acute relief of symptoms or on a scheduled basis to prevent or reduce symptoms.
- Formoterol and Salmeterol are long acting inhaled β_2 agonists that are dosed every 12 hours on a scheduled basis and provide bronchodilation throughout the dosing interval. In 2007, formoterol and arformoterol became available in the United States as nebulized solutions. Long acting inhaled β_2-agonists should be considered when patients demonstrate a frequent need for short acting agents. They are also useful to decrease nocturnal symptoms and improve quality of life. They are not indicated for acute relief of symptoms.

Anticholinergics

Mechanism of action:

- When given by inhalation, anticholinergic agents produce bronchodilation by competitively inhibiting cholinergic receptors in bronchial smooth muscle. This activity blocks acetylcholine, with the net effect being a reduction in cyclic guanosine monophosphate, which normally acts to constrict bronchial smooth muscle.

- Ipratropium bromide has a slower onset of action than short acting β_2 agonists (15 to 20 minutes *vs* 5 minutes for albuterol). For this reason, it may be less suitable for as-needed use, but it is often prescribed in this manner. Ipratropium has a more prolonged bronchodilator effect than short-acting β_2-agonists. Its peak effect occurs in 1.5 to 2 hours and its duration is 4 to 6 hours. The recommended dose *via* MDI is two puffs four times a day with upward titration often to 24 puffs/day. It is also available as a solution for nebulisation. The most frequent patient complaints are dry mouth, nausea and occasionally, metallic taste. Because it is poorly absorbed systemically, anticholinergic side effects are uncommon (e.g., blurred vision, urinary retention, nausea and tachycardia).
- Tiotropium bromide is a long-acting agent that protects against cholinergic bronchoconstriction for more than 24 hours. Its onset of effect is within 30 minutes with a peak effect in 3 hours.

Combination of Anticholinergics and Sympathomimetics

Mechanism of action:

- The combination of an inhaled anticholinergic and β_2-agonist is often used, especially as the disease progresses and symptoms worsen over time. Combining bronchodilators with different mechanisms of action allows the lowest effective doses to be used and reduces adverse effects from individual agents. Combination of both short and long acting β_2 agonists with ipratropium has been shown to provide added symptomatic relief and improvements in pulmonary function.
- A combination product containing Albuterol and Ipratropium is available as an MDI for chronic maintenance therapy of COPD. Other similar combination products may become available in the future Methylxanthines.
- Theophylline and Aminophylline may produce bronchodilation by inhibition of phosphodiesterase (thereby increasing cyclic adenosine monophosphate levels), inhibition of calcium ion influx into smooth muscle, prostaglandin antagonism, stimulation of endogenous catecholamine's, adenosine receptor antagonism and inhibition of release of mediators from mast cells and leukocytes.
- Chronic theophylline use in COPD has been shown to produce improvements in lung function, including vital capacity and FEV1. Subjectively, theophylline has been shown to reduce dyspnoea, increase exercise tolerance and improve respiratory drive. Nonpulmonary effects that may contribute to better functional capacity include improved cardiac function and decreased pulmonary artery pressure.
- Methylxanthines are no longer considered first-line therapy for COPD. Inhaled bronchodilator therapy is preferred over theophylline for COPD because of theophylline risk for drug interactions and the interpatient variability in dosage requirements. Theophylline may be considered in patients who are intolerant or unable to use an inhaled bronchodilator. Methylxanthines may also be added to the regimen of patients who have not achieved an optimal clinical response to an inhaled Anticholinergic and β_2- agonist.
- As with other bronchodilators in COPD, parameters other than objective measurements such as FEV1 should be monitored to assess efficacy. Subjective parameters, such as perceived improvements in dyspnoea and exercise tolerance, are important in assessing the acceptability of Methylxanthines for COPD patients.
- Sustained release theophylline preparations improve patient compliance and achieve more consistent serum concentrations than

rapid release theophylline and aminophylline preparations.

- The role of theophylline in COPD is as maintenance therapy in non-acutely ill patients. Therapy can be initiated at 200 mg twice daily and titrated upward every 3 to 5 days to the target dose; most patients require daily doses of 390 to 900 mg.

Adverse effects: The most common adverse effects of theophylline include dyspepsia, nausea, vomiting, diarrhoea, headache, dizziness and tachycardia. Arrhythmias and seizures may occur, especially at toxic concentrations.

- Factors that may decrease theophylline clearance and lead to reduced dosage requirements include advanced age, bacterial or viral pneumonia, heart failure, liver dysfunction, hypoxemia from acute decompensation and use of drugs such as cimetidine, macrolides and fluoroquinolones antibiotics. Factors that may enhance theophylline clearance and result in the need for higher doses include tobacco and marijuana smoking, hyperthyroidism and use of drugs such as phenytoin, phenobarbital and rifampin.

Corticosteroids

Mechanism of action:

- The anti inflammatory mechanisms whereby corticosteroids exert their beneficial effect in COPD include reduction in capillary permeability to decrease mucus, inhibition of release of proteolytic enzymes from leukocytes and inhibition of prostaglandins.
- The clinical benefits of systemic corticosteroid therapy in the chronic management of COPD are often not evident, and there is a high risk of toxicity. Consequently, chronic, systemic corticosteroids should be avoided if possible.
- Appropriate situations to consider corticosteroids in COPD include (1) short-term systemic use for acute exacerbations; and (2) inhalation therapy for chronic stable COPD.
- The role of inhaled corticosteroids in COPD is controversial. Major clinical trials have failed to demonstrate any benefit from chronic treatment in modifying long-term decline in lung function. However, other important benefits have been observed in some patients, including a decrease in exacerbation frequency and improvements in overall health status.
- Consensus guidelines indicate that inhaled corticosteroid therapy should be considered for symptomatic patients with stage III or IV disease (FEV1 less than 50%) that experience repeated exacerbations despite bronchodilator therapy.

Adverse effects:

- Adverse effects of inhaled corticosteroids are relatively mild and include hoarseness, sore throat, oral candidiasis and skin bruising. Severe side effects such as adrenal suppression, osteoporosis and cataract formation are reported less frequently than with systemic corticosteroids, but clinicians should monitor patients receiving high dose chronic inhaled therapy.
- Several studies have shown an additive effect with the combination of inhaled corticosteroids and long acting bronchodilators. Combination therapy with salmeterol plus fluticasone or formoterol plus budesonide is associated with greater improvements in FEV1, health status and exacerbation frequency than either agent alone. The availability of combination inhalers makes administration of both drugs convenient and decreases the total number of inhalations needed daily.

Antibiotics

The role of bacterial infections in COPD exacerbations is controversial and there are limited data on the efficacy of antibiotics in treating COPD exacerbations. Recent studies suggest that bacteria cause 40% to 50% of acute exacerbations. Antibiotics should be used in patients with COPD exacerbations who have either of the following characteristics: (1) at least two of three cardinal symptoms: increased dyspnea, sputum volume, or sputum purulence; or (2) a severe exacerbation requiring mechanical ventilation. The predominant bacterial organisms in patients with mild exacerbations are *Streptococcus pneumoniae, Haemophilus influenzae* and *Moraxella catarrhalis*. In patients with more severe underlying COPD, other bacteria, such as enteric gram negative bacilli (*Escherichia coli, Klebsiella pneumoniae and Enterobacter cloacae and Pseudomonas aeruginosa*) may be more common. Selection of empiric antibiotic therapy should be based on the most likely organism(s) thought to be responsible for the infection and on local resistance patterns. This approach is based on risk factors found to be predictive of treatment failure or early relapse. Patients at risk for poor outcome are candidates for more aggressive initial antibiotic treatment. Antibiotic treatment for most patients should be maintained for 3 to 10 days, until the patient has been a febrile for 3 consecutive days. Exacerbations due to certain infecting organisms (*P. aeruginosa, E. cloacae, and methicillin-resistant Staphylococcus aureus*), while not common, require more lengthy courses of therapy (21 to 42 days) when they occur. If there is worsening clinical status or inadequate clinical response in 48 to 72 hours, re evaluate the patient, consider sputum Gram's stain and culture if not already obtained and adjust antimicrobial therapy. If Gram's stain and culture results are available, narrow the antibiotic therapy according to cultured organism(s) and sensitivities. If no cultures have been obtained, or cultures remain negative, consider additional antibiotics and/ or change to antibiotics with a broader spectrum of activity.

Oxygen

The goal of oxygen therapy is to maintain PaO_2 above 60 mm Hg (8 kPa) or SaO_2 above 90% in order to prevent tissue hypoxia and preserve cellular oxygenation. Increasing the PaO_2 much further confers little added benefit and may increase the risk of CO_2 retention, which may lead to respiratory acidosis. An arterial blood gas should be obtained after 1 to 2 hours to assess for hypercapnia. In advanced COPD, caution should be used since overly aggressive administration of oxygen to patients with chronic hypercapnia may result in respiratory depression and respiratory failure. In these patients, mild hypoxemia, rather than carbon dioxide accumulation, triggers their drive to breathe.

Pharmacological Therapy of COPD Exacerbations

An exacerbation is a sustained worsening of the patient's symptoms from his or her usual stable state that is beyond normal day to-day variations. It is acute in onset and sufficient to warrant a change in management. Commonly reported symptoms are worsening of dyspnea, increased sputum production and change in sputum color. The most common causes of an exacerbation are respiratory infection and air pollution, but the cause cannot be identified in about one-third of severe exacerbations. Treatment depends on the symptoms and severity of the exacerbation. Mild exacerbations can often be treated at home with an increase in bronchodilator therapy with or without oral corticosteroids. Antibiotics are indicated only if there are clinical signs of airway infection (e.g., increased volume and change in color of sputum and/or fever). Moderate to severe exacerbations require management in the emergency department or hospital. Management should consist of controlled oxygen therapy, bronchodilators, oral or intravenous corticosteroids, antibiotics if indicated and consideration of mechanical ventilation (non invasive or invasive).

Cystic Fibrosis

Cystic fibrosis (CF) is an inherited multi organ system disorder affecting children and an ever growing adult population. It is the most common life threatening genetic disease among Caucasians and the major cause of severe chronic lung disease and pancreatic insufficiency in children. The disease generally manifests as mucosal obstruction of exocrine glands caused by defective ion transport within epithelial cells. Due to the array of affected organ systems and complicated medical therapies, appropriate CF treatment necessitates multidisciplinary team collaboration.

Epidemiology and Etiology

In the United States, CF most commonly occurs in the Caucasian population, ranging from 1 in 1900 to 3700 individuals. CF is less common in Hispanics (1 in 9000), African Americans (1 in 15,000), and Asian Americans (1 in 32,000). CF is inherited as an autosomal recessive trait and approximately 1 in 25 Caucasians are heterozygous carriers. For example, offspring of a carrier couple (each parent being heterozygous) have a one in four chance of having the disease (homozygous), a one in two chance of being a carrier (heterozygous) and a one in four chance of receiving no trait. The gene mutation is found on the long arm of chromosome 7 and encodes for the cystic fibrosis transmembrane regulator (CFTR) protein, which functions as a chloride channel to transport water and electrolytes. Over 1000 mutations have been described in the CF gene; however, the F508 mutation is the most common and is present in 70% to 90% of CF patients in the United States.

Pathophysiology

CF is a disease of exocrine gland epithelial cells where CFTR (Cystic fibrosis transmembrane conductance regulator) is largely expressed. Normally, these cells transport chloride through CFTR chloride channels with sodium and water accompanying this flux across the cell membrane. CFTR is regulated by protein kinases in response to varying levels of the intracellular second messenger cyclic adenosine monophosphate (cAMP). CFTR also down regulates the epithelial sodium channel, regulates calcium activated chloride and potassium channels and may function in exocytosis and formation of plasma membrane molecular complexes and proteins important in inflammatory responses. In CF, the CFTR chloride channel is dysfunctional and usually results in decreased chloride secretion and increased sodium absorption, leading to altered viscosity of fluid excreted by the exocrine glands and mucosal obstruction.

Pulmonary System

Chronic lung disease is a hallmark of CF, leading to death in 90% of patients. Pulmonary disease is characterized by thick mucus secretions, impaired mucus clearance, chronic airway infection and colonization, obstruction and an exaggerated neutrophil dominated infla-mmatory response. Over time, chronic obstruction and inflammation lead to air trapping, atelectasis, mucus plugging, bronchiectasis, cystic lesions, pulmonary hypertension and eventual respiratory failure. In the United States CF population, pulmonary function declines at an average yearly rate of 2%, as measured by forced expiratory volume in 1 second (FEV1). The rate in an individual patient may be higher or lower depending on severity of CFTR dysfunction and comorbidities. Patients may show a slow steady decline over time, or they may have stable lung function for several years and then experience periods of sharp decline. In the upper airways, sinusitis and nasal polyps are also common, and microbial colonization is similar to that of the lungs. Bacterial pathogens are often acquired in an age dependent sequence and prevalence is tracked in the Cystic Fibrosis Foundation Patient Registry. Early infection is most often caused by *Staphylococcus aureus* and non typeable *Haemophilus influenzae* (and thus is not prevented by childhood *H. influenzae* type b immunization). *Pseudomonas aeruginosa* infection also occurs early in life and is the most significant CF pathogen among all age groups. *P. aeruginosa* expresses extracellular toxins that perpetuate lung inflammation. Mucoid strains of *P. aeruginosa* produce an alginate biofilm layer that interferes with antibiotic penetration. Other organisms identified later in the disease course include *Stenotrophomonas maltophilia, Alcaligenes xylosoxidans, Burkholderia cepacia,* fungi including Candida and Aspergillus species, and non tuberculous mycobacteria. Other organisms may also present chronically or intermittently.

Similarly, cultured organisms may represent an initial infection, chronic colonization, or microbial overgrowth in an acute exacerbation.

Gastrointestinal System

Gastrointestinal involvement may present initially as small bowel obstruction shortly after birth (known as meconium ileus) due to abnormally thick meconium that cannot be passed. Older CF patients may develop distal intestinal obstruction syndrome (DIOS), formerly called meconium ileus equivalent, which occurs due to fecal impaction in the terminal ileum and cecum. Maldigestion due to pancreatic enzyme insufficiency is present in about 85% to 90% of CF patients. Thick pancreatic secretions and cellular debris obstruct the pancreatic ducts and lead to fibrosis. Volume and concentration of pancreatic enzymes and bicarbonate are reduced, leading to maldigestion of fat and protein. Subsequently, absorption of fat soluble vitamins (A, D, E and K) is often impaired. Maldigestion is characterized by abdominal distention, numerous large foul smelling loose stools (steatorrhea), flatulence and malnourishment and hunger despite voracious intake. Maldigestion is progressive and may develop later in a previously pancreatic sufficient patient. Other complications may include gastroesophageal reflux, dysmotility, intussusception, volvulus, atresia, rectal prolapse and complications related to corrective surgery for meconium ileus. Hepatobiliary disease occurs due to bile duct obstruction from abnormal bile composition and flow. Hepatomegaly, splenomegaly, and cholecystitis may be present. Hepatic steatosis may also be present due to effects of malnutrition. The progression from cholestasis (impaired bile flow) to portal fibrosis and to focal and multilobar cirrhosis, esophageal varices and portal hypertension takes several years. Many patients are compensated and asymptomatic but may be susceptible to acute decompensation in the event of extrinsic hepatic insult from viruses, medications, or other factors.

Endocrine System

CF related diabetes shares characteristics of both type 1 and type 2 diabetes mellitus but is categorized separately. The primary cause of CFRD is insulin deficiency resulting from both reduced functional pancreatic islet cells and increased islet amyloid deposition. Insulin secretion is delayed in response to glucose challenge, and absolute insulin secretion over time is reduced. Some insulin resistance may also be present in CFRD; however, sensitivity may be increased in CF patients without diabetes. Postprandial hyperglycemia is common, but because some basal insulin secretion is maintained, fasting hyperglycemia is less severe and ketosis is rare. Diet, acute and chronic infection, and corticosteroid use lead to fluctuations in glucose tolerance over time. CFRD is associated with greater nutritional failure, increased pulmonary disease and earlier death. The average age of onset is 18 to 21 years; but under diagnosis is thought to be common.

Reproductive System

CF patients often experience delayed puberty. In females, menarche occurs 18 months later than average, and menstrual irregularity is common. Females also have reduced fertility due to increased viscosity of cervical mucus. Due to increasing life expectancy, pregnancy is becoming more common; however, outcomes depend on pre-partum nutritional and pulmonary status. Almost all males with CF are azoospermic due to congenital absence of the vas deferens with resultant obstruction; however, conception still occurs occasionally. Conception can also occur through application of assisted reproductive technologies.

Musculoskeletal System

Several factors contribute to development of bone disease in CF: (1) malabsorption of vitamins D and K and calcium; (2) poor nutrition and decreased body mass; (3) physical inactivity; (4) corticosteroid therapy; and (5) delayed puberty. Chronic pulmonary infection, through release of inflammatory cytokines, can cause increased bone resorption and decreased formation. Osteopenia, osteoporosis, pathologic fractures, and kyphosis can then occur. Episodic or chronic arthritis and hypertrophic pulmonary osteoarthropathy may also occur due to immune complex formation in response to chronic inflammation. Digital clubbing is commonly observed and is a marker for hypoxia.

Hematologic System

Anemia may be present in some patients due to impaired erythropoietin regulation, nutritional factors (vitamin E and iron malabsorption), or chronic inflammation. With chronic pulmonary disease, increased cytokine production can lead to shortened red blood cell survival, reduced erythropoietin response and impaired mobilization of iron stores. Additionally, with chronic hypoxia, normal hemoglobin and hematocrit values may represent relative anemia. Increased red blood cell production is a physiologic response to hypoxia; however, this response may be blunted in CF and may result in symptoms of anemia despite normal lab values. Abnormal bleeding may also be observed as a result of vitamin K malabsorption or antibiotic associated depletion of gastro-intestinal flora and vitamin K synthesis.

Miscellaneous Systems

Abnormally high concentrations of sodium and chloride are found in sweat due to impaired reabsorption within the sweat duct from loss of CFTR channels. Patients are usually asymptomatic (other than a characteristic salty taste to the skin). In rare instances such as hot weather or excessive sweating during physical activity, patients may become dehydrated and experience symptoms of hyponatremia (nausea, headache, lethargy and confusion). Similar CFTR defects are also seen in the salivary glands, manifested by increased saliva viscosity and impaired salivary function.

Clinical Presentation and Diagnosis

Diagnosis

Diagnosis of CF is based on two separate elevated sweat chloride concentrations of greater than or equal to 60 mEq/L (or mmol/L) obtained through pilocarpine iontophoresis (referred to as the "sweat test"). Genetic testing (CFTR mutation analysis) may be performed to confirm the diagnosis, screen in utero, or detect carrier status. More than 70% of diagnoses are made by 12 months of age and almost all are made by age 12.

Clinical Presentation of Cystic Fibrosis

General

- CF is usually diagnosed in neonates or during early childhood. Some patients may present much later in life due to less severe symptoms or misdiagnosis.

Symptoms

- Pulmonary symptoms may include chronic cough, sputum production and decreased exercise tolerance.
- Patients with intestinal obstruction may complain of abdominal pain, abdominal distention, and/or decreased bowel movements.
- Maldigestion may be manifested by the presence of numerous large foul smelling loose stools (steatorrhea) and flatulence.
- Patients with vitamin A deficiency may report visual disturbances, night blindness, and dry skin.
- Acute infection may be marked by increased cough, changes in sputum (darker and thicker), dyspnea and fever.

Signs

- Signs of obstructive airway disease include tachypnea, dyspnea, cyanosis, wheezes, crackles, sternal retractions, digital clubbing and barrel chest.
- Infants and children with maldigestion may have evidence of failure to thrive (below age-based normals in both height and weight), and adults may be near or below their ideal body weight despite apparent adequate caloric intake.
- Salty taste to the skin may be noticed.
- Biliary cirrhosis may be asymptomatic or evidenced by hepatomegaly, splenomegaly, or prolonged bleeding.
- Recurrent pancreatitis (usually in pancreatic-sufficient patients) may present with episodes of epigastric abdominal pain, persistent vomiting and fever.

Laboratory Tests

- Maldigestion results in decreased serum levels of the fatsoluble vitamins A, D, E and K.
- Decreased vitamin K levels may result in elevated prothrombin time (PT) and International Normalized Ratio (INR).
- There may be glucose intolerance, as indicated by blood glucose between 140 and 199 mg/d*l* (7.77 to 11.04 mmol/L) 2 hours after an oral glucose tolerance test.
- Patients may have CFRD, as indicated by blood glucose greater than or equal to 200 mg/d*l* (greater than or equal to 11.1 mmol/*l*) 2 hours after an oral glucose tolerance test.
- Some patients have CFRD with fasting hyperglycemia (fasting blood glucose greater than or equal to 126 mg/dl (greater than or equal to 6.99 mmol/L) regardless of the post-glucose challenge level).
- Serum aspartate aminotransferase, alanine aminotransferase, alkaline phosphatase, glutamyl transferase, and bilirubin may be elevated in patients with hepotobiliary disease.
- White blood cell count with an associated increase in polymorphonuclear (PMN) leukocytes and bands may occur in acute pulmonary infection; however, infection may occur without these laboratory abnormalities.

Other Tests

- Pulmonary function tests (PFTs) indicate decreased forced expiratory volume in 1 second (FEV1), decreased forced vital capacity (FVC) and increased residual volume. Values are typically worse during acute pulmonary exacerbations.
- Chest X ray or chest computed tomography scan may reveal infiltrates, atelectasis, bronchiectasis and mucus plugging.
- Intestinal obstruction may be manifested as meconium ileus, distal intestinal obstruction syndrome, or intussusception on abdominal X ray or computed tomography scan. Rectal prolapse may be noted on physical exam.
- In recurrent pneumonia or sinusitis, *P. aeruginosa, S. aureus, S. maltophilia,* and other CF related organisms may be isolated in sputum, throat, or sinus cultures.

Clinical Course and Prognosis

Life expectancy has greatly increased from a predicted survival of 16 years in 1970 to more than 40 years for patients born in the 1990s. The average age of patients in the Cystic Fibrosis Foundation Registry is now more than 16 years, and many are living far into adulthood. More than 40% of CF patients in the 2004 Registry annual report are over 18 years old and the oldest is age 74. The clinical course varies greatly among patients because of the multiple genetic mutations and heterogeneous profile of the F508 mutation. Some patients develop severe lung disease early in childhood and reach end stage lung disease by their teens, whereas others maintain near normal lung function into adulthood. Newly diagnosed adults tend to present with chronic respiratory symptoms but usually have milder lung disease, less frequent Pseudomonas infection, and less severe pancreatic insufficiency. Life expectancy and quality of life are expected to continue to increase with aggressive treatment strategies, lung transplantation when appropriate and new therapies being investigated.

Treatment

Desired Outcomes

Therapeutic outcomes in CF care relate to both chronic and acute treatment goals. With chronic management, the primary goals are to delay disease progression and optimize quality of life. Maximizing nutritional status through pancreatic enzyme replacement and vitamin and nutritional supplements is necessary for normal growth and development and for maintaining long-term lung function. Reduction of airway inflammation and infection and aggressive preventive therapies minimize acute pulmonary exacerbations and delay pulmonary decline. In pulmonary exacerbations, therapy is directed toward reducing acute airway inflammation and obstruction. This is accomplished through more aggressive air clearance regimens and antibiotic therapy with a goal of returning lung function to pre-exacerbation levels or greater.

General approach to treatment: The intensity of the daily chronic maintenance regimen varies based on patient age, baseline lung function, other organ system involvement, and social factors such as time available for therapy and patient selected care choices. Generally, with more severe lung disease and multi organ system involvement, therapies become more complicated and time intensive. Additionally, therapy is intensified when pulmonary symptoms are increased with acute exacerbations or even mild viral upper respiratory illness such as the common cold. The approach to treatment is best described by the organ system affected.

Nonpharmacological Therapy

Airway clearance therapy: Airway clearance therapy is a necessary routine for all CF patients to clear secretions and control infection, even at diagnosis prior to becoming symptomatic. Waiting until development of a first pneumonia or until daily symptoms are present delays benefits and may contribute to a faster pulmonary decline.The traditional form of chest physiotherapy (CPT) is known as percussion and postural drainage. Areas of the patient's chest, sides and back are rapidly "clapped" by hand in different patient positions, followed by cough or forced expiration to mobilize secretions. Patients may also be taught autogenic drainage, which consists of deep breathing exercises followed by forced cough. Several devices are also available to promote airway clearance. Flutter valve devices employ oscillating positive expiratory pressure (OPEP) to cause vibratory air flow obstruction and an internal percussive effect to mobilize secretions. Intrapulmonary percussive ventilation (IPV) provides continuous oscillating pressures during inhalation and exhalation. Finally, the most commonly used technique is high frequency chest compression (HFCC) with an inflatable vest that provides external oscillation. Vest therapy is often preferred by patients because they can independently perform the therapy even from an early age. If performed appropriately, airway clearance techniques provide similar clearance results, so choice should be based on patient preference and compliance. Airway clearance therapy is typically performed once or twice daily for maintenance care and is increased to three or four times per day for acute exacerbations.

Nutrition

Most CF patients have an increased caloric need due to increased energy expenditure through increased work of breathing and increased basal metabolism. Prevention of malnutrition requires early nutritional intervention. In patients with mild lung disease and well controlled absorption, required caloric intake is approximately 100% to 120% of the recommended daily allowance (RDA) for age. As lung disease progresses, caloric requirements increase. Nutrition in malnourished patients consists of baseline required calories plus additional calories for weight gain. Even with aggressive diet and oral supplements, the caloric requirement may not be achieved. Placement of a gastrostomy or jejunostomy tube to allow for nighttime bolus or continuous formula feeds in addition to day time meals may be required to meet caloric goals. Patients with continued malabsorption on appropriate pancreatic enzyme supplementation or diabetes are especially challenging due to their unique caloric needs. Collaboration with a dietician specially trained in CF nutrition is essential.

Pharmacological Therapy

Pulmonary System

Treating obstruction and inflammation: Airway clearance therapy is usually accompanied by bronchodilator treatment [albuterol (also known as salbutamol outside the United States) by nebulizer or metered-dose inhaler] to stimulate mucociliary clearance and prevent bronchospasm associated with other inhaled agents. A mucolytic agent may be administered to reduce sputum viscosity and enhance clearance. Dornase alfa (Pulmozyme®) is a recombinant human (rh) DNAase that selectively cleaves extracellular deoxyribonucleic acid (DNA). This DNA is released during neutrophil degradation and contributes to the high viscosity of CF sputum. Nebulization of dornase alfa 2.5 mg once or twice daily improves daily pulmonary symptoms and function, reduces pulmonary exacerbations, and improves quality of life. N-acetylcysteine and hypertonic saline are other mucolytic agents that are occasionally used; however, they are not preferred agents due to a greater incidence of bronchospasm and unpleasant odour and taste. Many patients with CF also have a reactive airways component or concurrent asthma and benefit from long acting β_2 agonists. Patients with recurrent wheezing or dyspnoea who have demonstrated improvement with albuterol should be considered for maintenance therapy, as should patients with bronchodilator responsive pulmonary function tests. Inhaled corticosteroids may also attenuate reactive airways and reduce airway inflammation in some patients. While many patients appear to respond clinically to these agents, clear benefit in CF has not been established. Drug delivery to the site of inflammation is limited by the severity of lung disease, which may prevent maximal efficacy in CF. CF patients who are on inhaled corticosteroids and/or long acting agonists should be advised to administer these medications after airway clearance therapies to optimize drug delivery. Montelukast, antihistamines, and/or intranasal steroids are sometimes used for CF patients with a reactive airways or allergic rhinitis component to their disease. Several systemic therapies aim at reducing airway inflammation. Long term oral corticosteroids, namely prednisone and prednisolone, have been shown to reduce airway inflammation and improve lung function; however, beneficial effects diminish upon discontinuation. Concern for long term adverse effects including diabetes, osteoporosis, cataracts, cushingoid effects, growth suppression, and infection limits their use as maintenance therapy. In clinical practice, systemic steroids may be added for short courses in acute exacerbations or for longer treatment of the allergic response to Aspergillus colonization (allergic bronchopulmonary aspergillosis or ABPA); however, dose and duration of therapy should be minimized. High dose ibuprofen to achieve peak concentrations of 50 to 100 μ/m*l* (243 to 485 μmol/L) has been shown to slow progression of disease. At high doses, Ibuprofen inhibits the lipoxygenase pathway, reducing neutrophil migration and function as well as release of lysosomal enzymes. At the lower concentrations achieved with analgesic dosing, neutrophil migration increases, and potentially increasing inflammation. The greatest benefit with high dose ibuprofen is in children 5 to 13 years of age with mild lung disease (FEV1 greater than 60%). A dose of 20 to 30 mg/kg given twice daily is usually needed to attain these levels, but serum concentration monitoring is necessary due to interpatient variability. Due to the need for therapeutic drug monitoring and concerns regarding long-term safety and tolerability, only a few CF centers currently prescribe high-dose ibuprofen. Azithromycin is a macrolide antibiotic commonly used in CF as an anti-inflammatory agent. The exact mechanism for this activity is unclear, but azithromycin has been shown to improve overall lung function. Proposed mechanisms include interference with Pseudomonas alginate biofilm production, bactericidal activity during stationary Pseudomonas growth, neutrophil inhibition, interleukin-8 reduction and reduction in sputum viscosity. Due to its long tissue half-life, azithromycin is typically dosed 3 days per week (Monday, Wednesday and Friday), with a dose of 500 mg for patients weighing at least 40 kg and 250 mg for patients weighing 25 to 39 kg. Alternatively, patients may take 500 mg or 250 mg either every day or only Monday through Friday, based on the same weight parameters. To minimize the risk of selecting for macrolide resistant non tuberculous mycobacteria, patients should have a screening acid fast bacillus sputum culture obtained prior to starting therapy and then every 6 months. Confirmed mycobacterial colonization is usually a contraindication to chronic azithromycin therapy.

Antibiotic Therapy

Antibiotic therapy is used in three distinct clinical settings within the course of CF. First, in early lung disease, the primary goals are to detect infection early and institute appropriate antibiotic therapy to eradicate infection and delay colonization. Second, once colonization is present, chronic maintenance antibiotics are used to suppress bacterial growth. Third, in acute exacerbations, intensive antibiotics are administered in an attempt to drastically reduce bacterial load and return lung function to pre-exacerbation levels or greater. Antibiotic selection is based on periodic culture and sensitivity data, typically covering all organisms identified over the preceding year. If no culture data are available, empiric antibiotics should cover the most likely organisms for the patient's age group. Due to altered pharmacokinetics and microorganism resistance, care must be taken to ensure that optimal doses are prescribed. Severity of pulmonary symptoms also guides selection of antibiotic regimens for treatment of acute exacerbations. If symptoms are recent in onset and/or mild in severity (e.g., slight increase in cough and sputum production without fever), patients may be treated with oral and inhaled antibiotics for 14 to 21 days on an outpatient basis. Out patient fluoroquinolone use is common among CF patients infected with *P aeruginosa*, even in children. Despite concerns regarding cartilage and tendon toxicity in animal studies, clinical practice has not shown an increased risk in children. To prevent development of resistance and promote synergy, inhaled tobramycin or colistin is usually added to an oral fluoroquinolone for *P. aeruginosa* coverage. Methicillin sensitive *S. aureus* (MSSA) may be treated with oral amoxicillin clavulanic acid, dicloxacillin, first- or second generation cephalosporins, trimethoprim sulfamethoxazole, or clindamycin, depending on sensitivity. Likewise, methicillin resistant *S. aureus* (MRSA) may be treated with oral trimethoprim sulfamethoxazole, clindamycin, minocycline, or linezolid. *H. influenzae* often produces-lactamases but can usually be treated with amoxicillin clavulanic acid, a cephalosporin, or trimethoprim-sulfamethoxazole. Oral trimethoprim-sulfamethoxazole or minocycline may be used to treat *S. maltophilia*. For more severe infections or patients failing outpatient therapy, intravenous (i.v) antibiotic therapy is started and continued for 2 to 3 weeks. Most patients are admitted to the hospital for initiation of i.v antibiotics; however, depending on the availability of home health services, patients may be discharged to finish their course or even receive their entire course at home. Typical regimens for severe infections include an antipseudomonal β-lactam plus an aminoglycoside for added synergy and delay of resistance development. Cephalosporins tend to be better tolerated and offer the benefit of administration every 8 hours. Extended-spectrum penicillins have been associated with a higher incidence of allergy. Aztreonam offers the added benefit of little cross reactivity in penicillin- or cephalosporin allergic patients; however, it has no gram-positive coverage. Meropenem should be reserved for organisms resistant to all other antibiotics to minimize development of resistance in the carbapenem drug class, as it is the last line of defense against extended spectrum -lactamase (ESBL) producing organisms. Intravenous tobramycin is generally the first-line aminoglycoside. Isolates are usually resistant to gentamicin, and amikacin is reserved for tobramycin resistant strains. In general, higher peak serum concentrations are targeted in CF. As a result, lower serum trough levels are desirable to reduce toxicity. Some centers use once daily aminoglycoside dosing to achieve higher peaks and minimize troughs. Since aminoglycosides exhibit concentration dependent killing, once daily dosing may optimize this effect; however, time below the minimum inhibitory concentration (MIC) is prolonged with once daily administration, possibly leading to loss of synergy for a substantial portion of the dosing interval. With once daily administration, tobramycin is typically dosed at 10 to 15 mg/kg per day and amikacin at 35 mg/kg per day. Long term studies are needed to examine the efficacy and resistance patterns associated with once-daily aminogly-cosides in the CF population. Routine use of once-daily aminoglycosides in CF is not recommended and should be limited to adults and older teens, in whom the time below the MIC can be minimized. Due to a shorter half-life, once-daily aminoglycoside dosing does not appear to be optimal for use in younger children. Most other serious gram negative infections are also treated with combination therapy. *S. maltophilia* is highly resistant and is most often treated with trimethoprim sulfamethoxazole or ticarcillin clavulanate. *A xylosoxidans* and *B. cepacia* are also highly resistant and may have minimal therapeutic options. In some cases, fluoroquinolones may be substituted for aminoglycosides based on sensitivity data or if renal dysfunction is present. Due to excellent bioavailability, oral fluoroquinolones, trimethoprim-sulfamethoxazole, minocycline and linezolid should be used whenever possible. Due to toxicity risk, colistin and chloramphenicol are reserved for life-threatening, highly resistant infections. Additional combinations of two or three drugs may be used for highly resistant organisms based on synergy studies that test susceptibility of different antibiotic combinations. Inpatient treatment of methicillin resistant *S. aureus* can consist of i.v vancomycin or oral agents as described above, depending on the severity of infection and concomitant organisms. IV vancomycin may also be converted to oral stepdown therapy upon discharge. Chronic maintenance antibiotic therapy may be used in patients with Pseudomonas colonization in an attempt to prevent bacterial overgrowth. Some centers advocate regular scheduled CF "clean-outs" with i.v or oral antibiotics regardless of symptoms. However, long term systemic antibiotics are not recommended due to emergence of resistant isolates. Chronic or rotating inhaled antibiotic maintenance therapy has become a more common practice for preventing, treating and suppressing *P. aeruginosa* colonization. Inhaled tobramycin (TOBI®) is typically administered to patients 6 years of age and older in alternating 28-day cycles of 300 mg nebulized twice daily, followed by a 28-day washout or "off" period to minimize development of resistance. Longterm intermittent administration improves pulmonary function, decreases microbial burden and reduces the need for hospitalization for i.v therapy. Due to minimal systemic absorption, pharmacokinetic monitoring is not necessary with normal renal function. Lower doses of nebulized tobramycin solution for injection have been used in younger children, and studies are underway using 300 mg twice daily in children under age 6. Nebulized colistin using the i.v formulation may be an option in patients with tobramycin resistant strains or intolerance to inhaled tobramycin. Due to an increased risk of bronchoconstriction after colistin inhalation, patients should pre treat with albuterol and administer the first doses under medical observation. Inhaled antibiotics are typically stopped during an acute exacerbation requiring i.v therapy. Drug delivery is reduced with increased sputum production and concomitant use of i.v aminoglycosides may increase risk of toxicity.

Pharmacokinetic Considerations

CF patients have larger volumes of distribution of many antibiotics due to an increased ratio of lean body mass to total body mass and lower fat stores. CF patients also have an enhanced total body clearance, although the exact mechanism has not been determined. Increased renal clearance, increased glomerular filtration rate, decreased protein binding, increased tubular secretion, decreased tubular reabsorption, extrarenal elimination and increased metabolism have all been proposed as possible reasons for the increased clearance. As a result of these pharmacokinetic changes, higher doses of aminoglycosides are needed to achieve target serum levels and promote adequate tissue penetration. Higher doses of β-lactam antibiotics are also needed to achieve and sustain levels above the MIC. Trimethoprim-sulfamethoxazole displays enhanced renal clearance and hepatic metabolism in the CF population. Fluoroquinolones and vancomycin have fewer pharmacokinetic deviations in the CF population; however, higher doses are typically needed to attain inhibitory serum and tissue concentrations against CF pathogens. Although most CF patients have shorter half-lives and larger volumes of distribution than non-CF patients, some patients exhibit decreased clearance. Possible causes include concomitant use of nephrotoxic medications, presence of diabetic nephropathy, history of transplantation (with immunosuppressant use and/or procedural hypoxic injury) and age related decline in renal function in older adult patients. Additionally, CF patients are repeatedly exposed to multiple courses of i.v aminoglycosides, which can result in decreased renal function. Evaluation of previous pharmacokinetic parameters and trends, along with incorporation of new health information, is key to providing appropriate dosage recommendations.

Gastrointestinal System

Pancreatic enzyme replacement is the mainstay of gastrointestinal therapy. Most enzyme products are formulated as capsules containing enteric coated microspheres or microtablets to avoid inactivation of enzymes in the acidic stomach; instead, they dissolve in the more alkaline environment of the duodenum. Capsules may be opened and the microbeads swallowed with food, as long as they are not chewed. A powder form is available for patients unable to swallow the capsules or microbeads, but bioavailability is poor. While products may contain similar enzyme ratios, they are not bioequivalent and cannot be substituted. Generic enzyme products generally display poor dissolution and should not be used. Pancreatic enzyme doses are initiated at 500 to 1000 unit/kg per meal of lipase component with half-doses given with snacks. Infants are typically started at 1500 to 2500 units of lipase per 120 m*l* of formula or breast milk. Capsules may be opened and beads divided to obtain appropriate doses.

Endocrine System

Patients with mild CFRD may be managed with dietary modification if their nutritional status will allow carbohydrate control. However, most patients present with poor nutrition and weight loss and require more aggressive treatment. Because CFRD results from insulin insufficiency, exogenous insulin replacement is required in most cases. Many patients can be successfully managed by meal coverage with short or rapid acting insulin (regular, lispro, or aspart) dosed by carbohydrate counting. Patients with fasting hyperglycemia or patients receiving nighttime tube feedings typically also require longer acting basal insulin. Regular home glucose monitoring is essential to appropriate therapy. Little information is available regarding use of oral antidiabetic agents in CFRD and routine use is not recommended.

Musculoskeletal System

CF patients with low bone mineral density and low serum vitamin D levels may improve bone health through supplemental vitamin D analogs beyond those found in standard CF vitamins. The optimal dose and analog have not been determined. For ergocalciferol, a minimum of 400 IU and 800 IU should be taken daily by infants and patients over 1 year of age, respectively. Total weekly doses of 12,000 IU for children less than 5 years of age and 50,000 IU for patients 5 years of age and older may be required to achieve target vitamin D concentrations. Supplemental calcium should be provided if 1300 to 1500 mg of elemental calcium intake cannot be achieved through diet. Antiresorptive agents (oral or i.v bisphosphonates) may be used to treat adult CF patients with osteoporosis. Remaining upright for 30 minutes may be difficult in patients needing to perform airway clearance therapy, so once weekly dosing should be considered. A high incidence of gastroesophageal reflux and presence of cirrhosis-associated esophageal varices may also complicate therapy and increase the risk of erosive esophagitis. i.v pamidronate, dosed at 30 mg every 3 months, has increased bone mineral density in adult CF patients. Studies using i.v bisphosphonates in children with CF are underway. Androgen replacement in male CF patients with documented hypogonadism may also benefit bone health but should be decided on an individual basis. Short courses of non steroidal anti inflammatory drugs (NSAIDs) can be used to treat CF-related arthritis and hypertrophic pulmonary osteoarthropathy. The impact on neutrophil recruitment in the lung with long term NSAID therapy at lower analgesic doses is unknown.

Future Direction of Therapy

Significant strides have been made in past decades with development of new therapies that have led to the ever lengthening CF life span. Since the discovery of the CF gene and the CFTR protein defect, research has focused on gene therapy as a way to restore normal CFTR function through DNA transfer. Pharmacological approaches are being investigated to correct dysfunctional CFTR by suppressing premature stop codons in the CFTR gene and to activate alternative chloride channels, effectively bypassing dysfunctional CFTR. Additional research is being conducted with anti inflammatory therapies, antipseudomonal vaccines, and development of exogenous cationic antimicrobial peptides to mimic those found naturally in the lung. Development of more effective systemic and inhaled antibiotic agents continues to be a major focus as well.

References

2007 NHLBI Morbidity and Mortality Chart Book (PDF). Retrieved 2008-06-06.

Agarwal R, Aggarwal AN, Gupta D, Jindal SK (2010). Inhaled corticosteroids *vs* placebo for preventing COPD exacerbations: a systematic review and metaregression of randomized controlled trials. *Chest.* **137(2):** 318-325.

Shapiro SD, Reilly JJ Jr., Rennard SI (2010). Chronic bronchitis and emphysema. In: Mason RJ, Broaddus VC, Martin TR *et al.*, Murray & Nadel's Textbook of Respiratory Medicine. 5th ed. Philadelphia, Pa: Saunders Elsevier; chap 39.

What is COPD?. National Heart Lung and Blood Institute. U.S. National Institutes of Health. June 1, 2010.

CHAPTER

Respiratory Stimulants 4

These are referred to as "respiratory stimulants," which are drugs or chemical substances used to stimulate the respiratory system or restore normal breathing when the lungs are unable to exhale enough carbon dioxide or absorb enough oxygen molecules.

The term "CNS stimulator" refers to a class of medications used to stimulate the body's central nervous system (CNS). They also stimulate the body's chemo receptors and vasomotor centre, which controls blood vessel diameter. Finally, because the medications act as irritants, they irritate the epithelial lining of air passages like the bronchi, trachea, and lungs, stimulating the respiratory system

These medications' main effects include global CNS stimulation or enhancement of particular brain processes. The majority of CNS stimulants have a broad activity that, in high doses, might cause convulsions. These medications encourage breathing and may be useful for resuscitative care in cases of fainting or coma. In order to boost the need to breathe, a respiratory stimulant is typically employed as noninvasive ventilation, which supports a patient's ventilation through the upper airways. The amount of air that is inhaled or exhaled during a typical breath is referred to as tidal volume. It functions by stimulating the central nervous system, which increases respiratory rate.

The patient may experience convulsions while still in a coma, however they do induce respiration in sub convulsive doses. It is more efficient and secure to use mechanical respiration assistance and other circulation-improving methods.

Analeptics play a very small part in therapeutics. They may be used in the following circumstances:

(a) As a temporary solution in hypnotic drug intoxication while mechanical ventilation is being implemented.

(b) Suffocation upon drowning and severe respiratory failure.

(c) Infants born prematurely with apnea.

(d) Inability to breathe on one's own after general anaesthesia.

Example of Respiratory Stimulant Drugs

Doxapram

The only respiratory stimulant used regularly for acute ventilatory failure is doxapram. Both directly and indirectly, by stimulating peripheral chemoreceptors, it functions as a stimulant of the respiratory centre.

Mechanism of Action: Produces respiratory stimulation in the medulla through peripheral carotid chemoreceptors, which propagates stimulation to other regions of the brain and spinal cord.

Pharmacokinetics Onset: 20-40 sec Duration: 5-12 min (single IV injection) Peak Plasma Time: 1-2 min Half-life: 3.4 hr (2.4-4.1 hr)

Some individuals with acute ventilatory failure brought on by flare-ups of chronic bronchitis are treated with doxapram. Maintaining the patient's alertness and ability to cough efficiently in order to clear bronchial secretions is the first objective in this scenario. A choice must be taken regarding whether mechanical ventilation is necessary if the patient doesn't improve with conservative treatment, and if not, whether doxapram should be tried. The choice is made after considering a number of variables, including previous experience, available resources in the area, the reason for the current worsening, and other medical criteria. Doxapram only adds a slight boost to ventilation, and mechanical ventilation is typically a preferable option for individuals with issues that are unlikely to go away in a few hours. Doxapram is a short-term solution that can be used to try to avoid mechanical ventilation or in individuals for whom mechanical ventilation would not be acceptable. It can decrease the increased respiratory depression that occurs after oxygen therapy. It should typically only be used on individuals who are sleepy or whose PaC02 has risen to above 10 kPa due to its negative effects (75 mmHg). Doxapram has occasionally been used to alleviate excessive sedation after intravenous diazepam for endoscopy or after general anaesthesia.

Side-effects Doxapram seems to have less side effects than medications with only central effects, like nikethamide. However, it does result in some generalised activation of the vasomotor centre and other parts of the central nervous system. A metallic taste, tachycardia, mild hypertension, excitement, trembling, and a generalised warm feeling are some of the side effects. Hallucinations and vomiting are more severe signs. Patients with epilepsy, severe hypertension, coronary artery disease, and those using monoamine oxidase inhibitors should not take it. It has made asthmatic subjects' bronchioles contract.

Dosages: 1–5 mg/kg, IV, in dogs and cats, or 1–2 drops under the tongue of apneic neonates. In adult horses, the dosage is 0.5–1 mg/kg, IV, while foals are dosed carefully at 0.02–0.05 mg/kg/min, IV

Caffeine

Mechanism of Action

Methylxanthine improves medullary respiratory centre sensitivity to carbon dioxide, promotes cAMP (cyclic adenosine monophosphate) buildup by inhibiting phosphodiesterase, and may prevent apnea by acting as an adenosine receptor antagonist. The CNS stimulant impact of these medications also helps to improve renal and circulatory function in canine cardiac asthma, as well as respiratory function.

Pharmacokinetics

- Half-Life: 72-96hr
- Peak plasma time: 30-120 min
- Peak plasma concentration: 1.5-1.8 mcg/mL
- Protein Bound: 17-36%
- Vd: 0.6-0.9 L/kg
- Metabolism: hepatic CYP1A2
- Excretion: Urine

Dose: Respiratory Failure Caffeine and sodium benzoate: 250 mg IV/IM once

These are approved for treatment of

- Respiratory depression following anaesthesia;
- Drug-induced central nervous system depression;
- Chronic obstructive lung disease associated with hypercapnia (high blood carbon dioxide level);
- Tiredness and sleepiness
- A respiratory condition
- Newborn apnea (cessation of breathing in newborn)

References

Tattersfield, A.E., McNicol, M.W. (1987). Respiratory Stimulants. In: Respiratory Disease. Treatment in Clinical Medicine. Springer, London. https://doi.org/10.1007/978-1-4471-3132-8_20

Part - II

Drugs Affecting Gastrointestinal Tract

CHAPTER

Drugs Used to Treat Peptic, Ulcer Disease

5

A circumscribed ulceration of the gastrointestinal mucosa occurring in areas exposed to acid and pepsin and most often caused by *Helicobacter pylori* infection.

Classification by Region/Location

Types and location of ulcers are shown in Fig 5-1.

Stomach (called gastric ulcer)

Meckel's Diverticulum (called Meckel's Diverticulum Ulcer)

Esophagus (called Esophageal ulcer)

Duodenal Ulcers

Most common in middle age peak 30-50 years

Male to female ratio – 4:1

Genetic link: 3x more common in 1st degree relatives

More common in patients with blood group O

Associated with increased serum pepsinogen

H. pylori infection common up to 95%

Gastric Ulcers

Common in late middle age, incidence increases with age.

Male to female ratio – 2:1.

More common in patients with blood group A.

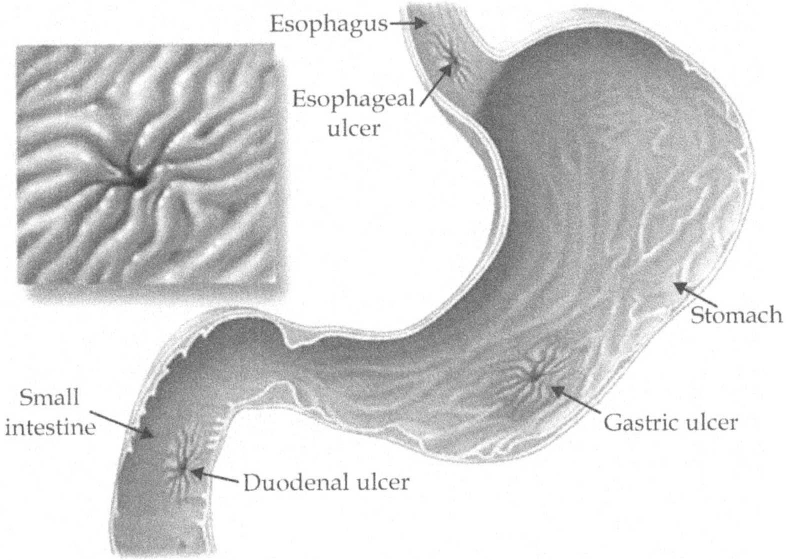

Fig 5-1: Types of ulcers and their location

Use of NSAIDs associated with a three to four fold increase in risk of gastric ulcer.

Less related to *H. pylori* (HP) than duodenal ulcers - about 80%.

10 - 20% of patients with a gastric ulcer have a concomitant duodenal ulcer.

Physiology of Acid Secretion

The physiology of acid secretion is shown in Fig 5-2. The parietal cell contains receptors for gastrin, histamine (H_2) and acetylcholine (muscarinic, M_3). When acetylcholine or gastrin bind to the parietal cell receptors, they cause an increase in cytosolic calcium, which in turn stimulates protein kinases that stimulate acid secretion from a H^+/K^+ ATPase (the proton pump) on the canalicular surface. In close proximity to the parietal cells are gut endocrine cells called enterochromaffin-like (ECL) cells. ECL cells have receptors for gastrin and acetylcholine and are the major source for histamine release. Histamine binds to the H_2 receptor on the parietal cell, resulting in activation of adenylyl cyclase, which increases intracellular cyclic adenosine monophosphate (cAMP). cAMP activates protein kinases that stimulate acid secretion by the H^+/K^+ ATPase. In humans, it is believed that the major effect of gastrin upon acid secretion is mediated indirectly through the release of histamine from ECL cells rather than through direct parietal cell stimulation.

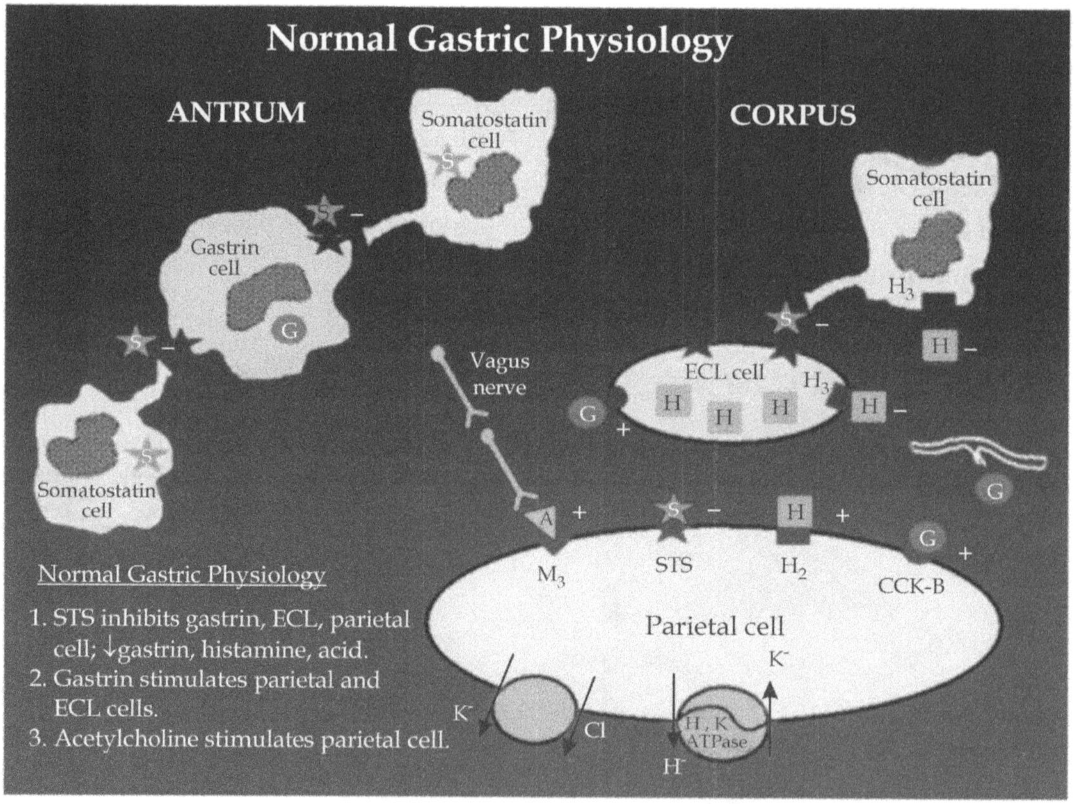

Fig 5-2: Physiology of acid secretion

Pathogenesis

With the exception of Zollinger–Ellison Syndrome (ZES) ulcer disease should be regarded as a reduction in normal mucosal defense. Considering the aggressive nature of acid pepsin environment, ulcer disease is surprisingly uncommon.

Factors such as *H. pylori*, NSAIDS disrupt these normal defense mechanisms. Smoking interferes with healing and secretory regulation.

The first line of defense is mucus and bicarbonate secretion. It stabilizes the pH between the lumen and the surface epithelial cells. Mucus gel in patients with HP infection was found to be structurally weak. Duodenal mucus as well as bicarbonate secretion is reduced in patients who smoke. The second line of defense is the intrinsic epithelial cell defense. The mucosal surface is a barrier to acid back diffusion thus maintaining normal intra cellular pH. The third line of defense is the rich mucosal blood flow. The blood provides a buffer for acid neutralization as well as adequate nutrition for the metabolic demand to maintain mucosal integrity.

Gastric mucosa has the ability to repair minor injury and therefore prevent progression to deep ulcers. Restitution has been evident within one hour. Peptic ulcers are produced by an imbalance between the gastro-duodenal mucosal defense mechanisms and damaging forces of gastric acid and pepsin, combined with superimposed injury from environmental or immunologic agents.

H. Pylori (HP) infection

H. pylori infection is present in almost all patients with duodenal ulcers and 70% cases with gastric ulcers.

Duodenal ulcers - Usually associated with gastritis confined to the antrum.

Gastric ulcers - Usually associated with pangastritis.

Mechanism: *Helico pylori* secretes urease (generates ammonia), protease (breaks down glycoprotein in the gastric mucus) or phospholipases. Bacterial lipopolysaccharide attracts inflammatory cells to the mucosa. Neutrophils release myeloperoxide. A bacterial platelet activating factor promotes thrombotic occlusion of surface capillaries. Mucosal damage allows leakage of tissue nutrients in the surface microenvironment, sustaining the bacillus. Damage of the protective mucosal layer. The epithelial cells are exposed to the damaging effect of acid-peptic digestion. Inflammation of the gastric mucosa.

Chronically inflamed mucosa more susceptible to acid peptic injury and prone to peptic ulceration. Ulcers occur at sites of chronic inflammation.

E.g., Antrum

Junction of antral and body fundic mucosa (division between the inflamed antral mucosa and normal acid secreting mucosa).

Pangastritis - When there is extensive gastritis, the ulcers are more proximally situated. In elderly patients gastric ulcers are more proximally situated as there is proximal migration of the antral-body mucosal junction.

NSAIDS

Nonsteroidal anti-inflammatory drugs (NSAIDs). Long term use of these pain relievers is the second most common cause of ulcers. These drugs block prostaglandins; substances in the stomach that help maintain blood flow and protect the area from injury. Some people are more susceptible to this side effect of NSAIDs than others. These drugs include ibuprofen (Advil, Motrin), naproxen (Aleve) and ketoprofen (OrudisKT), as well as prescription drugs.

Other Factors Causing Peptic Ulcer

Peptic ulcer caused due to high gastrin level and excess acid production. Gastrinoma may cause multiple peptic ulceration as in Zollinger Ellison syndrome. There is increased parietal cell mass. Peptic ulcers caused due to impaired mucosal defense. The gastric acid and pepsin levels are normal and no *H.pylori* are present. Repeated use of corticosteroid in high dose. Cigarette smoking impair healing and favour recurrences. Alcoholic cirrhosis. Personality, psychological stress, ischemia.

Signs and Symptoms

Abdominal pain with a burning or gnawing sensation

Pain 2 - 3 hours after eating

Pain is often made worse by an empty stomach; night time pain is common

Pain may be relieved by antacids or milk

Heartburn

Indigestion (dyspepsia)

Belching

Nausea

Vomiting

Poor appetite

Weight loss

Risk Factors

Heredity

Older age

Chronic pain from any cause such as arthritis, fibromyalgia, repetitive stress injuries (like carpal tunnel syndrome), or persistent back pain, causing long-term use of aspirin or NSAIDs

Alcohol abuse

Diabetes may increase your risk of having *H. pylori*

Lifestyle factors, including chronic stress, coffee drinking (even decaf), and smoking, may make you more susceptible to damage from NSAIDs or *H. pylori* if you are a carrier of this organism. But these factors do not cause an ulcer on their own.

Cigarette smoking

Complications

Gastrointestinal bleeding

Perforation

Penetration

Scarring and swelling due to ulcers causes narrowing in the duodenum and gastric outlet obstruction. Patient often presents with severe vomiting.

Cancer

Differential Diagnosis

Neoplasm of the stomach

Pancreatitis

Pancreatic cancer

Diverticulitis

Nonnuclear dyspepsia (also called functional dyspepsia)

Cholecystitis

Gastritis

GERD

Diagnostic Plan

Stool for fecal occult blood.

Lab tests: CBC (R/O bleeding), liver function test, amylase and lipase.

H. Pylori can be diagnosed by urea breath test, blood test, stool antigen assays and rapid urease test on a biopsy sample.

Upper GI Endoscopy.

Treatment

The treatment of ulcers are showin in Fig 5-3.

1. **Neutralization of gastric acid / Antacids**
   - **(a)** ***Systemic:*** Sodium bicarbonate ($NaHCO_3$)
   - **(b)** ***Non-Systemic:*** Magnesium hydroxide, Magnesium trisilicate, Aluminum hydroxide gel , Magaldrate calcium
2. **Reduction of gastric acid**
   - (a) *H_2 Anti Histamines:* Cimetidine, Ranitidine
   - (b) *Proton Pump Inhibitors:* Omeprazole, Lansoprazole, Pantoprazole, Rabeprazole
   - (c) *Anti Cholinergics:* Pirenzepine, Propantheline, Oxyphenonium
   - (di) *Prostaglandin Analogues:* Misoprostol

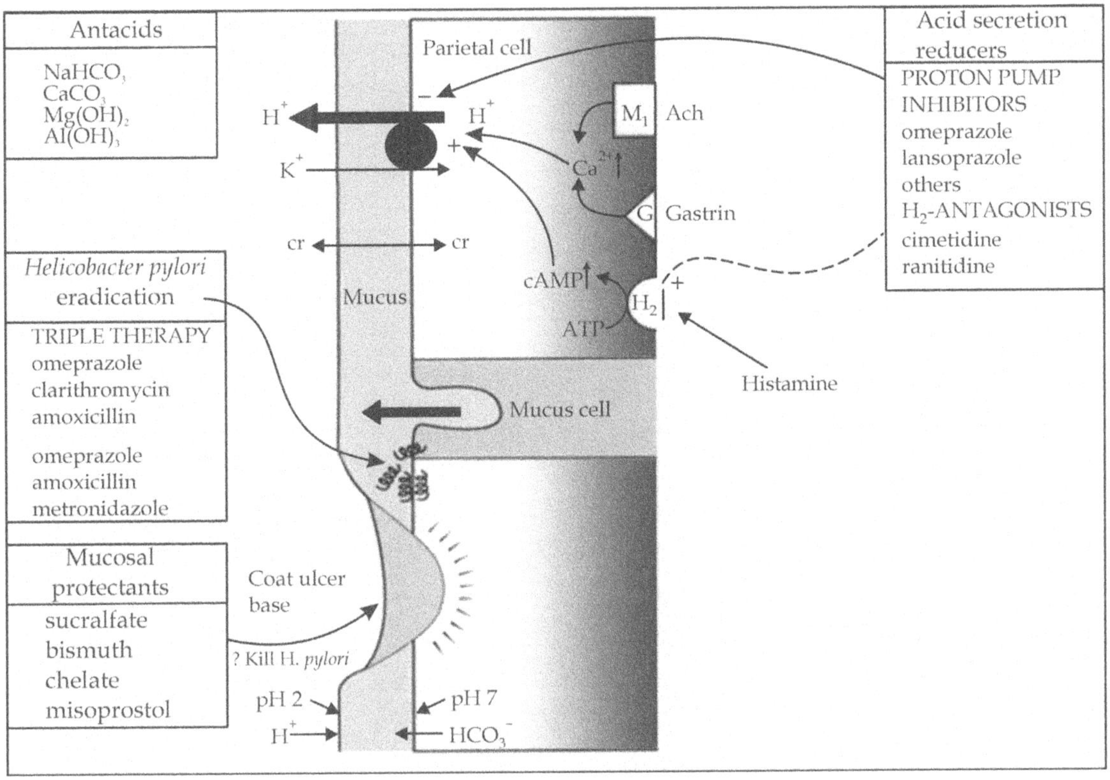

Fig 5-3: Sites of action of antiulcer drugs

3. **Mucosal protective agents:** Sucralfate, Colloidal bismuth sub citrate
4. **Ulcer healing**: Carbenoxolone sodium
5. **Anti-*H.pylori* drugs**: Amoxicillin, Clarithromycin, Metronidazole, Tinidazole Tetracycline

Neutralization of Gastric Acid/ Antacids

Antacids (Fig 5-4) either directly neutralize acidity, increasing the pH, or reversibly reduce or block the secretion of acid by gastric cells to reduce acidity in the stomach. When gastric hydrochloric acid reaches the nerves in the gastrointestinal mucosa, they signal pain to the central nervous system. This happens when these nerves are exposed. In addition to the reduction of gastric acidity, antacids also alter the profile of prostaglandins produced by gastroduodenal mucosa and this may promote mucosal healing and be related to its therapeutic effect.

Drug Types

- Sodium bicarbonate (Alka Seltzer)
- Calcium carbonate (Tums)
- Magnesium hydroxide
- Aluminum hydroxide (Amphojel)

Sodium bicarbonate: (E.g., baking soda, Alka Seltzer). It reacts rapidly with HCl to produce carbon dioxide and NaCl. Formation of carbon dioxide results in gastric distention and belching. Unreacted alkali is readily absorbed, potentially causing metabolic alkalosis when given in high doses or to patients with renal insufficiency.

Calcium carbonate: (E.g., Tums, Os-Cal). It is less soluble and reacts more slowly than sodium bicarbonate with HCl to form carbon dioxide and $CaCl_2$. Like sodium bicarbonate, calcium

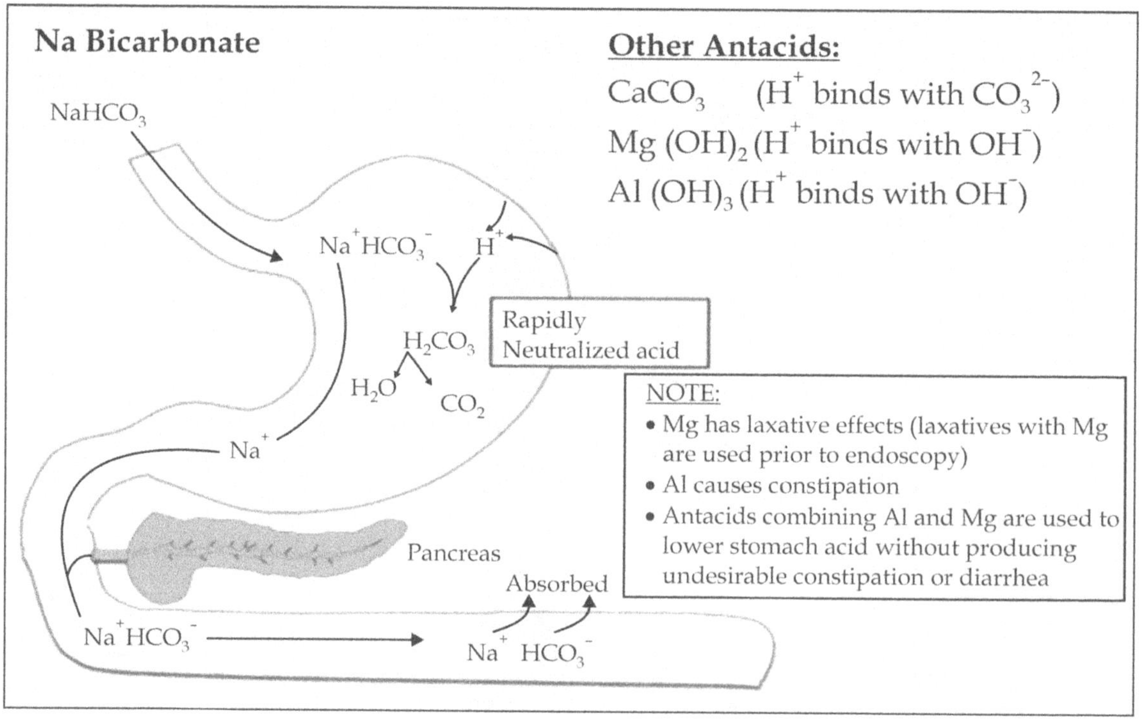

Fig 5-4: Antacids action

carbonate may cause belching or metabolic alkalosis. Calcium carbonate is used for a number of other indications apart from its antacid properties. Excessive doses of either sodium bicarbonate or calcium carbonate with calcium-containing dairy products can lead to hypercalcemia, renal insufficiency and metabolic alkalosis (milk-alkali syndrome).

Magnesium hydroxide or Aluminum hydroxide: These react slowly with HCl to form magnesium chloride or aluminum chloride and water. Because no gas is generated, belching does not occur. Metabolic alkalosis is also uncommon because of the efficiency of the neutralization reaction. Because unabsorbed magnesium salts may cause an osmotic diarrhea and aluminum salts may cause constipation, these agents are commonly administered together in proprietary formulations (e.g., Gelusil, Maalox, Mylanta) to minimize the impact upon bowel function.

Drug interactions: May affect the absorption of other medications by binding the drug, or by altering a drug's pH-dependent solubility (e.g., tetracyclines, flouroquinolone, itraconazole, iron).

Reduction of Gastric Acid

H_2-Receptor Antagonists

Histamine (H_2) antagonists (Fig 5-5) or blockers have been used for many years to treat peptic ulcer disease and symptoms of gastroesophageal reflux disease (GERD). Doses are often increased to two to four times normal when treating more severe cases of GERD.

Drugs: Cimetidine (Tagamet), Famotidine (Pepcid), Nizatidine (Axid), Ranitidine (Zantac)

Mechanism of Action

The H_2 antagonists are competitive antagonists of histamine at the parietal cell H_2 receptor. They suppress the normal secretion of acid by parietal cells and the meal-stimulated secretion of acid. They accomplish this by two mechanisms: Histamine released by ECL cells in the stomach is blocked from binding on parietal cell

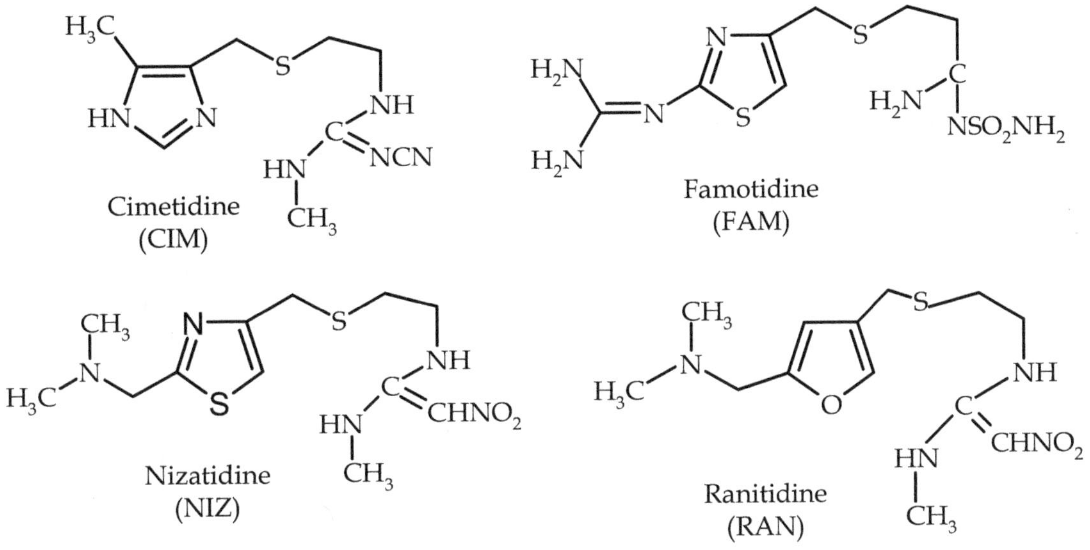

Fig 5-5: H_2-Receptor antagonists

H_2 receptors, which stimulate acid secretion; therefore, other substances that promote acid secretion (such as gastrin and acetylcholine) have a reduced effect on parietal cells when the H_2 receptors are blocked.

Chemistry and Pharmacokinetics

H_2 antagonists in clinical use: Cimetidine, ranitidine, famotidine and nizatidine. All four agents are rapidly absorbed from the intestine. Cimetidine, ranitidine, and famotidine undergo first-pass hepatic metabolism resulting in a bioavailability of approximately 50%. Nizatidine has little first pass metabolism and a bioavailability of almost 100%. The serum half-lives of the four agents range from 1.1–4 hours; however, duration of action depends on the dose.

H_2 antagonists are cleared by a combination of hepatic metabolism, glomerular filtration and renal tubular secretion. Dose reduction is required in patients with moderate to severe renal (and possibly severe hepatic) insufficiency.

Dosage

Ranitidine (Zantac)

Bolus i.v Dosing: 50 mg i.v q 6-8 hr, Continuous i.v Dosing: 6.25 mg/hr i.v, Oral Dosing: 150 mg P.O bid

Cimetidine (Tagamet)

Bolus parenteral dosing: 300 mg i.v or i.m q 6 hr, Continuous i.v Dosing: 37.5 mg/hr.

Oral Dosing: 400 mg PO bid

Famotidine (Pepcid)

Oral dosing: 20 to 40 mg PO bid

Nizatidine (Axid)

Oral dosing: 150 mg PO bid

Adverse Effects

Gynecomastia has been reported in patients who have been treated with cimetidine for one month or longer, reversible impotence. Impotence has been reported with the use of famotidine, ranitidine and nizatidine. Disturbances usually occur within two weeks of initiation of treatment and include the following reactions: confusion, disorientation, agitation, hostility, delirium, hallucinations, somnolence, mental status changes, psychosis, or paranoia.

Clinical Uses

Gastrointestinal conditions.

Peptic ulcer disease (PUD)

Gastroesophageal reflux disease (GERD/GORD)

Dyspepsia

Prevention of stress ulcer (a specific indication of ranitidine)

Drug Interactions

Drug interactions in this class occur mainly because of the inhibition of the cytochrome P450 system (CYP450). Cimetidine inhibits the CYP450 system which results in drug interactions. The most clinically significant drug interactions are with drugs that have a narrow therapeutic window. These drugs include phenytoin, theophylline and warfarin. Clinical significance of other drug interactions is unknown. Ranitidine also inhibits the CYP450 system but to a lesser degree than cimetidine. Drug interactions with ranitidine have been reported in case reports, but it is unknown if there is a causal relationship. Both nizatidine and famotidine do not inhibit the P450 system. Thus, these two agents do not cause drug interactions with drugs that are metabolized through the cytochrome P450 system.

All H_2 antagonists create an alkaline environment in the stomach that may interfere with the H_2 receptor antagonists. Absorption of certain drugs. Cimetidine and ranitidine have been shown to inhibit renal procainamide clearance *via* inhibition of tubular secretion. Clinical comparisons of these drugs listed in Table 5-1.

Proton Pump Inhibitors (PPIs)

The proton pump inhibitors are shown in Fig 5-6.

Table 5-1: Clinical comparisons of H_2 receptor blockers

Drug	Relative Potency	Inhibition for 10 hr	Usual dose for acute ulcer	Usual dose for GERD	Usual dose for prevention of stress related bleeding
Cimetidine	1	400-800 mg	800 mg HS or 400 mg bid	800 mg bid	50 mg/hr continuous infusion
Ranitidine	4-10 x	150 mg	300 mg HS or 150 mg bid	150 mg bid	6.2 mg/hr continuous infusion or 50 mg i.v every 6-8 hr
Nizatidine	4-10 x	150 mg	300 mg HS or 150 mg bid	150 mg bid	Not available
Famotidine	20-50 x	20 mg	40 mg HS or 20 mg bid	20 mg bid	20 mg i.v every 12 hr

BID, twice daily; HS, bedtime

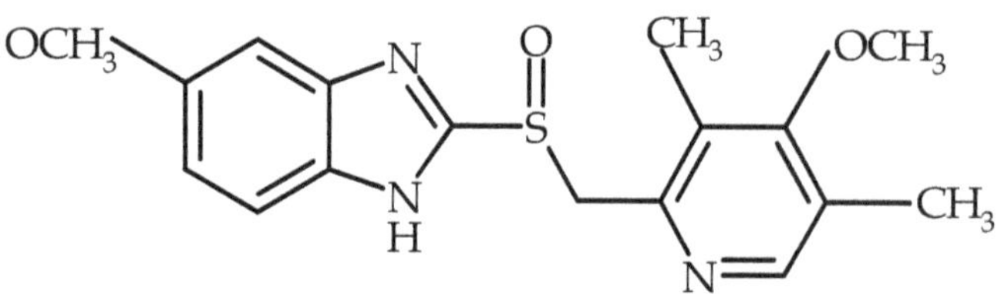

Omeprazole (OM)

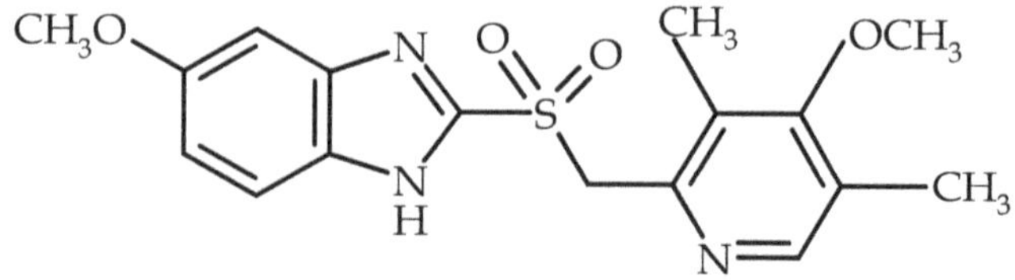

Omeprazole sulphone (OMS)

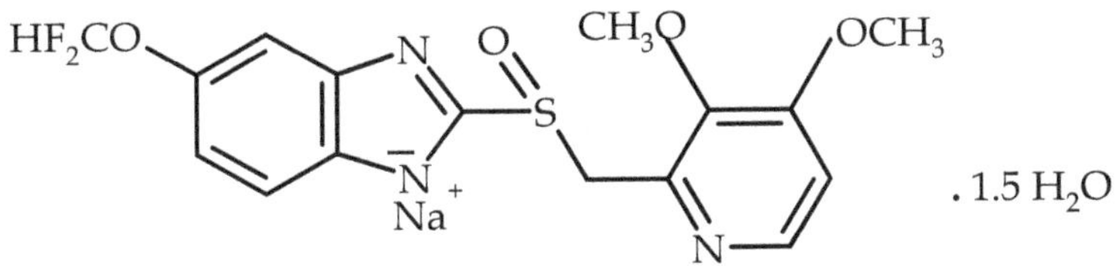

Pantoprazole sodium (PANa)

Fig 5-6: Proton pump inhibitors

Mechanism of Action

Proton pump inhibitors act by irreversibly blocking the hydrogen/potassium adenosine triphosphatase enzyme system (the H^+/K^+ ATPase, or more common gastric proton pump) of the gastric parietal cells. The proton pump is the terminal stage in gastric acid secretion, being directly responsible for secreting H^+ ions into the gastric lumen, making it an ideal target for inhibiting acid secretion. ("Irreversibility" refers to the effect on a single copy of the enzyme; the effect on the overall human digestive system is reversible, as the enzymes are naturally destroyed and replaced with new copies).

Targeting the terminal step in acid production, as well as the irreversible nature of the inhibition, results in a class of drugs that are significantly more effective than H_2 antagonists and reduce gastric acid secretion by up to 99%.

The proton pump inhibitors are given in an inactive form. The inactive form is neutrally charged (lipophilic) and readily crosses cell membranes into intracellular compartments (like the parietal cell canaliculus) that have acidic environments. In an acid environment, the inactive drug is protonated and rearranges into its active form.

Pharmacokinetics

The rate of omeprazole absorption, however, is decreased by concomitant food intake. In addition, the absorption of lansoprazole and esomeprazole is decreased and delayed by food.

It has been reported that these pharmacokinetic effects, however, have no significant impact on efficacy.

The elimination half-life of proton pump inhibitors ranges from 0.5–2 hours, however the effect of a single dose on acid secretion usually persists up to 2–3 days. This is because of accumulation of the drug in parietal cell canaliculi and the irreversible nature of proton pump inhibition.

Examples of proton pump inhibitors

Clinically used proton pump inhibitors:

Omeprazole (brand names: Losec, Prilosec, Zegerid, Ocid, Lomac, Omepral, Omez)

Lansoprazole (brand names: Prevacid, Zoton, Inhibitol, Levant, Lupizole)

Dexlansoprazole (brand name: Kapidex, Dexilant)

Esomeprazole (brand names: Nexium, Esotrex)

Pantoprazole (brand names: Protonix, Somac, Pantoloc, Pantozol, Zurcal, Zentro, Pan)

Rabeprazole (brand names: Zechin, Rabecid, Nzole-D).

Clinical Uses

Dyspepsia

Gastroesophageal reflux disease (GERD)

Peptic ulcer disease (PUD)

H. pylori–Associated ulcers

NSAIDs-Associated ulcers

Prevention of rebleeding from PUD

Non ulcer dyspepsia

Prevention of stress related mucosal bleeding

Gastrinoma and other hypersecretory conditions: Zollinger-Ellison syndrome

Adverse Effects

The most common side effects of proton pump inhibitors are headache, diarrhoea, constipation, abdominal pain, nausea, subnormal vit. B_{12} levels, Respiratory and enteric infections and rash.

Nevertheless, proton pump inhibitors generally are well tolerated. High doses and long-term use (1 year or longer) may increase the risk of osteoporosis-related fractures of the hip, wrist, or spine. Therefore, it is important to use the lowest doses and shortest duration of treatment necessary for the condition being treated.

Drug Interactions

Proton pump inhibitors interact with few drugs. The absorption into the body of some drugs is affected by the presence of acid in the stomach, and because PPIs reduce acid in the stomach, they may affect the absorption of these drugs. Specifically, PPIs reduce the absorption and concentration in the blood of ketoconazole (Nizoral) and increase the absorption and concentration of digoxin (Lanoxin). This may lead to reduced effectiveness of ketoconazole and an increase in digoxin toxicity.

Proton pump inhibitors can reduce the breakdown of some drugs by the liver and lead to an increase in their concentration in the blood. Omeprazole (Prilosec) is more likely than the other PPIs to reduce the breakdown of drugs by the liver. For example, omeprazole (Prilosec) may increase the concentration in the blood of diazepam (Valium), warfarin (Coumadin) and phenytoin (Dilantin).

Prostaglandin Analogues

The Prostaglandin Analogues are shown in Fig 5-7.

The term "cytoprotection" was coined by Jacobsonllfi and Robert" to denote the phenomenon by which the administration of prostaglandins confers gastric mucosa protection from ethanol, strong acids, strong alkali, or harmful physical agents. In the "cytoprotected" animals, the gastric mucosa remains remarkably intact after instillation of these agents which normally cause severe damage". In the present context, "cytoprotection" is used to mean protection of the gastric mucosa from gross or histologic damage. An agent is said to have a cytoprotective effect if it protects against damage at doses that are lower than the threshold dose for inhibition of acid secretion. Prostaglandins are one of several classes of compounds with cytoprotective action (Table 5-2).

Chemistry and Pharmacokinetics

Prostaglandins are 20-carbon oxygenated fatty acids. They are synthesized from dietary essential fatty acids through the action of cyclooxygenase. This cyclooxygenase pathway also results in the synthesis of prostacyclin and thromboxanes. All the prostaglandins have a cyclopentane ring, and, depending on the structure of the ring, they are classified as prostaglandin A, B, C, D, E and F. The compounds also have upper and lower carbon side-chains. Depending on the number of double-bonds present in the upper and lower side-chains, the prostaglandins are further designated 1, 2, and 3. The prostaglandins of

Misoprostol
$C_{22}H_{38}O_5$

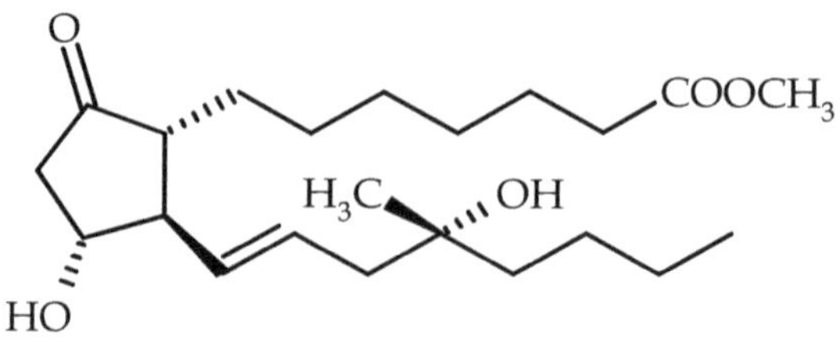

Fig 5-7: Misoprostol

medical interest are of the E-type and the important molecules are prostaglandin E l-3, i.e., PGE-1, PGE-2 and PGE-3. Analogues of PGE-1 and the naturally occurring PGE-2 have been developed for possible clinical use. To date, only three prostaglandin analogues have been subjected to double-blind controlled clinical trials. These are Misoprostil, Enprostil and Orbaprostil .

Table 5-2: Cytoprotective agents

Drugs
Prostaglandins
Colloidal bismuth
Carbenoxolone
Sucralfate
Mechanism of cytoprotection
Bicarbonate secretion
Reduction in H^+ back diffusion
Mucus secretion
Increased blood flow
Rapid renewal of surface epithelial cells

Two mechanisms of action in healing ulcers are proposed for these drugs:

1. Inhibition of acid secretion (antisecretory effect); and
2. Cytoprotective effect which can occur at doses lower than the antisecretory dose. It appears that antisecretory doses are required to heal ulcers, although cytoprotective doses may protect against aspirin injury.

Naturally occurring prostaglandins have very short half-lives in the blood and are rapidly inactivated by enzymes in human tissue. The synthetic prostaglandin analogues resist rapid degradation and, when administered orally, are effective in inhibiting acid secretion stimulated by histamine, pentagastrin or food for up to 2 hours. Although their precise mechanism of action in inhibiting acid secretion is unknown, the compounds do not interact with the cell-surface receptors for histamine, gastrin, or acetylcholine. They also do not appear to interfere with the activity of the H^+/K^+ ATPase.

Clinical Uses

More than 3,000 patients in 20 countries have been enrolled in controlled ulcer trials of Misoprostil and Enprostil. Misoprostil, administered at a dose of 200 mg 4 times daily, causes endoscopic duodenal ulcer healing at 4 weeks in 63% of patients, compared to the healing rate for cimetidine of 72%. In studies comparing Enprostil (70 mg, twice daily), duodenal ulcer healing rates at 4 weeks were 40% for placebo, 75% for cimetidine and 80% for Enprostil. In a European study, comparing Orbaprostil with placebo, the 4-week healing rates of duodenal ulcer were 67% and 40%, respectively. Both Misoprostil and Enprostil have also been shown to heal over 80% of gastric ulcers in patients treated for 6 to 8 weeks. In erosive gastro duodenal disease, low doses of prostaglandins have been shown convincingly to prevent gastric mucosal damage and gastrointestinal blood loss in subjects receiving aspirin and non steroidal anti inflammatory drugs.

The clinical applications and implications of prostaglandin therapy in patients with acid peptic disease are summarized in Table 5-3.

Table 5-3: Prostaglandin therapy in acid peptic disease

Useful compounds
PGE-1 (Misoprostol)
PGE -2 (Enprostil, Orbaprostil)
Mechanism of action
Inhibition of acid secretion
Cytoprotection
Clinical efficacy
Similar to H_2 receptor antagonist
May be useful in erosive gastritis
Side effects
Diarrhoea
Uterine bleeding
Abortifacient property
PGE-1= Prostaglandin E-1

Side Effects

The major side effect of prostaglandin therapy is diarrhoea. Some 30% to 40% of patients will experience some loosening of their stool but diarrhoea occurs only in about 5%. The diarrhoea in most cases has been transient and has stopped despite continued administration of the drug. In less than 0.5% of patients, prostaglandin analogues have to be stopped because of severe diarrhoea. The other two side effects of prostaglandins are uterine bleeding and the potential for spontaneous abortions. In West German study in which 56 women received two 400 mg doses of Misoprostol 5 hours apart on the evenings before a scheduled abortion, 6 (11%) had partial or total abortion. This potential abortifacient property of prostaglandins is of major concern both in terms of danger to pregnant women and in terms of potential abuse by those wanting to terminate pregnancy.

Mucosal Protective Agents

The gastro duodenal mucosa has evolved a number of defense mechanisms to protect itself against the noxious effects of acid and pepsin. Both mucus and epithelial cell-cell tight junctions restrict back diffusion of acid and pepsin. Epithelial bicarbonate secretion establishes a pH gradient within the mucous layer in which the pH ranges from 7 at the mucosal surface to 1–2 in the gastric lumen. Blood flow carries bicarbonate and vital nutrients to surface cells. Areas of injured epithelium are quickly repaired by restitution, a process in which migration of cells from gland neck cells seals small erosions to re-establish intact epithelium. Mucosal prostaglandins appear to be important in stimulating mucus and bicarbonate secretion and mucosal blood flow. A number of agents that potentiate these mucosal defense mechanisms are available for the prevention and treatment of acid peptic disorders.

Sucralfate

Sucralfate (Fig 5-8) is the basic aluminium salt of sulfated sucrose. In the acid medium of the stomach, it becomes viscous and adheres to defective mucosa to form a protective barrier. Thus, the ulcer bed becomes protected from continuing exposure to acid and pepsin. In addition to this barrier action, sucralfate possesses several potentially beneficial actions: (1) It neutralizes small amounts of acid (1 gm of sucralfate buffers 13 mEq of H^+ at pH 4.01); (2) It inhibits the action of pepsin; (3) It binds bile-salts, leading to their depletion from the gastric lumen; (4) It stimulates mucus secretion. Sucralfate is one of the drugs said to have "cytoprotective" properties. Whether this property is due solely to these listed actions of the drug, or whether it also has additional effects on the rate of renewal of surface epithelial cells and prostaglandin synthesis, has not been conclusively shown.

Sucralfate
$C_{12}H_{54}Al_{16}O_{25}S_8$

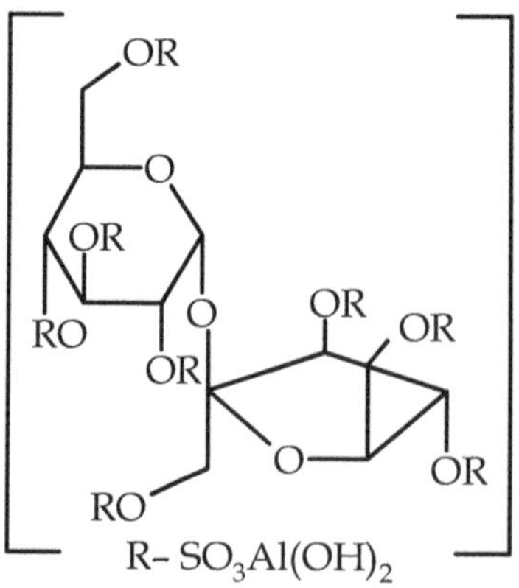

$[Al(OH)_3]$ X [H2o]Y
(X = 8 to 10 and Y = 22 to 31)

Fig 5-8: Sucralfate

Pharmacodynamics

Sulfated polysaccharide has been known for a long time to possess an inhibitory action on proteolytic activity of pepsin and a preventive action on experimental peptic ulcerations. Sucralfate, a disaccharide sulfate, has been shown to have a strong antipepsin and antiulcer action. Contrary to the more polymerized saccharides, sucralfate is devoid of any anti-coagulant activity. Moreover, it has been found that enhanced antiulcerogenic activity was more pronounced with the aluminum salt of the disaccharide sucralfate. *In vitro* and clinical studies have shown that sucralfate is not an antacid. Sucralfate has no effect on the cardiovascular system or central nervous system and on the hematopoietic system including blood coagulation factors.

Sucralfate produces distinct morphologic and functional changes in the normal gastric mucosa: mucus release, changes in ion transport and increased release of luminal prostaglandins. Several studies have shown that it can increase the synthesis and release of prostaglandin E_2 from the mucosa. This mechanism may in part explain its effective cytoprotective properties.

Results of *in vivo* and *in vitro* studies show that sucralfate produced an adherent and cytoprotective barrier at the ulcer site which resisted degradation by acid and pepsin.

Laboratory and clinical studies indicate that sucralfate promotes the healing of gastric and duodenal ulcers by a three-way action:

1. Formation of a chemical complex that binds to the ulcer site to establish a protective barrier.
2. Direct inhibition of the action of pepsin and bile.
3. Blockage of the back diffusion of gastric acid across the barrier.

Clinical Uses

Sucralfate is the first cytoprotective drug commercially available in the United States for the treatment of ulcer. Several studies have shown sucralfate therapy to be efficacious in the treatment of duodenal ulcer. Sucralfate has been demonstrated to heal gastric ulcers better than placebo (50% to 71% *vs* 13% to 40% at 4 weeks). Sucralfate therapy has also been shown to be effective in preventing gastric ulcer relapse. Sucralfate has been reported to protect against gastric mucosal injury by aspirin, ethanol and concentrated acid or concentrated alkali. In addition, sucralfate has been shown to be as effective as antacids in the prevention of stress ulceration in critically ill patients. The drug has also been used with reported efficacy in reflux esophagitis and gastritis.

Side Effects

Side effects are mild and infrequent with the use of sucralfate, occurring in less than 5% of patients. The reported side effects include constipation, dizziness, dry mouth, skin rash, headache, diarrhoea, nausea and abdominal discomfort. This safety factor makes sucralfate attractive to medical practitioners for long term maintenance use.

Colloidal Bismuth Compounds

Chemistry and Pharmacokinetics

Tripotassium dicitrate bismuthate, a colloidal bismuth compound, has been shown in rats to reduce the incidence of acute gastric ulcers induced by restraint, pyloric ligation, histamine, aspirin, or cortisone.

Pharmacodynamics

Colloidal bismuth compounds promote healing by binding to protein and necrotic debris at the ulcer base to form a coating impermeable to acid. An acid medium is presumably required for colloidal bismuth to chelate to the protein components of the ulcer bed to create an insoluble coagulum. Both light and electron microscopy have shown an increase in the number of bismuth-laden macrophages recruited to the area of injury. The influx of these macrophages may expedite healing and the microvilli of epithelial cells at the duodenal ulcer edge have been shown to return more quickly to their normal size in patients treated with bismuth as compared to patients treated with cimetidine. In addition to the protective coagulum which colloidal bismuth compounds form in the ulcer bed, other beneficial actions of these drugs have been cited. Tripotassium dicitra to bismuthate has been shown to have antipepsin activity and to stimulate the release of gastric mucus.

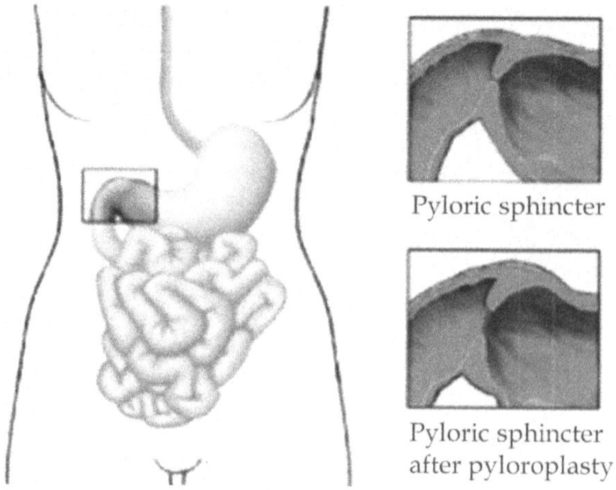

Fig 5-9: Pyloroplasty

Clinical Uses

In controlled clinical trials, colloidal bismuth compounds have been shown to cause healing rates comparable to cimetidine. The major difference between colloidal bismuth and cimetidine is the significantly lower ulcer recurrence rate after cessation of bismuth therapy relative to that observed of cessation of cimetidine. This observation suggests that colloidal bismuth may be capable of changing the natural history of duodenal ulcer disease in a manner not observed with cimetidine. Both bictropeptide bismuthate and tripotassium dicitratobismuthate have been shown to heal gastric ulcers significantly better than placebo (79% to 90% *vs* 30% to 35% at 4 weeks). While there is anticipation that colloidal bismuth may provide a more effective therapy of gastric ulcer than cimetidine, significantly large clinical trials are not available to sustain this assumption.

Adverse Effects

No serious side effects have been reported with the use of colloidal bismuth compounds. However, bismuth causes blackening of the stools which may be confused with melena. It also causes the tongue to turn black. Although innocuous, this side effect is cosmetically unappealing.

Surgery

People who do not respond to medication, or who develop complications may undergo surgery.

Vagotomy: Cutting the vagus nerve to interrupt messages sent from the brain to the stomach to reducing acid secretion.

Antrectomy: Remove the lower part of the stomach (antrum), which produces a hormone that stimulates the stomach to secrete digestive juices. A vagotomy is usually done in conjunction with an antrectomy.

Pyloroplasty: The opening into the duodenum and small intestine (pylorus) are enlarged, enabling contents to pass more freely from the stomach. May be performed along with a vagotomy (Fig 5-9).

References

Debas HT (1987). Peripheral regulation of gastric acid secretion, in Johnson LK (ed): Physiology of the Gastrointestinal Tract. New York, Raven Press, pp 931-946.

Debas HT, Mulholland MW (1986). New horizons in the pharmacologic management of peptic ulceration. *Am J Surg* **151:** 422-430.

Mendeloff A (1974). What has been happening to duodenal ulcer? *Gastroenterology* **67:** 1020-1022.

Price WA, Grizzle JA, Postlewait RW, *et al.,* (1970). Results of operation for duodenal ulcer. *Surg Gynecol Obstet* **131:** 233-244.

Monson RR, McMahon B (1969). Peptic ulcer in Massachusetts physicians. *N Ensl J Med* **281:** 11-15.

CHAPTER

Drugs Used in Constipation

6

Introduction

Constipation (also known as **costiveness, dyschezia and dyssynergic defaecation**) refers to bowel movements that are infrequent or hard to pass. Constipation is a common cause of painful defecation. Severe constipation includes obstipation (failure to pass stools or gas) and fecal impaction.

The definition of constipation includes the following:

- Infrequent bowel movements (typically three times or fewer per week)
- Difficulty during defecation (straining during more than 25% of bowel movements or a subjective sensation of hard stools), or
- The sensation of incomplete bowel evacuation.

Causes

The causes of constipation can be divided into congenital, primary and secondary. The most common cause is primary and not life threatening. In the elderly, causes include: insufficient dietary fiber intake, inadequate fluid intake, decreased physical activity, side effects of medications, hypothyroidism and obstruction by colorectal cancer.

Primary

Primary or functional constipation is ongoing symptoms for greater than six months not due to any underlying cause such as medication side effects or an underlying medical condition. It is not associated with abdominal pain thus distinguishing it from irritable bowel syndrome. It is the most common cause of constipation.

Diet

Constipation can be caused or exacerbated by a low fiber diet, low liquid intake, or dieting.

Medication

Many medications have constipation as a side effect. Some include (but are not limited to); opioids (e.g., common pain killers), diuretics, antidepressants, antihistamines, antispasmodics, anticonvulsants and aluminium antacids

Metabolic and Muscular

Metabolic and endocrine problems which may lead to constipation include: hypercalcemia, hypothyroidism, diabetes mellitus, cystic fibrosis and celiac disease. Constipation is also common in individuals with muscular and myotonic dystrophy.

Structural and Functional Abnormalities

Constipation has a number of structural (mechanical, morphological, anatomical) causes, including: spinal cord lesions, Parkinson's disease, colon cancer, anal fissures and pelvic floor dysfunction.

Drugs Associated with Constipation

Anticholinergics

Antidepressants

Antihistamines

- Anticonvulsants
- Antipsychotics
- Calcium channel blockers
- Clonidine (Catapress)
- Diuretics
- Iron
- Levodopa
- NSAIDs
- Opioids
- Psychotropics

Treatment

Non Pharmacological Measures

Physical Activity

Low physical activity is associated with a twofold increased risk of constipation. Patients who are sedentary are more likely to complain of constipation. Prolonged bed rest and immobility are often associated with constipation.

Bowel Training

Having a bowel movement may partly be a conditioned reflex. Most patients with a regular bowel pattern report that they empty their bowels at approximately the same time every day. The optimal times to have a bowel movement are soon after waking and soon after meals, when colonic transit is greatest. Most importantly, patients should recognize and promptly respond to the urge to defaecate. Failure to do so can result in a build up of faeces that continue to have water absorbed from them, making them increasingly more difficult to pass.

Toileting Position

A study on a small series of comparative positions for defaecation suggests that patients should be encouraged to adopt a "semi-squatting" position to defecate. Most people aren't good at squatting, but you can get closer to the proper position by using a footstool and leaning forward on the toilet. A pillow can also help brace abdominal muscles.

Fluid Intake

Fluid intake is the key to treatment. Patients should be advised to drink at least 8 glasses of water daily. In some patient fluids consists of coffee, tea or alcohol. This practice is counterproductive because of the diuretic effects of the products. They should decrease consumption of coffee, tea and alcohol as much as possible, and they should consume extra glass of water for every drink of coffee, tea or alcohol.

Fibre

Increasing fibre intake is commonly recommended for the initial treatment for constipation. This is can be accomplished by recommending the patients eat high fibre foods (fruits, vegetables) or taking fibre/bulk supplements Psyllium (ispaghula husk), methylcellulose, polycarbophil, or bran. However, patients must be counselled that they may need to continue such therapy for 2-3 months before they experience any measurable symptom relief. Despite the widespread use of fibre supplementation, this approach is effective in only a subset of patients and clinical trial evidence supporting the use of fibre intake is limited. Several studies that have looked at dietary fibre intake by people with chronic constipation did not find any difference in fiber intake compared with controls. It should be emphasized that a diet poor in fibre should be assumed to be the cause of chronic constipation. It was found that many patients with severe constipation deteriorated when dietary fibre is increased. In Germany 149 patients were treated with *Plantago ovata* seeds, 15-30 gm/day for a period of six weeks. They found that 80% of patients with slow transit and 63% of patients with a disorder of defecation did not improve with the additional dietary fibre. A prospective crossover trial comparing ispaghula husk with lactulose in Singapore resulted in a significantly higher bowel frequency and less bulking consistency. The adverse effects were similar. More patients preferred the use of lactulose (61.5%) over fibre (35.9%) to ease constipation.

Pharmacological Measures

The agents available for relieving constipation can be classified into bulk laxatives, osmotic laxatives,stimulant laxatives, other agents, and novel agents.

Drugs Available to Treat Constipation

Bulk Forming Laxatives

Psyllium (ispaghula husk), methylcellulose, polycarbophil, bran.

Osmotic Laxatives

Poorly absorbed sugars: lactulose, sorbitol, mannitol; Saline products; salts of magnesia, sulphate, phosphate, polyethylene glycol.

Stimulant Laxatives

Surface acting docusates, bile salts; Antraquinolones (Senna, cascara); Diphenylmethane-derivatives (e.g., bisacodyl); Ricinoleic acid (Castor oil).

Enemas

Phosphates

Lubricants

Liquid paraffin

Other Drugs

Probiotics: E.g. *Lactobacillus rhamnosus* GG, *L.plantarum* 299v, *L. casei* Shirota

Misoprostol, colchicine, botulinium toxin

Novel agents

Chloride Channel Activator

Lubiprostone

Seratonin 5HT$_4$-Receptor Agonists

Prucalopride

In many cases, constipation can be corrected by adherence to a fiber-rich (20 to 30 gm daily) diet, adequate fluid intake, appropriate bowel habits and training and avoidance of constipating drugs. However, the association between constipation and either fluid intake or exercise has not withstood scientific scrutiny. Constipation related to medications can be corrected by use of alternative drugs where possible, or adjustment of dosage. If Nonpharmacological measures alone are inadequate or unrealistic (e.g., because of elderly age or infirmity), they may be supplemented with bulk forming agents or osmotic laxatives. When stimulant laxatives are used, they should be administered at the lowest effective dosage and for the shortest period of time to avoid abuse.

In addition to treating constipation, laxatives frequently are employed before surgical, radiological and endoscopic procedures where an empty colon is desirable.

The terms laxatives, cathartics, purgatives, aperients and evacuants often are used interchangeably. There is a distinction, however, between laxation (the evacuation of formed fecal material from the rectum) and catharsis (the evacuation of unformed, usually watery fecal material from the entire colon). Most of the commonly used agents promote laxation, but some are actually cathartics that act as laxatives at low doses.

Laxatives generally act in one of the following ways:

1. Enhancing retention of intraluminal fluid by hydrophilic or osmotic mechanisms;
2. Decreasing net absorption of fluid by effects on small- and large-bowel fluid and electrolyte transport; or
3. Altering motility by either inhibiting segmenting (nonpropulsive) contractions or stimulating propulsive contractions.

A variety of laxatives, both osmotic agents and stimulants, increase the activity of NO synthase and the biosynthesis of platelet activating factor in the gut. Platelet activating factor is a phospholipid proinflammatory mediator that stimulates colonic secretion and GI motility. Nitric oxide also may stimulate intestinal secretion and inhibit segmenting contractions in the colon, thereby promoting laxation. Agents that reduce the expression of NO synthase or its activity can prevent the laxative effects of castor oil, cascara, and bisacodyl (but not senna), as well as magnesium sulfate.

Bulk-Forming Laxatives

The principal fibre and bulk forming laxatives are psyllium (ispaghula husk), methylcellulose, and polycarbophil. They increase the weight and water-absorbent properties of the stool, thereby increasing fecal bulk and accelerating luminal propulsion. Increased gastrointestional motility results in more rapid colonic transit time and increased frequency of bowel movements.

Osmotic Laxatives

The colon can neither concentrate nor dilute fecal fluid: fecal water is isotonic throughout the colon. Osmotic laxatives are soluble but nonabsorbable compounds that result in increased stool liquidity due to an obligate increase in fecal fluid.

Nonabsorbable Sugars or Salts

These agents may be used for the treatment of acute constipation or the prevention of chronic constipation. **Magnesium oxide (milk of magnesia)** is a commonly used osmotic laxative. **Sorbitol** and **lactulose** are nonabsorbable sugars that can be used to prevent or treat chronic constipation. These sugars are metabolized by colonic bacteria, producing severe flatulent and cramps. These hyperosmolar agents cause secretion of water into the intestinal lumen by osmotic activity. They have been associated with electrolyte imbalance within the colonic lumen and may precipitate hypokalaemia, fluid and salt overload and diarrhoea. They should be used carefully in patients with congestive heart failure and chronic renal insufficiency, with hypermagnesemia.

High doses of osmotically active agents produce prompt bowel evacuation (purgation) within 1–3 hours. The rapid movement of water into the distal small intestine and colon leads to a high volume of liquid stool followed by rapid relief of constipation. The most commonly used **purgatives** are **magnesium citrate** and **sodium phosphate.** These Hyperosmolar agents may lead to intravascular volume depletion and electrolyte fluctuations; hence they should not be used in patients who are frail, elderly, have renal insufficiency, or have significant cardiac disease.

Alternative hyperosmolar laxatives are sorbitol, lactulose and polyethylene glycol (PEG) 3350. Poor absorption of these agents may lead to flatulence and abdominal distension.

Balanced Polyethylene Glycol

Lavage solutions containing **polyethylene glycol (PEG)** are used for complete colonic cleansing prior to gastrointestinal endoscopic procedures. These balanced, isotonic solutions contain an inert, nonabsorbable, osmotically active sugar (PEG) with sodium sulfate, sodium chloride, sodium bicarbonate and potassium chloride. The solution is designed so that no significant intravascular fluid or electrolyte shifts occur. Therefore, they are safe for all patients. The solution should be ingested rapidly (4 L over 2–4 hours) to promote bowel cleansing. For treatment or prevention of chronic constipation, smaller doses of PEG powder may be mixed with water or juices (17 gm/8 oz) and ingested daily. In contrast to sorbitol or lactulose, PEG does not produce significant cramps or flatus.

Stimulant Laxatives

Stimulant laxatives (cathartics) induce bowel movements through a number of poorly understood mechanisms. Stimulant laxatives increase intestinal motility and secretions. They may be recommended if osmotic laxatives fail. They exert their effects *via* alteration of electrolyte transport by the intestinal mucosa; they also increase intestinal motor activity. They work within hour and may cause abdominal cramps. These include direct stimulation of the enteric nervous system and colonic electrolyte and fluid secretion. There has been concern that long-term use of cathartics could lead to dependence and destruction of the myenteric plexus, resulting in colonic atony and dilation. More recent research suggests that long-term use of these agents probably is safe in most patients. Cathartics may be required on a long-term basis, especially in patients who are neurologically impaired and in bed-bound patients in long-term care facilities.

Excessive use of these agents may be associated with side effects, including hypokalemia, protein losing enteropathy and salt overload . Melanosis coli may develop in patients who take stimulant laxatives containing anthra-quinolones. This does not lead to cancer development and it decreases over time on discontinuation of the responsible drug.

Stool Surfactant Agents (Softeners)

These agents soften stool material, permitting water and lipids to penetrate. They may be administered orally or rectally. Common agents include **docusate** (oral or enema) or **glycerine suppository.** In hospitalized patients, docusate is commonly prescribed to prevent constipation and minimize straining. **Mineral oil** is clear, viscous oil that lubricates fecal material, retarding water absorption from the stool. It is used to prevent and treat fecal impaction in young children and debilitated adults. It is not palatable but may be mixed with juices. Aspiration can result in a severe lipid pneumonitis. Long term use can impair absorption of fat soluble vitamins (A, D, E and K).

Anthraquinone Derivatives

Aloe, senna and **cascara** occur naturally in plants. These laxatives are poorly absorbed and after hydrolysis in the colon, produce a bowel movement in 6–12 hours when given orally and within 2 hours when given rectally. Chronic use leads to a characteristic brown pigmentation of the colon known as "melanosis coli". There has been some concern that these agents may be carcinogenic, but epidemiologic studies do not suggest a relationship to colorectal cancer.

Diphenylmethane Derivatives

Phenolphthalein, once among the most popular components of laxatives, has been withdrawn from the market in the United States because of potential carcinogenicity. **Oxyphenisatin,** another older drug, was withdrawn due to Hepatotoxicity. **Sodium picosulfate** (LUBRILAX, SUR-LAX) is a diphenylmethane derivative widely available outside of the United States. It is hydrolyzed by colonic bacteria to its active form, and hence acts locally only in the colon. Effective doses of the diphenylmethane derivatives vary as much as four- to eightfold in individual patients.

Bisacodyl is the only Diphenylmethane derivative available in the United States. It is marketed as an enteric coated preparation (DULCOLAX, CORRECTOL, others) and as a suppository for rectal administration. The usual oral daily dose of Bisacodyl is 10 to 15 mg for adults and 5 to 10 mg for children ages 6 to 12 years old. The drug requires hydrolysis by endogenous esterases in the bowel for activation, and so the laxative effects after an oral dose usually are not produced in less than 6 hours; taken at bedtime, it will produce its effect the next morning. Suppositories work much more rapidly, within 30 to 60 minutes.

Bisacodyl is mainly excreted in the stool; about 5% is absorbed and excreted in the urine as a Glucuronide. Over dosage can lead to catharsis and fluid and electrolyte deficits. The Diphenylmethane can damage the mucosa and initiate an inflammatory response in the small bowel and colon. To avoid drug activation in the stomach with consequent gastric irritation and cramping, patients should swallow tablets without chewing or crushing and avoid milk or antacid medications within 1 hour of the ingestion of Bisacodyl.

Castor Oil

An age-old home remedy, castor oil (PURGE, NEOLOID, others) is derived from the bean of the castor plant, *Ricinus communis*, and contains two well-known noxious ingredients: an extremely toxic protein, ricin, and an oil composed chiefly of the triglyceride of ricinoleic acid. The triglyceride is hydrolyzed in the small intestine by the action of lipases into glycerol and the active agent, ricinoleic acid, which acts primarily in the small intestine to stimulate secretion of fluid and electrolytes and speed intestinal transit. When taken on an empty stomach, as little as 4 ml of castor oil may produce a laxative effect within 1 to 3 hours; however, the usual dose for a cathartic effect is 15 to 60 ml for adults.

Other Drugs

Probiotics

Probiotics has been shown to improve the frequency in patients with constipation as lactic acid producing bacteria has been shown to improve intestinal motility and transit time. However, the trials reported in the studies did not reach statistical significance.

Colchicine and Misoprostol

Both of these agents accelerate colonic transit time and increase stool frequency in patients with constipation, although neither has been approved by the U.S. Food and Drug Administration for this indication.

Novel Agents

Chloride Channel Activator

Lubiprostone is a recently approved prostanoic acid derivative labelled for use in chronic constipation. It is reported to act by stimulating chloride channel opening in the intestine. This increases liquid secretion into the intestine and shortens intestinal transit time. The drug also delays gastric emptying, which may cause nausea. This is a locally acting chloride channel activator that enhances chloride rich intestinal fluid secretion. It works by activating type-2 chloride channels on the surface of intestinal epithelial cells to enhance intestinal fluid secretion and integrity of the epithelial tight junctions. It is the only agent for chronic constipation that is FDA approved for patients > 65 years. Its approval was based upon two placebo controlled trials. The recommended dose for chronic constipation is 24 mg twice daily. Those patients receiving active treatment achieved the primary endpoint (an increase in spontaneous bowel movements to at least three per week) during each week of observation. Corresponding improvements was observed for abdominal bloating, discomfort, stool frequency and straining. The use of this drug is best reserved for patients with severe constipation in whom other approaches have been unsuccessful.

Serotonin 5-HT$_4$-Receptor Agonists

Pharmacokinetics and Pharmacodynamics

Tegaserod is a serotonin 5-HT$_4$ partial agonist that resembles serotonin in structure. It has high affinity for 5-HT$_4$ receptors but no appreciable binding to 5-HT$_3$ or dopamine receptors. As discussed earlier, stimulation of 5-HT$_4$ receptors on the presynaptic terminal of submucosal intrinsic primary afferent nerves enhances the release of their neurotransmitters, including calcitonin gene related peptide, that stimulate second-order enteric neurons to promote the peristaltic reflex. These enteric neurons stimulate proximal bowel contraction (*via* acetylcholine and substance P) and distal bowel relaxation (*via* nitric oxide and vasoactive intestinal peptide). Tegaserod promotes gastric emptying and enhances small and large bowel transit but has no effect upon oesophageal motility. Stimulation of 5-HT$_4$ receptors also activates cAMP-dependent chloride secretion from the colon, leading to increased stool liquidity.

Tegaserod has a bioavailability of only 10%. It should be taken before meals because food further reduces bioavailability by 50%. The drug is metabolized both by gastric acid-catalyzed hydrolysis and hepatic Glucuronidation. Approximately 66% of drug is excreted unchanged in the feces and 33% as a metabolite in the urine. It should not be given to patients with severe hepatic or renal impairment.

Clinical Uses

Chronic Constipation

Tegaserod is approved for the treatment of patients with chronic constipation. In controlled trials, 40% of patients treated with tegaserod, 2–6 mg twice daily, had a significant increase in the number of spontaneous bowel movements compared with 25% receiving placebo. Responders also reported reduced bloating, straining, and stool hardness, and enhanced satisfaction. The effect of tegaserod on bowel activity is usually noted within 48 hours. Given its high cost, tegaserod should be reserved for patients with chronic constipation who have failed or are intolerant of other less expensive therapies.

Other Uses

The role of Tegaserod in the treatment of other gastrointestinal motility disorders, such as non ulcer dyspepsia, gastroparesis, and chronic constipation, is under investigation. The use of Tegaserod in the treatment of irritable bowel syndrome.

Adverse Effects

Tegaserod appears to be an extremely safe agent. diarrhoea occurs in 9% of patients within the first few days of treatment but resolves in the majority of patients. Less than 2% of patients discontinue the drug because of diarrhea. Although it is stated that the drug does not cross the blood-brain barrier (and does not affect central serotonin receptors), headache may occur.

Drug Interactions

Tegaserod has no known effects on cytochrome P450 enzymes and no reported drug interactions.

Prucalopride: This is a highly selective 5-HT_4 agonist that has been shown to increase bowel movements by initiating peristalsis in the intestines. It appears to be effective in the treatment of chronic constipation.

References

Locke GR, Pemberton JH and Phillips SF (2000). AGA Technical review on constipation. American Gastroenterological Association. *Gastroenterology* **119(6):** 1766-78.

Mohsen A and Wilkinson M (2007). Current management options for chronic constipation. *Prescriber* **118(21):** 23-38.

Wald A, Talley NJ and Bonis PAL. Etiology and evaluation of chronic constipation in adults.

CHAPTER 7

Emetics and Antiemetic Drugs

Emesis (Vomiting)

Vomiting (known medically as emesis) is the forceful expulsion of the contents of the stomach through the mouth and sometimes the nose. The feeling that one is about to vomit is called nausea, which usually precedes, but does not always lead to, vomiting.

Nausea and vomiting may be manifestations of many conditions. A useful mnemonic for remembering causes of nausea and vomiting is VOMIT.

Vestibular

Obstruction (opiates)

Mind (dysmotility)

Infection (irritation of gut)

Toxins (taste and other senses)

Rational (valuable) reflex

1. Prevention of ingestion of noxious substances (sight, smell, taste, texture)
2. Local gut reflexes stimulate vomiting e.g., toxins
3. Backup blood monitoring system, should former two protective reflexes be breached

Irrational reflexes

1. labyrinth
2. pregnancy
3. Visual nasties!

Control of Vomiting

1. Vomiting centre (VC)

   Respond to inputs from
   - Vestibular system.
   - Periphery (Pharynx, GIT).
   - Higher brain stem and cortical structures.
   - CTZ stimulation.
   - Muscarinic, histaminergic, serotoninergic receptors.
2. Chemoreceptor Trigger Zone (CTZ)
   - CTZ includes nucleus ambiguous, nucleus of solitary tract and nucleus of the vague.
   - CTZ is physiologically outside BBB (chemical stimuli in blood, CSF).
   - D_2, 5-HT_3 receptors.

There are five sources of the afferent input to the vomiting centre (Fig 7-1):

1. The chemoreceptor trigger zone has numerous dopamine D_2 receptors, serotonin -5-HT_3 receptors, opioid receptors, acetylcholine receptors.
2. Cranial nerve X which is activated when the pharynx is irritated, leading to a gag reflex.
3. The vestibular system which sends information to the brain *via* cranial nerve VIII (vestibulocochlear nerve). It plays a major role in motion sickness and is rich in muscarinic receptors and histamine H_1 receptors.
4. Vagal and enteric nervous system inputs that transmit information regarding the state of the gastrointestinal system. Irritation of the GI mucosa by chemotherapy, radiation,

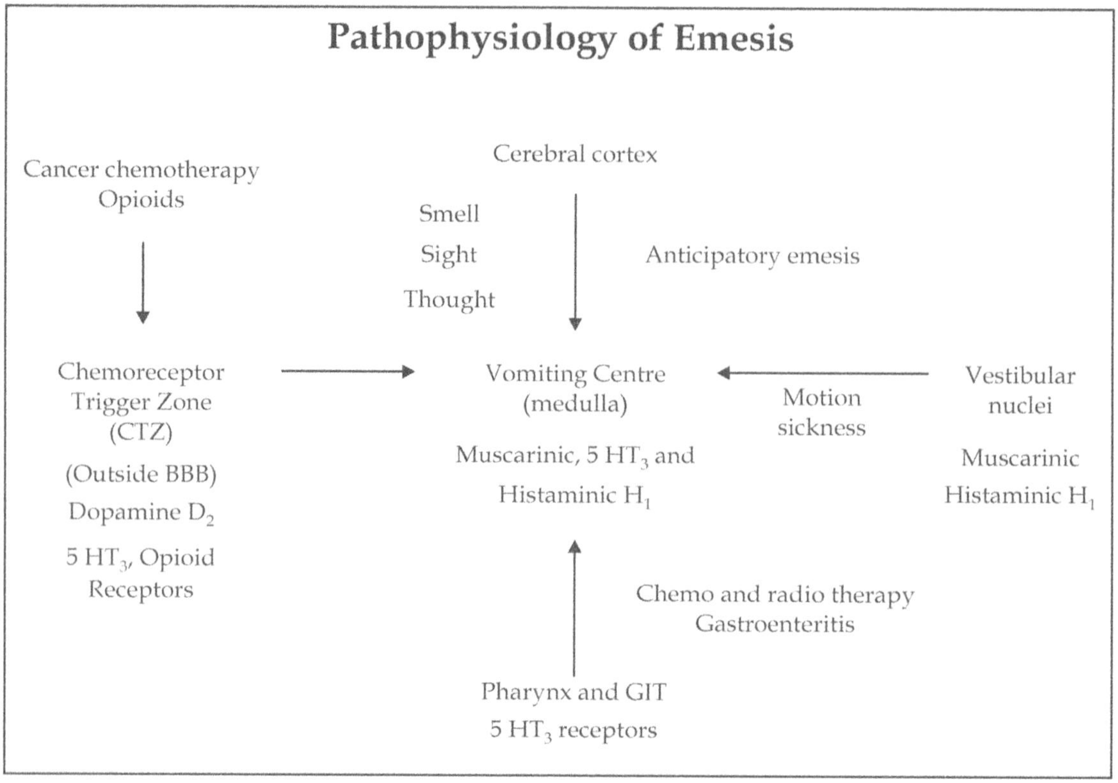

Fig 7-1: Pathophysiology of emesis and site of action of antiemetics

distention, or acute infectious gastroenteritis activates the 5-HT_3 receptors of these inputs.

5. The CNS mediates vomiting arising from psychiatric disorders and stress from higher brain centres.

Causes

Causes in the Digestive Tract

1. Gastritis (inflammation of the gastric wall, usually by viruses).
2. Gastroenteritis.
3. Bowel obstruction.
4. Overeating.
5. Food allergies.
6. Food poisoning.

Pregnancy

Causes in the sensory system

Movement: motion sickness

Causes in the brain

1. Cerebral haemorrhage
2. Migraine
3. Brain tumours

Metabolic Disturbances

(these may irritate the stomach and the brain that coordinate vomiting)

1. Hypercalcemia, hypoglycemia, hyperglycemia
2. Uraemia
3. Adrenal insufficiency

Drug Reaction

1. Alcohol
2. Opioids
3. Selective serotonin reuptake inhibitors
4. Many chemotherapy drugs

5. Digoxin
6. Antiparkinsonian drugs (dopaminergic drugs)

Emetics

They are required when an undesirable substance has been ingested. Drugs which induce vomiting are called emetics.

Emetic Drugs – Uses

1. May be used to cause the expulsion of foreign bodies such as pieces of gristle or meat which has become impacted in the upper part of the esophagus, and by pressing on the larynx, are giving rise to suffocation.
2. May be used to remove the contents of the stomach when these, instead of undergoing digestion and absorption in a normal manner, have undergone fermentative changes and become acid, acrid and irritating, giving rise to pain either in the stomach itself , or in some other organ as in the head.
3. Emetics remove the poison from the stomach in cases where it had been swallowed Mustard and water, Copper Sulfate and Zinc Sulfate.
4. To expel BILE from the gall bladder and may remove jaundice due to obstruction.
5. To remove bile from the body in cases of biliousness, fevers and ague.
6. To remove obstructions from air passages such as false membranes from the trachea and bronchia or diphtheria or the over abundant secretion which is clogging the bronchi and interfering with respiration in bronchitis and more rarely in phthisis.

Emetic Drugs

Centrally acting: Apomorphine

Directly stimulate the CTZ or VC

Reflexly acting: Ipecacuanha

Stimulate the VC by irritating gastric and duodenal mucosa which stimulate afferent fibres of vagus nerve.

Locally acting: Alum, Sodium Chloride (Concentrated Solution).

Other Drugs as Adverse Effect: Morphine, Digitalis, Emetine, Aspirin, Quinine and Anticancer drugs.

Apomorphine

Semi synthetic derivative of morphine. Given i.m or s.c. Dose is 6 mg (2-8 mg). Induces vomiting in 5-10min. CNS depressant contraindicated in respiratory depression. Dose required is high so not given orally.

Ipecacuanha

Contains two alkaloids emetine and cephaeline. Used as syrup ipecac and produces effect in 15 min. Acts by irritating gastric mucosa and through CTZ centre.

Dose: 5 ml for infants

10-15 ml for children

15-20 ml for adults

Contraindications

Corrosive poisoning

CNS stimulant drug poisoning

Kerosene poisoning

Unconscious patients

Morphine poisoning

Xylazine

An α_2- adrenergic agonist used primarily for its sedative and analgesic action. A reliable emetic which stimulates the CTZ.

Hydrogen Peroxide (3%) or Salt

Stimulates vomiting *via* cranial nerve. Small doses (5-10 ml) of hydrogen peroxide can be administered *via* oral syringe until emesis occurs causes severe aspiration pneumonia.

Tartar Emetic

Tartrate of antimony and potassium. Too severe.

Mineral Emetics

Zinc sulfate, copper sulfate etc.

Handy Emetics

Mustard (a teaspoonful) or salt (a tablespoonful), in a teacupful of warm water.

Let it be swallowed all at once and follow it in ten minutes with another teacupful of warm water if in that time, it has not taken effect.

Emetics are Not Used For

Not used to treat poisoning by strong acids or alkalis, petroleum distillates such as kerosene or substances causing convulsions.

Emetic Drugs – contraindications

Hernias

Aneurysm

Severe heart diseases

Peptic ulcer

Hypertension

Pulmonary TB

Prolapse of rectum or uterus

Threatened abortion

Weak/Debilitated persons

Antiemetics

Introduction

A group of drugs which are used to control nausea and vomiting, provide symptomatic relief and helpful in removal of causative factor to have ultimate relief.

Emesis is controled by two centres

Two centres: Emetic centre (EC) and chemoreceptor trigger zone (CTZ).

Both near the floor of the fourth ventricle, close to the vital centres.

EC is within the blood brain barrier (BBB)

CTZ outside in the area postrema

They are connected together

Classification - Antiemetic Drugs

H_1 antihistamines

Meclizine, Cinnarizine, Cyclizine, Dimenhydrinate and Diphenhydramine.

Muscarinic Antagonist

Hyoscine (Scopolamine).

Selective 5-HT_3 Antagonists

Ondansetron, Granisetron, Palonosetron and Dolasetron.

D_2 Antagonists

1. **Substituted Benzamides**

   Metoclopramide, Trimethobenzamide

2. **Butyrophenones**

   Domperidone, Droperidol

3. **Phenothiazines**

   Prochlorperazine, Promethazine and Thiethylperazine.

Cannabinoids

Dronabinol, Nabilone

Glucocorticoids

Dexamethasone, Methylprednisolone

Benzodiazepines

Diazepam, Lorazepam

Neurokinin-I Antagonist

Aprepitant (oral formulation), Fosaprepitant (IV formulation)

H_1 Antihistamines and Muscarinic Antagonists

H_1 antihistamines

Meclizine, Cinnarizine, Cyclizine and Diphenhydramine and its salt Dimenhydrinate.

Muscarinic Antagonist

Hyoscine (Scopolamine).

Vestibular system is important in motion sickness *via* cranial nerve VIII - rich in Cholinergic M_1 and Histamine H_1 receptors

Most effective drugs for motion sickness

Scopolamine (Hyoscine) – used as Transdermal patch for motion sickness

Mechanism of Action (MOA)

They have Anticholinergic and H_1 antagonist sedating properties (1st generation).

They produce specific depression of conduction in vestibulocerebellar pathway.

Therapeutic Uses

Effective for nausea and vomiting associated with motion sickness.

Vestibular disorders (Meniere's disease)

Meclizine is longer acting so useful in sea sickness

Cinnarizine also has antivertigo effect. Act by inhibiting influx of calcium to vestibular sensory cells from endolymph.

Selective 5-HT_3 Antagonists

Ondansetron, Granisetron, Dolasetron and Palonosetron

Mechanism of Action (MOA)

Act as anti-emetic by selectively blocking central 5-HT_3 receptors in vomiting center and CTZ and mainly by blocking Periphery 5-HT_3 receptors on intestinal vagal and spinal afferent fibers. Antiemetic action is restricted to emesis caused by vagal stimulation (e.g., post op) and chemotherapy.

Palonosetron: Newer with greater affinity for 5-HT_3 receptor and comparatively longer half life

No effect on Dopamine/muscarinic receptors

Pharmacokinetics - Selective 5-HT_3 Antagonists

High first pass metabolism

$t_{1/2}$: 4-9 hr (Ondansetron, Granisetron and Dolasetron).

40 hr (Palonosetron)

Given once or twice daily - orally or intravenously

Excreted by liver and kidney

No dose reduction in renal insufficiency but needed in hepatic insufficiency (Ondansetron) .

Therapeutic Uses

Chemotherapy- Induced Nausea and Vomiting

Primary Agents - prevention of acute chemotherapy induced nausea and vomiting. Effective alone in most of the cases. Efficacy is enhanced in combination. Can be given i.v 1/2 hr before chemotherapy.

To prevent delayed nausea and vomiting occurring after 24 hr of Cancer chemotherapy in combination with Dexamethasone and NK_1 receptor antagonist.

To prevent and treat post operative and post radiation Nausea and vomiting

Adverse Effects

Excellent safety profile but causes

Headache, dizziness and constipation

All four drugs cause prolongation of QT interval, but more pronounced with dolasetron.

Drug Interactions

Hepatic clearance may decrease by enzyme inhibitors.

D_2 Antagonists

Substituted Benzamides

Metoclopramide

Chemistry: Substituted Benzamide

Mechanism of Action: Metoclopramide acts centrally by blocking dopamine D_2 receptors in the CTZ and peripherally by enhancing the action of acetylcholine at muscarinic nerve endings in the gut. It relaxes the pyloric antrum and increases peristalsis and emptying of the upper gut. If an opioid has been given, metoclopramide may fail to overcome the opioid-induced inhibition of gastric emptying and thus the risk of vomiting and inhaling gastric contents remains. The action of metoclopramide is terminated by metabolism in the liver ($t_{1/2}$ 4 hr).

As antiemetic: It has potent antiemetic and antinausea effect.

The effects of Metoclopramide is shown in Fig 7-2.

Blocks D_2 receptors in CTZ of the medulla (area postrema).

As prokinetic agent: It can selectively stimulate gut motor function.

Blocks D_2 receptor in GIT and blocks the normal inhibitory effect of Dopamine on cholinergic smooth muscle stimulation and increases motility.

Therapeutic uses: Potent antiemetic controls/ reduces vomiting due to Uremia, Radiation, Viral gastroenteritis, hepatic biliary disease, Anticancer drugs, Migraine, Post operatively and pre operatively.

As prokinetic agent useful in Gastroesophageal reflux disease (GERD)

Only symptomatic relief. May be combined with anti- secretory agents in refractory cases.

Impaired GI emptying

After surgery (vagotomy, antrectomy)

Diabetic gastropresis

To promote advancement of nasoenteric feeding tube from stomach to intestine.

Non ulcer dyspepsia

Only symptomatic relief in chronic dyspepsia

Pharmacokinetics: Rapidly absorbed from GIT after oral administration. Undergoes a high degree first pass metabolism. It is excreted in the urine as free and as metabolites. It is also excreted in the breast milk.

DOSE: 10-20 mg orally or i.v every 6 hr.

Adverse effects: Adverse reactions are characteristic of dopamine receptor antagonists and include Extra pyramidal reactions with facial and skeletal muscle spasms- restlessness, dystonias, parkinsonian symptoms (Occulogyric crises). More common in young and very old. Usually occur shortly after staring treatment and subside within 24 hours of stopping the drug. Bowel upsets, diarrhea, drowsiness and fatigue, dizziness, restlessness and anxiety. Metoclopramide stimulates prolactin release and may cause gynaecomastia, galactorrhea, impotence and menstrual disorders.

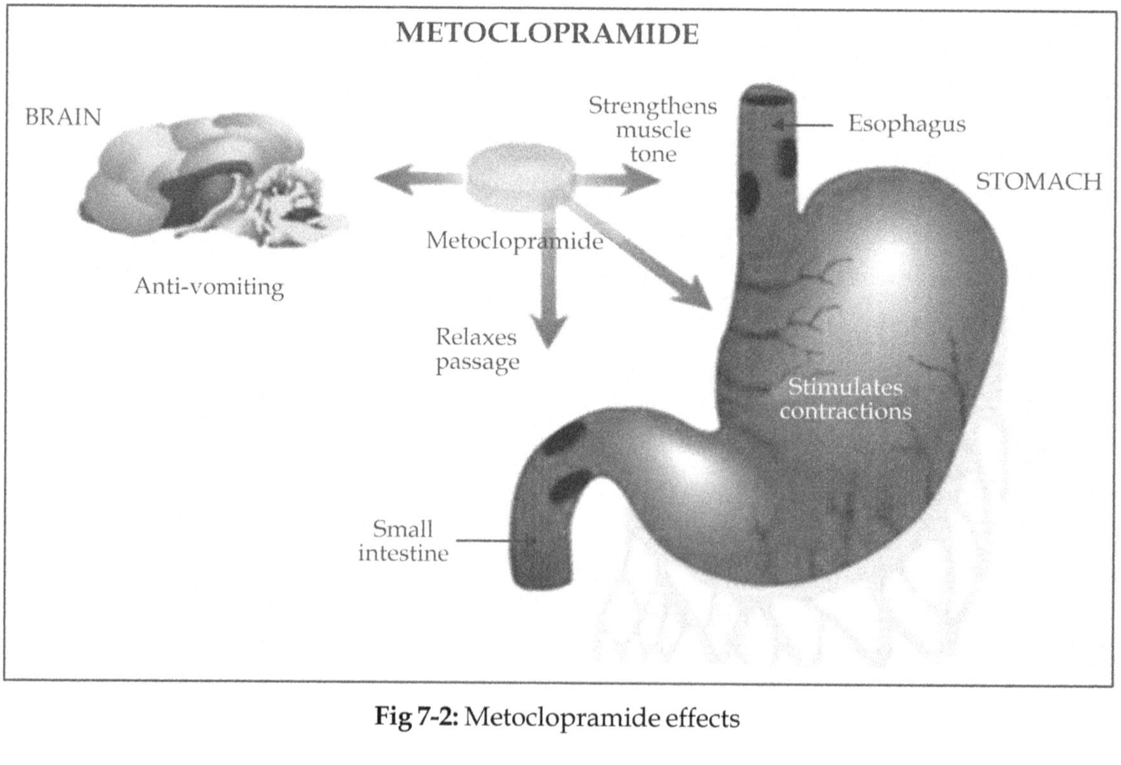

Fig 7-2: Metoclopramide effects

Trimethobenzamide

Substituted Benzamide. Antiemetic like Metoclopramide. D_2 Antagonist & mild anti-histaminic activity.

DOSE: 250 mg orally, 200 mg rectally, 200 mg i.m.

Phenothiazines

Prochlorperazine, Promethazine and Thiethyl-perazine

Phenothiazines are antipsychotics with potent antiemetic property due to D_2 antagonism and anti muscarinic properties. Phenothiazines are antipsychotic agents that can be used for their potent antiemetic and sedative properties. The antiemetic properties of phenothiazines are mediated through inhibition of dopamine and muscarinic receptors. Mainly used as anti emetic in severe nausea and vomiting. Main adverse effects are *Extra Pyramidal Side effects* (EPS), sedation, postural hypotension.

Butyrophenones

Antipsychotic drugs, D_2 antagonists

Droperidol

Central D_2 antagonist. Droperidol used for postoperative nausea and vomiting. Main adverse effects are postural hypotension and cause ECG -QT prolongation.

Domperidone

Domperidone is a selective dopamine D_2 receptor antagonist; unlike metoclopramide it does not possess an acetylcholine-like effect. The $t_{1/2}$ is 7 hr. Domperidone does not readily penetrate the blood-brain barrier; this does not limit its therapeutic efficacy, for the CTZ is functionally out with the barrier, but there is less risk of adverse effects in the central nervous system.

Uses: Domperidone is used for nausea or vomiting associated with gastrointestinal disorders and with cytotoxic and other drug treatment. It may cause gynaecomastia.

Which is a better antiemetic - Metoclopramide or Domperidone ?

As CTZ is outside BBB both have antiemetic effects.

But as metoclopramide crosses BBB it has adverse effects like extrapyramidal side effects.

Domperidone is well tolerated.

Cannabinoids (Dronabinol, Nabilone)

Dronabinol

Tetrahydrocannabinol (THC) main psychoactive chemical in marijuana.

Pharmacokinetics

Complete absorption on oral administration, significant 1st pass effect, metabolites excreted slowly over days to weeks in faeces and urine

Mechanism of Action (MOA)

Act as antiemetic and appetite stimulant in addition to psychoactive action.

Cancer chemotherapy induced nausea & vomiting with Phenothiazines - synergistic effect but AEs are added - not used as better drugs are available.

Nabilone

Nabilone is a synthetic cannabinoid and has properties similar to tetrahydrocannabinol (the active constituent of marijuana) which has an antiemetic action. It is used to relieve nausea or vomiting caused by cytotoxic drugs.

Adverse Effects

Dry mouth, decreased appetite, dizziness, euphoria, postural hypotension, confusion and psychosis. These may be reduced if prochlorperazine is given concomitantly.

Glucocorticoids

Dexamethasone, Methylprednisolone

The structure of Glucocorticoids are shown in Fig 7-3.

Enhance action of 5-HT_3 antagonists in Cancer chemotherapy induced nausea & vomiting. Corticosteroids have antiemetic properties. These agents appear to enhance the

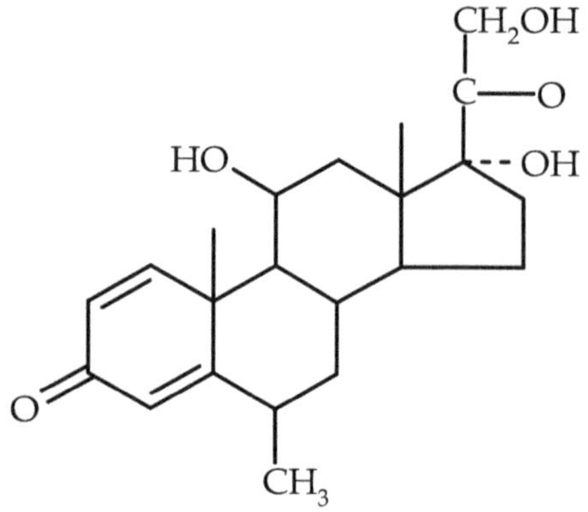

Methylprednisolone

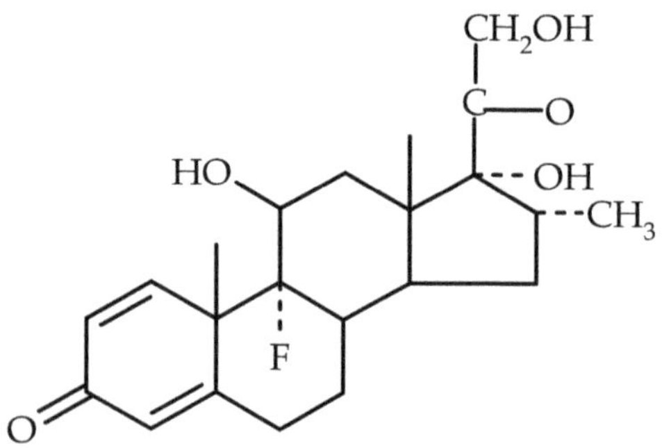

Dexamethasone

Fig 7-3: Glucocorticoids

efficacy of 5-HT_3-receptor antagonists for prevention of acute and delayed nausea and vomiting in patients receiving moderately to highly emetogenic chemotherapy regimens. Although a number of corticosteroids have been used, dexamethasone 8-20 mg intravenously before chemotherapy, followed by 8 mg/d orally for 2-4 days, is commonly administered.

Benzodiazepines

Diazepam, Lorazepam

Benzodiazepines such as lorazepam, diazepam (Fig 7-4) and midazolam are used prior to the initiation of chemotherapy to reduce vomiting caused by anxiety. Combination with 5-HT_3 antagonists is very effective in post operative vomiting used prior to Cancer chemotherapy to reduce anticipatory vomiting. Vomiting caused by anxiety.

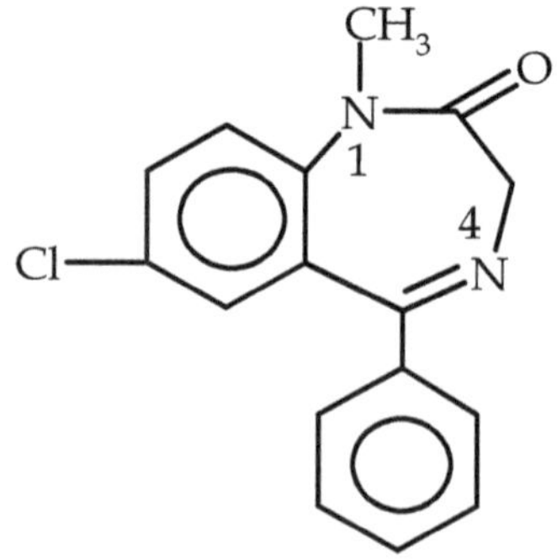

Fig 7-4: Diazepam

Neurokinin-1 (NK_1) Antagonists

Aprepitant, Fosaprepitant

Pharmacokinetics

Given orally Bioavailability is 65%, Crosses BBB.

$t_{1/2}$: 12 hr, Metabolized by hepatic CYP3A4.

MOA

Act as Antiemetic: Selectively block NK_1 receptor in area postrema.

No effect on Serotonin, Dopamine or Corticoid receptors

Aprepitant

A protein called substance P is involved in transmitting nerve messages to the vomiting centre. Substance P acts on neurokinin-1 receptors that are found in the vomiting centre in the brain. Chemotherapy causes substance P to activate these neurokinin-1 receptors, resulting in feelings of sickness. Aprepitant, which is a type of medicine called a neurokinin receptor antagonist. It is used to prevent nausea and vomiting that can be caused by chemotherapy treatment for cancer. Aprepitant works by blocking the neurokinin-1 receptors in the brain. This stops substance P from acting on them and so prevents nausea and vomiting. Aprepitant is used to prevent acute and delayed sickness that can be caused by chemotherapy, in particular by a medicine called cisplatin. It is given in combination with a steroid, e.g., dexamethasone, and a 5-HT_3 antagonist, e.g., ondansetron.

Pharmacokinetics

Enzyme inhibition: Metabolized by CYP3A4 and may inhibit metabolism of many anticancer drugs (Docetaxel, Paclitaxel, Etoposide, Vinblastine, Imatinib) increase levels toxicity.

Metabolism of Aprepitant may be inhibited by Ketoconazole, Ciprofloxacin, Clarithromycin, Nafazodone, Ritonavir, Nelfinavir, Verapamil and Quinidine.

Therapeutic Uses

Used in combination with 5-HT$_3$ antagonists and corticosteroids for prevention of acute and chronic nausea and vomiting from Cancer chemotherapy

Adverse Effects

Fatigue, dizziness and diarrhea. Decrease prothrombin time in Warfarin treated patients.

Therapeutic Uses of Antiemetics

Motion sickness: Hyoscine

Vestibular disorders (Menieres, disease): Cinnerazine

Vomiting due to Uremia, Radiation, Viral gastro enteritis, Liver disease, Migraine, Prochlor-perazine, Metroclopramide

Vomiting due to pregnancy (hyperemesis gravi-darum): Meclizine with vit. B$_6$ (Navidoxine)

Table 7-1: Antiemetic drugs

Neurotransmitter	Drug	Good for use in	Side effects	Beware
Histamine (H_1 antagonists)	Cyclazine Promethazine	Post-op N and V Vestibular/labyrinthine disorders	Sedation Antimuscarinic effects e.g., blurred vision, urinary retention, dry mouth	Avoid in: IHD, heart failure Caution in: BPH, glaucoma
Dopamine (D_2 antagonists)	Metoclopramide Prochloperazine	GI causes, drugs Drugs, post-op, chemo/radiotherapy	↑ Prolactin ↓ BP ↓seizure threshold Extrapyramidal side effects	Caution in: CV disease, respiratory disease, epilepsy, Parkinson's disease
Serotonin (5-HT_3 antagonists)	Ondansetron Granisetron	Severe/refractory N and V Chemo/radiotherapy	Minimal side effects Constipation Headache	Long QT
Acetylcholine (muscarinic antagonists)	Hyoscine	Motion sickness Prophylaxis against post-op N and V (given as patch prior to surgery)	Antimuscarinic effects	Avoid in: IHD, Ischaemic Heart Disease (IHD), heart failure Caution in: BPH, Benign prostatic hyperplasia (BPH) glaucoma
Unknown action	Dexamethasone	Chemo/radiotherapy CNS disease	Corticosteroid effects	Avoid in: Peptic ulcers, Cushung's Syndrome

Vomiting due to cytotoxic anticancer drugs: 5-HT_3 Antagonists, Metroclopramide, Cannabinoids, corticosteroids, Aprepitant

Anticipatory Vomiting due to Cytotoxic Anticancer drugs. Benzodiazepines (Diazepam)

Post operative vomiting: Metoclopramide, Prochlorperazine, Dimenhydrinate, 5-HT_3 Antagonists (Ondensetron)

References

Aapro M (2005). 5-HT_3-receptor antagonists in the management of nausea and vomiting in cancer and cancer treatment. *Oncology* **69:** 97.

Apfel CC *et al.,* (2004). A factorial trial of six interventions for the prevention of postoperative nausea and vomiting. *N Engl J Med* **350:** 24.

Hasler WL and Chey WD (2003). Nausea and vomiting. *Gastroenterology* **125:** 1860.

Sharma R, Tobin P and Clarke SJ (2005). Management of chemotherapy-induced nausea, vomiting, oral mucositis, and diarrhoea. *Lancet Oncol* **6:** 93.

CHAPTER 8

Drugs Used in Diarrhoea

Introduction

Diarrhoea (or **diarrhoea**) is the condition of having three or more loose or liquid bowel movements per day. The loss of fluids through diarrhea can cause dehydration and electrolyte disturbances such as potassium deficiency or other salt imbalances.

Diarrhoea is defined by the World Health Organization as "having three or more loose or liquid stools per day, or as having more stools than is normal for that person".

Types of Diarrhoea

Secretory Diarrhoea

Secretory diarrhoea means that there is an increase in the active secretion, or there is an inhibition of absorption. There is little to no structural damage. The most common cause of this type of diarrhoea is a cholera toxin that stimulates the secretion of anions, especially chloride ions. Therefore, to maintain a charge balance in the lumen, sodium is carried with it, along with water.

Osmotic Diarrhoea

Osmotic diarrhoea occurs when too much water is drawn into the bowels. If a person drinks solutions with excessive sugar or excessive salt, these can draw water from the body into the bowel and cause osmotic diarrhoea. Osmotic diarrhoea can also be the result of maldigestion (e.g., pancreatic disease or coeliac disease), in which the nutrients are left in the lumen to pull in water or it can be caused by osmotic laxatives (which work to alleviate constipation by drawing water into the bowels). In healthy individuals, too much magnesium or vitamin C or undigested lactose can produce osmotic diarrhea and distention of the bowel. A person who has lactose can have difficulty absorbing lactose after an extraordinarily high intake of dairy products. In persons who have fructose malabsorption, excess fructose intake can also cause diarrhoea. High-fructose foods that also have high glucose content are more absorbable and less likely to cause diarrhoea. Sugar alcohols such as sorbitol (often found in sugar free foods) are difficult for the body to absorb and, in large amounts, may lead to osmotic diarrhea.

Exudative Diarrhoea

Exudative diarrhoea occurs with the presence of blood and pus in the stool. This occurs with inflammatory bowel diseases, such as Crohn's disease or ulcerative colitis, and other severe infections such as *E. coli* or other forms of food poisoning.

Motility Related Diarrhoea

Motility related diarrhoea is caused by the rapid movement of food through the intestines (hypermotility). If the food moves too quickly through the gastrointestinal tract, there is not enough time for sufficient nutrients and water to be absorbed. This can be due to a vagotomy or diabetic neuropathy, or a complication of menstruation. Hyperthyroidism can produce hypermotility and lead to pseudodiarrhoea and occasionally real diarrhoea. Diarrhoea can be treated with antimotility agents (such as loperamide). Hypermotility can be observed in people who have had portions of their bowel removed, allowing less total time for absorption of nutrients.

Inflammatory Diarrhoea

Inflammatory diarrhoea occurs when there is damage to the mucosal lining or brush border, which leads to a passive loss of protein-rich fluids, and a decreased ability to absorb these lost fluids. Features of all three of the other types of diarrhoea can be found in this type of diarrhea. It can be caused by bacterial infections, viral infections, parasitic infections, or autoimmune problems such as inflammatory bowel diseases. It can also be caused by tuberculosis, colon cancer and enteritis.

Dysentery

Generally, if there is blood visible in the stools, it is not diarrhea, but dysentery. The blood is trace of an invasion of bowel tissue. Dysentery is a symptom of, among others, Shigella, *Entamoeba histolytica* and Salmonella infection.

Diarrhoea is most commonly due to viral gastroenteritis with rotavirus, which accounts for 40% of cases in children under five. In travellers however bacterial infections predominate. Various toxins such as mushroom poisoning and drugs can also cause acute diarrhea.

Chronic diarrhoea can be the part of the presentations of a number of chronic medical conditions affecting the intestine. Common causes include colitis, Crohn's, microscopic colitis, celiac disease, irritable bowel syndrome and bile acid malabsorption.

Differential Diagnosis

Infections

There are many causes of infectious diarrhoea, which include viruses, bacteria and parasite, norovirus is the most common cause of viral diarrhoea in adult, but rotavirus is the most common cause in children under five years old. Adenovirus types 40 and 41 and astroviruses cause a significant number of infections.

The bacterium Campylobacter is a common cause of bacterial diarrhea, but infections by Salmonellae, Shigella and some strains of *Escherichia coli* (*E.Coli*) are frequent.

In the elderly, particularly those who have been treated with antibiotics for unrelated infections, a toxin produced by *Clostridium difficile* often causes severe diarrhea.

Parasites do not often cause diarrhea except for the protozoan Giardia, which can cause chronic infections if these are not diagnosed and treated with drugs such as metronidazole, and *Entamoeba histolytica*.

Other infectious agents such as parasites and bacterial toxins also occur. In sanitary living conditions where there is ample food and a supply of clean water, an otherwise healthy person usually recovers from viral infections in a few days. However, for ill or malnourished individuals, diarrhea can lead to severe dehydration and can become life threatening.

Malabsorption

Malabsorption is the inability to absorb food fully, mostly from disorders in the small bowel, but also due to maldigestion from diseases of the pancreas.

Causes Include

- Enzyme deficiencies or mucosal abnormality, as in food allergy and food in tolerance, e.g., celiac disease (glutenin tolerance), lactose-intolerance (intolerance to milk sugar, common in non-Europeans) and fructose malabsorption.
- Pernicious anemia, or impaired bowel function due to the inability to absorb vitamin B_{12}.
- Loss of pancreatic secretions, which may be due to cystic fibrosis or pancreatitis.
- Structural defects, like short bowel syndrome (surgically removed bowel) and radiation fibrosis, such as usually follows cancer treatment and other drugs, including agents used in chemotherapy.
- Certain drugs, like Orlistat, which inhibits the absorption of fat.

Irritable Bowel Syndrome

Another possible cause of diarrhoea is irritable bowel syndrome (IBS) which usually presents with abdominal discomfort relieved by defecation and unusual stool (diarrhoea or constipation) for at least 3 days a week over the previous 3 months. Symptoms of diarrhoea predominant IBS can be managed through a combination of dietary changes, soluble fiber supplements, and/or medications such as loperamide or codeine.

Other Causes

- Diarrhoea can be caused by chronic ethanol ingestion.
- ***Ischemic bowel disease:*** This usually affects older people and can be due to blocked arteries.
- Microscopic colitis, a type of inflammatory bowel disease where changes are only seen on histological examination of colonic biopsies.
- Bile salt malabsorption (primary bile acid diarrhea) where excessive bile acids in the colon produce a secretory diarrhea.
- ***Hormone secreting tumours:*** Some hormones (e.g., serotonin) can cause diarrhea if excreted in excess (usually from a tumor).
- Chronic mild diarrhea in infants and toddlers may occur with no obvious cause and with no other ill effects; this condition is called toddler's diarrhea.

Treatment

In many cases of diarrhea, replacing lost fluid and salts is the only treatment needed. This is usually by mouth - oral rehydration therapy - or, in severe cases, intravenously. Medications such as loperamide (Imodium) and bismuth subsalicylate may be beneficial. The treatment of diarrhoea is shown in Fig 8-1.

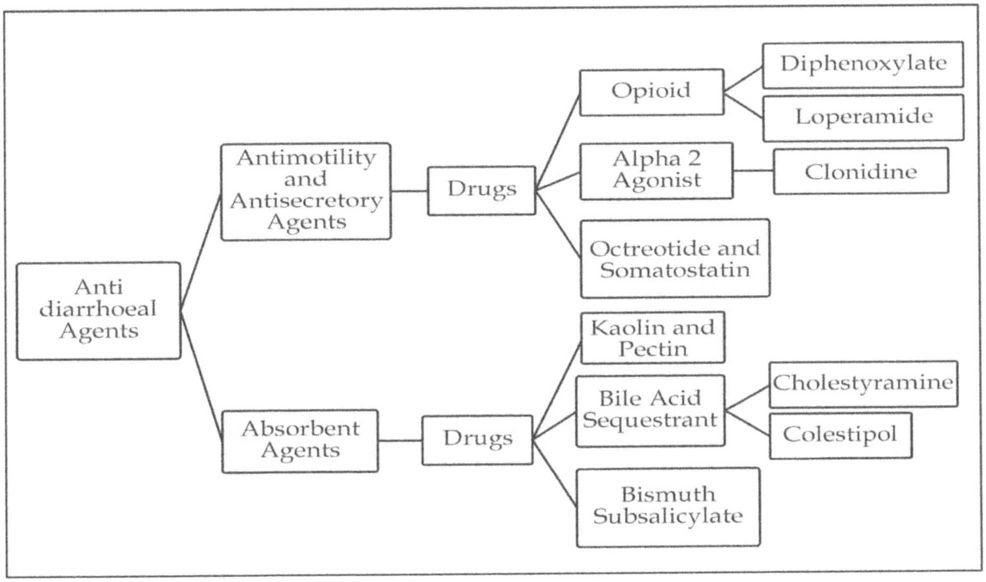

Fig 8-1: Classification of Antidiarrhoeals.

Oral Rehydration Therapy

Oral Rehydration Therapy (ORT) is a simple treatment for dehydration associated with diarrhoea, particularly gastroenteritis or gastro-enteropathy, such as that caused by cholera or rotavirus. ORT consists of a solution of salts and sugars that is taken by mouth. Rehydrating a dehydrated person through oral route is called as ORT.

Principle Glucose when given orally enhances the intestinal absorption of salt and water. Thus it can correct electrolyte and water deficit.

Types of ORS

Sodium bicarbonate based

Trisodium citrate based

Reduced osmolarity ORS

Super ORS

Antimotility and Antisecretory Agents

Opioids

Opioids (Fig 8-2) continue to be widely used in the treatment of diarrhea. They act by several different mechanisms, mediated principally through either μ- or δ -Opioid receptors on enteric nerves, epithelial cells, and muscle. These mechanisms include effects on intestinal motility (μ receptors), intestinal secretion (δ receptors), or absorption (μ and δ receptors). Commonly used antidiarrheal such as diphenoxylate, difenoxin and loperamide act principally *via* peripheral μ -Opioid receptors and are preferred over opioids that penetrate the CNS.

Loperamide

Loperamide (IMODIUM, IMODIUM A-D, others), a piperidine butyramide derivative with μ-receptor activity, is an orally active antidiarrheal agent. The drug is 40 to 50 times more potent than morphine as an antidiarrheal agent and penetrates the CNS poorly. It increases small intestinal and mouth-to-cecum transit times. Loperamide also increases anal sphincter tone, an effect that may be of therapeutic value in some patients who suffer from anal incontinence. In addition, loperamide has antisecretory activity against cholera toxin and

Loperamide
$C_{29}H_{33}ClN_2O_2$

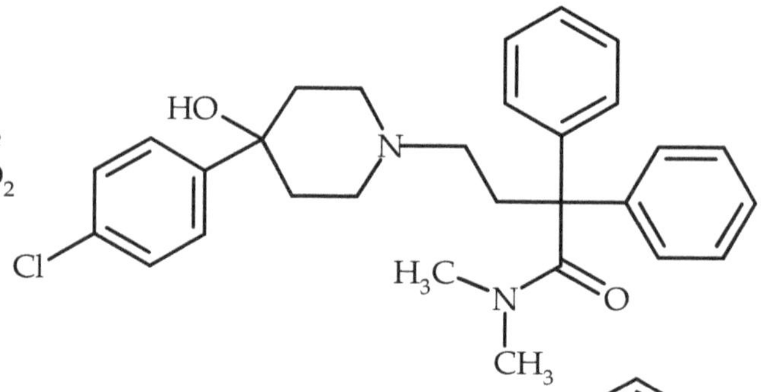

Diphenoxylate
$C_{30}H_{32}N_2O_2$

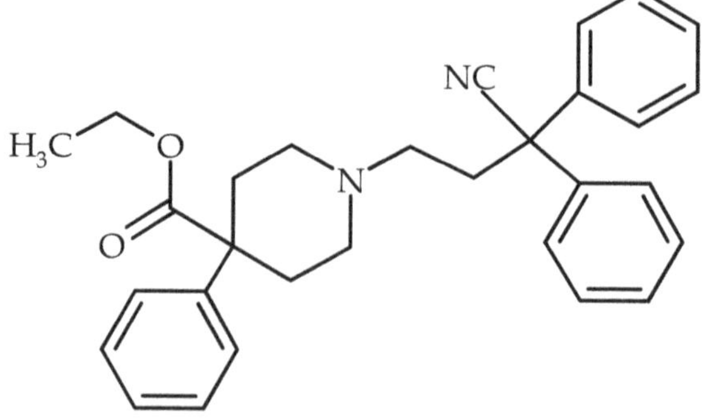

Fig 8-2: Opioid drugs.

some forms of *E. coli* toxin, presumably by acting on Gi-linked receptors and countering the increase in cellular cyclic AMP generated in response to the toxins.

Because of its effectiveness and safety, loperamide is marketed for over-the-counter distribution and is available in capsule, solution and chewable forms. It acts quickly after an oral dose, with peak plasma levels achieved within 3 to 5 hours. It has a half-life of about 11 hours and undergoes extensive hepatic metabolism. The usual adult dose is 4 mg initially followed by 2 mg after each subsequent loose stool, upto 16 mg per day. If clinical improvement in acute diarrhea does not occur within 48 hours, loperamide should be discontinued. Recommended maximum daily doses for children are 3 mg for ages 2 to 5 years, 4 mg for ages 6 to 8 years and 6 mg for ages 8 to 12 years. Loperamide is not recommended for use in children younger than 2 years of age.

Loperamide has been shown to be effective against traveller's diarrhea, used either alone or in combination with antimicrobial agents (trimethoprim, trimethoprim-sulfamethoxazole, or a fluoroquinolones). Loperamide also has been used as adjunct treatment in almost all forms of chronic diarrheal disease, with few adverse effects. Loperamide lacks significant abuse potential and is more effective in treating diarrhea than diphenoxylate. Overdosage, however, can result in CNS depression (especially in children) and paralytic ileus. In patients with active inflammatory bowel disease involving the colon, loperamide should be used with great caution, if at all, to prevent development of toxic megacolon.

Loperamide N-oxide, an investigational agent, is a site-specific prodrug; it is chemically designed for controlled release of loperamide in the intestinal lumen, thereby reducing systemic absorption.

Diphenoxylate and Difenoxin

Diphenoxylate and its active metabolite Difenoxin (diphenoxylic acid) are piperidine derivatives that are related structurally to meperidine. As antidiarrheal agents, diphenoxylate and Difenoxin are somewhat more potent than morphine. Both compounds are extensively absorbed after oral administration, with peak levels achieved within 1 to 2 hours. Diphenoxylate is rapidly deesterified to Difenoxin, which is eliminated with a half-life of about 12 hours. Both drugs can produce CNS effects when used in higher doses (40 to 60 mg per day) and thus have a potential for abuse and/or addiction. They are available in preparations containing small doses of atropine (considered sub therapeutic) to discourage abuse and deliberate overdosage: 25 μg of atropine sulfate per tablet with either 2.5 mg diphenoxylate hydrochloride (LOMOTIL) or 1 mg of Difenoxin hydrochloride (MOTOFEN). The usual dosage is two tablets initially and then one tablet every 3 to 4 hours. With excessive use or overdose, constipation and (in inflammatory conditions of the colon) toxic megacolon may develop. In high doses, these drugs cause CNS effects as well as anticholinergic effects from the atropine (dry mouth, blurred vision, etc.).

Other opioids used for diarrhea include codeine (in doses of 30 mg given three or four times daily) and opium containing compounds.

Paregoric (camphorated opium tincture) contains the equivalent of 2 mg of morphine per 5 ml (0.4 mg/ml); deodorized tincture of opium, which is 25 times stronger, contains the equivalent of 50 mg of morphine per 5 ml (10 mg/ml). The two tinctures sometimes are confused in prescribing and dispensing, resulting in dangerous overdoses. The antidiarrheal dose of opium tincture for adults is 0.6 ml (equivalent to 6 mg morphine) four times daily; the adult dose of paregoric is 5 to 10 ml (equivalent to 2 or 4 mg morphine) one to four times daily. Paregoric is used in children at a dose of 0.25 to 0.5 ml/kg (equivalent to 0.1 to 0.2 mg morphine/kg) one to four times daily.

Enkephalins are endogenous opioids that are important enteric neurotransmitters. Enkephalins inhibit intestinal secretion without affecting motility. Racecadotril (acetorphan), a dipeptide inhibitor of enkephalinase, reinforces the effects of endogenous Enkephalins on the δ -opioid receptor to produce an antidiarrheal effect.

α_2 Adrenergic Receptor Agonists

α_2 Adrenergic receptor agonists such as clonidine (Fig 8-3) can interact with specific receptors on enteric neurons and enterocytes, thereby stimulating absorption and inhibiting secretion of fluid and electrolytes and increasing intestinal transit time. These agents may have a special role in diabetics with chronic diarrhea, in whom autonomic neuropathy can lead to loss of noradrenergic innervation. Oral clonidine (beginning at 0.1 mg twice a day) has been used in these patients; the use of a topical preparation (e.g., CATAPRES TTS, two patches a week) may result in more steady plasma levels of the drug. Clonidine also may be useful in patients with diarrhea caused by opiate withdrawal. Side effects such as hypotension, depression, and perceived fatigue may be dose limiting in susceptible patients.

Clonidine
Hydrochloride
$C_9H_9Cl_2N_3 . HCl$

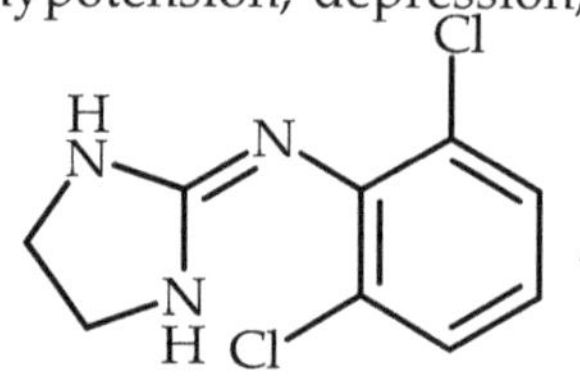

. HCl

Fig 8-3: Clonidine

Octreotide and Somatostatin

Octreotide (SANDOSTATIN) is an octapeptide analogue of somatostatin that is effective in inhibiting the severe secretory diarrhea brought about by hormone-secreting tumours of the pancreas and the gastrointestinal tract. Its mechanism of action appears to involve inhibition of hormone secretion, including serotonin and various other GI peptides (e.g., gastrin, vasoactive intestinal polypeptide, insulin, secretin, etc.). Octreotide has been used, with varying success, in other forms of secretory diarrhea such as chemotherapy induced diarrhea, diarrhea associated with human immunodeficiency virus (HIV), and diabetes associated diarrhea. Its greatest utility, however, may be in the "dumping syndrome" seen in some patients after gastric surgery and Pyloroplasty. In this condition, Octreotide inhibits the release of hormones (triggered by rapid passage of food into the small intestine) that are responsible for distressing local and systemic effects.

Octreotide has a half-life of 1 to 2 hours and is administered either subcutaneously or intravenously as a bolus dose. Standard initial therapy with octreotide is 50 to 100 μg, given subcutaneously two or three times a day, with titration to a maximum dose of 500 μg three times a day based on clinical and biochemical responses. A long acting preparation of octreotide acetate enclosed in biodegradable microspheres (SANDOSTATIN LAR DEPOT) is available for use in the treatment of diarrhoeas associated with carcinoid tumours and vasoactive intestinal peptide–secreting tumours, as well as in the treatment of acromegaly. This preparation is injected intramuscularly once per month in a dose of 20 or 30 mg. Side effects of Octreotide depend on the duration of therapy. Short term therapy leads to transient nausea, bloating, or pain at sites of injection. Long term therapy can lead to gallstone formation and hypo- or hyperglycemia. Another long-acting somatostatin analogue, lanreotide (SOMATULINE, others), is available in Europe but not in the United States; another, vapreotide, is under development.

Absorbent Agents

Bulk-Forming and Hydroscopic Agents

Hydrophilic and poorly fermentable colloids or polymers such as carboxymethylcellulose and calcium polycarbophil absorb water and increase stool bulk (calcium polycarbophil absorbs 60 times its weight in water). They usually are used for constipation but are sometimes useful in mild chronic diarrhoeas in patients suffering with irritable bowel syndrome. The mechanism of this effect is not clear, but they may work as gels to modify stool texture and viscosity and to produce a perception of decreased stool fluidity. Some of these agents also may bind bacterial toxins and bile salts. Clays such as kaolin (a hydrated aluminium silicate) and other silicates such as attapulgite (magnesium aluminium disilicate; DIASORB) bind water avidly (attapulgite absorbs eight times its weight in water) and also may bind enterotoxins. However, this effect is not selective and may involve other drugs and nutrients; hence these agents are best avoided within 2 to 3 hours of taking other medications. A mixture of kaolin and pectin (a plant polysaccharide) is a popular over-the counter remedy (KAOPECTOLIN) and may provide useful symptomatic relief of mild diarrhea.

Bile Acid Sequestrants

The structures of Bile acid Sequesterants are shown in Fig 8-4.

Cholestyramine, Colestipol and Colesevelam

There are effectively binds bile acids and some bacterial toxins. Cholestyramine is useful in the treatment of bile salt–induced diarrhea, as in patients with resection of the distal ileum. In these patients, there is partial interruption of the normal enterohepatic circulation of bile salts, resulting in excessive concentrations reaching the colon and stimulating water and electrolyte secretion. Patients with extensive ileal resection (usually more than 100 cm) eventually develop net bile salt depletion, which can produce steatorrhea because of inadequate micellar formation required for fat absorption. In such patients, the use of cholestyramine will aggravate the diarrhea. The drug also had an historic role in treating mild antibiotic associated diarrhea and mild colitis due to *Clostridium difficile*. However, its use in infectious diarrheas generally is discouraged, as it may decrease clearance of the pathogen from the bowel.

In patients suspected of having bile salt–induced diarrhea, a trial of cholestyramine can be given at a dose of 4 gm of the dried resin (contained in either 9 gm (QUESTRAN, others) or 5 gm (QUESTRAN LIGHT, others) of powder) four times a day. If successful, the dose may be titrated down to achieve the desired stool frequency.

Cholestyramine resin also is helpful for the relief of pruritus associated with partial biliary obstruction and in conditions such as primary biliary cirrhosis. In such conditions, excessive bile acids are thought to be deposited in the skin and cause irritation. Cholestyramine increases fecal excretion of bile acids and reduces

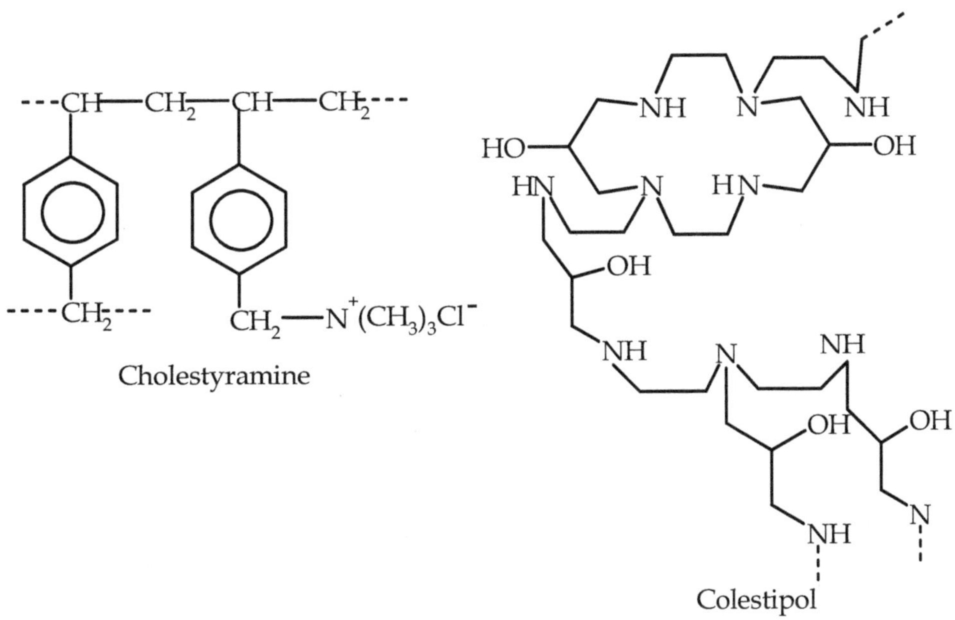

Fig 8-4: Bile acid sequestrants.

circulating and eventually systemic levels with relief of pruritus in about 1 to 3 weeks.

Bismuth

Bismuth compounds have been used to treat a variety of gastrointestinal diseases and symptoms for centuries, although their mechanism of action remains poorly understood. PEPTO-BISMOL (bismuth subsalicylate) is an over-the-counter preparation estimated to be used by 60% of American households. It is a crystal complex consisting of trivalent bismuth and salicylate suspended in a mixture of magnesium aluminium silicate clay. In the low pH of the stomach, the bismuth subsalicylate reacts with hydrochloric acid to form bismuth oxychloride and salicylic acid. While 99% of the bismuth passes unaltered and unabsorbed into the feces, the salicylate is absorbed in the stomach and small intestine. Thus, caution should be used in patients taking salicylates for other indications.

Bismuth is thought to have antisecretory, anti inflammatory and antimicrobial effects. Nausea and abdominal cramps also are relieved by bismuth. The clay in PEPTO-BISMOL also may have some additional benefits in diarrhea, but this is not clear. Bismuth subsalicylate has been used extensively for the prevention and treatment of traveller's diarrhea, but it also is effective in other forms of episodic diarrhea and in acute gastroenteritis. Today, the most common antibacterial use of this agent is in the treatment of *Helicobacter pylori* . A recommended dose of the bismuth subsalicylate (30 ml of regular strength PEPTO-BISMOL liquid or 2 tablets) contains approximately equal amounts of bismuth and salicylate (262 mg each). For control of indigestion, nausea, or diarrhea, the dose is repeated every 30 to 60 minutes, as needed, up to eight times a day. Bismuth products have a long track record of safety at recommended doses, although impaction may occur in infants and debilitated patients. Dark stools (sometimes mistaken for melena) and black staining of the tongue in association with bismuth compounds are caused by bismuth sulphide formed in a reaction between the drug and bacterial sulphides in the gastrointestinal tract.

Other Agents

Calcium channel blockers such as verapamil and nifedipine reduce motility and may promote intestinal electrolyte and water absorption. Constipation, in fact, is a significant side effect of these drugs. However, because of their systemic effects and the availability of other agents, they seldom if ever are used for diarrheal illnesses. Berberine is a plant alkaloid that has been used for millennia in traditional Indian and Chinese medicine. It is produced by several genera of the families Ranuculaceae and Berberidaceae (e.g., Berberis, Mahonia and Coptis) and has complex pharmacological actions that include antimicrobial actions, stimulation of bile flow, inhibition of ventricular tachyarrhythmia's and possible antineoplastic activity. It is used most commonly in bacterial diarrhea and cholera, but it is also apparently effective against intestinal parasites. The antidiarrheal effects in part may be related to its antimicrobial activity, as well as its ability to inhibit smooth muscle contraction and delay intestinal transit by antagonizing the effects of acetylcholine (by competitive and non-competitive mechanisms) and blocking the entry of Ca^{2+} into cells. In addition, it inhibits intestinal secretion. Chloride channel blockers are effective antisecretory agents *in vitro* but are too toxic for human use and have not proven to be effective antidiarrheal agents *in vivo*. Calmodulin inhibitors, which include chlorpromazine, also are antisecretory. Zaldaride maleate, a new drug in this class, may be effective in traveller's diarrhea by reducing secretion without affecting intestinal motility.

Alternative Therapies

Zinc supplementation benefits children suffering from diarrhea in developing countries, but only in infants over six months old.

Probiotics reduce the duration of symptoms by one day and reduced the chances of symptoms lasting longer than four days by 60%. The probiotic lactobacillus can help prevent antibiotic associated diarrhoea in adults but possibly not children. For those who with lactose intolerance, taking digestive enzymes containing lactase when consuming dairy products is recommended.

Table 8-1: Antidiarrhoeal Drugs.

<table>
<tr><th colspan="5">Antimotility and Antisecretory Agents</th></tr>
<tr><td colspan="5">Opioid agonists</td></tr>
<tr><th>Drugs</th><th>Pharmacokinetics</th><th>Mechanism of action</th><th>Clinical uses</th><th>Adverse effects</th></tr>
<tr><td rowspan="3">Loperamide</td><td rowspan="3">Absorption
• Poorly absorbed orally
Distribution
• Does not cross the BBB unless in a very high dose, therefore doesn't lead to opioid dependency
• 97% bound to plasma protein
Metabolism
• Hepatic metabolism
Excretion
• Urine
• Bile</td><td rowspan="3">• Opioid receptor agonist
▪ Bind to μ receptor on the Myenteric Plexus of GIT
• Stimulation of this receptor will lead to
▪ Decrease the tone of longitudinal smooth muscle cells
▪ Increase transit time
▪ Increase the tone of circular smooth muscle cells
▪ Increase the time for and capacity of intestine to absorb water
▪ Inhibition of Gastrocolic reflex
• All and all, it reduces GIT motility and increase transit time</td><td>• Travellers diarrhea
• Chronic diarrhea</td><td>• Abdominal pain
• Bloating
• Nausea
• Vomiting
• Constipation
•</td></tr>
<tr><th>Contraindication</th><th>Drug drug Reaction</th></tr>
<tr><td>Children less in 2 years of age
▪ Risk of fatal Paralytic Ileus
• Diarrhea associated with organism that may penetrate the gut wall
▪ E. coli
▪ Salmonella
• Symptomatic Pseudomembranous Colitis
▪ Risk of toxin retention
▪ Precipitate Toxic Megacolon
• Hepatic failure
▪ Precipitate Hepatic Encephalopathy</td><td>• If administered together with
▪ Quinidine
▪ Omeprazole
▪ Ritonavir
• These are all CYP450 inhibitors which may elevate the plasma level of Loperamide to as high as 3 folds
• These drugs enable Loperamide to pass the BBB and lead to sedative effects of Opioid agonists</td></tr>
</table>

Table 8-1 Contd...

Antimotility and Antisecretory Agents				
Opioid agonists				
Drugs	**Pharmacokinetics**	**Mechanism of action**	**Clinical uses**	**Adverse effects**
Diphenoxylate	**Absorption** • Good upon oral administration **Distribution** • Active metabolite Difenoxin may pass the BBB **Metabolism** • Hepatic **Excretion** • Urine • Bile			**Inclusion of Atropine** • Atropine is an Anticholinergic agent • It synergizes the activity of Diphenoxylate in reducing GIT motility and increasing transit time • Since Difenoxin is 3 to 4 times more potent than Diphenoxylate, it increases the potency of getting Dependency • Atropine will reduce the dose required for Diphenoxylate
Alpha 2 Agonists				
Clonidine	**Absorption** • Good upon oral administration **Distribution** • Plasma protein bound **Metabolism** • Hepatic **Excretion** • Urine	• Binds to presynaptic Alpha 2 Adrenergic receptor • It leads to reduction in the release of Neurotransmitters by inhibition • Adenylate Cyclase exerts its antidiarrheal effects through • Reducing GIT motility by ▪ Increasing transit time ▪ Increase GIT capacity ▪ Absorption of electrolytes and fluids ▪ Reducing secretion of fluid	• Diarrhea in Diabetic patient • Diarrhea due to withdrawal of Opioid	Rebound hypertension Depression

Table 8-1 Contd...

Antimotility and Antisecretory Agents				
Octreotide and Somatostatin				
Drugs	**Pharmacokinetics**	**Mechanism of action**	**Clinical uses**	**Adverse effects**
• Octreotide is a synthetic analogue for Somatostatin • Octeretide has 400-500 more potency compared to Somatostatin	**Absorption** • Complete absorption after S.C administration **Distribution** • Distributed across body compartment **Metabolism** • Unknown **Excretion** • Urine	• Resembles the activity of Somatostatin • Inhibits the release of various hormones ▪ GIT hormones ▪ Gastrin ▪ CCK-PZ ▪ Secretin ▪ Pancreatic Polypeptide ▪ Vasoactive Intestinal Peptide ▪ Other Hormones ▪ Insulin ▪ Glucagon ▪ TSH ▪ Growth Hormone • Reduces fluid and electrolyte secretion from the Intestine • Reduces GIT motility • Vasoconstriction in the blood vessels	• Secretory diarrhea due to ▪ Hormone secreting tumor of Pancreas or Intestine ▪ Chemotherapy ▪ HIV ▪ Diabetes Mellitus	• Hypothyroidism Hypo/Hyper-glycaemia • Reduce Insulin release • QT prolongation • Gallstones formation • Bradycardia

Absorbent Agents			
Bulk-Forming and Hydroscopic Agents			
Drugs	**Mechanism of action**	**Clinical uses**	**Adverse effects**
• Kaolin ▪ Naturally occurring hydrated Magnesium Aluminum Silicate • Pectin ▪ Indigestible carbohydrate derived from apples.	• May work as gels to modify stool texture and viscosity • Produce a perception of decreased stool fluidity • May bind bacterial toxins especially Enterotoxin • May bind to bile salts	• Symptomatic relieve of ▪ Acute diarrhea ▪ Chronic diarrhea	• Interfere with many oral drugs absorption in the GIT

Table 8-1 Contd...

Absorbent Agents			
Bile Acids Sequestrants			
Drugs	**Mechanism of action**	**Clinical uses**	**Adverse effects**
• Cholestyramine • Cholestipol	• Bile salt binding in the intestine • Leading to increase in bulk of the stool • Make the stools less watery	• Bile salt-induced diarrhea ▪ In patients with resection of the distal ileum	• Hypertriglyceridaemia • Constipation • Bloating • Flatulence • Heartburn • Diarrhea • Steatorrhea • Malabsorption of Vitamin K ▪ Hypoprothrombinaemia • Gallstones formation
Bismuth Subsalicylate			
	• Retarding the expulsion of fluids into the digestive system by irritated tissues, by "coating" them. • Stimulation of absorption of fluids and electrolytes by the intestinal wall (antisecretory action) • Reducing inflammation/ irritation of stomach and intestinal lining through inhibition of prostaglandin G/H Synthase 1/2 • Reduction in hyper-motility of the stomach • Binding of toxins produced by *E. coli* • Bactericidal action	• Prophylaxis for Traveller's diarrhea Treatment of *H.pylori* infection	• Dark stools (sometimes mistaken for melena) • Black staining of the tongue

References

Camilleri M (2004). Chronic diarrhea: A review of pathophysiology and management for the clinical gastroenterologist. *Clin Gastroenterol Hepatol* **2:** 198.

Schiller L (2004). Chronic diarrhea. *Gastroenterology* **127:** 287.

CHAPTER

Digestants and GERD 9

Digestants

These drugs are used to promote digestion of food as a replacement therapy in condition of their deficiency especially in atrophic gastritis, gastric carcinoma, pernicious anaemia or pancreatic insufficiency etc. Various proteolytic (pepsin, papain), lipolytic (lipases) and amylolytic (diastase and takadiastase) enzymes are used in combination as appetite stimulants and health tonics. Dilute hydrochloric acid (HCl) is advocated in severe achlorhydria. These are beneficial only when deficiency of these are marked, otherwise their routine use is irrational and unwarranted. Digestive drugs (digestants) aid digestion in the patient whose missing enzymes or other substances needed to digest food. Digestants that function in the GI tract, liver and pancreas include:

- Pancreatin
- Pancrelipase
- lipase
- protease
- amylase (pancreatic enzymes)

Pharmacokinetics

Digestants are not absorbed. They act locally in the GI tract and are excreted in feces.

Pharmacodynamics

The action of digestants resembles the action of the body substances they replace. Dehydrocholic acid, a bile acid, increases the output of bile in the liver. The pancreatic enzymes pancreatin and pancrelipase replace normal pancreatic enzymes. Digestants contain trypsin to digest proteins, amylase to digest carbohydrates and lipase to digest fats.

Pharmacotherapeutics

Because their action resembles the action of the body substances they replace, each digestant has its own indication. Dehydrocholic acid, a bile acid, provides temporary relief from constipation and promotes the flow of bile. Pancreatic enzymes are given to patients with insufficient levels of pancreatic enzymes, such as those with pancreatitis and cystic fibrosis. They may also be used to treat steatorrhea (disorder of fat metabolism characterized by fatty, foul-smelling stools).

Examples of Digestants

Glutamic Acid Hydrochloride

Glutamic acid hydrochloride is used in the treatment of patients who are either secreting no stomach acid (achlorhydria) or secreting little stomachacid (hypochlorhydria). Once prepared, the cid solution is sipped through a glass straw in order to minimize damage to the teeth.

Dehydrocholic acid, NF

Dehydrocholic acid is used to increase the volume of bile produced and secreted in the digestive system. It is used to relieve excessive constipation as well as to remove fragments of gallstones from the body. The usual dose of this drug is 3 to 5 millilitres of a 20 percent solution administered intrave-nously.

Pancrelipase (Cotazyme)

This product is used as a pancreatic enzyme supplement. The usual dosage of pancrelipase is one to three capsules or one to twopackets of the powder before or with meals. The preparation is available in both capsule or powder (regular and cherry flavor). When you dispense the granules, tell the patient to mix the granules with food or with water.

Pancreatin (Panteric)

Pancreatin is used as pancreatic enzyme supplement. The usual dosage of the product is one to three tablets with meals. Other examples of these digestants are:

1. Ox bile extract.
2. Ox bile extract, pancreatin, pepsin, glutamic acid, hydrochloride and cellulose (kanulase)

Drug Interactions

Antacids reduce the effects of pancreatic enzymes and shouldn't be given at the same time. Pancreatic enzymes may decrease the absorption of folic acid and iron.

Digestants in Gastric Dysfunction

1. Hydrochloric acid- 5 to 10 ml of 10% HCl, diluted further in 100-200 ml of water may be sipped with a straw (to avoid direct contact with teeth) during meals. When taken in sufficient quantity HCl will help in enhancing the activity of pepsin (both of endogenous/exogenous source) and may prevent bacterial growth in stomach during achlorhydria.
2. Pepsin it may be used with HCl in condition of deficiency. Dose- 20 to 100 mg/day in divided doses contained in various marketed enzyme preparations.
3. Papain raw papaya contains papain which has got proteolytic activity. Dose- 30-60 mg/day as advocated in different enzyme preparations.

Digestants in Pancreatic Insufficiency

1. Diastase/takadiastase: These are amylolytic enzymes obtained from fungus *Aspergillus oryzae*.

   Dose: Takadiastase-150-160 mg/day and diastase-around 20 mg/day in various marketed preparations.
2. Pancreatin: It is a mixture of various pancreatic enzymes like amylase, trypsin and lipase, generally obtained from hog/pig pancreas. It reduces fecal fat and nitrogen content. It should be given by enteric coated capsule to prevent its own digestion in stomach by pepsin. It can produce adverse reactions like nausea, diarrhea and uric acid renal stones.

   Dose: 150-250 mg/day in various marketed preparations with simethicone (25 mg) or tauroglycocholate (50 mg).

Side Effects

The most common side effects of digestive drugs are cramping, nausea and diarrhoea. A relaxing massage may help to calm these effects, especially a massage using the systemic reflex strokes that can help the body to relax. Other adverse effects, such as epigastric pain, may indicate gallstones and must be referred to a physician for evaluation and massage withheld.

GERD

Gastroesophageal reflux disease (GERD) refers to symptoms or mucosal damage resulting from the abnormal retrograde movement of gastric contents from the stomach into the esophagus. When the esophagus is repeatedly exposed to refluxed material for prolonged periods, inflammation of the esophagus (reflux esophagitis) can occur and in some cases it progresses to erosion of the squamous epithelium (erosive esophagitis). Severe reflux symptoms associated with normal endoscopic findings are referred to as "symptomatic GERD", nonerosive reflux disease, or endoscopy negative reflux disease.

Pathophysiology

The key factor in the development of GERD is the abnormal reflux of gastric contents from the stomach into the esophagus. In some cases, gastroesophageal reflux is associated with defective lower esophageal sphincter (LES) pressure or function. Patients may have decreased LES pressures related to spontaneous transient LES relaxations, transient increases in intraabdominal pressure, or an atonic LES. Problems with other normal mucosal defense mechanisms may also contribute to the development of GERD, including prolonged acid clearance time from the esophagus, delayed gastric emptying and reduced mucosal resistance. Aggressive factors that may promote esophageal damage upon reflux into the esophagus include gastric acid, pepsin, bile acids and pancreatic enzymes. The composition and volume of the refluxate and the duration of exposure are the most important aggressive factors in determining the consequences of gastro esophageal reflux.

Signs and Symptoms

The hallmark symptom of gastroesophageal reflux and esophagitis is heartburn, or pyrosis. It is classically described as a substernal sensation of warmth or burning that may radiate to the neck. It is waxing and waning in character and is often aggravated by activities that worsen gastroesophageal reflux (e.g., recumbent position, bending over, eating a high-fat meal). Other symptoms include water brash (hypersalivation), belching and regurgitation. Atypical symptoms include nonallergic asthma, chronic cough, hoarseness, pharyngitis, dental erosions and chest pain that mimics angina. Inadequately treated GERD may lead to complications from long-term acid exposure such as continual pain, dysphagia and odynophagia. Other severe complications include esophageal strictures, hemorrhage, Barrett's esophagus and esophageal adenocarcinoma.

Diagnosis

The most useful tool in the diagnosis of gastroesophageal reflux is the clinical history, including both presenting symptoms and associated risk factors. Patients with mild, typical reflux symptoms do not usually require invasive evaluation; a clinical diagnosis of GERD can be assumed in patients who respond to appropriate therapy. Further diagnostic evaluation should be performed in those who do not respond to therapy, who present with alarm symptoms (e.g., dysphagia, weight loss), or who have long-standing GERD symptoms. Endoscopy is the preferred technique for assessing the mucosa for esophagitis and complications such as Barrett's esophagus. It enables visualization and biopsy of the esophageal mucosa, but the mucosa may appear relatively normal in mild cases of GERD. A camera-containing capsule swallowed by the patient is a new technology for visualizing the esophageal mucosa (PillCam ESO). The procedure is less invasive than endoscopy and takes about 20 minutes to perform in the clinician's office. Images of the esophagus are downloaded through sensors placed on the patient's chest that are connected to a data collector. The camera-containing capsule is passed in the stool. Barium radiography is less expensive than endoscopy but lacks the sensitivity and specificity needed to accurately determine the presence of mucosal injury or to distinguish Barrett's esophagus from esophagitis. Twenty-four-hour ambulatory pH monitoring is useful in patients who continue to have symptoms without evidence of esophageal damage, patients who are refractory to standard treatment and patients who present with atypical symptoms (e.g., chest pain or pulmonary symptoms). The test helps to correlate symptoms with abnormal esophageal acid exposure, documents the percentage of time the intraesophageal pH is low and determines the frequency and severity of reflux. **Omeprazole** given empirically in standard or double doses as a "therapeutic trial" for diagnosing GERD may be as beneficial as ambulatory P^H monitoring while also being less expensive, more convenient and more readily available. However, there is no standard dosing regimen; standard dose or double-dose omeprazole has been used. Esophageal manometry to evaluate motility should be performed in any patient who is a candidate for antireflux surgery. It is useful in determining which surgical procedure is best for the patient.

Treatment

Therapeutic modalities are targeted at reversing the pathophysiological abnormalities. These include decreasing the acidity of the refluxate, decreasing the gastric volume available to be refluxed, improving gastric emptying, increasing LES pressure, enhancing esophageal acid clearance and protecting the esophageal mucosa (Fig. 9-1).

Treatment is categorized into the following modalities:

Phase I: Lifestyle changes and patient directed therapy with **antacids** and/or non prescription **histamine receptor antagonists (H_2-RA)** or **proton pump inhibitors (PPIs)**.

Phase II: Pharmacological interventions with standard or high-dose acid suppressing agents.

Phase III: Interventional therapies (antireflux surgery or endoluminal therapies).

The initial therapeutic modality depends in part on the patient's condition (symptom frequency, degree of esophagitis, presence of complications). Historically, a step-up approach has been used, starting with phase I and then progressing through phases II and III if necessary.

Antacids and Antacid-Alginic Acid Products

Antacids provide immediate, symptomatic relief for mild GERD and are often used concurrently with other acid-suppressing therapies. Patients who require frequent use for chronic symptoms should receive prescription-strength, acid suppressing therapy instead.

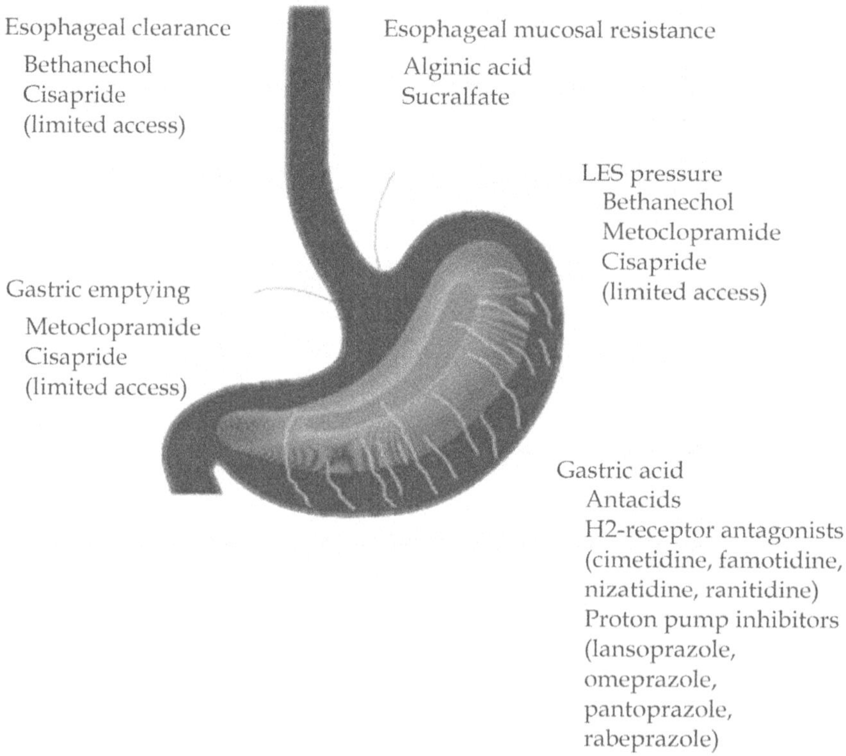

Fig 9-1: Therapeutic interventions in the management of gastroesophageal reflux disease. Pharmacological interventions are targeted at improving defence mechanisms or decreasing aggressive factors (LES, lower esophageal sphincter).

An **antacid with alginic acid** (Gaviscon) is not a potent acid-neutralizing agent, but it does forms a viscous solution that floats on the surface of the gastric contents. This serves as a protective barrier for the esophagus against reflux of gastric contents and reduces the frequency of reflux episodes. The combination product may be superior to antacids alone in relieving symptoms, but efficacy data indicating endoscopic healing are lacking. Antacids have a short duration, which necessitates frequent administration throughout the day to provide continuous acid neutralization. Typical doses are two tablets or 1 tablespoonful four times daily (after meals and at bedtime). Night time acid suppression cannot be maintained with bedtime doses of antacids.

H_2-Receptor Antagonists (H_2RAs)

Cimetidine, Ranitidine, Famotidine and Nizatidine

The H_2RAs in divided doses are effective for treating mild to moderate GERD. Low-dose non prescription products may be beneficial for symptomatic relief of intermittent heartburn and for preventing meal-provoked heartburn in patients with mild disease. For nonerosive disease, H_2RAs are given in standard doses twice daily. For non responding patients and those with erosive disease, higher doses and/or four times daily dosing provide better acid control .The efficacy of H_2RAs in GERD is highly variable; although standard doses produce symptomatic improvement in about 60% of patients, endoscopic healing rates average only about 50%. The more severe the esophageal damage, the poorer the response. Higher doses and prolonged courses (8 weeks or more) are frequently required. The H_2RAs are generally well tolerated. The most common adverse effects are headache, somnolence, fatigue, dizziness, and either constipation or diarrhea. Cimetidine may inhibit the metabolism of theophylline, warfarin, phenytoin, nifedipine and propranolol, among other drugs.

Proton Pump Inhibitors (PPIs)

Esomeprazole, Lansoprazole, Omeprazole, Pantoprazole and Rabeprazole

PPIs block gastric acid secretion by inhibiting hydrogen potassium adenosine triphosphatase in gastric parietal cells, which results in profound and long-lasting antisecretory effects. PPIs are superior to H_2RAs in patients with moderate to severe GERD, including those with erosive esophagitis, complicated symptoms (Barrett's esophagus, strictures) and nonerosive GERD with moderate to severe symptoms. Relapse is common in these patients and long-term maintenance therapy is generally indicated. Symptomatic relief is achieved in approximately 83% of patients and endoscopic healing rates are about 78% at 8 weeks. PPIs are also efficacious in patients refractory to H_2RAs in patients with severe disease. PPIs are usually well tolerated. Potential adverse effects include headache, dizziness, somnolence, diarrhoea, constipation, nausea and vitamin B_{12} deficiency. All PPIs can decrease the absorption of drugs such as Ketoconazole or itraconazole that require an acidic environment for absorption. Other drug interactions vary with each agent. The PPIs degrade in acidic environments and are therefore formulated in delayed-release capsules or tablets. Lansoprazole, esomeprazole and omeprazole contain enteric coated (pH-sensitive) granules in a capsule form. In patients unable to swallow the capsules, the contents can be mixed in apple sauce or placed in orange juice. In patients with nasogastric tubes, the contents should be mixed in 8.4% sodium bicarbonate solution. Esomeprazole granules can be dispersed in water. Lansoprazole is also available in packets for oral suspension and delayed release orally disintegrating tablets; the packet for oral suspension should not be placed through nasogastric tubes. Patients taking pantoprazole or rabeprazole should be instructed not to crush, chew, or split the delayed release tablets. Lansoprazole, esomeprazole and pantoprazole are available in IV formulations for patients who cannot take oral medications, but they are not more efficacious than oral preparations and are significantly more expensive. Patients should be instructed to take oral PPIs in the morning 15 to 30 minutes before breakfast to maximize efficacy, because these agents inhibit only actively secreting proton pumps. If dosed twice daily, the second dose should be taken approximately 10 to 12 hours after the morning dose and prior to a meal or snack.

Promotility Agents

Promotility agents may be useful as adjuncts to acid suppression therapy in patients with a known motility defect (e.g., LES incompetence, decreased esophageal clearance, delayed gastric emptying). However, these agents are generally not as effective as acid suppression therapy and have undesirable side effects. Cisapride has comparable efficacy to H_2RAs in patients with mild esophagitis. It is no longer available for routine use because of life-threatening arrhythmias when combined with certain medications and other disease states. Metoclopramide, a dopamine antagonist, increases LES pressure in a dose related manner and accelerates gastric emptying. Unlike cisapride, it does not improve esophageal clearance. Metoclopramide provides symptomatic improvement for some patients with GERD, but substantial evidence of endoscopic healing is lacking. Tachyphylaxis and side effects limit its usefulness. Commonly reported adverse reactions include somnolence, nervousness, fatigue, dizziness, weakness, depression, diarrhoea and rash. Bethanechol has very limited value and is not routinely recommended for the treatment of GERD because of unwanted side effects.

Mucosal Protectants

Sucralfate is a nonabsorbable aluminium salt of sucrose octasulfate that has limited value and is not routinely recommended for treatment of GERD.

Combination Therapy

Combination therapy with an acid-suppressing agent and a prokinetic agent or mucosal protectant seems logical, but data supporting such therapy are limited. This approach should be reserved for patients who have esophagitis plus concurrent motor dysfunction or for those who have failed high-dose PPI therapy.

References

A. Savitri, T. N. Bhavanishankar and H. S. R. Desikachar (1986). Effect of spices on *in vitro* gas production by *Clostridium perfringens. Food Microbiology* **3:** 195-199.

S. K. Garg, A. C. Banerjea, J. Verma and M. J. Abraham. Effect of Various Treatments of Pulses on *In Vitro* Gas Production by Selected Intestinal *Clostridia. Journal of Food Science* **45(6):** 1601-1602.

CHAPTER 10

Appetite Stimulants and Suppressants

Appetite Stimulants

Appetite stimulants act by increasing food intake in people who have lost weight abnormally or have cachexia (loss of weight due to diseased conditions like cancer, AIDS etc.)

This condition is termed as *Anorexia.*

Anorexia is most commonly seen in the following conditions,

- Emotional upset, Nervousness, Loneliness, Boredom.
- Tension, Anxiety, Depression
- Acute and Chronic infections
- Pregnancy
- Hypothyroidism
- Usage of chemotherapeutic agents

Drugs used as Appetite stimulants:

- Alcohol
- Megestrol
- Dronabinol
- Vitamin B12, zinc
- Dexamethasone
- Cyproheptadine.

Alcohol (10%)

- Given in small quantities before meals.
- It act primarily by increasing the gastric secretions both reflex and also by stimulating the taste buds.
- Alcohol stands as a major constituent in many appetite stimulants and tonics.
- Repeated ingestion leads to gastritis and diminution in appetite.
- Use of alcohol as an appetite stimulant is limited because of its abuse.

Magestrol

- It is a progesterone derivative.
- Commonly used as an appetite stimulant in people with cancer.
- Weight gain with megestrol is because of water or fat gain but not because of gain lean body mass.
- After prolonged therapy patients become unresponsive to megestrol and develop anorexia.

Dronabinol

- It is an FDA approved tetrahydrocannabinol derivative.
- It posses antiemetic properties and serves as an appetite booster.

Dexamethasone

- It is found to be effective as an appetite stimulant. If used as an appetite stimulant, dexamethasone exhibits many side effects such as immunosuppression, steroids inducesmyopathy, etc.

Vitamin B12, zinc

- Loss of appetite is a symptom of vitamin B12 deficiency,
- Zinc, vitamins are the major ingredients in appetite boosters.

Appetite Suppressants/ Anorexiants

- Anorexiants, anorexigenics or Appetite suppressants are dietary supplements or drugs that act primarily by reducing the appetite.
- These are used in the treatment of obesity.
- Anorexiants generally act by reducing the food intake.

Classification: centrally acting

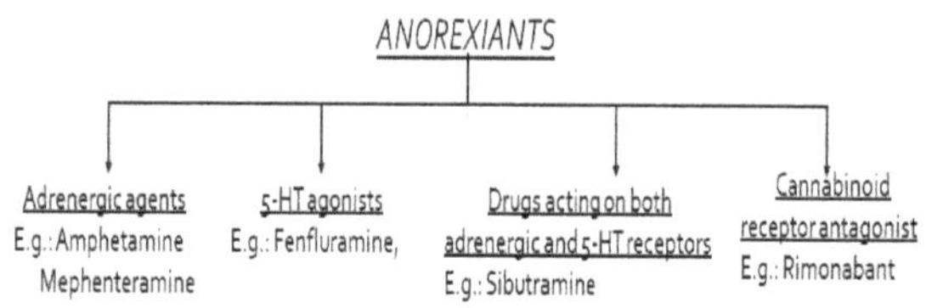

Classification: Drugs acting on GIT

Anorexiants

- Bulk anorexiants

  E.g.: Methylcellulose, Dietary fibre.
- Non-absorbable fat substitutes

  E.g.: Olestra.
- Lipase inhibitors

  E.g.: Orlistat

Centrally Acting Anorexiants

Adrenergic agents

This class of drugs act by enhancing the release of dopamine and norepinephrine from adrenergic cells.

Amphetamine

- Amphetamine is also known as Benzedrine.
- Which is an indirectly acting sympathomimetic.
- It acts either by stimulating NE release or blocking its reuptake.
- Amphetamine is known to exhibit anorexiant effect, i.e., body weight decreases as a result of less food intake.
- Amphetamine cannot used in the treatment of obesity due to rapid development of tolerance.

5-HT Agonists

This class of drugs act by enhancing 5-HT levels in brain, by stimulating their release and reducing reuptake.

Fenfluramine

- Fenfluramine in combination with phenteramine is widely used as an anti-obesity medication. This combination is known as "FEN-PHEN".
- It is found to be effective in the management of exogenous obesity and as an adjunct in the treatment of weight reduction based on caloric restriction.
- Most common adverse effects of fenfluramine includes drowsiness, diarrhoea and dry mouth.
- It is no longer used because of wide profile of unwanted effects which include heart valve disease, pulmonary hypertension and cardiac fibrosis.

Drugs acting on both Adrenergic and 5-HT Receptors

This class of drugs exhibit their action by inhibiting the reuptake of serotonin and norepinephrine.

Sibutramine

- Sibutramine exerts its action by inhibiting the reuptake of the neurotransmitters like serotonin, norepinephrine and dopamine leading to enhanced levels of the neurotransmitters in the synaptic cleft. Enhanced level of neurotransmitters stimulates satiety centre. Anorexiant effect of sibutramine is due to its serotonergic action.
- It is rapidly metabolized by cytochrome P450 isozyme CYP3A4 to yield secondary (M1) and primary (M2) metabolites which are pharmacologically active in nature.
- Side effects include headache, insomnia, dry mouth, nausea, constipation, tachycardia, rise in BP and rarely arrhythmias.
- It is contraindicated in uncontrolled hypertension, stroke, hepatic failure and obesity of endocrine and psychiatric origin.

Cannabinoid Receptor Antagonists

This class of drugs exhibit their action by selectively antagonizing cannabinoid (CB1) receptors.

Rimonabant

- It acts by inhibiting lipogenesis and increasing the production of adinopectin, resulting in decreased food intake and consequent weight loss. It also enhances high density lipid (HDL-C) levels and decrease low density lipids (LDL-C).
- It is also found to be effective in improving short term memory.
- Side effects include dizziness, nausea, diarrhoea, upper respiratory tract infections, depression etc.
- The drug is still under FDA consideration.

Anorexiant Acting on GIT

Bulk Anorexiant

This class of drugs act by increasing the bulk in diet.

Methylcellulose

- MC is a non-digestible polysaccharide which swells in the stomach, their by increasing the bulk in the diet. It is used as a low calorie diet.
- It is an important ingredient of many commercial preparations used for the treatment of obesity.
- It is also used in the treatment of constipation and diarrhoea.

Non-Absorbable Fat Substitutes

Olestra

- It consist of a mixture of sucrose and fatty acid esters which is neither digested nor absorbed from the GIT.
- It enhances bowel function and forms bulky faeces.
- It is recommended as a fat substitute in cooking.
- It is expensive and its long term health effects are yet to be explored.

Lipase Inhibitors

Orlistat

- It exerts its action by suppressing pancreatic and other lipases thereby preventing the degradation and subsequent absorption of $1/3^{rd}$ of the dietary fat.
- It also reduces total cholesterol and LDL cholesterol in plasma.
- Most common side effects are abdominal pain and augmented defecation of fatty stools with anal leaking.
- It is contraindicated in chronic diarrhoea.

CHAPTER

Carminatives

11

Introduction

These medications warm and comfort the epigastrium while promoting the ejection of gases from the gastrointestinal tract. They increases gas ejection from GIT and prevents gas formation.

Plants called carminative herbs have historically been employed for their pharmacological effects on improving human health. They include volatile chemicals. These herbs' phytonutrients primarily assist digestive health and have positive impacts on general wellbeing.

Hippocrates even made mention of peppermint, one of the most widely utilised carminatives today, in his writings when he refers to its botanical name, Mentha Piperita L.

Today, there are numerous uses for carminatives, including gum, bitter liqueurs, food preparation, toothpaste, and herbal teas.

Reduced gas, bloating after meals, nausea, and other problems can be greatly improved by include carminative herbs in your diet and even in the air you breathe.

Commonly used drugs are:

Sodium bicarbonate: 0.6–1.5 g

Oil Peppermint: 0.06–0.1 ml

Tincture Cardamom Co.: 1–2 ml

Oil of dil: 0.06–0.2 ml

Tincture ginger: 0.6–1 ml

Gastric HCl and sodium bicarbonate combine to form CO_2, which rapidly expands the stomach, relaxes the LES, and causes eructation.

The other types of food are seasonings and spices that contain volatile oils that, through their mild irritating effects and flavour, relax the LES and improve gastrointestinal motility. They cause the stomach to feel warm and cosy.

Used for:

flatulent dyspepsia.

Part - III

Chemotherapeutic Drugs

CHAPTER

General Principles of Chemotherapy 12

Chemotherapy: Treatment of infectious diseases or malignancy with drugs to destroy microorganisms or cancer cells with minimal damage to host cells

- Bacteria
- Virus
- Fungi
- Protozoa
- Helminths.

Definitions

- Antibiotics: chemical substances obtained from microorganisms that kill or suppress the growth of other microorganisms at a very low concentration.
- Antimicrobials: synthetic as well as naturally obtained drugs that act against microorganisms.
- Bacteriocidal: They kills & destroys microorganisms. Eg.Penicillin, Cephalosporins , Aminoglycosides.
- Bacteriostatic: they inhibit the growth & multiplication of microorganisms.

  Eg. sulphonamides, tetracyclines, chloramphenicol
- Minimum inhibitory concentration (MIC): Is the minimum concentration of antibiotic that prevents visible growth of a microorganism.

Classification

(A) Chemical structure

(1) b- lactam antibiotics- b lactam ring e.g.- Penicillin –usually end by cillin. Cephalosporins

(2) Aminoglycosides – Streptomycin, Gentamicin

(3) Macrolides – Erythromycin, Roxithromycin

(4) Quinolones – Nalidixic acid

(B) Mechanism of action

- Inhibit cell wall synthesis- Penicillin, Vancomycin, Bacitracin.
- Cause leakage from cell membrane- Amphotericin B, Nystatin, Polymyxins.
- Inhibit protein synthesis-Tetracycline, Erythromycin, chloramphenicol.
- Misreading of m RNA and affect permeability- Aminoglycosides.
- Antimetabolite action (interfere with intermediary metabolism)- Sulfonamide, Trimethoprim, Pyrimethamine.
- Interfere with DNA function – Rifampin, Metronidazole.
- Interfere with DNA synthesis-Acylovir, Zidovudine.
- Inhibit DNA gyrase-Fluoroquinolones.

(C) Types of organisms against which primarily active-

-Antibacterial, Antifungal, Antiviral.

(D) Spectrum activity-

- Narrow spectrum- Penicillin G, Streptomycin.
- Broad spectrum -Tetracycline, chloramphenicol.

(E) Types of action-

- Bacteriostatic - Inhibiting growth e.g. Sulfonamide, Tetracycline, Erythromycin, Ethambutol, Chloramphenicol.
- Bactericidal- Destroying the organism e.g. Penicillin, Fluoroquinolones, Cotrimoxazole.

(F)Antibiotic are obtained from-

- Fungi -Penicillin, Griseofulvin.
- Bacteria- Bacitracin, Polymyxin B,Azteronam.
- Actinomycetes- Macrolides, Tetracyclines, Aminoglycosides.

Problems with Antimicrobials

1. **Toxicity-**

- Local irritancy at Oral - gastric irritation, IM-pain & abscess formation, IV-thrombophlebitis.
- Systemic toxicity - some have high therapeutic index.

  e.g. Penicillin, other have low therapeutic index ® watched for toxicity

  Aminoglycosides -Nephrotoxicity

  Chloramphenicol- Bone marrow depression

2. **Hypersensitivity reactions-**

   Unpredictable & unrelated to dose, rashes to anaphylactic shock. All Antimicrobial agents may cause hypersensitivity reaction but most common with Penicillins, Sulfonamides.

3. **Drug resistance**

I. **Unresponsiveness of microorganisms to an AMA Naturally resistant -** due to lack of target site e.g. - outer membrane of Gm – Ve bacteria is act as barrier and thus became ineffective to Penicillin.

II. **Acquired resistance -** development of resistance by organism use of AMA over period of time.

- Resistance may be acquired by **mutation** ® Gyras e gene mutation - Quinolone resistant, RNA polymerase gene mutation- Rifampin resistant.
- More commonly resistance is acquired by horizontal transfer of resistant determinants from a donor cell, often to another bacterial species by Transduction, Transformation, Conjugation, Gene transfer.

Resistance of microorganism can be

1. **Drug tolerance**

   Loss of affinity of the target biomolecule of the microorganism for a particular AMA.

   - Penicillin resistant due to alternation of penicillin binding protein.

   - Drug destroying - b lactamases are produced by Staphylococci, Gonococci which inactivate penicillin G.

2. **Drug impermeable**

   In Gram -ve bacteria hydrophilic antibiotic gain access into bacterial cell through specific channels formed by protein called PORINS loss of appropriate porins channel-drug delivery to target site become ineffective.

   Eg: Aminoglycosides resistant with Gm -ve bacteria

3. **Cross Resistance**

- Acquisition of resistance to one AMA conferring resistance to another AMA, to which the organism has not been exposed, is called cross resistance.
- More commonly seen in chemically related drugs. Eg: One sulphonamide resistant to all other sulphonamide.
- Unrelated drugs show partial cross resistance Eg: Between tetracycline &Chloramphenicol.

4. **Superinfection**

- Appearance of new infection as a result of antimicrobial therapy.
- Normal flora contributes host defense by elaborating substance called bacteroc in which inhibit pathogenic organism.
- Broad spectrum antibiotic suppress the pathogenic organism & normal flora in absence of bacteriocin *Candida albicans, pseudomonas* infection will appear.

Principles

- **I. Make a diagnosis-** Define site of infection
  - organism responsible & their sensitive to drugs
  - Biological sample send to lab before start T/t
- **II. Remove barriers to cure- Incision &.** drainage of abscesses, removal of infected I.V. catheter.
- **III. Select the best drug –** Specificity- Given drug has status of first line.
  - Indiscriminate use of broad pectrum drug promote Antimicrobial resistance.
  - But absence of precise diagnosis best guess chemotherapy or broad pectrum antibiotic may be given.

  Pharmacokinetic factors- Drug is capable to reaching site of infection in adequate amount e.g. By crossing Blood Brain Barrier.

  The patients- Previously allergy to particular drug -renal disease, hepatic disease.
- **IV. Administer the drug –** By optimum dose and most appropriate route & duration of T/t.
- **V. Test for cure-** Sign & symptoms disappear before eradication of organism e.g. Microbiological culture done after T/t of UTI.

Principle of Antibiotic Dosing

- Some antibiotics are much more effective if higher blood concentrations are reached periodically.
- These exhibit concentration-dependent killing (CDK).
- Rate and extent of killing action increases with increasing drug concentration.
- Eg. Aminoglycosides, Fluoroquinolones and Metronidazole
- Time- dependent killing.
- Effective if blood levels are maintained above the MIC for as long a duration as possible.
- These exhibit time-dependent killing (TDK).
- Eg. B-lactams and vancomycin

Combined use of Antimicrobials

- Done only for specific purpose.

1. **To achieve synergism-**
   - Two bacteriostatic agent often additive, sometimes supraadditive e.g. Sulfamethoxazole + Trimethoprim =Cotrimoxazole.
   - Two bactericidal drug often additive.
   - Eg. - Rifampin + Isoniazid in Tuberculosis

     -Ampicillin +Gentamicin in *Enterococcal* Subacute bacterial endocarditis.
2. **To reduce severity of adverse effect-**
   - Dose can be reduce.e.g.-Streptomycin +Penicillin in SABE due to *Streptococcus faecalis.*
3. **To prevent emergence of resistance-**
   - Mutation conferring resistance to one AMA but may sensitive to other e.g. Treatment of tuberculosis, HIV.
4. **Broaden spectrum of antimicrobial-**
   - For T/t of mixed infection e.g. Peritonitis.

Disadvantages of Combination

- Emergence of organism resistant to the multiple drugs used by using non synergistic drug.
- Increased incidence and variety of adverse effects.
- Increased chances of superinfections.
- Increased cost of therapy.

CHAPTER

Sulfonamides, Trimethoprim and Cotrimoxazole 13

Sulfonamides

Sulfonamides were the first successful selectively toxic antibacterial drugs. Prontosil (see below Fig 13-1) was discovered by Gerhard Domagk in 1936 and used to successfully treat puerperal sepsis (childbirth fever) in London. Prontosil is converted by cellular enzymes to sulfanilamide, the prototype of all sulfonamides.

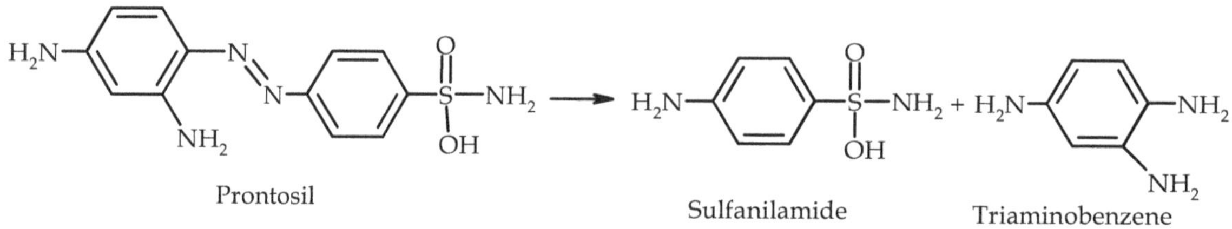

Fig 13-1: Conversion of prontosil

Mechanism of Action

Both sulfonamides and trimethoprim (not a sulfonamide) sequentially interfere with folic acid synthesis by bacteria. Folic acid functions as a coenzyme in the transfer of one-carbon unit, required for the synthesis of thymidine, purines and some amino acids and consists of three components like a pteridine moiety, Para-aminobenzoic Acid (PABA), and glutamate (Fig. 13-2). The sulfonamides, as structural

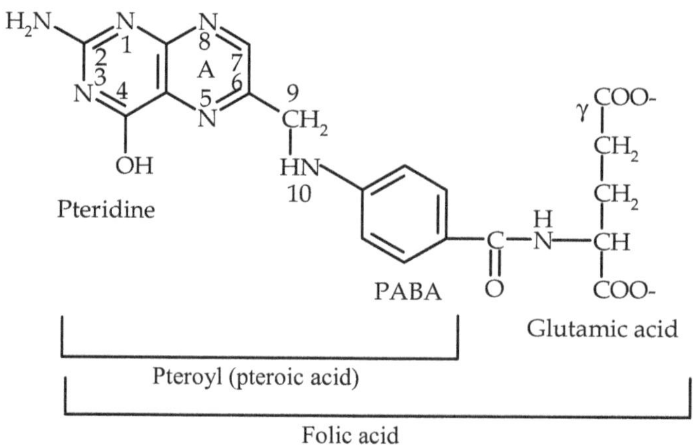

Fig 13-2: Structure of folic acid.

analogues, competitively block PABA incorporation. Sulfonamides inhibit the enzyme (Fig 13-3)dihydropteroate synthatase, which is necessary for PABA to be incorporated into dihydropteroic acid, an intermediate compound in the formation of folinic acid. Since the sulfonamides reversibly block the synthesis of folic acid, they are bacteriostatic drugs. Humans cannot synthesize folic acid and acquire from the diet thus, the sulfonamides selectively inhibit microbial growth. Resistance to the sulfonamides can be the result of decreased bacterial permeability to the drug, increased production of PABA, or production of an altered dihydropteroate synthetase that exhibits low afûnity for sulfonamides. The latter mechanism of resistance is plasmid mediated. Active efûux of the sulfonamides has also been reported to play a role in resistance. The inhibitory effect of the sulfonamides also can be reversed by the presence of pus, tissue ûuids and drugs that contain releasable PABA.

Resistance

Resistance occurs as the result of one or more alterations in the cellular metabolism of the bacteria; both mutation and plasmid-mediated resistance occurs. These changes, which can be irreversible, include alterations in the physical or enzymatic characteristics of the enzyme or enzymes that metabolize PABA and participate in the cellular synthesis of tetrahydrofolic acid.

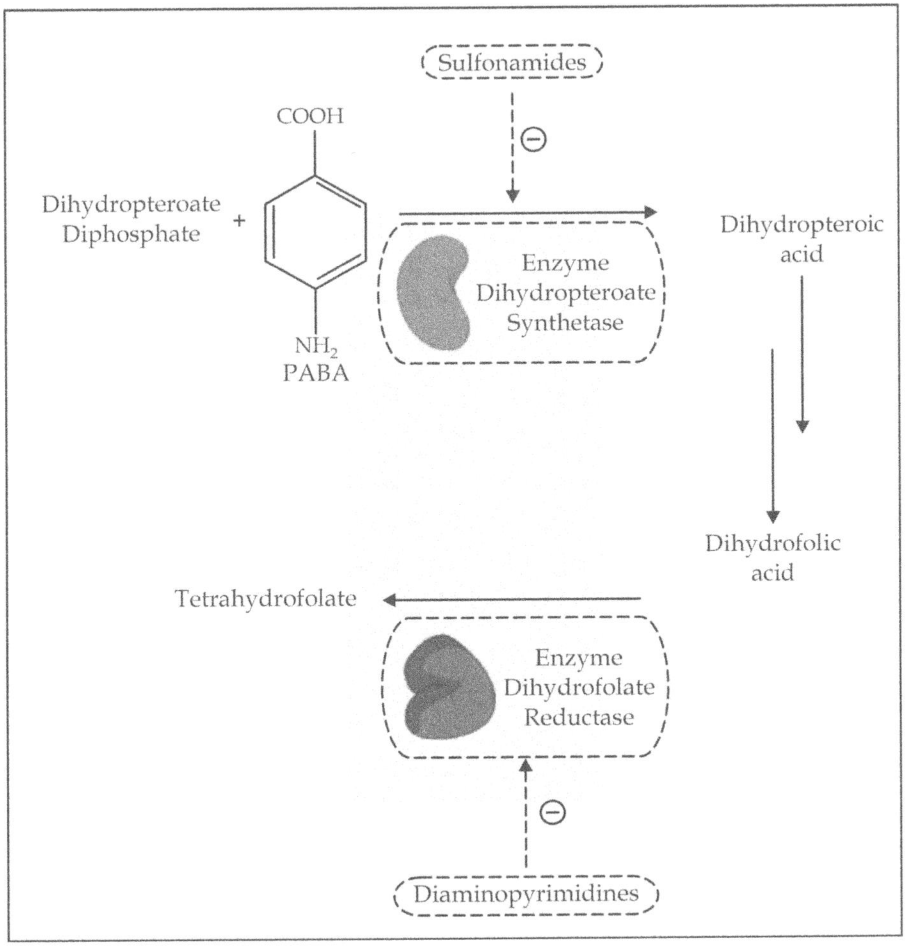

Fig 13-3: Mechanism of action of sulfonamides.

The appearance of alternative pathways for PABA synthesis within the bacteria or the development of an increased capacity to inactivate or eliminate the sulfonamide also may contribute to bacterial cell resistance. Bacteria that can use preformed folate are not inhibited by sulfonamides.

Antibacterial Spectrum

The sulfonamides are broad-spectrum antimicrobials that are effective against gram-positive and some gram negative organisms of the *Enterobacteriaceae*. There is good activity against *Escherichia coli*, moderate activity against *Proteus mirabilis* and *Enterobacter spp.*; poor activity against indole-positive *Proteus* and *Klebsiella spp.*, and no inhibitory activity against *Pseudomonas aeruginosa* and *Serratia spp.* They are also effective against Chlamydia spp., but superior drugs are now available. Sulfonamides are used in treating infections caused by *Toxoplasma gondii* and occasionally chloroquine-resistant Plasmodium falciparum.

Classification

The classification of Sulfonamides are shown in Fig 13-4.

General Properties

The sulfonamides are derivatives of sulfanilamide. All have the same nucleus to which various functional groups have been added to the amido group or in which various substitutions on the amino group are made. These changes produce compounds with varying physical, chemical, pharmacological, and antibacterial properties. Although amphoteric, sulfonamides generally behave as weak organic acids and are much more soluble in an alkaline than in an acidic environment. Those of therapeutic interest have pK_a values of 4.8–8.6. Water-soluble sodium or disodium salts are used for parenteral administration. Such solutions are highly alkaline, somewhat unstable and readily precipitate with the addition of polyionic electrolytes. In a mixture of sulfonamides (eg, the sulfa-pyrimidine group), each component drug has its own solubility; therefore, a combination of sulfonamides is more

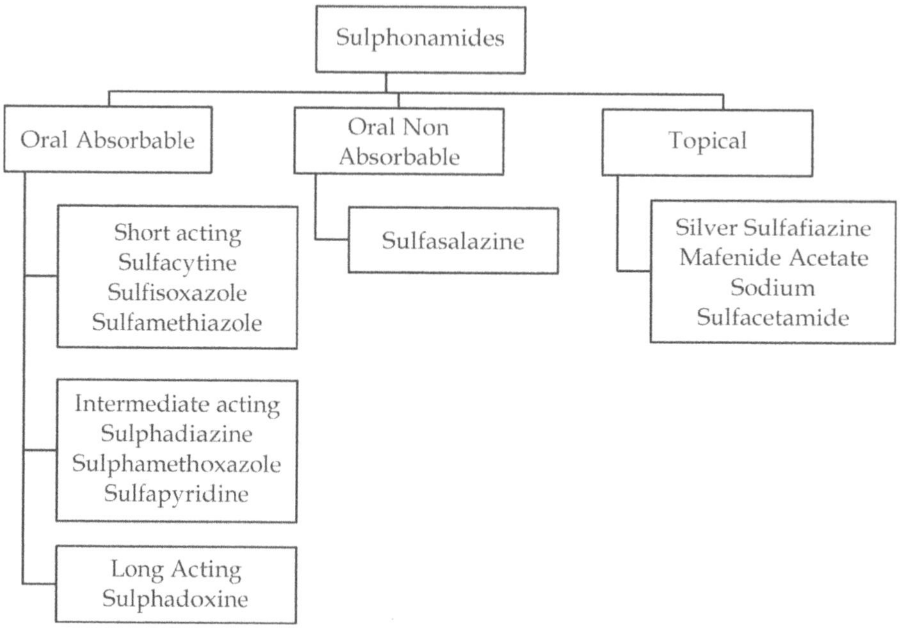

Fig 13-4: Sulphonamide classification.

water-soluble than a single drug at the same total concentration. This is the basis of triple sulfonamide mixtures used clinically. The N-4 acetylated sulfonamides, except for the sulfapyrimidine group (sulfamethazine, sulfamerazine, sulfadiazine), are less water-soluble than their non-acetylated forms. This has bearing in the development of sulfonamide crystalluria. The highly insoluble sulfonamides (phthalylsulfathiazole and succinyl-sulfathiazole) are retained in the lumen of the GI tract for prolonged periods and are known as "gut-active" sulfonamides.

Chemistry

A sulfonamide is a chemical entity characterized by a sulfur dioxide (SO_2) and nitrogen (N) moiety directly linked to a benzene ring (Fig 13-5). Many medication classes contain this chemical entity, including sulfonamide antimicrobials (e.g., sulfamethoxazole, sulfadiazine, sulfacetamide), carbonic anhydrase inhibitors (e.g., acetazolamide, methazolamide), sulfonylureas (e.g., glyburide, glipizide), diuretics (e.g., hydrochlorothiazide, chlorthalidone, furosemide, bumetanide), uricosurics (e.g., probenecid), drugs for

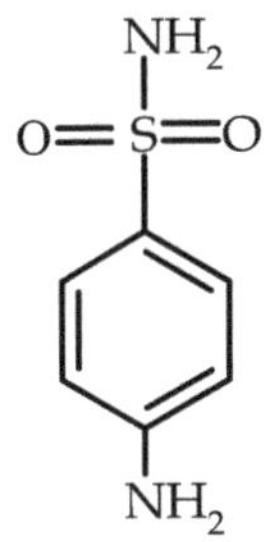

Sulfanilamide
(Basic-Sulfonamide Structure)

Structures of Sulfonamide Antimicrobials (All contain an Arylamine Group)

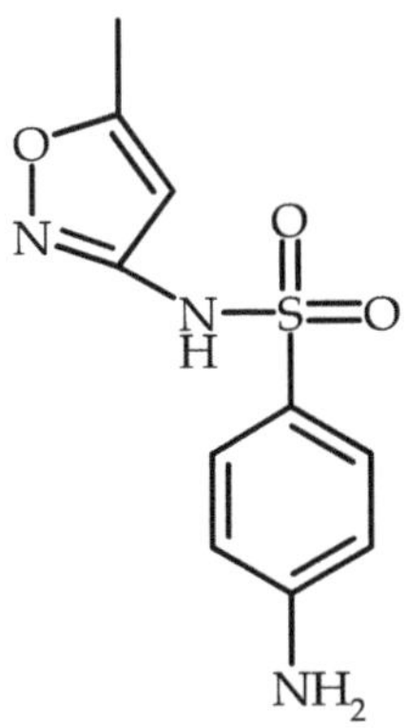

Sulfamethoxazole

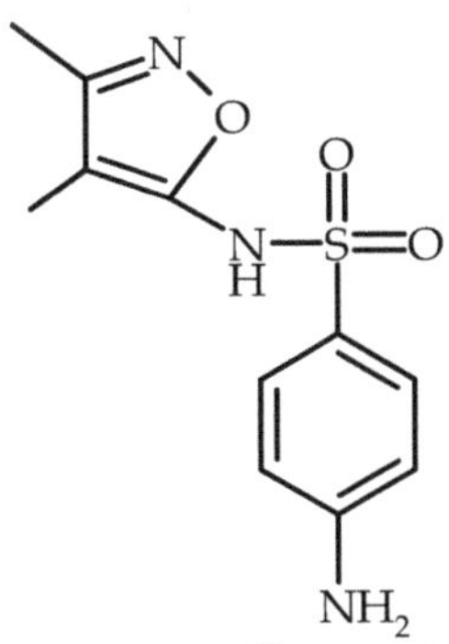

Sulfisoxazole

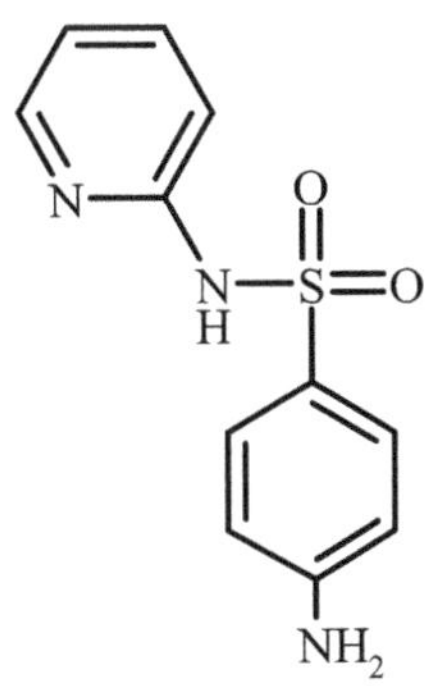

Sulfapyridine

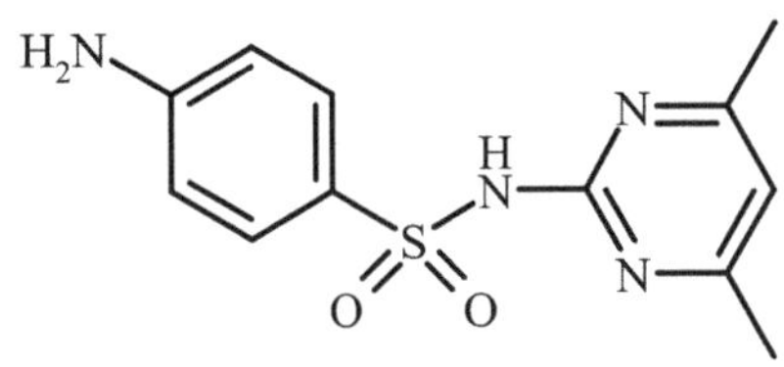

Sulfamethazine

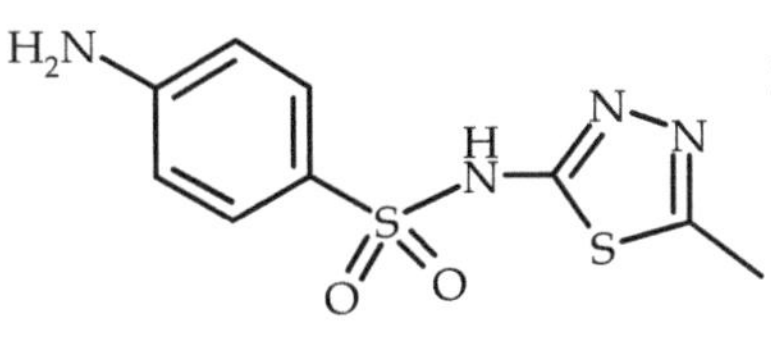

Sulfamethizole

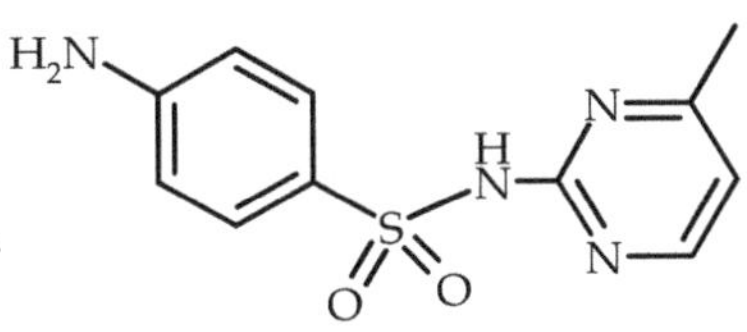

Sulfamerazine

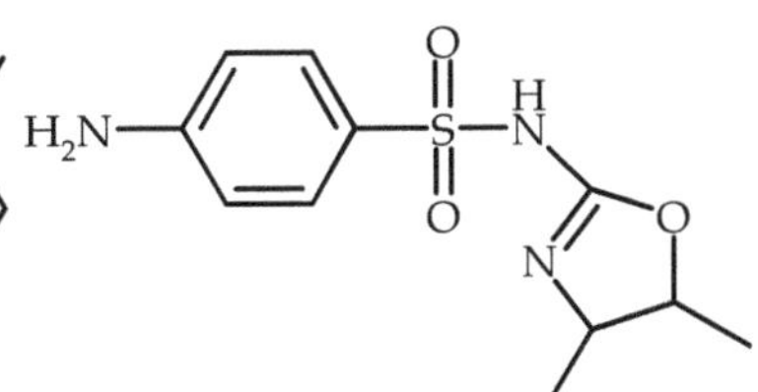

Sulfamoxole

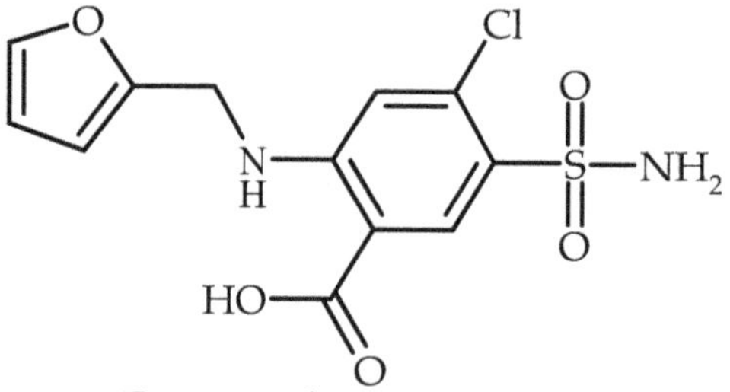

Furosemide

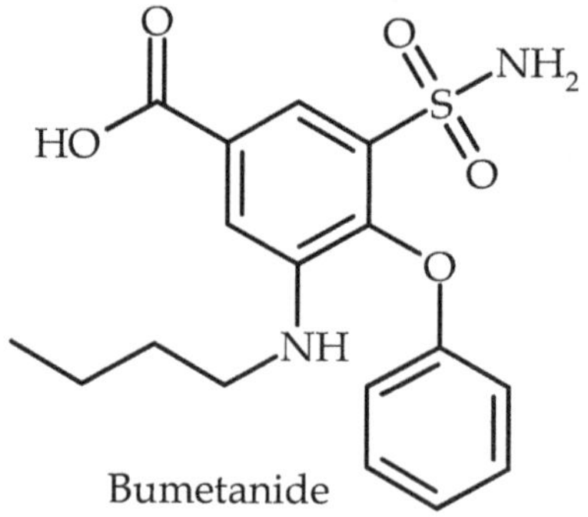

Bumetanide

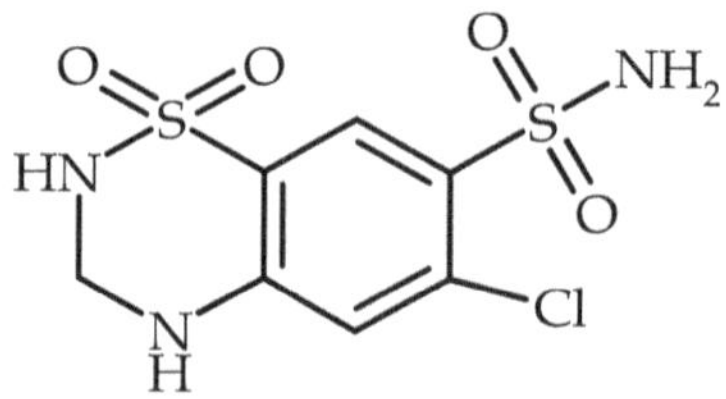

Hydrochlorothiazide

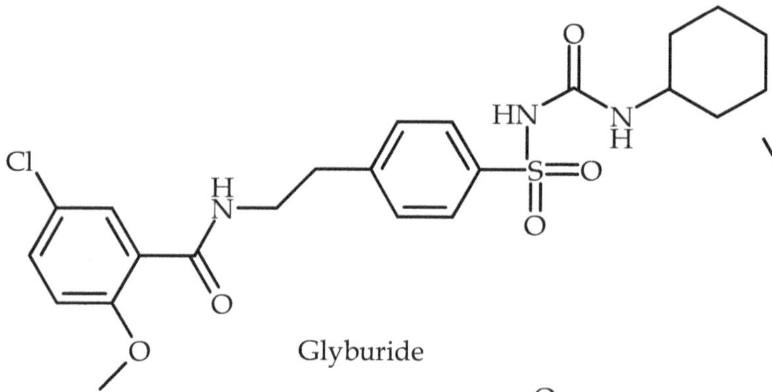

Glyburide

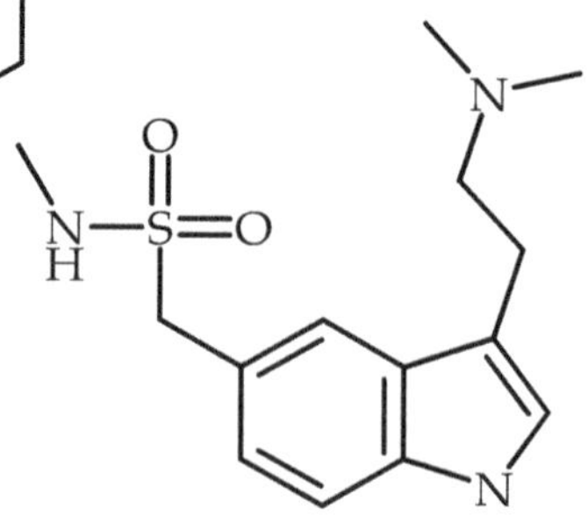

Sumatriptan

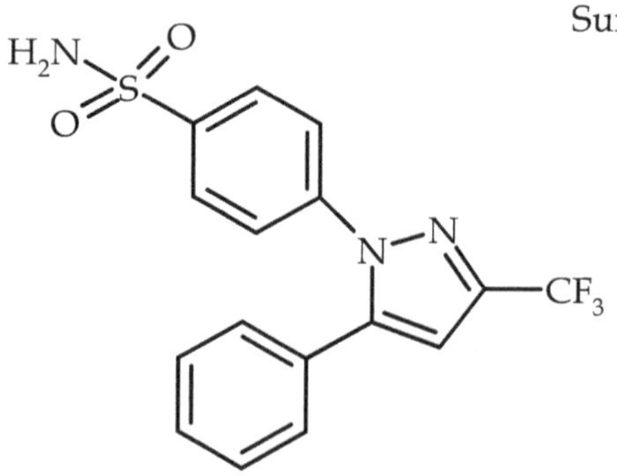

Celecoxib

Fig 13-5: Structures of sulphonamides.

Structures of Other Sulfonamide-Containing Compounds (None contain an Arylamine Group) inflammatory bowel disease (e.g., sulfasalazine), selective serotonin-1 receptor agonists (e.g., sumatriptan), and the specific cyclooxygenase-2 inhibitor celecoxib. Several structural differences exist among these medication classes. A major difference between sulfonamide antimicrobials and other sulfonamide-containing medications is the presence of an arylamine group (NH_2) at the N^4 position. It has been hypothesized that the arylamine group is critical in producing hypersensitivity reactions. Only sulfonamide antimicrobials contain this group.

Pharmacokinetic Properties

Absorption

Sulfonamides are usually given orally, although the soluble sodium salts can be given parenterally, a route that is infrequently used. Except for compounds designed for local gut effects, the sulfonamides are rapidly absorbed from the intestinal tract, primarily from the small intestine. They can usually be found in serum and urine within 30 minutes after ingestion. Peak serum levels are obtained in 2 to 6 hours; urine levels can reach above 500 µg/ml. Although absorption can occur via other routes (e.g., burned and/or abraded skin, stomach), the amounts absorbed are usually low and unpredictable. A burn area larger than 20% of total body surface can absorb enough drug to result in toxicity, especially if accompanied by renal dysfunction.

Distribution

Systemically absorbed sulfonamides readily distribute throughout body fluids. They pass the placental barrier and enter the cerebrospinal fluid (CSF) even in the absence of inflammation. The degree of protein binding, the half-life, and the drug's solubility in urine will vary considerably from one sulfonamide to another. Half life range from 2.5 to 17 hours, the latter exhibited by sulfadiazine. Sulfadiazine and sulfacetamide tend to have lower protein binding (about 20–30%) than the other major systemic sulfonamides, whose binding ranges from 80 to 90% (e.g., sulfamethoxazole, sulfisoxazole). The effects of high protein binding by a sulfonamide become almost negligible in body fluids with a paucity of protein (e.g., synovial, peritoneal, ocular); thus, the drug in these sites is primarily in the active unbound form. Most drugs with protein binding above 30% do not cross the placenta; while this reduces toxic potential, it concomitantly lowers drug antibacterial activity.

Metabolism and Excretion

The sulfonamides are degraded in the liver by acetylation and oxidation; metabolites have reduced bacteriological activity. The parent compound and the metabolites are excreted in the urine, primarily by glomerular filtration followed by tubular reabsorption. Most sulfonamides are excreted primarily in the urine. Bile, feces, milk, and sweat are excretory routes of lesser significance. Glomerular filtration, active tubular secretion, and tubular reabsorption are the main processes involved. The proportion reabsorbed is influenced by the inherent lipid solubility of individual sulfonamides and their metabolites and by urinary pH. Urinary pH, renal clearance, and the concentration and solubility of the respective sulfonamides and their metabolites determine whether solubilities are exceeded and crystals precipitate. This can be prevented by alkalinizing the urine, increasing fluid intake, reducing dose rates in renal insufficiency and using triple-sulfonamide or sulfonamide-diamino-pyrimidine combinations. The metabolism of Sulfonamide is shown in Fig 13-6.

Therapeutic uses

The sulfonamides are commonly used to treat or prevent acute systemic or local infections. Disease syndromes treated with sulfonamides include actinobacillosis, coccidiosis, mastitis, metritis, colibacillosis, pododermatitis, polyarthritis, respiratory infections and toxoplasmosis.

Sulfonamides are more effective when administered early in the course of a disease. Chronic infections, particularly with large amounts of exudate or tissue debris present, often are not responsive. In severe infections, the initial dose should be administered i.v to reduce the lag time between dose and effect. For drugs

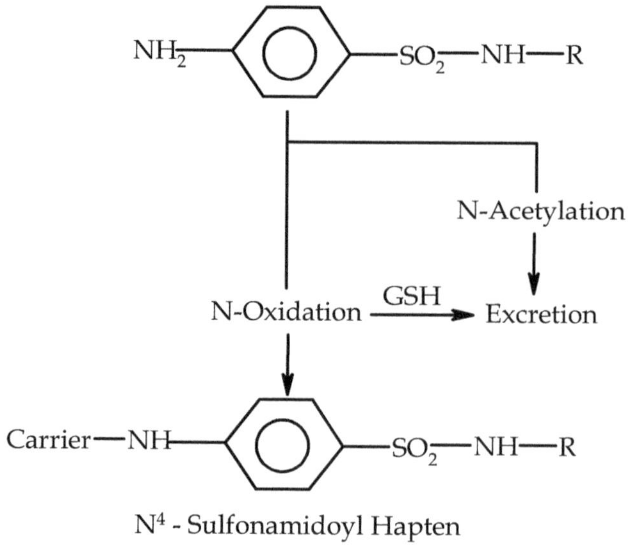

Fig 13-6: Metabolism of sulfonamide.

with a long elimination half-life, the initial dose should be double the maintenance dose. Adequate drinking water should be available at all times, and urine output monitored. A course of treatment should not exceed 7 days under usual circumstances. If a favorable response is seen within 72 hr, treatment should be continued for 48 hr after remission to prevent relapse and the emergence of resistance. The ability to mount an immune response must be intact for successful sulfonamide therapy.

Adverse Effects and Toxicity

Adverse reactions to sulfonamides may be due to hypersensitivity or direct toxic effects. Possible hypersensitivity reactions include urticaria, angioedema, anaphylaxis, skin rashes, drug fever, polyarthritis, hemolytic anemia, and agranulocytosis. Crystalluria with hematuria, and even tubular obstruction, is not common in veterinary medicine. Acute toxic manifestations may be seen after too rapid i.v administration or if an excessive dose is injected. Clinical signs include muscle weakness, ataxia, blindness, and collapse. GI disturbances, in addition to nausea and vomiting, may occur when sulfonamide concentrations are sufficiently high in the tract to disturb normal micro-floral balance and vitamin B synthesis. Sulfonamides depress the cellulolytic function of ruminal microflora, but the effect is usually transient (unless excessively high concentrations are reached). Several adverse effects have been reported after prolonged treatment, including bone marrow depression (aplastic anemia, granulocytopenia, thrombocytopenia), hepatitis and icterus, peripheral neuritis and myelin degeneration in the spinal cord and peripheral nerves, photosensitization, stomatitis, conjunctivitis, and keratitis sicca. Mild follicular thyroid hyperplasia may be associated with prolonged administration of sulfonamides in sensitive species such as dogs, and reversible hypothyroidism can be induced after treatment with high doses in dogs. Several sulfonamides can lead to decreased egg production and growth. Topically, the sulfonamides retard healing of uncontaminated wounds.

Interactions

Sulfonamide solutions are incompatible with calcium- or other polyionic containing fluids as well as many other preparations. Sulfonamides may be displaced from their plasma-protein-

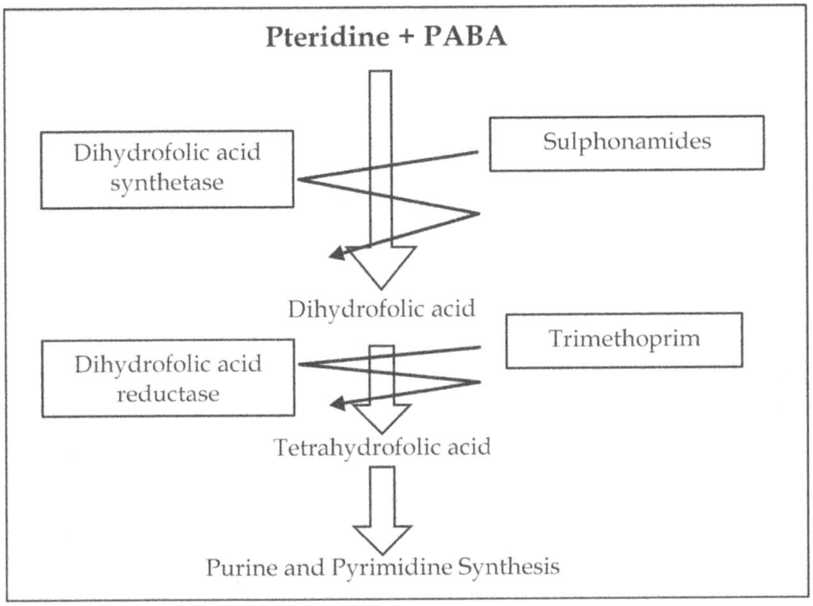

Fig 13-7: Mechanism of trimethoprim and sulfamethoxazole.

binding sites by other acidic drugs with higher binding affinities. Antacids tend to inhibit the GI absorption of sulfonamides. Alkalinization of the urine promotes sulfonamide excretion and urinary acidification increases the risk of crystalluria. Some sulfonamides act as microsomal enzyme inhibitors, which may lead to toxic manifestations of concurrently administered drugs such as phenytoin.

Trimethoprim–Sulfamethoxazole

Sulfamethoxazole, a structural analogue of para-aminobenzoic acid, interferes with the production of dihydrofolate. Trimethoprim is a pyrimidine derivative that competitively inhibits the production of dihydrofolate reductase. Fig 13-8 and 13-9.

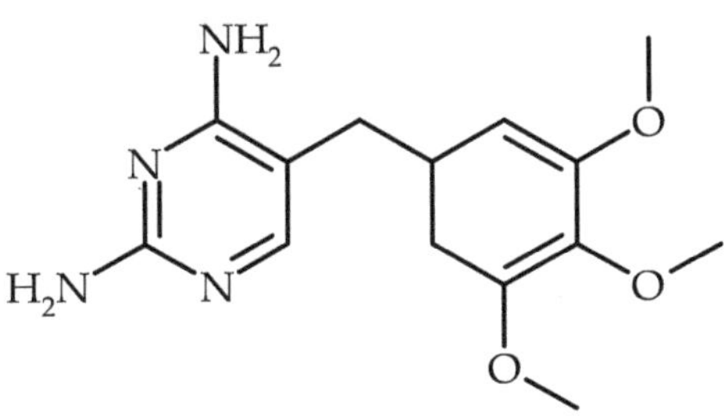

Fig 13-8: Structure of trimethoprim.

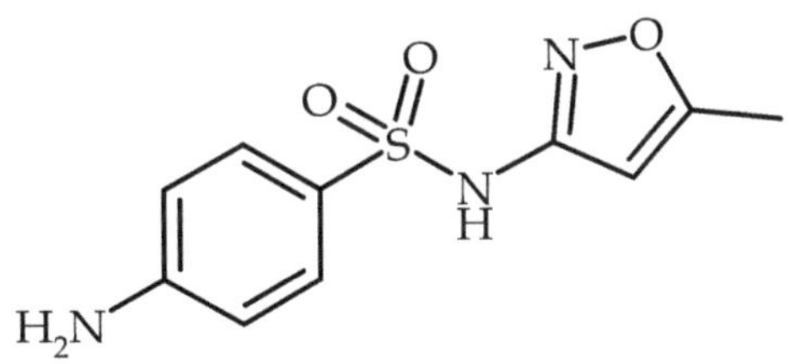

Fig 13-9: Structure of sulfamethoxazole.

Mechanism of Action

Sulfamethoxazole, a structural analogue of para aminobenzoic acid, interferes with the production of dihydrofolate. Trimethoprim binds to dihydrofolate reductase and inhibits the reduction of dihydrofolic acid (DHF) to tetrahydrofolic acid (THF). Trimethoprim binds much more avidly to bacterial dihydrofolate reductase than to the mammalian enzyme. The drug's overall effect is based on a sequential blockade of the various steps involved in microbial folate synthesis, which is necessary for the formation of purines and ultimately of deoxyribonucleic acid (Fig 13-7). The key action of Trimethoprim–Sulfamethoxazole (TMP-SMX) appears to be its inhibition of thymidine synthesis, since small concentrations of this nucleoside are capable of reversing the drug's action *in vitro*. Although SMX alone is bacteriostatic, the combination of SMX and TMP is bactericidal against most organisms *in vitro*.

Pharmacokinetics

Trimethoprim–Sulfamethoxazole (TMP-SMX) is commercially available in several forms various oral suspensions, tablets, and intravenous solutions (Table 13-1). Both TMP and SMX are efficiently absorbed after oral administration. Peak serum levels of 1.1 μg/mL of TMP and 20.3 μg/mL of SMX are achieved after a single oral dose of double strength TMP-SMX. Intravenous administration of 80 mg of TMP and 400 mg of SMX every 12 hours results in a steady state on the 4th day, with peak serum levels of 5.9 μg/mL of TMP and 178 μg/mL of SMX. Commercially available preparations of TMP-SMX are characterized by a 1:5 ratio of TMP to SMX. The volume of distribution of TMP (2 L/kg) exceeds that of SMX (360 ml/kg) because of TMP's lipophilic properties. This fixed ratio of TMP to SMX provides a peak serum TMP:SMX ratio of between 1:15 and 1:22, which is within the range of optimal antibacterial activity for most microorganisms. Tissue concentrations of the drug's components can vary widely. TMP-SMX penetrates well into tissues, in both the presence and the absence of inflammation. Cerebrospinal-fluid levels vary from 13% to 53% of serum levels for TMP and from 19% to 63% of serum levels for SMX. Diffusion of SMX into the cerebrospinal fluid is slow; peak concentrations occur 6 hours after administration. Concentrations of TMP in saliva, prostatic tissue, sputum, urine, bile, and vaginal secretions equal or exceed serum concentrations of the drug. Sulfamethoxazole concentrations in these tissues are usually lower than concurrent serum levels. Peritoneal dialysis is ineffective for elimination. The half-life of TMP-SMX is also age-dependent, being much shorter in children.

Table 13-1: Commercially available fixed-combination trimethoprim-sulphamethoxazole.

Form	Dosage
Oral suspension	8 mg TMP/40 mg SMX per ml
Tablets	80 mg TMP/400 mg SMX, 160 mg TMP/800 mg SMX per ml
Intravenous Solution	80 mg TMP/400 mg SMX per 5 ml

Spectrum of Activity

TMP-SMX has activity against a wide range of microorganisms, including gram-positive and gram-negative aerobic bacteria, *Nocardia, Legionella, Chlamydia,* non tuberculous mycobacteria (*Mycobacteriium kansasii, M. marinum, M. fortuitum, M. scrofulaceum, and M. avium-intracellulare*) and various protozoa (*Pneumocystis carinii, Plasmodium species and Toxoplasma gondii*). Notably, TMP-SMX has good activity against aerobic gram-negative bacilli such as *Flavobacterium meningosepticum, Brucella species, Pseudomonas pseudomallei, Pseudomonas maltophilia and Acinetobacter species,* which are usually resistant to the 3rd-generation cephalosporins. Although TMP-SMX displays good activity against some anaerobic bacteria in vitro, there is no clinical evidence of its efficacy against these organisms. Similarly, although enterococci appear to be susceptible to TMP-SMX in vitro, the drug may not be effective against clinical infections. Antimicrobial susceptibility testing for TMP-SMX, in order to be reproducible, requires a standardized inoculum size and a medium that does not contain end products of folate metabolism (Para-aminobenzoic acid, thymine, or thymidine). Most organisms are more sensitive to TMP alone than to SMX alone. Resistance to TMP is 30 times more common in SMX resistant than in SMX-sensitive strains. Sixty to eighty percent of TMP is excreted in the urine within 24 hours, either as unchanged drug or as biologically inactive urinary metabolites. Sulfamethoxazole is metabolized to a greater extent, undergoing acetylation and glucuronidation in the liver. The relatively long half-life of both drugs (11 hours for TMP and 9 hours for SMX) permits doses to be given every 8 to 12 hours. Renal clearance of SMX, a weak acid, increases as the urine becomes more alkaline. Conversely, urine acidity enhances TMP excretion. The half-life of both components correlates directly with the serum creatinine level. Metabolites may accumulate during renal insufficiency, necessitating a dosage reduction in patients with decreased renal function. The manufacturers recommend that the dose be halved in patients with creatinine clearances of 15 to 30 ml/min and that it be avoided in patients with creatinine clearances of less than 15 ml/min. Hemodialysis removes significant amounts of both TMP and SMX; however,

The drug reaches supraserum levels in prostatic tissues and has been used in the therapy of acute and chronic bacterial prostatitis. Secretory dysfunction of the prostate, resulting in increased alkalinity of secretions, may adversely affect the drug's accumulation and account for failure of therapy in some instances. TMP-SMX plays several roles in the therapy of sexually transmitted diseases. In a dosage of 2 double strength tablets twice daily, the drug is as effective as single-dose ampicillin and probenecid for the treatment of uncomplicated genital gonorrhea in women; it may be more effective than these drugs in treating pharyngeal gonorrhoea. Chlamydia trachomatis which often coexists with Neisseria gonorrhoea infection, is also inhibited by TMP-SMX, although there does not appear to be true synergy *in vitro*. TMP-SMX is active against the causative agents of chancroid (Haemophilus ducreyi) and lymphogranuloma venereum (Chlamydia trachomatis). Because the drug has no activity against Treponema pallidum, symptoms of syphilis will not be masked by TMP-SMX therapy.

Resistance

Clinically important TMP-SMX resistance is uncommon and development of resistance during therapy is rare. In hospitalized transplant patients receiving TMP-SMX prophylaxis, however, 39% of the fecal isolates have proved resistant to the drug. Resistance depends on several potential mechanisms. The intrinsic resistance of bacteria such as Pseudomonas aeruginosa may be related to the bacterial cell wall's relative permeability to TMP. Mutant organisms resistant to TMP can be produced in a heavy inoculum in media that contain increasing TMP concentrations. The addition of a sulfonamide sometimes prevents the development of TMP resistance in this setting. "Resistance can also be due to mutants that have lost the capacity to synthesize thymidine and are dependent on exogenous sources of the nucleoside". This situation generally occurs only with prolonged TMP-SMX therapy. Perhaps the mechanism of greatest clinical importance is the production of plasmid-derived TMP-resistant forms of dihydrofolate reductase.

Clinical Uses

Genitourinary Infection TMP-SMX displays good activity against most genitourinary pathogens. Acute lower and upper urinary tract infections caused by susceptible organisms are effectively treated with either oral or intravenous therapy. Single-dose TMP-SMX has been shown to have a 93% success rate in the therapy of uncomplicated lower urinary tract infections in women. In addition, oral TMP-SMX is an effective, well-tolerated agent for long-term prophylaxis against recurrent urinary tract infections. The clinical uses of TMP-SMX are shown in Table 13-2.

Gastrointestinal Infections

TMP-SMX is active against a number of enteropathogens, including enterotoxigenic *Escherichia coli*, *Shigella species* and *Salmonella typhi*. It is considered the drug of choice for treating shigellosis in areas where multiply-resistant Shigella strains are common. TMP-SMX is a satisfactory alternative in the therapy of typhoid fever and is particularly useful against chloramphenicol-resistant strains or in patients who cannot tolerate chloramphenicol. A recent report suggests that ciprofloxacin may be more effective than TMP-SMX in the empiric therapy of outpatient-acquired acute diarrhea. Ericsson and colleagues have shown TMP-SMX to be efficacious in the therapy of traveler's diarrhea in adults. A more recent randomized trial by the same group of investigators has indicated that the combination of TMP-SMX (1 double-strength tablet twice daily for 3 days) and loperamide hydrochloride rapidly relieves traveler's

Table 13-2: Indications and suggested dosages for trimethoprim-sulfamethoxazole.

	Dosage				
Infection	Oral Tablets frequency	Intravenous Trimethoprim equivalent (mg / kg / day)	Frequency		Duration***
Genitourinary tract					
Upper urinary tract pyelonephritis	1 DS	Every 12 hr	8-10	Every 6 hr	10-14 days
Lower urinary tract					
Cystitis					
Single dose, female	2 DS	Once			
Conventional, female or male	1 DS	Every 12 hr			7-10 days
Urinary tract prophylaxis	½/2 SS	Every day			Variable
	or 1 SS	Every other day			Variable
Asymptomatic bacteriuria (when treatment is indicated)	1DS	Every 12 hr			7-10 days
Prostatitis					
Acute	1 DS	Every6 hr			7-10 days
	then 1 DS	Every 12 hr	10	Every 6 hr	14-35days
Chronic	1 DS	Every 12 hr			Up to 12 weeks
Venereal disease					
Neisseria gonorrhoeae	4 DS	Once			5 days
(urethritis, cervicitis)	or 2 DS	Every 12 hr			
Lymphogranuloma Venereum	1 DS or 3SS	Every 12 hr			7-10 days
Chancroid (Haemophilus ducreyi)	1 DS	Every 12 hr			10 days
Gastrointestinal tract		Every 6 hr			
Shigella	1 DS	Every 6 hr			5-7 days
Salmonella enteric	1 DS		8-10	Every 6 hr	10-14 days
Fever			8-10	Every 6 hr	
Enteropathogenic Escherichia coli					5-7 days
Adults	1 DS	Every 12 hr			
Children	5-7 mg/kg/day (liquid)	Every 6 hr	5-7	Every 6 hr	
Traveler's diarrhea prophylaxis	1 DS	Every 24 hr			Duration of Exposure
Respiratory tract					
Otitis media					
Adults	1 SS	Every 6 hr			7-10 days
Children	8-10 mg/kg/day (liquid)	Every 8-12 hr			7-10 days
Acute bronchitis	1 SS	Every 6 hr			7-10 days
Prophylaxis against acute infectious exacerbations in chronic bronchitis	1 SS	Daily			7 days/mo or alternate weeks

Table 13-2 Contd...

	Dosage				
Infection	Oral Tablets frequency	Intravenous Trimethoprim equivalent (mg / kg / day)	Frequency		Duration***
Pneumocystic carinii Pneumonia	2 DS	Every 6 hr	20	Every 6 hr	2 wks (non-AIDS) 3 wks (AIDS)
Nocardia asteroides infections	3 SS or 1 DS	Every 6 hr	10-15	Every 6 hr	6 mo-1 yr

*All doses are for adults unless otherwise specified. Oral doses: 1 single-strength tablet = 80 mg of trimethoprim and 400 mg of sulfamethoxazole. 1 double-strength tablet = 160 mg of trimethoprim and 800 mg of sulfamethoxazole

** DS = double strength; SS = single strength

*** Duration refers to the entire length of the treatment regimen, whether the initial treatment is intravenous and the subsequent

treatment is oral or the entire treatment regimen is oral or intravenous therapy alone.

AIDS = acquired immunodeficiency syndrome

(From: Cockerill and Edson,24 with permission from the Mayo Clinic Proceedings.)

diarrhea. The loperamide hydrochloride is given in a 4 mg oral loading dose followed by 2 mg after each loose stool (maximum daily dose, 16 mg). In half of the patients treated with this combination regimen, the symptoms lasted for less than 1 hour.

Respiratory Infections

TMP-SMX penetrates well into tracheobronchial secretions and has good activity against a number of agents commonly responsible for respiratory infection (*Streptococcus pneumoniae, Moraxella catarrbalis, and Haemopbilus species,* including ampicillin resistant strains). The drug has been used successfully to manage bacterial exacerbations of chronic. Bronchitis, otitis media and lower respiratory tract infections. The use of TMP-SMX for streptococcal pharyngitis is not recommended, because of a high incidence of bacteriologic failure with this agent. Perhaps one of the most rapidly growing indications for the use of TMP-SMX is the prophylaxis and therapy of *Pneumocystis carinii* pneumonia (PCP) in immunosuppressed patients, particularly those with the human immunodeficiency virus. In a review of 80 confirmed cases of PCP in patients with acquired immunodeficiency syndrome (AIDS), TMP-SMX had a 67.5% overall success rate; the success rate in patients who received therapy for at least 9 days was 85.5%. Prospective randomized trials comparing TMP-SMX with pentamidine for 1st-episode PCP in AIDS patients have shown that the 2 agents have essentially equal rates of response and toxicity. Chemoprophylaxis with TMP-SMX has proved efficacious in preventing PCP, both in AIDS patients and in those with immunosuppression related to a hematologic malignancy. Central Nervous System Infections TMP-SMX has both favourable penetration into the cerebrospinal fluid and satisfactory activity against a wide range of gram-positive and gram-negative bacteria that commonly cause meningitis. The drug has been used clinically to treat community-acquired meningitis resulting from *Streptococcus pneumoniae, Neisseria meningitidis and Haemophilus influenzae.* Nevertheless, because there is a much greater accumulation of experience with agents such as penicillin G and chloramphenicol in this situation, TMP-SMX cannot be considered the drug of choice for community- acquired meningitis. Other central nervous system indications for TMP-SMX therapy include *Staphylococcus aureus* meningitis after neurosurgical procedures, *Listeria monocytogenes* meningitis and gram-negative bacillary meningitis related to head trauma or neurosurgical procedures. The drug may be especially important in the management of meningitis associated with β -lactam-resistant organisms and in patients with serious -lactam allergies. TMP-SMX has good in vitro activity against *Toxoplasma gondii*. Successful TMP-SMX therapy of toxoplasmic encephalitis in AIDS patients has been reported.

The TMP-SMX may be useful in the treatment of infections in patients with a malignancy, particularly when the drug is combined with anti-pseudomonal penicillins or aminoglycosides. The response rate is highest in patients who have rising granulocyte counts during therapy. The prophylactic oral TMP-SMX can decrease the incidence of fever and infection associated with gram-negative bacteria in granulocytopenic patients. The newer quinolone derivatives may prove superior to TMP-SMX in this setting. Nocardia Infections, Prolonged TMP-SMX therapy is considered the treatment of choice for infections secondary to Nocardia species, although the superiority of the combination drug over SMX alone has not been proved. Synergistic activity occurs in vitro, with an 8-fold decrease in the mean inhibitory concentration of SMX against Nocardia organisms after the addition of TMP. The overall rate of cure or improvement in patients with Nocardia infections treated with TMP-SMX is 89%. Miscellaneous Indications TMP-SMX has been used for a variety of other indications, including brucellosis, malaria, and leishmaniasis. Spiera and colleagues recently reported symptomatic improvement of Wegener's granulomatosis, with normalization of hematologic and radiographic abnormalities, in a patient treated with TMP-SMX.

Adverse Reactions

The toxicity profile of TMP-SMX is very favorable. Fifty percent of these reactions occurred within the 1st 3 days of therapy, and the rest appeared within 14 days after the initiation of therapy. A significantly higher number of adverse reactions were encountered in women (11%) than in men (5%). Mild gastrointestinal symptoms have been reported by 3% to 4% of the patients treated with TMP-SMX. Nausea and vomiting are the most common findings; diarrhea and abdominal pain occur in a much smaller percentage of patients. Antimicrobial associated colitis (AAC) is rarely encountered in patients receiving TMP-SMX. Allergic skin reactions occur in 3% to 4% of patients. TMP-SMX has been associated infrequently with serious skin reactions, including erythema multiforme, Lyell's syndrome and Stevens-Johnson syndrome. If a skin reaction occurs, therapy should be discontinued immediately. An increase in the serum creatinine level without a concomitant decrease in glomerular function has been noted in patients receiving TMP-SMX; this occurs because TMP interferes with creatinine secretion. Interstitial nephritis and tubular necrosis are infrequently reported and are more common in patients with underlying renal insufficiency. In TMP-SMX recipients, adequate fluid intake should be maintained to prevent crystalluria secondary to excretion of the insoluble acetylated metabolite of SMX. Hematologic abnormalities, including thrombocytopenia, leukopenia, agranulocytosis, anemia, and eosinophilia are encountered in less than 0.5% of adults who receive oral TMP-SMX. These hematologic abnormalities do not appear to be related to changes in human folate metabolism. Nevertheless, patients with documented megaloblastic anemia probably should not be given this agent. Although folinic acid can reverse these hematologic effects without inhibiting antimicrobial activity, it should be reserved for patients who develop cytopenias during therapy. TMP-SMX rarely causes hemolysis in glucose- 6-phosphate dehydrogenase-deficient patients; this is probably due to the relatively low serum concentrations of SMX. Mild central nervous system findings, including headache, confusion, or hallucinations, have been encountered during TMP-SMX therapy. Drug-related aseptic meningitis has been reported and is believed to be hypersensitivity-mediated. Other infrequent reactions include hypoglycemia, hepatitis, necrotizing vasculitis, and drug-induced polyarteritis nodosa. Patients with AIDS have a much higher incidence of adverse reactions. The most common finding in these patientsis a diffuse erythematous maculopapular rash, often associated with fever. Neutropenia or thrombocytopenia may occur in as many as 50% of the patients.

Azotemia and hepatitis have also been reported. The use of TMP-SMX in near-term pregnant women is discouraged because of the risk of hemolysis, jaundice, and kernicterus in the neonate. For the same reason, TMP-SMX is not recommended for infants less than 2 months old. Several potential drug interactions have been associated with the use of TMP-SMX. Decreased metabolism and displacement of oral anticoagulants may result in an increased anticoagulant effect. Because patient response is highly variable, prothrombin times should be monitored, at least initially. Any of the sulfonamides can accentuate the hypoglycemic effects of oral sulfonylurea agents. The effects of phenytoin and methotrexate may also be increased, although the clinical significance of this increase is unclear.

References

Bushby SRM and Hitchings GH (1968). Trimethoprim, a sulphonamide potentiator. *Br J Pharmacol Chemother* **33:** 72-90.

Burchall JJ and Hitchings GH (1965). Inhibitor binding analysis of dihydrofolate reductases from various species. *Mol Pharmacol* **1:** 126-36.

Kaplan SA, Weinfeld RE, Abruzzo CW, McFaden K, Jack ML and Weissman L (1973). Pharmacokinetic profile of trimethoprim-sulfamethoxazole in man. *J Infect Dis* **128 (Suppl):** S547-55.

Patel RB and Welling PG (1980). Clinical pharmacokinetics of co-trimoxazole (trimethoprim-sulphamethoxazole). *Clin Pharmacokinet* **5:** 405-23.

Spicehandler J, Pollock AA, Simberkoff MS, RahaljJJJr. Intra- venous pharmacokinetics and in vitro bactericidal activity of trimethoprim-sulfamethoxazole. Rev Infect Dis 1982; 4:562-5.

Then R and Angehm P (1973). Nature of the bactericidal action of sulfonamides and trimethoprim, alone and in combination. *J Infect Dis* **128(Suppl):** S498-501.

CHAPTER

Cell Wall Inhibitors 14

Some antimicrobial drugs selectively interfere with synthesis of the bacterial cell walls a structure that mammalian cells do not possess. The cell wall is composed of a polymer called peptidoglycan that consists of glycan units joined to each other by peptide cross-links. To be maximally effective, inhibitors of cell wall synthesis require actively proliferating microorganisms; they have little or no effect on bacteria that are not growing and dividing. The most important members of this group of drugs are the β-Lactam antibiotics (named after the β-Lactam ring that is essential to their activity) and vancomycin.

Classification of Agents Affecting Cell Wall Synthesis

The classification of Cell Wall synthesis inhibitors are shown in Fig 14-1.

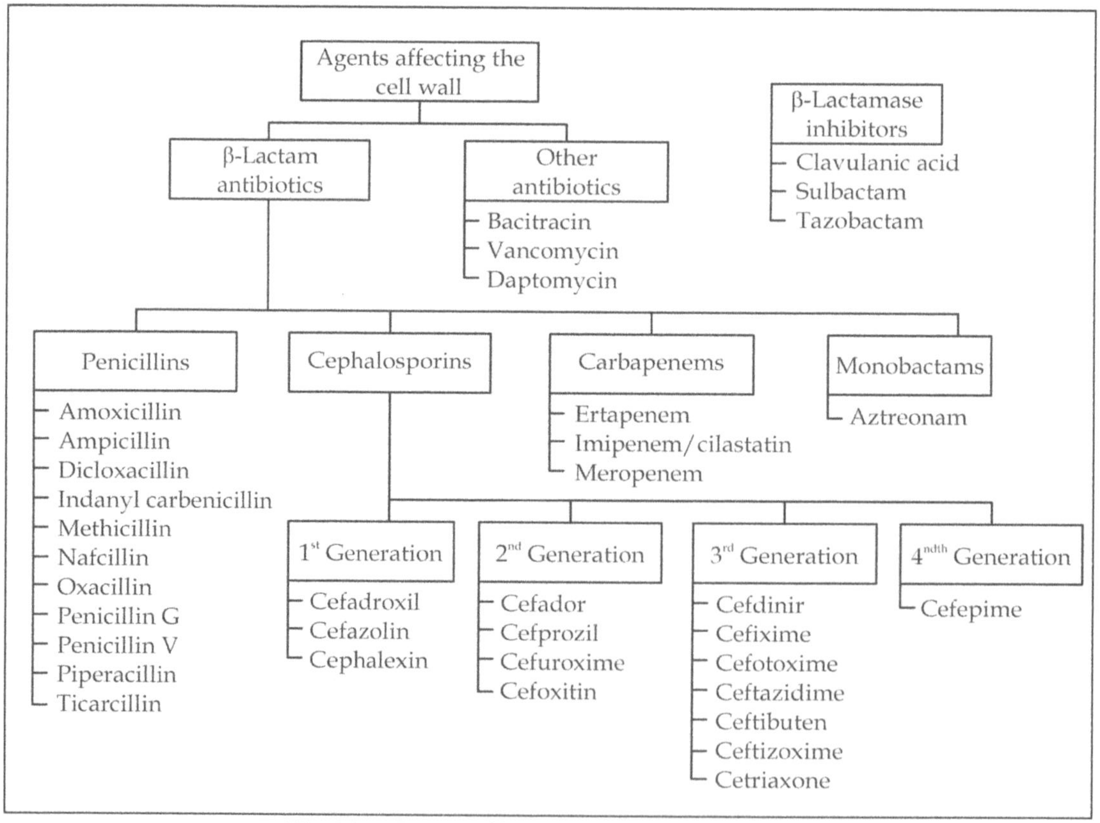

Fig 14-1: Drugs effecting cell wall synthesis.

β-Lactam Antibiotics

β-lactam antibiotics, named after the active chemical component of the drug, include the 6-membered ring-structured penicillins, monobactams and carbapenems; and the 7-membered ring-structured cephalosporins and cephamycins. In addition to their chemical structure, the major difference between these two subclasses of β-lactams is their susceptibility to β-lactamase destruction, with the cephalosporins, in general, being more resistant.

Antimicrobial Activity

Mode of Action

β-lactams impair the development of bacterial cell walls by interfering with transpeptidase enzymes responsible for the formation of the cross-links between peptidoglycan strands. These enzymes are associated with a group of proteins in both gram-positive and gram-negative bacteria called the penicillin-binding proteins (PBP). During bacterial cell growth, while the peptidoglycan structure is being formed, autolysins continuously cleave the lattice to provide acceptor sites for new strands. Normal bacterial growth depends on a balance between cell wall deposition and autolysis. Interaction between a β-lactam and a PBP inhibits synthetic enzymes, causing defective cell walls to be formed and subsequent abnormal elongation of cells, formation of spheroplasts, or osmotic lysis. The effect of the β-lactams when present in sufficient concentrations is generally bactericidal. At concentrations lower than minimal inhibitory concentrations (MIC), β-lactam antibiotics do exert residual effects on bacterial structure and function that, in turn, promote phagocytosis.

β-lactam antibiotics have little influence on formed bacterial cell walls and even susceptible organisms must be actively multiplying or growing. β-lactams are most active during the logarithmic phase of bacterial growth. They also tend to be somewhat more active in a slightly acidic environment (pH 5.5–6.5), perhaps because of enhanced membrane penetration.

Efficacy of the β-lactams is related to the time that plasma or tissue drug concentrations exceed the MIC of the infecting organism. Generally, concentrations should remain above the MIC for about 1/4 (carbapenems) to 2/3 of the dosing interval.

Bacterial Resistance

Only microorganisms that have cell walls are susceptible to the action of β-lactam antibiotics. Within this range of bacteria, resistance to β-lactams is well recognized and takes a number of forms.

Permeability Barrier

In gram-positive organisms, capsular materials may hinder access to the cytoplasmic membrane, but this rarely limits the diffusion of the cell-wall inhibitors. Gram-negative bacteria have a restricting sieving mechanism (porins) in their outer membranes (external to the cell wall), which reduces the penetration of several types of antibiotics. Different species of gram-negative bacteria exhibit varying permeability barriers to β-lactam antibiotics and these impair access of the antibiotics to the membrane-associated binding proteins. For example, the permeability barrier of *Haemophilus influenzae* is readily crossed by β-lactam antibiotics, *Escherichia coli* presents a greater obstacle to these agents, and the outer membranes of *Pseudomonas aeruginosa* are penetrated with great difficulty by most β-lactam compounds. Penicillins, aminopenicillins, first- and second-generation cephalosporins and selected other β-lactams cannot penetrate the outer membrane of *Pseudomonas aeruginosa*. Further, porins are frequently associated with efflux proteins that effectively remove drug which has successfully penetrated the lipopolysaccharide covering of gram-negative organisms.

The chemical nature of β-lactams (penicillins, cephalosporins and the β-lactamase inhibitors), as well as their concentration gradients, also greatly influence their penetration of bacteria to their targets at the surface of the cytoplasmic membrane, giving rise to the differences between anti-bacterial spectra of the various classes of penicillin. β-Lactams are often used in combination with other antibiotics that disrupt the integrity of the membranes and thereby facilitate access by β-lactams. The genetic loci controlling permeability generally have been considered to be chromosomally located, but they also may be plasmid-specified genes.

Specific Bacterial Binding Proteins

Resistance to β-lactam antimicrobial agents can be acquired by alterations in the PBP targets of these drugs. A loss or decrease in affinity of crucial PBP can lead to a significant increase in penicillin resistance. Changes in PBP-2 of Staphylococcus sp render the organism resistant to all β-lactams.

L-Forms of Bacteria

A phenotypic form of resistance can occur when spheroplasts (incomplete cell wall) or protoplasts (absence of cell wall) are present. These so-called "L-forms" must be present in a hyperosmotic environment (e.g., the renal medulla) to survive; otherwise, they will lyse. The clinical significance of this form of resistance is unclear.

Quiescent Organisms

In any bacterial population, a few organisms will always be quiescent. Because the β-lactams are active only against growing bacteria, the static organisms are unaffected and may persist. These "persisters" may then develop normally after the antibiotic is removed.

Tolerance

Some bacterial isolates, when treated with inhibitors of cell-wall synthesis, undergo inhibition of growth but not lysis at usual concentrations. These "tolerant" organisms are defective in their production or use of autolytic enzymes and can survive exposure to β-lactam antibiotics. Clinically, relapses and failures in serious infections due to tolerant organisms may be prevented by the frequently synergistic effect of the aminoglycosides with β-lactam antibiotics.

β-Lactamase (Penicillinase) Resistance

The most important mechanism of bacterial resistance to penicillins and the other β-lactam antibiotics is enzymatic inactivation. There are at least 6 major types of β-lactamase enzymes that can cleave the β-lactam ring, rendering the drug inactive. β-Lactamases are produced by gram-positive organisms (Staphylococcus aureus, S epidermidis), and 5 of the 6 types of β-lactamases are produced by gram-negative organisms. Some of these enzymes are active exclusively against penicillins, others are principally active against cephalosporins, and several types hydrolyze both equally. The type and concentration of β-lactamases are also bacterial species-specific. Gram-positive generally are excreted into the external environment as exoenzymes, produced in large quantity, plasmid-mediated (single determinant), usually inducible (rarely constitutive), unable to initiate self-transmission (rely principally on transduction), and active primarily against penicillins. Staphylococcal strains are the main gram-positive bacteria in which β-lactamase resistance develops, often very quickly. Gram-negative β-lactamases generally are heterogenous (wide range), retained within the periplasmic space, produced in small quantity, often constitutive (less often inducible), able to initiate self-transmission (conjugation mechanisms), and active against both penicillins and cephalosporins. Gram-negative bacteria capable of resistance as a result of β-lactamase production include Escherichia, Haemophilus, Klebsiella, Pasteurella, Proteus, Pseudomonas, and Salmonella spp; resistance may take longer to develop in some of these strains. The development of newer extended-spectrum cephalosporins resistant to β-lactamase, destruction has been associated with the recent emergence of extended β-lactamases, particularly by E coli, Klebsiella, and Proteus. These enzymes may not be produced during routine culture and susceptibility testing, causing the isolate to appear susceptible.

β-Lactamase-induced resistance is widespread. Of veterinary isolates, <"50–60% of Staphyl-ococcus spp strains and 40–70% of E coli strains are resistant to penicillin G; 15–40% of E coli strains from companion and farm animals may also be resistant to ampicillin.

Penicillin's

General Properties

Chemical Properties

Penicillin's are derivatives of benzyl penicillin, from which the methyl benzene radical is split off by amidase producing 6-aminopenicillanic acid, the parent compound of all semisynthetic pencillins. The compound consists of 2 basic structures: Fig 14-2

1. Thiazolidine Ring (A)
2. Beta-Lactam Ring (B)

Mechanisms of Action

All penicillin derivatives produce their bactericidal effects by inhibition of bacterial cell wall synthesis. Specifically, the cross linking of peptides on the mucosaccharide chains is prevented. If cell walls are improperly made cell walls allow water to flow into the cell causing it to burst. Resemblances between a segment of penicillin structure and the backbone of a peptide chain have been used to explain the mechanism of action of beta-lactam antibiotics. Gram-positive bacteria possess a thick cell wall composed of a cellulose-like structural sugar polymer covalently bound to short peptide units in layers. The polysaccharide portion of the peptidoglycan structure is made of repeating units of N-acetylglucosamine linked β-1,4 to N-acetylmuramic acid (NAG-NAM). The peptide varies, but begins with L-Ala and ends with D-Ala. In the middle is a dibasic amino acid, diaminopimelate (DAP). DAP (orange) provides a linkage to the D-Ala (gray) residue on an adjacent peptide.

The bacterial cell wall synthesis is completed when a cross link between two peptide chains attached to polysaccharide backbones is formed. The cross linking is catalyzed by the enzyme transpeptidase. First the terminal alanine from each peptide is hydrolyzed and secondly one alanine is joined to lysine through an amide bond. Penicillin binds at the active site of the transpeptidase enzyme that cross-links the peptidoglycan strands. It does this by mimicking the D-alanyl-D-alanine residues that would normally bind to this site. Penicillin irreversibly inhibits the enzyme transpeptidase by reacting with a serine residue in the transpeptidase. This reaction is irreversible and so the growth of the bacterial cell wall is inhibited. Since mammal cells do not have the same type of cell walls, penicillin specifically inhibits only bacterial cell wall synthesis.

Classification

The structures of Pencillins are shown in Fig 14-3.

Penicillins

1. Natural - derived from *Penicillium sp.* (Pen G or Benzylpenicillin)
2. Penicillinase Stable (Resistant) Penicillins (Methicillin, Nafcillin)
   (a) Isoxazolyl Penicillins (Oxacillin)
3. Extended Spectrum Penicillins
   (a) Aminopenicillins (Ampicillin, Amoxicillin)
   (b) Carboxypenicillins (Carbenicillin, Ticarcillin)

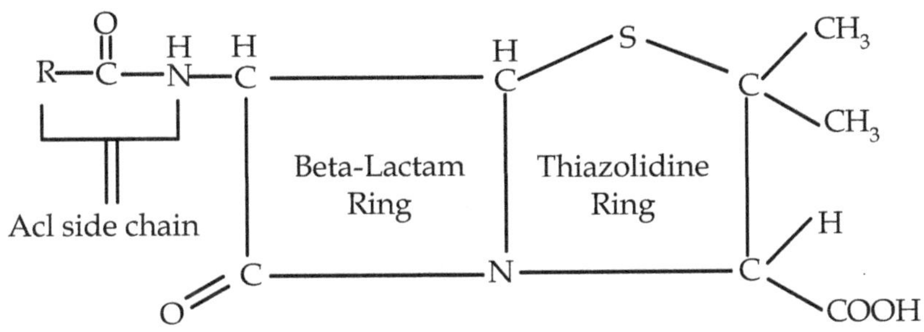

Fig 14-2: General structure of penicillin.

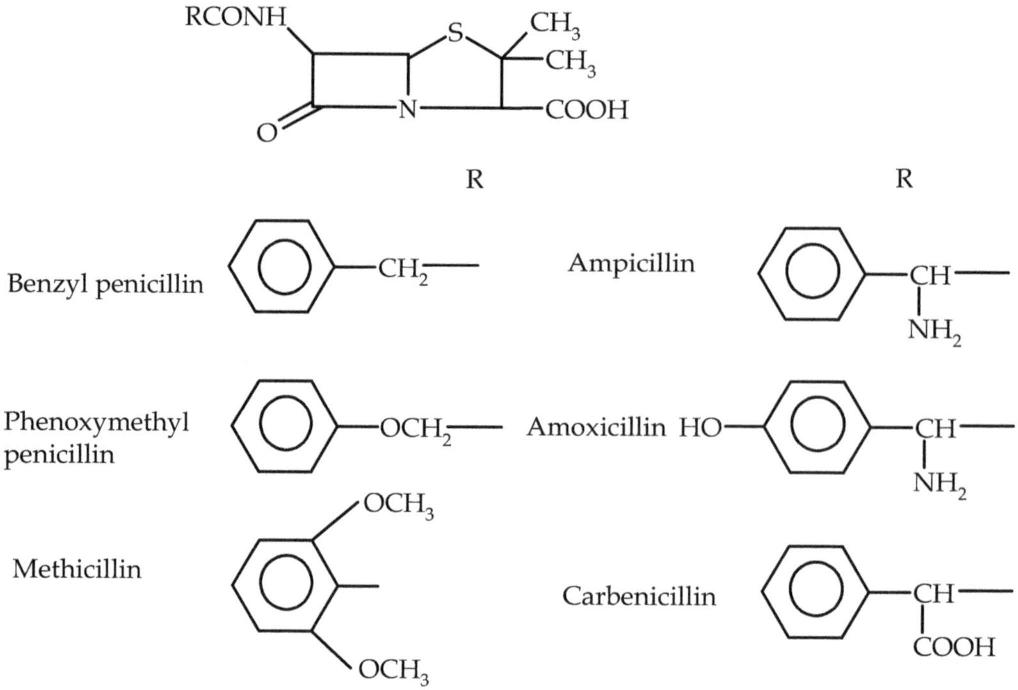

Fig 14-3: Penicillin structures.

(c) Ureidopenicillins (Azlocillin, Mezlocillin, Piperacillin)

4. Beta-lactamase Inhibitor Combinations (BLI)

   (Amp/Sul, Amox/Clav, Pip/Tazo, Ticar/Clav)

5. Amidinopenicillin (Mecillinam)

General Properties

The penicillins are somewhat unstable, being sensitive to heat, light, extremes in pH, heavy metals and oxidizing and reducing agents. Also, they often deteriorate in aqueous solution and require reconstitution with a diluent just before injection. Penicillins are poorly soluble, weak organic acids that are administered parenterally either as suspensions in water or oil or as water-soluble salts. For example, sodium or potassium salts of penicillin G are highly water soluble and are absorbed rapidly from injection sites, whereas organic esters in microsuspension such as procaine penicillin G or benzathine penicillin G are gradually absorbed over 1–3 (or even more) days, respectively. The trihydrate forms of the semisynthetic penicillins have greater aqueous solubility than the parent compounds and are usually preferred for both parenteral and oral use.

Penicillins contain a β-lactam nucleus that when cleaved by a β-lactamase enzyme (penicillinase) produces penicilloic acid derivatives that are inactive but may act as the antigenic determinants for penicillin hypersensitivity. Modification of the 6-aminopenicillanic acid nucleus, either by biosynthetic or semisynthetic means, has produced the array of penicillins used clinically. These differ in their antibacterial spectra, pharmacokinetic characteristics and susceptibility to microbial enzymatic degradation.

Antibacterial Spectra

Penicillin G and its oral congeners (e.g., penicillin V) are active against both aerobic and anaerobic gram-positive bacteria and with a few exceptions (*Haemophilus* and *Neisseria spp* and strains of Bacteroides other than B fragilis) are inactive against gram-negative organisms at usual concentrations. Organisms usually sensitive *in vitro* to penicillin G include streptococci, penicillin-sensitive staphylococci, *Arcano-bacterium pyogenes, Clostridium spp, Erysipelothrix rhusiopathiae, Actinomyces bovis, Leptospira canicola, Bacillus anthracis, Fusiformis nodosus, and Nocardia spp.*

The semisynthetic β-lactamase-resistant penicillins, such as oxacillin, cloxacillin, floxacillin and nafcillin, have spectra similar to those noted above (although often at higher MIC) but also include many of the β-lactamase-producing strains of staphylococci (especially S aureus and S epidermidis).

A large number of gram-positive and gram-negative bacteria (but not β-lactamase-producing strains) are sensitive to the semisynthetic broad-spectrum penicillins (ampicillin and amoxicillin). Susceptible genera include *Staphylococcus, Streptococcus, Arcanobacterium, Clostridium, Escherichia, Klebsiella, Shigella, Salmonella, Proteus, and Pasteurella*. While bacterial resistance is widespread, the combination of β-lactamase inhibitors and broad-spectrum penicillins markedly enhances the spectrum and efficacy against both gram-positive and gram-negative pathogens. Clavulanate-potentiated amoxicillin is an excellent example of such a synergistic association.

The anti-Pseudomonas and other extended-spectrum penicillins are active against most of the usual penicillin-sensitive bacteria. They often have a degree of β-lactamase resistance and are usually active against one or more characteristic penicillin-resistant organisms. Yet, as a class, they remain susceptible to destruction by β-lactamases. Examples include the use of carbenicillin, ticarcillin and piperacillin against Pseudomonas aeruginosa and several Proteus strains and the use of piperacillin against Pseudomonas aeruginosa, several Shigella and Proteus strains and some Citrobacter and Enterobacter spp. *Streptococcus faecalis* is often resistant to these new extended-spectrum penicillins. Imipenem and meropenem are relatively resistant to β-lactamase destruction. Their spectrum includes a wide variety of aerobic and anaerobic microorganisms, including most strains of *Pseudomonas, streptococci, enterococci, staphylococci, and Listeria. Anaerobes, including Bacteroides fragilis,* are highly susceptible.

Mechanisms of Resistance

Mutations in PBP's: Bacteria spontaneously undergo mutation at a frequency of approximately 10. In the presence of an antibiotic, mutations that enhance survival are selected and eventually organisms with these mutations can predominate. *Streptococcus pneumoniae*, a very common Gram positive respiratory pathogen, can accumulate mutations in the PBP's and become relatively or absolutely resistant to penicillin. When these organisms die and lyse, their DNA is taken up by other streptococci (they are naturally transformable) and in the presence of antibiotic selective pressure, the now transformed penicillin-resistant organisms are maintained in the population. A DNA cassette which encodes a mutant PBP2 in *S. aureus* is also a common clinical problem and causes methicillin resistant *S. aureus* (MRSA).

β-lactamase production: Both Gram positive and Gram negative organisms can produce β-lactamases that cause clinically significant antibiotic resistance. In Gram positives, this is a major problem with *S. aureus* which classically produces a penicillinase. In some recent outbreaks, staphylococci were found to be producing β-lactamases with cephalosporinase activity as well. Again, there can be mutations in the β-lactamase genes that alter the activity of the enzyme, and in the presence of selective pressure, these mutants flourish. Gram negative bacteria can express both chromosomal β-lactamases as well as plasmid mediated enzymes with a wide variety of activities.

Permeability: The expression of efflux pumps in both Gram negative and in Gram positive bacteria is a major cause of antibiotic resistance. The drugs are rapidly removed from the cell by an inducible pump system. In Gram negative organisms, such as *P. aeruginosa*, there are >20 different efflux systems that have been identified.

Natural Penicillins

Penicillin G (benzylpenicillin) is an acid-labile compound having variable bioavailability after oral administration. Consequently, penicillin G is most appropriate for intramuscular or intravenous therapy.

The drug distributes to most tissues and serosa-lined cavities, although low concentrations appear in breast milk and cerebrospinal fluid. When the meninges are inflamed, cerebrospinal fluid concentrations of penicillin G approximate 5% of the serum concentration. In inflamed joints, concentrations of the drug approach serum levels. Penicillin G is excreted by the kidneys, with 90% of renal elimination occurring via tubular secretion and 10% by glomerular filtration. Probenecid blocks tubular secretion and has been used to increase the serum concentration and prolong the half-life of penicillin G and other penicillins.

The clinical uses of penicillin G include endocarditis caused by *S. viridans* (or *Streptococcus bovis*), pharyngitis (group A β-hemolytic streptococci), cat bite cellulitis (*Pasteurella multocida*) and syphilis (*Treponema pallidum*). Depot intramuscular formulations of penicillin G, including procaine penicillin and benzathine penicillin have decreased solubility, delayed absorption and a prolonged half-life. Drug concentrations are detectable 24 hours after injection of procaine penicillin and low levels of benzathine penicillin (0.003 units/ml) are detectable 4 weeks after injection. When prescribing one of the penicillin G depot formulations, practitioners must individualize treatment to clinical and microbial conditions. Some long-acting formulations may not maintain adequate plasma and tissue concentrations to treat specific organisms or infections. For acute streptococcal meningitis, the goal is rapid achievement of high antibiotic concentrations in the cerebrospinal fluid. Consequently, depot formulations are inappropriate for meningitis. Intravenous penicillin G is among the antibiotics of first choice for therapy of meningitis caused by susceptible *S. pneumoniae*. In contrast, a depot formulation of benzathine penicillin G suffices for rheumatic fever prophylaxis. Penicillin V is an orally administered phenoxymethyl congener of penicillin G having an antibacterial spectrum of activity that is similar to that of penicillin G. Penicillin V is used to treat streptococcal infections when oral therapy is appropriate and desirable.

Antistaphylococcal (Penicillinase-Resistant) Penicillins

Nafcillin, oxacillin, cloxacillin and dicloxacillin are more resistant to bacterial β-lactamases than is penicillin G. Consequently, these antibiotics are effective against streptococci and most community-acquired penicillinase-producing staphylococci. For historical reasons, staphylococci resistant to oxacillin or nafcillin are labeled methicillin resistant. Many hospitals are reservoirs for MRSA and methicillin-resistant *Staphylococcus epidermidis* (MRSE). These nosocomial pathogens are resistant *in vitro* to all β-lactam antibiotics. For parenteral therapy, nafcillin and oxacillin offer comparable efûcacy and antimicrobial spectra of activity.

Although both drugs undergo hepatic metabolism, only nafcillin requires dose adjustment in patients with combined hepatic and renal insufficiency. Indications for nafcillin or oxacillin include severe staphylococcal infections like cellulitis, empyema, endocarditis, osteomyelitis, pneumonia, septic arthritis and toxic shock syndrome.

For oral therapy, cloxacillin and dicloxacillin are comparable alternatives. Both undergo hepatic metabolism and neither drug requires dose adjustment in patients with hepatic insufficiency. Indications for cloxacillin or dicloxacillin include clinically mild staphylococcal infections like impetigo.

Aminopenicillins

The pharmacokinetics of ampicillin and amoxicillin are similar. Both have good oral bioavailability; ampicillin is also bioavailable after intramuscular injection. Concomitant ingestion of food decreases the bioavailability of ampicillin but not amoxicillin. Consequently, oral doses of ampicillin should be given on an empty stomach. Ampicillin achieves therapeutic concentrations in the cerebrospinal fluid only during inflammation. Therefore, ampicillin is effective treatment for meningitis caused by *Listeria monocytogenes*. Amoxicillin does not reach adequate concentrations in the central nervous system and is not appropriate for meningitis therapy. Other indications for ampicillin include serious infections like enterococcal endocarditis and pneumonia caused by β-lactamase-negative H. influenzae. Amoxicillin oral therapy is appropriate for clinically acute nonserious bacterial infections like Otitis media and sinusitis. Amoxicillin also has use in multidrug regimens for the eradication of Helicobacter pylori in duodenal and gastric ulcers.

Antipseudomonal Penicillins

Mezlocillin, piperacillin and ticarcillin are parenteral antibiotics formulated as sodium salts. when administering them to patients with congestive heart failure. During their distribution phase, antipseudomonal penicillins achieve only low concentrations in the cerebrospinal fluid. Consequently, antipseudomonal penicillins are not among the drugs of first choice for meningitis therapy. The antipseudomonal penicillins undergo renal elimination. Piperacillin and ticarcillin have minimal hepatic metabolism. In contrast, mezlocillin has significant hepatic metabolism and requires dose adjustment in patients with hepatic insufficiency. The antipseudomonal penicillins have comparable spectra of activity against many gram-positive and gram-negative pathogens, including most anaerobes. Mezlocillin, piperacillin and ticarcillin have similar clinical outcomes in patients with known or suspected *P. aeruginosa* infections. Antipseudomonal penicillins are used to treat pneumonias associated with cystic fibrosis or mechanical ventilation. Carbenicillin indanyl sodium is an antipseudomonal penicillin formulated for oral administration. The drug achieves negligible carbenicillin concentrations in the urine of patients with renal failure. Consequently, carbenicillin is not appropriate for patients with renal failure. In patients with normal renal function, however, carbenicillin indanyl sodium is used to treat urinary tract infections caused by *P. aeruginosa, Proteus spp. and Escherichia coli.*

β-Lactamase Inhibitor Combinations

Several formulations combine a β-lactam antibiotic with a β-lactamase inhibitor (ampicillin-sulbactam [Unasyn], ticarcillin-clavulanic acid [Timentin], piperacillin-tazobactam [Zosyn] and amoxicillin–clavulanic acid [Augmentin]). All of the β-lactamase inhibitor combinations except amoxicillin-clavulanic acid are parenteral formulations. Amoxicillin–clavulanic acid is the only combination drug with oral bioavailability. Elimination of the combination drugs occurs primarily by renal excretion. Therefore, all of the β-lactamase inhibitor combinations require dose adjustments in patients with renal insufficiency. The addition of the β-lactamase inhibitor significantly broadens the spectrum of antibacterial activity against β-lactamase-producing organisms. Consequently, these drugs have clinical use in treating infections with known or suspected mixed bacterial flora, such as biliary infections, diabetic foot ulcers, endomyometritis and peritonitis.

Routes of Administration and Dosage

Penicillin G: For bacterial infections: For oral dosage form (oral solution, oral suspension, and tablets): Adults: 200,000 to 500,000 Units every four to six hours. Infants and children less than 12 years of age: Dose is based on body weight - 4000 to 30,000 Units per kilogram (kg) of body weight every four to eight hours. For benzathine Penicillin (injection): Adults : 1,200,000 to 2,400,000 Units injected intramuscular as a single dose. Infants and children: 300,000 to 1,200,000 Units injected intramuscular as a single dose; or 50,000 Units per kg of body weight injected intramuscular as a single dose. For injection dosage forms (potassium and sodium salts): Adults: 1,000,000 to 5,000,000 Units, injected intravenous or intramuscular every four to six hours. Older infants and children : The usual dose is 8000 to 25,000 Units per kg of body weight, injected intravenous or intramuscular every four to six hours. Premature infants and newborns : The usual dose is 30,000 Units per kg of body weight, injected i.v. or i.m. every twelve hours. For Procaine Penicillin (injection) : Adults and teenagers : 600,000 to 1,200,000 Units injected i.m. once a day. Children: The usual dose is 50,000 Units per kg of body weight, injected i.m.once a day. For penicillin V: For bacterial infections: For the benzathine salt oral dosage form (oral solution): Adults: 200,000 to 500,000 Units every six to eight hours.Children: 100,000 to 250,000 Units every six to eight hours. For the potassium salt oral dosage: Adults and teenagers : 125 to 500 milligrams (mg) every six to eight hours. Children :The usual dose is 2.5 to 16 mg per kilogram (kg) of body weight every four to eight hours.

Pharmacokinetics

The pharmacokinetics of the many penicillins differ substantially. The general guidelines below emphasize singularly significant aspects.

Absorption

Most penicillins in aqueous solution are rapidly absorbed from parenteral sites. Absorption is delayed when the inorganic penicillin salts are suspended in vegetable oil vehicles or when the sparingly soluble repository organic salts (e.g., procaine penicillin G and benzathine penicillin G) are administered parenterally. Although prolonged absorption results in longer persistence of plasma and tissue drug concentrations, peak concentrations may not be sufficiently high to be effective against organisms unless MIC are low. The penicillin G repositol salts should never be injected i.v Only selected penicillins are acid stable and can be administered PO at standard doses. Absorption from the upper GI tract differs markedly in amount and rate among the various penicillins. Penicillin V must be given at high oral doses. The aminopenicillins are orally bioavailable, although food impairs the absorption of ampicillin. The indanyl form of carbenicillin is orally bioavailable, but effective concentrations are likely to be achieved only in the urine. Serum concentrations of penicillins generally peak within 2 hr of PO administration. Penicillins may also be absorbed after intrauterine infusion.

Distribution

After absorption, penicillins are widely distributed in body fluids and tissues. The volume of distribution tends to reflect extracellular compartmentalization, although some penicillins penetrate into tissues quite well. Potentially therapeutic concentrations of the various penicillins are generally found in the liver, bile, kidneys, intestines, muscle and lungs, but only very low concentrations are found in poorly perfused areas such as the cornea, bronchial secretions, cartilage and bone. The diethylamino salt of penicillin G produces particularly high concentrations in pulmonary tissue. The penicillins usually do not readily cross the normal blood-brain, placental, mammary or prostatic barriers unless massive doses are given or inflammation is present. Selected penicillins are able to penetrate nonchronic abscesses and pleural, peritoneal, or synovial fluids. Penicillins are reversibly and loosely bound to plasma proteins. The extent of this binding varies with particular penicillins and their concentration, e.g., ampicillin is usually <20% bound and cloxacillin may be <80% bound. Pregnancy increases the volume of distribution, which has the effect of lowering the concentration of drug produced by a given dose.

Biotransformation

Penicillins are generally excreted unchanged, but fractions of a given dose may undergo metabolic transformations by unknown mechanisms (usually <20% metabolized). Penicilloic acid derivatives that are formed tend to be allergenic.

Excretion

Most (60–90%) of a parenterally administered penicillin is eliminated in the urine within a short time (e.g., up to 90% of penicillin G within 6 hr), which results in high concentrations in urine. About 20% of renal excretion occurs by glomerular filtration and <80% by tubular secretion—a process that may be deliberately inhibited (to prolong effective concentrations in the body) by probenecid and other weak organic acids. Anuria may increase the half-life of penicillin G (normally <30 min) to 10 hr. The biliary route also may be a major excretory pathway for the broad-spectrum semisynthetic penicillins. Clearance is considerably lower in neonates than in adults. Penicillins are also eliminated in milk, although often only in trace amounts in the normal udder, and may persist for up to 90 hr. Penicillin residues in milk also have been found after intrauterine infusion.

Adverse Effects:

1. Hypersensitivity reactions
   - most common adverse effects - cause the highest incidence of antibiotic allergy.
     (a) Major antigenic determinant- penicilloyl metabolite skin testing (penicilloyl polylysine (PPL))
     (b) Signs and symptoms:
       - varied skin rashes and purpuric reactions
       - angioedema and anaphylactic reactions
       - fever
       - Eosinophilia
       - interstitial nephritis
2. Gastrointestinal disturbances after oral administration.
3. Convulsions following rapid i.v admini- stration.
4. Accidental injection into the sciatic nerve - severe pain and nerve Dysfunction persisting for weeks.
5. Chronic use may cause hepatitis Over growth of minor/atypical organisms following use of broad spectrum preparations.
6. Specific toxicities:
   (a) Procaine Penicillin G after accidental IV injection: Pulmonary embolism acute psychotic reactions.
   (b) Oxacillin and Nafcillin hepatitis, Granulocytopenia, bone marrow depressionc.
   (c) Disodium Carbenicillin and high dose Penicillin G Na-Hypernatremia.
   (d) Penicillin G Potassium hyperkalemia with high doses.
   (e) Penicillin G Sodium Jarisch_herxheimer reaction with high doses in secondary syphilis.
   (f) Carbenicillin and Ticarcillin bleeding, diathesis.
   (g) Methicillin interstitial nephritis.
   (h) Ampicillin Associated with pseudomem branous colitis.

Contra Indications

Contra indicated in Renal failure, Lactation, Hypersenitivity to penicillin and penicillinase producing organisms.

Precautions

In Allergy: Patients with a history of general allergies may be more likely to have a severe reaction to penicillin.

Renal disease: Patients with renal disease may have an increased chance of side effects.

Mononucleosis: Patients with mononucleosis may have an increased chance of skin rash when receiving penicillin.

Stomach or intestinal disease (especially colitis, including colitis caused by antibiotics): Patients with a history of stomach or intestinal disease may be more likely to develop colitis while taking penicillin.

Drug Interactions

Oral contraceptives containing estrogen : Use of Penicillins together with estrogen-containing oral contraceptives may prevent oral contraceptives from being effective, increasing the chance of pregnancy.

Methotrexate: Use of methotrexate with penicillin may increase the chance of side effects of methotrexate.

Probenecid: Probenecid causes penicillin to build up in the blood. This may increase the chance of adverse effects.

Cephalosporins

Chemistry

Cephalosporins Fig 14-4 are β-lactam antibiotics that differ from the penicillins in that the B ring is a 6-membered dihydrothiazine ring. Variations among the cephalosporins are made on either the acyl side chain at the 7-position to change antibacterial activity or at the 3-position to alter the pharmacokinetic profile. Cephalosporin C was first isolated in 1948 by Dr. Abraham from a fungus, *Cephalosporium acremonium*, collected in seawater near a sewage outlet in Sardinia by Professor Guiseppe Brotzu in 1945.

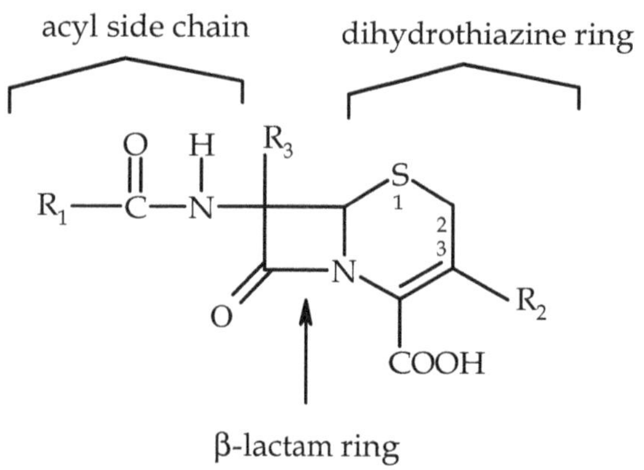

Fig 14-4: General structure of cephalosporins.

General Properties

The physical and chemical properties of the cephalosporins are similar to those of the penicillins, although the cephalosporins are somewhat more stable to pH and temperature changes. Cephalosporins are weak acids derived from 7-aminocephalosporanic acid. They are used either as the free base form for PO administration (if acid stable) or as sodium salts in aqueous solution for parenteral delivery (sodium salt of cephalothin contains 2.4 mEq sodium/g). Cephalosporins also contain a β-lactam nucleus that is susceptible to β-lactamase (cephalosporinase) hydrolysis. These β-lactamases may or may not also attack penicillins. Modifications of the 7-amino-cephalosporanic acid nucleus and substitutions on the sidechains by semisynthetic means have produced differences among cephalosporins in antibacterial spectra, β-lactamase sensitivities, and pharmacokinetics.

Classification

The structures of Cephalosphorins are shown in Fig 14-5.

Based on antimicrobial spectrum and pharmacokinetic properties they are classified as

A. First Generation
   1. Cephaloridine
   2. Cephalothin
   3. Cephalexin
   4. Cefazolin
   5. Cephradine
   6. Cepharpirin
   7. Cephadroxil
B. Second Generation
   1. Cefaclor
   2. Cefoxitin
   3. Cefuroxime
   4. Cefonicid
   5. Cefotetan
   6. Cefamdandole
   7. Cefprozil
   8. Loracarbef
   9. Cefmetazole
   10. Ceforanide
C. Third Generation
   1. Cefotaxime
   2. Cefoperazone
   3. Moxolactam
   4. Ceftizoxime
   5. Ceftriaxone

6. Ceftazidime
7. Cefotiam
8. Cefixime
9. Cefetamet
10. Cefpodoxime
11. Ceftibuten
12. Cefdinir
13. Cefditoren

D. Fourth Generation

1. Cefepime
2. Cefpirome

First-Generation

Cephalexin, cefadroxil, cefazolin and cephradine are first-generation cephalosporins, all with good efficacy versus gram-positive organisms and only marginal efficacy versus gram-negative organisms. These cephalosporins are generally effective against methicillin-sensitive *Staph aureus*, as well as *Streptococcus* spp. Cefazolin (100 mg/ml diluted to 50 mg/ml) in particular is used in the treatment of corneal ulcers due to its good Gram-positive spectrum, however *Strep. pneumoniae* and viridans streptococci are developing increasing resistance in such infections, which is a cause for concern. Following subconjuntival injection in humans and rabbits and intravenous administration in dogs, cefazolin reaches therapeutic anterior chamber concentrations.

Second-Generation

Cefaclor, cefprozil, cefuroxime, cefoxitin and cefotetan are members of the second-generation class of cephalosporins, which have increased gram-negative activity relative to those in the first generation.

Third-Generation

Cefixime, cefdinir, cefotaxime, ceftriaxone and ceftazidime are third-generation cephalosporins with increased activity versus enteric gram-negative bacteria. Ceftazidime is used in human ophthalmology via intravitreal injection as treatment for endophthalmitis, due in part to excellent activity versus *Pseudomonas aeruginosa*. Use of these medications in veterinary ophthalmology is rarely justified.

Fourth-Generation

Cefepime has a broad spectrum versus both gram-positive and gram-negative organisms.

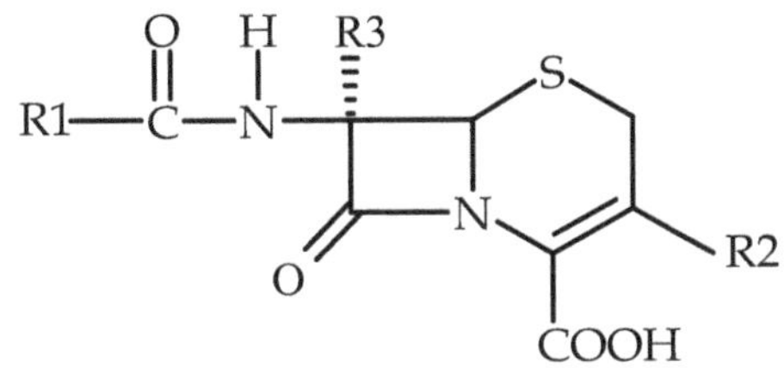

Cepalosporin	R1	R2	R3
Cefazolin	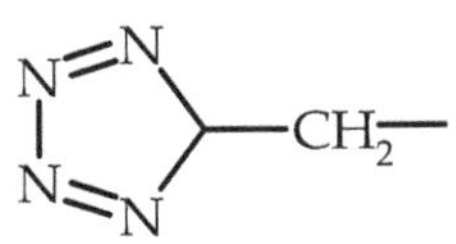	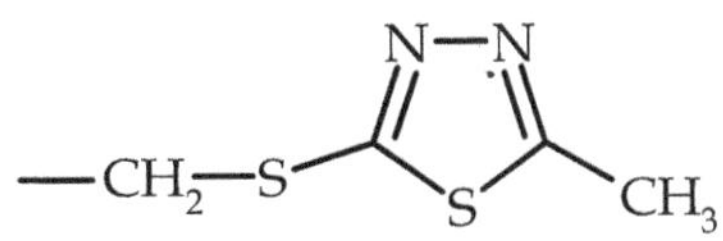	H
Cephalexin	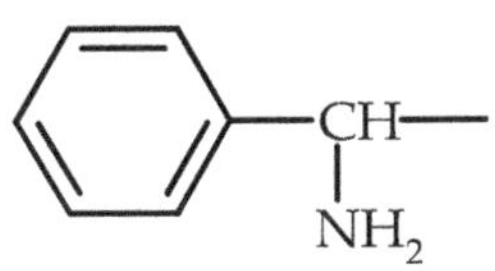	CH3	H

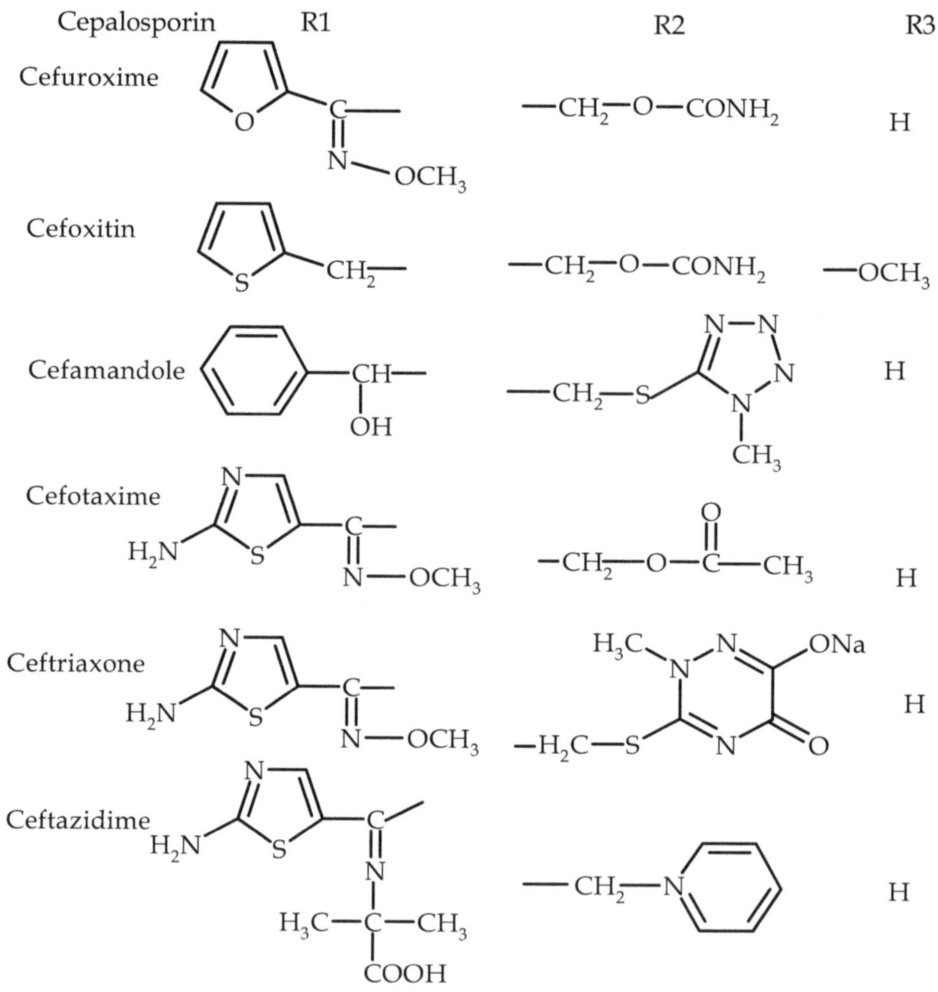

Fig 14-5: Cephalosporins structures.

Antimicrobial Activity

Bacterial Resistance

Resistance to the cephalosporins includes mechanisms described in general for β-lactams. Cephalosporins generally are stable against the plasmid-mediated β-lactamases produced by gram-positive bacteria such as *Staphylococcus aureus*. Several types of inducible β-lactamases produced by gram-negative organisms may be mediated by either plasmids or chromosomally and may hydrolyze either or both penicillins and cephalosporins (cross-resistance). Second and particularly third-generation cephalosporins have greater stability against gram-negative β-lactamases.

Antibacterial Spectra

The first generation cephalosporins are generally effective against most gram-positive aerobic cocci and several of the gram-negative bacteria, including E coli and *Proteus, Klebsiella, Salmonella, Shigella and Enterobacter spp.* Cefazolin is more effective against E coli compared to cephalexin. Cephalosporinase-producing organisms are not susceptible. The second generation cephalosporins have greater activity against gram-negative organisms but are somewhat less active against gram-positive species. An exception is cefoxitin, which has excellent efficacy against gram-positive bacteria and potentially *Pseudomonas spp*. It is difficult to identify trends among third and fourth-generation cephalosporins. Some (e.g., cefotaxime, ceftazidime) have an extensive gram-negative spectrum, which may include P aeruginosa. Ceftiofur is a third-generation cephalosporin with a gram-negative spectrum that is more similar to first generation cephalosporins. However, unlike first generation cephalosporins, efficacy against *Staphylococcus spp* is not predictable. Cefpodoxime and cefovicin are particularly effective against *Staphylococcus intermedius*, while retaining fair efficacy toward gram-negative organisms such as *E coli, Klebsiella and Proteus*. The later generation cephalosporins may be effective against anaerobic bacteria, except for *Bacteroides fragilis*, which is susceptible only to certain cephalosporins (e.g., cefoxitin). The newest members of this group are also highly resistant to β-lactamase, although cephalosporins (and to a lesser degree cephamycins) are susceptible to destruction by extended spectrum β-lactamases.

Pharmacokinetic Features

Absorption

Only a few cephalosporins are acid stable and thus effective when administered PO (e.g., cephalexin, cephradine, cefadroxil, cefpodoxime, and cefachlor). They are usually well absorbed and bioavailability values are 75–90%. The others are administered either i.v or i.m with plasma concentrations peaking <30 min after injection. Ceftiofur is available in a sustained-release form; its duration of action is extended by administration at the base of the ear in food animals.

Distribution

Cephalosporins are distributed into most body fluids and tissues, including kidneys, lungs, joints, bone, soft tissues, and the biliary tract, but in general, the volume of distribution is <0.3 l/kg. However, poor penetration into the CSF, even in inflammation, is a notable feature of the standard cephalosporins. Cephalosporins are substrates for p-glycoprotein efflux from the CNS. The third generation cephalosporins (e.g., moxalactam) may achieve good penetration into the CSF. The degree of plasma-protein binding is variable (e.g., 20% for cefadroxil and 80% for cefazolin). The high degree of protein binding of cefovecin contributes to its long elimination half-life . However, drug concentrations in transudate remain above the MIC_{90} of both Staphyloccocus intermedius and E coli for up to 14 days.

Biotransformation

Several cephalosporins (such as cephalothin, cephapirin, ceftiofur, cephacetrile, and cefotaxime) are actively deacetylated, primarily in the liver but also in other tissues. The deacetylated derivatives are much less active with the exception of ceftiofur. Ceftiofur is metabolized to several active metabolites that can contribute significantly to efficacy. Few of the other cephalosporins are metabolized to any appreciable extent.

Excretion

Most cephalosporins, including cefpodoxime and cefovecin are renally excreted. Tubular secretion predominates, although glomerular filtration is important in some cases (cephalexin and cefazolin). In renal failure, dose rates should be reduced. Biliary elimination of the newer cephalosporins (e.g., cefoperazone) may be significant. Generally, these β-lactam antibiotics maintain effective blood concentrations for only 6–8 hr. Exceptions include ceftiofur, cefpodoxime and cefovecin.

Clinical Uses

First Generation Cephalosporins - Uses

1. Upper respiratory tract infections due to *Staph.* and *Strep.*
2. Lower respiratory tract infections due to susceptible bacteria e.g., *Strep. pneumoniae* in penicillin-allergic patient (previous rash).
3. Uncomplicated urinary tract infections (Cephalexin).
4. Surgical prophylaxis for orthopedic and cardiovascular operations.

   (cefazolin preferred because of longer half-life).
5. Staphylococcal infections of skin and skin structure.

Second Generation Cephalosporins – Uses

1. Community-acquired pneumonia - Cefuroxime is widely used for empiric therapy. Has activity vs. many ampicillin-resistant *H. influenzae* strains.
2. Skin and soft tissue infection.
3. Urinary tract infections.
4. Upper respiratory tract infections (otitis media, sinusitis). Some resistance to *H. influenzae* to cefaclor (20-30%).
5. Mixed aerobic & anaerobic infections - Cefoxitin & Cefotetan. Resistance to *B. fragilis* is increasing.
6. Surgical prophylaxis - Cefoxitin or cefotetan are widely used in cases where mixed aerobic and anaerobic infections may occur, especialls intra-abdominal, colorectal and gynecologic operations. For cardiovascular and orthopedic procedures, cefuroxime and others may be used, but cefazolin is cheaper and appears to work well.

Third Generation Cephalosporins - Uses

1. Gram negative septicemia & other serious Gm - infections.
2. *Pseudomonas aeruginosa* infections (Ceftazidime - 90% effective).
3. Gram negative meningitis - Cefotaxime, Ceftriaxone, Cefepime. For empiric therapy add vancomycin ± rifampin to cover resistant *Strep. pneumoniae.*
4. Gonorrhea - Single shot of Ceftriaxone is drug of choice. Oral cefixime and ceftibuten are also OK.
5. Complicated urinary tract infections, pyelonephritis
6. Osteomyelitis - Ceftriaxone in home health care situations.
7. Lyme disease - ceftriaxone in home health care situations.

Inappropriate Uses (yet widely prescribed)

1. Surgical prophylaxis (use 1st or 2nd generation agents).
2. Otitis media, URIs - Cefixime (Suprax), ceftibuten have poor Gm + activity.
3. Uncomplicated UTIs.

Adverse Effects

The cephalosporins have good safety profiles. The overall incidence of adverse events attributed to cephalosporins is between 1 and 10%. The most common adverse drug reactions are rashes (1–5%), eosinophilia (3–10%), gastrointestinal symptoms (3%), hematological abnormalities (1–2%), phlebitis (2%) and fever (<1%). Anaphylactic reactions to cephalosporins are rare (<0.02%). Because of cross-reactions between cephalosporins and penicillins, caution should be used when prescribing cephalosporins to patients with penicillin allergy. If a patient had anaphylaxis, angioedema, or urticaria following penicillin use, cephalosporins should be avoided. Among patients with morbilliform rashes (resembling measles) after penicillin, the majority (95%) will tolerate cephalosporins without adverse effects and with no increased risk of anaphylaxis. When evaluating patients with histories of allergic penicillin reactions, practitioners may order penicillin skin tests to screen potential cephalosporin recipients.The frequency of allergic reactions to cephalosporins is 1.7% in patients with histories of type I penicillin reactions and negative penicillin skin tests. Most patients with negative penicillin skin tests may receive cephalosporins safely. The cephalos porins are valuable because of their broad spectrum of antimicrobial activity. However, their bactericidal action alters gut flora and selects for overgrowth of resistant organisms. Cephalosporins have been associated with superinfections with *Clostridium difficile,* enterococci, coagulasenegative staphylococci, *P. aeruginosa,* and *Candida albicans.* Overgrowth by toxigenic *C. difficile* occasionally causes pseudomembranous colitis in patients treatedwith cephalosporins. Some third-generation cephalosporins induce production of extended-spectrum β-lactamases (ESBLs) in

P. aeruginosa. The ESBLs can transfer to various Enterobacteriaceae and produce organisms resistant to almost all β-lactam antibiotics. Bleeding is an uncommon but serious side effect of some cephalosporins. The *N*-methylthiotetrazole (MTT) side chain on the R_substituent inhibits production of active vitamin K. Cephalosporins with the MTT side chain (cefamandole, cefmetazole, cefoperazone, cefotetan) are associated with hypoprothrombinemia, coagulation abnormalities and bleeding. In addition, the MTT cephalosporins increase the effect of oral anticoagulants.

Bleeding or coagulation abnormalities caused by MTT cephalosporins can be treated or prevented with supplemental vitamin K. Additional bleeding problems may result from antiplatelet effects. The MTT side chain confers a structure and activity similar to that of disulfiram, so patients taking MTT cephalosporins who also ingest alcohol may develop symptoms similar to the disulfiram reaction. Children and adults receiving high doses of ceftriaxone may develop gallbladder sludge (pseudolithiasis). While most patients with sludge have no symptoms, occasionally the sludge identified by abdominal ultrasonography has led to laparotomy. Biliary sludge usually disappears after discontinuation of ceftriaxone.

Monobactams

The natural monobactams have little antimicrobial activity. A synthetic derivative, Aztreonam (*Azactam*), Fig 14-6 has excellent activity against gram-negative organisms, including *P. aeruginosa*. Aztreonam has low affinity for penicillin-binding proteins in streptococci, staphylococci and anaerobes and therefore has no significant activity against gram-positive bacteria or anaerobes. Specific activity against gram-negative organisms relates to the aminothiazolyl oxime moiety on the acyl side chain. Addition of two methyl groups and a carboxylic acid group on the oxime side chain enhances activity gainst *P. aeruginosa*. Aztreonam is stable to most β-lactamases (chromosomal and plasmid). The pharmacokinetic properties of aztreonam are similar to those of the parenteral cephalosporins. Aztreonam is not bioavailable after oral administration. During its distribution phase, the drug can achieve therapeutic concentrations in cerebrospinal fluid in the presence of inflamed meninges. Consequently, aztreonam is an alternative antibiotic to the cephalosporins for the therapy of meningitis caused by gram-negative bacilli. Aztreonam may be used as a substitute for an aminoglycoside in the treatment of infections caused by susceptible gram-negative organisms. Most of the adverse effects of aztreonam are local reactions at the site of injection. Interestingly, aztreonam rarely causes allergic reactions in patients with a history of type I hypersensitivity to other β-lactam antibiotics.

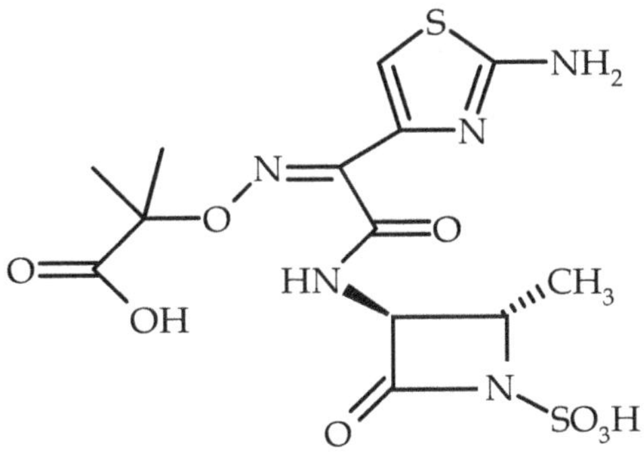

Fig 14-6: Structure of aztreonam.

β-lactamase Inhibitors (Clavulanic Acid, Sulbactam and Tazobactam)

β-Lactamase Inhibitors

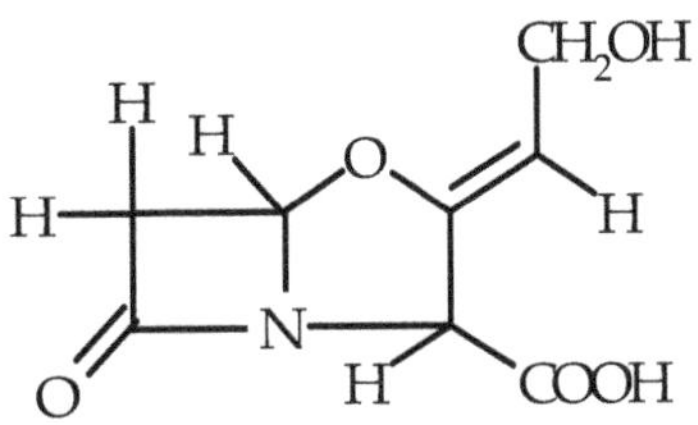

Clavulanic acid

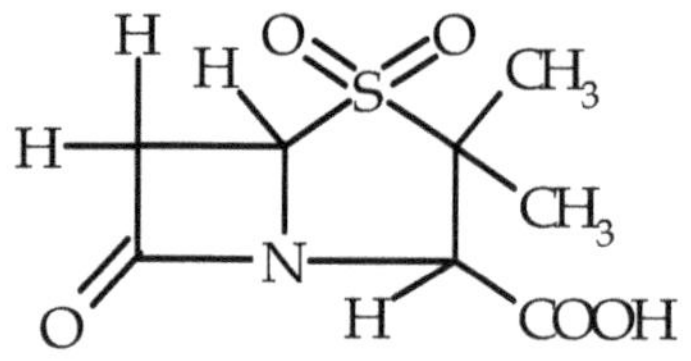

Sulbactam

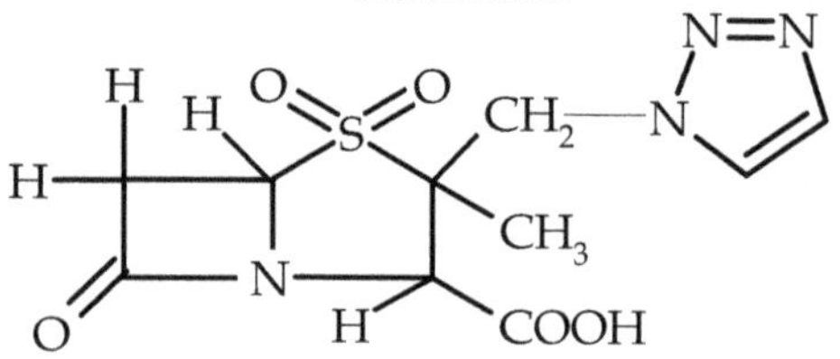

Tazobactam

Fig 14-7: Structure of beta lactamases inhibitors.

A successful strategy for combating β-lactamase mediated resistance is the use of agents designed to bind at the active site, which are frequently β-lactams. This strategy can take two forms: (i) create substrates that reversibly and/or irreversibly bind the enzyme with high affinity but form unfavorable steric interactions as the acyl-enzyme or (ii) develop mechanism based or irreversible "suicide inhibitors" Examples of the former are extended-spectrum cephalosporins, monobactams or carbapenems which form acyl-enzymes and adopt catalytically incompetent conformations that are poorly hydrolyzed .

Irreversible "suicide inhibitors" can permanently inactivate the -lactamase through secondary chemical reactions in the enzyme active site. The general mechanism of irreversible inhibitors (I) leading to permanent enzyme inactivation. Examples of these inactivators are the commercially available class A inhibitors clavulanic acid, sulbactam and tazobactam.

β-Lactamase Inhibitors in Clinical Practice

Clavulanic acid, sulbactam and tazobactam

Clavulanic acid, the first β-lactamase inhibitor introduced into clinical medicine, was isolated from *Streptomyces clavuligerus*. Clavulanate (the salt form of the acid in solution) showed little antimicrobial activity alone, but when combined with amoxicillin, clavulanate significantly lowered the amoxicillin MICs against *S. aureus*, *K. pneumoniae*, *Proteus mirabilis* and *E. coli* . All three -lactamase inhibitor compounds share structural similarity with penicillin; are effective against many susceptible organisms expressing class A β-lactamases (including CTX-M and the ESBL derivatives of TEM-1, TEM-2, and SHV-1); and are generally less effective against class B, C, and D β-lactamases. The efficacy of the mechanism-based inhibitors can vary within and between the classes of β-lactamases. The strcuture of β-lactamase inhibitors are shown in Fig 14-7.

Mechanism of inhibition

Evidence from X-ray crystallography, UV difference spectra, isoelectric focusing, mass spectrometry (MS), and Raman microscopy suggests that the inactivators of class A β–lactamases undergo complex reaction schemes with branch points after formation of the acyl-enzyme. Kinetic and mass spectrometry analysis of inactivation mechanisms, combined with crystallographic studies, suggests that clavulanate, sulbactam and tazobactam follow similar reaction pathways, beginning with formation of an acylenzyme species. After acylation, opening of the five membered ring leads to formation of a transient imine intermediate. This imine species is likely the common intermediate preceding the chemical conversions that lead to transient enzyme inhibition. Depending on the properties of the enzyme and inhibitor, the reaction will ultimately proceed to deacylation or irreversible (prolonged) inactivation. In the case of deacylation of the enamine intermediate, the acyl-enzyme undergoes decarboxylation and ester bond hydrolysis, regenerating the active β-lactamase, albeit very slowly.

The duration of transient inhibition is determined, in part, by the stability of the intermediate species. Preceding acylation of the inhibitor, a persistent noncovalent Michaelis complex may account for inhibition of enzyme activity. Following formation of the acyl-enzyme, stabilization of the enamine intermediate is a significant factor in prolonged enzyme inhibition. The *trans*-enamine intermediate of tazobactam, as opposed to the *trans* enamine intermediates of clavulanate and sulbactam, may be stabilized by intra and intermolecular interactions. These interactions between the sulfone and triazolyl moieties of the tazobactam intermediate and the enzyme active site may explain, in part, tazobactam's potent *in vitro* and *in vivo* inhibition of many serine β-lactamases . Studies of SHV-1 in complex with each of the mechanism based inhibitors revealed that tazobactam forms a predominant population of *trans*-enamine, as opposed to clavulanate and sulbactam, which form a mixture of *trans*-enamine and the more chemically labile *cis*- enamine and imine species .

β-Lactam–β-lactamase inhibitor combinations: clinical use

Generally, the inhibitors do not inactivate PBPs, but notable exceptions include

(i) the intrinsic activities of sulbactam against *Bacteroides spp., Acinetobacter spp.,* and *N. gonorrhoea*

(ii) clavulanate action against *Haemophilus influenza* and *N. gonorrhoea*; and

(iii) tazobactam inhibition of PBPs in *Borrelia burgdorferi* .

As these "antibacterial effects" are relatively weak, the inhibitors are always combined with - lactam antibiotics for clinical use. Currently, there are five β-lactam–β-lactamase inhibitor formulations available. Amoxicillin-clavulanate, ticarcillin-clavulanate, ampicillin-sulbactam and piperacillin-tazobactam are available. Importantly, as in clinical usage, the lactamase inhibitors are combined with β-lactams for *in vitro* susceptibility testing. The composition of these formulations can have a major impact on susceptibility results, which may or may not reflect clinical efficacy example, the ticarcillin clavulanate preparation for parental administration is 3.0 g-0.1 g, while ampicillin-sulbactam is at a 2.0 g-1.0 g ratio. However, both combinations are tested at a 2:1 ratio *in vitro*, and since clavulanate has higher "gram-for-gram" potency than sulbactam, clavulanate may "test better" in MIC profiling. However, clinically ampicillin-sulbactam may retain efficacy because of the relatively large amount of inhibitor delivered relative to the-lactam and relative to the amount of β-lactamase in the cell. This scenario illustrates an important issue in susceptibility testing and its correlate to clinical efficacy.

(i) Amoxicillin-clavulanate

Amoxicillin-clavulanate was the first β-lactam–β-lactamase inhibitor combination introduced into clinical practice and remains the only combination available for oral use. The activity of amoxicillin against susceptible bacteria that do not possess a β-lactamase (e. g., streptococci, enterococci, *E. coli*, and *Listeria* spp.) is not improved by the use of clavulanate. However, the addition of clavulanate significantly expands amoxicillin's spectrum to include penicillinase-producing *S. aureus, H. influenzae, Moraxella catarrhalis, Bacteroides* spp., *N. gonorrhoeae, E. coli, Klebsiella* spp., and *P. mirabilis*. The oral availability of amoxicillin-clavulanate makes it well suited for the outpatient clinic and this β-lactam–β-lactamase inhibitor combination exerted its greatest impact on the treatment of community acquired respiratory infections. Additionally, amoxicillin clavulanate is sometimes used as an oral equivalent ("stepdown therapy") of ampicillin-sulbactam or ticarcillin clavulanate in the treatment of skin, soft tissue, abdominal and gynecological infections.

(ii) Ticarcillin-clavulanate

Ticarcillin-clavulanate was the first β-lactam–β-lactamase inhibitor combination available for parenteral administration. Similar to the case for amoxicillin, the addition of clavulanate does not increase activity against pathogens for which ticarcillin alone is effective, such as non-β-lactamase-producing *Haemophilus* spp., *E. coli, Proteus* spp., *Enterobacter* spp.,

Morganella spp., *Providencia* spp., and *P. aeruginosa*. However, the combination of ticarcillin and clavulanate does increase activity against β-lactamase-producing staphylococci, *E. coli*, *H. influenzae*, *Klebsiella* spp., *Proteus* spp., *Pseudomonas* spp., *Providencia* spp., *N. gonorrhoeae*, *Moraxella catarrhalis* and *Bacteroides* spp. Surprisingly, ticarcillin-clavulanate exhibits activity against the multidrug-resistant, non-lactose-fermenting *S. maltophilia* and the use of this combination in addition to other antimicrobials (e.g., aztreonam or trimethoprim-sulfamethoxazole) leads to synergistic killing. This phenomenon may represent a very interesting opportunity to study the activity of ticarcillin-clavulanate against *S. maltophilia*. Clavulanate induces the expression of chromosomally mediated AmpC β-lactamases in many *Enterobacteriaceae* and can antagonize the antibacterial effects of ticarcillin as a partner β-lactam. This ticarcillin antagonism was observed in laboratory checkerboard studies with *E. cloacae* and *Morganella morganii* strains

(iii) Ampicillin-sulbactam

Ampicillin shows activity against most streptococci, enterococci, *Listeria* spp., and strains of *S. aureus*, *H. influenzae*, *E. coli*, *P. mirabilis*, *Salmonella* spp., and *Shigella* spp. that are devoid of β-lactamases (an important exception are ampicillin-resistant strains of *H. influenzae* that do not contain a β-lactamase and often have substitutions in PBP sequences). In combination with sulbactam, the activity extends to β-lactamase-containing *S. aureus*, *H. influenzae*, *M. catarrhalis*, *E. coli*, *Proteus* spp., *Klebsiella* spp., and anaerobes .When the combination of ampicillin at 2.0 g and sulbactam at 1.0 g was marketed in 1987, this broad-spectrum activity made ampicillin-sulbactam ideal therapy for polymicrobial infections such as abdominal and gynecological surgical infections, aspiration pneumonia, odontogenic abscesses, and diabetic foot infections. The early clinical success of this combination (and susceptibility of many pathogens to ampicillin-sulbactam and ticarcillin-clavulanate) established confidence in the role of β-lactam–β-lactamase inhibitor therapy. Unfortunately, the resistance to ampicillin-sulbactam among clinical isolates of *E. coli* is increasing. Sulbactam is not well absorbed orally and must be administered parenterally. However, the intravenous ampicillin-sulbactam combination is well tolerated, with very few reported side effects.

(iv) Piperacillin-tazobactam

Piperacillin in combination with tazobactam became available in the United States in 1993. Piperacillin is a broad-spectrum penicillin that is bactericidal against many Gram-positive and Gram-negative aerobes and anaerobes. As a single agent, piperacillin demonstrates activity against *P. aeruginosa*, pneumococci, streptococci, anaerobes and *Enterococcus faecalis*, and this activity is retained in combination with tazobactam. Clinicians must remember that the addition of tazobactam does not always increase susceptibility of *P. aeruginosa* and other Gram-negative bacilli expressing AmpC -lactamases. However, tazobactam does extend piperacillin's activity against most β-lactamase producing strains of *Enterobacteriaceae*, *H. influenzae*, *N. gonorrhoeae* and *M. catarrhalis* and has the potential to lower MICs against these strains expressing ESBLs (Extended Spectrum Beta Lactamases). Several observational studies have strongly suggested that the replacement of extended-spectrum cephalosporins with piperacillin-tazobactam can help lower the rates of infection from Gram-negative ESBL producers and vancomycin-resistant *Enterococcus* spp. While the mechanism for decreasing ESBL-producing isolates is not clear, it must be noted that the efficacy of β-lactam–β-lactamase inhibitor combinations may be reduced for organisms producing multiple ESBLs, particularly if they also have an AmpC β -lactamase.

Carbapenems

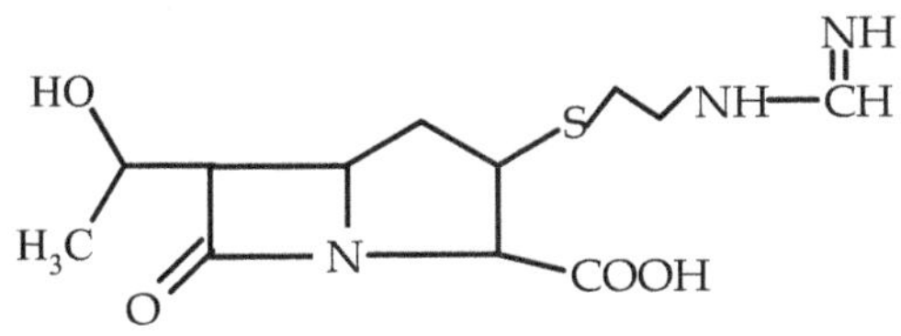

Imipenem
(N-formimidoyithienamycin)

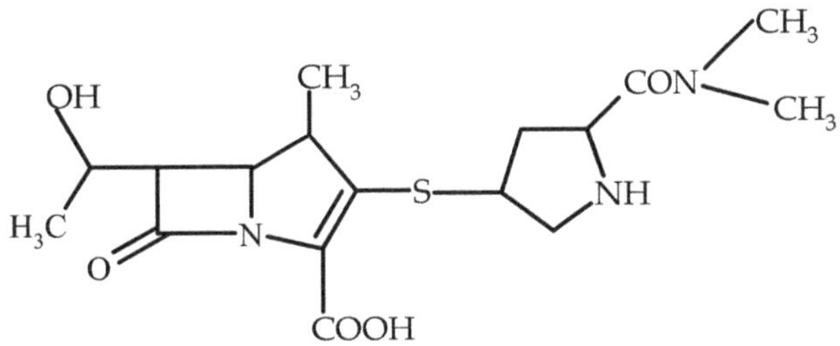

Meropenem

Fig 14-8: Structure of carbapenems.

The newest classes of β -lactam antibiotics are the carbapenems arbacephems. Their mechanism of action is the same as those of the other β-lactam antibiotics. The structures of Carbepenems are shown in Fig 14-8.

Imipenem

The first carbapenem, imipenem–cilastatin (Primaxin), is a chemically stable analogue of thienamycin produced by *Streptomyces cattleya.* The antibacterial spectrum of imipenem is among the broadest of all of the β-lactam antibiotics. Imipenem is active against most gram-positive, gram-negative, and anaerobic bacteria. When compared with the *in vitro* activities of third generation cephalosporins, imipenem is more potent against *E. faecalis, B. fragilis* and *P. aeruginosa.* Imipenem's stability against β -lactamases is attributable to the trans position of the 6-hydroxyethyl side chain on the β -lactam ring. Organisms resistant to imipenem include *E. faecium and Stenotrophomonas maltophilia.*

Imipenem–cilastatin is only available for intramuscular or intravenous administration because oral bioavailability is poor. The enzyme, dehydropeptidase I, present in renal tubules, converts imipenem to an inactive metabolite. To decrease metabolic clearance, imipenem is combined with cilastatin, an inhibitor of dehydropeptidase I.

Imipenem–cilastatin is one of the drugs of first choice for the empirical therapy of many polymicrobial pulmonary, intraabdominal, and soft tissue infections. The notable adverse effect of imipenem–cilastatin is seizures affecting 1% of patients. Risk factors for seizures are old age, head trauma, previous seizure disorder, cerebrovascular accident, and renal failure. Among patients with a history of penicillin allergy, 10% are cross-sensitive to imipenem–cilastatin.

Meropenem

Meropenem (*Merrem*) is another carbapenem antibiotic with a broad spectrum of activity comparable to that of imipenem. A methyl group attached at oneposition on the five-member ring confers stability to dehydropeptidase I. Consequently, meropenem does not require administration with cilastatin.When compared in human trials, imipenem–cilastatin and meropenem achieve similar clinical outcomes in patients with serious intraabdominal and soft tissue infections. Both imipenem–cilastatin and meropenem are used to treat infections caused by highly resistant *Klebsiella pneumonia* producing ESBLs.The major clinically relevant distinction between imipenem–cilastatin and meropenem is the lower likelihood of seizures associated with meropenem.

Loracarbef

Loracarbef (*Lorabid*) is a synthetic β-lactam antibiotic of the carbacephem class. The chemical structure of loracarbef is similar to that of cefaclor. Loracarbef's spectrum of antibacterial activity resembles those of the second-generation cephalosporins. Comparative clinical trials reveal similar outcomes in patients treated with cefaclor, cefprozil, and loracarbef.

Other Cell Wall Synthesis Inhibitors

Vancomycin and Teicoplanin

Structure and Mechanism of Action

Vancomycin (*Vancocin*) is a complex tricyclic glycopeptides antibiotic produced by *Streptomyces orientalis,* while teicoplanin (*Targocid*) is derived from *Actinoplanes* (*Actinomyces*) *teichomyceticus.* Teicoplanin has two major components: a phosphoglycolipid (A1) and five chlorine-containing glycopeptides (A2). It is available as an investigational drug. The glycopeptides are inhibitors of cell wall synthesis. They bind to the terminal carboxyl group on the D alanyl- D-alanine terminus of the *N*-acetylglucosamine- *N*-acetylmuramic acid peptide and prevent polymerization of the linear peptidoglycan by peptidoglycan synthase.They are bactericidal *invitro.*

Antimicrobial Spectrum

The glycopeptides are narrow-spectrum agents that are active against gram-positive organisms. Like vancomycin, teicoplanin is bacteriostatic against staphylococci, streptococci and enterococci. Gram-positive rods, such as *Bacillus anthracis, Corynebacterium diphtheriae, Clostridium tetani,* and *Clostridium perfringens,* are also sensitive to the glycopeptides. The glycopeptides are not effective against gram-negative rods, mycobacteria, or fungi.

Absorption, Distribution and Excretion

Vancomycin is poorly absorbed from the gastrointestinal tract, resulting in high concentrations in the feces. In neutropenic patients and others with altered gastrointestinal mucosa with denudation, significant oral absorption of vancomycin may occur and may be accompanied by additive toxicity if rapid infusion or large parenteral doses of the drug are given concomitantly. Except for the treatment of staphylococcal enterocolitis and pseudo-membranous colitis, it is administered intravenously. Peak serum levels are achieved 2 hr after intravenous (i.v) administration, and about 55% is bound to serum protein. The therapeutic range is a trough concentration between 5 and 15 μg/ml, and the peak should stay below 60 μg/ml to avoid side effects. In normal adults the serum half-life is 5 to 11 hours. With impaired renal function, the half-life is 7 to 9 days. The dose of vancomycin must be carefully adjusted to avoid toxicity or ineffective treatment, especially in patients undergoing hemodialysis. Pediatric oncology patients with normal renal function may require vancomycin dosage regimens that are substantially greater than predicted. Similar studies in adult patients with hematological malignancies have suggested a larger dosage requirement as well, owing to an increased volume of distribution. After i.v administration, vancomycin diffuses into serous cavities and across inflamed but not normal meninges. It can be used in the treatment of meningitis with susceptible organisms. It is also given via ventriculoatrial or ventriculo-peritoneal shunts when these become infected. Renal excretion is predominant, with 80 to 90% of an administered dose eliminated in 24 hours. Only small amounts appear in the stool and bile after intravenous administration. Teicoplanin, like vancomycin, is not absorbed from the intestinal tract. Peak plasma levels are achieved about 2 hours after intramuscular administration. The drug distributes widely in tissues; plasma protein binding is about 90%.The half-life approximates 50 hours, which is considerably longer than that of vancomycin, and may make it useful for outpatient administration. Like vancomycin, teicoplanin is excreted by the kidneys.

Clinical Uses

Vancomycin and teicoplanin display excellent activity against staphylococci and streptococci, but because of the wide availability of equally effective and less toxic drugs, they are *second-line drugs in the treatment of most infections.* As antistaphylococcal agents they are less effective than β -lactam cephalosporin antibiotics, such as nafcillin and cefazolin. They have attained much wider use in recent years as a consequence of the emergence of methicillin-resistant *S. aureus* (MRSA) infections, in particular the growing importance of *Staphylococcus epidermidis* infections associated with the use of intravascular catheters and in patients with peritonitis who are on continuous ambulatory peritoneal dialysis. Vancomycin is also an effective alternative therapy for the treatment of staphylococcal enterocolitis and endocarditis. The combination of vancomycin and either streptomycin or gentamicin acts synergistically against enterococci and is used effectively for the treatment or prevention of enterococcal endocarditis. Teicoplanin demonstrates similar synergy. Staphylococcal vascular shunt infections in persons undergoing renal dialysis have been successfully treated with vancomycin. Vancomycin in oral form can also be used in patients in whom *C. difficile* colitis is not responding to metronidazole. Teicoplanin, although not available in the United States, has been used to treat a wide range of gram-positive infections, including endocarditis and peritonitis. It is not as effective as the β -lactams, but its actions are similar to those of vancomycin against staphylococcal infections. High-grade resistance of pneumococci to penicillin may also necessitate vancomycin therapy. Enterococci that are resistant to vancomycin are emerging as major nosocomial pathogens. These strains are generally resistant to a number of other antibiotics, such as penicillin, ampicillin, and gentamicin, which limits treatment options. The possibility of transferring these resistance determinants to other gram-positive organisms, like *S. aureus,* is a valid concern. It is therefore necessary to limit the use of vancomycin to treatment of serious infections caused by methicillin-resistant staphylococci and situations in which allergies preclude the use of other antibiotics.

Adverse Effects

The major adverse effect associated with vancomycin therapy is ototoxicity, which may result in tinnitus, hightone hearing loss, and deafness in extreme instances. More commonly, the intravenous infusion of vancomycin can result in chills, fever and a maculopapular skin rash often involving the head and upper thorax (red man syndrome). Red man syndrome is associated with increased levels of serum histamine.Vancomycin is rarely nephrotoxic when used alone. Teicoplanin rarely causes red man syndrome or nephrotoxicity.

Bacitracin

Structure and Mechanism of Action Bacitracin is a mixture of polypeptide antibiotics produced by *Bacillus subtilis.* As with penicillin, it contains a thiazolidine nucleus attached through L-leucine to a peptide composed of both D- and L-amino acids. However, it does not contain a β-lactam ring. *Bacitracin prevents cell wall synthesis by binding to a lipid pyrophosphate carrier that transports cell wall precursors to the growing cell wall.* Bacitracin inhibits the dephosphorylation of this lipid carrier, a step essential to the carrier molecule's ability to accept cell wall constituents for transport.

Antimicrobial Spectrum

Bacitracin inhibits gram-positive cocci, including *Staphylococcus aureus,* streptococci, a few gram-negative organisms and one anaerobe, *Clostridium difficile.* The bacitracins are not absorbed from the gastrointestinal tract following oral administration.

Clinical Uses

Bacitracin is highly active against staphylococci, *Streptococcus pyogenes,* and *C. difficile.* Its high degree of activity against the group A streptococci is used in the laboratory as a means of differentiating between the Lancefield group A streptococci and other streptococci. Bacitracin is well tolerated topically and orally and is frequently used in combination with other agents (notably polymyxin B and neomycin) in the form of creams, ointments and aerosol preparations. Hydrocortisone has been added to the combination for its antiinflammatory effects. Bacitracin preparations are effective in the treatment of impetigo and other superficial skin infections. However, poststreptococcal nephritis has followed the topical treatment of impetigo, and therefore oral penicillin therapy is preferred.

Bacitracin has been used with limited success for eradication of *S. aureus* in the nares. Because of the risk of serious nephrotoxicity, the *parenteral use of bacitracin is not justified.*

References

Balbisi. EA, Cefditoren, a new aminothiazolyl cephalosporin. Pharmacology 2002;22:1278.

Centers for Disease Control and Prevention: Vancomycin resistant *Staphylococcus aureus*. Pennsylvania, 2002. JAMA 2002;288:2116.

Chow. JW, et al. *Enterobacter* bacteremia: Clinical features and emergence of antibiotic resistance during therapy. Ann Intern Med 1991; 115:585.

Fowler VG et al. Daptomycin versus standard therapy for bacteremia and endocarditis caused by *Staphylococcus aureus*. N Engl J Med 2006; 355:653.

Hiramatsu K et al. Methicillin resistant *Staphylococcus aureus* clinical strain with reduced vancomycin susceptibility. J Antimicrob Chemother 1997; 40:135.

Jacoby GA, Munoz-Price LS. The new beta-lactamases. N Engl J Med 2005;352:380.

Keating GM, Perry CM. Ertapenem: A review of its use in the treatment of bacterial infections. Drugs 2005; 65:2151.

Park MA, Li JT. Diagnosis and management of penicillin allergy. Mayo Clin Proc 2005; 80:405.

Perry CM, Scott LJ. Cefdinir: A review of its use in the management of mild-to-moderate bacterial infections. Drugs 2004; 64:1433.

CHAPTER 15

Protein Synthesis Inhibitors

A number of antibiotics fig 15-1 exert their antimicrobial effects by targeting the bacterial ribosome, which has components that differ structurally from those of the mammalian cytoplasmic ribosome. In general, the bacterial ribosome is smaller (70S) than the mammalian ribosome (80S) and is composed of 50S and 30S subunits (as compared to 60S and 40S subunits). The mammalian mitochondrial ribosome, however, more closely resembles the bacterial ribosome. Thus, although drugs that interact with the bacterial target usually spare the host cells, high levels of drugs such as chloramphenicol or the Tetracyclines may cause toxic effects as a result of interaction with the host mitochondrial ribosomes.

Aminoglycosides

The chemical structures of aminoglycosides are similar. All of them are organic alkalis with a high dissociation and low lipid diffusion, and do not easily transport across membranes.

Classification

The structures of Amino glycosides are shown in Fig 15-2.

- Older Aminoglycosides:
  - Streptomycin
  - Kanamycin
- Newer Aminoglycosides:
  - Gentamicin
  - Tobramycin
  - Neomycin
  - Amikacin
  - Netilmicin
  - Sisomicin

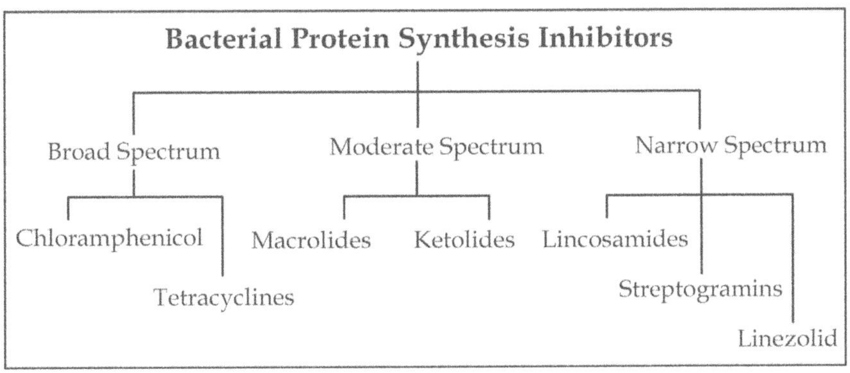

Fig 15-1: Bacterial protein synthesis inhibitors.

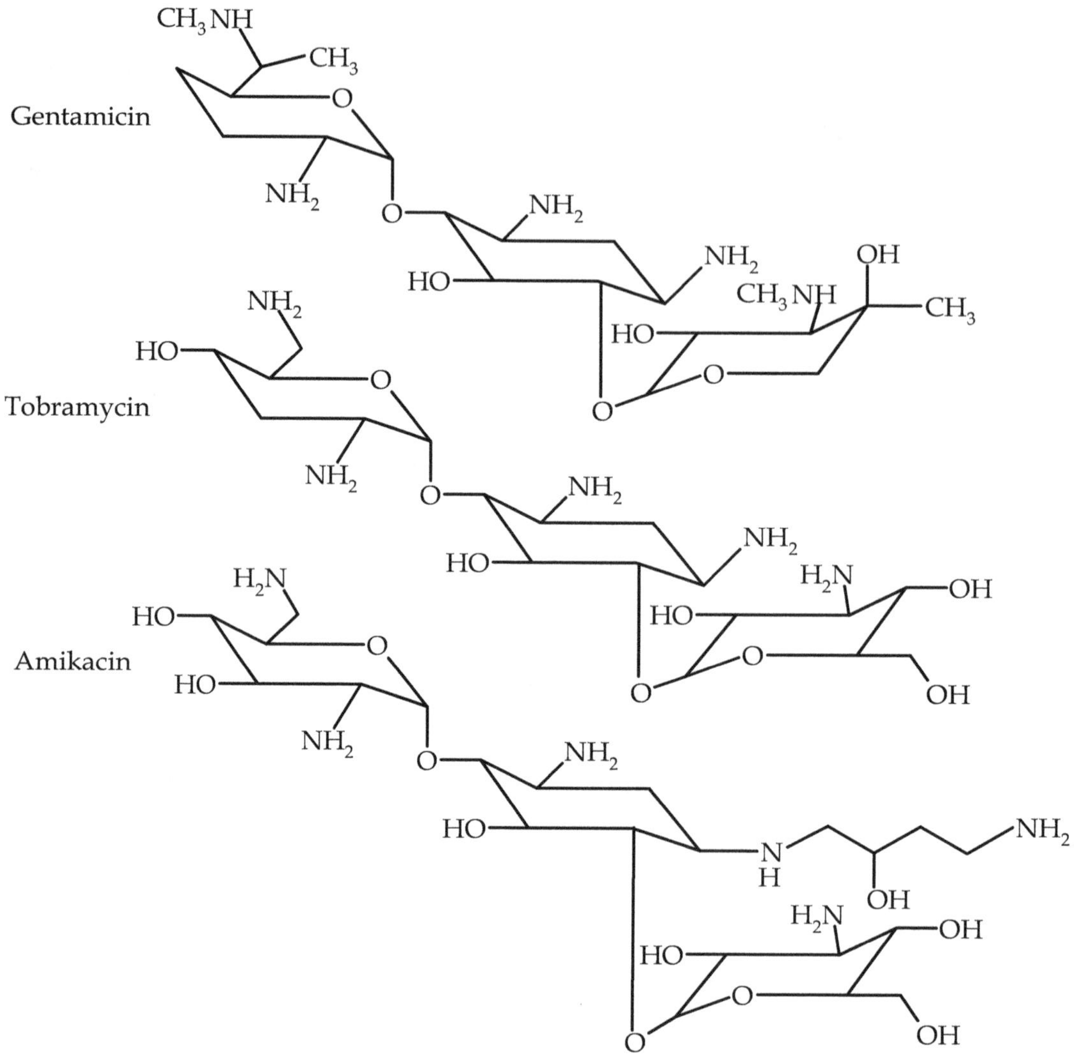

Fig 15-2: Aminoglycosides.

Antimicrobial Spectrum: Aminoglycosides are useful for infections caused by aerobic gram-negative bacilli, particularly the more resistant bacteria associated with hospital-acquired infections. While aminoglycosides are also active against aerobic gram-negative bacilli that cause community-acquired infections, their toxicities and the availability of other less toxic antimicrobials would not make them the drugs of choice for these infections.

Aerobic gram-negative bacilli. Very active, including Enterobacteriaceae *(Escherichia coli, Klebsiella, Proteus), Pseudomonas aeruginosa, Acinetobacter, Providencia*. Minimally active against Hemophilus.

Gram-positive aerobes. Though active against Staphylococci, Streptococci (e.g., Enterococci, Group B streptococci, viridans streptococci) aminoglycosides are not the preferred agents.

Aminoglycosides (particularly gentamicin, streptomycin) may be used in combination with cell-wall active drugs such as β-lactams and vancomycin for synergy against Staphylococci and Streptococci. Importantly, only low levels of aminoglycoside (peak levels of 3-4 mcg/ml and trough levels less than 1 mcg/ml) are generally recommended when used for synergy.

Anaerobes are not susceptible because they lack the necessary system that transports aminoglycosides to their target site.

Other Mycobacterium tuberculosis (amikacin, streptomycin) and Mycobacterium-avium intracellular (amikacin).

Mechanism of Action

The antibacterial actions of the aminoglycosides involve two possibly synergistic effects. First, the positively charged aminoglycoside binds to negatively charged sites on the outer bacterial membrane, thereby disrupting membrane integrity. It is likely that the aminoglycoside-induced bacterial outer membrane degradation accounts for the rapid concentration dependent bactericidal effect of these compounds. Second, aminoglycosides bind to various sites on bacterial 30S ribosomal subunits, disrupting the initiation of protein synthesis and inducing errors in the translation of messenger RNA to peptides. They also bind to sites on bacterial 50S ribosomal subunits, although the significance of this binding is uncertain. In addition, they have a postantibiotic effect; that is, they continue to suppress bacterial regrowth even after removal of the antibiotic from the bacterial microenvironment. It is likely that ribosome disruption accounts for this postantibiotic activity.

The postantibiotic effect is characterized by prolonged suppression of bacterial regrowth after the initially high aminoglycoside concentration has fallen to a subinhibitory level. Perhaps resumption of bacterial ribosomal function requires the time-consuming synthesis of new ribosomes after their disruption by aminoglycosides. The postantibiotic effect explains why aminoglycosides can be given in single daily doses despite their short half-life. Penetration of aminoglycosides through the outer bacterial membrane occurs both by outer membrane disruption and by diffusion through outer membrane porins. Penetration through the inner bacterial membrane occurs in two phases. The first requires that the cytosol have a negative electron potential and therefore be inhibited by the presence of a low pH. The second phase depends on aerobic bacterial metabolism and therefore will be inhibited by low oxygen tension. The latter two observations are of considerable clinical relevance, since both a low pH and a low oxygen tension frequently occur in bacterial abscesses. Administration of β-lactam antibiotics will reverse the negative effects of both low pH and low oxygen tension on the ability of aminoglycosides to penetrate into bacteria; this ability accounts in part for the synergism that occurs between aminoglycoside and β-lactam antibiotic drugs.

Microbial Resistance

Resistant aerobic gram-negative bacilli to aminoglycosides are problematic in some areas. Cross-resistance between aminoglycosides is not always complete.

Mechanisms of resistance

1. **Aminoglycoside modifying enzymes** that inactivate the aminoglycoside

Adenyltransferase → adenylation of a hydroxyl group

Acetyltransferase → acetylation of an amino group

Phosphotransferase → phosphorylation of a hydroxyl group

2. **Amikacin is less susceptible to aminoglycoside-modifying enzymes** because of protective side chains and therefore may still be useful when resistance to gentamicin or tobramycin develops.
3. Altered ribosome binding sites.
4. Altered aminoglycoside uptake, cross resistance to all aminoglycosides occurs.

Kinetics

Absorption: Aminoglycoside are poorly absorbed from the G.I tract. Absorption by i.m route is rapid and complete, however in critically ill patients i.m absorption can vary considerably. Peak serum concentrations of aminoglycosides are reached within 30-120 minutes after i.m. injection. Therapeutic or toxic concentrations may be obtained by i.p route. The aminoglycosides are usually administered by parenteral routes: 30-60 minutes intravenous infusion or intramuscular injection.

Distribution: Aminoglycosides are polar drugs and their distribution is mainly restricted to extracellular fluids. Protein binding of these antibiotics is less than 10%. Aminoglycosides distribute well in synovial, peritoneal, ascitic and pleural fluids. High concentrations of aminoglycosides are obtained in renal tissue especially in renal cortex. Penetration of these drugs is poor in eye and central nervous system. Concentrations of aminoglycosides in biliar and bronchial secretions are variable.

The distribution volume of aminoglycosides approximates to the extracellular fluid (20-25% of body weight). Modifications of the distribution coefficient of aminoglycosides occur in some kind of patients as those suffering from gram negative sepsis, dehydrated, febrile, critically ill, hematological, burned patients, etc.

Elimination: Aminoglycosides are primarily excreted unchanged through the kidney by glomerular filtration. The 80-90% of the administered dose is excreted in the urine resulting in high urinary concentrations. A small amount of aminoglycoside is excreted by bile. Serum half-life in patients with normal renal function is about 2-3 hours. Linear correlations are obtained between the clearance or the elimination constant of aminoglycoside and creatinine clearance of the patient.

Dose Conventional: The goal of conventional dosing of aminoglycosides is to achieve peak drug levels between 4-10 mcg/ml and trough concentrations less than 2.0 mcg/ml. Higher levels are used for serious infections or infections caused by resistant bacteria, while lower levels were generally used for less serious infections, infections at sites where aminoglycosides are highly concentrated (e.g., urinary tract) or when used in combination with other antibiotics for synergy.

Dose: (gentamicin, tobramycin, netilmicin) 1-2 mg/kg (lean body weight) hours in patients with normal renal function.

Amikacin: 5-7.5 mg/kg (lean body weight) Q8-12 hours in adults with normal renal function.

Dosage adjustments are necessary in patients with renal dysfunction and who are obese.

Once daily dosing. A single daily dose (4-7 mg/kg of gentamicin, tobramycin) is administered once daily. Since aminoglycosides display concentration dependent bactericidal activity and a post-antibiotic effect, these traits would theoretically provide for a more effective and less toxic regimen. Various nomograms are available for once-daily dosing of aminoglycosides. There is a lack of data on the efficacy and safety of once-daily dosing of aminoglycosides in certain patient populations and certain types of infections.

Clinical Uses

1. Aminoglycosides are excellent agents for infections due to aerobic gram-negative bacteria, particularly those associated with hospital-acquired infections. They are commonly used in combination with cell-wall active antibiotics (e.g., beta-lactams) because combinations such as these are generally synergistic against aerobic gram negative bacilli (e.g., Pseudomonas aeruginosa, Enterobacteriaceae).
2. Empiric therapy for serious or life-threatening infection, or infection that is presumed to be due to resistant aerobic gram negative bacilli. These circumstances are likely to be encountered in patients who are hospitalized patients, have recently been hospitalized, have recently received antibiotics or are immunocompromised.
3. Septicemia.

4. Intraabdominal infections. In combination with other antibiotics active against anaerobes. Activity of aminoglycoside may be limited by: 1) anaerobic environment and low pH in an abscess, 2) necrotic tissue that may contain divalent cations.
5. Complicated urinary tract infections.
6. Complicated, skin and soft tissue infections (in combination with other appropriate antibiotics (e.g., diabetic ulcer).
7. Endocarditis. When used in combination with a cell wall active drug (e.g., beta-lactam, vancomycin) for endocarditis due to gram positive cocci (Staphylococci, Enterococci, Viridans streptococci), low levels (peak 3-4 mcg/ml, and trough <1.0 mcg/ml) are generally recommended.
8. Osteomyelitis/septic arthritis.
9. Lower respiratory tract. (e.g., pneumonia), although the low pH of bronchial secretions may inhibit the activity of aminoglycosides.

Toxicity

Nephrotoxicity is a major toxicity (5-10%). Risk factors for nephrotoxicity include prolonged duration of therapy, increased age, preexisting renal insufficiency, recent aminoglycoside therapy, concurrent use of other nephrotoxins (e.g., amphotericin b, vancomycin, others), volume depletion, liver disease. Toxicity is due to **accumulation of aminoglycosides in proximal tubular cells of the kidney**, and is **usually reversible** since proximal tubular cells can regenerate.

Some studies have suggested than netilmicin and tobramycin are less nephrotoxic than gentamicin; however, other studies have been unable to find a difference between aminoglycosides.

Ototoxicity, including vestibular (1-3%) and auditory (2-14%) is a major toxicity and is **usually irreversible** and can occur after the end of treatment. Risk factors for ototoxicity include dose and duration of therapy, repeated exposure to aminoglycosides, loop diuretics, vancomycin, hypovolemia, liver dysfunction, increased age, higher blood levels, renal impairment.

Clinical symptoms of cochlear toxicity include **tinnitus**; and of vestibular toxicity, **headache, nausea, and vomiting.**

Neuromuscular blockade may be problematic particularly in situations where neuromuscular transmission is already compromised (e.g., myasthenia gravis, administration of D-tubocuare, succinylcholine) is reversed by intravenous calcium gluconate.

Drug Interactions

Penicillins

Coadministration of aminoglycosides with penicillin result in inactivation of the aminoglycoside. This interaction may be minimized by not drawing aminoglycoside blood levels immediately after administration of the penicillin.

Heparin

Heparin will also decrease the measured aminoglycoside blood levels. Management includes proper flushing of intravenous lines containing heparin before drawing aminoglycoside blood levels.

Individual Agents

Streptomycin

Ribosomal resistance to this agent develops readily, limiting its role as a single agent mainly used as a second line agent for treatment of tuberculosis given at 0.5-1g/d (7.5-15 mg/kg/day for children) i.m or i.v should be used only in combination with other agents to prevent emergence of resistance. In plague, tularemia and sometimes brucellosis, 1 g/d (15 mg/kg/day for children) i.m or i.v + oral tetracycline+Penicillin; effective for enterococcal endocarditis and 2 week therapy of viridans streptococcal endocarditis. Can cause fever, skin rashes and other allergic reactions, pain at injection site, vestibular dysfunction – most serious toxic effect, if given during pregnancy, can cause deafness in the newborn.

Gentamicin

Employed mainly in severe infections (sepsis and pneumonia) caused by gram (-) bacteria in combination with a cephalosporin or a penicillin may be life saving given at 5-6 mg/kg/day i.v in three equal doses + Penicillin G for bactericidal activity in endocarditis due to viridans streptococci or enterococci and in combination with Nafcillin in selected cases of staphylococcal endocarditis. Serum concentrations and renal function should be monitored if administered for more than a few days or if renal function is changing (e.g., Sepsis; often complicated by acute renal failure). Gentamicin sulfate 0.1% -0.3% cream, ointment - for the treatment of infected burns, wounds, or skin lesions and the prevention of intravenous catheter infections. Topical Gentamicin is partly inactivated by purulent exudates. Ten milligrams can be injected sub conjunctivally for treatment of ocular infections. Nephrotoxicity is reversible and usually mild; Irreversible ototoxicity manifested as vestibular dysfunction, hypersensitivity reactions are uncommon

Tobramycin

Antimicrobial spectrum and pharmacokinetic properties virtually identical to Gentamicin. Given at 5-6 mg/kg i.m or i.v into three equal amounts every 8 hours. Blood levels should be monitored in renal insufficiency. Slightly more active against pseudomonas but not E. faecium, Ototoxic and Nephrotoxic.

Amikacin

Semi synthetic derivative of kanamycin. Resistant to many inactivating enzymes for tuberculosis; given at 7.5 - 15 mg/kg/d as a once daily or 2-3 weekly. Serum concentrations should be monitored. Nephrotoxic and ototoxic.

Netilmicin

Shares many characteristics with gentamicin and Tobramycin. Dosage and the routes of administration are the same, completely therapeutically Interchangeable with gentamicin or tobramycin and has similar toxicities

Kanamycin and Neomycin

Paromomycin is also a member of this group and all have similar properties. There is complete cross-resistance between kanamycin and neomycin. Not significantly absorbed from the GIT; excretion of any absorbed drug is mainly through GF into the urine. Too toxic for parenteral use, now limited to topical and oral use

Solutions 1-5 mg/ml - used on infected surfaces or injected into joints, pleural cavity, tissue spaces or abscess cavities where infection is present (15 mg/kg/day)

Ointments (Neomycin-Polymyxin-Bacitracin combination) applied to infected skin lesions or in the nares for suppression of staphylococci

In preparation for elective bowel surgery, 1 g of Neomycin given orally q 6-8 hours + 1 g of erythromycin base;

Paromomycin, 1 g q 6 hours orally for 2 weeks; effective in intestinal amebiasis

Sudden absorption of postoperatively instilled kanamycin from the peritoneal cavity (3-5 g) has resulted in curare-like neuromuscular blockade and respiratory arrest (Calcium gluconate and neostigmine can act as antidotes)

Prolonged application to skin and eyes- severe allergic reactions

Spectinomycin

Chemically related to the aminoglycosides binds at the 30 S subunit (bacteriostatic).

Dispensed as the dihydrochloride pentahydrate for i.m injection

Used almost solely as an alternative treatment for gonorrhea inpatients who are allergic to penicillin or whose gonococci are resistant to other drugs.

Single dose of 2 g (40 mg/kg).

Tetracycline's

Chlortetracycline was the first tetracycline discovered, in 1948. Since then five additional tetracyclines have been isolated or derived (oxytetracycline, tetracycline, demeclocycline, doxycycline and minocycline), but only the last four are available for systemic use in the United States. Of these four agents, doxycycline and minocycline are the most frequently prescribed. Research to find tetracycline analogues lead to the development of the glycylcyclines. Tigecycline is the first of this new class of agents and exhibits broad-spectrum antibacterial activity similar to the tetracyclines .

Doxycycline is one of the most active tetracyclines and is the most often used clinically since it possesses many advantages over traditional tetracycline and minocycline. Doxycycline can be administered twice daily, has both intravenous (i.v) and oral (PO) formulations, achieves reasonable concentrations even if administered with food and is less likely to cause photosensitivity. Doxycycline may be an alternative for use in children since it binds calcium to a lesser extent than tetracycline, which can cause tooth discoloration and bony growth retardation.

Classification

The structures of Tetracylines are shown in Fig 15-3.

- Short Acting:

  Tetracyline, Oxytetracycline, Chlortetracycline

- Intermediate Acting:

  Demeclocycline, Methacycline

- Long Acting:

  Doxycycline, Minocycline

Origin

Tetracycline, oxytetracycline isolated from Streptomyces.

Minocycline, doxycycline are synthetic.

At present, for many reasons such as toxicity, drug resistance, the development of more effective, the uses of tetracyclines have been largely declined.

Tetracycline is limited for a few infections and is being gradually substituted by some semisynthetic tetracyclines such as minocycline and doxycycline.

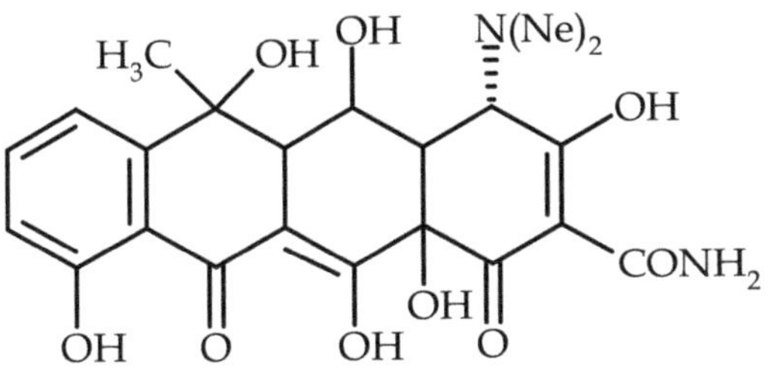

Oxytetracycline

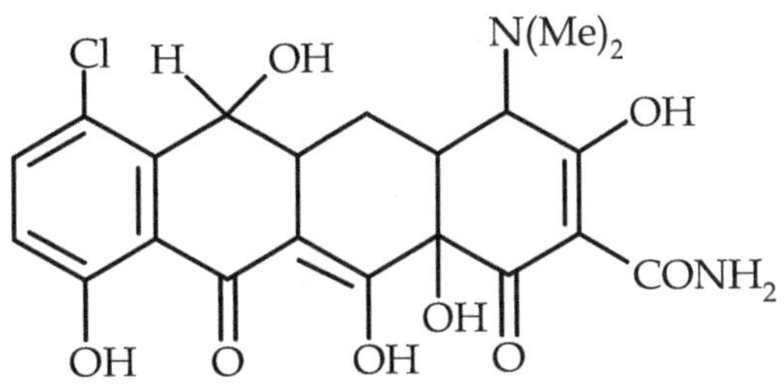

Demeclocycline

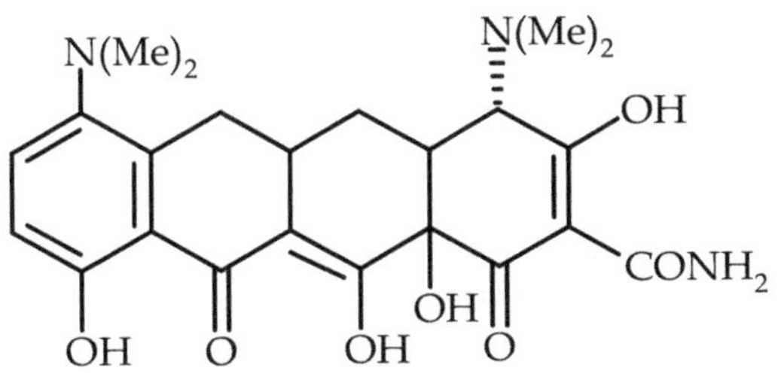

Minocycline

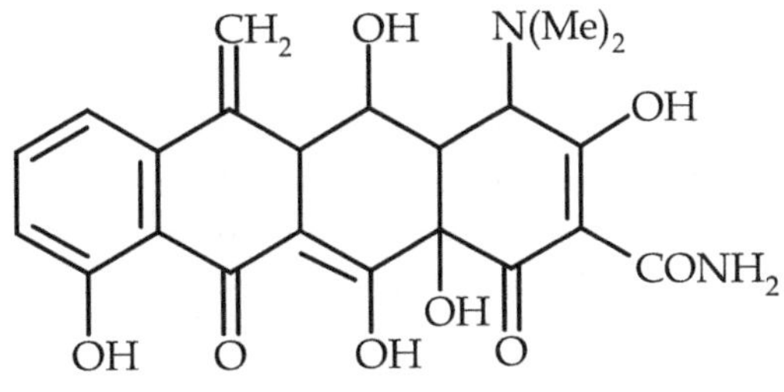

Methacycline

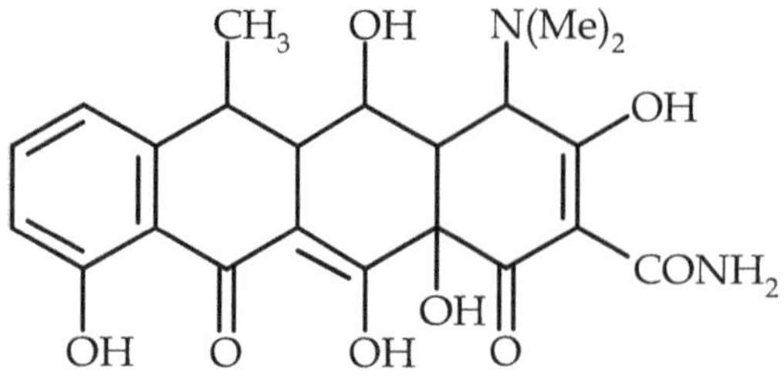

Doxycycline

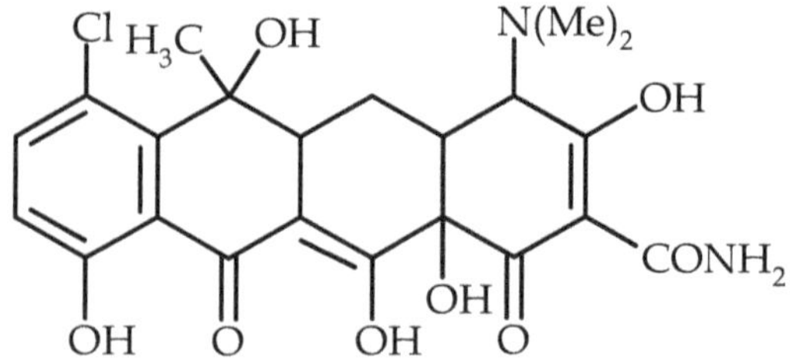

Chlortetracycline

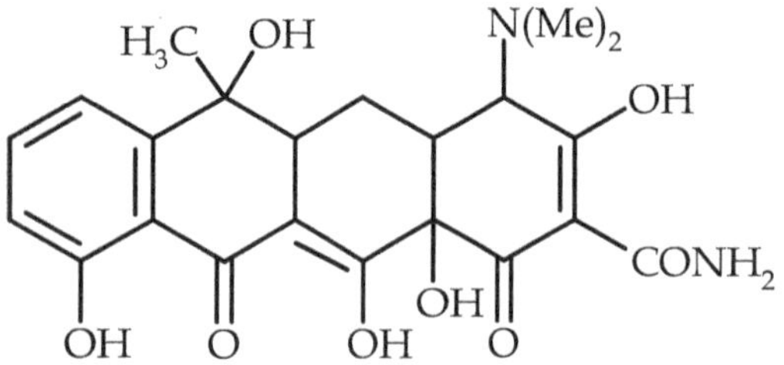

Tetracycline

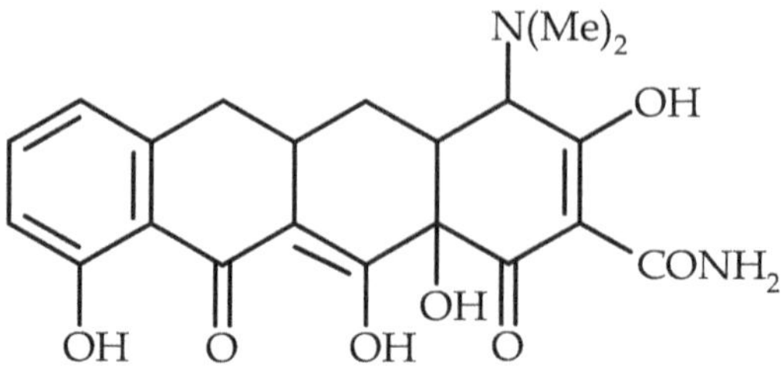

Sancycline

Fig 15-3: Structures of tetracyclines.

Antimicrobial Spectrum: The tetracyclines display broad spectrum activity and are effective against both gram-positive and gram-negative bacteria, including *Rickettsia, Coxiella, Mycoplasma* and *Chlamydia* spp. Tetracycline resistance has increased among pneumococci and gonococci, which limits their use in the treatment of infections caused by these organisms. Although several congeners of the tetracyclines are available, they all have a similar spectrum of *invitro* activity. Minocycline is somewhat more active and oxytetracycline and tetracycline are somewhat less active than other members of this group.

Mechanism of Action

Although all tetracyclines have a similar mechanism of action, they have different chemical structures and are produced by different species of *Streptomyces.* In addition, structural analogues of these compounds have been synthesized to improve pharmacokinetic properties and antimicrobial activity. While several biological processes in the bacterial cells are modiûed by the tetracyclines, their primary mode of action is inhibition of protein synthesis. Tetracyclines bind to the 30S ribosome and thereby prevent the binding of aminoacyl transfer RNA (tRNA) to the A site (acceptor site) on the 50S ribosomal unit. The tetracyclines affect both eukaryotic and prokaryotic cells but are selectively toxic for bacteria, because they readily penetrate microbial membranes and accumulate in the cytoplasm through an energy dependent tetracycline transport system that is absent from mammalian cells.

Resistance: Decreased intracellular accumulation due to impaired influx or increased efflux by an active transport protein pump ribosome protection due to production of proteins that interfere with tetracycline binding to the ribosome enzymatic inactivation.

Pharmacokinetics

These antibiotics are partially absorbed from the stomach and upper gastrointestinal tract. Food impairs absorption of all tetracyclines except doxycycline and minocycline.

Absorption of doxycycline and minocycline is improved with food. Since the tetracyclines form insoluble chelates with calcium (such as are found in many antacids), magnesium and other metal ions, their simultaneous administration with milk (calcium), magnesium hydroxide, aluminum hydroxide, or iron will interfere with absorption.

Because some of the tetracyclines are not completely absorbed, any drug remaining in the intestine may inhibit sensitive intestinal microorganisms and alter the normal intestinal flora. The tetracyclines are distributed throughout body tissues and fluids in concentrations that reflect the lipid solubility of each individual agent. Minocycline and doxycycline are the most lipid soluble, while oxytetracycline is the least lipid soluble. The tetracyclines penetrate (but somewhat unpredictably) the uninflamed meninges and cross the placental barrier. Peak serum levels are reached approximately 2 hours after oral administration; cerebrospinal fluid (CSF) levels are only one-fourth those of plasma. Significant differences in serum half-life allow the grouping of the tetracyclines into subclasses: short acting (tetracycline, chlortetracycline and oxytetracycline), intermediate acting (demeclocycline and methacycline) and long acting (minocycline and doxycycline). The tetracyclines are metabolized in the liver and are concentrated in the bile. Bile concentrations can be up to five times those of the plasma. Doxycycline, minocycline, and chlortetracycline are excreted primarily in the feces. The other tetracyclines are eliminated primarily in the urine by glomerular ûltration. Obviously, these tetracyclines have greater urinary antibacterial activity than those (e.g., doxycycline) that are excreted by nonrenal mechanisms.

Clinical Uses

It is the drug of choice in the treatment of infections caused by Chlamydia (trachoma, psittacosis, salpingitis, nongonococcal urethritis, inclusion conjunctivitis, and lymphogranuloma venereum), Rickettsia (including Q-fever, Rocky Mountain spotted fever, typhus), Mycoplasma e.g., *Mycoplasma pneumoniae* (respiratory and genital infections).

1. Spirochetal infections (relapsing fever - *Borrelia burgdorferi* - Lyme disease), leptospirosis in penicillin hypersensitivity (as an alternative to erythromycin),

   Syphilis (in penicillin hypersensitivity patients).
2. Amebiasis.
3. Gram negative bacterial infections (e.g., brucellosis, shigellosis, cholera,

   Gonorrhea [in penicillin hypersensitivity patients], granuloma inguinale, tularemia).
4. Gram positive infections (e.g., tetanus).
5. Used orally and topically (solution) for inflammatory acne vulgaris.
6. Topical ointment used for superficial skin infections.
7. Ophthalmic use.
8. Exacerbation of chronic bronchitis (because of their activity against *Haemophilus influenzae*).
9. As a sclerosing agent for pleural effusions due to malignancy or cirrhosis.

Adverse effects

Oral administration can cause nausea, vomiting, epigastric burning, stomatitis and glossitis and an intravenous injection can cause phlebitis. When given over long periods, use of these agents can result in a negative nitrogen balance, which may lead to elevated blood urea nitrogen.

Hepatotoxicity occurs infrequently but is particularly severe during pregnancy, when the combination of uremia and increasing jaundice can be fatal. In addition, these antibiotics are occasionally Nephrotoxic and should not be administered with other potentially nephrotoxic drugs. Staining of both the deciduous and permanent teeth and retardation of bone growth can occur if tetracyclines are administered after the fourth month of gestation or if they are given to children less than 8 years of age.

Photosensitivity, observed as abnormal sunburn reaction, is particularly associated with demeclocycline and doxycycline administration. Superinfection may result in oral, anogenital, and intestinal *Candida albicans* infections, whereas *Staphylococcus aureus* or *Clostridium difûcile* overgrowth may cause enterocolitis. Minocycline can produce vertigo.

Minocycline is frequently used in the treatment of chronic facial dermatoses. Increased usage has resulted in local skin pigmentation, particularly at sites of previous tissue trauma that is unrelated to the photosensitization phenomenon characteristic of this class of drug. This effect does not appear to be dose dependent and usually resolves in months to years following drug discontinuation.

Other significant side effects of minocycline may make it unsuitable for some light-skinned patients. In particular, dark bone pigmentation is severe enough to be visible through the mucosa of the alveolar ridges in the mouth and other areas where bone directly adheres to skin (black bone disease). Thyroid staining is visible through the overlying skin of the neck but does not affect the endocrine function of the gland.

Pulmonary eosinophilic syndrome, characterized by extreme hypoxemia, eosinophilia, interstitial pneumonitis, hilar lymphadenopathy and pleural effusions, can be severe and can occur with as little as 7 to 9 days of therapy with the tetracyclines. In severe cases steroid therapy is required, but the outcome following drug discontinuation is nearly always good.

Pseudotumor cerebri is another potential complication of chronic use of these agents, particularly in individuals treated for severe cystic acne with simultaneous use of isotretinoin. This complication can be induced within several days of initiation of therapy and usually resolves with cessation of treatment.

Chronic use always predisposes to the development of fungal esophagitis, which may be so severe as to require treatment with antifungal therapy. Prompt recognition of dysphagia and cessation of treatment are usually curative.

Routes of Administration and Dosage

Oral dose; 250 to 500 mgs qid or tds .

Drug interactions in Table 15-1

Table 15-1: Drug interactions of tetracyclines.

Overview of Tetracyclines Drug-Drug Interactions	
Drug	**Interaction**
Antacids	Calcium, magnesium bind to tetracycline in the gut and decrease its absorption.
Antidiarrheal agents	Kaolin and pectin may decrease Tetracycline (TC) absorption.
Food	Dairy products and iron supplements decrease tetracycline absorption. Space administration within 2 hrs. of tetracycline intake.
Methoxyflurane	May produce fatal nephrotoxicity. Avoid concomitant use.
Oral anticoagulants	Coadministration may potentiate hypoprothrombinemia.
Oral contraceptives	Effectiveness of oral contraceptives (OC) decreases. Backup methods should be used.
Penicillin	Bacteriostatic drugs (e.g., tetracycline) may interfere with the bactericidal action of penicillins; avoid concomitant administration.

Chloramphenicol

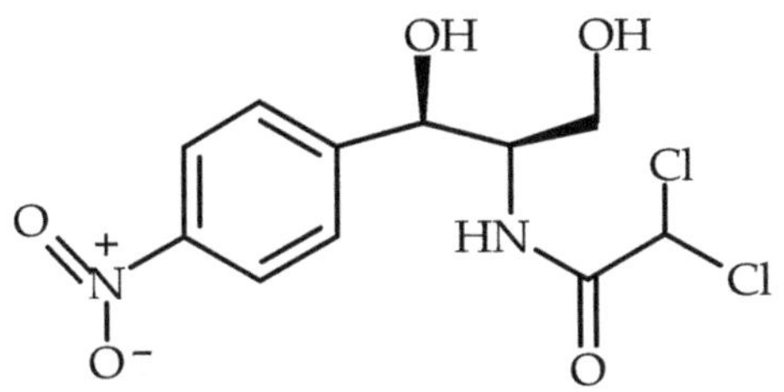

Fig 15-4: Structure of chloramphenicol.

Mechanism of Action

Chloramphenicol Fig 15-4 (*Chloromycetin*) is a nitrobenzene derivative that affects protein synthesis by binding to the 50S ribosomal subunit and preventing peptide bond formation. It prevents the attachment of the amino acid end of aminoacyl-tRNA to the A site, hence the association of peptidyl transferase with the amino acid substrate. Resistance due to changes in the ribosome binding site results in a decreased affinity for the drug, decreased permeability and plasmids that code for enzymes that degrade the antibiotic. The drug-induced inhibition of mitochondrial protein synthesis is probably responsible for the associated toxicity.

Spectrum: Chloramphenicol is a broad spectrum antibiotic that is effective against gram positive and gram negative bacteria, including *Rickettsia, Mycoplasma,* and *Chlamydia* spp. Chloramphenicol is also effective against most anaerobic bacteria, including *Bacteroides fragilis.*

Pharmacokinetics

Chloramphenicol is rapidly and completely absorbed from the gastrointestinal tract and is not affected by food ingestion or metal ions. Parenteral administration is generally reserved for situations in which oral therapy is contraindicated, as in the treatment of meningitis and septicemia or when vomiting prohibits oral administration. The biological half-life of chloramphenicol is 1.5 to 3.5 hours. Although up to 60% of the drug is bound to serum albumin, it penetrates the brain and CSF and crosses the placental barrier. Chloramphenicol is inactivated in the liver by glucuronosyl transferase and is rapidly excreted (80–90% of dose) in the urine. About 5 to 10% of the administered drug is excreted unchanged. Renal elimination is by tubular secretion and glomerular filtration. Other degradation pathways are known to exist and may account for some of the toxicity seen in neonates and children.

Clinical Uses

Sometimes used for ricketssial infections

Infections caused by anaerobes like *B. fragilis.*

Commonly used as topical agent.

Backup drug for severe infections caused by salmonella.

Treatment of pneumococcal and meningococcal meningitis in beta-lactam-sensitive persons.

Adverse effects

There are three major side effects of chloramphenicol, but all are extremely rare and are generally not considered a significant factor when managing a life-threatening illness. One of these three, bone marrow suppression, is usually reversible when therapy is ceased. The other two warrant mentioning in more detail. They are chloramphenicol induced aplastic anaemia (CIAA) and the grey baby syndrome. CIAA could occur after the first, second or even third exposure, even if there was a considerable time lapse between courses. Since then, the use has largely been restricted to severe and life-threatening illness, primarily in developing countries. Death usually followed an overwhelming infection or haemorrhage or both. The grey baby syndrome is a rare condition almost exclusively seen in neonates and very young infants. Toxic blood levels of chloramphenicol secondary to neonatal hepatic enzyme immaturity leads to circulatory collapse and the signs of cardiac shock. The infant is cyanosed, is acidotic, has cold peripheries and has the signs of all of marked hyponia, poor feeding, vomiting, loose stools and a distended abdomen. Because of this, it is recommended that chloramphenicol not been to be given to neonates or to young infants, but if given should be administered in low doses (25 mg/kg/day in four divided doses) as noted previously.

Less severe side effects are seen with chloramphenicol but some of these (peripheral neuritis, optic neuritis) only occur with prolonged treatment, which is irrelevant to this report and the management of BM. Other side effects such as nausea, vomiting, diarrhoea, headache, fever and skin rashes are reported with chloramphenicol, but these are not unique to chloramphenicol and can be easily managed. Anaphylaxis has been reported when treating typhoid fever with chloramphenicol. Acute psychosis has been reported in adults. Both chloramphenicol and ceftriaxone have insignificant side effects when weighed up against their use for managing a life-threatening illness.

Macrolides

Macrolide Fig 15-5 antibiotics include erythromycin, clarithromycin, azithromycin, dirithromycin and troleandomycin. These may be bacteriostatic or bactericidal depending on factors such as drug concentration. Macrolides are weak bases, their activity increases in alkaline pH. This is important when using for UTI. They enter pleural fluid, ascitic fluid, middle ear exudates and sputum. Erythromycin is the most commonly used macrolide.

Chemistry

Erythromycin is a macrolide antibiotic whose structure consists of a macrocyclic 14-membered lactone ring attached to two sugar moieties (a neutral sugar, cladinose, and an amino sugar, desosamine). In the acidic environment of the stomach, it is rapidly degraded to the 8,9-anhydro-6,9hemiketal and then to the 6,9,9,12-spiroketal form. The hemiketal intermediate may be responsible for the gastrointestinal adverse effects associated with erythromycin.

Clarithromycin (6-O-methylerythromycin) is synthesized by substituting a methoxy group for the C-6 hydroxyl group of erythromycin. This substitution creates a more acid-stable antimicrobial and prevents the degradation of the erythromycin base to the hemiketal intermediate. The increased acid stability of clarithromycin results in improved oral bioavailability and reduced gastrointestinal intolerance. Clarithromycin is available as immediate-release tablets (250 or 500 mg); extended-release tablets (500 mg); and granules for oral suspension (125 or 250 mg per 5 mL).

Azithromycin (9-deoxo-9a-aza-9a-methyl-9a-homoerythromycin) is formed by inserting a methyl-substituted nitrogen in place of the carbonyl group at the 9a position of the aglycone ring. The resulting dibasic 15membered ring macrolide derivative is more appropriately referred to as an ''azalide.'' This structural change makes the compound more stable in acid, significantly increases the serum half-life and tissue penetration and results in increased activity against gram negative organisms and decreased activity against some gram positive organisms when compared with erythromycin . Azithromycin is available as 250, 500, or 600 mg tablets; oral suspension (100–200 mg per 5 ml); and intravenous preparation (lyophilized 500 mg per10 ml vial).

Ketolides, a new group of 14- embered macrolides, are synthesized by substituting a keto function for the a-L cladinose moiety at position 3 of the 14-membered erythronolide A ring . This change promotes greater acid stability and prevents induction of macrolide-lincosamide-streptogramin B resistance. Additionally, the hydroxyl group at position 6 of the erythronolide A ring is replaced by a methoxy group. Telithromycin is synthesized by cycling of the C11-12 positions to form a carbamate ring with an imidazo-pyridyl group attachment. The 11,12 carbamate extension enhances binding to the bacterial ribosome and in vitro activity.

Classification

Old Generation: Erythromycin, Oleandomycin, Troleandomycin, Spiramycin, Josamycin

New Generation: Rosaramycin, Roxithromycin, Clarithromycin, Azithromycin, Dirithromycin

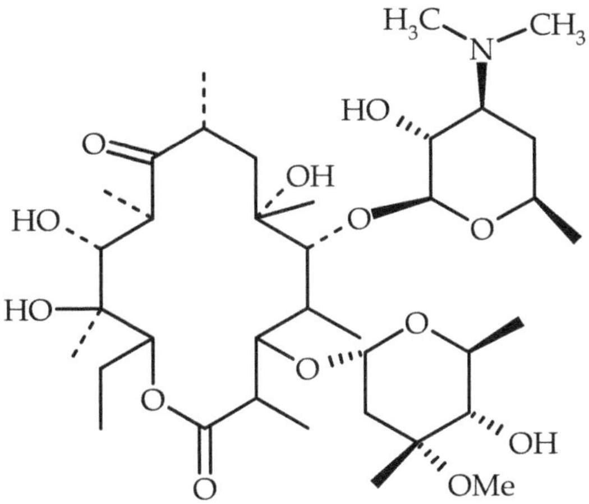

Erythromycin A

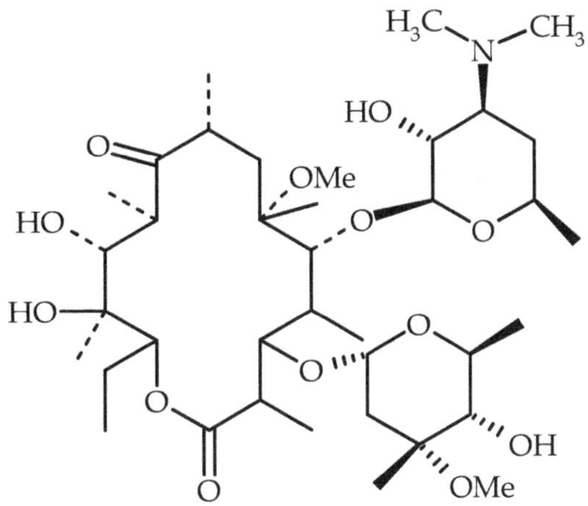

Clarithromycin

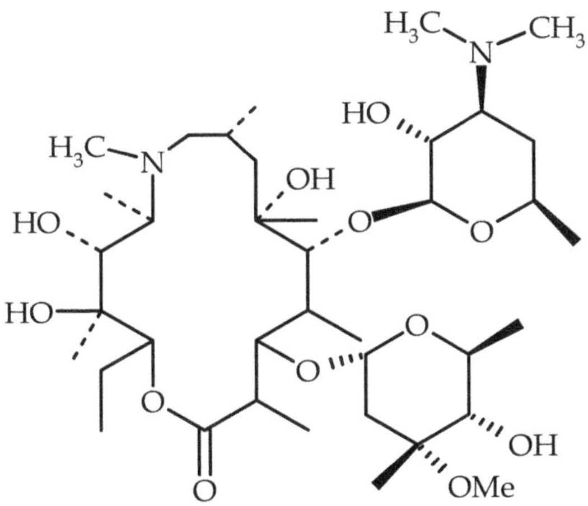

Azithromycin

Fig 15-5: Structures of macrolides.

Mechanism of Action

Macrolides bind to the 50S ribosomal subunit of bacteria but not to the 80S mammalian ribosome; this accounts for its selective toxicity. Binding to the ribosome occurs at a site near peptidyltransferase, with a resultant inhibition of translocation, peptide bond formation and release of oligopeptidyl tRNA. However, unlike chloramphenicol the macrolides do not inhibit protein synthesis by intact mitochondria and this suggests that the mitochondrial membrane is not permeable to erythromycin.

Resistance: Reduced permeability of the cell membrane or active efflux production (by Enterobacteriaceae) of esterase's that hydrolyze Macrolides modification of the ribosomal binding site by chromosomal mutation.

Spectrum: The macrolides are effective against a number of organisms, including *Mycoplasma* spp., *H. inffuenzae, Streptococcus* spp. (including *S. pyogenes* and *S. pneumoniae*), staphylococci, gonococci, *Legionella pneumophila* and other *Legionella* spp. There has been increasing resistance of *S. pneumoniae* to macrolides worldwide. This is true especially if the strain is resistant to penicillin. This resistance includes not only erythromycin but also clarithromycin and azithromycin. Approximately 10 to 15% of *S. pneumoniae* in the United States show complete resistance to macrolides. Staphylococci resistant to erythromycin are resistant to all macrolides. The hemolytic streptococci also exhibit varying degrees of cross-resistance to the macrolides and to lincomycin and clindamycin, although the macrolides are chemically unrelated to the last two agents.

There are only minor variations in the antibacterial spectrum of the newer macrolides. Clarithromycin is very active against *H. influenzae, Legionella* and *Mycobacterium avium-intracellulare,* whereas azithromycin is superior against *Branhamella, Neisseria* and *H. influenzae* but less active against mycobacterial species. Clarithromycin and azithromycin have signiûcant activity against *Mycobacterium avium* complex (MAC) and it is one of the drugs of choice in treating disseminated MAC. Both azithromycin and clarithromycin can be used prophylactically in HIV and AIDS patients to help prevent disseminated MAC.

Pharmacokinetics

The macrolides are absorbed from the intestinal tract, although the presence of food interferes with absorption and part of the dose is destroyed because of the relative acid lability of these antimicrobials. To minimize destruction and enhance absorption, erythromycin is administered as a stearate or oleate salt or is enteric coated. Because stearate and estolate erythromycins are not acid labile, the administration of these formulations results in higher blood levels. The O-methyl substitution of erythromycin that results in clarithromycin also confers acid stability and better absorption with food. The macrolides diffuse readily into tissues and cross placental membranes. CSF levels are about 20% of plasma levels, while biliary concentrations are about 10 times plasma levels. Although the serum levels of clarithromycin and azithromycin are low, these antibiotics concentrate in tissue and reach high levels. Erythromycin and azithromycin are excreted primarily in active form in bile, with only low levels found in urine. Clarithromycin is metabolized to the biologically active 14-OH metabolite and is eliminated largely by the kidney. The half-life of erythromycin is approximately 1.4 hours, whereas the half-life of clarithromycin is 3 to 7 hours and that of azithromycin approaches 68 hours.

Clinical uses

Respiratory tract infections

Upper respiratory tract infections

Clarithromycin, azithromycin and telithromycin are effective against the most frequently isolated bacterial causes of pharyngitis, otitis media, and sinusitis. A 5-day course of either the extended-release formulation of clarithromycin, azithromycin, or telithromycin is equally as effective as a 10day course of penicillin for the treatment of streptococcal pharyngitis Clarithromycin has been shown to have equivalent eûcacy for the treatment of acute sinusitis compared with cefuroxime axetil, levoûoxacin, sparfloxacin, or ciproûoxacin . A 14-day course of either the immediate-release or extended-release formulations of clarithromycin was comparable in the treatment of acute maxillary sinusitis in adults. A 3day regimen of azithromycin (500 mg daily) was equally as efficacious as a 10-day course of amoxicillin- clavulanate in acute sinusitis. Clarithromycin is approved for the treatment of pharyngitis caused by S pyogenes; the recommended dose is 250 mg every 12 hours for 10 days. Dosage for treatment of acute maxillary sinusitis is either 500 mg every 12 hours with the immediate-release tablets .

Lower respiratory tract infections

Clarithromycin and azithromycin are used for the treatment of lower respiratory tract infections including acute bronchitis, acute exacerbation of chronic bronchitis (AECB) and community-acquired pneumonia (CAP). Azithromycin (500 mg on day 1 followed by 250 mg daily for 4 days) has been found to be equivalent to cefaclor in patients with outpatient CAP. The use of a 3-

day course of azithromycin (500 mg daily) for the treatment of lower respiratory tract infections seems to have equivalent efficacy compared with longer courses of other antimicrobial agents. Telithromycin has demonstrated excellent clinical efficacy in the outpatient treatment of CAP . Telithromycin was equally as effective when compared with either a 10day course of high-dose amoxicillin, twice-daily clarithromycin, or a 7 to 10 day course of trovafloxacin (clinical cure rates 88%–95%). Azithromycin and clarithromycin have also been shown to be effective in the treatment of CAP in patients requiring hospitalization. Monotherapy with intravenous azithromycin was equally as eûective as cefuroxime plus or minus erythromycin followed by their oral equivalents to complete a 7 to 10 day course of therapy.

Sexually transmitted diseases

The use of the advanced macrolides in the treatment of sexually transmitted diseases has focused primarily on azithromycin. The unique pharmacokinetics of azithromycin, including high tissue concentrations and a prolonged tissue half-life, allows single-dose treatment courses, directly observed therapy and improved patient compliance.

Skin and soft tissue infections

Azithromycin and clarithromycin have been approved for use in skin and soft tissue infections. Azithromycin (1.5 g administered over 3 or 5 days) was equivalent to a 7-day course of dicloxacillin or a 10-day course of cephalexin in the treatment of adult skin and soft tissue infection . Similarly in children, azithromycin was equally as effective as either dicloxacillin or cefaclor. Clarithromycin was equivalent to erythromycin or cefadroxil in the treatment of skin infections.

Helicobacter pylori infections

Antibiotic therapy for H pylori–associated peptic ulcer disease decreases ulcer recurrence and promotes healing. Several dual treatment regimens (clarithromycin 500 mg three times a day, in combination with either ranitidine bismuth citrate or omeprazole) have received FDA approval.

Mycobacterium avium complex and HIV infection

Clarithromycin and azithromycin have been shown to be effective in preventing and treating disseminated M avium complex disease in HIV infected patients. Azithromycin is effective as prophylaxis against disseminated M avium complex disease in patients with CD4 counts less than 100 cells/mm^3. Compared with placebo, a 1200-mg weekly dose decreased the incidence of disseminated M avium complex from 24.7% to 10.6% .

Adverse effects

Azithromycin, clarithromycin and telithromycin are well tolerated. Gastrointestinal intolerance is the primary adverse side effect of these agents, but occurs at a significantly reduced rate when compared with erythromycin . The most common adverse eûects reported with Azithromycin were diarrhoea (3.6%); nausea (2.6%); abdominal pain (2.5%); and headache or dizziness (1.3%). Laboratory abnormalities were infrequent and minor including transient increases in transaminases in 1.5% of patients. Only 0.7% of patients discontinued azithromycin therapy compared with 2.6% of patients receiving comparative medications. Adverse events related to the intravenous infusion of azithromycin were pain at the injection site (6.5%) and local inflammation (3.1%) . The most common adverse reactions reported with clarithromycin were similar (e.g., nausea [3.8%], diarrhea [3%], abdominal pain [1.9%], and headache [1.7%]). There was no diûerence in the spectrum and frequency of adverse reactions between the extended release or immediate release formulations of clarithromycin. Gastrointestinal adverse events with the extended-release formulation, however, tended to be less severe and resulted in fewer discontinuations of the medication.

Drug interactions

Clarithromycin, like erythromycin, is oxidized by the cytochrome P-450 system, primarily the

CYP3A4 subclass of hepatic enzymes. This converts clarithromycin to a nitrosalkalane metabolite that forms an inactive metabolite-enzyme complex by binding to the iron of the CYP3A4 enzyme. This interaction inhibits the CYP3A4 enzymes resulting in decreased clearance of other agents given concurrently that are metabolized by the same enzyme system. Clarithromycin is a less potent inhibitor of the CYP3A4 enzymes than erythromycin and azithromycin interferes poorly with this system. Appropriate dose reductions and clinical and therapeutic drug level monitoring are necessary when drugs metabolized by the CYP3A enzymes are given concurrently with clarithromycin. The concurrent use of cisapride, pimozide, terfenadine and astemizole with clarithromycin is contraindicated because of the possible cardiotoxic effects of these agents and the occurrence of torsades de pointes. Other medications, such as benzodiazepines (triazolam, midazolam and alprazolam), 3-hydroxy-3methylglu-taryl–coenzyme A reductase inhibitors (lovastatin, simvastatin, and atorvastatin), class 1A antiarrhythmic agents (quinidine, disopyramide), theophylline, carbamazepine, warfarin, ergots, and cyclosporine should be used cautiously when given with clarithromycin. These drug drug interactions are less likely to occur with azithromycin because it is not a potent inhibitor of the CYP3A enzymes .Both clarithromycin and azithromycin have been associated with digoxin toxicity. In a study of healthy volunteers, coadministration of clarithromycin with oral digoxin resulted in a 1.7-fold increase in the AUC of digoxin and a reduction of the nonglomerular renal clearance of digoxin, but after intravenous administration of digoxin, the digoxin AUC increased only 1.2-fold. The clarithromycin inhibits intestinal and renal P-glycoprotein (an ATP-dependent effux drug transporter) resulting in increased oral bioavailability and reduced nonglomerular renal clearance of digoxin.

The potential for telithromycin to inhibit the CYP3A4 pathway is comparable with clarithromycin even though metabolism of telithromycin does not result in the formation of nitrosalkalene metabolite. Telithromycin also competitively inhibits the CYP2D6 system.

Clindamycin/Lincomycin

Mechanism of Action

The lincosamide fig 15-6 family of antibiotics includes Lincomycin (*Lincocin*) and clindamycin (*Cleocin*), both of which inhibit protein synthesis. They bind to the 50S ribosomal subunit at a binding site close to or overlapping the binding sites for chloramphenicol and erythromycin. They block peptide bond formation by interference at either the A or P site on the ribosome.

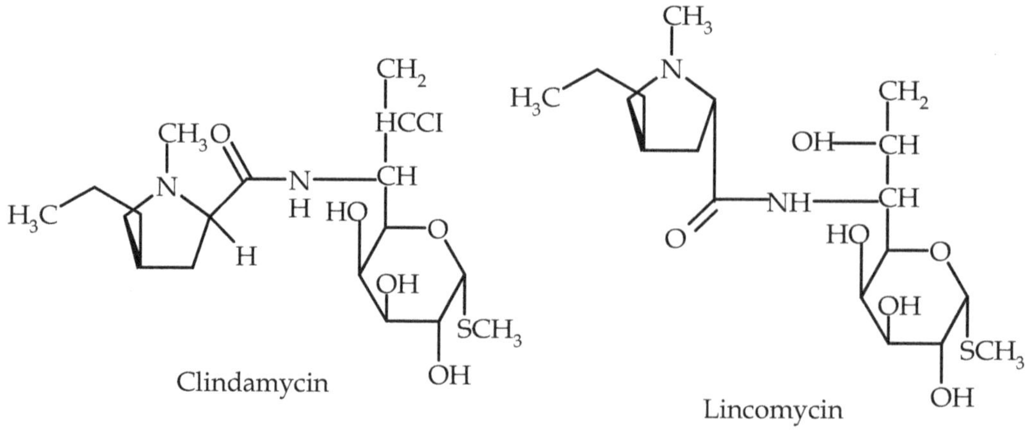

Fig 15-6: Structures of clindamycin and lincomycin.

Spectrum : Narrow Gram (+) spectrum, excellent activity against anaerobic bacteria; strep, pneumococci, staphylococci

Resistance: Mutation of the ribosomal receptor site modification of the receptor by a constitutively expressed methylase enzymatic inactivation.

Pharmacokinetics

Clindamycin is more clinically used than Lincomycin:

Excellent absorption given at 150-300 mg Q - adults; 10-20 mg/kg/d for children, low concentration in CSF,well bone penetration, excreted mainly via the liver, bile and urine, half life is 2.5 hours normally and 6 hours in patients with anuria, more toxic than erythromycin, prophylaxis of endocarditis in patients with valvular heart disease for dental procedures.

Clinical uses

Most important indication is the treatment of severe anaerobic infection caused by Bacteroides and other anaerobes that often participate in mixed infections -aminoglycoside or cephalosporin used to treat penetrating wounds of the abdomen and the gut Septic abortion, pelvic abscesses, aspiration pneumonia-primaquine - effective alternative to trimethoprim sulfamethoxazole for moderate to moderately severe Pneumocystis carinii pneumonia in AIDS patients - Pyrimethamine for AIDS - related toxoplasmosis of the brain.

Adverse Effects

The major adverse reactions reported are hypersensitivity rashes and diarrhea. The rash is usually itchy, morbilliform and general. Gastrointestinal intolerance with abdominal pain, nausea and vomiting occurs infrequently. Hepatotoxicity and bone marrow suppression have been noted. It is important to differentiate between gastrointestinal irritation and pseudomembranous colitis. In its most extreme form, the colitis results in mucosal ulceration and bleeding and infrequently may necessitate colectomy. On rare occasions it has been fatal.

Streptogramins

Quinupristin-Dalfopristin (Synercid)

Mechanism of action

Action is similar to Macrolides except bactericidal for staph and most organisms except Enterococcus faecium. prolonged post antibiotic effect up to 10 h for Staph. Aureus.

Pharmacokinetics

Administered i.v at 7.5 mg/kg Q 8-12 hr. Eliminated through fecal route, < 20% urine. inhibits CYP 3A4, which metabolizes warfarin, diazepam, astemizole, terfenadine, cisapride, Nonnucleoside reverse transcriptase inhibitors and cyclosporine.

Clinical Uses

infections caused by Vancomycin resistant strains of *E.faecium* but not E. faecalis bacteremis or respiratory tract infections caused by methicillin-resistant staphylococci and penicllin susceptibe and resistant strains of S. pheumonia.

Adverse effects

Infusion related events, pain at the injection site, arthralgia, myalgia.

Oxazoladinones: Linezolide (Zyvox)

Mechanism of action

Inhibits protein synthesis by preventing formation of the ribosome complex that initiated protein synthesis.Its unique binding site located on 23 S ribosomal RNA of the 50 S subunit, results in no cross resistance with other drug classes.

Pharmacokinetics

Has high oral bioavailability, half life of 4-6 hr.

Clinical Uses

Treatment of infections caused by vancomycin resistant *E. faecium* and other infections caused by multiple drug resistant organisms staph, strep, enterococci, G(+) anaerobic cocci, G (+) rods, Corynebacterium, L. monocytogenes

References

Fraschini F, Scaglione F, Pintucci G, et al. (1991). The diûusion of clarithromycin and roxithromycin into nasal mucosa, tonsil and lung in humans. J Antimicrob Chemother **27 (Suppl A):** 61–5.

Namour F, Wessels DH, Pascual MH, et al. (2001). Pharmacokinetics of the new ketolide telithromycin (HMR 3647) administered in ascending single and multiple doses. *Antimicrob Agents Chemother* **45:** 170–5.

Rodvold KA, Gotfried MH, Danziger LH, et al. (1997). Intrapulmonary steady-state concentrations of clarithromycin and azithromycin in healthy adult volunteers. *Antimicrob Agents Chemother* **41:** 1399–402.

Similak JD (1999). Symposium on antimicrobial agents: Part X. The tetracyclines. *Mayo Clin Proc.* **74:** 727–729.

Standiford HC (2000). Tetracyclines and chloramphenicol. In Mandell GL, Bennett JE, and Dolin R (eds.). Principles and Practice of Infectious Diseases (5th ed.). *Philadelphia*: Churchill Livingstone.

CHAPTER

Quinolones and Urinary Antiseptics 16

Quinolones

Introduction

The first quinolone, nalidixic acid (NegGram), was introduced in 1962. Since then, structural modifications have resulted in second, third and fourth generation fluoroquinolones, which have improved coverage of gram positive organisms. The structures of Fluoroquinolones are shown in Fig 16-1.

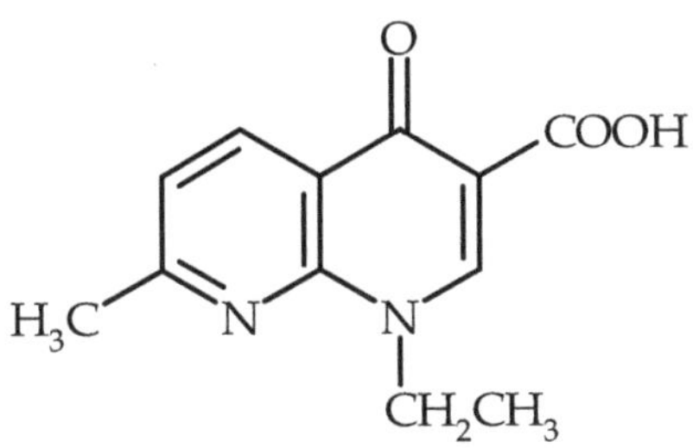

Nalidixic acid

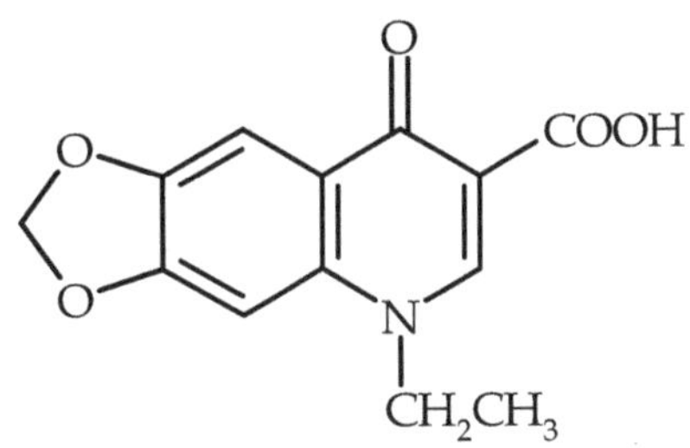

Oxolinic acid

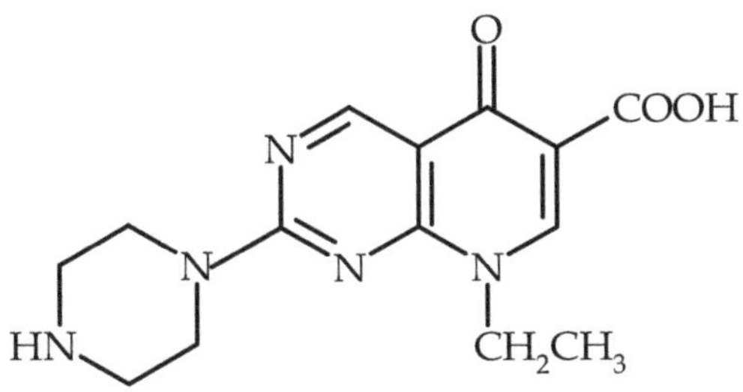

Pipemidic acid

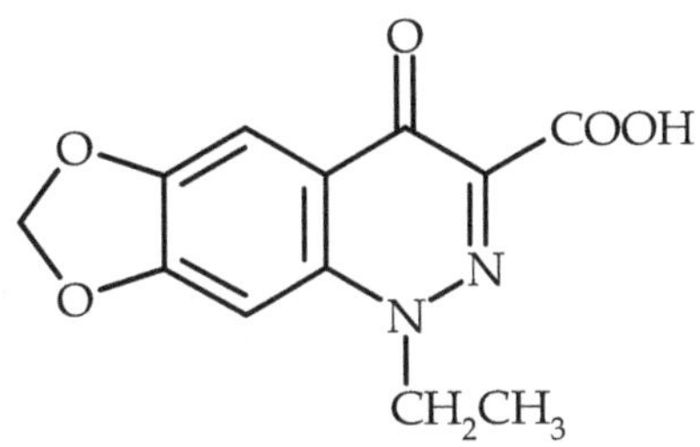

Cinoxacin

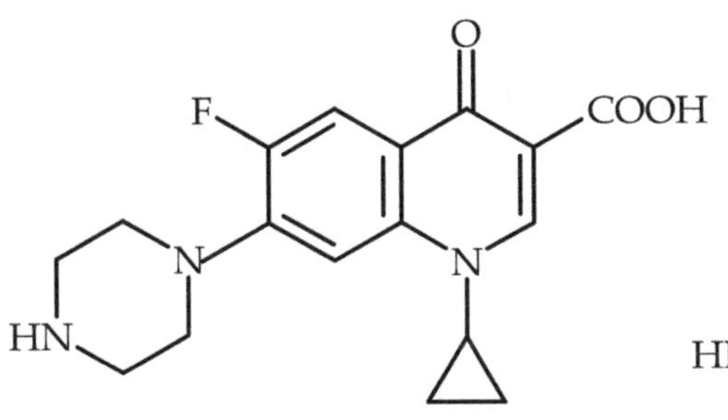

Ciprofloxacin

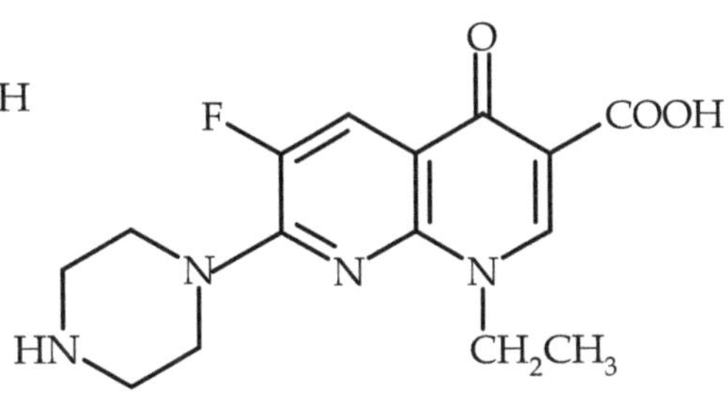

Norfloxacin

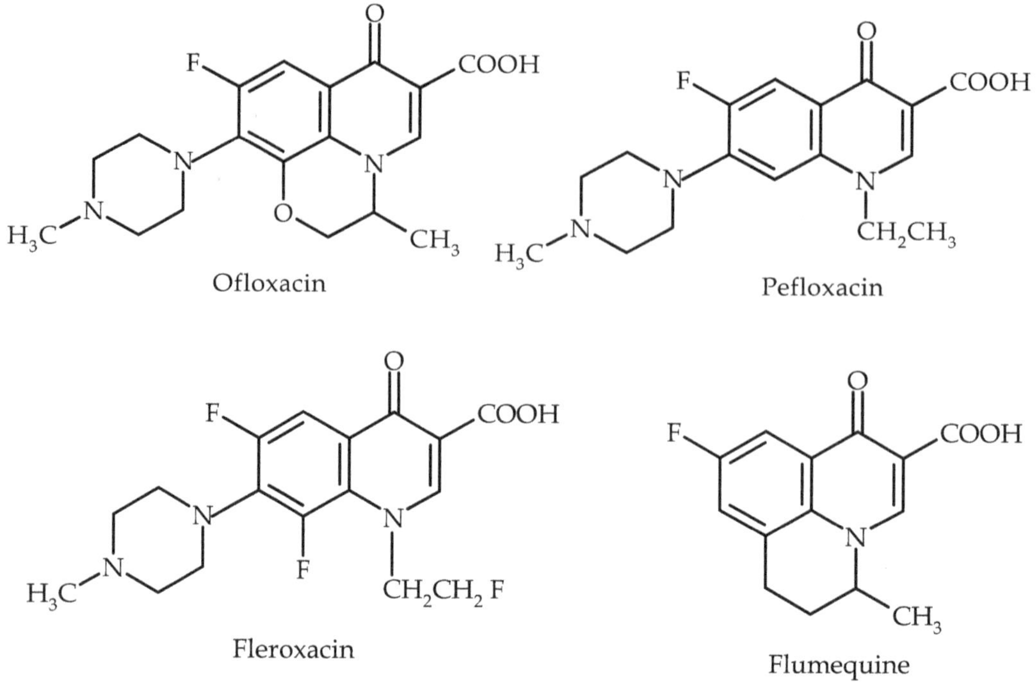

Fig 16-1: Structures of fluoroquinolones.

Mechanism of Action

All clinically approved quinolones in use contain a carboxylic acid moiety in the 3-position of the basic ring structure (the 4-quinolones). The 4-quinolones inhibit DNA synthesis through their specific action on DNA gyrases, which are composed of two A and two B subunits. DNA subunits A (gyrase A gene) have a strand cutting function to prevent overwinding (supercoiling) of the DNA strands during separation and eventual replication of the mirror strand. The A subunits are the site of action for the 4-quinolones, recently a second target, unique to the fluoroquinolones has been identified as topoisomerase type IV. This enzyme is responsible for separating the daughter cells following replication. The DNA gyrases and type IV topoisomerase both belong to the general class of DNA enzymes called topoisomerases. The effect of quinolones on these DNA enzymes is initially bacteriostatic but becomes bactericidal when bacteria are unable to repair the DNA lesions. These drug targets may be primary or secondary depending upon the organism; this observation can affect the bacterial potential for the development of drug resistance; this may require the use of another drug with a different specificity and spectrum of activity.

General Properties

Within the diversity of their various ring structures, the quinolones have a number of common functional groups that are essential for their antimicrobial activity. For example, the quinolone nucleus contains a carboxylic acid group at position 3 and an exocyclic oxygen at position 4 (hence the term 4-quinolones), which are believed to be the active DNA gyrase binding sites. Various modifications have produced compounds with differing physical, chemical, pharmacokinetic and antimicrobial properties. For example, the side chain attached to the nitrogen at position 1 affects potency. Replacement of the ethyl group at this position with a bulkier group (e.g., the cyclopropyl group of ciprofloxacin and similar drugs) enhances gram-negative and positive spectra. Addition of a fluorine atom at position 6 profoundly enhances the gram positive spectrum, whereas the addition of a (heterocyclic nitrogen containing) piperazyl ring at position 7 enhances bacterial penetration and potency, including toward *Pseudomonas aeruginosa*. Substitutions on the piperazyl (e.g., ofloxacin and its L isomer, levofloxacin; sparfloxacin) enhance gram positive penetration, while substitutions at position 8 enhance anaerobic activity (e.g., sparfloxacin, pradofloxacin, moxifloxacin). If the substitution is with a methoxy group (rather than a halogen), the risk of phototoxicity is reduced.

The quinolones are amphoteric and, with a few exceptions, generally exhibit poor water solubility at pH 6–8. In concentrated acidic urine, some quinolones form needle-shaped crystals, although this apparently has not been reported with clinical use. Liquid formulations of various quinolones for PO or parenteral administration usually contain freely soluble salts in stable aqueous solutions. Solid formulations (e.g., tablets, capsules or boluses) contain the active ingredient either in its betaine form or, occasionally, as the hydrochloride salt.

Pharmacokinetics

Like aminoglycosides, the Quinolones exhibit concentration-dependent bacterial killing. Bactericidal activity becomes more pronounced as the serum drug concentration increases to approximately 30 times the Minimum Inhibitory Concentration (MIC). Higher drug concentrations paradoxically inhibit RNA and protein synthesis, thereby reducing bactericidal activity. Quinolones have a post antibiotic effect of about one to two hours. When used in combination with agents from other antibiotic classes, such as beta lactams and aminoglycosides, the Quinolones are not predictably synergistic. Although the effects of most combinations are indifferent or additive, ciprofloxacin (Cipro) and rifampin (Rifadin) appear to be antagonistic against Staphylococcus aureus. Quinolones are well absorbed following oral administration, with moderate to excellent bioavailability. Serum drug levels achieved after oral administration are comparable to those with intravenous dosing, which allows an early transition from intravenous to oral therapy and a potential reduction of treatment costs. Food does not impair the absorption of most Quinolones. However, Quinolones chelate with cations such as aluminum, magnesium, calcium, iron and zinc. This interaction significantly reduces absorption and bioavailability, resulting in lower serum drug concentrations and less target-tissue penetration. Elimination half life for the Quinolones vary from 1.5 to 16 hours. Therefore, most of these drugs are administered every 12 to 24 hours. The Quinolones are eliminated by renal and nonrenal routes. To avoid toxicity dosages often need to be adjusted in patients with renal or hepatic impairment. The majority of Quinolones are excreted renally; however, sparfloxacin (Zagam), moxifloxacin (Avelox) and trovafloxacin (Trovan) are excreted hepatically. Quinolones are widely distributed throughout the body. Tissue penetration is higher than the concentration achieved in plasma, stool, bile, prostatic tissue and lung tissue. Intracellular concentration is exceptional in neutrophils and macrophages. Quinolones also penetrate well in urine and kidneys when renal clearance is the route of drug elimination. Penetration into prostatic fluid, saliva, bone and cerebrospinal fluid does not exceed serum drug levels. Because cerebrospinal fluid levels of Quinolones are predictably poor, these agents are inadequate for first-line treatment of meningitis.

Antimicrobial Activity

The Quinolones can be classified into four generations based on antimicrobial activity.

First generation agents, which are used less often today, have moderate gram negative activity and minimal systemic distribution.

Second generation Quinolones have expanded gram negative activity and a typical pathogen coverage, but limited gram-positive activity. These agents are most active against aerobic gram-negative bacilli. Ciprofloxacin remains the quinolone most active against Pseudomonas aeruginosa.

Third generation Quinolones retain expanded gram negative and a typical intracellular activity but have improved gram-positive coverage.

Finally, fourth generation agents improve gram positive coverage, maintain gram negative coverage and gain anaerobic coverage.

Marginal susceptibility and acquired resistance limit the usefulness of second generation quinolones in the treatment of staphylococcal, streptococcal and enterococcal infections.

The presently available fluoroquinolones with *in vitro* activity against Streptococcus pneumoniae (including current penicillin resistant strains) are levofloxacin (Levaquin), sparfloxacin, gatifloxacin (Tequin), moxifloxacin and trovafloxacin. Levofloxacin and sparfloxacin exhibit inferior *in vitro* streptococcal activity compared with gatifloxacin, moxifloxacin and trovafloxacin. Gatifloxacin is two to four times more active than levofloxacin against *S. pneumoniae in vitro* and moxifloxacin is four to eight times more active.

Compared with ciprofloxacin and levofloxacin, the fluoroquinolones gatifloxacin, moxifloxacin and trovafloxacin have greater in vitro activity against *S. aureus* and some Enterococcus strains.

Table 16-1: Classification of quinolones.

Quinolone generations	Microbiologic activity	Administration and characteristics	Indications
First generation Nalidixic acid (NegGram) Cinoxacin (cinobac)	Enterobacteriaceae	Oral administration Low serum and tissue drug concentrations Narrow gram negative coverage	Uncomplicated urinary tract infections Not for use in systemic infections
Second generation **Class I** Lomefloxacin (Maxaquin) Norfloxacin (Noroxin) Enoxacin (Penetrex)	Enterobacteriaceae	Oral administration Low serum and tissue drug concentrations Improved gram-negative coverage compared with first generation quinolones Limited gram-positive coverage	Uncomplicated urinary tract infections Not for use in systemic infections
Class II Ofloxacin (Floxin) Ciprofloxacin (Cipro)	Enterobacteriaceae atypical pathogens: Pseudomonas aeruginosa	Oral and intravenous administration Higher serum, tissue, and intracellular drug concentrations compared with class I agents Coverage of atypical pathogens	Complicated urinary tract and catheter related infections Gastroenteritis With severe diarrhea Prostatitis Nosocomial infections Sexually transmitted diseases Not for use in community-acquired pneumonia because of associations with pneumococcal bacteremia and meningeal seeding due to poor pneumococcal susceptibility)

Table 16-1 Contd...

Quinolone generations	Microbiologic activity	Administration and characteristics	Indications
Third generation. Levofloxacin (Levaquin) Sparfloxacin (Zagam) Gatifloxacin (Tequin)Moxifloxacin (Avelox)	Enterobacteriaceae, atypical pathogens, streptococci	Oral and intravenous administration Similar to class II second generation quinolones but with modest streptococcal' coverage. Increase hepatic metabolism (sparfloxacin and moxifloxacin)	Similar indications as for second generation quinolones Community-acquired pneumonia in hospitalized patients if atypical pathogens are strongly suspected Community-acquired pneumonia in non hospitalized patients with risk factors for resistant pneumococcal infection.
Fourth generation Trovafloxacin (Trovari)*	Enterobacteriaceae, *P* aeruginosa (reduced or absent), atypical pathogens, methicillin-susceptibie *Staphylococcus* aureus streptococci, anaerobes	Oral and intravenous administration Similar to third-generation quinolones but with improved gram-positive coverage and added anaerobic coverage.	Consider for treatment of intra-abdominal infections

*—Sparfloxacin and trovafloxacin have significant non renal elimination pathways; these agents should not be used to treat urinary tract infections.

Resistance to Quinolones

Chromosomal mutational resistance to the original fluoroquinolones was considered to be low in frequency and plasmid mediated resistance nonexistent. However, resistance is increasingly being recognized, indicating that therapy based on culture and susceptibility is prudent. In general, cross resistance should be anticipated among the more closely related members of this class.

Gram-negative bacteria more commonly target DNA gyrase; emerging resistance is more often associated with changes in the GyrA compared to the GyrB subunit. In contrast, the primary target of gram positive organisms tends to be topoisomerase IV, with resistance mechanisms targeting it followed by changes in DNA gyrase. Use of the drug selects for resistance. High level resistance (3–4 × the breakpoint MIC) generally reflects a second step mutation that leads to changes in the amino acid sequence of subsequent topoisomerase targets. Newer drugs, including gemifloxacin, trovafloxacin, gatifloxacin, or pradofloxacin, may target both DNA gyrase and topoisomerase IV and thus may lead to less resistance.

Another mechanism of resistance is the combined effect of increased efflux pumps and decreased porins that act in concert to reduce intracellular concentrations. Virulence of refractory mutants may not diminish.

Therapeutic Uses of Quinolones

Genitourinary Infections

Because of their extensive gram negative coverage, quinolone antibiotics were initially used to treat urinary tract infections. The higher genitourinary drug concentrations that occur with renally cleared quinolones promote their effectiveness in the treatment of genitourinary infections.

Given in three- to 10-day courses, most quinolones are as effective as trimethoprim-sulfamethoxazole (Bactrim, Septra) in treating uncomplicated urinary tract infections caused by susceptible *Escherichia coli*.

Complicated urinary tract infections include those in patients with stones or obstructive uropathies and in patients with catheter related infections. These infections are often associated with nosocomial, antibiotic-resistant gram negative pathogens and gram-positive bacteria and with Candida species. Because ciprofloxacin, ofloxacin, lomefloxacin (Maxaquin), enoxacin (Penetrex), levofloxacin, and gatifloxacin have higher renal clearance and greater renal concentration, they are optimal choices for the treatment of complicated urinary tract infections.

Ciprofloxacin has been shown to be more effective than trimethoprim-sulfamethoxazole and aminoglycosides in 7 to 10 day courses for the treatment of complicated urinary tract infections. However, few patients maintain sterile urine six weeks after any antibiotic therapy.

A 7 to 10 day course of orally administered norfloxacin (Noroxin) or ofloxacin has been successful in the treatment of uncomplicated pyelonephritis, with a bacteriologic cure rate equal to that for trimethoprim-sulfamethoxazole.

In the treatment of acute uncomplicated pyelonephritis in nonpregnant women, similar efficacy has been shown for levofloxacin, in a dosage of 250 mg per day for seven to 10 days, and ciprofloxacin, in a dosage of 500 mg twice daily for 10 days.

Gatifloxacin, in a dosage of 400 mg per day, has compared favourably with ciprofloxacin, in a dosage of 500 mg twice daily, in the treatment of complicated urinary tract infections and pyelonephritis, with cure rates of 93 percent and 91 percent, respectively Fluoroquinolones, especially levofloxacin and ciprofloxacin, are valuable in the treatment of complicated urinary tract infections and pyelonephritis.

Prostatitis

Quinolones are effective in the treatment of prostatitis because of their excellent penetration into prostatic tissue. When taken for four to six weeks, norfloxacin, ciprofloxacin, levofloxacin and ofloxacin have eradication rates of 67 to 91 percent.

Levofloxacin is an excellent first line agent in the treatment of prostatitis. Ciprofloxacin should be reserved for use in patients with resistant gram-negative, pseudomonal, and enterococcal prostatitis, because of its superior activity against *P. aeruginosa* and *enterococci*.

Respiratory Diseases

Acute bacterial sinusitis may be the complication of an initial viral illness. The primary bacterial isolates are *S. aureus*, *S. pneumoniae*, Haemophilus influenza and Moraxella catarrhalis.

The U.S. Food and Drug Administration (FDA) has labeled gatifloxacin, moxifloxacin, sparfloxacin and levofloxacin for use in the treatment of acute bacterial sinusitis.

However, we believe that quinolones should not be used as first line agents in the treatment of acute bacterial sinusitis because of the potential for development of bacterial resistance.

Acute bronchitis may follow a viral illness, but antimicrobial therapy generally is not warranted unless the patient has underlying pulmonary disease. Fluoroquinolone therapy for acute bacterial bronchitis has been effective against *H. influenzae* and *M. catarrhalis*, the primary pathogens.

The use of ciprofloxacin for *S. pneumoniae* and *P. Aeruginosa* bronchitis has resulted in clinical treatment failures and the development of bacterial resistance.

Generally, levofloxacin, sparfloxacin, ofloxacin, gatifloxacin and moxifloxacin have compared favorably with cefuroxime, cefaclor (Ceclor), amoxicillinclavulanate potassium and amoxicillin.

S. pneumoniae, H. influenzae and *M. pneumoniae* are the pathogens most commonly identified in community acquired pneumonia; less commonly isolated pathogens include viruses, *S. aureus, C. pneumoniae, M. catarrhalis, Klebsiella pneumoniae* and *L. pneumophila*.

The pathogens most often responsible for death in patients with community-acquired pneumonia are *S. pneumoniae, S. aureus* and *L. pneumophila*.

Listed antibiotic choices for outpatient treatment included macrolides, doxycycline (Vibramycin) and fluoroquinolones. Antibiotic choices for hospitalized patients included fluoroquinolones or extended-spectrum penicillins (piperacillin [Pipracil], piperacillin-tazobactam [Zosyn] or ampicillin-sulbactam [Unasyn]), carbapenems (meropenem [Merrem] and imipenem-cilastatin [Primaxin]) and cephalosporins, plus adjunctive macrolides, aminoglycosides, clindamycin (Cleocin) or metronidazole (Flagyl).

For treatment of community-acquired pneumonia in patients hospitalized in a general ward, antibiotics like macrolide with an extended-spectrum cephalosporin (cefotaxime [Claforan] or ceftriaxone [Rocephin]) or a beta-lactam/beta lactamase inhibitor combined with a macrolide or a fluoroquinolone alone (levofloxacin, gatifloxacin or moxifloxacin.

For the treatment of patients hospitalized in an intensive care unit, the drugs are macrolide or a fluoroquinolone (levofloxacin, gatifloxacin or moxifloxacin) plus an extended-spectrum cephalosporin (cefotaxime or ceftriaxone) or a beta-lactam/beta lactamase inhibitor.

For the treatment of atypical pneumonias, macrolides are likely to be equivalent to fluoroquinolones and are currently more cost-effective. Quinolones provide exceptional coverage against atypical pathogens when infection with these organisms is suspected in patients with community-acquired pneumonia. Compared with other quinolones, moxifloxacin and gatifloxacin have been shown to have superior *in vitro* activity against pneumococci.

Of the fluoroquinolones, ciprofloxacin and trovafloxacin have been studied most extensively in the treatment of nosocomial pneumonia. Ciprofloxacin has been found to be comparable in efficacy to imipenem-cilastatin in mechanically ventilated patients, especially those infected with pathogens from the Enterobacteriaceae family, but it has also been associated with poorer responses and higher clinical failure rates in patients with nosocomial pneumonia caused by *S. Aureus* or *P. aeruginosa*.

At present, quinolones are best used in combination antimicrobial therapy for nosocomial pneumonia.

Sexually Transmitted Diseases

Ceftriaxone is the agent of choice for treatment of uncomplicated Neisseria gonorrhoeae urethritis and cervicitis. A single dose of ciprofloxacin or ofloxacin should be considered as alternative treatment in, for example, patients with penicillin allergy. Recently, gatifloxacin was reported to be as effective as ofloxacin against *N. gonorrhoeae*. A sevenday course of ofloxacin or sparfloxacin has been found to be as effective as doxycycline in the treatment of *C. trachomatis* infections. Finally, ciprofloxacin has been reported to be as effective as trimethoprim-sulfamethoxazole for treating chancroid caused by Haemophilus ducreyi. Pelvic inflammatory disease is a polymicrobial infection. Quinolone treatment options include ofloxacin plus metronidazole, ofloxacin plus cefoxitin (Mefoxin) and ciprofloxacin plus clindamycin.

Gastroenteritis

Prophylactic antimicrobial therapy is not recommended for the prevention of diarrhea in travelers. Norfloxacin or ciprofloxacin has been found to be comparable to trimethoprim-sulfamethoxazole in the treatment of traveler's diarrhea caused by Shigella species, enterotoxigenic *E. coli*, or Campylobacter jejuni. Ciprofloxacin and ofloxacin are the agents of choice for treatment of enteric typhoid fever. Norfloxacin has been found to be superior to both trimethoprim-sulfamethoxazole and doxycycline in the treatment of Vibrio cholerae infection.

Skin and Soft Tissue Infections

Diabetic foot infections, which are polymicrobial, can be treated with Quinolones in combination with other antibiotics.

Adverse Events

In general, the quinolones and fluoroquinolones are well tolerated. The most frequently reported side effects (Table 16-2) are associated with the GI tract (2–13%); these include nausea, vomiting, diarrhea, and abdominal pain. CNS effects (1–8%), such as drowsiness, weakness, headache, dizziness and in severe cases, convulsions and toxic psychosis have been reported. Some side effects such as photosensitivity, correlate with specific chemical structures including the halogen substitution on the eighth position, as found in sparfloxacin and lomefloxacin. Adverse cardiovascular effects (6–7%; vascular embolism, cardiac insufficiency, hypotension) also occur with sparfloxacin. Sparfloxacin, moxifloxacin and gatifloxacin can exacerbate QT prolongations. Fulminant hepatotoxicity associated with trovafloxacin has resulted in acute liver failure and the FDA has recommended limiting therapy to life-threatening infections. The use of the quinolones in pregnant or breastfeeding women and children whose epiphysial plates have not closed is generally contraindicated. Their use for treating young cystic fibrosis children infected with *Pseudomonas* spp. is an exception; the patient should be monitored carefully for untoward effects.

Drug Interactions

Clinically significant drug interactions are known to occur with all quinolones (Table 16-3). When products containing multivalent cations (calcium, aluminum, magnesium, iron, zinc), including sucralfate (Carafate), antacids, nutritional supplements and multivitamin and mineral supplements, are taken within two to four hours of an orally administered quinolone, the maximum serum concentration of the quinolone may be reduced by 25 percent to approximately 90 percent.

Table 16-2: Adverse effects of fluoroquinolones.

Adverse Effects of Quinolones *
Gastrointestinal: nausea, vomiting, diarrhea, abdominal pain
CNS : headache, dizziness, drowsiness,, confusion, insomnia, fatigue, malaise, depression, somenolence, seizures, vertigo, lightheadedness, restlessness, tremor
Dermatologic : rash, photosensitivity reactions, pruritus
Other : QTc prolongation, hepatotoxicity, abnormal or bitter taste, tendon rupture

CNS = central nervous system; QTc = corrected QT Interval.

* – because Quinolones have been associated with arthropathy and chondrotoxicity in immature animals, they are not recommended for use in children and adolescents younger than 18 years of age or in pregnant or breastfeeding women.

Table 16-3: Drug interactions of quinolones .

Any quinolone
Decreased absorption of quinolones if didanosine (videx) or multivalent cations are administered concomitantly or less than two hours before of after a quinolone.
May increase anticoagulant effects of warfarin (Coumadin)
May increase caffeine levels
May increase cyclosporine (Sandimmune) levels
May increase theophline levels
May prolong QTc if used concomitantly with antiarrhythmics (e.g., class IA and III agents) or with cisapride (Propulsid)
May increase risk of CNS stimulation and convulsions if used concomitantly with nonsteroidal antiinflammatory drugs
May lead to hypoglycemia and/or hyperglycemia if used concomitantly with antidiabetic aents (oral hypoglycemic of insulin)

QTc = corrected QT interval; CNS = central nervous system.

Applications of Fluoroquinolones in Biologic Warfare

Bacillus anthracis (anthrax) spores have recently been deployed as a biologic weapon in the United States. Fluoroquinolones have a role in postexposure prophylaxis and chemotherapy for specific agents that could be used in biologic warfare (Table 16-4).

Specific fluoroquinolones are indicated for prophylaxis or treatment of anthrax, cholera, plague, brucellosis and tularemia. Ciprofloxacin is the drug of choice for postexposure prophylaxis for anthrax until sensitivities are available. Although penicillin resistance has only rarely occurred in the natural setting of anthrax, the former Soviet Union developed a B. anthracis strain that was resistant to both penicillin and tetracycline.

Table 16-4: Selected potential biologic pathogens: post exposure prophylaxis and treatment.

Selected Potential Biologic Pathogens: Post exposure Prophylaxis and Treatment		
Pathogen	**Post exposure Prophylaxis**	**Treatment**
Bacillus anthracis (antharax)	Agent of choice : ciprofloxacin (Cipro)* Alternative : doxycycline (Vibramycin)	Agents of choice;ciprofloxacin, doxycycline Alternative if organisms are penicillin sensitive: penicillin G
Vibrio cholera (cholera)	Not available	Agents of choice oral rehydration therapy, tetracycline, doxycycline, ciprofloxacin, norfloxacin (Noroxin)
Yersinia pestis (plague)	Agents of choice doxycycline, ciprofloxacin Alternative: Tetracycline	Agents of choice streptomycin, gentamicin, ciprofloxacin Alternative doxycycline
Brucell melitensis (brucellosis)	Agents of choice: doxycycline plus rifampin (Rifadin)	Agents of choice streptomycin Alternative gentamicin, ciprofloxacin
*-Levofloxacin (Levaquin) and oflaxacin are alternatives for postexposure prophylaxis in mass casualty		

Urinary Antiseptics

Urinary tract infections (most commonly uncomplicated acute cystitis and pyelonephritis) in women of child bearing age and in the elderly are one of the most common problems seen by primary care physicians. *Escherichia coli* is the most common pathogen, causing about 80 percent of uncomplicated upper and lower UTIs. Staphylococcus saprophyticus is the second most common bacterial pathogen causing UTIs, with other common causes including Klebsiella pneumoniae and Proteus mirabilis These infections may be treated with any one of a group of agents called urinary tract antiseptics, including methenamine, nitrofurantoin and the quinolone nalidixic acid. These drugs do not achieve antibacterial levels in the circulation, but because they are concentrated in the urine, microorganisms at that site can be effectively eradicated.

Methenamine

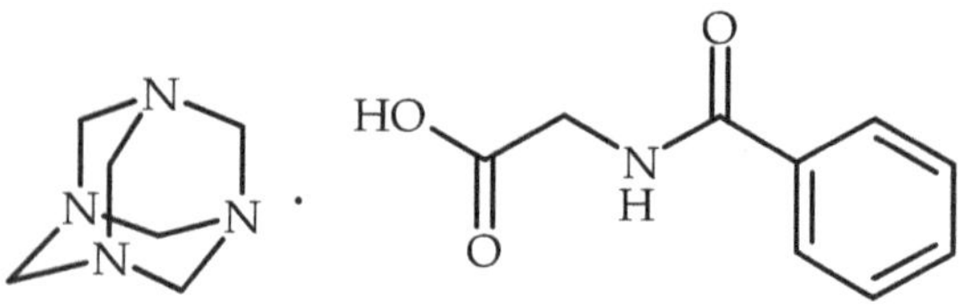

Fig 16 -2: Structure of methenamine.

Mechanism of Action

To act, methenamine (Fig 16-2) must decompose at an acidic pH of 5.5 or less in the urine, thus producing formaldehyde, which is toxic to most bacteria . The reaction is slow, requiring 3 hours to reach 90 percent decomposition. Methenamine should not be used in patients with indwelling catheters. Bacteria do not develop resistance to formaldehyde. [Note: Methenamine is frequently formulated with a weak acid, such as mandelic acid or hippuric acid.]

Antibacterial spectrum: Methenamine is primarily used for chronic suppressive therapy. Urea splitting bacteria that alkalinize the urine, such as Proteus species, are usually resistant to the action of methenamine. Methenamine is used to treat lower UTIs but is not effective in upper UTIs.

Pharmacokinetics

Methenamine is administered orally. In addition to formaldehyde, ammonium ion is produced in the bladder. Because the liver rapidly metabolizes ammonia to form urea, methenamine is contraindicated in patients with hepatic insufficiency, in which elevated levels of circulating ammonium ions would be toxic to the CNS. Methenamine is distributed throughout the body fluids, but no decomposition of the drug occurs at pH 7.4. Thus, systemic toxicity does not occur. The drug is eliminated in the urine.

Adverse effects

The major side effect of methenamine treatment is gastrointestinal distress, although at higher doses, albuminuria, hematuria and rashes may develop. Methenamine mandelate is contraindicated in patients with renal insufficiency, because mandelic acid may precipitate.

Nitrofurans (Nitrofurantoin)

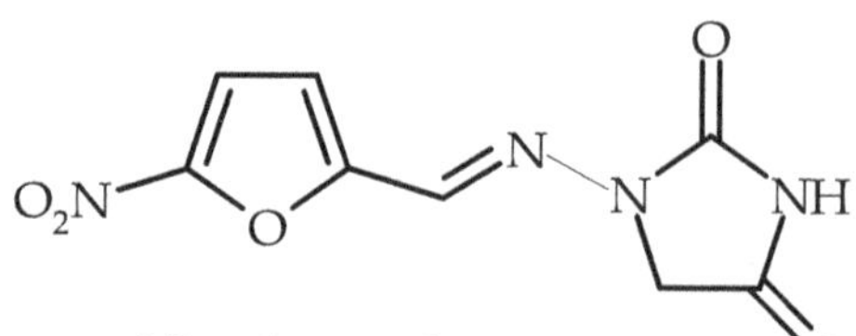

Nitrofurantoin

Fig 16-3: Structure of nitrofurantoin.

Chemistry and Mechanism of Action

A number of 5-nitro-2-furaldehyde derivatives, called nitrofurans (Fig 16-3), are used in the treatment and/or prophylaxis of microbial infections, primarily in the urinary tract. Recent evidence suggests that the reduction of the 5-nitro group to the nitro anion results in bacterial toxicity. Intermediate metabolites modify various bacterial macromolecules that affect a variety of biochemical processes (e.g.,

DNA and RNA synthesis, protein synthesis); this observation may explain the lack of resistance development to these drugs. Evidence also indicates that the nitro anion undergoes recycling with the production of superoxide and other toxic oxygen compounds. It is presumed that the nitrofurans are selectively toxic to microbial cells because in humans, the slower reduction by mammalian cells prevents high serum concentrations.

Antibacterial Spectrum and Resistance

Nitrofurantoin (*Furadantin, Macrodantin*) is primarily active against gram negative bacteria (*E. coli, P. mirabilis* is variable) and some susceptible gram-positive organisms, such as *S. aureus* and *Enterococcus faecalis. In vitro* activity is demonstrated against *Staphylococcus saprophyticus* and *Staphylococcus epidermidis*, but it may not be helpful in predicting patient response; the same applies for certain species of *Klebsiella* and *Citrobacter.* Most *Proteus* (indole positive), *Serratia* and *Pseudomonas* spp. are resistant. Development of resistant strains is virtually unknown and crossresistance with other antimicrobials has not been reported.

Absorption, Metabolism and Excretion

Nitrofurantoin is administered orally and is rapidly and almost completely absorbed from the small intestine; only low levels of activity are achieved in serum because the drug is rapidly metabolized. Relatively high protein binding (about 70%) also affects serum levels, reducing potential for systemic toxicity and alteration of intestinal flora. Relative tissue penetration is much lower than other antimicrobials for UTIs and therefore, nitrofurantoin is not indicated in the therapy of infections such as pyelonephritis and renal cortical or perinephric abscesses. Nitrofurantoin is rapidly excreted by glomerular filtration and tubular secretion to yield effective urinary levels. In moderate to severe renal dysfunction, toxic blood levels may occur while urinary levels may be inadequate. The drug is inactivated in the liver. Nitrofurazone (*Furacin*) is used topically and is not readily absorbed from the skin.

Clinical Use

The singular indication for nitrofurantoin is the treatment and long term prophylaxis of lower UTIs caused by susceptible bacteria; it is not used as a bacterial suppressant. It is often used prophylactically post intercourse in women with chronic UTIs. Although serum drug concentrations are low, concentrations (100–200 g/mL) are found in urine that are well above the minimum inhibitory concentration for susceptible bacteria. The bacteriostatic or bactericidal activity of nitrofurantoin is concentration dependent; a urinary concentration greater than 100 μg/mL ensures bactericidal activity. Because nitrofurantoin lacks the broad tissue distribution of other antimicrobial agents, urine cultures should be obtained before and after therapy. Alkalinization of the urine increases urinary concentrations of the drug but decreases its antibacterial efficacy; acidifying agents, including cranberry juice, can be useful. Nitrofurazone, a topical antibiotic, is occasionally used in the treatment of burns or skin grafts in which bacterial contamination may cause tissue rejection.

Adverse Effects and Drug Interactions

Nausea and vomiting are the most commonly observed adverse effects. Pulmonary hypersensitivity reactions can result in chronic morbidity, usually after therapy lasting at least 6 months. Findings can include chronic desquamative interstitial pneumonia with fibrosis. Resolution may not occur with discontinuation of therapy; fever is absent. Reactions may also be acute or subacute. Patients may present acutely with findings resembling acute respiratory distress syndrome. Infiltrates (especially at the base of the lung) and/or effusions may develop but are usually reversible when the drug is stopped; fever is a common finding. In contrast, resolution of pulmonary disease may require several months, especially in subacute reactions, with which fever is not frequent. These reaction types have all been reported as contributing factors in mortality. When a patient taking nitrofurantoin develops pulmonary symptoms, a suspicion of drug-associated toxicity must be entertained. Intrahepatic cholestasis and hepatitis similar to that seen in chronic active hepatitis can rarely occur; fatalities have been reported. Nitrofurantoin can interfere with immature red blood cell enzyme systems found in babies less than 1 month of age and in nursing infants. This leads to cellular damage and anemia. Nitrofurantoin use is also contraindicated in pregnant women near term. *In vitro* antagonism between nitrofurantoin and the quinolones has been shown, but a demonstration of clinical relevance warrants further study. Certain drugs used in treating gout, which inhibit tubular secretion, can affect UTI therapy by raising serum levels of nitrofurantoin with concomitant diminished urinary levels. Nitrofurazone is a relatively safe topical agent. Skin sensitization has been reported.

Fosfomycin

Antibacterial Spectrum

Fosfomycin tromethamine is a phosphonic acid derivative useful in the treatment of uncomplicated urinary tract infection. The spectrum of activity includes *E coli*, including extended spectrum β-lactamase producing isolates, *E faecalis* and other gram negative aerobic urinary pathogens but not *P. aeruginosa.*

Available as a 3-g sachet, fosfomycin may be useful for the single-dose treatment of the above organisms. Like nitrofurantoin, fosfomycin should not be used for systemic infection. However, the increased concentrations in urine allow for its use in uncomplicated bacteriuria. Considering the increased resistance associated with *E. coli* in the treatment of urinary tract infection, fosfomycin has increased its utility in this disease state.

Adverse effects

The most frequently reported adverse effects include diarrhea, headache and nausea.

References

Alghasham AA and Nahata M (1999). Trovafloxacin: a new fluoroquinolone. *Ann Pharmacother* **33:** 48-60.

Falagas ME et al (2010). Fosfomycin for the treatment of multidrug-resistant, including extended-spectrum beta-lactamase producing, Enterobacteriaceae infections: a systematic review. *Lancet Infect Dis. Jan* **10(1):** 43–50.

Hackbarth CJ, Chambers HF and Sande MA (1986). Serum bactericidal activity of rifampin in combination with other antimicrobial agents against Staphylococcus aureus. *Antimicrob Agents Chemother* **29:** 611-3.

Hooper DC (1999). Mode of action of fluoroquinolones. *Drugs,* **58 (suppl 2):** 6-10.

Hooper D (2000). Quinolones. In: Mandell GL, Bennett JE, Dolin R. Mandell, Douglas, and Bennett's Principles and practice of infectious diseases. 5th ed. *Philadelphia: Churchill Livingstone,* 404-23.

Hooper DC (2000). New uses for new and old quinolones and the challenge of resistance. *Clin Infect Dis* **30:** 243-54.

Hooper DC and Wolfson JS (1993). Mechanisms of quinolone action and bacterial killing. In: Quinolone antimicrobial agents. 2nd ed. Washington, D.C. *American Society for Microbiology,* 53-7.

Owens RC Jr and Ambrose PG (2000). Clinical use of the fluoroquinolones. *Med Clin North Am* **84:** 1447-69.

Turnidge J (1999). Pharmacokinetics and pharmacodynamics of fluoroquinolones. *Drugs,* **58 (suppl 2):** 29-36.

Walker RC (1999). The fluoroquinolones. *Mayo Clin Proc* **74:** 1030-7.

CHAPTER

Antimycobacterials 17

An **antimycobacterial** is a type of drug used to treat Mycobacteria infections.

Types include:

Tuberculosis treatments

Leprostatic agents

Tuberculosis

Tuberculosis or TB (short for *tubercles bacillus*) is a common and often deadly infectious disease caused by various strains of Mycobacteria, usually *Mycobacterium tuberculosis* in humans. Tuberculosis usually attacks the lungs but can also affect other parts of the body.

Other names: "Consumption", "white plague", "pott`s disease", "wasting disease".

Transmission

There are two possible ways a person can become sick with TB disease.

The first applies to a person who may have had been infected with TB but is perfectly healthy. The person can get infected again if they have another disease such as HIV or cancer or they may get infected if they use drugs/alcohol.

The other way it TB can develop, happens much more quickly. Sometimes when a person first breathes in the TB germs, the body is unable to protect itself against the disease. The germs then develop into active TB disease within weeks.

Signs and Symptoms

When the disease becomes active, 75% of the cases are pulmonary TB, that is, TB in the lungs. Symptoms include chest pain, coughing up blood and a productive, prolonged cough for more than three weeks. Systemic symptoms include fever, chills, night sweats, appetite loss, weight loss, pallor and often a tendency to fatigue very easily.

In the other 25% of active cases, the infection moves from the lungs, causing other kinds of TB, collectively denoted extra pulmonary tuberculosis. Extra pulmonary infection sites include

Pleura in tuberculosis pleurisy

Central nervous system in meningitis

Lymphatic system in scrofula of the neck

Bones and joints in Pott's disease of the spine.

Genitourinary system in urogenital tuberculosis.

An especially serious form is disseminated TB, more commonly known as miliary tuberculosis.

Cause

The primary cause of TB, *Mycobacterium tuberculosis*, is a small aerobic non-motile bacillus. Since MTB has a cell wall but lacks a phospholipid outer membrane, it is classified as a Gram positive bacterium. However, if a Gram stain is performed, MTB either stains very weakly Gram positive or does not retain dye due to the high lipid & mycolic acid content of its cell wall.

MTB retains certain stains after being treated with acidic solution, it is classified as an acid-fast bacillus (AFB). The most common acid-fast staining technique, the Ziehl-Neelsen stain, dyes AFBs a bright red that stands out clearly against a blue background. Other ways to visualize AFBs include an auramine-rhodamine stain and fluorescent microscopy.

The *M. tuberculosis* complex includes four other TB-causing mycobacteria: *M. bovis*, *M. africanum*, *M. canetti* and *M. microti*, *M. africanum* is not widespread, but in parts of Africa it is a significant cause of tuberculosis. *M. bovis* was once a common cause of tuberculosis, but the introduction of pasteurized milk has largely eliminated this as a public health problem in developed countries. *M. canetti* is rare and seems to be limited to Africa, although a few cases have been seen in African emigrants. *M. microti* is mostly seen in immunodeficient people.

Other known pathogenic mycobacteria include *Mycobacterium leprae*, *Mycobacterium marinum*, *Mycobacterium avium* and *M. kansasii*. The last two are part of the nontuberculous mycobacteria (NTM) group. Nontuberculous mycobacteria cause neither TB nor leprosy, but they *do* cause pulmonary diseases resembling tuberculosis

Who Gets Tuberculosis?

Anyone can get tuberculosis. Some people are at higher risks than others. The people who have more of a chance getting TB are:

People who share same breathing space

Poor people/homeless people

Prisoners

Alcoholics or Drug users

People with medical conditions (cancer, diabetes)

Specially people with aids

Risk factors

Persons with silicosis

Low body weight

Diabetes mellitus

Prolonged corticosteroid therapy and other immunosuppressive therapy

Rheumatoid arthritis

Stages

There are three stages in the disease of tuberculosis. These three stages are identified from mild to extreme danger which is death.

The first mild stage can get cured easily as long as the patient gets medication on time and takes good care.

The second stage is more dangerous and the patient has to be really careful and that is where the symptoms should be considered.

The third stage is extremely dangerous and there is no cure which means death. The third stage is the stage where nothing should go wrong and the patient will slowly begin to vomit blood and eventually die.

Diagnostic Tests

Complete blood count test

Chest x-ray

Sputum culture test

Tuberculin skin test

Treatment

Drugs {Multiple drug therapy}

Dots

Alternate therapies

Drugs {Multiple Drug Therapy}

The structures and classification of Anti TB drugs are shown in Fig 17-1, 17-2.

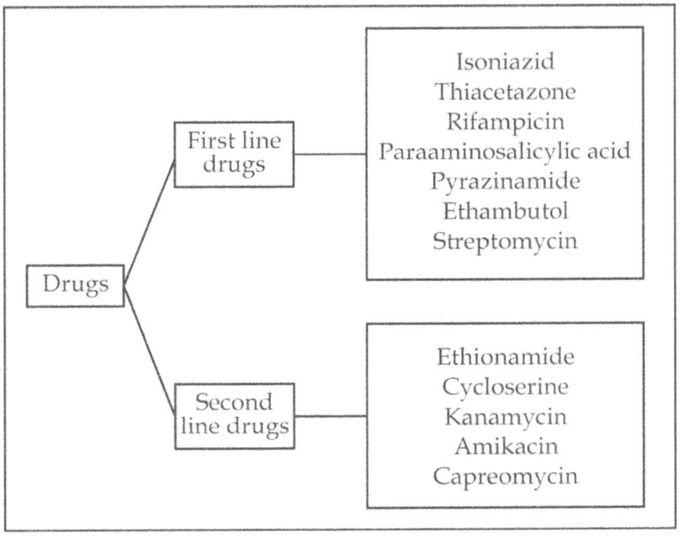

Fig 17-1: Antitubercular drugs.

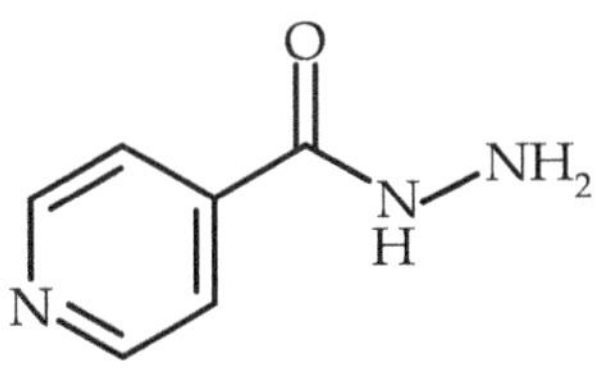

Isoniazid

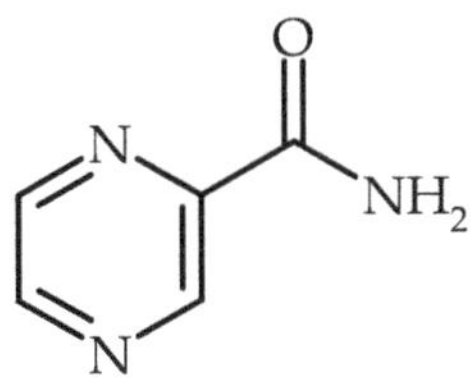

Pyrazinamide

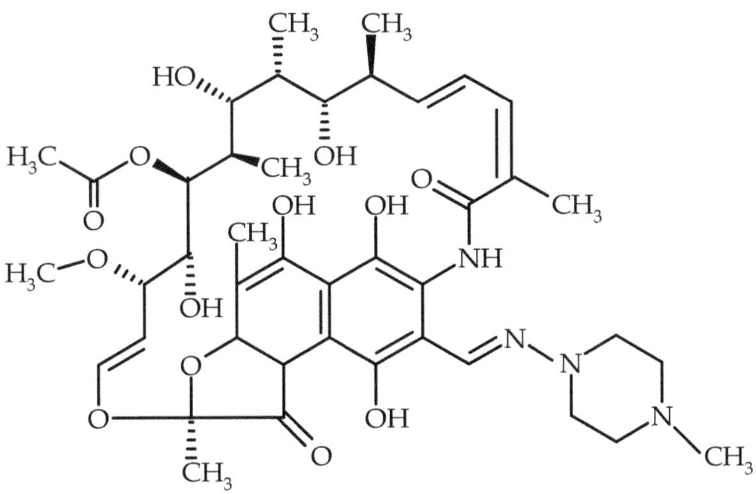

Rifampin

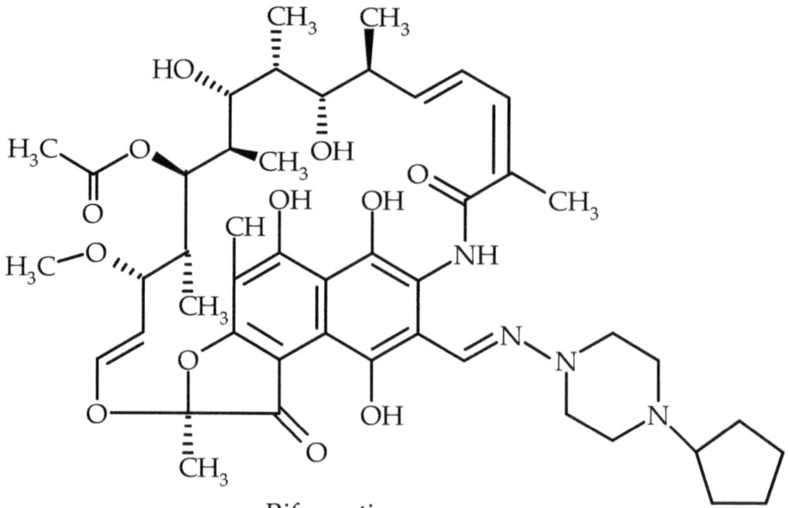

Rifapentine

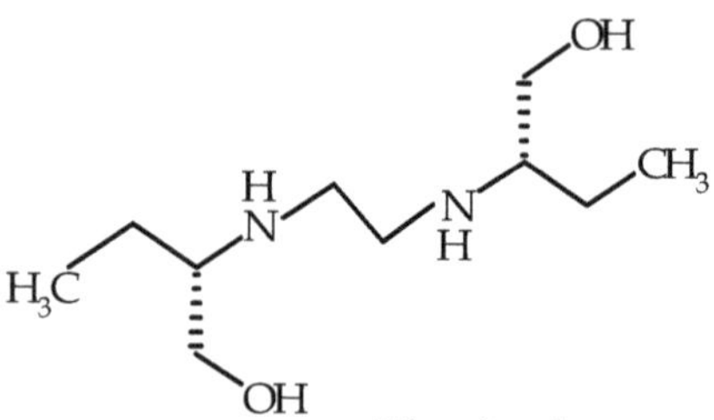

Ethambutol

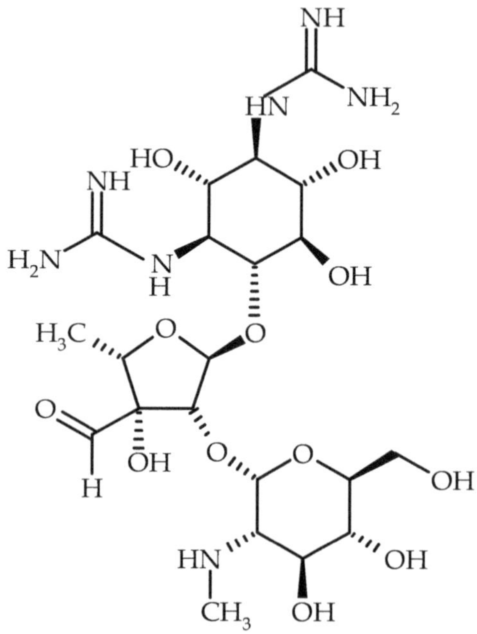

Streptomycin

Fig 17-2: Structures of anti TB drugs.

Isoniazid

Isoniazid, the hydrazide of isonicotinic acid, is a synthetic analog of pyridoxine (Vit-B6).

Most potent of the Antitubercular drugs.

But it is never given as a single agent in the treatment of active tuberculosis.

Mechanism of Action

Inhibits synthesis of mycolic acids, which are essential components of mycobacterial cell walls. INH is a prodrug that is activated by KatG (the mycobacterial catalase peroxidase). At least two different target enzymes for Isoniazid which are involved in the production of mycolic acids. The activated drug covalently binds to and inhibits these enzymes, which are essential for the synthesis of mycolic acid. Decreased mycolic acid synthesis corresponds with the loss of acid-fastness after exposure to Isoniazid.

Antibacterial spectrum

For bacilli in the stationary phase, INH is bacteriostatic, but for rapidly dividing organisms, it is bactericidal.

It is effective against intracellular bacteria.

Isoniazid inhibits most tubercle bacilli in a concentration of 0.2 μg/mL or less.

Resistance

Treatment with INH alone leads to development of resistance, occurs within a few weeks after therapy is started.

This is associated with several different chromosomal mutations.

Drug resistant mutants are normally present in susceptible mycobacterial.

Pharmacokinetics

Metabolism of Isoniazid, especially acetylation by liver N-acetyltransferase, is genetically determined.

Sub therapeutic concentrations may occur if drug is administered as a once-weekly dose or if there is malabsorption.

Metabolites and a small amount of unchanged drug are excreted mainly in the urine.

Adverse effects

Peripheral neuritis

Hepatitis and idiosyncratic Hepatotoxicity

Mental abnormalities, convulsions in patients prone to seizures, optic neuritis have been observed. Hypersensitivity reactions include rashes and fever.

Hematologic abnormalities, provocation of pyridoxine deficiency anemia, tinnitus, and gastrointestinal discomfort etc.

Drug Interactions

Because Isoniazid inhibits metabolism of phenytoin, Isoniazid can potentiate the adverse effects of that drug.

Rifampicin

Rifampin is a semi synthetic derivative of rifamycin, an antibiotic produced by *Streptomyces mediterranei.*

Mechanism of action & resistance

Rifampin binds to the α subunit of bacterial DNA-dependent RNA polymerase and thereby inhibits RNA synthesis. Resistance results from any one of several possible point mutations in the gene for the â subunit of RNA polymerase. These mutations result in reduced binding of rifampin to RNA polymerase. Human RNA polymerase does not bind rifampin and is not inhibited by it.

Antibacterial spectrum

Rifampin is bactericidal for both intracellular and extracellular mycobacteria, including M. tuberculosis and atypical Mycobacteria such as *M. kansasii.* Effective against many gram positive and gram negative organisms.

Pharmacokinetics

Rifampin is well absorbed after oral administration and excreted mainly through the liver into bile.

It then undergoes enterohepatic recirculation, with the bulk excreted in feces and a small amount in the urine.

Distributed widely in body fluids and tissues. It is relatively highly protein-bound and adequate cerebrospinal fluid concentrations are achieved only in the presence of Meningeal inflammation.

Clinical uses

Used against persisters.

Adverse Reactions

Rifampin imparts a harmless orange color to urine, sweat, tears and contact lenses (soft lenses may be permanently stained).

Occasional adverse effects include rashes, thrombocytopenia and nephritis. May cause Cholestatic jaundice and occasionally hepatitis.

Commonly causes light-chain proteinuria.

If administered less often than twice weekly, rifampin causes a flu-like syndrome characterized by fever, chills, myalgia, anemia, Thrombocytopenia and sometimes is associated with acute tubular necrosis.

Drug interactions

Strongly induces most cytochrome P450 isoform which increases the elimination of numerous other drugs including methadone, anticoagulants, cyclosporine, some anticonvulsants, protease inhibitors, some Non-nucleoside reverse transcriptase inhibitors, contraceptives and a host of others.

Should be used with caution in patients who are alcoholic, elderly, or have chronic liver disease due to the increased incidence of severe hepatic dysfunction.

Ethambutol

Ethambutol is a synthetic, water-soluble, heat-stable compound.

Antibacterial Spectrum

Susceptible strains of Mycobacterium tuberculosis and other Mycobacteria are inhibited *invitro* by Ethambutol, 1-5 µg/mL.

Mechanism of Action and Resistance

Ethambutol inhibits mycobacterial arabinosyl transferases, involved in the polymerization reaction of arabinoglycan, an essential component of the mycobacterial cell wall. Resistance to Ethambutol is due to mutations.

Pharmacokinetics

Ethambutol accumulates in renal failure, and the dose should be reduced by half if creatinine clearance is less than 10 mL/min.

Ethambutol crosses the blood-brain barrier only if the meninges are inflamed.

Clinical Use

Tuberculous meningitis.

Adverse Reactions

The most common serious adverse event is retrobulbar neuritis, resulting in loss of visual acuity and red-green color blindness. Ethambutol is relatively contraindicated in children too young to permit assessment of visual acuity and red-green color discrimination.

Pyrazinamide

Pyrazinamide (PZA) is a relative of Nicotinamide, stable, and slightly soluble in water. Inactive at neutral pH, but at pH 5.5, it inhibits tubercle bacilli and some other mycobacteria.

The drug is taken up by macrophages and exerts its activity against Mycobacteria residing within the acidic environment of lysosome.

Mechanism of action

Pyrazinamide is converted to pyrazinoic acid, the active form of the drug by mycobacterial pyrazinamidase and makes surrounding environment of bacteria unsuitable for its survival.

Resistance

May be due to impaired uptake of Pyrazinamide or mutations that impair conversion of Pyrazinamide to its active form.

Pharmacokinetics

Pyrazinamide is well absorbed from the gastrointestinal tract and widely distributed in body tissues, including inflamed meninges. The half-life is 8-11 hours.

Metabolized by the liver, but metabolites are renally cleared; therefore, pyrazinamide should be administered at 25-35 mg/kg three times weekly (not daily) in hemodialysis patients and those in whom the creatinine clearance is less than 30 mL/min.

Adverse Reactions

Major adverse effects of Pyrazinamide include Hepatotoxicity (in 1-5% of patients), nausea, vomiting, drug fever, and hyperuricemia (level of uric acid in the blood that is abnormally high).

The latter occurs uniformly and is not a reason to halt therapy. Hyperuricemia may provoke acute gouty arthritis.

Streptomycin

First clinically effective drug to become available for the treatment of TB. Irreversible inhibitors of protein synthesis. Protein synthesis is inhibited by amino glycosides in at least three ways

1. interference with the initiation complex of peptide formation;
2. misreading of mRNA, which causes incorporation of incorrect amino acids into the peptide, resulting in a nonfunctional or toxic protein;
3. breakup of polysomes into nonfunctional monosomes.

Resistance

Resistance is due to a point mutation in either the gene encoding the S12 ribosomal protein gene or the gene encoding 16S ribosomal rRNA, which alters the ribosomal binding site. Streptomycin penetrates into cells poorly and is active mainly against extracellular tuberclebacilli. Streptomycin crosses the blood-brain barrier and achieves therapeutic concentrations with inflamed meninges.

Clinical Use in Tuberculosis

Streptomycin sulfate is used when an injectable drug is needed or desirable, principally in individuals with severe, possibly life-threatening forms of tuberculosis, e.g., meningitis and disseminated disease and in treatment of infections resistant to other drugs.

Adverse Reactions

Streptomycin is ototoxic and Nephrotoxic.

Vertigo and hearing loss are the most common side effects and may be permanent.

Toxicity is dose-related, and the risk is increased in the elderly. As with all aminoglycosides, the dose must be adjusted according to renal function.

Cycloserine

Mode of Action

The terminal two amino acid residues of the murein precursor lipid II consist of D-alanine, which is produced by the enzyme alanine racemase; the two residues are joined by D-alanine ligase. Both enzymes are competitively inhibited by Cycloserine.

Uses

It is also being trialed as an adjuvant to exposure therapy for anxiety disorders (e.g., phobias), depression, obsessive-compulsive disorder and schizophrenia

Recent research suggests that D-Cycloserine (d-4-amino-3-isoxazolidinone) may be effective in treating chronic pain.

Adverse Effects

Mainly central nervous system (CNS) manifestations, i.e., headache, irritability, depression, psychosis convulsions. Co-administration of pyridoxine can reduce the incidence of some of the CNS side effects (e.g., convulsions).

These psychotropic responses are related to D-cycloserine's action as a partial agonist of the neuronal NMDA receptor for glutamate and have been examined in implications with sensory-related fear extinction in the amygdala, and extinction of cocaine seeking in the nucleus accumbens.

D-cycloserine is a partial agonist at the glycine receptor and has been shown to have cognition-enhancing properties for models of Parkinsons disease.

The dosages of Anti TB drugs are shown in Table 17-1, 17-2.

Table 17-1: Dosages of first-line anti-TB agents.

Drugs	Daily doses (mg/kg)	Route	Thrice weekly Dosage (mg/kg/dose)
Isoniazid (H)	5 (4-6)	Oral	10 (8-12)
Rifampin (R)	10 (8-12)	Oral	10 (8-12)
Ethambutol (E)	15 (15-20)	Oral	30 (25-35)
Pyrazinamide (Z)	25 (25-30)	Oral	35 (30-40)
Streptomycin (S)	15 (12 - 18)	Oral	15 (12-18)

Table 17-2: Dosages of second-line anti-TB agents.

Drugs	Daily doses (mg/kg)	Route	Maximum daily dose
Kanamycin (K)	15	IM	Up to 1 g
Amikacin (A)	15	IM	Up to 1 g
Ethionamide (Eto)	10-15	Oral	Up to 1 g
Cycloserine (Cs)	10	Oral	Up to 1 g
Para amino salicylic acid (PAS)	250	Oral	Up to 1 g
Ofloxacin (Ofx)	15-20	Oral	800-10000 mg
Levofloxacin	7.5-10	Oral	750-1000 mg
Moxifloxacin	7.5-10	Oral	400 mg

DOTS

DOTS (directly observed treatment, short-course), is the name given to the World Health Organization-recommended tuberculosis control strategy that combines five components:

Government commitment (including both political will at all levels and establishing a centralized and prioritized system of TB monitoring, recording and training)

Case detection by sputum smear microscopy.

Standardized treatment regimen directly observed by a healthcare worker or community health worker for at least the first two months.

A regular, uninterrupted drug supply.

A standardized recording and reporting system that allows assessment of treatment results.

Prevention

BCG vaccine: Bacillus Calmette-Guérin (or Bacille Calmette-Guérin, BCG) is a vaccine against tuberculosis that is prepared from a strain of the attenuated (weakened) live bovine tuberculosis bacillus, *Mycobacterium bovis*, that has lost its virulence in humans by being specially subcultured (230 passages) in an artificial medium for 13 years and also prepared from *Mycobacterium tuberculosis*. The bacilli have retained enough strong antigenicity to become a somewhat effective vaccine for the prevention of human tuberculosis. At best, the BCG vaccine is 80% effective in preventing tuberculosis for a duration of 15 years.

It is recommended the BCG vaccination be given intradermally by a nurse skilled in the technique.

Leprosy

Introduction

Caused by *Mycobacterium leprae*. Chronic granulomatous infection mainly involving the skin, peripheral nerves, the mucosa of the upper respiratory tract and testes. Its distribution is global and almost exclusively affects individuals in the "developing world".

Prodromal symptoms are generally so mild that the disease is not recognized until a cutaneous eruption is present.

The clinical syndromes of leprosy represent a spectrum that reflects the cellular immune response to *Mycobacterium leprae* and the unique tropism for peripheral nerves.

The less severe end of the spectrum is tuberculoid leprosy and the most severe is lepromatous leprosy.

Gram Positive, Obligate, Intracellular, Acid-Fast Bacilli.

Differs from all other mycobacterium in that it cannot be cultured *in vitro*.

Organism grows at 27-30 degrees C; Thus it grows best in the cooler areas of the body.

Skin, peripheral nerves, anterior chamber of the eye, upper respiratory tract and testes.

Has an affinity for macrophages and Schwann cells.

For Schwann cells in particular, the mycobacterium binds to the G domain of the alpha chain of laminin 2 (found only in peripheral nerves) in the basal lamina.

Its slow replication within the Schwann cell will eventually stimulate a cell-mediated immune response, which creates a chronic inflammatory reaction.

As a result, swelling occurs in the perineurium, leading to ischemia, fibrosis and axonal death.

Classification Schemes for Leprosy

Ridley-Jopling Classification: based on clinical manifestation (Fig 17-3)

Tuberculoid (TT)

Lepromatous (LL)

Intermediate Classifications

Borderline Tuberculoid (BT)

Midborderline (BB)

Borderline Lepromatous (BL)

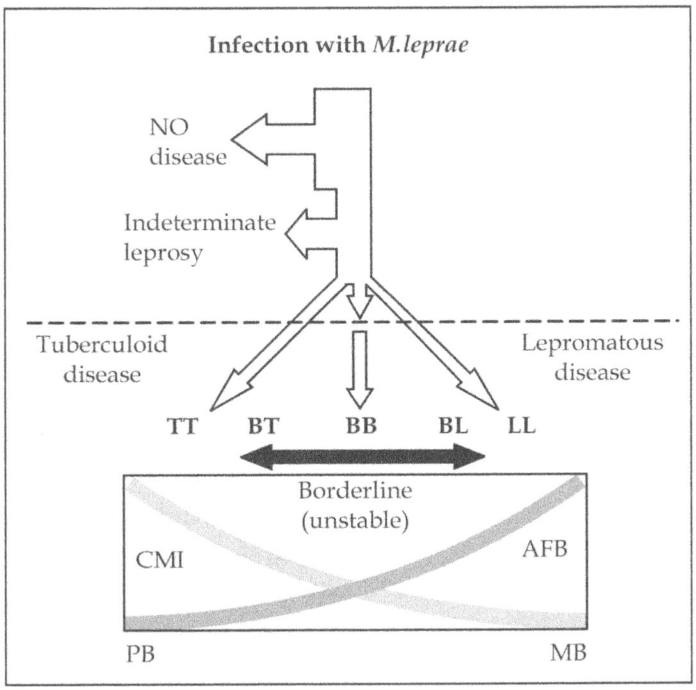

Fig 17-3: Classification of leprosy.

WHO Classification: Based on number of lesions and presence of bacilli on a skin smear.

Paucibacillary: 5 or few lesions with absence of organisms on smear. Usually includes tuberculoid and borderline tuberculoid forms.

Multi-bacillary: Marked by 6 or more lesion with possible visualization of bacilli on smear Includes the Lepromatous, borderline lepromatous and midborderline forms.

Tuberculoid/Paucibacillary

Occurs in individuals who have a vigorous cellular immune response to the organism.

Host cell mediated immune responses are intact.

Disease usually involves the skin and peripheral nerve.

Skin often has one or a few well-demarcated, hypopigmented, or erythematous, hypoesthetic or anesthetic lesions, often with raised, active spreading edges and central clearing.

Characterized by the presence of non necrotizing granulomas in the dermis and peripheral nerves with acid fast bacilli absent or few in number.

Nerve involvement is usually asymmetric.

Low numbers of bacteria in skin lesions (<5 skin lesions, with absence of organisms on smear).

Signs of Tuberculoid Leprosy

Skin Lesions

Sharply demarcated, hypopigmented macules

Enlarged peripheral nerves

Neuropathy

Ulnar nerve

Superficial Radial Cutaneous

Median nerve

Common Peroneal nerve

Greater Auricular

Hypoesthesia

Temperature is the first sensation that is lost. Patients cannot sense extremes of hot or cold.

Lepromatous/Multibacillary

Occurs in individuals who have a minimal.

The loss of ability to kill bacteria appears to be specific for *M. leprae*.

Mycobacterium leprae specific, cell-mediated immunity is diminished greatly, but serum antibody responses to *M.Leprae* derived antigens may occur or titers to non-specific antibodies (such as RF or non-treponenemal tests) may be increased.

Patients with lepromatous leprosy are not unusually susceptible to opportunistic infections, cancer or AIDS and maintain delayed type hypersensitivity to Candida, Trichophyton, mumps, tetanus toxoid and tuberculin.

Disease usually has extensive skin involvement.

Skin lesions are described as infiltrated nodules and plagues and occur in cooler regions of body, with sparing of axilla, groin and scalp.

Nerve involvement is usually symmetric.

High numbers of bacteria in skin lesions (>6 skin lesions, with possible visualization of organisms on smear).

Results of skin tests with antigen from killed organisms (lepromin) are nonreactive and there is a predominance of suppressor CD8+ over CD4+ T lymphocytes.

Physical Findings in Lepromatous Disease

Skin lesions

Poorly defined borders

Raised, indurated lesions

Affects Face, Ears, Wrists, Elbows, Buttocks and Knees

Hoarseness

Loss of eyebrows (madarosis)

Nasal collapse

Lagophthalmos (inability to close the eye), a late finding in LL, results from involvement of the zygomatic and temporal branches of the facial nerve (cranial nerve [CN] VII).

Involvement of the ophthalmic branch of the trigeminal nerve (CN V2) can result in reduced corneal reflex, leaving dry eyes and reduced blinking.

Keratitis, Glaucoma, Iridocyclitis, Leonine facies - skin of the face becomes thickened and corrugated.

Axillary and inguinal LAD.

Borderline (Dimorphous)

Single or multiple well-defined skin lesions similar to tuberculoid lesions but with a raised center and delayed development of dysesthesia.

Often subdivided into borderline lepromatous and borderline tuberculoid.

Indeterminate Leprosy

Early form of leprosy that may develop into any other form.

Typified by hypopigmented macule with indistinct edges and no associated dysesthesia.

Bone Changes in Leprosy

Bone changes in leprosy occur in a high percentage of cases and account for much physical disability and psychosocial distress in these patients.

Various studies have shown incidence of overall bone changes in leprosy to be ranging from 82.9 percent to 91 percent.

The common sites of predilection for bone damage in leprosy are the small bones of hands and feet followed by bones of the face.

In today's clinical era of improved case detection and prompt treatment with effective multidrug regimens, advanced bone changes are rarely encountered.

Transmission of Leprosy

Not a highly infectious disease.

Route of transmission has not be definitely established.

Nasal secretions from patients with untreated lepromatous, borderline lepromatous or borderline disease from whom organisms are secreted in large numbers is probably the most significant source of infectious material.

Little shedding of *M.Leprae* occurs from involved intact skin.

Infectivity of lepromatous patients probably ceases a few days or weeks after initiating rifampin therapy or approximately 3 months after initiating therapy with dapsone or clofazamine.

Contaminated soil or insect vectors may play a role in disease transmission.

Diagnostic Tests

Organisms have not been cultured successfully *in vitro.*

Skin biopsy, nasal smears, or both for acid-fast bacilli using Fite stain.

AFB may be found in biopsy specimens of skin lesions of LL but rarely from Tuberculoid and indeterminate forms.

Histopathologic examination is best method for diagnosis and is the basis of the classification of leprosy; the presence of an inflamed nerve in a skin biopsy is considered the criterion standard for diagnosis.

PCR for *M.Leprae* is available from the National Hanson's Disease Program.

Used to identify the mycobacterium in biopsy samples, skin and nasal smears, and blood and tissue sections.

Histamine testing: Used to diagnose postganglionic nerve injury.

Histamine diphosphate is dropped on normal skin and affected skin, and a pinprick is made through each site. The site forms a wheal on normal skin but none where nerve damage is present.

Histological Testing

TT form: Well-developed epithelioid granulomas are observed in the papillary dermis, often around neurovascular structures.

The granulomas are surrounded by lymphocytes, which extend into the epidermis. Langhans giant cells are common.

Dermal nerves are destroyed or swollen because of the granulomas.

Acid-fast bacilli are not observed.

LL form: A diffuse infiltrate of foamy macrophages is present in the dermis below a subepidermal grenz zone.

An enormous number of acid-fast bacilli develop within the foamy macrophages, singly or in clumps called globi.

Lymphocytes are scant, and giant cells are typically absent.

Numerous bacilli invade the nerves, but these are fairly well preserved with little infiltrate.

Immunologic tests: Lepromin skin test (not available in the U.S.)

Not diagnostic of exposure or infection with *M leprae.*

Assesses a patient's ability to mount a granulomatous response against a skin injection of killed *M leprae*.

Patients with Tuberculoid or borderline lepromatous leprosy typically have a positive response (>5 mm). Patients with lepromatous leprosy typically have no response.

PGL-1: This is A specific serologic test based on the detection of antibodies to phenolic glycolipid-1 (PGL-1).

This test has a sensitivity of 95% for the detection of lepromatous disease but only 30% for tuberculoid disease.

Lymphocyte Migration Inhibition Test (LMIT): Cell-mediated immunity to *M leprae* is absent in the lepromatous form of disease but present in the tuberculoid form of disease.

Treatment

Multi-Drug Treatment is recommended for prevention of resistance

Main Therapeutics

Dapsone

Rifampin

Clofazamine

The length of treatment ranges from 6 months to 2 years.

Patients are considered noninfectious within 1-2 weeks of treatment (usually after the first dose).

Other Drugs with activity against *M.Leprae*

Ofloxacin

Levofloxacin

Minocycline

Clarithyromycin

Natural Remedy

Gotu Kola

Centella asiatica

Other names: brahma-buti, centella, centellase, gotu cola, gotu kola, hydrocotyle, indian pennywort, indian water navelwort, marsh penny, talepetrako, tungchian, white rot.

Perennial herb native to swamps of Sri Lanka, India, South Africa and tropical regions.

Extract is primarily used for dermatologic problems – skin inflammation, burns, wounds, scars, leprosy.

Proposed mechanism of action – stimulate type I collagen production and increases collagen and fibronectin synthesis during wound healing.

Table 17-3: Multi-drug treatment of leprosy.

Type of Leprosy	Daily, Self-Administered	Monthly Supervised	Months of Treatment
Paucibacillary	Dapsone 100 mg	Rifampicin 600 mg	6-12 months
Multibacillary	Dapsone 100 mg	Rifampicin 600 mg	24 months
	Clofazimine 50 mg	Clofazimine 300 mg	
Pediatric	Dapsone 2 mg/kg	Rifampicin 10 mg/kg	Same as in adults
	Clofazimine 1 mg/kg	Clofazimine 6 mg/kg	

US regimens emphasize the use of rifampin, which is the most bactericidal drug used to treat leprosy. Although a single dose of 600 mg once monthly (the WHO standard) is considered bactericidal, treatment plans in the United States may include 600 mg/day doses.

Patients with Paucibacillary leprosy should receive Dapsone 100 mg/day unsupervised plus rifampin 600 mg/day supervised for 6-12 months. This regimen should be followed by treatment with dapsone as monotherapy for 3 years for tuberculoid leprosy and 5 years for borderline lepromatous leprosy.

Patients with multibacillary leprosy should receive (1) dapsone 100 mg/day plus clofazimine 50 mg/day unsupervised or (2) rifampin 600 mg/day plus clofazimine 300 mg every month supervised for 24 months.

Clofazamine

Phenazine dye used as an antimycobacterial and anti-inflammatory agent.

Binds preferentially to mycobacterial DNA and inhibits reproduction and growth.

Bactericidal against *M. tuberculosis* and *M. marinum* and slowly bactericidal against *M. Leprae.*

Bacteriostatic against other mycobacterium.

Much lower activity against other bacteria and none against fungi or protozoa.

Clofazimine
$C_{27}H_{22}Cl_2N_4$

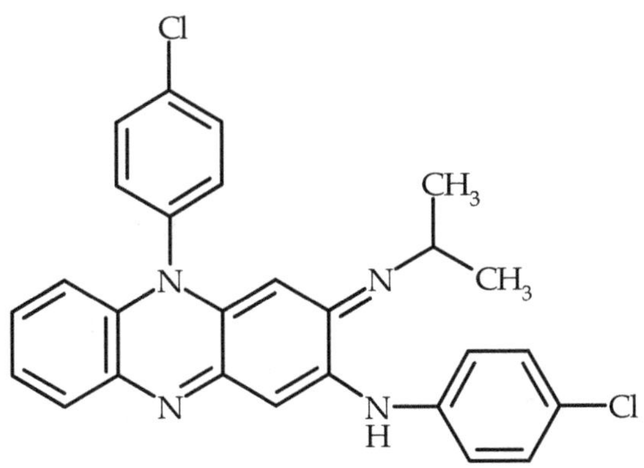

Fig 17-4: Structure of clofazamine.

Dapsone

Synthetic sulfone.

Inhibits Dihyropteroate synthase.

For many years, dapsone was the main therapy for leprosy.

Unfortunately, years of monotherapy has lead to significant resistance in this organism.

Resistance to *M. Leprae* develops in 2-10% of patients after prolonged administration.

MDT Side-Effects

Red coloured urine: This is due to Rifampicin. Lasts only for few hours. Reassure the patient that this is harmless.

Darkening of skin: This is due to clofazamine. Reassure the patient that this will disappear after treatment is completed.

Severe itching of skin: This is due to allergy to one of the drugs (commonly to dapsone). Stop all medicines and refer to hospital.

Complications of Medical Therapy

Careful attention to the development of reversal reactions during treatment and prompt and proper management minimizes long term neurologic sequelae.

Type 1 reaction

Reversal reaction, or leprae type 1 reaction.

A delayed type hypersensitivity reaction that arises when a borderline case shifts toward borderline lepromatous with treatment.

Reflect the development of an appropriate immune response and the local generation of tumor necrosis factor-alpha and interferon-gamma.

The reaction is characterized by edema and erythema of existing skin lesions, the formation of new skin lesions, neuritis and additional sensory and motor loss.

Treatment includes nonsteroidal anti-inflammatory drugs (NSAIDs) and high dose steroids.

Prednisone is given at a dose of 40-60 mg/day with a decreasing taper of 5 mg every 2-4 weeks.

Type 2 reaction

Erythema nodosum leprosum (ENL), also known as lepra type 2 reaction.

A complication of the lepromatous form of the disease.

It is characterized by the development of inflamed subcutaneous nodules accompanied at times by fever, lymphadenopathy and arthralgias.

Treatment includes prednisolone, clofazimine, or thalidomid.

Mild ENL reactions are treated with aspirin 600-1200 mg/day in 4-6 doses per day

Severe ENL reactions are treated with prednisone 60-80 mg/day with a slow taper, reducing by 5-10 mg every 2-4 weeks, depending on response and severity, to prevent residual deformity and nerve damage.

Alternatively, thalidomide 100 mg PO 4 times per day (if available and if no contraindications) can be used in cases that involve large subcutaneous plaques, arthritis and temperature of more than 38.8 °C.

Lucio phenomenon: A severe complication of multibacillary leprosy that is marked by blue hemorrhagic plaques and necrotic ulcerations.

The bacilli may extend to the endothelial cells along with the appearance of necrotic epidermis and vasculitis with thrombus formation and endothelial proliferation.

Surgical Treatments

Most surgery aims to remedy motor paralysis due to primary nerve impairment.

Claw hands are repaired with arthrodesis or with a tendon transfer to 1 of 4 insertion sites on the finger.

Tendon transfers are also used to repair abduction and opposition of the thumb, dorsiflexion of the foot and flexion and extension of the metacarpophalangeal and proximal interphalangeal joints, respectively.

Contractures of the hand, such as the thumb web contracture, can be repaired with Z-plasty, and joint stability can be improved with tenodesis.

Amputation is the last resort.

Eye procedures: Loss of eyelid function may be treated with passing a strip from the temporalis muscle through the eyelid and connecting it to the inner canthus.

Cosmetic surgery: After the disease is controlled medically, the following cosmetic procedures may also be considered:

Nasal reconstruction

Removal of excess skin

Replacement of eyebrows using transplants of scalp hair.

References

Anonymous (1997). Diagnosis and treatment of disease caused by nontuberculous mycobacteria. *Am J Respir Crit Care Med* **156(2 Part 2):** S1.

Anonymous (2000). Targeted tuberculin testing and treatment of latent tuberculosis infection. *Am J Respir Crit Care Med* **161(4 Part 2):** S221.

Gillespie SH et al (2005). Early bactericidal activity of a moxifloxacin and isoniazid combination in smear-positive pulmonary tuberculosis. *J Antimicrob Chemother* **56:** 1169. [PMID: 16223939]

Jasmer RM, Nahid P and Hopewell PC (2002). Latent tuberculosis infection. *N Engl J Med* **347:** 1860. [PMID: 12466511]

Kinzig-Schippers M et al (2005). Should we use *N*-acetyltransferase type 2 genotyping to personalize isoniazid doses? *Antimicrob Agents Chemother* **49:** 1733. [PMID: 15855489]

Sulochana S, Rahman F and Paramasivan CN (2005). *In vitro* activity of fluoroquinolones against *Mycobacterium tuberculosis*. *J Chemother* **17:** 169.[PMID: 15920901]

von der Lippe B, Sandven P and Brubakk O (2006). Efficacy and safety of linezolid in multidrug resistant tuberculosis (MDR-TB) — a report of ten cases. *J Infect* **52:** 92.

CHAPTER

Antifungal Drugs 18

Introduction

Human fungal infections have increased dramatically in incidence and severity in recent years, owing mainly to advances in surgery, cancer treatment and critical care accompanied by increases in the use of broad spectrum antimicrobials and the HIV epidemic. These changes have resulted in increased numbers of patients at risk for fungal infections.

Pharmacotherapy of fungal disease has been revolutionized by the introduction of the relatively nontoxic oral azole drugs and the echinocandins. Combination therapy is being reconsidered and new formulations of old agents are becoming available. Unfortunately, the appearance of azole resistant organisms, as well as the rise in the number of patients at risk for mycotic infections, has created new challenges.

Types of Fungal Infections - Mycoses

Superficial mycoses

Affect the skin, hair and nails

Subcutaneous mycoses (tropical)

Affect the muscle and connective tissue immediately below the skin

Systemic (invasive) mycoses

Involve the internal organs

Primary vs. opportunistic

Allergic mycoses

Affect lungs or sinuses

Patients may have chronic asthma, cystic fibrosis or sinusitis.

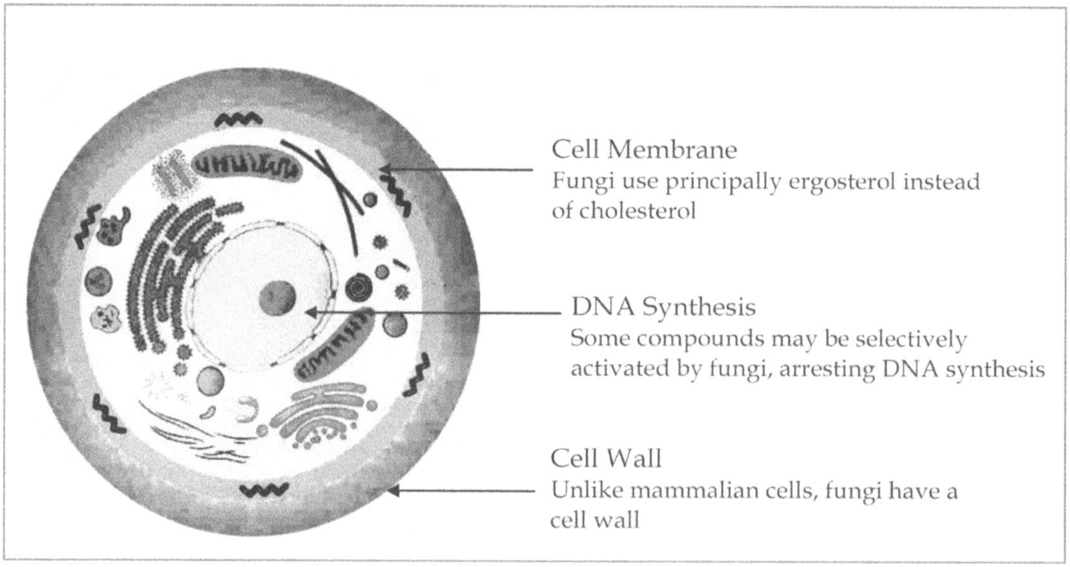

Fig 18-1: Targets for antifungal therapy.

Classification of Antifungals

Targets and classification of Antifungals are shown in Fig 18-1, 18-2.

1. **Drugs acting on Cell membrane**

   Polyene antibiotics

   Amphotericin B, lipid formulations

   Nystatin (topical)

   Azole antifungals

   Ketoconazole

   Itraconazole

   Fluconazole

   Voriconazole

   Miconazole, clotrimazole (and other topicals)

2. **Drugs acting on cell wall**

   Echinocandins

   Caspofungin acetate (Cancidas)

3. **DNA/RNA synthesis**

   Pyrimidine analogues

   Flucytosine

4. **Squalene epoxide inhibitors**

   Terbinafine, naftifine,butenafine

Azole Antifungals for Systemic Infections

Ketoconazole (Nizoril) - Imidazole

Itraconazole (Sporanox) ⎤ Triazoles
Fluconazole (Diflucan) ⎦

Voriconazole (Vfend) -"2nd generation triazole"

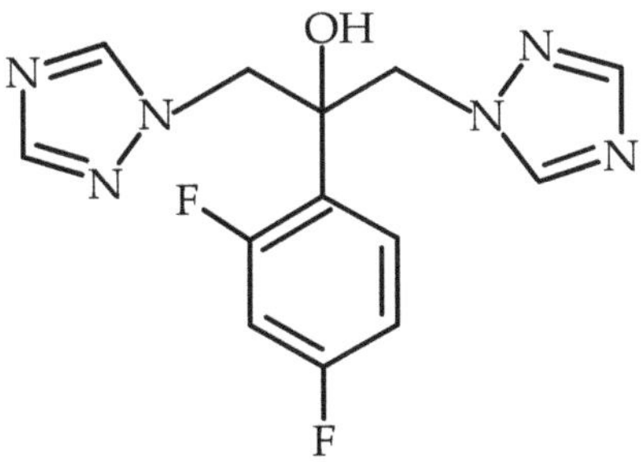

Fluconazole

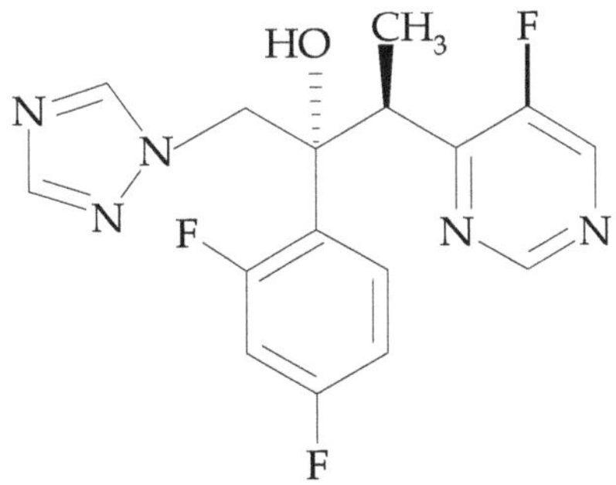

Voriconazole

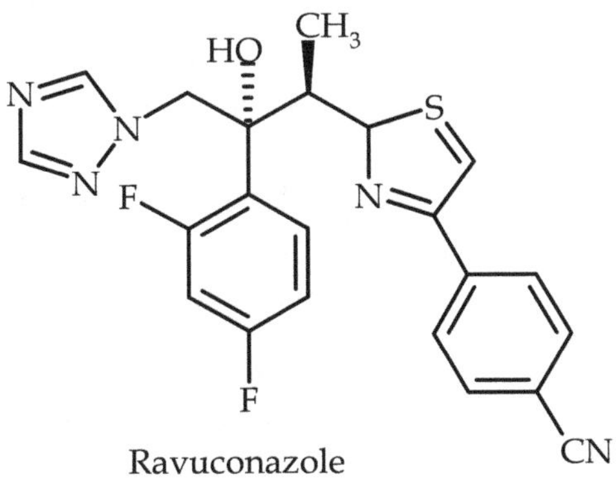

Ravuconazole

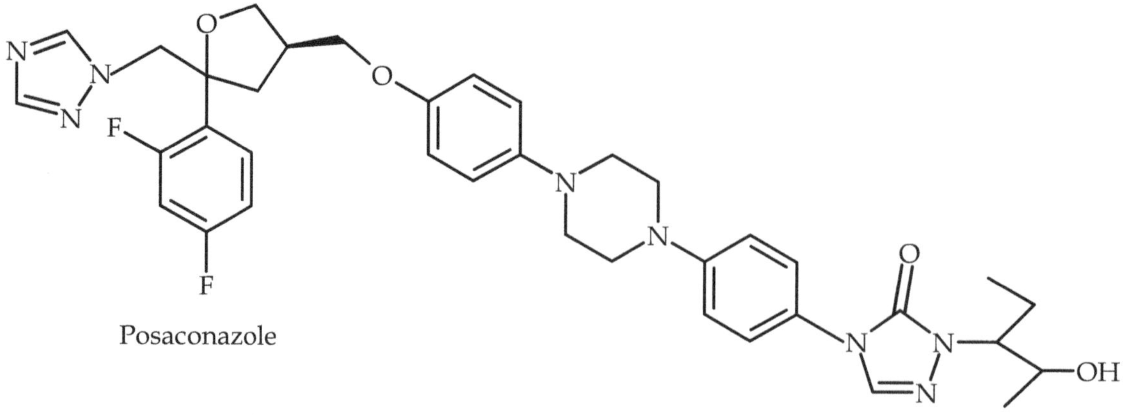

Posaconazole

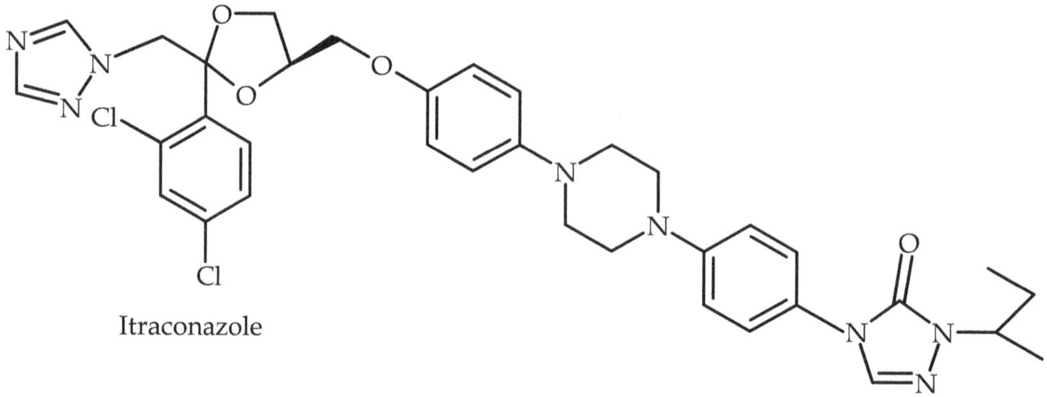

Itraconazole

Fig 18-2: Azole antifungal drugs.

Azoles – Mechanism

In fungi, the cytochrome P450-enzyme lanosterol 14-α demethylase is responsible for the conversion of lanosterol to ergosterol. Azoles bind to lanosterol 14-α demethylase inhibiting the production of ergosterol. The mechanism of Action of Azoles are shown in Fig 18-3.

Pharmacodynamics

Concentration independent fungistatic agents .

Dosage escalation may be necessary when faced with more resistant fungal species (e.g., *Candida glabrata*). Goal of dosing is to maintain AUC:MIC >50 i.e., maintain concentrations 1-2 x MIC for the entire dosing interval.

Spectrum of activity

Broad spectrum of activity against

- Candida.
- Cryptococcus neoformans
- Endemic mycosis (Blastomycosis, histoplasmosis)
- Dermatophytes.
- Asperigllus infection (voriconazole and itraconazole)

Ketoconazole

Ketoconazole (Fig 18-4) was the first orally active azole available for the treatment of systemic mycoses.

Mechanism of action

Azoles are predominantly fungistatic. They inhibit C-14 α-demethylase (a cytochrome P450 [CYP450] enzyme), thereby blocking the demethylation of lanosterol to ergosterol, the principal sterol of fungal membranes. This inhibition disrupts membrane structure and function, which in turn, inhibits fungal cell growth. The drug also inhibits human gonadal

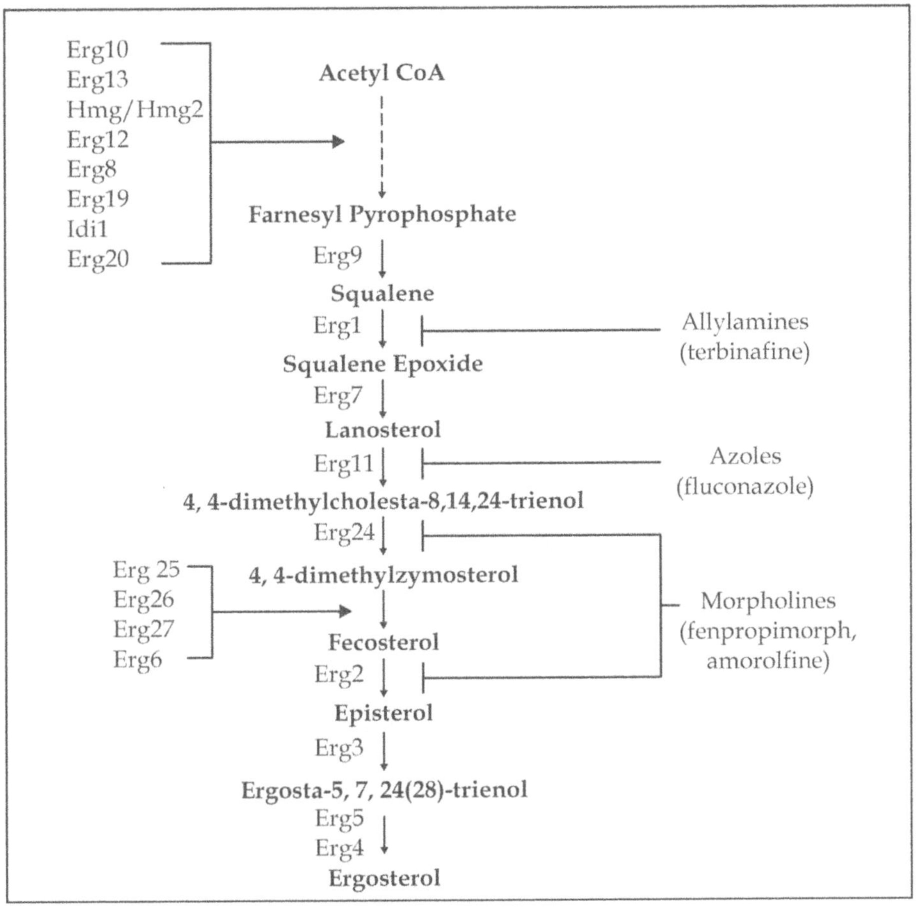

Fig 18-3: Mechanism of action of azoles.

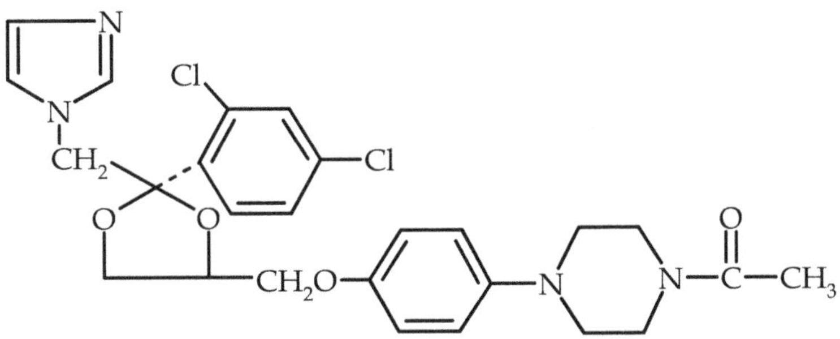

Fig 18-4: Ketoconazole structure.

and adrenal steroid synthesis, leading to decreased testosterone and cortisol production.

Antifungal spectrum: Oral ketoconazole is active against many fungi, including Histoplasma, Blastomyces, Candida and Coccidioides, but not aspergillus species. Itraconazole has largely replaced ketoconazole in the treatment of most mycoses because of its broader spectrum, greater potency and fewer adverse effects. Topical ketoconazole is used to treat tinea corporis, tinea cruris and tinea pedis. Also, topical ketoconazole is used to treat tinea versicolor, cutaneous candidiasis caused by Candida species. It is also used topically in the treatment of seborrheic dermatitis and dandruff.

Resistance: Identified mechanisms of resistance include mutations in the C-14 α-demethylase gene, which cause decreased azole binding. Additionally, some strains of fungi have developed the ability to pump the azole out of the cell.

Pharmacokinetics

When ketoconazole is administered orally, it requires gastric acid for dissolution and is absorbed through the intestinal mucosa. Administering acidifying agents before taking the drug can improve absorption in patients with achlorhydria. Ketoconazole is extensively bound to plasma proteins. Extensive metabolism occurs in the liver and excretion is primarily through the bile. (Table 18-1).

Adverse Effects

In addition to allergies, dose-dependent gastrointestinal disturbances, including nausea, anorexia and vomiting, are the most common adverse effects of ketoconazole treatment. Endocrine effects, such as gynecomastia, decreased libido, impotence, and menstrual irregularities, result from the blocking of androgen and adrenal steroid synthesis by ketoconazole. Frank hepatitis occurs rarely, but requires immediate cessation of ketoconazole treatment.

Drug interactions and contraindications

By inhibiting CYP450, ketoconazole can potentiate the toxicities of drugs such as cyclosporine. Rifampin, an inducer of the CYP450 system, can shorten the duration of action of ketoconazole. Drugs that decrease gastric acidity, such as H2-receptor blockers, antacids and proton-pump inhibitors, can decrease absorption of ketoconazole. Finally, ketoconazole is teratogenic in animals and it should not be given during pregnancy.

Fluconazole

Fluconazole is a member of the triazole class of antifungal products. It is clinically important because of its lack of the endocrine side effects of ketoconazole and its excellent penetrability into the CSF of both normal and inflamed meninges. Fluconazole is employed prophylactically, with

Table 18-1: Key biopharmaceutical characteristics of the triazole antifungals.

	Fluconazole	Itraconazole	Voriconazole
Spectrum vs. Candida and Aspergillus	C. albicans, C. tropicalis +/- C. glabrata Not Aspergillus	Similar Candida coverage as fluconazole, + Aspergillus	Broad, includes most Candida spp., Aspergillus, Fusarium sp. Not Zygomycoses
Oral formulation (% bioavailibility)	Tablet (>90%)	Capsule (6-25%) Solution (20-60%)	Tablet (>90%)
Intravenous formulation	Available, no solubilizer	Available, cyclodextrin	Available, cyclodextrin
Clearance	Renal (80%)	Hepatic 3A4	Hepatic 2C19, 3A4
Serum half life (hr)	24	24-30	6-24
CSF penetration	Excellent	Poor	Excellent
CYP 3A4 inhibition	Weak	Strong	Moderate-Strong
Adverse effects	Hepatic	Diarrhea (solution), hepatic, CHF	Visual disturbances, hepatic, rash

some success, for reducing fungal infections in recipients of bone marrow transplants. It inhibits the synthesis of fungal membrane ergosterol in the same manner as ketoconazole and is the drug of choice for Cryptococcus neoformans after therapy with amphotericin B, for most candidemias and for coccidioidomycosis. Fluconazole is effective against most forms of mucocutaneous candidiasis. Fluconazole is administered orally or intravenously. For the treatment of vaginal candidiasis, the dose is 150 mg as a single oral dose. The adverse effects caused by fluconazole treatment are less of a problem than those with ketoconazole. However, it can inhibit the P450 cytochromes that metabolize other drugs. Nausea vomiting, and rashes are a problem. There is a caution for patients with liver dysfunction. Fluconazole is teratogenic, as are other azoles and should not be used in pregnancy.

Itraconazole

Itraconazole is an antifungal agent with a broad antifungal spectrum. Like fluconazole, it is a synthetic triazole and also lacks the endocrinologic side effects of ketoconazole. Its mechanism of action is the same as that of the other triazoles. Itraconazole is the drug of choice for the treatment of blastomycosis, sporotrichosis, paracoccidioidomycosis and histoplasmosis. Itraconazole is well absorbed orally, but it requires acid for dissolution. Food increases the bioavailability of some preparations. Adverse effects include nausea and vomiting, rash, hypokalemia, hypertension, edema and headache. Itraconazole should be avoided in pregnancy. The capsules should not be taken by patients with evidence of ventricular dysfunction.

Voriconazole

Voriconazole, a triazole, has the advantage of being a broad spectrum antifungal agent. It is available for both i.v and oral administration and is approximately 96 percent bioavailable. Voriconazole is approved for the treatment of invasive aspergillosis and has replaced amphotericin B as the treatment of choice for this indication. Voriconazole is also approved for treatment of serious infections. Side effects are similar to those of the other azoles. High trough concentrations are associated with visual and auditory hallucinations.

Posaconazole

A triazole, is a new oral, broadspectrum antifungal agent with a chemical structure similar to that of itraconazole: It was approved in 2006 to prevent Candida and Aspergillus infections. Due to its spectrum of activity, posaconazole could possibly be used in the treatment of fungal infections caused by Mucor species and other zygomycetes. To date, amphotericin B formulations are the only other antifungal agents available for treatment of zygomycete infections. The most common side effects observed were gastrointestinal issues (nausea, vomiting, diarrhea and abdominal pain) and headaches. Rare cases of hemolytic uremic syndrome, thrombotic thrombocytopenic purpura and pulmonary embolus have been reported. To be effective, posaconazole must be administered with a high fat meal.

Amphotericin B

Amphotericin B (Fig 18-5) is a naturally occurring polyene macrolide antibiotic produced by Streptomyces nodosus. In spite of its toxic potential, amphotericin B is the drug of choice for the treatment of life threatening systemic mycoses.

Mechanism of Action

Several amphotericin B molecules bind to ergosterol in the plasma membranes of sensitive fungal cells. There, they form pores (channels). The pores disrupt membrane function, allowing electrolytes (particularly potassium) and small molecules to leak from the cell, resulting in cell death.

Antifungal Spectrum

Amphotericin B is either fungicidal or fungistatic, depending on the organism and the concentration of the drug. It is effective against a wide range of fungi, including Candida albicans, Histoplasma capsulatum, Cryptococcus neoformans, Coccidioides immitis, Blastomyces dermatitidis, and many strains of Aspergillus.

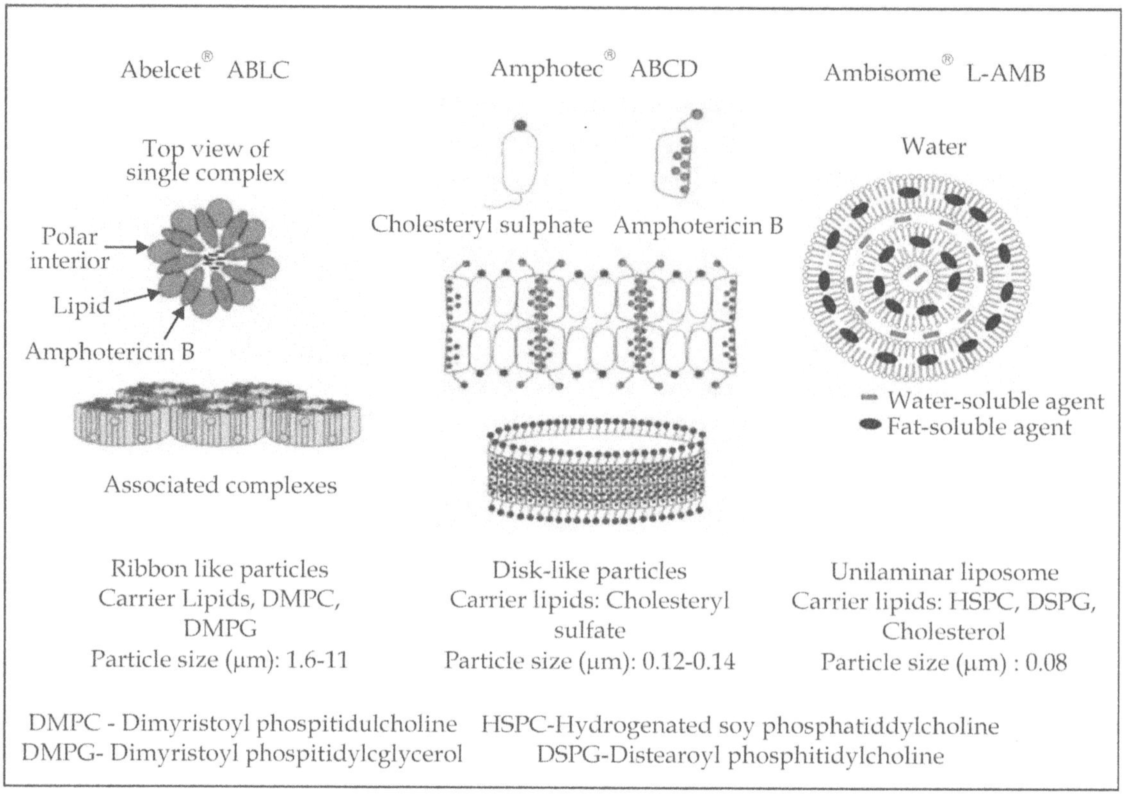

Fig 18-5: Lipid amphotericin B formulations.

[Note: Amphotericin B is also used in the treatment of the protozoal infection leishmaniasis.]

Resistance

Fungal resistance, although infrequent, is associated with decreased ergosterol content of the fungal membrane.

Pharmacokinetics

Amphotericin B is administered by slow, intravenous (i.v) infusion. The three amphotericin B lipid formulations marketed in the United States are AMPHOTEC, ABELCET and AMBISOME. These liposomal preparations have the primary advantage of reduced renal and infusion toxicity. Amphotericin B is extensively bound to plasma proteins and is distributed throughout the body. To minimize nephrotoxicity, alternatives including sodium loading with infusions of normal saline and the lipid-based amphotericin B products are used.

Classic Amphotericin B deoxycholate (Fungizone™) formulation: serious toxic side effects.

Less toxic preparations:

1. Liposomal Amphotericin B
2. Amphotericin B colloidal dispersion
3. Amphotericin B lipid complex

Dosing and Administration

"Test dose" 1.0 mg in 25-100 ml 5% dextrose infused over 10 minutes used to evaluate possibility of anaphylactic reaction. No longer recommended, current product has fewer impurities. Current recommendation is to Start with ~30% of target dose, infuse for 15 minutes, stop infusion and monitor patient for adverse effects before resuming infusion. With leads to escalate to full dosages within 48-72 hours. Delay in giving full dose = worse clinical outcome

Clinical Uses

The drug of choice for: Cryptococcal meningitis, Mucormycosis (zygomycosis) and Invasive fungal infection.

Adverse effects

Amphotericin B has a low therapeutic index. The total adult daily dose should not exceed 1.5 mg/kg. Small test doses may be administered to assess the degree of negative responses, such as anaphylaxis or convulsions. Other toxic manifestations include the following.

(a) ***Fever and chills:*** These occur most commonly 1 to 3 hours after starting the IV administration, but they usually subside with repeated administration of the drug.

(b) ***Renal impairment:*** Despite the low levels of the drug excreted in the urine, patients may exhibit a decrease in glomerular filtration rate and renal tubular function. Creatinine clearance can drop and potassium and magnesium are lost.

(c) ***Hypotension:*** A shock-like fall in blood pressure accompanied by hypokalemia may occur, requiring potassium supplementation.

(d) ***Anemia:*** Normochromic, normocytic anemia caused by a reversible suppression of erythrocyte production may occur.

(e) ***Neurologic effects:*** Intrathecal administration can cause a variety of serious neurologic problems.

(f) ***Thrombophlebitis:*** Adding heparin to the infusion can alleviate this problem.

Drug Interactions

Enhanced nephrotoxicity occurs with Nephrotoxic drugs like Cyclosporine, aminoglycosides, foscarnet, pentamidine and Antineoplastic agents like Cisplatin, nitrogen mustards

Flucytosine

Flucytosine was synthesized in 1957 as an antitumor agent. It was inactive but it was found to have antifungal activity.

Mechanism of Action

The drug enters the fungal cell through active transport on ATPases that normally transport pyrimidines. Once inside cells, fungal cytosine deaminase convert the drug to active 5-

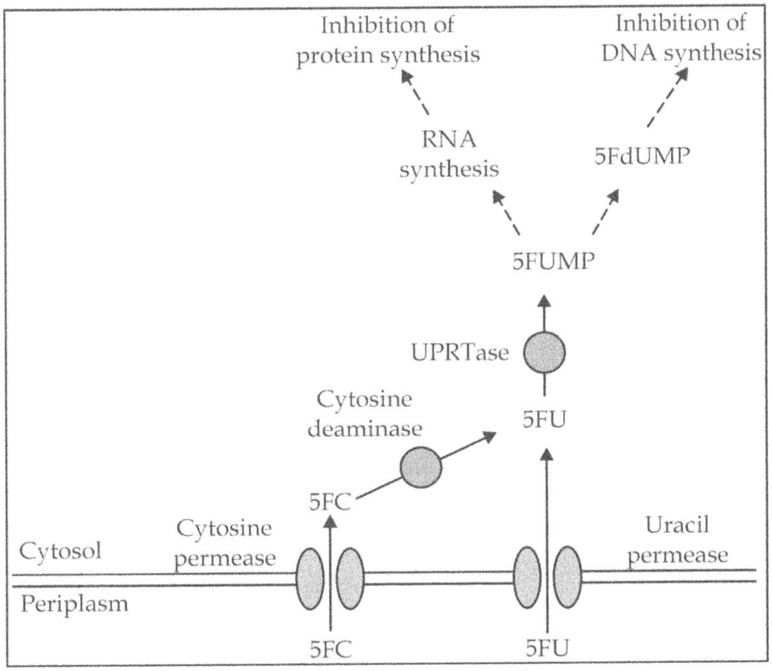

Fig 18-6: Mechanism of action of flucytosine.

fluorouracil (5FU, a very effective antitumor agent, by the way!) which is incorporated into RNA causing faulty RNA synthesis and also is a strong, non competitive inhibitor of thymidylate synthesis interrupting the one carbon pool substrate. Mammalian cells do not contain cytosine deaminase. The mechanism of Action of Flucytosine is shown in Fig 18-6.

Resistance

Resistance develops rapidly and occurs on many levels e.g., transport into the cell and cytosine deaminase steps. After a few dosing intervals the drug is essentially useless. To avoid rapid resistance, combination with Amphotericin B and the combination is synergistic.

Pharmacokinetics

The drug is well absorbed and well distributed. CSF levels are 65-90% of plasma levels. Is eliminated unchanged largely in the urine (Table 18-2).

Table 18-2: Pharmacokinetics of flucytosine

Clinical Uses

It is also synergistic with itraconazole and fluconazole and interest in these combinations for treatment of systemic Candida infections is increasing. Amphotericin B damaged membranes are thought to allow better entry of flucytosine. Used (with Amp. B) for Cryptococcal meningitis, systemic Candida infections and some other systemic fungal infections. This is an oral drug. Good also for fungal UTI.

Adverse Effects

GI upset, hepatic involvement seen in the increase in transaminases, Hematologic involvement include anemia, leucopenia. Thrombocytopenia is the major complication of therapy and may be due to low levels of 5-FU circulating.

Squalene Epoxidase Inhibitors

These agents act by inhibiting squalene epoxidase, resulting in the blocking of the biosynthesis of ergosterol, an essential component of fungal cell membrane.

Terbinafine

Oral terbinafine (Fig 18-7) is the drug of choice for treating dermatophytoses and especially, onycho-mycoses (fungal infections of nails). It is better tolerated, requires shorter duration of therapy and is more effective than either itraconazole or griseofulvin.

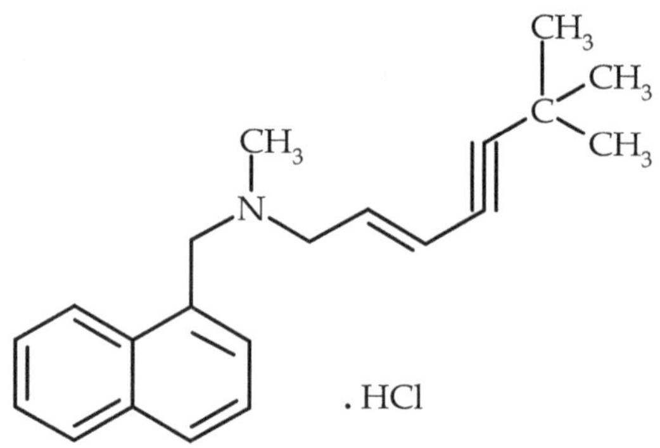

Fig 18-7: Structure of terbinafine.

Mechanism of Action

Terbinafine inhibits fungal squalene epoxidase, thereby decreasing the synthesis of ergosterol. This plus the accumulation of toxic amounts of squalene result in the death of the fungal cell.

Antifungal Spectrum

The drug is primarily fungicidal. Topical terbinafine is active against Trichophyton. It may also be effective against Candida albicans, Epidermophyton floccosum. Topical terbinafine 1% cream and solution are used to treat tinea pedis, tinea corporis and tinea cruris. Therapy is prolonged (usually about 3 months) but considerably shorter than that with griseofulvin.

Pharmacokinetics

Terbinafine is available for oral and topical administration, although its bioavailability is only 40 percent due to first pass metabolism. Absorption is not significantly enhanced by food. Terbinafine is greater than 99 percent bound to plasma proteins. It is deposited in the skin, nails and fat. Terbinafine accumulates in breast milk and should not be given to nursing mothers. A prolonged terminal half-life of 200 to 400 hours may reflect the slow release from these tissues.

Adverse Effects

The most common adverse effects from terbinafine are gastrointestinal disturbances (diarrhea, dyspepsia and nausea), headache, and rash. Taste and visual disturbances have been reported. Rarely, terbinafine may cause hepatotoxicity and neutropenia.

Naftifine: Naftifine is active against Trichophyton and Epidermophyton floccosum. Naftifine 1% cream and gel is used for topical treatment of tinea corporis, tinea cruris, and tinea pedis.

Butenafine: Butenafine is active against Trichophyton, Epidermophyton and Malassezia. Butenafine 1% cream is used for topical treatment of tinea corporis, tinea cruris, interdigital tinea pedis and tinea versicolor.

Griseofulvin

It is an antifungal produced from *Penicillium griseofulvin*. Therapy must continue until new tissue replaces old diseased tissue. When given orally, plasma-borne griseofulvin becomes incorporated into keratin precursor cells and ultimately into kearatin that cannot support fungal growth. Griseofulvin has been largely replaced by oral terbinafine for the treatment of dermatophytic infections of the nails, although it is still used for ringworm and dermatophytosis of the skin and hair.

Mechanism of Action

Griseofulvin inhibits microtubule polymerization thus inhibiting the formation of the mitotic spindle.

Pharmacokinetics

Griseofulvin requires treatment of 6 to 12 months in duration. Griseofulvin absorption is enhanced by high fat meals. Griseofulvin induces hepatic CYP450 activity. It also increases the rate of metabolism of a number of drugs, including anticoagulants.

Adverse Effects

Headache is a common adverse effect. May cause aplastic anemia. Being gradually replaced by newer agent.

Nystatin

Mechanism of Action

Nystatin is a polyene macrolide much like amphotericin B. Binds to ergosterol in fungal membrane causing membrane to become leaky.

Pharmacokinetics

It is too toxic for parenteral administration and is only used topically. Nystatin is currently available in creams, ointments, suppositories and other forms for application to skin and mucous membranes. It is not absorbed to a significant degree from skin, mucous membranes, or the gastrointestinal tract. As a result, nystatin has little toxicity, although oral use is often limited by the unpleasant taste. Nystatin will treat gut candidiasis and is used in a "swish and swallow" routine for oral candidiasis.

Clinical Uses

Nystatin is active against most candida species and is most commonly used for suppression of local candidal infections. Some common indications include oropharyngeal thrush, vaginal candidiasis and intertriginous candidal infections.

Adverse Effects

No significant adverse effects with these uses, however itching, irritation and burning may occur. Rarely nystatin can cause diarrhea and nausea Nystatin can be combined with tetracycline to prevent monilial overgrowth caused by the destruction of bacterial microflora of the intestine during tetracycline therapy

Ciclopirox

Ciclopirox (Fig 18-8) is a topical solution used to treat fungal infections of the nails and hair. It is a broad spectrum antifungal medication that also has antibacterial and anti-inflammatory properties.

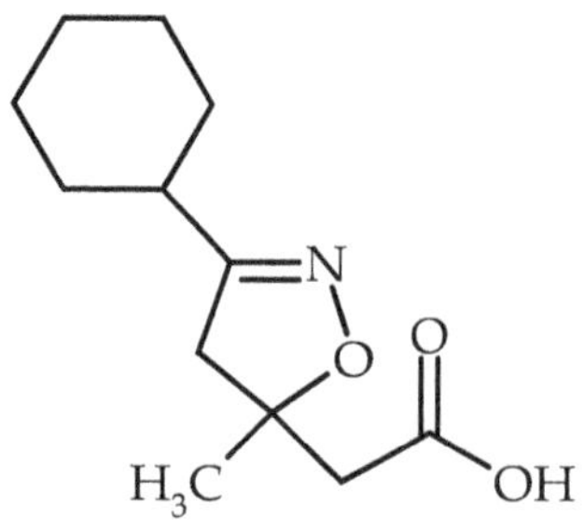

Fig 18-8: Structure of ciclopirox.

Mechanism of Action

Its main mode of action is thought to be its high affinity for trivalent cations, which inhibit essential co factors in enzymes. Ciclopirox is thought to act through the chelation of polyvalent metal cations, such as Fe^{3+} and Al^{3+}. These cations inhibit many enzymes, including cytochromes, possibly disrupting the biosynthesis of ergosterol. Ciclopirox also appears to modify the plasma membrane of fungi, resulting in the disorganization of internal structures.

Spectrum of Activity

Ciclopirox exhibits either fungistatic or fungicidal activity in vitro against a broad spectrum of fungal organisms, such as dermatophytes, yeasts, dimorphic fungi, eumycetes and actinomycetes. In addition to its broad spectrum of action, ciclopirox also exerts antibacterial activity against many Gram positive and Gramnegative bacteria. Ciclopirox is active against Trichophyton, Epidermophyton, Microsporum, Candida albicans and Malassezia.

Clinical Uses

The anti inflammatory effects of ciclopirox have been demonstrated in human polymorphonuclear cells, where ciclopirox has inhibited the synthesis of prostaglandin and leukotriene. Ciclopirox can also exhibit its anti inflammatory effects by inhibiting the formation of 5 lipoxygenase and cyclooxygenase. Ciclopirox 1% shampoo is used for treatment of seborrheic dermatitis. Ciclopirox 0.77% gel is used for treatment of interdigital tinea pedis, tinea corporis and seborrheic dermatitis. Ciclopirox 8% solution is used for treatment of onychomycosis of nails without lanula involvement. Ciclopirox 0.77% cream and suspension is used for treatment of dermatomycosis, candidiasis and tinea versicolor.

Adverse Effects

Redness, irritation, burning, blistering or swelling at the site of application and discoloration of the nails or surrounding area. Treated nails may become ingrown.

Tolnaftate

Tolnaftate distorts the hyphae and stunts mycelial growth in susceptible fungi. Tolnaftate is active against Epidermophyton, Microsporum and Malassezia furfur. [Note: Tolnaftate is not effective against Candida.] Tolnaftate is used to treat tinea pedis, tinea cruris and tinea corporis. It is available as a 1% solution, cream and powder.

Cell Wall Inhibitors

Echinocandins - Pharmacology

Cyclic lipopeptide antibiotics that interfere with fungal cell wall synthesis by inhibition of β-(1,3) D-glucan synthase. Loss of cell wall glucan results in osmotic fragility. Caspofungin, micafungin and anidulafungin are available for i.v adminstration once daily.

Spectrum

Candida species including non albicans isolates resistant to Fluconazole. *Aspergillus spp.* but not activity against other moulds (Fusarium, Zygomycosis). No coverage of Cryptococcus neoformans

Caspofungin: Caspofungin is the first approved member of the echinocandins class of antifungal drugs. Caspofungin has activity against Aspergillus and most Candida species, including those species resistant to azoles. Adverse effects include fever, rash, nausea and phlebitis. Flushing occurs. The dose of caspofungin does not need to be adjusted in renal impairment but is warranted with moderate hepatic dysfunction. Caspofungin is a second line antifungal for those who have failed or cannot tolerate amphotericin B or an azole. (Table 18-3)

Micafungin and Anidulafungin: Micafungin and Anidulafungin (Table 18-4) are the newer members of the echinocandins class of antifungal drugs. Micafungin and anidulafungin have similar efficacy against Candida species. The dose of micafungin and anidulafungin does not need to be adjusted in renal impairment or mild to-moderate hepatic dysfunction. Also, they are not substrates for CYP450 enzymes and do not have any associated drug interactions.

Undecylenic Acid

It is widely used topically as the zinc salt in OTC preparations for topical treatment of infections by dermatophytes.

Mechanism of Action

This organic acid will interact non specifically with components in the cell membrane. It can be used in concentrations up to 10% in solution, powder and emulsions.

The drugs of Antifungals are shown in Table 18-5.

Traditionally used for athlete's foot (tinea pedis) although cure rates are low.

Adverse effects are rare. Skin irritation has been reported.

Table 18-3: Pharmacokinetics of caspofungin.

Absorption	< 2%
Distribution (Vd)	9.67 L
Protein binding	97% albumin
Major metabolic pathway	Peptide hydrolysis, SlowN acetylation
t 1/2	9-11 hours
CNS penetration Dosage adjustment	Probably poor Moderate-severe hepatic dysfunction
Drug Drug interactions	Significant interactions CSA, FK-506, Mycophenolate, Inducers of 3A4.

Table 18-4: Comparative pharmacokinetics of echinocandins.

	Caspofungin	Micafungin	Anidulafungin
Administration	i.v Only	i.v Only	i.v Only
$T_{1/2}$	9-11 hr	11-15 hr	24-48 hr Longest
Uses	Mucocutaneous candidiasis Invasive aspergillosis Febrile neutropenia	Mucocutaneous candidiasis prophylaxis in bone marrow transplants	Esophageal & invasive candidiasis
	elevated liver enzymes with cyclosporine	elevated plasma levels of cyclosporine, sirolimus, nifedipine	histamine release upon i.v infusion

Table 18-5: Dosages of antifungals.

Polyenes	
Amphotericin B deoxycholate	1 mg/kg/day i.v
Lipo-AMB (AmBisome)	3 mg/kg/day i.v
ABLC (Abelcet)	5 mg/kg/day i.v
Amphocil	3 mg/kg/day i.v
Triazoles	
Fluconazole	400/800 mg i.v
Itraconazole	400 mg i.v
Voriconazole	4 mg/kg i.v
Echinocandins	
Caspofungin	50 mg i.v x 1 day,

Other Inhibitors of Fungal Cell Wall Synthesis: Under Development

Other β-1,3 glucan synthetase inhibitors: Papulacandins - glycolipid antifungal produced by *papularia sp.* Loss of β-glucan results in weakening of the cell wall, thus internal pressures can cause the cells to lyse

Chitin Synthase inhibitors: Polyoxins and Nikkomycins- nucleoside peptides. Chitin is also a major component to the cell wall and its loss will also weaken the cell walls.

C Mannan binding antifungals: Pradimicins and benanomicins. *C mannan* is a cell wall glycoprotein that combats the host immune response through disruption of cytokine response and possibly T-lymphocyte action.

References

Diekema DJ et al (2003). Activities of caspofungin, itraconazole, posaconazole, ravuconazole, voriconazole and amphotericin B against 448 recent clinical isolates of filamentous fungi. *J Clin Microbiol* **41:** 3623.

Groll A, Piscitelli SC and Walsh TJ (1998). Clinical pharmacology of systemic antifungal agents: A comprehensive review of agents in clinical use, current investigational compounds and putative targets for antifungal drug development. *Adv Pharmacol* **44:** 343.

Herbrecht R et al (2002). Voriconazole versus amphotericin B for primary therapy of invasive aspergillosis. *N Engl J Med* **347:** 408.

Sheehan DJ, Hitchcock CA and Sibley CM (1999). Current and emerging azole antifungal agents. *Clin Microbiol Rev* **12:** 40.

Wiederhold NP and Lewis RE (2003). The echinocandin antifungals: An overview of the pharmacology, spectrum and clinical efficacy. *Expert Opin Investig Drugs* **12:** 1313.

CHAPTER

Antiprotozoal Drugs 19

Protozoal Infections

Protozoal infections are a major cause of disease in many parts of the world. Although some of these diseases are endemic to the United States or can be found in migrant workers or individuals returning from an endemic area, many other such infections are rarely seen in the United States. However, physicians should be aware of these diseases and seek advice from those experienced in their diagnosis and treatment. Some of the protozoal infections includes

Malaria

Leishmaniasis

Amebiasis

Giardiasis

Trichomoniasis

Malaria

Cause

Four species of plasmodium typically cause human malaria:

Plasmodium falciparum

P vivax

P malariae,

P ovale.

A fifth species, P knowlesi, is primarily a pathogen of monkeys, but has recently been recognized to cause illness, including severe disease, in humans in Asia.

Although all of the species may cause significant illness, *P falciparum* is responsible for the majority of serious complications and deaths.

Drug resistance is an important therapeutic problem, most notably with P. falciparum.

Parasite Life Cycle

Life cycle of Malarial Parasite is shown in Fig 19-1.

An anopheles mosquito/infected syringe inoculates plasmodium sporozoites to initiate human infection.

Circulating sporozoites rapidly invade liver cells and exoerythrocytic stage tissue schizonts mature in the liver.

Merozoites are subsequently released from the liver and invade erythrocytes. Only erythrocytic parasites cause clinical illness.

Repeated cycles of infection can lead to the infection of many erythrocytes and serious disease.

Sexual stage gametocytes also develop in erythrocytes before being taken up by mosquitoes, where they develop into infective sporozoites.

In P falciparum and P malariae infection, only one cycle of lever cell invasion and multiplication occurs and liver infection ceases spontaneously in less than 4 weeks.

Thus, treatment that eliminates erythrocytic parasites will cure these infections.

In P vivax and P ovale infections, a dormant hepatic stage, the hypnozoite, is not eradicated by most drugs and subsequent relapses can therefore occur after therapy directed against erythrocytic parasites.

Eradication of both erythrocytic and hepatic parasites is required to cure these infections.

Anti malarial Drugs may be selected for: Prevention of clinical attacks(Chemoprophylaxis)

Treatment of clinical attack

Radical cure

Classification of Anti Malarial Drugs according to Site of Action

Tissue Hepatic Schizonticides/Acting on Hepatic cycle

Drug effective against primary tissue forms **Pre erythrocytic stage/for Causal prophylaxis.** *Proguanil*

Drug effective against developing or dormant tissue forms/**for Terminal prophylaxis or Radical cure**. *Primaquine*

Blood Schizonticides/Drug acting on Erythrocytic parasites/ for Suppressive cure

Rapidly acting Blood Schizonticides

Chloroquine

Amodiaquine

Piperaquine

Quinine

Mefloquine

Halofantrine

Artemisinin (Qinghaosu) and its derivatives i.e., Artemether, Artesunate, dihydro artemisinin

Slower acting Blood Schizonticides

Proguanil

Doxycycline

Pyrimethamine

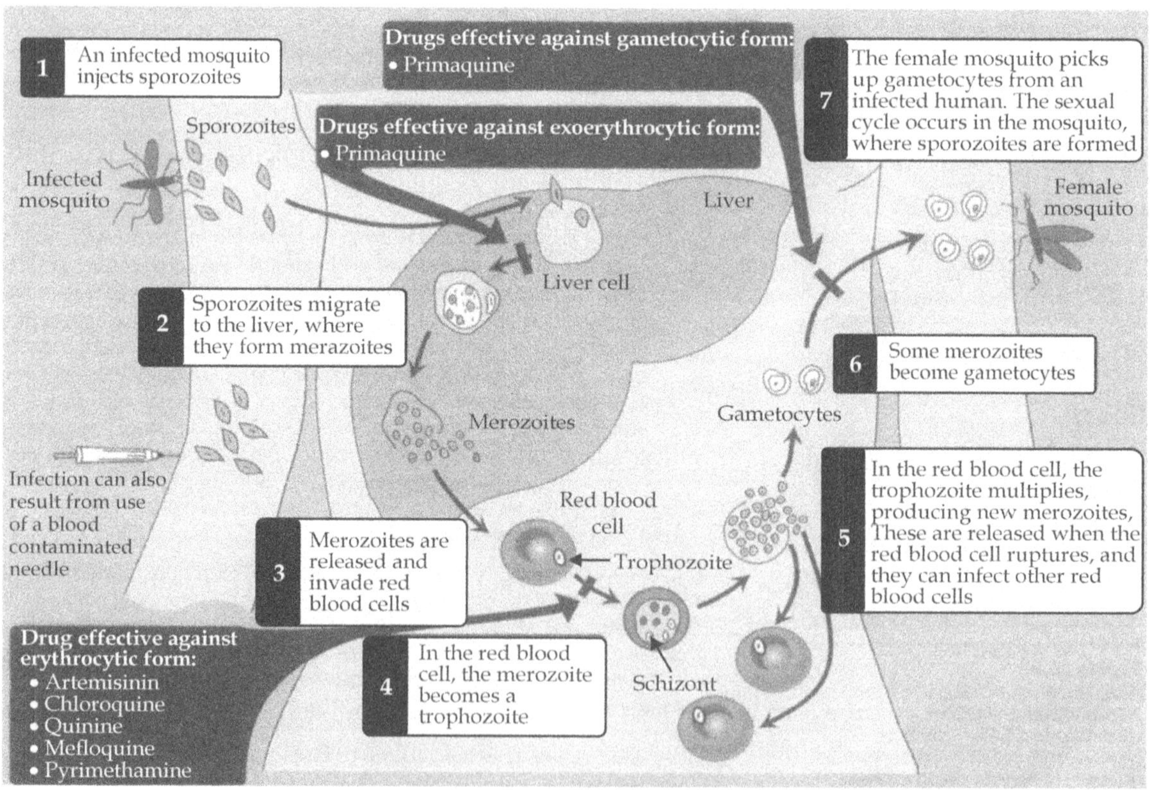

Fig 19-1: Life cycle of malarial parasite plasmodium falciparum, showing the sites of antimalarial drugs.

Gametocides/against sexual Erythrocytic forms

Primaquine is used against *P. Falciparum*, Chloroquine, Quinine used against *P Vivax, P Ovale*. They kills sexual forms and prevents transmission to mosquitoes.

Chloroquine

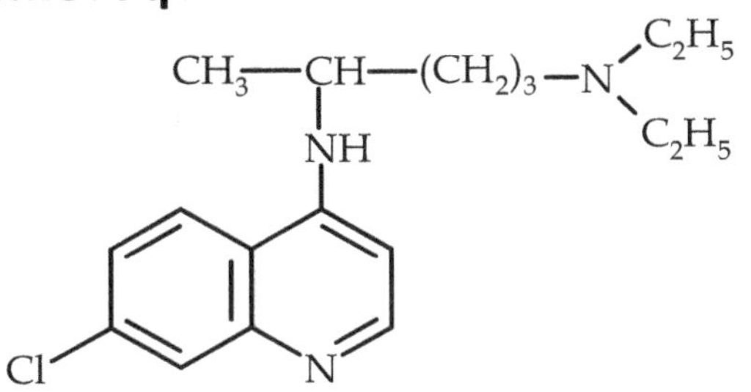

Fig 19-2: Structure of chloroquine.

Chloroquine (*Aralen*) Fig 19-2 is one of several 4-aminoquinoline derivatives that display antimalarial activity. Chloroquine is particularly effective against intraerythrocytic forms because it is concentrated within the parasitized erythrocyte. This preferential drug accumulation appears to occur as a result of speciûc uptake mechanisms in the parasite. It is highly effective blood schizonticide.

Mechanism of action

Chloroquine probably acts as follows: Chloroquine is a weak base; it is concentrated in parasite's food vacuoles by ion trapping. Malarial Parasites utilize hemoglobin as food, it is broken down in to heme which is toxic but it is polymerized into harmless hemozoin by enzyme haem polymerase. Chloroquine prevents biocrystallization of heme in to Hemozoin, by inhibiting Haem polymerase. Increased pH and accumulation of toxic heme, produces oxidative damage to the membranes, leading to lysis of both the Malarial Parasites & RBCs.

Pharmacokinetics

The absorption of chloroquine from the gastrointestinal tract is rapid and complete. Aborption is well & almost complete from GIT and it is decreased by Kaolin and antacids containing Calcium and Magnesium.

The drug is distributed widely and is extensively bound to body tissues, with the liver containing 500 times the blood concentration. Such binding is reflected in a large volume of distribution (V_d). The drug is concentrated in RBCs, liver, spleen, kidney, lung, melanin containing tissues. It also penetrates into the CNS & traverses placenta.

The drug is very slowly released & metabolized in the liver. Desethylchloroquine is the major metabolite formed following hepatic metabolism.

The parent compound and its metabolites are slowly eliminated by renal excretion. The half life of the drug is 6 to 7 days. Excretion rate is enhanced if urine is acidified. Initial $t_{½}$: 1-2 days and terminal elimination $t_{½}$: 1-2 months

Dose: Chloroquine Phosphate tablet is administered orally. (tab 250 mg, Chloroquine base is 150 mg), 4 tablets (1mg)starting Then 2 tab(500mg) at 6, 24, 48 hrs.

Resistance to chloroquine

Resistance is very commonly seen in P falciparum. In *P falciparum*, it has been correlated with mutations in a transporter, PfCRT. There is decreased accumulation of drug in malaria parasite. It can be reversed by verapamil, desipramine and chlorpheniramine, clinical value not established.

Therapeutic uses

1. ***Acute attack of Malaria:*** Chloroquine is safe & cost effective. It terminates fever rapidly in 24-48 hr. Clears parasitemia in 48-72 hr. It is highly effective blood schizonticide for all species. It is a moderate Gametocide for P vivax, P. ovale & P. malariea. It has no effect on liver stages, so primaquine is added for radical cure. Safe to use in pregnant women & in young children.
2. ***Chemoprophylaxis of Malaria:*** The drug is effective against all four types of malaria with the exception of chloroquine resistant *P. falciparum*. Chloroquine destroys the blood

stages of the infection and therefore ameliorates the clinical symptoms seen in *P. malariae, P. vivax, P. ovale* and sensitive *P. falciparum* forms of malaria. The disease will return in *P. vivax* and *P. ovale* malaria, however, unless the liver stages are sequentially treated with primaquine after the administration of chloroquine. Chloroquine also can be used prophylactically in areas where resistance does not exist. In addition to its use as an antimalarial, chloroquine has been used in the treatment of rheumatoid arthritis and lupus erythematosus, extraintestinal amebiasis and photoallergic reactions. They improve symptoms but do not alter bony damage in Rheumatoid arthritis.

Dose: 500 mg weekly begin 1-2 week before departure and continue for 4 weeks after leaving the endemic area.

Adverse Effects

1. **After oral doses for Acute attack of Malaria:** ***Common adverse effects:*** Pruritis (Primarily In Africans)Sometimes With Urticaria, Nausea, Vomiting, Abdominal Pain, Anorexia, Headache, Blurring of Vision.

   Other Adverse effects are: Haemolysis in G6PD deficiency, Impaired Hearing, confusion, Psychosis, Seizures, Agranulocytosis, Exfoliative Dermatitis, Alopecia, Bleaching of Hair. Hypotension. ECG Changes(QRS widening and T wave changes).
2. ***Chronic use of high daily doses in Rheumatoid diseases:*** Discoloration of nail beds and mucus membranes, Bleaching of hair & Alopecia Irreversible Ototoxicity, Retinopathy, myopathy and Peripheral Neuropathy. It can exacerbate dermatitis produced by gold / phenylbutazone therapy.
3. Large i.m or Rapid i.v administration cause Excessive hypotension, respiratory and cardiac arrest.

Contraindications and Precautions

Contraindicated in Psoariasis, Porphyria- acute attack may be precipitated.

With retinal or visual field abnormalities.

Caution

Patients with G6PD deficiency, Hepatic diseases, Neurological and blood diseases.

Amodiaquine

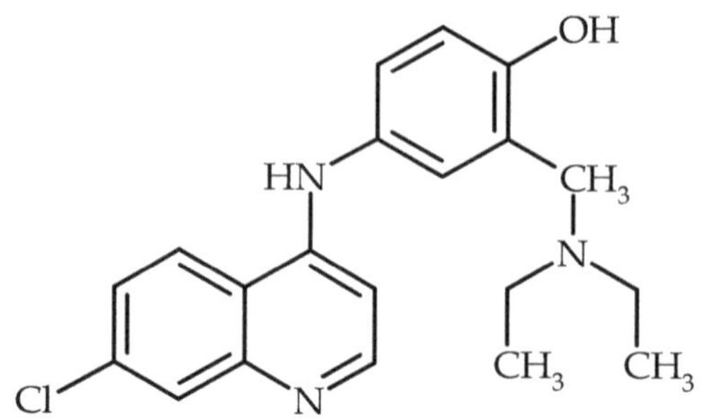

Fig 19-3: Structure of amodiaquine.

Amodiaquine (*Camoquin*) (Fig 19-3) is another 4-aminoquinoline derivative whose antimalarial spectrum and adverse reactions are similar to those of chloroquine, although chloroquine resistant parasites may not be amodiaquine-resistant to the same degree. There is a 1:2000 risk of agranulocytosis and hepatocellular dysfunction when the drug is used prophylactically.

Adverse Effects

Prolonged treatment with amodiaquine may result in pigmentation of the palate, nail beds and skin. Agranulocytosis aplastic anemia & hepatotoxicity are seen rarely.

Therapeutic Uses

Treatment of malaria with chloroquine resistant P falciparum in combination:

Amodiaquine with Artesunate (Coarsucam). It is first line therapy in many African countries.

Piperaquine

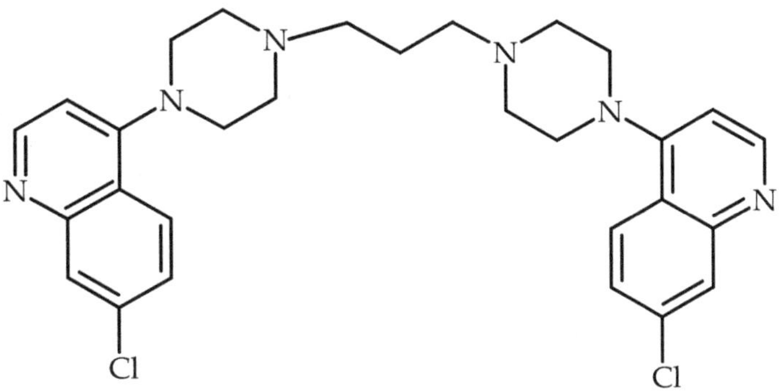

Fig 19-4: Structure of piperaquine.

Piperaquine Fig 19-4 was used for treatment of malaria rfom1970s-1980s in China, the use waned due to resistance. Chemically it is Bisquinoline. Now it is combined with Dihydroartemisinins. Piperaquine & Dihydroartemisinins **(Artikin)**–are used as first line therapy for falciparum malaria, without apparent resistance.

It has longer half life 28 days so longer period of post treatment prophylaxis than other combinations of artemisinins.

Artemisinin (Qinghaosu) and its Derivatives

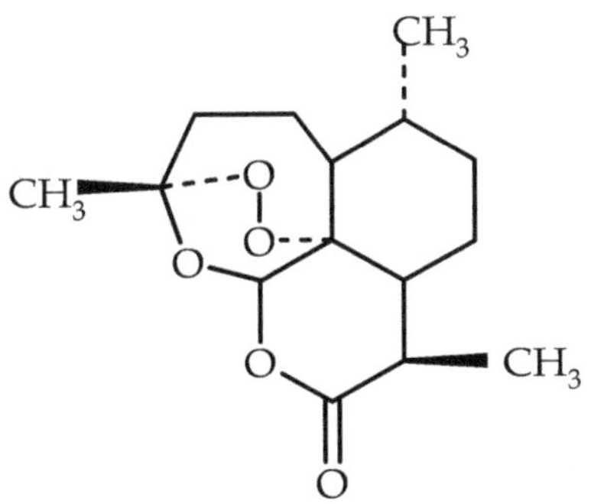

Fig 19-5: Structure of artemisinin.

Artemisinin(Fig 19-5)

It is Sesquiterpene lactone endoperoxide, active compound of a Herbal medicine used in China for 2000 yrs. Insoluble so only used orally.

Analogs: Artesunate and Artemether

Artesunate: Water soluble, useful for oral i.v, i.m and rectal administration.

Artemether: Lipid soluble, useful for oral i.m and rectal administration .

Dihydroartimisinin: Water soluble, useful for oral administration.

Mechanism of action

It is a rapidly acting blood schizonticide acts against all four species of malarial parasites. It has no effect on hepatic stages. They act by producing free radicals due to iron catalyzed cleavage of the artemisinin endoperoxide bridge in the parasite food vacuole or Inhibition of a parasite calcium ATPase.

Pharmacokinetics of Artemisinin (Qinghaosu) and its Analogs

Absorption: When given orally it is well absorbed and almost completely from GIT. Distribution is Rapid and wide. Metabolised in liver. Artesunate and Artemether are metabolized to active metabolite dihydroartimisinin. The $t_{1/2}$ is 1-3 hrs and peak plasma levels: 1-2 hrs.

Therapeutic Uses

Commonly used in treatment of uncomplicated *P. falciparum* malaria. Combination is preferred as standard treatment: Artemether in combination with lumefantrine. Artesunate in combination with Mefloquine/ Amodiaquine/

Sulfadoxime and Pyrimethamine. Dihydroartemisinins with Piperaquine **(Artikin)** is used for treatment of complicated P. falciparum malaria. i.v Artemether and Artesunate i.v Artemether has efficacy like Quinine and i.v. Not useful for prophylaxis due to short half life.

Adverse Effects

The most common adverse effects are nausea, vomiting, diarrhea and dizziness. Rarely toxicities like Neutropenia, anemia, hemolysis, elevated liver enzymes and Allergic reactions are noticed. It causes irreversible neurotoxicity in animals at high doses and teratogenic in animals. However WHO has recommended use of i.v artisunate in pregnanct women, for treatment of severe Falciparum malaria.

Quinine and Quinidine

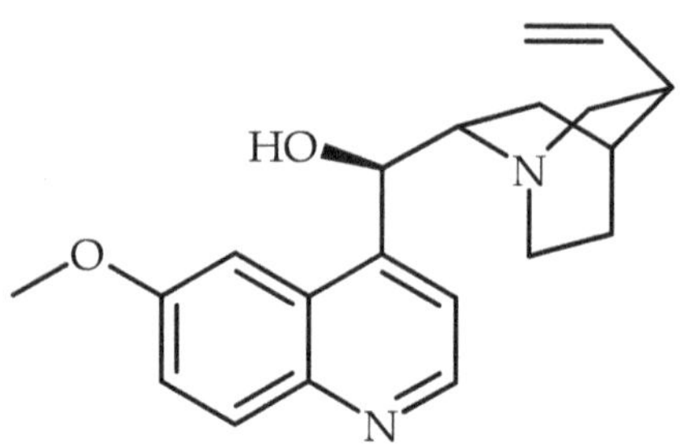

Fig 19-6: Structure of quinine.

Quinine(Fig 19-6) is one of several alkaloids derived from the bark of the cinchona tree. Quinidine is the dextrorotatory stereoisomer of quinine. It is a Quinoline methanol derivative.

Mechanism of action

The mechanism by which it exerts its antimalarial activity is not known. It does not bind to DNA at antimalarial dosages. It may poison the parasite's feeding mechanism and it has been termed a general protoplasmic poison, since many organisms are affected by it. It is a rapidly acting Blood schizonticide, highly effective against four species of human M. Parasites. It shows gameticidal activity against P. vivax and P. ovale but not P. falciparum.

Therapeutic Uses

The primary present day indication for quinine and its isomer, quinidine, is in the intravenous treatment of severe manifestations and complications of chloroquine- resistant malaria caused by *P. falciparum* orally Quinine sulfate in combination with Doxycycline/Clindamycin. Prophylaxis of malaria is generally not used. Babesiosis is treated with clindamycin for infection with Babesia microti

Severe or complicated infections with P falciparum: During severe or complicated infections with *P. falciparum* Cardiac monitoring is mandatory and a Slow i.v infusion or i.m loading dose is given which is changed to oral as patient recovers.

Preparations available

Quinidine gluconate 10mg/kg i.v over 1-2 hrs, then 0.02 mg/kg i.v/min or 15 mg/kg i.v over 4 hrs, then 7.5 mg/kg i.v over 4 hrs every 8 hrs

Adverse Effects

Cinchonism describes the toxic state induced by excessive plasma levels of free quinine. Symptoms include sweating, ringing in the ears, impaired hearing, blurred vision, nausea, vomiting and diarrhea. Quinine is a potent stimulus to insulin secretion and irritates the gastrointestinal mucosa. Also, a variety of relatively rare hematological changes occur, including leukopenia and agranulocytosis. Quinine is potentially neurotoxic in high dosages, thrombophlebitis and severe hypotension may follow its rapid intravenous administration. Other adverse effects generally seen are Haemolytic anaemia (in G6PD deficiency), Leucopenia, agranulocytosis, thrombocytopenia and Hypersensitivity reactions like skin rashes, urticaria, angioedema, bronchospasm.

Black Water Fever is other adverse effect of Qunines. This is rare and serious characterized by Hemolysis, haemolytic anemia & Hemoglobinuria(hypersensitivity reaction).

In some cases abortion is observed as it stimulates uterine contractions.

Drug interactions

Aluminium containing antacids delay the absorption.

It may decrease the renal clearance of Digoxin and warfarin which increases their levels in the body thus causes toxicity.

Contraindications and cautions

- Patients having visual and auditory disturbances.
- Discontinue on severe Cinchonism.
- G6PD deficient patient.
- Cardiac abnormalities.
- Contraindicated taking along with Mefloquine.
- Dose reduction in renal insufficiency.

Therapeutic Uses

Used for Chemoprophylaxis & in the treatment of P. falciparum malaria.

Adverse Effects

Among its side effects are vertigo, visual alterations, vomiting and such CNS disturbances as psychosis, hallucinations, confusion, anxiety and depression.

Contraindications

It should not be used concurrently with compounds known to alter cardiac conduction or prophylactically in patients operating dangerous machinery. It should not used to treat severe malaria, as there is no intravenous formulation.

Mefloquine

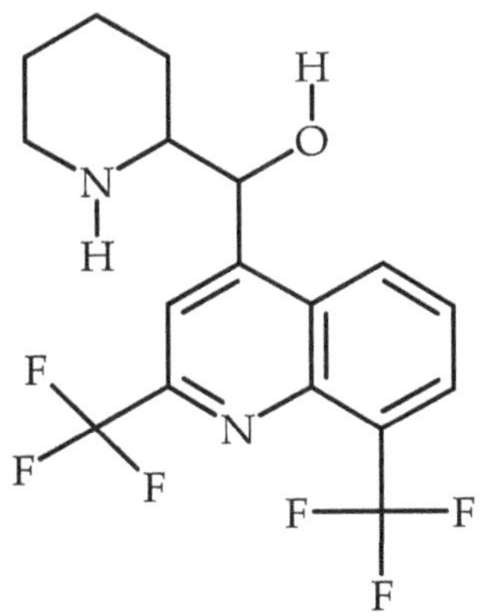

Fig 19-7: Structure of mefloquine.

Mefloquine (*Lariam*) (Fig 19-7) is a 4 quinolinemethanol derivative used both prophylactically and acutely against resistant *P. falciparum* malaria. It is ineffective against the liver stage of *P. vivax* malaria.

Mechanism of Action

While its detailed mechanism of action is unknown, it is an effective blood schizonticide; that is, it acts against the form of the parasite responsible for clinical symptoms.

Pharmacokinetics

Orally administered mefloquine is well absorbed and has an absorption half life of about 2 hours; the elimination half life is 2 to 3 weeks.

Primaquine

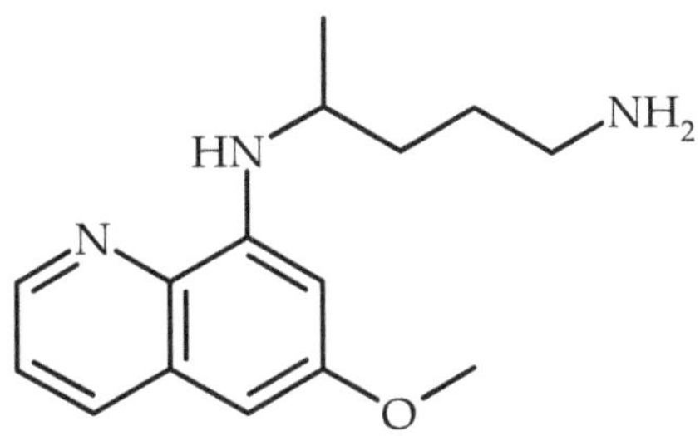

Fig 19-8: Structure of primaquine.

Primaquine (Fig 19-8) is the least toxic and most effective of the 8 aminoquinoline antimalarial compounds.

Mechanism of action

The mechanism by which 8 aminoquinolines exert their antimalarial effects is thought to be through a quinoline-quinone metabolite that inhibits the coenzyme Q-mediated respiratory chain of the exoerythrocytic parasite.

Pharmacokinetics

Primaquine is readily absorbed from the gastrointestinal tract and in contrast to chloroquine, it is not bound extensively by tissues. It is rapidly metabolized and the metabolites are reported to be as active as the parent drug itself. Peak plasma levels are reached in 4 to 6 hours after an oral dose, with almost total drug elimination occurring by 24 hours. The half-life is short and daily administration is usually required for radical cure and prevention of relapses.

Therapeutic Uses

Primaquine is an important antimalarial because it is essentially the only drug effective against the liver (exoerythrocytic) forms of the malarial parasite. The drug also kills the gametocytes in all four species of human malaria. Primaquine is relatively ineffective against the a sexual erythrocyte forms. Primaquine finds its greatest use in providing a radical cure for *P. vivax* and *P. ovale* malaria.

Adverse Effects

Although primaquine has a good therapeutic index, a number of important side effects are associated with its administration. In individuals with a genetically determined glucose 6-phosphate dehydrogenase deficiency, primaquine can cause lethal hemolysis of red cells. This genetic deficiency occurs in 5 to 10% of black males, in Asians and in some Mediterranean peoples. With higher dosages or prolonged drug use, gastrointestinal distress, nausea, headache, pruritus and leukopenia, haemolytic anaemia and Methaemoglobinaemia (in G6PD deficiency) andrarely Leucopenia, agranulocytosis and Cardiac arrhythmias can occur.

Contraindications and cautions

Never given parenterally as it causes marked hypotension. Contraindicated in Patients with Myelosuppression, pregnancy.

Atovaquone

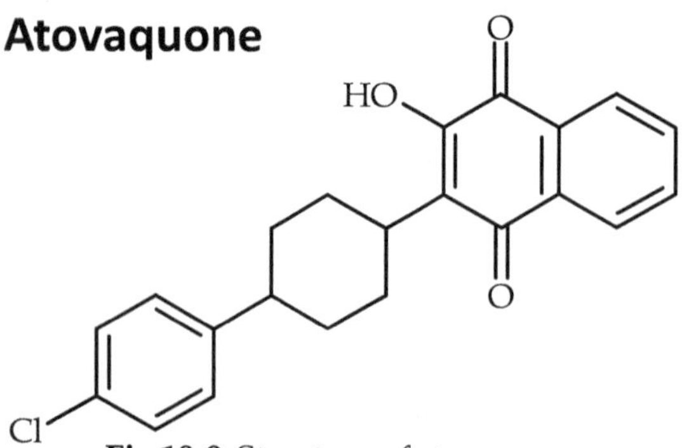

Fig 19-9: Structure of atovaquone.

Mechanism of action

Atovaquone is a naphthoquinone(Fig 19-9) whose mechanism of action involves inhibition of the mitochondrial electron transport system in the protozoa. Malaria parasites depend on de novo pyrimidine biosynthesis through dihydroorotate dehydrogenase coupled to electron transport. Plasmodia are unable to salvage and recycle pyrimidines as do mammalian cells.

Pharmacokinetics

Atovaquone is poorly absorbed from the gastrointestinal tract, but absorption is increased with a fatty meal. Excretion of the drug, mostly unchanged, occurs in the feces. The elimination half-life is 2 to 3 days. Low plasma levels persist for several weeks. Concurrent administration of metoclopramide, tetracycline, or rifampin reduces atovaquone plasma levels by 40 to 50%.

Therapeutic Uses

Atovaquone has good initial activity against the blood but not the hepatic stage of *P. vivax* and *P. ovale* malaria parasites. It is effective against erythrocytic and exoerythrocytic *P. falciparum* and therefore, daily suppressive doses need to be taken for only 1 week upon leaving endemic areas. When used alone, it has an unacceptable (30%) rate of recrudescence and selects for resistant organisms. It and proguanil are synergistic when combined and no atovaquone resistance is seen. This combination (*Malarone*) is significantly more effective than mefloquine, amodiaquine, chloroquine and combinations of chloroquine, pyrimethamine and sulfadoxine. In addition to using the combination of atovaquone and proguanil for the treatment and prophylaxis of *P. falciparum* malaria, atovaquone is also used for the treatment and prevention of *P. carinii* pneumonia and babesiosis therapy.

Adverse Effects

Atovaquone is well tolerated and produces only rare instances of nausea, vomiting, diarrhea, abdominal pain, headache and rash of mild to moderate intensity

Atovaquone (250mg) and Proguanil. (100mg)

Alternate therapy for Pneumocystis jevorici infection.

Pyrimethamine

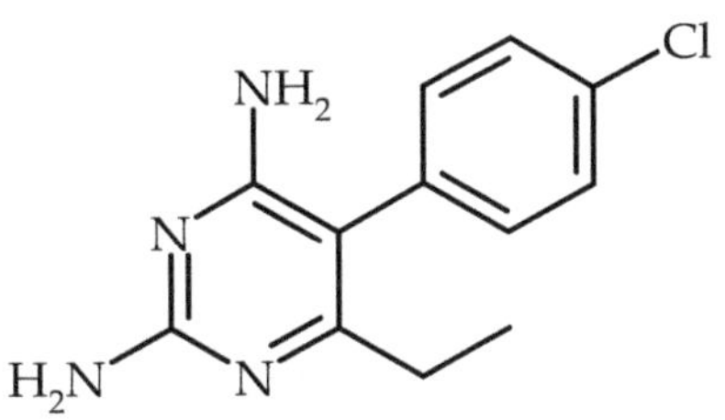

Fig 19-10: Structure of pyrimethamine.

Pyrimethamine (*Daraprim*)(Fig 19-10) is the best of a number of 2,4- diaminopyrimidines that were synthesized as potential antimalarial and antibacterial compounds. Trimethoprim (*Proloprim*) is a closely related compound.

Mechanism of action

The only antimalarial drugs whose mechanisms of action are reasonably well understood are the drugs that inhibit the parasite's ability to synthesize folic acid. Parasites cannot use preformed folic acid and therefore must synthesize this compound from the following precursors obtained from their host: p-aminobenzoic acid (PABA), pteridine and glutamic acid. The dihydrofolic acid formed from these precursors must then be hydrogenated to form tetrahydrofolic acid. The latter compound is the coenzyme that acts as an acceptor of a variety of one carbon units. The transfer of one carbon units is important in the synthesis of the pyrimidines and purines, which are essential in nucleic acid synthesis. Whereas the sulfonamides and sulfones inhibit the initial step whereby PABA and the pteridine moiety combine to form dihydropteroic acid, pyrimethamine and trimethoprim inhibit the conversion of dihydrofolic acid to tetrahydrofolic acid, a reaction catalyzed by the enzyme dihydrofolate reductase. The basis of pyrimethamine selective toxicity resides in the preferential binding of the drug to the parasite's reductase enzyme.

Pharmacokinetics

Pyrimethamine is well absorbed after oral administration, with peak plasma levels occurring within 3 to 7 hours. An initial loading dose to saturate nonspecific binding sites is not required, as it is with chloroquine. However, the drug binds to tissues and therefore, its rate of renal excretion is slow. Pyrimethamine has a half-life of about 4 days. Although the drug does undergo some metabolic alterations, the metabolites formed have not been totally identified.

Therapeutic Uses

The combined use of sulfonamides or sulfones with dihydrofolate reductase inhibitors, such as trimethoprim (*Bactrim, Septra*) or pyrimethamine (*Fansidar*), is a good example of the synergistic possibilities that exist in multipledrug chemotherapy. This type of impairment of the parasite's metabolism is termed sequential blockade. Using drugs that inhibit at two different points in the same biochemical pathway produces parasite lethality at lower drug concentrations than are possible when either drug is used alone. Pyrimethamine has been recommended for prophylactic use against all susceptible strains of plasmodia; however, it should not be used as the sole therapeutic agent for treating acute malarial attacks. As mentioned previously, sulfonamides should always be coadministered with pyrimethamine (or trimethoprim), since the combined antimalarial activity of the two drugs is significantly greater than when either drug is used alone. Also, resistance develops more slowly when they are used in combination. Sulfonamides exert little or no effect on the blood stages of *P. vivax* and resistance to the dihydrofolate reductase inhibitors is widespread. In addition to its antimalarial effects, pyrimethamine is indicated (in combination with a sulfonamide) for the treatment of toxoplasmosis. The dosage required is 10 to 20 times higher than that employed in malarial infections.

Adverse Effects

Relatively few side effects are associated with the usual antimalarial dosages. However, signs of toxicity are evident at higher dosages, particularly those used in the management of toxoplasmosis. Many of these reactions reflect the interference of pyrimethamine with *host* folic acid metabolism, especially that occurring in rapidly dividing cells. Toxic symptoms include anorexia, vomiting, anemia, leukopenia, thrombocytopenia and atrophic glossitis. CNS stimulation, including convulsions, may follow an acute overdose. The side effects associated with the pyrimethamine-sulfadoxine combination include those associated with the sulfonamide and pyrimethamine alone. In addition, there is evidence of a greater incidence of allergic reactions, particularly toxic epidermal necrolysis and Stevens-Johnson syndrome, with the combination. This carries an estimated mortality of 1:11,000 to 1:25,000 when used as a chemoprophylactic.

Combinations

Pyrimethamine 25 mg and Sulfadoxine 500 mg (Fansidar).

Mefloquine , Pyrimethamine and Sulfadoxine (Fansimef).

Artesunate in combination Sulfadoxime and Pyrimethamine.

Atovaquone and Proguanil (Malarone).

Pyrimethamine and Dapsone (Maloprim).

Presumptive treatment of P falciparum in travelers.

Toxoplasmosis: Pyrimethamine & Sulfadiazine, add folinic acid.

Pneumocystosis jiroveci: Trimethoprim and Sulfamethoxazole.

Proguanil: Chloroguanide

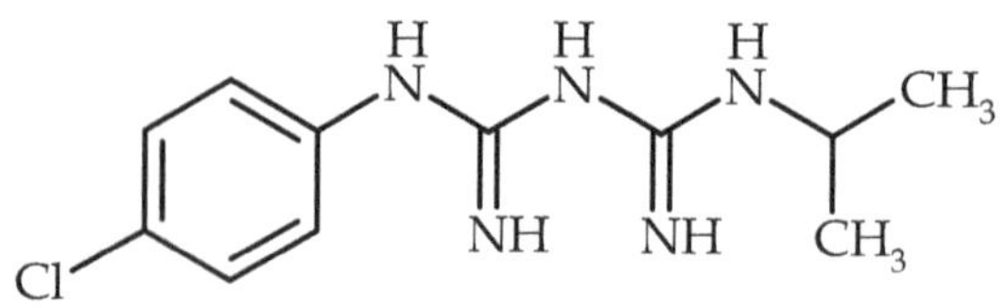

Fig 19-11: Structure of proguanil.

Chloroguanide hydrochloride (*Paludrine*) (Fig 19-11) is activated to a triazine metabolite, cycloguanil.

Mechanism of action

It is a dihydrofolate reductase inhibitor that interferes with parasite folic acid synthesis. It is used for the prophylaxis of malaria caused by all susceptible strains of plasmodia.

Pharmacokinetics

Chloroguanide is rapidly absorbed from the gastrointestinal tract. Peak plasma levels occur 2 to 4 hours after oral administration and the drug is excreted in the urine with an elimination half-life of 12 to 21 hours.

Adverse Effects

Its side effects and spectrum of antimalarial activity are quite similar to those of pyrimethamine. The conversion of chloroguanide to the active metabolite is decreased in pregnancy and also as a result of genetic polymorphism in 3% of whites and Africans and 20% of Asians.

Proguanil causes mouth ulcers and Alopecia.

Antibiotics

Doxycycline

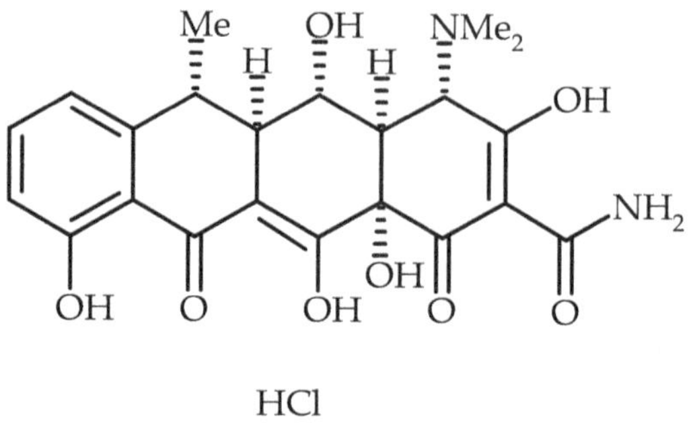

Fig 19-12: Structure of doxycycline.

Doxycycline (Fig 19-12) prophylaxis should begin 1–2 days before travel to malarious areas. It should be continued once a day, at the same time each day, during travel in malarious areas and daily for 4 weeks after the traveler leaves such areas. Insufficient data exist on the antimalarial prophylactic efficacy of related compounds such as minocycline (commonly prescribed for the treatment of acne). People on a long term regimen of minocycline who need malaria prophylaxis should stop taking minocycline 1–2 days before travel and start doxycycline instead.

Adverse effects

Doxycycline can cause photosensitivity, usually manifested as an exaggerated sunburn reaction. The risk for such a reaction can be minimized by avoiding prolonged, direct exposure to the sun and by using sunscreen. In addition, doxycycline use is associated with an increased frequency of vaginal yeast infections. Gastrointestinal side effects (nausea or vomiting) may be minimized by taking the drug with a meal or by specifically prescribing doxycycline monohydrate or the enteric coated doxycycline hyclate, rather than the generic doxycycline hyclate, which is often less expensive. To reduce the risk for esophagitis, travelers should be advised to swallow the medicine with sufficient fluids and not to take doxycycline before going to bed.

Contraindications

Doxycycline is contraindicated in people with an allergy to tetracyclines, during pregnancy and in infants and children aged <8 years. Vaccination with the oral typhoid vaccine Ty21a should be delayed for ee24 hours after taking a dose of doxycycline.

Reasons to consider use of this drug:

- Tends to be the least expensive antimalarial
- People who are already taking doxycycline chronically to prevent acne do not have to take an additional medicine
- Doxycycline also can prevent some additional infections (such as rickettsial infections and leptospirosis), so it may be preferred by people planning to hike, camp and swim in fresh water

For chemoprophylaxis of chloroquine/ Mefloquine resistant malaria

For treatment of P. falciparum malaria with quinine/quinidine.

Clindamycin: Slow blood schizonticide used with quinine/quinidine if doxycycline is contraindicated.

Azithromycin: Under study for chemoprophylaxis.

Halofantrine and Lumefantrine

Halofantrine(Fig 19-13) is related to quinine. It is effective against most chloroquine resistant P. falciparum blood schizonticide. Its use limited, because of cardiac conduction defects and it is found to be Teratogenic.

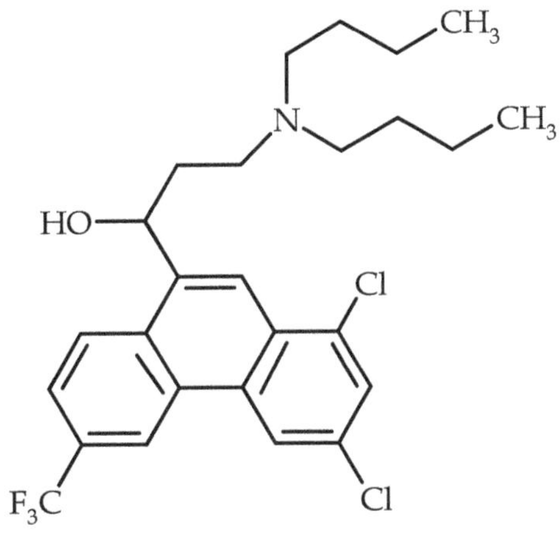

Fig 19-13: Structure of halofantrine.

Lumefantrine(Fig 19-14) is related to halofantrine. Used in combination with artemether Coartem as first line drug for resistant Falciparum malaria. It is not cardiotoxic.

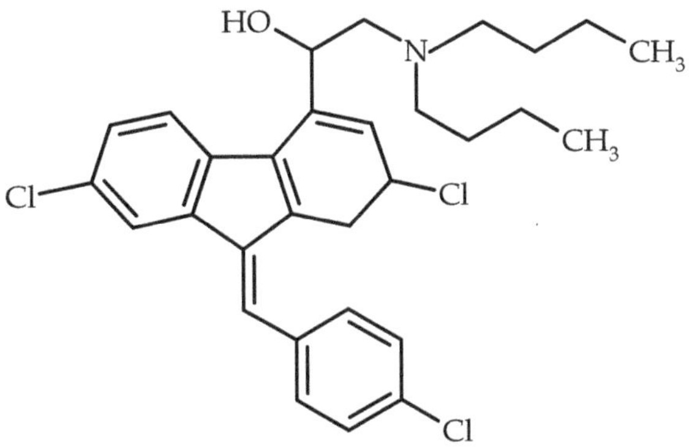

Fig 19-14: Structure of lumefantrine.

Standard Regimens for Prophylaxis (start one week before travel and continue for 4 weeks after)

Exception: (start 2 days before travel for Doxycycline and Malarone and continue for 1 week after, for Malarone.)

Chloroquine 500 mg weekly

(Areas without resistant *P. falciparum*)

Mefloquine 250 mg weekly

(Areas with chloroquine resistant *P. falciparum*)

Doxycycline – 100 mg daily

(Areas with multidrug resistant *P. falciparum*)

Malarone 1 Tab daily (250 mg atovaquone/ 100 mg proguanil daily)

(Areas with chloroquine resistant *P. falciparum*)

Primaquine 15 mg base daily for 14 days after travel.(G6PD status should be determined.) for radical cure/terminal prophylaxis of *P vivax* and *P ovale* infections .

Combination Therapy for Chloroquine Resistant Malaria

Artemether in combination with lumefantrine. (Coartem)

Artesunate in combination with Mefloquine / Amodiaquine(Coarsucam)/Sulfadoxime and Pyrimethamine.

Dihydroartemisinins with Piperaquine **(Artikin)**

Pyrimethamine and Sulfadoxine **(Fansidar)**

Pyrimethamine and Dapsone **(Maloprim)**

Mefloquine, Pyrimethamine & Sulfadoxine **(Fansimef)**

Amodiaquine with Sulfadoxine Pyrimethamine

Atovaquone and Proguanil **(Malarone)**

Quinine and Doxycycline

Quinine and Clindamycin

Treatment of Complicated P. falciparum

Malaria

i.v administration Artemether and Artesunate is used in combination to treat complicated P.falciparum malaria.

Anti-Amoebic Drugs

Amoebiasis caused by *Entamoeba histolytica*, is a major public health problem in developing countries. Entamoeba histolytica, associated with high morbidity and mortality continues to be a major public health problem throughout the world. Asymptomatic individuals account for almost 90 percent of the infections. Poverty, ignorance, overcrowding, poor sanitation and malnutrition favour transmission and increased disease burden. Prevalence varies from country to country and within a country 3-6. In India, it was estimated to be 2-55 percent in early nineties. Identification of two morphologically similar Entamoeba spp., pathogenic *E. histolytica* and non pathogenic *E. dispar* responsible for asymptomatic infection, have raised the question of treating all such cases. The recommendation is that *E. histolytica* should be specifically identified, treated with antiamoebic drugs. In individuals with only *E. dispar*, the treatment is unnecessary. Treating asymptomatic individuals indiscriminately may lead to drug resistance. Though it does not appear to be a serious problem now, reports of failed treatment with metronidazole and differences in drug susceptibilities do suggest that this could probably herald the development of drug resistance clinically. Therefore, understanding the mechanisms involved in multi drug resistance of different antiamoebic drugs is essential.

Life Cycle of *E. histolytica*

Entamoeba histolytica (Fig 19-15) exists in two forms: cysts that can survive outside the body and labile but invasive trophozoite that do not persist outside the body. Cysts, ingested through feces contaminated food or water, pass into the lumen of the intestine, where the trophozoites

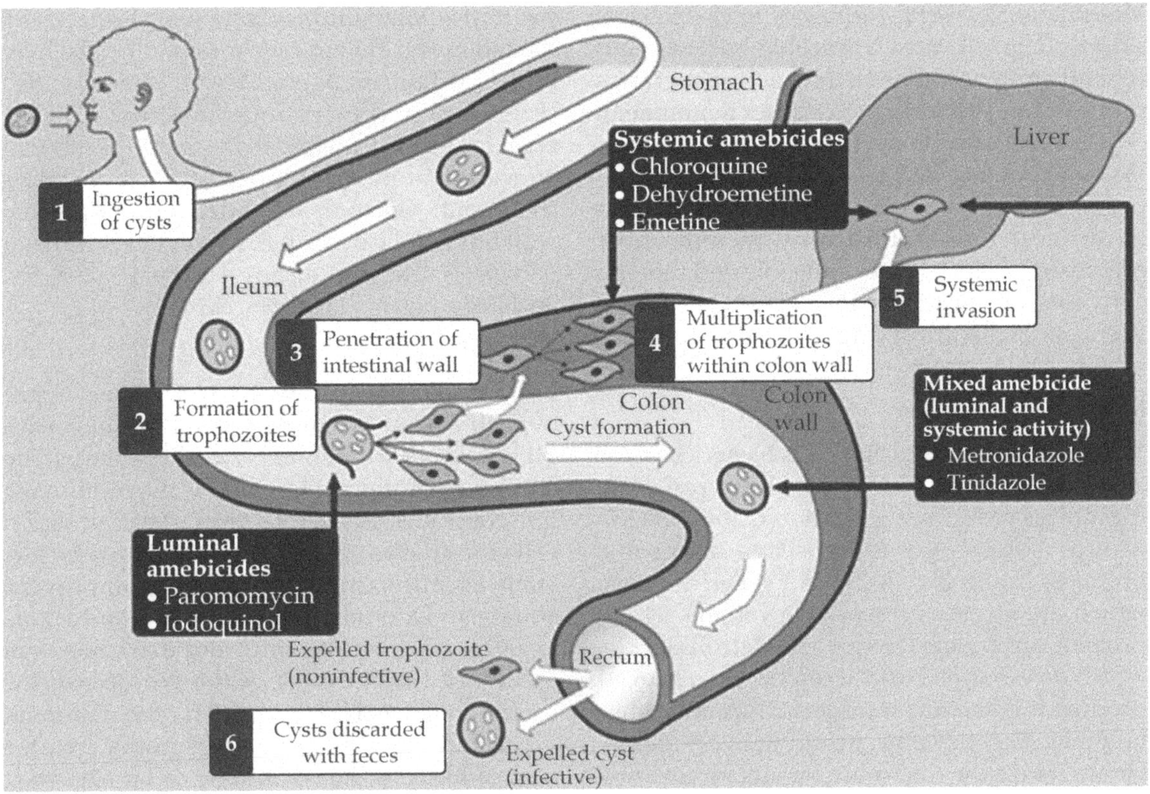

Fig 19-15: Life cycle of E. histolytica.

are liberated. The trophozoites multiply and they either invade and ulcerate the mucosa of the large intestine or simply feed on intestinal bacteria. [Note: One strategy for treating luminal amebiasis is to add antibiotics, such as tetracycline, to the treatment regimen, resulting in a reduction in intestinal flora the ameba's major food source.] The trophozoites within the intestine are slowly carried toward the rectum, where they return to the cyst form and are excreted in feces.

Therapeutic Classification of Anti-Amoebic Drugs

Luminal Amoebicides (Drugs effective in Luminal Infection only)

Dichloroacetamides: Diloxanide Furoate

Halogenated Hydroxyquinolines: Idoquinol (Diiodohydroxyquine)

Antibiotics: Tetracyclines, Paromomycin

Oral Bismuth Salt: Emetine Bismuth Iodide

Extra-Luminal Amoebicides

A: Systemic or Tissue Amoebicides
Chloroquine
Emetines : Emetine, Dehydroemetine

B: Mixed Amoebicides /Drugs effective in systemic & Intestinal Amoebiasis. (Not reliably effective against luminal infections as luminal concentrations are too low for single drug treatment)
Nitroimidazoles, Metronidazole, Tinidazole, Secnidazole.

Metronidazole (Flagyl)

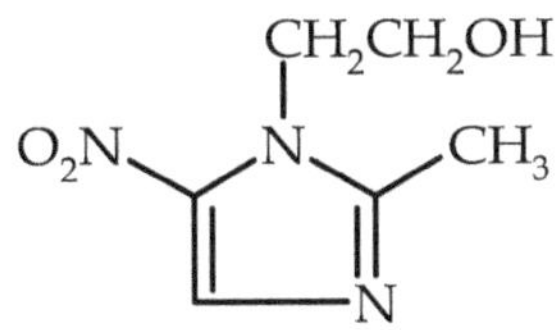

Fig 19-16: Structure of metronidazole.

Metronidazole (*Flagyl, Metrogel*) Fig 19 -16 exerts activity against most anaerobic bacteria and several protozoa. The drug freely penetrates protozoal and bacterial cells but not mammalian cells. Metronidazole can function as an electron sink and because it does so, its 5-nitro group is reduced. The enzyme, pyruvate-ferredoxin oxidoreductase, found only in anaerobic organisms, reduces metronidazole and thereby activates the drug. Reduced metronidazole disrupts replication and transcription and inhibits DNA repair.

Mechanism of action

Metronidazole kills protozoa is bactericidal for anaerobic bacteria. Metronidazole is a pro drug. It requires reductive activation of the NITRO group. This occurs in sensitive anaerobic protozoa anaerobic bacteria by Ferredoxins; which are electron transport proteins. These proteins can donate electrons to Metronidazole, which serves as electron acceptor. The reduced product is cytotoxic; it targets DNA and other biomolecules/proteins, resulting in cell death. Hence it kills the micro-organisms excreted by the kidneys, although small amounts can be found in saliva and breast milk. Dose reduction is generally unnecessary in renal failure.

Antimicrobial Spectrum

Metronidazole inhibits *E. histolytica, G. lamblia, T. vaginalis, Blastocystis hominis* and the helminth *Dracunculus medinensis.* It is also bactericidal for obligate anaerobic gram positive and gram negative bacteria except *Actinomyces* spp. It is not active against aerobes or facultative anaerobes. Drug resistance is infrequent; the mechanism of resistance is not understood. Tinidazole, a 5-nitroimidazole closely related to metronidazole, is effective against vaginal trichomoniasis resistant to metronidazole.

Pharmacokinetics

Absorption from the intestinal tract is usually good. Food delays but does not reduce absorption. The drug is distributed in body fluids and has a half-life of about 8 hours. High levels are found in plasma and cerebrospinal fluid (CSF). Less than 20% binds to plasma proteins. Metronidazole is metabolized by oxidation and glucuronide formation in the liver and is primarily Mixed tissue Amoebicides (Intestinal and extra Intestinal) not reliably effective against amebae in the lumen as luminal concentrations are too low for single drug treatment. Kills only trophozoites in intestinal wall but not the cysts of E. histolytica. The drug is majorly excreted through urine. $t_{1/2:}$ 7.5 hrs and Peak plasma levels:1- 3 hrs

Therapeutic Uses

Metronidazole is the most effective agent available for the treatment of individuals with all forms of amoebiasis, with perhaps the exception of the person who is asymptomatic but continues to excrete cysts. That situation calls for an effective intraluminal amoebicide, such as diloxanide furoate, paromomycin sulfate, or Diiodohydroxyquin. Metronidazole is active against intestinal and extraintestinal cysts and trophozoites. Although quinacrine hydro-chloride has been used for the treatment of giardiasis, many physicians prefer metronidazole. Furazolidone is an alternate choice. Metronidazole is the drug of choice in Europe for anaerobic bacterial infections; concern about possible carcinogenicity has led to some caution in its use in the United States. Recently it has been found to be effective in treating *D. medinensis* (Guinea worm) infections and *Helicobacter pylori.*

Amoebiasis: Drug of choice in all tissue infections. Used in the treatment of Acute intestinal Amoebiasis/Amoebic colitis with dysentery. Administered for 10 days along with a luminal amebicide.It is not reliably effective against parasites in lumen, Hepatic Amoebiasis: 10 day course cures 95 % cases. For cases in which initial therapy fails - Aspiration of abscess and addition of Chloroquine/ Dehydroemetine or Emetin toxic.

Trichomoniasis: Treatment of choice single dose of 2g.

Vaginal and urethral Trichomoniasis. Can be used topically.

Giardiasis: Treatment of choice is single dose shows 90% efficacy.

Bacterial vaginosis: Can be used topically as a gel.

Eradication of H. Pylori in Peptic ulcer a component of 14 days triple therapy regimen. Metronidazole 500 mg twice a day along with a proton pump inhibitor, Clarithromycin 500 mg is taken twice a day.

It is drug of choice for Pseudomembranous enterocolitis caued by Clostridium difficile. (Vancomycin is the drug of second choice)

It is also used in the treatment of Brain abscess, Acute Ulcerative Gingivitis.It also facilitates extraction of adult guinea worm in Dranculosis.

Adverse Effects

The most frequently observed adverse reactions to metronidazole include nausea, vomiting, cramps, dry mouth, diarrhea and a metallic taste. The urine is often dark or redbrown. Less frequently, unsteadiness, vertigo, ataxia, paresthesias, peripheral neuropathy, encephalopathy and neutropenia have been reported. Since metronidazole is a weak inhibitor of alcohol dehydrogenase, alcohol ingestion should be avoided during treatment. A psychotic reaction also may be produced. Metronidazole interferes with the metabolism of warfarin and may potentiate its anticoagulant activity. Phenobarbital and corticosteroids lower metronidazole plasma levels by increasing its metabolism, whereas cimetidine raises levels by impairing metronidazole metabolism. The drug is not recommended for use during pregnancy.

Preparations: Oral, i.v infusion, topical gel, cream.

Resistance

Not a therapeutic problem. Some strains of T. vaginalis are becoming resistance.

Drug interactions

Potentiate Anticoagulant effect of Warfarin. Metabolism of Metronidazole induced by Phenytoin and Phenobarbitone andCimetidine may inhibit it. Metronidazole increases Lithium toxicity.

Contraindications

Patient with active disease of the CNS.

Hepatic Disease/Renal disease, dose adjustment should be done.

Pregnancy/Nursing Mothers.

Tinidazole

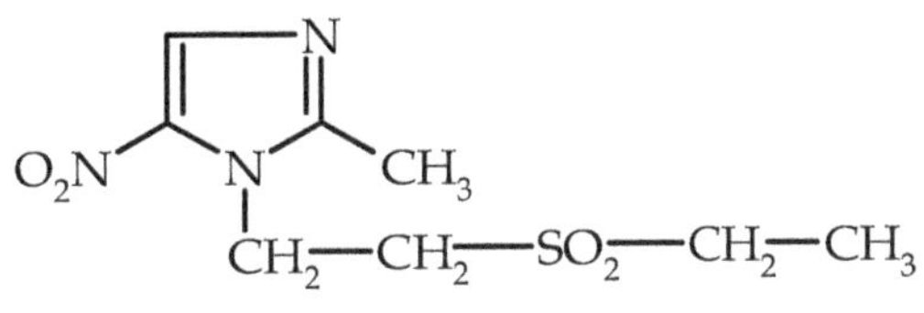

Fig 19-17: Structure of tinidazole.

Tinadazole (Fig 19-17) is a second generation Nitroimidazole and a Congener of Metronidazole. It is similar to Metronidazole in spectrum of activity, MOA, absorption, adverse effects and drug interactions. It is also effective against cysts of *E.histolytica.*

It is longer acting hence administered once daily.

Secnidazole: Longer acting, Single 2 gm dose is given

Emetines

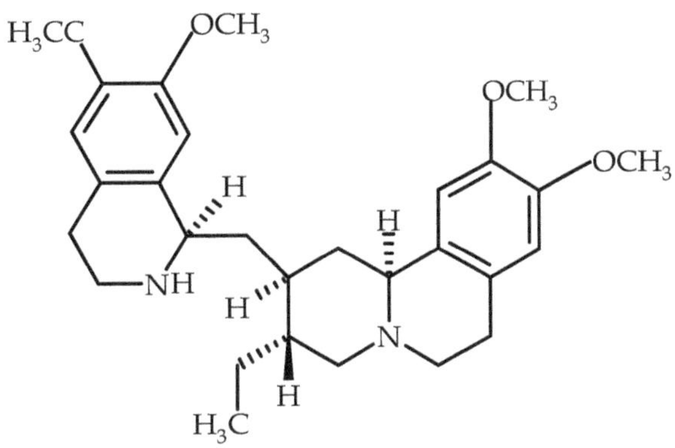

Fig 19-18: Structure of emetines.

Emetine (Fig 19-18) is an Alkaloid of Ipecacuanna (Ipecac). It is mostly concentrated in Liver, Lungs, Spleen, Kidney, Cardiac muscle and Intestinal wall.It is metabolized and excreted slowly via kidney so it has a cumulative effect. Trace amounts could be detected in urine 1-2 month after last dose. Therefore it should not be used for more than 10 days (usually 3-5 days).

Pharmacological Actions

Act on trophozoites causing irreversible block of protein synthesis. Depress cardiac conduction & contraction arrhythmia, heart failure and death.Antiadrenergic action may lead to hypotension.Nausea and vomiting of central origin. Decreases serum potassium.

Clinical Uses

Amoebic liver abscess. Intestinal wall infections. Severe forms of acute amoebic dysentery dehydroemetine + tetracycline for a short period followed by metronidazole.

Adverse Effects

Dehydroemetine is less toxic than emetine pain at site of injection, abcesses. GIT: nausea, vomiting, diarrhoea. Neuromuscular weakness, Serious toxicities like cardiotoxicity cardiac arrhythmias, Hypotension congestive heart failure are seen.

Contraindications

Heart disease

Kidney disease

Pregnancy

Children

Dehydroemetineis a Synthetic analog of Emetine. It is Effective against the trophozoites of Entamoeba histolytica.

Therapeutic Uses

Limited use: Only when Metronidazole cannot be used in :

Severe Amoebic dysentry

Hepatic Amebiasis

Dehydroemetine is preferrd– better toxic profile

Drug should be used S.C or I.M injection in a supervised setting

Adverse Effects

Mild when used for 3-5 days, increase with time Diarrhea.

Central nausea & vomiting

Pain & tenderness at site of injection/ sterile abscess.

Muscle weakness & discomfort.

Minor ECG changes

Serious toxicity: Hypotension, Cardiac arrhythmias, Cardiac failure.

Contraindications

Cardiac/renal disease, Young children, pregnancy.

Chloroquine

Antimalarial drug–already discussed.

Tissue Amoebicide especially against Amoebic Hepatitis and Liver Abscess.

Concentrated in liver; kills trophozoites of E. histolytica.

Not effective for amoebic colitis or luminal amoebae because absorbed in upper intestine.

Therapeutic Use

Hepatic amoebiasis/abscess; not responding to Metronidazole.

Diloxanide Furoate (Luminal Amebicide)

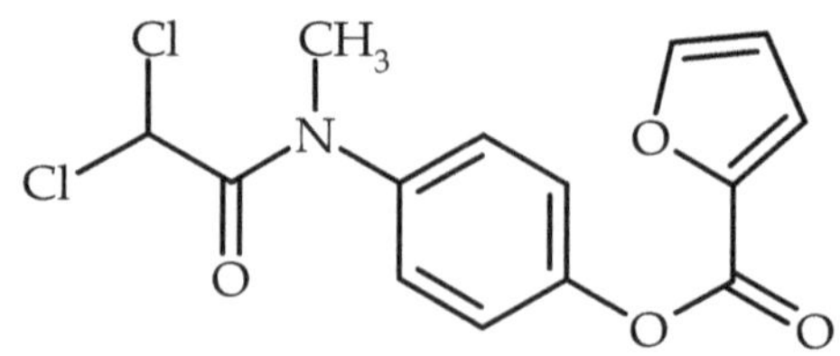

Fig 19-19: Structure of diloxanide furoate.

Diloxanide furoate (*Furamide*) (Fig 19-19) is an amebicide that is effective against trophozoites in the intestinal tract. In mild or asymptomatic infections, cures of 83 to 95% have been achieved; in patients with dysentery, cure rates may be less impressive.

Mechanism of action

Luminal Amebicide. The mechanism of action of Diloxanide is unknown. This agent destroys the trophozoites of *E. histolytica* that eventually form into cysts. The cysts are then excreted by persons infected with asymptomatic amebiasis. Unabsorbed Diloxanoid is directly amebicidal against amebea in lumen but not those in intestinal wall.

Pharmacokinetics

The drug is administered only orally and is rapidly absorbed from the gastrointestinal tract following hydrolysis of the ester group, in gut splits into Diloxanoid and furoic acid. 90% Diloxanoid is absorbed and conjugated to form Glucuronide and excreted in urine

Therapeutic uses

Drug of choice for Asymptomatic Luminal Amoebiasis (cyst passers).

It is given along with tissue amebicide in severe intestinal and extra intestinal amebiasis.

Adverse effects

It is remarkably free of side effects, but occasionally flatulence, abdominal distention, anorexia, nausea, vomiting, diarrhea, pruritis and urticaria may occur.

Precautions

It is contraindicated in Pregnancy.

Iodoquinol

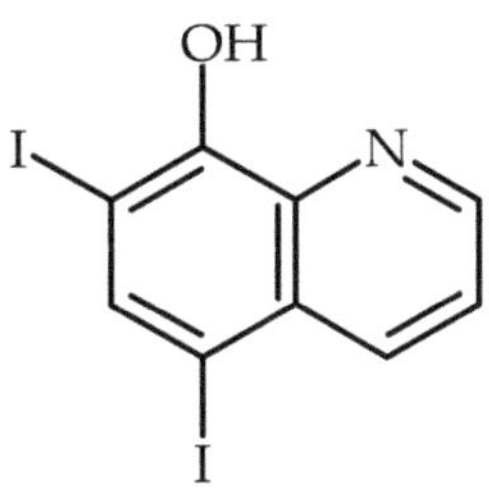

Fig 19-20: Structure of iodoquinol.

Iodoquinol (Diiodohydroxyquine) Fig 19-20 is a halogenated hydroxyquinoline. An effective luminal amoebicide used with metronidazole to treat amebic infections. It is only effective against trophozoites in lumen.

Pharmacokinetics

The pharmacokinetics are poorly understood and 90%of the drug is unabsorbed and acts as amoebicide and 10% is absorbed which is metabolized to Glucronides and excreted in urine. Half life is about 11-14 hrs.

Adverse Effects

Diarrhoea, anorexia, nausea, vomiting, abdominal pain, Headache.The increased intake of the dug leads to a condition called "Iodism". Which results in Dermatitis, urticaria, pruritis, fever. Some idoquinol can produce severe neurotoxicity on prolonged use and high dose. So high doses should be used with caution.

Precautions

Should be careful when taking along with meals and in conditions like optic neuropathy, Non amebic Hepatic disease, and Renal or Thyroid disease.

Contraindicated in patient who are intolerant to Iodine.

Antibiotics

The common antibiotics used are Paromomycin and Tetracyclines. These drugs are generally used for luminal amebicides , Asymptomatic infection (Carriers) and also used along with extra luminal amebicides in serious infections.

Paromomycin Sulphate

It is an aminoglycoside antibiotic. Not significantly absorbed from the gut. Used as Luminal amebicide and less toxic than other agents. It is superior to Diloxanide Furoate in clearing asymptomatic infections. It has no effect on extra intestinal amebic infections. Also used in visceral leishmeniasis .

Adverse effects

Abdominal distress and diarrhea.

Tetracyclines

Tetracyclines are broad spectrum antibiotics. Used in resistant cases and does not kill bacteria directly but disturbs the symbiosis between normal intestinal flora and *E histolytica.* The amebae grow at expense of normal intestinal flora. Used as Luminal amebicide.

Treatment of Specific Forms of Amebiasis

These are used in treating asymptomatic intestinal infection. Generally not treated in endemic area.In non endemic area treated with luminal amebicides like Dolixanide furoate, Iodoquinol and Paromomycin. Some times may be combined with tetracyclines.

Amebic Colitis with dysentery

In case of mild to moderate intestinal infection the combination of Metronidazole and Luminal agent is used and as an alternative Dolixanide furoate, Iodoquinol, Paromomycin + Tetracycline/Erythromycin are used.

Where as in severe intestinal infection, Metronidazole and Luminal agentis used and as an alternative Dolixanide furoate, Iodoquinol, Paromomycin + Tetracycline/dehydroemetine or emetine.

Hepatic abscess, ameboma and other Extra intestinal Infections

Generally for these type of infections Metronidazole and luminal agent are used but for unusual cases which are not responding to metronidazole the drugs like Chloroquine + Luminal agent/ Dehydroemetine or emetine are use.

Chemotherapy for Trypanosomiasis

Trypanosomiasis refers to two chronic and eventually, fatal diseases caused by species of Trypanosoma: African sleeping sickness and American sleeping sickness.

In African sleeping sickness, the causative organisms, Trypanosoma brucei gambiense and Trypanosoma brucei rhodiense, initially live and grow in the blood.

The parasite invades the CNS, causing an inflammation of the brain and spinal cord that produces the characteristic lethargy and eventually, continuous sleep. Chagas' disease (American sleeping sickness) is caused by Trypanosoma cruzi and occurs in South America.

Treatment

Melarsoprol

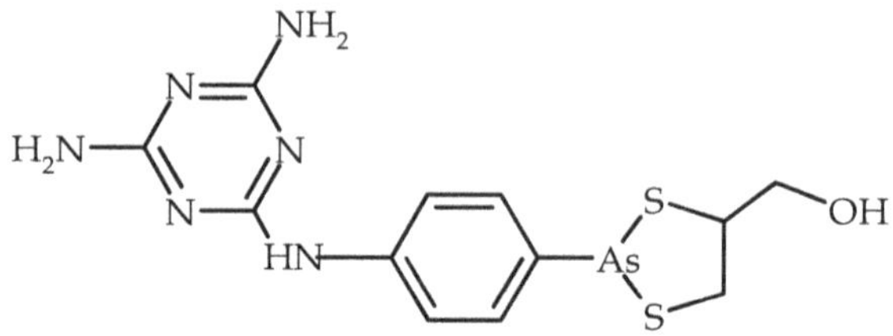

Fig 19-21: Structure of melarsoprol.

Melarsoprol(Fig 19-21) is a derivative of mersalyl oxide, a trivalent arsenical. Its use is limited to the treatment of trypanosomal infections usually in the late stage with CNS involvement and it is lethal to these parasites.

Mechanism of Action

The drug reacts with sulfhydryl groups of various substances, including enzymes in both the organism and host. The parasite's enzymes may be more sensitive than those of the host. There is evidence that mammalian cells may be less permeable to the drug and thus, are protected from its toxic effects. Trypanosomal resistance may also be due to decreased permeability of the drug.

Pharmacokinetics

Melarsoprol usually is slowly administered intravenously through a fine needle, even though it is absorbed from the gastrointestinal tract. Because it is very irritating, care should be taken not to infiltrate surrounding tissue. Adequate trypanocidal concentrations appear in the CSF, in contrast to nonpenetration of the CSF by pentamidine. Melarsoprol is therefore the agent of choice in the treatment of *T. brucei rhodesiense*, which rapidly invades the CNS, as well as for meningoencephalitis caused by *T. brucei* gambiense. The host readily oxidizes melarsoprol to a relatively nontoxic, pentavalent arsenic compound. The drug has a very short half-life and is rapidly excreted into the urine.

Adverse Effects

CNS toxicities are the most serious side effects of melarsoprol treatment. Encephalopathy may appear soon after the first course of treatment but usually subsides. It may, however, be fatal. Hypersensitivity reactions may also occur and fever may follow injection. Gastrointestinal disturbances, such as severe vomiting and abdominal pain, can be minimized if the patient is in the fasting state during drug administration and for several hours thereafter. Melarsoprol is contraindicated in patients with influenza. Hemolytic anemia has been seen in patients with glucose 6-phosphate dehydrogenase deficiency.

Pentamidine Isethionate

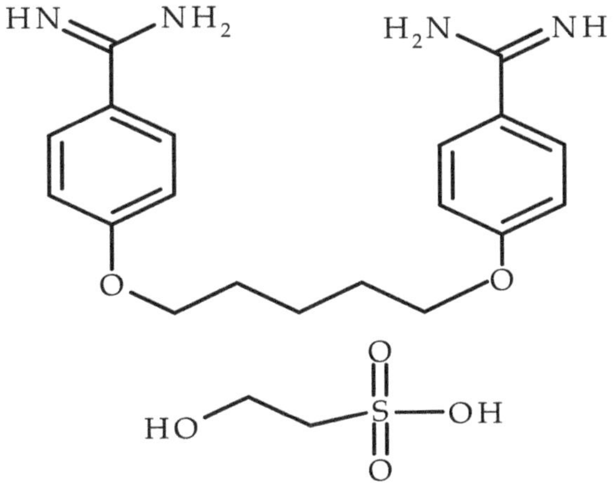

Fig 19-22: Structure of pentamidine isethionate.

Pentamidine (Fig 19-22) is active against a variety of protozoal infections, including many trypanosomes, such as *T. brucei* gambiense, for which pentamidine is used to treat and prevent the organism's hematologic stage. However, some trypanosomes, including *T. cruzi*, are resistant. Pentamidine is also effective in the treatment of systemic blastomycosis (caused by the fungus Blastomyces dermatitidis) and in treating infections caused by Pneumocystis jiroveci (formerly called Pneumocystis carinii a name now used to refer to the organism in animals). [Note: It is now considered to be a fungus, but it is not susceptible to antifungal drugs. Trimethoprim-sulfamethoxazole is preferred in the treatment of *P. jiroveci* infections. However, pentamidine is the drug of choice in treating patients with pneumonia caused by *P. jiroveci* who have failed to respond to trimethoprim-sulfamethoxazole. The drug is also used in treating *P. jiroveci* infected individuals who are allergic to sulfonamides. Because of the increased incidence of pneumonia caused by this organism in immunocompromised patients, such as those infected with human immunodeficiency virus, pentamidine has assumed an important place in chemotherapy.] Pentamidine is also an alternative drug to stibogluconate in the treatment of leishmaniasis.

Mechanism of Action

Trypanosoma brucei concentrates pentamidine by an energy dependent, high affinity uptake system. [Note: Resistance is associated with an inability of the trypanosome to concentrate the drug.] Although its mechanism of action has not been defined, evidence exists that the drug binds to the parasite's DNA and interferes with the synthesis of RNA, DNA, phospholipid and protein by the parasite.

Pharmacokinetics

Fresh solutions of pentamidine are administered intramuscularly or as an aerosol. [Note: The intravenous route is avoided because of severe adverse reactions, such as a sharp fall in blood pressure and tachycardia.] The drug is concentrated and stored in the liver and kidney for a long period of time. Because it does not enter the CSF, it is ineffective against the meningoencephalitic stage of trypanosomiasis. The drug is not metabolized and it is excreted very slowly into the urine. Its half life in the plasma is about 5 days.

Adverse Effects

Serious renal dysfunction may occur, which reverses on discontinuation of the drug. Other adverse reactions are hypotension, dizziness, rash and toxicity to Î^{2} cells of the pancreas.

Nifurtimox

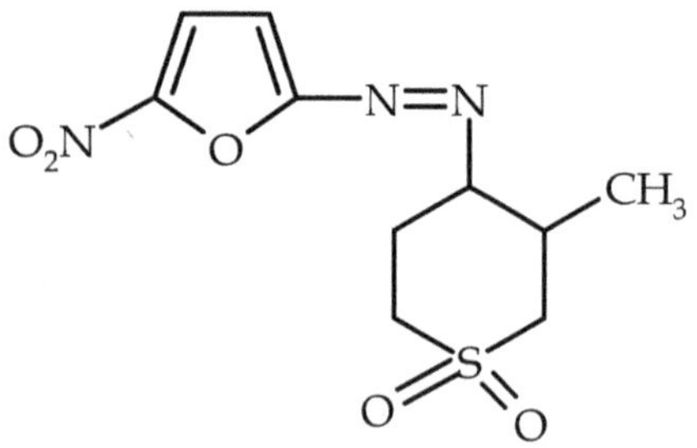

Fig 19-23: Structure of nifurtimox.

Nifurtimox(Fig 19-23) has found use only in the treatment of acute *T. cruzi* infections (Chagas' disease), although treatment of the chronic stage of such infections has led to variable results.

Mechanism of Action

Being a nitroaromatic compound, nifurtimox undergoes reduction and, eventually, generates intracellular oxygen radicals, such as superoxide radicals and hydrogen peroxide. These highly reactive radicals are toxic to *T. cruzi*, which lacks catalase.

Pharmacokinetics

Nifurtimox is administered orally, and it is rapidly absorbed and metabolized to unidentified products that are excreted in the urine.

Adverse Effects

Adverse effects are common following chronic administration, particularly among the elderly. Major toxicities include immediate hypersensitivity reactions such as anaphylaxis, delayed hypersensitivity reactions such as dermatitis and icterus and gastrointestinal problems that may be severe enough to cause weight loss. Peripheral neuropathy is relatively common and disturbances in the CNS may also occur. In addition, cell mediated immune reactions may be suppressed.

Suramin

Suramin(Fig 19-24) is used primarily in the early treatment and especially, the prophylaxis of African trypanosomiasis.

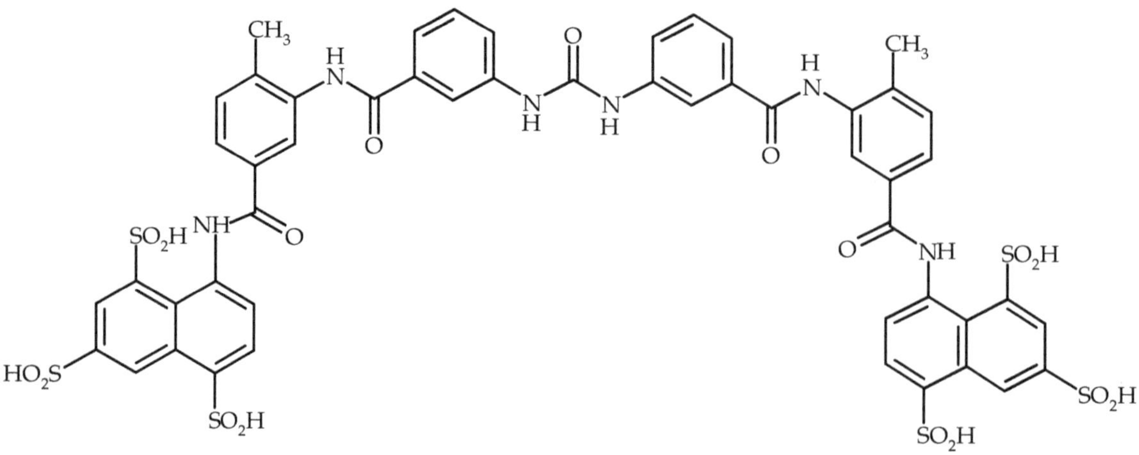

Fig 19-24: Structure of suramin.

Mechanism of Action

It is very reactive and inhibits many enzymes, among them those involved in energy metabolism (for example, glycerol phosphate dehydrogenase), which appears to be the mechanism most closely correlated with trypanocidal activity.

Pharmacokinetics

The drug must be injected intravenously. It binds to plasma proteins and remains in the plasma for a long time, accumulating in the liver and in the proximal tubular cells of the kidney.

Adverse Effects

Although infrequent, adverse reactions include nausea and vomiting (which cause further debilitation of the patient), shock and loss of consciousness, acute urticaria and neurologic problems, including paresthesia, photophobia, palpebral edema (edema of the eyelids) and hyperesthesia of the hands and feet. Albuminuria tends to be common, but when cylindruria (the presence of renal casts in the urine) and hematuria occur, treatment should cease.

Benznidazole

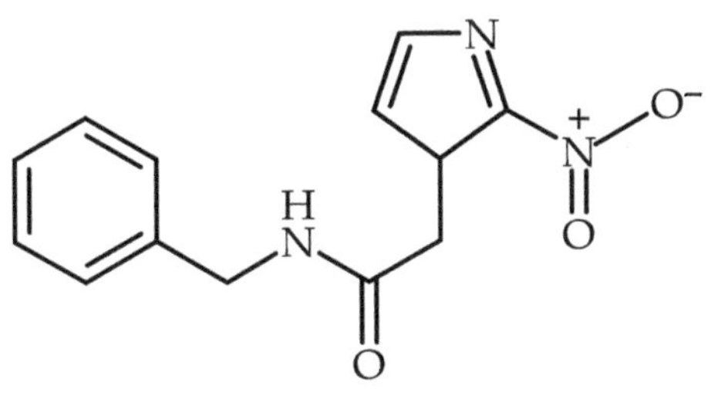

Fig 19-25: Structure of benznidazole.

Benznidazole (Fig 19-25) is a nitroimidazole derivative that inhibits protein synthesis and ribonucleic acid synthesis in the *T. cruzi* cells. It is an alternative choice for treatment of acute and indeterminate phases of Chagas' disease, but therapy with benznidazole does not offer any significant efficacy or toxicity advantages over that with nifurtimox. However, benznidazole is recommended as prophylaxis for preventing infections caused by *T. cruzi* among hematopoietic stem cell transplant, recipients because treatment in potential donors is not always effective.

Chemotherapy for Leishmaniasis

There are three types of leishmaniasis: cutaneous, mucocutaneous and visceral. In the visceral type (liver and spleen), the parasite is in the bloodstream and can cause very serious problems. Leishmaniasis is transmitted from animals to humans (and between humans) by the bite of infected sandflies. The diagnosis is established by demonstrating the parasite in biopsy material and skin lesions. The treatments of leishmaniasis and trypanosomiasis are difficult, because the effective drugs are limited by their toxicities and failure rates. Pentavalent antimonials, such as sodium stibogluconate, are the conventional therapy used in the treatment of leishmaniasis, with pentamidine and amphotericin B as backup agents. Allopurinol has also been reported to be effective (it is converted to a toxic metabolite by the amastigote form[7] of the organism).

Life Cycle of the Causative Organism: Leishmania Species

The sandfly transfers the flagellated promastigote form of the protozoa, which is rapidly phagocytized by macrophages.

In the macrophage, the promastigotes rapidly change to nonflagellated amastigotes and multiply, killing the cell.

The newly released amastigotes are again phagocytized, and the cycle continues.

Treatment

Sodium stibogluconate

Mechanism of Action

Sodium stibogluconate (Fig 19-26) is not effective invitro. Therefore, it has been proposed that reduction to the trivalent antimonial compound

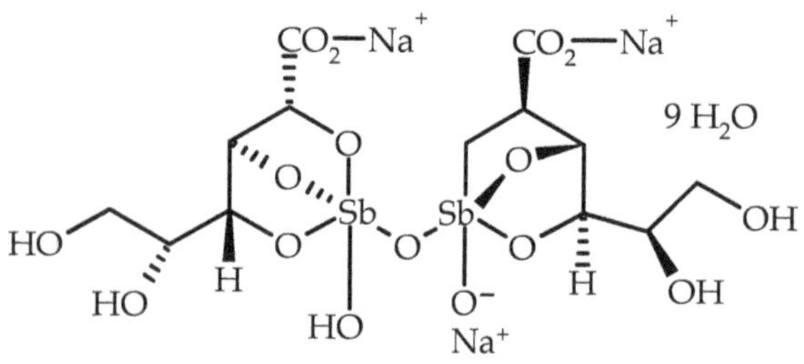

Fig 19-26: Structure of sodium stibogluconate.

is essential for activity. The exact mechanism of action has not been determined. Evidence for inhibition of glycolysis in the parasite at the phosphofructokinase reaction has been found.

Pharmacokinetics

Because it is not absorbed on oral administration, sodium stibogluconate must be administered parenterally, and it is distributed in the extravascular compartment. Metabolism is minimal and the drug is excreted in the urine.

Adverse Effects

Adverse effects include pain at the injection site, gastrointestinal upsets, and cardiac arrhythmias. Renal and hepatic function should be monitored periodically.

Chemotherapy for Toxoplasmosis

One of the most common infections in humans is caused by the protozoan Toxoplasma gondii, which is transmitted to humans when they consume raw or inadequately cooked, infected meat. An infected pregnant woman can transmit the organism to her fetus. Cats are the only animals that shed oocysts, which can infect other animals as well as humans. The treatment of choice for this condition is the antifolate drug pyrimethamine. A combination of sulfadiazine and pyrimethamine is also efficacious. Leucovorin is often administered to protect against folate deficiency. Other inhibitors of folate biosynthesis, such as trimethoprim and sulfamethoxazole, are without therapeutic efficacy in toxoplasmosis. At the first appearance of a rash, pyrimethamine should be discontinued, because hypersensitivity to this drug can be severe.

Chemotherapy for Giardiasis

Giardia lamblia is the most commonly diagnosed intestinal parasite . It has only two life-cycle stages: the binucleate trophozoite with four flagellae and the drug-resistant, four-nucleate cyst . Ingestion, usually from contaminated drinking water, leads to infection. The trophozoites exist in the small intestine and divide by binary fission. Occasionally, cysts are formed that pass out in the stool. Although some infections are asymptomatic, severe diarrhea can occur, which can be very serious in immune suppressed patients. The treatment of choice is metronidazole for 5 days. One alternative agent is tinidazole, which is equally effective as metronidazole in treatment of giardiasis but with a much shorter course of treatment (2 given once). Nitazoxanide [nye-ta-ZOX-a-nide], a nitrothiazole derivative structurally similar to aspirin, was recently approved for treatment of giardiasis. Nitazoxanide is also equally efficacious as metronidazole and, in comparison, has a 2 day shorter course of therapy

References

Mutabingwa TK et al (2001). Chlorproguanil dapsone for treatment of drug resistant falciparum malaria in Tanzania. *Lancet* **358:** 1218.

Mutabingwa TK et al (2005). Amodiaquine alone, amodiaquine+sulfadoxine-pyrimeth-amine, amodiaquine+artesunate, and artemether-lumefantrine for outpatient treatment of malaria in Tanzanian children: A four-arm randomised effectiveness trial. *Lancet* **365**: 1474.

Nosten F, Brasseur P(2002). Combination therapy for malaria. *Drugs* **62**: 1315.

Olliaro P (2002). Mode of action and mechanisms of resistance for antimalarial drugs. *Pharmacol Ther* **89**: 207.

Ridley RG (2002). Medical need, scientific opportunity and the drive for antimalarial drugs. *Nature* **415**: 686.

CHAPTER

Anthelmintic Drugs 20

Helmintic Infections

Humans are the primary host for most helminthic infections. Most worms produce eggs and larva. These pass out of human body and infect secondary host. Immature forms invade humans via skin or GIT.

Types of Worms

Worms live in host's alimentary canal.

Worms or larvae live in muscles, viscera, meninges, lungs and Subcutaneous tissues.

Intestinal Worms

(a) Round Worms (Nematodes)

Ascaris lmubricods (common)

Enterobius vermicularis (pin worm)

Trichris trichuria (whip worm)

Strongyloids stercoralis (thread worm)

Ankylostoma dudenale (hook worm)

(b) Tape Worms (Cestodes)

- Taenia saginata (Beef)
- Taenia solium (pork)

Humans become infected by eating raw or under cooked meat containing larvae of infected cattle or pig.

- In some cases the larva gets encysted in muscles, viscera, brain, eye resulting in **cysticercosis**.

(c) Tissue Worms

- **Filariae** (bancrofti, loa loa): Adult filariae live in the lymphatics, causing lymphadenitis, swelling of limb. Microfilariae goes to blood stream to be ingested by mosquitoes.
- **Trichnella spiralis :** Larva migrats from intestine to tissues of leg or foot producing ulcer.

Anthelmintic Drugs

Anthelmintics are drugs that are used to treat infections with parasitic worms. This includes flat worms, e.g., flukes, tapeworms and round worms, i.e., nematodes. They are of huge importance for human tropical medicine and for veterinary medicine. Parasitic worms also infect livestock and crops, affecting food production with a resultant economic impact. Also of importance is the infection of domestic pets. Indeed, the companion animal market is a major economic consideration for animal health companies undertaking drug discovery programmes. Despite the prevalence of parasitic worms, Anthelmintic drug discovery is the poor relation of the pharmaceutical industry. The anthelminthic drugs are shown in Table 20-1.

Anthelminthic drugs may act by causing:

- Paralysis of the worm.
- Damaging the worm leading to partial digestion or rejection by immune mechanisms.
- Interfere with the metabolism of the worm.

Table 20-1: Key drugs registered for the treatment of parasitic worms in humans.

Schistosomiasis (blood fluke)	**Intestinal round worms**
Antimonials	Piperazine
Metrifonate	Benzimidazoles
Oxamnaquine	Morantel
Praziquantel	Pyrantel
	Levamisole
Cestodiasis (tape worm)	Avermectins and milbemycins
Niclosamide	Closantel (and halogenated salicylamides)
Benzimidazoles	Emodepside
Praziquantel	
Fasciolasis (liver fluke)	**Filariasis (tissue round worms)**
Praziquantel	Diethylcarbmazine
Closantel	Suramin
(and halogenated salicylamides)	Ivermectin

Classification

- **Benzimidazoles:**
  - **Albendazole** – effective against thread worms, roundworms, whipworms, tapeworms, hookworms.
  - **Mebendazole** – effective against pinworms, roundworms and hookworms.
  - **Thiabendazole** – effective against roundworms, hookworms.
  - **Fenbendazole** – effective against gastrointestinal parasites.
  - **Triclabendazole** – effective against liver flukes.
  - **Flubendazole** – effective against most intestinal parasites.
- **Abamectin** – effective against most common intestinal worms, except tapeworms, for which praziquantel is commonly used in conjunction with abamectin.
- **Diethylcarbamazine** – effective against *Wuchereria bancrofti, Brugia malayi, Brugia timori*, tropical pulmonary eosinophilia, loiasis.
- **Niclosamide** – effective against tapeworms.
- **Ivermectin** – effective against most common intestinal worms (except tapeworms).
- **Suramin**
- **Pyrantel pamoate** – effective against most nematode infections.
- **Levamisole**
- **Praziquantel** – effective against cestodes, some trematodes.

Piperazine

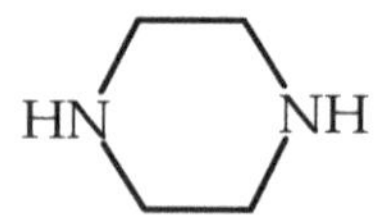

Fig 20-1: Structure of piperazine.

It is the most popular and readily used drug for the treatment of parasite infection. Piperazine was first used as an anthelmintic in 1950s and it is still the active constituent as over the counter drug and is used in the remedies for thread worm infection in children.

Mechanism of Action

Piperazine (Fig 20-1) (*Vermizine*) contains a heterocyclic ring that lacks a carboxyl group. It acts on the musculature of the helminths to cause reversible flaccid paralysis mediated by chloride dependent hyperpolarization of the muscle membrane. This results in expulsion of the worm. Piperazine acts as an agonist at gated chloride channels on the parasite muscle.

Pharmacokinetics

Piperazine is administered orally and is readily absorbed from the intestinal tract. Most of the drug is excreted in the urine within 24 hours.

Clinical Uses

Piperazine has been used with success to treat *A. lumbricoides* and *E. vermicularis* infections, although mebendazole is now the agent of choice. Piperazine is an appropriate alternative to Mebendazole for the treatment of ascariasis, especially in the presence of intestinal or biliary obstruction. Cure rates of more than 80% are obtained following a 2-day regimen.

Adverse Effects

Side effects occasionally include gastrointestinal distress, urticaria and dizziness. Neurological symptoms of ataxia, hypotonia, visual disturbances and exacerbations of epilepsy can occur in patients with pre existing renal insufficiency. It should not be used in pregnant women because of the formation of a potentially carcinogenic and teratogenic nitrosamine metabolite. Concomitant use of piperazine and chlorpromazine or Pyrantel should be avoided.

Benzimidazoles

Several benzimidazoles are in use for the treatment of helminthic infections. Three of these, mebendazole, thiabendazole and albendazole, are described in this section. They have a broad range of activity against many nematode and cestode parasites, including cutaneous larva migrans, trichinosis, disseminated strongyloidiasis and visceral larva migrans. A fourth, triclabendazole, is considered as the drug of choice for *Fasciola hepatica* therapy.

Albendazole

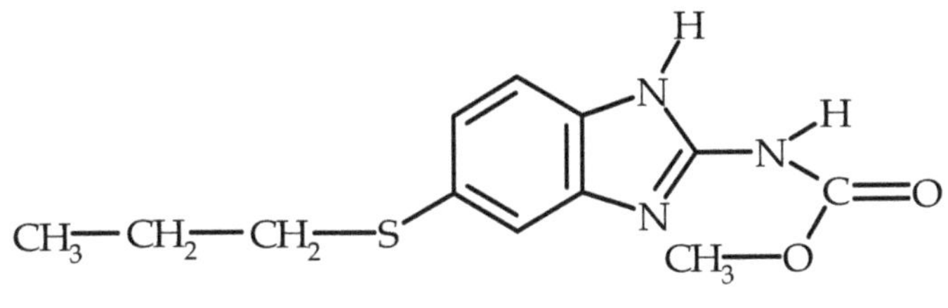

Fig 20-2: Structure of albendazole.

Mechanism of Action

Albendazole (Fig 20-2) appears to cause cytoplasmic microtubular degeneration, which in turn impairs vital cellular processes and leads to parasite death. There is some evidence that the drug also inhibits helminth specific ATP generation by fumarate reductase.

Pharmacokinetics

Albendazole is given orally and is poorly and variably absorbed (5%) because of its poor water solubility. Oral bioavailability is increased as much as five times when the drug is given with a fatty meal instead of on an empty stomach. Concurrent treatment with corticosteroids increases plasma concentrations of albendazole. The drug is rapidly metabolized in the liver to an active sulfoxide metabolite. The half life of the metabolites is 8 to 12 hours.

Clinical Uses

Albendazole has a broad spectrum of activity against intestinal nematodes and cestodes, as well as the liver flukes *Opisthorchis sinensis, Opisthorchis viverrini,* and *Clonorchis sinensis.* It also has been used successfully against Giardia lamblia. Albendazole is an effective treatment of hydatid cyst disease (echinococcosis), especially when accompanied with praziquantel. It also is effective in treating cerebral and spinal neurocysticercosis, particularly when given with dexamethasone. Albendazole is recommended for treatment of gnathostomiasis.

Mebendazole

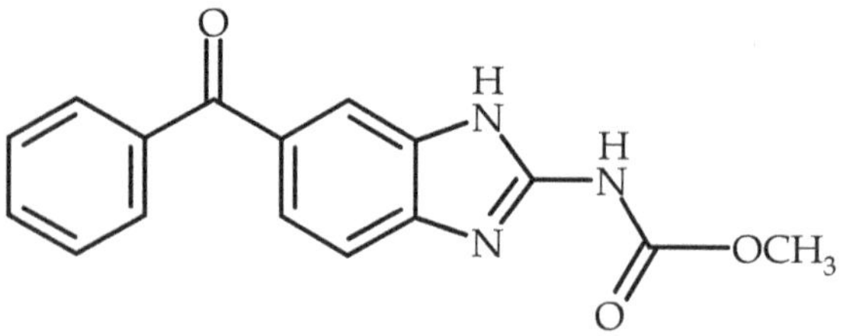

Fig 20-3: Structure of mebendazole.

Mechanism of Action

Unlike thiabendazole, mebendazole (*Vermox*) (Fig 20-3) does not inhibit fumarate reductase. While mebendazole binds to both mammalian and nematode tubulin, it exhibits a differential affinity for the latter, possibly explaining the selective action of the drug. The selective binding to nematode tubulin may inhibit glucose absorption, leading to glycogen consumption and ATP depletion.

Pharmacokinetics

Mebendazole is given orally; it is poorly soluble and very little is absorbed from the intestinal tract. About 5 to 10%, principally the decarboxylated derivatives, is recovered in the urine; most of the orally administered drug is found in the feces within 24 hours.

Clinical Uses

Mebendazole is used primarily for the treatment of *A. lumbricoides, T. trichiura, E. vermicularis,* and hookworm infections, in which it produces high cure rates. It is an alternative agent for the treatment of trichinosis and visceral larva migrans. Owing to its broad spectrum anthelmintic effect, mixed infections (ascariasis, hookworm infestation, or enterobiasis in association with trichuriasis) frequently respond to therapy. High doses have been used to treat hydatid disease, but Albendazole is now thought to be superior.

Adverse Effects

Abdominal discomfort and diarrhea may occur when the worm load is heavy. Its use is contraindicated during pregnancy.

Thiabendazole

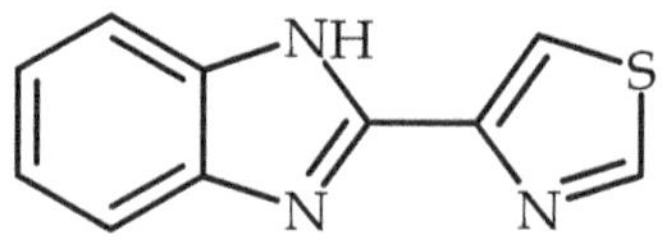

Fig 20-4: Structure of thiabendazole.

Mechanism of Action

Thiabendazole (*Mintezol*) (Fig 20-4) inhibits fumarate reductase and electron transport–associated phosphorylation in helminths. Interference with ATP generation decreases glucose uptake and affects the energy available for metabolism.

Benzimidazole anthelmintics as a class (e.g., thiabendazole, mebendazole and albendazole), bind selectively to tubulin of nematodes (roundworms), cestodes (tapeworms) and trematodes (flukes). This inhibits microtubule assembly, which is important in a number of helminth cellular processes, such as mitosis, transport and motility.

Pharmacokinetics

Thiabendazole is administered orally and is rapidly absorbed from the intestinal tract, with peak plasma levels achieved in 1 to 2 hours. The drug is metabolized in the liver and excreted in urine within 24 to 48 hours as glucuronide and sulfate esters. Approximately 10% is found in feces.

Clinical Uses

Thiabendazole shows a broad spectrum of activity against the following nematodes: *A. lumbricoides, N. americanus, A. duodenale, E. vermicularis, S. stercoralis* and *Trichuris trichiura* (whipworm). It has largely been replaced with safer drugs for all but *Strongyloides* spp. At present, thiabendazole is the drug of choice for the treatment of cutaneous larva migrans (creeping eruption), strongyloidiasis, tricho-strongyliasis and trichinosis.

Adverse Effects

Anorexia, nausea, vomiting, drowsiness and vertigo occur in up to one third of patients.

Diarrhea, pruritus, rash, hallucinations, crystalluria and leukopenia are less common; shock, hyperglycemia, lymphadenopathy and Stevens Johnson syndrome are rare. Some patients report that their urine smells like asparagus, a reaction related to excretion of the metabolite asparagine.

Diethylcarbamazine

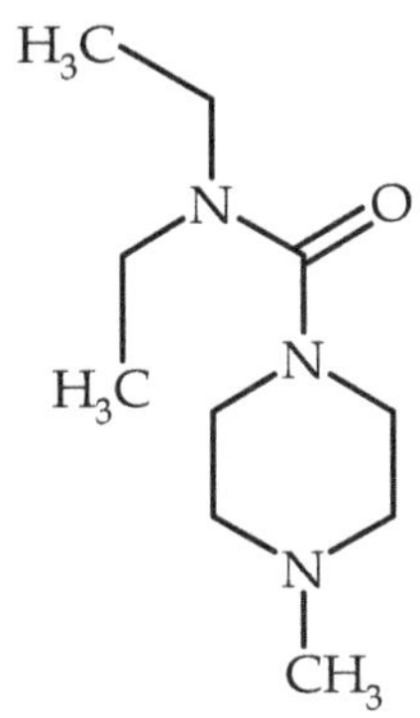

Fig 20-5: Structure of diethylcarbamazine.

Diethylcarbamazine citrate (*Hetrazan*) (Fig 20-5) is active against several microfilaria and adult filarial worms.

Mechanism of Action

It interferes with the metabolism of arachidonic acid and blocks the production of prostaglandins, resulting in capillary vasoconstriction and impairment of the passage of the microfilaria. Diethylcarbamazine also increases the adherence of microfilariae to the vascular wall, platelets and granulocytes.

Pharmacokinetics

Diethylcarbamazine is absorbed from the gastrointestinal tract and peak blood levels are obtained in 4 hours; the drug disappears from the blood within 48 hours. The intact drug and its metabolites are excreted in the urine.

Clinical Uses

Diethylcarbamazine is the drug of choice for certain filarial infections, such as *Wuchereria bancrofti, Brugia malayi* and *Loa loa.* Since diethylcarbamazine is not universally active against filarial infections, a specific diagnosis based on blood smears, biopsy samples and a geographic history is important. Dosage should be adjusted in patients with renal impairment. Caution is necessary when using this agent, particularly when treating onchocerciasis.

Adverse Effects

The sudden death of the microfilariae can produce mild to severe reactions within hours of drug administration. These are manifested by fever, lymphadenopathy, cutaneous swelling, leukocytosis and intensification of any pre existing eosinophilia, edema, rashes, tachycardia and headache. If microfilariae are present in the eye, further ocular damage may result. Other side effects are relatively mild and range from malaise, headache and arthralgias to gastrointestinal symptoms.

Niclosamide

Mechanism of Action

For many years, niclosamide (*Niclocide*) (Fig 20-6) was widely used to treat infestations of derived from anaerobic metabolism. It may also have adenosine triphosphatase. Niclosamide is a chlorinated salicylamide that inhibits the production of energy (cestodes ATPase) stimulating properties. Inhibition of anaerobic incorporation of inorganic phosphate into ATP is detrimental to the parasite. Niclosamide can uncouple oxidative phosphorylation in mammalian mitochondria, but this action requires dosages that are higher than those commonly used in treating worm infections. The drug affects the scolex and proximal segments of the cestodes, resulting in detachment of the scolex from the intestinal wall and eventual evacuation of the cestodes from the intestine by the normal peristaltic action of the host's bowel. It is absorbed by intestinal cestodes but not nematodes. A single dose is usually adequate to produce a cure rate of 95%. With *H. nana* (dwarf tapeworm), a longer treatment course (up to 7 days) is necessary.

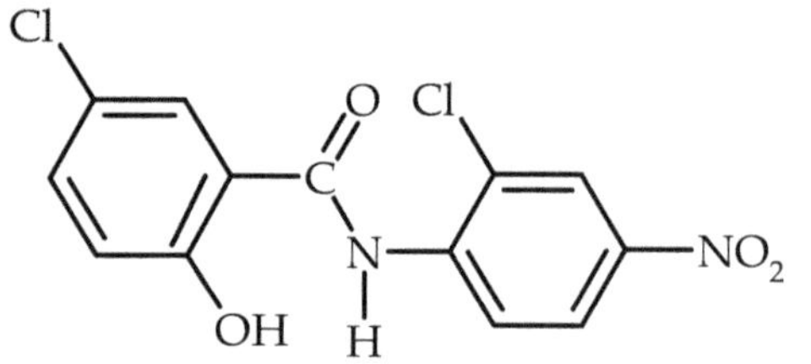

Fig 20-6: Structure of niclosamide.

Pharmacokinetics

Niclosamide is administered orally after the patient has fasted overnight and may be followed in 2 hours by purging (magnesium sulfate 15–30 gm to encourage complete expulsion of the cestode, especially *T. solium,* although this is not always considered necessary. Cure is assessed by follow up stool examination in 3 to 5 months. With the availability of other agents, niclosamide is no longer widely used. The most widely employed agents are praziquantel and the benzimidazoles. Because niclosamide is not absorbed from the intestinal tract, high concentrations can be achieved in the intestinal lumen. The drug is not ovicidal.

Clinical Uses

Niclosamide has been used extensively in the treatment of tapeworm infections caused by *Taenia saginata, Taenia solium, Diphyllobothrium latum, Fasciolopsis buski* and *Hymenolepis nana.* It is an effective alternative to praziquantel for treating infections caused by *T. saginata* (beef tapeworm), *T. solium* (pork tapeworm) and *D. latum* (fish tapeworm) and is active against most other tapeworm infections.

Adverse Effects

No serious side effects are associated with niclosamide use, although some patients report abdominal discomfort and loose stools.

Ivermectin

Ivermectin is a semi synthetic derivative of avermectin which is introduced as anthelmintic in the 1980s by Merck contains large macrocyclic lactone fermented product of the micro organism Streptomyces avermitilis. It is a potent drug and its discovery led to the development of ivermectin analogues which include moxidectin, milbemycin oxime, doramectin, selamectin, abamectin and eprinomectin.

Mechanism of Action

Ivermectin (Fig 20-7) causes the paralysis of pharyngeal and body wall musculature. It has been shown to interact with a range of ligand gated ion channels acetylcholine gated chloride channels, GABA gated chloride channels, histamine gated chloride channels and glycine receptors. Nematode glutamate gated chloride channels (GluCl) has high affinity which is correlated with its potent anthelmintic activity.

Ivermectin (*Mectizan*) acts on parasite specific inhibitory glutamate gated chloride channels that are phylogenetically related to vertebrate GABA-gated chloride channels. Ivermectin causes hyperpolarization of the parasite cell membrane and muscle paralysis. At higher doses it can potentiate GABA-gated chloride channels. It does not cross the blood-brain barrier and therefore has no paralytic action in mammals, since GABA-regulated transmission occurs only in the central nervous system (CNS).

Pharmacokinetics

Ivermectin is administered by the oral and subcutaneous routes. It is rapidly absorbed. Most of the drug is excreted unaltered in the feces. The half-life is approximately 12 hours.

Clinical Uses

Ivermectin has broad spectrum activity in that it can affect nematodes, insects and acarine parasites. It is the drug of choice in onchocerciasis and is quite useful in the treatment of other forms of filariasis, strongyloidiasis, ascariasis, loiasis and cutaneous larva migrans. It is also highly active against various mites. It is the drug of choice in treating humans infected with *Onchocerca volvulus,* acting as a microfilaricidal drug

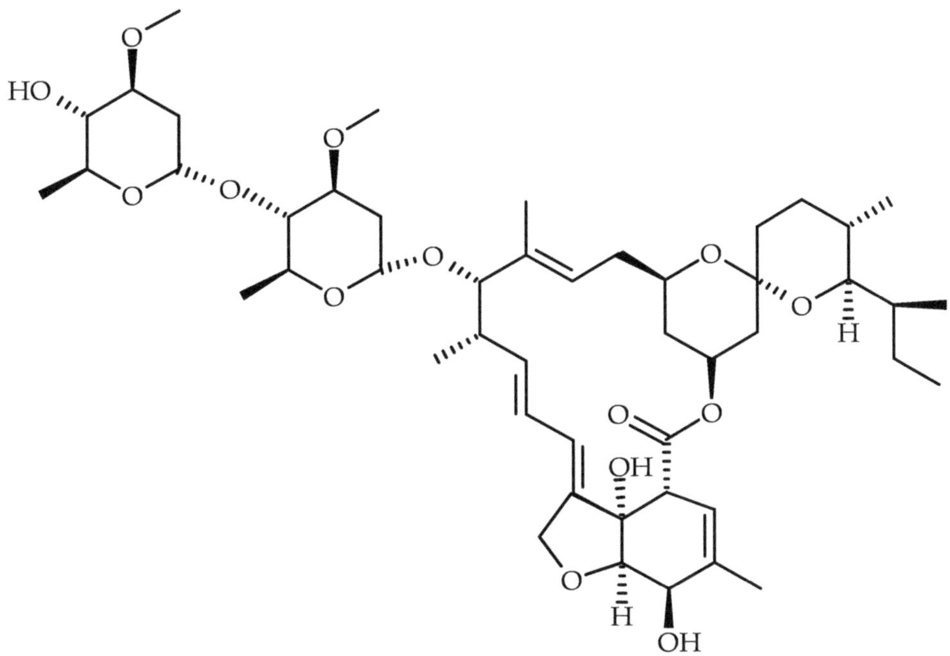

Fig 20-7: Structure of ivermectin.

against the skin dwelling larvae (microfilaria). Annual treatment can prevent blindness from ocular onchocerciasis. Ivermectin is clearly more effective than diethylcarbamazine in bancroftian filariasis and it reduces microfilaremia to near zero levels. In brugian filariasis diethylcar-bamazine induced clearance may be superior. It is also used to treat cutaneous larva migrans and disseminated strongyloidiasis. Its safe use in pregnancy has not been fully established.

Adverse Effects

The side effects are minimal, with pruritus, fever and tender lymph nodes occasionally seen. The side effects are considerably less than those associated with diethylcarbamazine administration.

Suramin

Suramin (Fig 20-8) is widely used as a macro-filaricide in human onchocerciasis and its action on microfilariae also is considerable. It is also useful in the treatment of the hemolym-phatic stage of African trypanosomiasis. Early treatment of the infection with suramin clears trypanosomes from the blood and lymphatics within 30 minutes and keeps them clear for approximately 3 months.

Mechanism of Action

Suramin inhibits a number of filarial enzymes involved with carbohydrate metabolism as well as the production of adenosine triphosphate (ATP). It is 35 times more inhibitory to the dihydrofolate reductase of *O. volvulus* than to the same enzyme in human tissue. It is a potent inhibitor of reverse transcriptase, the DNA polymerase of retroviruses and also has some effects on the infective and cytopathic effects of HIV.

Clinical Uses

It is being evaluated as an anticancer drug, reducing pain and delaying progression in hormone refractory prostate cancer. Its most significant toxicity has been the development of severe polyradiculoneuropathy.

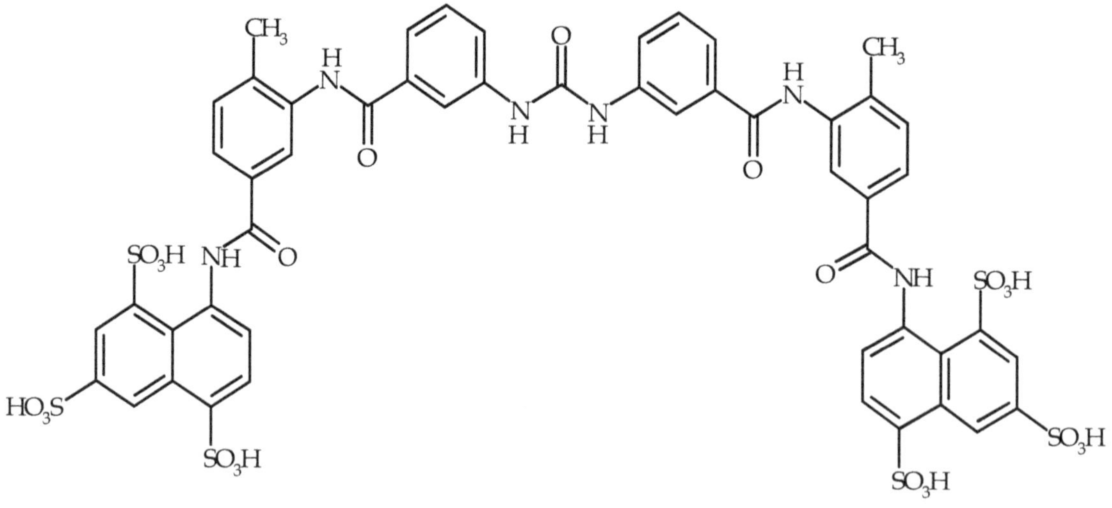

Fig 20-8: Structure of suramin.

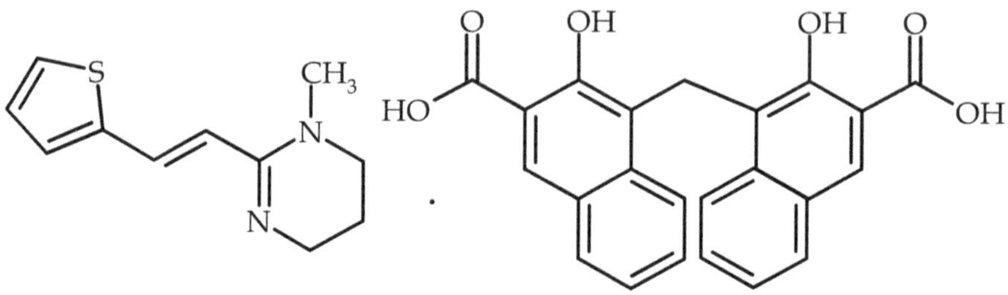

Fig 20-9: Structure of pyrantel pamoate.

Pyrantel Pamoate

Mechanism of Action

Pyrantel pamoate (*Antiminth*) (Fig 20-9) is a agonist at the nicotinic acetylcholine receptor and its actions result in depolarization and spastic paralysis of the helminth muscle. Its selective toxicity occurs primarily because the neuromuscular junction of helminth muscle is more sensitive to the drug than is mammalian muscle.

Pharmacokinetics

This drug is administered orally and because very little is absorbed, high levels are achieved in the intestinal tract. Less than 15% of the drug and its metabolites are excreted in urine.

Clinical Uses

Pyrantel pamoate is active against several roundworms: *A. lumbricoides, Ancylostoma duodenale, Necator americanus* and *E. vermicularis.* Pyrantel is an alternative drug of choice in treating infections with *A. lumbricoides, E. vermicularis* (pinworms) and hookworms (*N. americanus* and *A. duodenale*).

Adverse Effects

It is not recommended for pregnant patients or for children under age 1 year. Although most of the drug remains in the intestinal lumen, enough can be absorbed systemically to cause headache, dizziness and drowsiness. No major adverse effects have been reported on renal, hepatic or haematological systems.

Paraherquamide

Paraherquamide is a drug of oxindole alkaloid family and marcfortine A are isolated from Penicillium paraherquei and Penicillium roqueforti, respectively. Paraherquamide, (Fig 20-10) its derivative, 2 deoxy paraherquamide, induces flaccid paralysis in parasitic nemato-des.

Mechanism of Action

Paraherquamide also block the action of nicotinic agonists but not equipotently. This antagonist has greater affinity to distinguish the nicotinic receptor sub types on the muscle but for the receptors mediating the response to

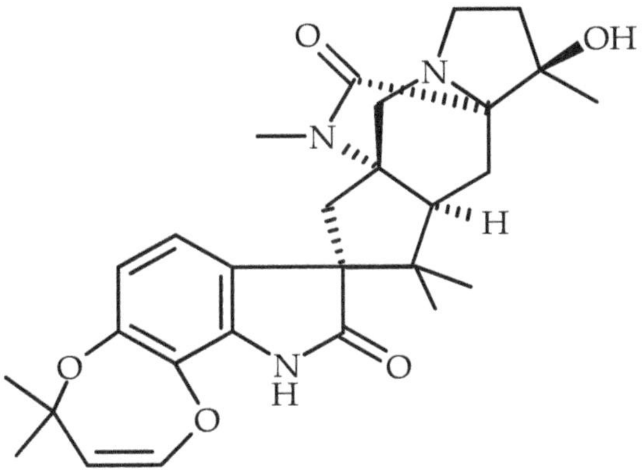

Fig 20-10: Structure of paraherquamide.

levamisole and pyrantel. Paraherquamide was found to be an effective antagonist of the levamisole selective receptor on *C. elegans* body wall muscle and the mode of action of this drug was to interfere with cholinergic transmission, levamisole, is act as competitive antagonists rather than cholinomimetics. It is a competitive inhibitor of the body wall nACh receptor as it would increase transmitter release.

Praziquantel

Mechanism of Action

The neuromuscular effects of praziquantel (*Biltricide*)(Fig 20-11) appear to increase parasite motility leading to spastic paralysis. The drug increases calcium permeability through parasite

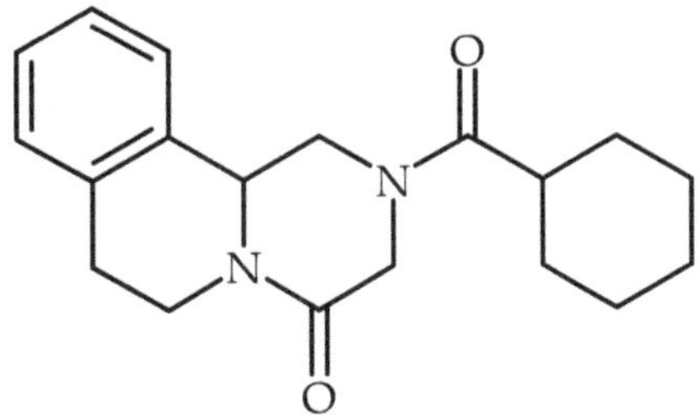

Fig 20-11: Structure of praziquantel.

specific ion channels, so that the tegmental and muscle cells of the parasite accumulate calcium. This action is followed by vacuolization and the exposure of hitherto masked tegmental antigens, lipidanchored protein and actin. Insertion of the drug into the fluke's lipid bilayer causes conformational changes, rendering the ûuke susceptible to antibody and complement mediated assault.

Pharmacokinetics

Praziquantel is readily absorbed (80% in 24 hours) after oral administration, with serum concentrations being maximal in 1 to 3 hours; the drug has a half-life of 0.8 to 1.5 hours. Its bioavailability is reduced by phenytoin or carbamazepine and increased by cimetidine. Dexamethasone decreases plasma praziquantel levels by 50%. Praziquantel is excreted by the kidneys.

Clinical Uses

Praziquantel is an extremely active broad spectrum anthelmintic that is well tolerated. It is the most effective of the drugs used in the treatment of schistosomiasis, possessing activity against male and female adults and immature stages. Unlike other agents, it is active against all three major species (*S. haematobium, S. mansoni* and *S. japonicum*). In addition, it has activity against other flukes, such as *C. sinensis, Paragonimus westermani, O. viverrini* and the tapeworms (*D. latum, H. nana, T. saginata,* and *T. solium*). It is not as effective against *F. hepatica*. It is used effectively in the treatment of clonorchiasis and paragonimiasis and is an effective alternative agent to niclosamide in the treatment of tapeworm infestations.

Adverse Effects

Adverse reactions tend to occur within a few hours of administration. They include gastrointestinal intolerance with nausea, vomiting and abdominal discomfort. This may be due to the liberation of helminth proteins from dead worms rather than any direct effect of the drug.

Oxamniquine

Mechanism of Action

Oxamniquine (*Vansil*) (Fig 20-12) is a tetrahydroquinoline that stimulates parasite muscular activity at low concentrations but causes paralysis at higher concentrations. The drug may act by esterification and binding of DNA, leading to the death of the schistosome by interruption of its nucleic acid and protein synthesis. The fluke may esterify oxamniquine to produce a reactive metabolite that alkylates parasite DNA. Resistance results from absent or defective esterifying activity of the drug. Oxamniquine has a restricted range of efficacy, being active only against *S. mansoni* infections.

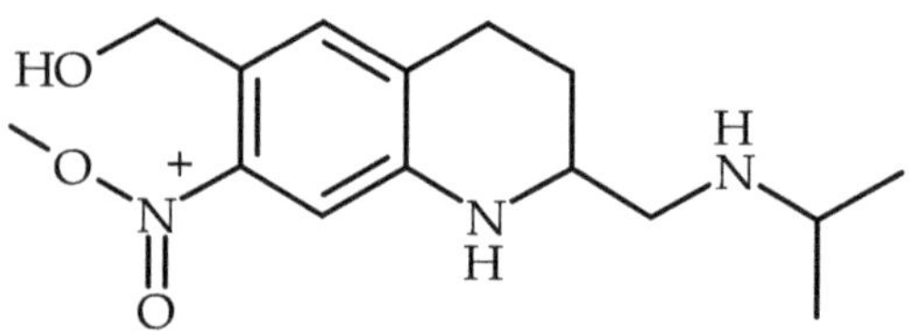

Fig 20-12: Structure of oxamniquine.

Pharmacokinetics

Oxamniquine is given orally and is readily absorbed from the intestinal tract. Peak concentrations in plasma are obtained in about 3 hours. The drug is excreted in urine mostly as a 6-carboxyl derivative.

Adverse Effects

Side effects include CNS toxicity with unsteadiness and occasionally seizures, especially in patients with a history of seizures. It is contraindicated in pregnancy.

Bithionol

Mechanism of Action

Bithionol (*Actamer*) (Fig 20-13) is a phenolic derivative whose mode of action is related to uncoupling of parasite specific fumarate reductase-mediated oxidative phosphorylation.

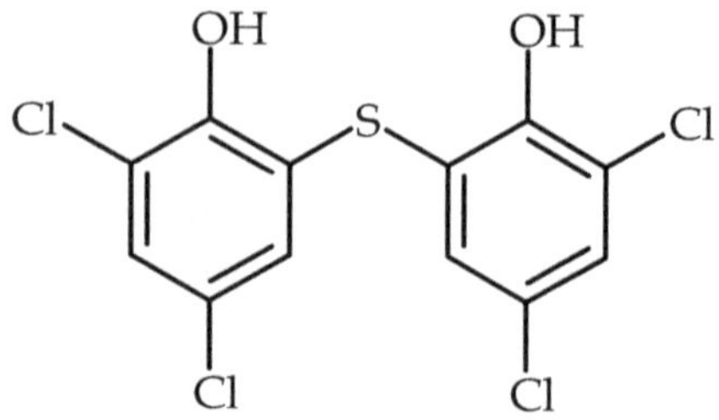

Fig 20-13: Structure of bithionol.

Pharmacokinetics

The drug is administered orally and is absorbed from the intestinal tract. Peak blood levels are achieved in 4 to 8 hours. Excretion is mainly by the kidneys.

Bithionol is used in treatment of *F. hepatica* infections and as an alternative to praziquantel in the treatment of infestation by *P. westermani*. It is highly active against the adult worm but exerts no action against the migratory stages. A second course of treatment is required for complete cure in 20 to 30% of patients.

Adverse Effects

Side effects are generally mild and transient; they include nausea, vomiting, diarrhea, headache, dizziness, urticaria and other skin rashes in 50% of patients.

Metrifonate

Mechanism of Action

Metrifonate (Fig 20-14) is an organophosphorous compound that is effective only in the treatment of S. *haematobium*. The active metabolite, dichlorvos, inactivates acetylcholinesterase and potentiates inhibitory cholinergic effects. The schistosomes are swept away from the bladder to the lungs and are trapped.

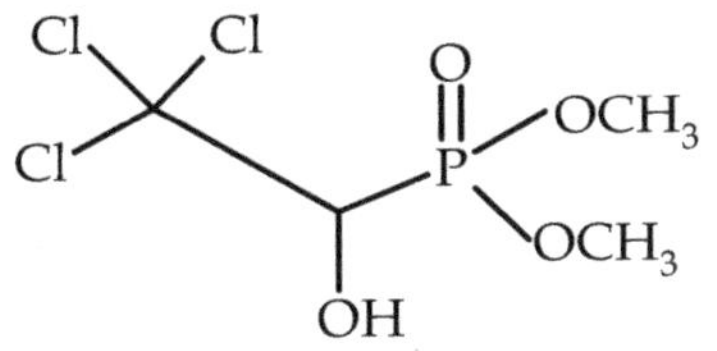

Fig 20-14: Structure of metrifonate.

Adverse Effects

Therapeutic doses produce no untoward side effects except for mild cholinergic symptoms. It is contraindicated in pregnancy, previous insecticide exposure, or with depolarizing neuromuscular blockers. Metrifonate is not available in the United States.

Emodepside

Emodepside is cyclodepsipeptide molecule and semi synthetic derivative. A product obtained through fermentation from the fungus, Mycelia sterilia. Its discovery and anthelmintic activity has recently been discovered. It is effective against isolates of parasites that are resistant to the molecule having pore forming properties. Planar lipids does not appear to be an important inanthelmintic potency, as an optical isomer of emodepside with similar pore forming properties does not shows anthelmintic action. Thus it may act through the stereo specific binding to a receptor. The receptors for the cyclo depsipeptides have been cloned from a H. contortus cDNA library by immuno screening with an antibody. This receptor has been designated in the cells and showed gate calcium flux in a dependent manner. Its homology is like mammalian latrophilins, which is a class of G protein coupled receptors which bind to the neurotoxin, latrotoxin. Latrotoxin paralyze the mammals by triggering neurotransmitter release and thus the identification of latrophilin as an emodepside receptor raised the possibility that emodepside causes paralysis by stimulating excessive neurotransmitter release at neuro-muscular sites thus showing effects such as slowed development, inhibition of pharyngeal pumping, decreased locomotion and inhibition of egg laying in adult hermaphrodites which showed that emodepside exerts its pleiotropic actions. The use of the latrophilins in

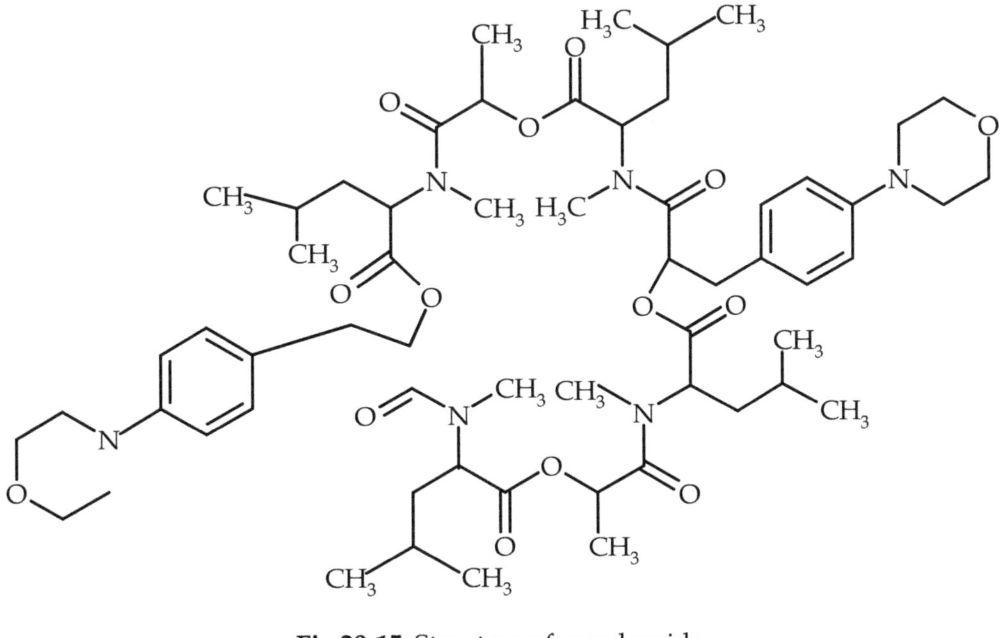

Fig 20-15: Structure of emodepside.

mediating the inhibitory effects of emodepside showed its effects on feeding and locomotion using RNA and genes. The pharyngeal system of mutants showed a reduced sensitivity in the favor of emodepside but its locomotors activity is inhibited. Emodepside does not show its inhibitory effect on locomotion through the other latrophilins mutants which respond just like wild animals. There is no redundancy function in terms of effect of emodepside on locomotion, as the double mutant's responds to emodepside in a similar fashion because emodepside has latrophilin independent actions. Emodepside activates the slo-1 gene which behaves in the same manner as the treated animals thus bring about the neuromuscular inhibition. The structure of Emodepside is shown in Fig 20-15.

Nitazoxanide

Nitazoxanide (Fig 20-16) is a pyruvate ferred oxin oxidoreductase inhibitor which acts

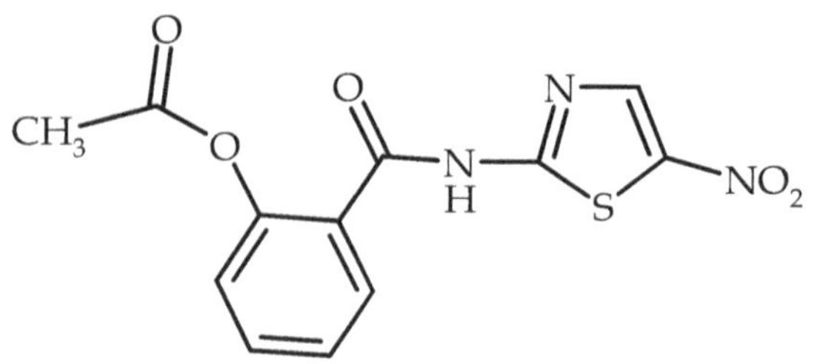

Fig 20-16: Structure of nitazoxanide.

against broad spectrum of protozoa and helminths that occur in the intestinal tract. It is currently used for the treatment of protozoal infections.

The mechanism of action of this compound has not been found in nematodes anaerobic electron transport enzymes are the potential target. After seven days of culture, nitazoxanide reduces population growth by 33%. In contrast mebendazole and albendazole reduced the growth over 90%. Nitazoxanide had no effect on either embryonation or hatching in Heligmosomo idespolygyrus. Therefore the efficacy of this compound is relatively low as compared to other anthelmintic agents.

References

Ammann RW and Eckert J. Cestodes: Echinococcus. Gastroenterol Clin North Am 1996; 25:655–689.

Cook GC. Manson's Tropical Diseases (20th ed.). London: Saunders, 1996. Drugs for parasitic infections. Med Lett Drugs Ther 2000; 42:1–12.

Frayha GJ et al. The mechanisms of action of antiprotozoals and anthelmintic drugs in man. Gen Pharmacol 1997; 28:273–299.

Gilbert DN, Moellering RC Jr, and Sande MA. The Sanford Guide to Antimicrobial Therapy (32nd ed.). Hyde Park, VT: Antimicrobial Therapy, 2002.

Graham CS, Brodie SB, and Weller PF. Imported *Fasciola hepatica* infection in the United States and treatment with triclabendazole. Clin Infect Dis 2001; 33:1–5.

CHAPTER

Antiviral Drugs 21

Introduction

Viruses are obligate intracellular parasites; their replication depends primarily on synthetic processes of the host cell. Therefore, to be effective, antiviral agents must either block viral entry into or exit from the cell or be active inside the host cell. As a corollary, nonselective inhibitors of virus replication may interfere with host cell function and produce toxicity.

Progress in antiviral chemotherapy began in the early 1950s, when the search for anticancer drugs generated several new compounds capable of inhibiting viral DNA synthesis. The two first-generation Antivirals, 5-iododeoxyuridine and trifluorothymidine, had poor specificity (i.e., they inhibited host cell DNA as well as viral DNA) that rendered them too toxic for systemic use. However, both agents are effective when used topically for the treatment of herpes Keratitis.

Recent research has focused on the identification of agents with greater selectivity, *In vivo* stability, and lack of toxicity. Selective antiretroviral agents that inhibit a critical HIV-1 enzyme such as reverse transcriptase or the protease required for final packaging of the virus particle have become available. However, because replication of the virus peaks at or before the manifestation of clinical symptoms in many viral infections, chemoprophylaxis or early initiation of therapy may be key. In chronic illnesses such as viral hepatitis or HIV infection, potent inhibition of viral replication is crucial in limiting the extent of systemic damage.

Viral replication consists of several steps (Fig 21-1).

1. Attachment of the virus to the host cell;
2. Entry of the virus through the host cell membrane;
3. Uncoating of viral nucleic acid;
4. Synthesis of early regulatory proteins, e.g, nucleic acid polymerases;
5. Synthesis of RNA or DNA;
6. Synthesis of late, structural proteins;
7. Assembly (maturation) of viral particles; and
8. Release from the cell. Antiviral agents can potentially target any of these steps.

Research in Antiviral Chemotherapy

In the early 1950s, IdUR and Trifluorothymidine.

In the mid 1970s, Adenine arabinoside (Vidarabine,ara-A,).

In the late 1970s, Acyclovir.

With the appearance of AIDS epidemic in the 1990s, Inhibitor reverse transcriptase or the protease.

Antiviral Agents

The structures of Antiviral agents are shown in Fig 21-2.

Agents to treat Herpes Simplex Virus (HSV) and Varicella Zoseter Virus (VZV) infections

Acyclovir

Valcyclovir

Famciclovir

Penciclovir

Trifluridine

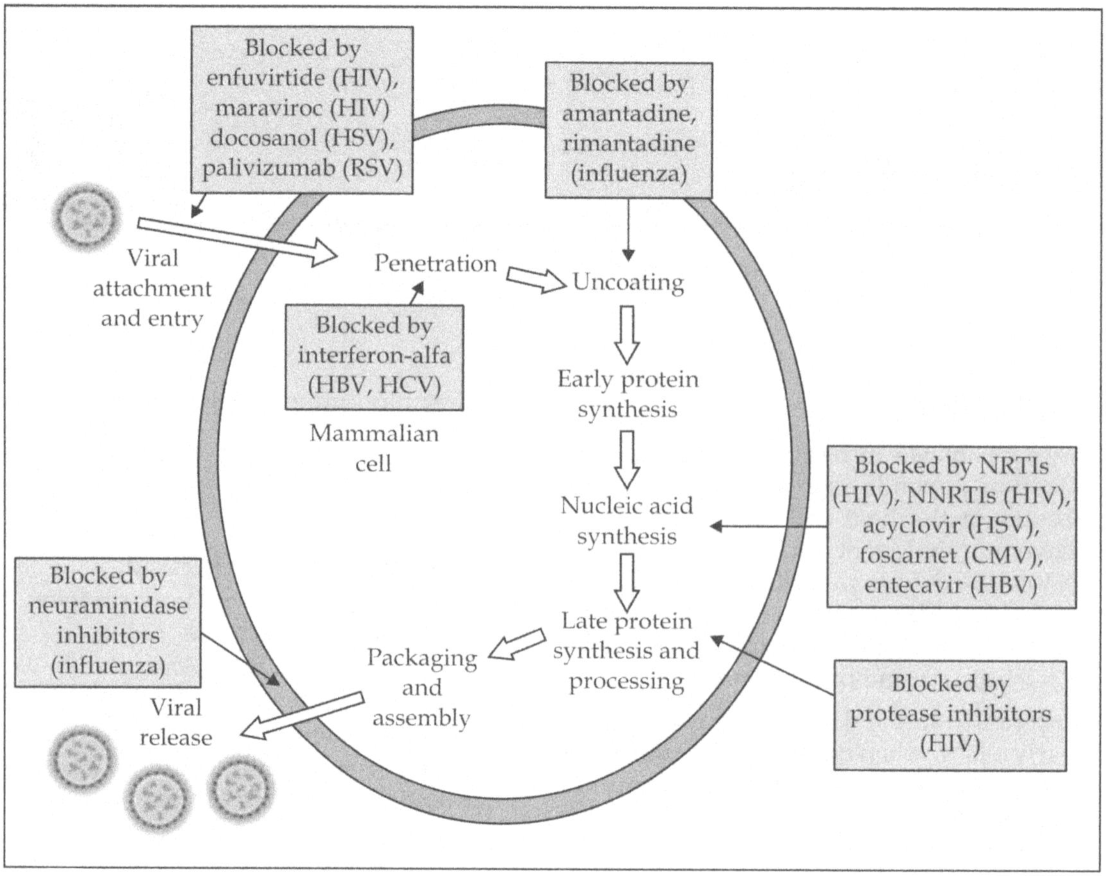

Fig 21-1: Viral replication steps.

Agents to treat Cytomegalovirus (CMV) infections

- Ganciclovir
- Valganciclovir
- Cidofovir
- Foscarnet
- Fomivirsen

Anitretroviralagents: Nucleoside Reverse Transcriptase Inhibitors (NRTIs)

- Zidovudine
- Didanosine
- Lamivudine
- Zalcitabine
- Stavudine
- Abacavir

Nucleotide inhibitors

Tenofovir

NonNucleoside Reverse Transcriptase Inhibitors (NNRTIs)

- Nevirapine
- Delaviridine
- Efavirenz

Protease Inhibitors

- Saquinavir
- Ritonavir
- Lopinavir
- Ritonavir
- Indinavir
- Nelfinavir
- Ampernavir

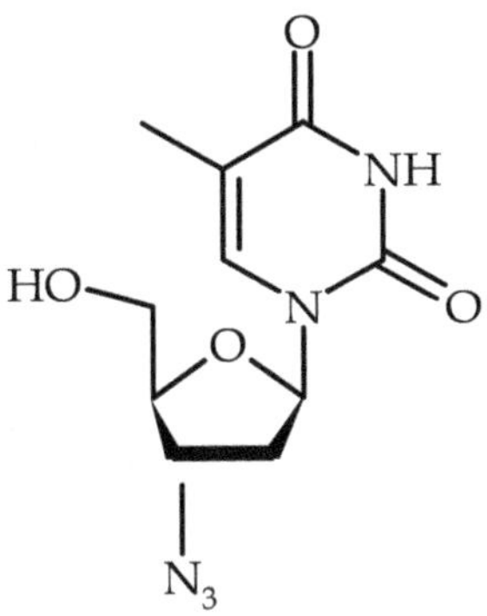

Zidovudine (AZT)

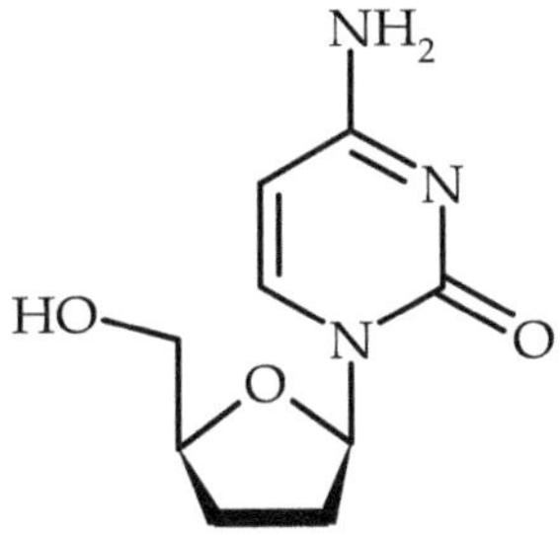

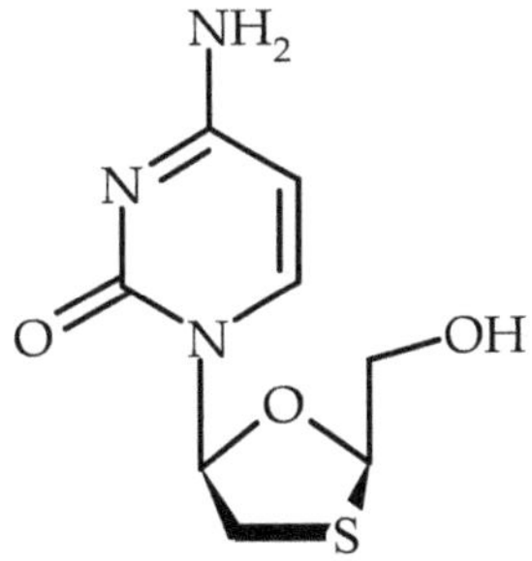

Zalcitabine (ddC) Lamivudine (3TC)

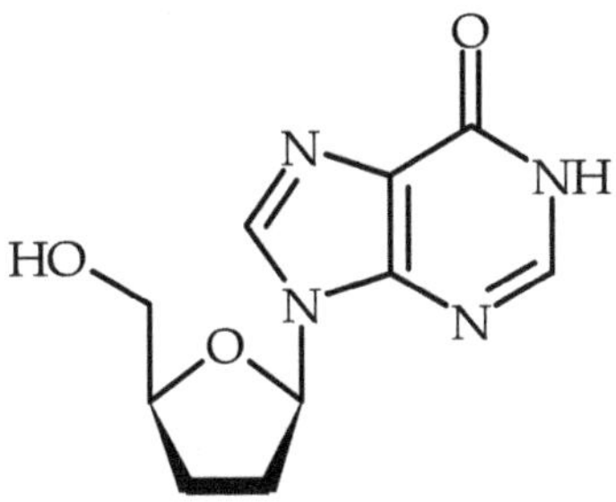

Didanosine (ddl)

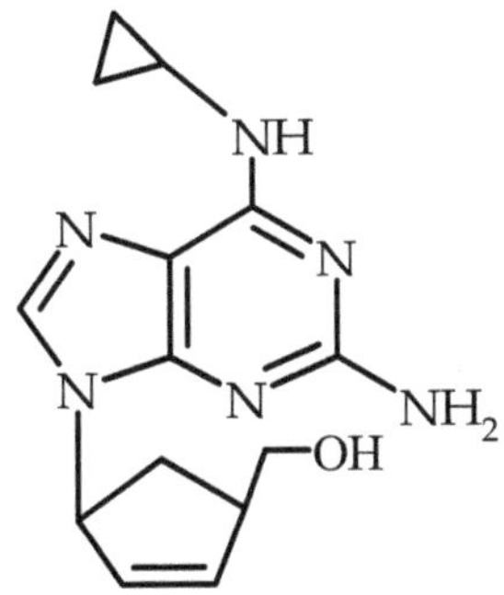

Abacavir

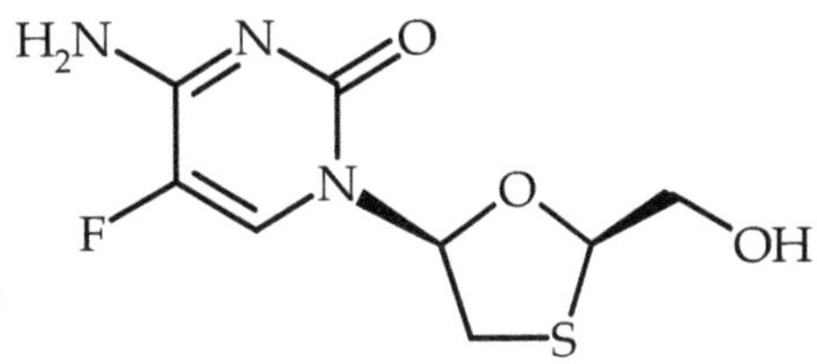

Emtricitabine

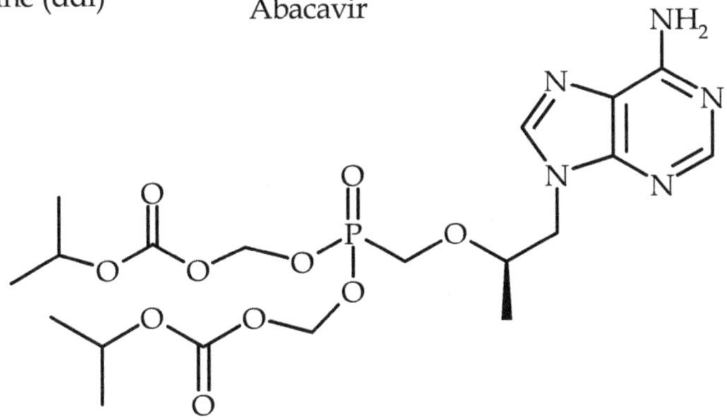

Tenofovir disoproxil

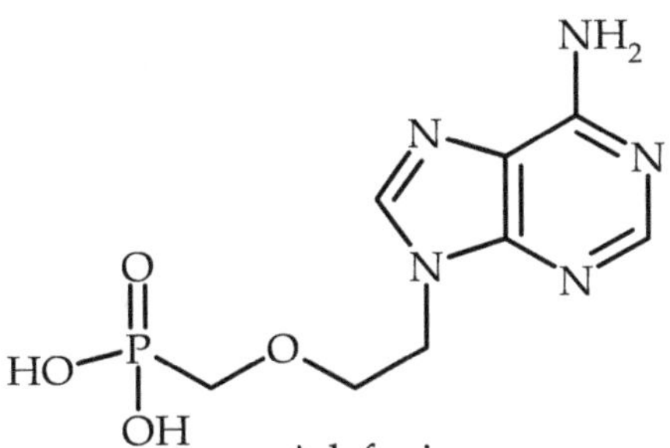

Adefovir

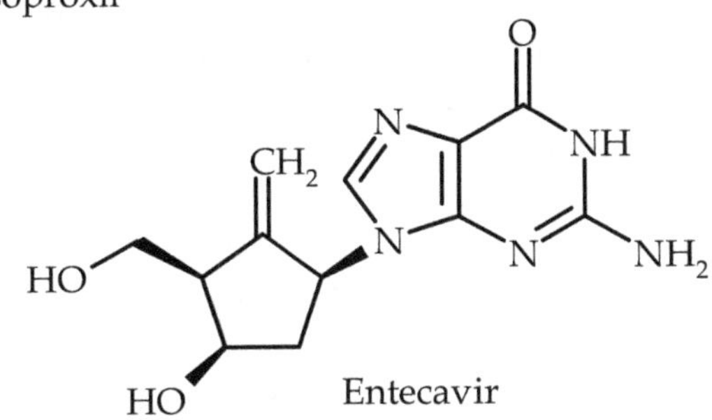

Entecavir

Fig 21-2: Chemical structures of some antiviral nucleoside and nucleotide analogues.

Fusion Inhibitors

Enfuvirtide (HIV)

Docosanol (HSV)

Anti-Hepatitis Agents

Lamivudine

Adefovir

Interferon alpha

Pegylated interferon alpha

Ribavirin

Anti-Influenza Agents

Amantadine

Rimantadine

Zanamivir

Oseltamivir

Other Antiviral Agents

Palivizumab

Imiquimod

Antiviral Drugs: General Features

Many antiviral drugs are purine or pyrimidine analogs.

Many antiviral drugs are prodrugs.

They must be phosphorylated by viral or cellular enzymes in order to become active.

Antiviral drugs typically have a restricted spectrum of antiviral activity and inhibit a specific viral protein, most often an enzyme involved in viral nucleic acid synthesis.

Single nucleotide changes leading to critical amino acid substitutions in a target protein often are sufficient to cause antiviral drug resistance.

Current agents inhibit active replication but do not eliminate nonreplicating or latent viruses so that viral growth may resume after drug removal. Effective host immune response remain essential for recovery from infection.

Antiviral drugs may have antiviral synergistic effects when given concomitantly (i.e. gancyclovir and foscarnet, zidovudine and didanosine, zidovudine and protease inhibitors, etc.). In other cases toxic synergistic effects preclude concurrent administration of two antiviral drugs (i.e., zidovudine and acyclovir, zidovudine and gancyclovir, etc.)

Clinical efficacy of antiviral drugs depends on achieving inhibitory concentrations within infected cells. Therefore a clear relationship between blood concentration and clinical response have not been established for most antiviral agents.

Amantadine and Congeners

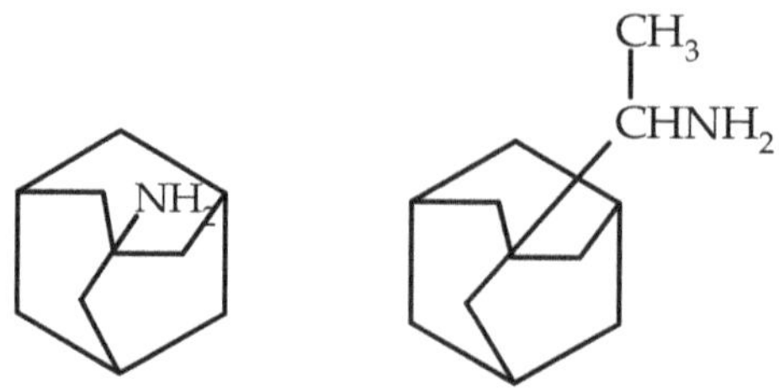

Amantadine Rimantadine

Fig 21-3: Structures of amantadine and congeners.

Amantadine (Symmetrel) (Fig 21-3) is a synthetic tricyclic amine and rimantadine (Flumadine) is its α-methyl derivative. Both drugs inhibit the replication of the three antigenic subtypes of influenza A (H1N1, H2N2 and H3N2) and have negligible activity against influenza B. Their mechanism of action involves inhibition of the viral M2 protein, an integral membrane protein that acts as a H^+ channel. Blockade of the M2 protein prevents the acid-mediated dissociation of the ribonucleoprotein complex that occurs early in replication. In certain strains, the pH changes that result from M2 inhibition alter the conformation of hemagglutinin, hence inhibit viral assembly. Viral resistance develops rapidly in approximately 30% of individuals treated with amantadine or rimantadine. Resistant viruses are associated with the failure of drug prophylaxis in close contacts of infected individuals who have been treated with these antiviral agents. Mutation in the transmembrane domain of the M2 protein is the most frequent cause of resistance to amantadine and rimantadine.

Absorption, Metabolism and Excretion

Amantadine is rapidly and completely absorbed from the gastrointestinal tract and peak blood levels are achieved in 2 to 5 hours.The serum half-life of amantadine averages 17 hours in young adults and 29 hours in the elderly. Most of the drug (90%) is eliminated unchanged by glomerular filtration and tubular secretion. Rimantadine is well absorbed following oral administration, with peak blood levels achieved in 5 to 7 hours. Its elimination half-life averages 25 hours in young adults and 32 hours in the elderly. Less than 25% of the dose is excreted in the urine as unchanged drug; the remainder is eliminated as hydroxylated or conjugated metabolites.

Clinical Uses

Amantadine and rimantadine are used for the treatment of diseases caused by influenza A strains. When these agents are administered within 48 hours of the onset of symptoms, they reduce the duration of fever and systemic complaints by 1 to 2 days and may decrease the duration of viral shedding. Evidence is insufficient to suggest that treatment with these drugs will prevent the development of influenza A virus pneumonitis or other complications in high-risk patients. The Centers for Disease Control's (CDC) Immunization Practices Advisory Committee recommends annual vaccination as the method of choice in the prevention of influenza infection. However, when vaccination is contraindicated or early vaccination is not possible, amantadine and rimantadine are effective prophylactic agents that have been shown to protect approximately 70 to 90% of patients from influenza A infection. Since these drugs do not prevent the host immune response to influenza A, they may be used to prevent infection during the 2- to 4-week period required to develop immunity following vaccination. An additional use of amantadine, unrelated to its antiviral activity, is in the therapy of Parkinson's disease.

Adverse Effects, Contraindications and Drug Interactions

The most frequently reported side effects of amantadine and rimantadine are nausea, anorexia, dizziness and insomnia. These effects are dose related and are more common with amantadine than rimantadine. Depression, impaired coordination, confusion, anxiety, light-headedness, urinary retention and dry mouth are also more frequent with amantadine. High doses of amantadine may produce cardiac arrhythmias, delirium, hallucinations and suicidal ideation; long term treatment may cause peripheral edema, orthostatic hypotension and rarely, congestive heart failure. Abrupt withdrawal of amantadine may produce a neuroleptic malignant syndrome. Both drugs can produce seizures or worsen preexisting seizure disorders. Neither drug should be given during pregnancy and lactation. Individuals with congestive heart failure, edema, orthostatic hypotension, seizure disorders, or uncontrolled psychosis should be closely monitored during therapy with amantadine. The dosage of rimantadine must be decreased in cases of renal or hepatic impairment, whereas amantadine requires dosage adjustment only when renal impairment is present. The elderly are more susceptible to the central nervous system (CNS) and gastrointestinal effects of these drugs; rimantadine is generally better tolerated in this population.

Several drug interactions involving amantadine and rimantadine are clinically significant. Anticholinergic drugs can potentiate the toxicity of amantadine. Thiazide–triamterene, trimethoprim–sulfamethoxazole, quinine and quinidine increase plasma amantadine levels. Cimetidine decreases rimantadine clearance and aspirin and acetaminophen decrease rimantadine plasma levels.

Ribavirin

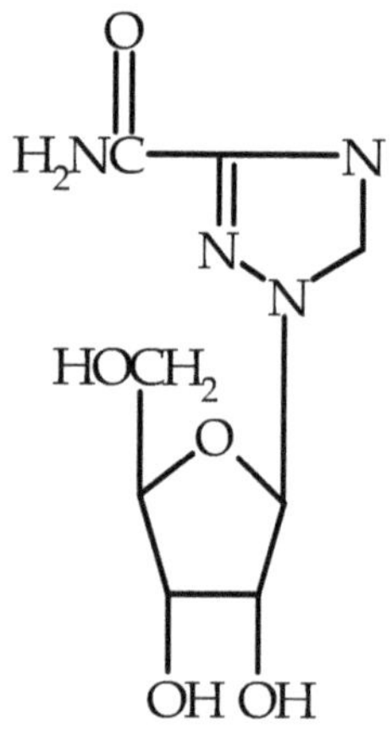

Fig 21-4: Structure of ribavirin.

Ribavirin (Fig 21-4) is a synthetic guanosine analogue that possesses broad antiviral inhibitory activity against many viruses, including influenza A and B, parainfluenza, RSV, HCV, HIV-1 and various herpesviruses, arenaviruses and paramyxoviruses. Its exact mechanism of action has not been fully elucidated; however, it appears to inhibit the synthesis of viral mRNA through an effect on nucleotide pools. Following absorption, host cell enzymes convert ribavirin to its monophosphate, diphosphate, and triphosphate forms. Ribavirin monophosphate inhibits the guanosine triphosphate (GTP) synthesis pathway and subsequently inhibits many GTP-dependent processes. Ribavirin triphosphate inhibits the 5 capping of viral mRNA with GTP and specifically inhibits influenza virus RNA polymerase. Ribavirin may also act by increasing the mutation rate of RNA viruses, leading to the production of nonviable progeny virions.

Absorption, Metabolism and Excretion

Ribavirin can be administered as an aerosol using a small particle aerosol generator. When administered by this route, the drug has only minimal systemic absorption, with drug concentrations in respiratory tract secretions approximately 100 times as high as those found in plasma. Oral absorption is rapid and first pass metabolism is extensive; ribavirin's oral bioavailability is 64% and can be increased by administration with a high fat meal. Steady state levels are reached after 4 weeks.

Ribavirin is reversibly phosphorylated by all nucleated cells. It is also metabolized in the liver to a triazole carboxylic acid metabolite that is eliminated in the urine along with the parent compound. The plasma half life of ribavirin is 9.5 hours when it is administered by aerosol (2.5 hours/day for 3 days), whereas its half-life is around 12.5 days at steady state. The drug accumulates in erythrocytes, with a half-life of 40 days.

Clinical Uses

Ribavirin aerosol (*Virazole*) is indicated in the treatment of high risk infants and young children with severe bronchiolitis or pneumonia due to RSV infection. Treatment is most effective if begun within 3 days of the onset of symptoms. Although ribavirin monotherapy is ineffective against HCV, oral ribavirin in combination with interferon-α (*Rebatron*) is approved for this indication and is effective in patients resistant to interferon therapy alone. Intravenous ribavirin may be useful in the therapy of Hantaan virus infection, Crimean or Congo virus hemorrhagic fever, Lassa fever and severe adenovirus infection.

Adverse Effects, Contraindications and Drug Interactions

Most adverse effects associated with aerosol ribavirin are local. Pulmonary function may decline if aerosol ribavirin is used in adults with chronic obstructive lung disease or asthma. Deterioration of pulmonary and cardiovascular function has also been seen in severely ill infants given this preparation. Rash, conjunctivitis and rare cases of anemia have been reported. Oral and intravenous ribavirin are associated with additional adverse effects. When given via these routes, ribavirin can produce hemolytic anemia that is reversible following dosage reduction or cessation of therapy. When given in combination with interferon-α, ribavirin increases the incidence of many of its side effects, such as fatigue, nausea, insomnia, depression, and anemia, and may cause fatal or nonfatal pancreatitis. Ribavirin is mutagenic, teratogenic, and embryotoxic in animals at doses below the therapeutic level in humans.

It is contraindicated in pregnant women and in the male partners of pregnant women. Women of childbearing potential and male partners of these women must use two effective forms of contraception during ribavirin treatment and for 6 months post therapy. Pregnant women should not directly care for patients receiving ribavirin.

Ribavirin is contraindicated in patients with sickle cell anemia and other hemoglobinopathies because of its propensity to cause anemia. Similarly, persons with coronary disease should not use ribavirin, because anemia may cause deterioration of cardiac function. Oral ribavirin should not be given to individuals with severe renal impairment; no dosage adjustment is necessary for the inhaled formulation. However, patients with hepatic impairment may require dosage adjustment. Little information on the drug interactions of ribavirin is available. *In vitro*, ribavirin inhibits the phosphorylation reactions that are required for activation of zidovudine and stavudine.

Acyclovir and Congeners

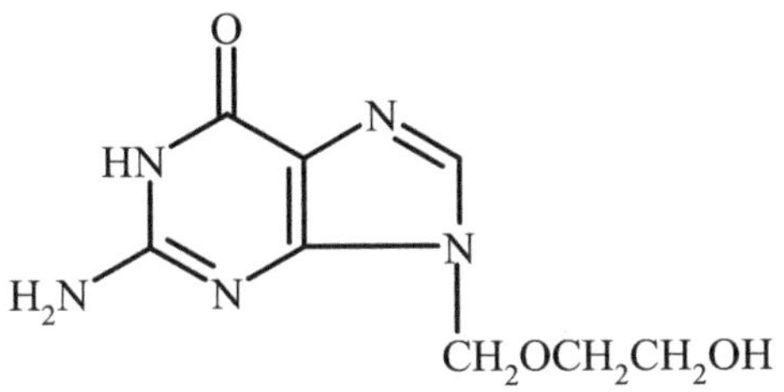

Fig 21-5: Structure of acyclovir.

Acyclovir (*Zovirax*) (Fig 21-5, 21-6) is a guanine nucleoside analogue most effective against HSV-1 and HSV-2, but it has some activity against VCV, CMV and EBV.

Valacyclovir (*Valtrex*) is the L valine ester prodrug of acyclovir. Acyclovir is converted to its active metabolite via three phosphorylation steps. First, viral *thymidine kinase* converts acyclovir to acyclovir monophosphate. Next, host cell enzymes convert the monophosphate to the diphosphate and then to the active compound, acyclovir triphosphate. Because viral thymidine kinase has a much greater affinity for acyclovir triphosphate than does mammalian thymidine kinase, acyclovir triphosphate accumulates only in virus infected cells. The active metabolite of acyclovir inhibits herpesvirus DNA replication in two ways. Acyclovir triphosphate acts as a competitive inhibitor for the incorporation of deoxyguanosine triphosphate (dGTP) into the viral DNA. In addition, acyclovir that is incorporated into viral DNA acts as a chain terminator because it lacks the 3-hydroxy group necessary for further chain elongation.

Viral DNA polymerase becomes irreversibly bound to an acyclovir-terminated DNA chain and is unavailable for further replicative activity. The effect of acyclovir on host cell DNA synthesis is much smaller than its effect on the viral enzyme. Concentrations of acyclovir significantly beyond the therapeutic range are required to inhibit host cell growth. In HSV and VZV, the most common mechanism of resistance to acyclovir involves mutations that result in decreased thymidine kinase activity. Therefore, these viral mutants exhibit cross-resistance to other antiviral agents that require thymidine kinase activation, such as famciclovir, ganciclovir, and valacyclovir. Less commonly, thymidine kinase mutations result in altered substrate specificity. A rare mechanism of acyclovir resistance involves decreased affinity of viral DNA polymerase for the drug.

Absorption, Metabolism and Excretion

Valacyclovir is rapidly and completely converted to acyclovir by intestinal and hepatic first pass metabolism. The bioavailability of acyclovir following oral valacyclovir dosing is three to five times that resulting from oral acyclovir administration and is comparable to that of intravenous acyclovir. Acyclovir absorption is variable and incomplete following oral administration. It is about 20% bound to plasma protein and is widely distributed throughout body tissues. Significant amounts may be found in amniotic fluid, placenta, and breast milk. Acyclovir is both filtered at the glomeruli and actively secreted. Most of the dose is excreted in the urine as unchanged drug; a small portion is excreted as an oxidized inactive metabolite. The plasma half life of acyclovir is 3 to 4 hours in patients with normal kidney function and up to 20 hours in patients with renal impairment.

Clinical Uses

Oral acyclovir is useful in the treatment of HSV-1 and HSV-2 infections, such as genital herpes, herpes encephalitis, herpes keratitis, herpes labialis and neonatal herpes. In initial episodes of genital herpes, oral acyclovir has been found to reduce viral shedding, increase the speed of healing of lesions and decrease the duration of pain and new lesion formation. Acyclovir appears to be less effective in the treatment of recurrent herpes genitalis but may be used for the long term suppression of recurrent HSV. Intravenous acyclovir is used in the treatment of herpes simplex encephalitis, neonatal HSV infection and mucocutaneous HSV infection in immunocompromised individuals. Acyclovir ointment is used in the treatment of initial genital herpes but is not effective for recurrent disease. Ophthalmic acyclovir formulations, although not available in the United States, are effective in the treatment of herpes keratoconjunctivitis. Acyclovir reduces the extent and duration of VZV lesions in adults and children, although higher doses are required than for the treatment of HSV infection. Although not recommended for the routine treatment of uncomplicated varicella in children, acyclovir may be used for chickenpox treatment and prophylaxis in high risk individuals. Acyclovir accelerates healing in patients with herpes zoster (shingles), but it does not affect postherpetic neuralgia. Immunocompromised individuals and patients receiving immunosuppressive drugs or cancer chemotherapy have a high incidence of severe reactivated HSV and VZV infections. In these patients, acyclovir has been shown to be effective for the prophylaxis and therapy of HSV and

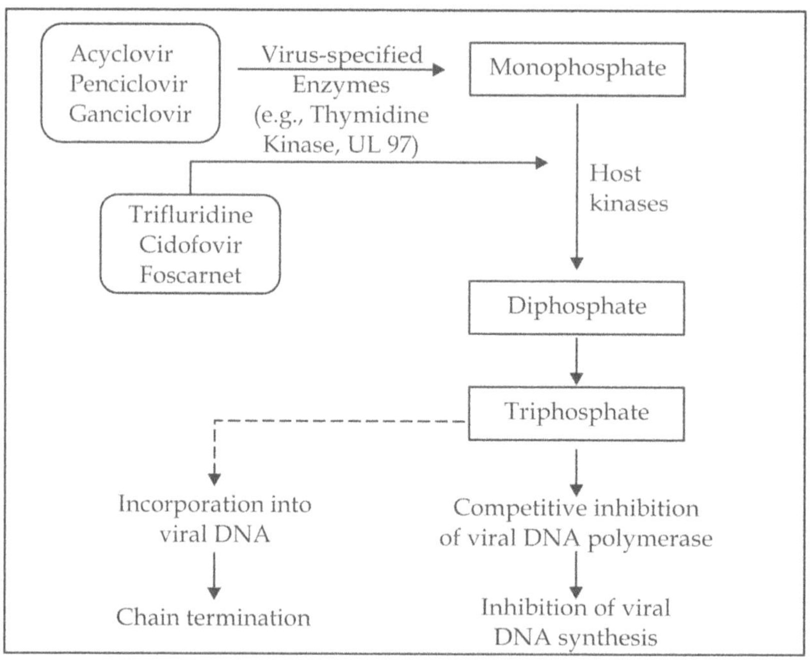

Fig 21-6: Mechanism of action of antiherpes agents.

VZV. Valacyclovir demonstrates efficacy similar to that of acyclovir but requires less frequent oral dosing. While indicated for the treatment of herpes zoster and the treatment and suppression of HSV, it is not approved for use in immunocompromised individuals or for the therapy of disseminated herpes zoster.

Adverse Effects, Contraindications and Drug Interactions

The adverse effects of valacyclovir and acyclovir are similar. Toxicity is generally minimal, consisting largely of headache, nausea, and diarrhea. Less frequently observed are skin rash, fatigue, fever, hair loss and depression. Reversible renal dysfunction (azotemia) and neurotoxicity (tremor, seizure, delirium) are doselimiting toxicities of intravenous acyclovir. Adequate hydration and slow drug infusion can minimize the risk of renal toxicity. Aside from drug hypersensitivity, there are no absolute contraindications to the use of acyclovir and valacyclovir. Adjustment of drug dosage is required in patients with renal impairment. A potentially fatal disorder, thrombotic thrombocytopenic purpura hemolytic uremic syndrome (TTP-HUS), has been reported in immunocompromised individuals. Animal studies have demonstrated no teratogenic or embryotoxic effects of valacyclovir and acyclovir. Although there are no large, controlled studies of the safety of these drugs in pregnant women, a prospective epidemiological registry of acyclovir use during pregnancy showed no increase in the incidence of common birth defects. The potential for drug interactions, particularly with other drugs that are actively secreted by the proximal tubules, should be considered. Probenecid has been shown to inhibit the renal clearance of acyclovir. Cyclosporine and other nephrotoxic agents may increase the risk of renal toxicity of acyclovir.

Vidarabine

Vidarabine (adenine arabinoside, Vira-A) (Fig 21-7) is an adenine nucleoside analogue containing arabinose in place of ribose. It is obtained from cultures of Streptomyces antibiotics and has activity against HSV-1, HSV-2, VZV, CMV, HBV, poxviruses, hepadnaviruses, rhabdoviruses and certain RNA tumor viruses. Cellular enzymes convert this drug to a triphosphate that inhibits DNA polymerase activity.

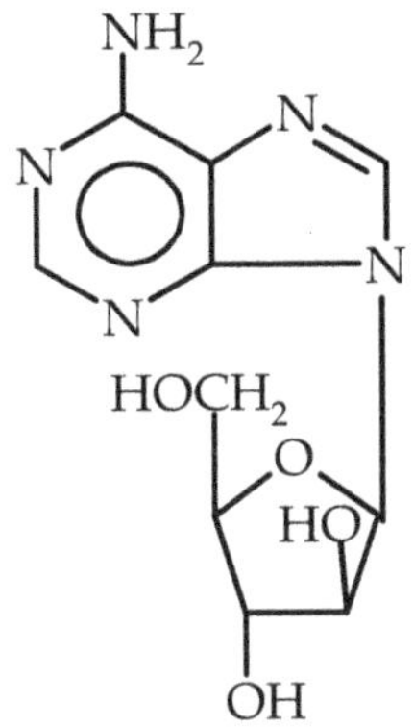

Fig 21-7: Structure of vidarabine.

Vidarabine triphosphate competes with deoxyadenosine triphosphate (dATP) for access to DNA polymerase and also acts as a chain terminator. Although vidarabine is incorporated into host DNA to some extent, viral DNA polymerase is much more susceptible to inhibition by vidarabine. Vidarabine also inhibits ribonucleoside reductase and other enzymes. Resistance occurs as a result of DNA polymerase mutation. Absorption, Metabolism, and Excretion Vidarabine is administered only as a topical ophthalmic ointment. It has relatively limited solubility and is not significantly absorbed after application to the eye. Within the tissues, it is rapidly deaminated to its principal metabolite, arabinosyl hypoxanthine, which retains some degree of antiviral activity.

Clinical Uses

The principal use of vidarabine is in the treatment of HSV keratoconjunctivitis. It is also used to treat superficial keratitis in patients unresponsive or hypersensitive to topical idoxuridine.

Adverse Effects, Contraindications and Drug Interactions

The most commonly observed side effects associated with vidarabine are lacrimation, burning, irritation, pain and photophobia. Vidarabine has oncogenic and mutagenic potential; however, the risk of systemic effects is low because of its limited absorption. It should not be used in conjunction with ophthalmic corticosteroids, since these drugs increase the spread of HSV infection and may produce side effects such as increased intraocular pressure, glaucoma, and cataracts.

Idoxuridine and Trifluridine

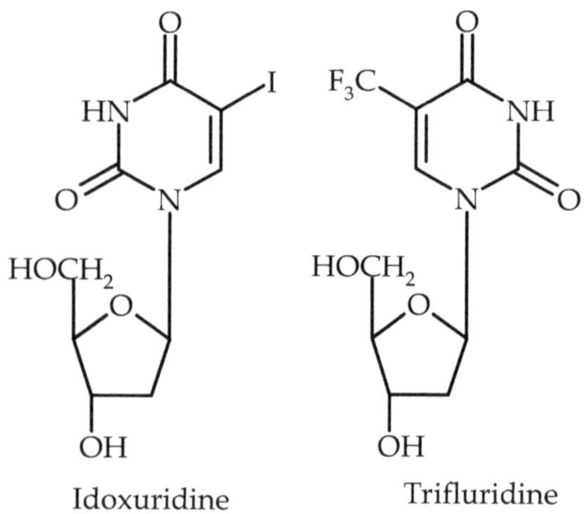

Fig 21-8: Structure of idoxuridine and trifluridine.

Idoxuridine

Idoxuridine (Herplex) (Fig 21-8) is a water soluble iodinated derivative of deoxyuridine that inhibits several DNA viruses including HSV, VZV, vaccinia, and polyoma virus. The triphosphorylated metabolite of idoxuridine inhibits both viral and cellular DNA synthesis and is also incorporated into DNA. Such modified DNA is susceptible to strand breakage and causes aberrant viral protein synthesis. Because of its significant host cytotoxicity, idoxuridine cannot be used to treat systemic viral infections. The development of resistance to this drug is common.

Absorption, Metabolism and Excretion

Idoxuridine is marketed strictly for topical ophthalmic use and systemic exposure is insignificant. However, after oral dosing, the drug is rapidly metabolized and excreted. It tends not to accumulate in body tissues.

Clinical Uses

The only FDA-approved use of idoxuridine is in the treatment of herpes simplex infections of the eyelid, conjunctiva and cornea. It is most effective against surface infections because it has little ability to penetrate the tissues of the eye. intravenous idoxuridine was designated an orphan drug for the treatment of soft tissue sarcoma.

Adverse Effects, Contraindications and Drug Interactions

Idoxuridine may cause local irritation, mild edema, itching and photophobia. Corneal clouding and small punctuate defects in the corneal epithelium have been reported. Allergic reactions are rare.

Trifluridine

Trifluridine (Viroptic) is a fluorinated pyrimidine nucleoside that has *invitro* activity against HSV-1 and HSV- 2, vaccinia and to a lesser extent, some adenoviruses. Activation of trifluridine requires its conversion to the 5 monophosphate form by cellular enzymes. Trifluridine monophosphate inhibits the conversion of deoxyuridine monophosphate (dUMP) to deoxythymidine monophosphate (dTMP) by thymidylate synthetase. In addition, it competes with deoxythymidine triphosphate (dTTP) for incorporation by both viral and cellular

DNA Polymerases

Trifluridine resistant mutants have been found to hav e alterations in thymidylate synthetase specificity.

Absorption, Metabolism and Excretion No detectable trifluridine is found in the blood following topical instillation of trifluridine into the eyes. Its half-life is approximately 12 minutes.

Clinical Uses

Trifluridine is administered as a topical ophthalmic solution for the treatment of primary keratoconjunctivitis and recurrent keratitis due to HSV-1 or HSV-2. It is not effective in the prophylaxis of these infections; however, it is effective in treating patients who were unresponsive or intolerant to topical idoxuridine or vidarabine.

Adverse Effects, Contraindi-cations and Drug Interactions

The most frequent adverse reactions to trifluridine administration are transient burning or stinging and palpebral edema. Other adverse reactions include superficial punctate keratopathy, epithelial keratopathy, hypersensitivity, stromal edema, irritation, keratitis sicca, hyperemia and increased intraocular pressure. Trifluridine is mutagenic *in vitro* and carcinogenic and teratogenic when administered subcutaneously to animals. Topical trifluridine was not teratogenic in animal studies. Because it is applied topically in humans, the likelihood of systemic effects is low.

Foscarnet

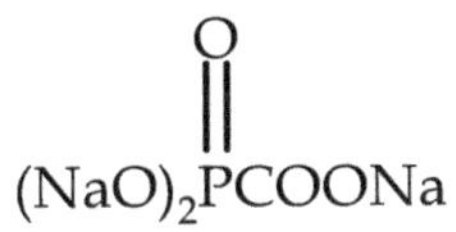

Fig 21-9: Structure of foscarnet sodium.

Foscarnet (*Foscavir*) (Fig 21-9) is an inorganic pyrophosphate analogue that acts *invitro* against HSV-1, HSV-2, VZV, CMV, EBV, HBV, and HIV. It acts as a noncompetitive inhibitor of viral DNA polymerase and reverse transcriptase by reversibly binding to the pyrophosphate binding site of the viral enzyme and *preventing the cleavage of pyrophosphate from deoxynucleoside triphosphates*

Resistance to foscarnet may result from mutation of viral DNA polymerase. Because this drug does not require phosphorylation for activation, thymidine kinase–deficient mutants should not be resistant to foscarnet.

Absorption, Metabolism and Excretion

Because of its poor oral bioavailability, foscarnet is administered intravenously. Following intravenous infusion, 14 to 17% of foscarnet is bound to plasma proteins. The concentration of this compound in the vitreous humor is approximately the same as its plasma level. Foscarnet accumulates in bone; this property may prolong terminal elimination half-life of 45 to 130 hours. Foscarnet is eliminated primarily as unchanged drug via glomerular filtration and active tubular secretion.

Clinical Uses

Foscarnet is indicated for the treatment of CMV retinitis in AIDS patients. Its effectiveness is comparable to that of ganciclovir; these drugs are synergistic when given to counteract refractory retinitis. A decreased incidence of Kaposi's sarcoma has been observed in AIDS patients who have undergone foscarnet therapy. Foscarnet is approved for the treatment of acyclovir resistant mucocutaneous HSV infections in immunocompromised individuals. A clinical study indicated that it is more effective than vidarabine. Foscarnet has also been used for the treatment of acyclovir resistant VZV and nonretinitis forms of CMV infection, although its efficacy is not so well established.

Adverse Effects, Contraindications and Drug Interactions

The most clinically significant adverse effect of foscarnet is renal impairment. Nephrotoxicity is most likely to occur during the second week of induction therapy but may occur at any time during induction or maintenance therapy. Serum creatinine levels may be elevated in up to 33 to 50% of patients; this effect is usually reversible upon drug discontinuation. Dehydration, previous renal impairment and concurrent administration of other nephrotoxic drugs increase the risk of renal toxicity. Infusion of fluids along with foscarnet decreases the likelihood of renal impairment to about 12%. Dosage adjustment is required for patients with renal insufficiency. Foscarnet is also associated with adverse effects on a variety of other organ systems. It may induce changes in serum electrolytes, including hypocalcemia, hypophosphatemia, hyperphosphat emia, hypomagnesemia and hypokalemia. Neurological and cardiovascular signs such as paresthesia, tetany, arrhythmias and seizures may result from these mineral imbalances. Anemia and granulocytopenia occur fairly commonly but seldom require discontinuation of therapy. Headache, vomiting and diarrhea also occur with regularity. Genital ulceration has been reported and is likely due to high levels of ionized drug in the urine. While studies in rats indicate a lack of carcinogenicity, cell culture studies suggest a mutagenic effect. The safety of foscarnet during childhood, pregnancy and lactation has not been established. Foscarnet should not be used in combination with drugs that cause renal toxicity (e.g., acyclovir, aminoglycosides, amphotericin B, NSAIDs). Abnormal renal function has been noted when foscarnet is used with ritonavir or ritonavir and saquinavir. Pentamidine may increase the risk of nephrotoxicity, hypocalcemia, and hypomagnesemia. Caution should be used when foscarnet is given in combination with agents that can cause mineral imbalances.

Zidovudine

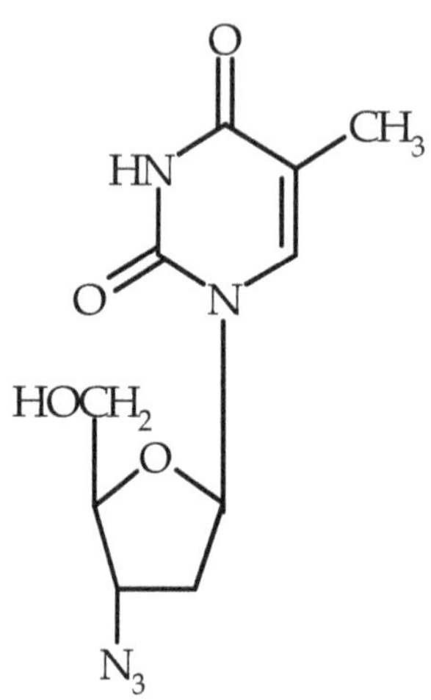

Fig 21-10: Structure of zidovudine.

Zidovudine (AZT, ZDV) (Fig 21-10) was the first antiviral drug used against HIV. It is a thymidine analogue that is effective against HIV-1, HIV-2, and human T-cell lymphotrophic virus (HTLV) I and II. It is available as a single agent (*Retrovir*) or in fixed combinations with lamivudine (*Combivir*) or lamivudine and abacavir (*Trizivir*). Zidovudine, in combination with one or more other antiretroviral agents, is approved for the treatment of HIV infection in adults and children and for postexposure prophylaxis. It is used alone or in combination for the prevention of prenatal and perinatal transmission to the baby by HIV-infected pregnant women.

The most common adverse reactions to zidovudine are headache, nausea, vomiting and anorexia. Fatigue, confusion, insomnia, malaise, hepatitis, myopathy and myositis may also occur. Bone marrow toxicity occurs in up to 30% of patients taking zidovudine; anemia, neutropenia and other hematological abnormalities can necessitate a dosage reduction, drug discontinuation, or therapy with erythropoietin or colony stimulating factors. Cross resistance to multiple nucleoside analogues has been documented.

Caution should be exercised when zidovudine is administered to patients with preexisting anemia or neutropenia and to those with advanced cases of AIDS. Dosage adjustment is required for patients with significant renal impairment and may also be necessary in those with hepatic impairment.

Zidovudine should be used cautiously with any other agent that causes bone marrow suppression, such as interferon-α trimethoprim-sulfamethoxazole, dapsone, foscarnet, flucytosine, ganciclovir and valganciclovir. Probenecid inhibit the elimination of zidovudine; therefore, a dosage reduction of zidovudine is necessary when the drugs are administered concurrently. Ribavirin inhibits the phosphorylation reactions that activate zidovudine and zidovudine similarly inhibits the activation of stavudine; thus, the coadministration of zidovudine with ribavirin or stavudine is contraindicated.

Deoxynucleosides used in AIDS

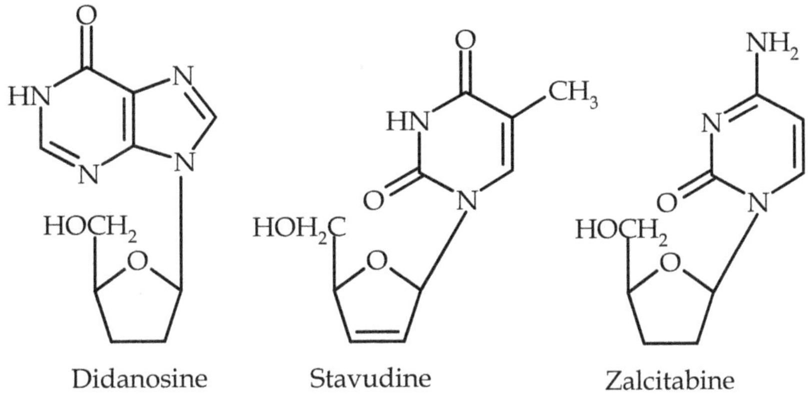

Fig 21-11: Structure of didanosine, stavudine and zalcitabine.

Stavudine

Stavudine (d4T, *Zerit*) (Fig 21-11) is a thymidine nucleoside analogue that is active against HIV-1 and HIV-2. It is approved for the therapy of HIV infection as part of a multidrug regimen and is also used for postexposure prophylaxis.

The adverse effects with which stavudine is most frequently associated are headache, diarrhea, skin rash, nausea, vomiting, insomnia, anorexia, myalgia, and weakness. Peripheral neuropathy consisting of numbness, tingling or pain in the hands or feet is also common with higher doses of the drug. Significant elevation of hepatic enzymes may be seen in approximately 10 to 15% of patients. Lactic acidosis occurs more frequently with stavudine than with other NRTIs. Viral resistance to stavudine may develop and cross resistance to zidovudine and didanosine may occur.

Stavudine should be used with caution in patients at risk for hepatic disease and those who have had pancreatitis. Persons with peripheral neuropathy, the elderly, and those with advanced HIV disease are at increased risk for neurotoxicity. Dosage adjustment is required for patients with renal insufficiency. Stavudine possesses several clinically significant interactions with other drugs. Although hydroxyurea enhances the antiviral activity of stavudine and didanosine, combination therapy that includes stavudine and didanosine, with or without hydroxyurea, increases the risk of pancreatitis. Combinations of stavudine and didanosine should not be given to pregnant women because of the increased risk of metabolic acidosis. Zidovudine inhibits the phosphorylation of stavudine; thus, this combination should be avoided.

Didanosine

Didanosine (ddI, *Videx*) is an adenosine analogue with activity against HIV-1, HIV-2 and HTLV-I. It is approved as part of a multidrug regimen for the therapy of HIV infection and is also used as postexposure HIV prophylaxis.

The most common adverse effect produced by didanosine is diarrhea. Abdominal pain, nausea, vomiting, anorexia and dose related peripheral neuropathy may occur. Pancreatitis occurs rarely, as do hyperuricemia, bone marrow suppression, retinal depigmentation and optical neuritis. Resistance to didanosine appears to result from mutations different from those responsible for zidovudine resistance.

Didanosine should be used with great caution in individuals who have a history of pancreatitis. Didanosine tablets contain phenylalanine and should not be taken by phenylketonurics. Didanosine should be used cautiously in patients with gout, peripheral neuropathy and advanced AIDS.

Buffering agents that are compounded with didanosine to counteract its degradation by gastric acid may interfere with the absorption of other drugs that require acidity (e.g., indinavir, delavirdine, ketoconazole, fluoroquinolones, tetracyclines, dapsone). An enteric coated formulation (*Videx EC*) that dissolves in the basic pH of the small intestine is not susceptible to these interactions. Ganciclovir and valganciclovir can increase blood levels of didanosine.The use of zalcitabine with didanosine is not recommended because that combination carries an additive risk of peripheral neuropathy. The combination of didanosine with stavudine increases the risk of pancreatitis, hepatotoxicity and peripheral neuropathy. Stavudine should not be given with didanosine to pregnant women because of the increased risk of metabolic acidosis.

Lamivudine

Lamivudine (3TC, *Epivir*) is a cytosine nucleoside analogue with activity against HIV-1, HIV-2 and hepatitis B virus. It is approved as part of a multidrug regimen for the therapy of HIV infection in adults and children and has been used for HIV postexposure prophylaxis. Combination products contain lamivudine with either zidovudine (*Combivir*) or zidovudine and abacavir (*Trizivir*). The use of low dose lamivudine in the treatment of chronic hepatitis B is described in Chapter 50.

Lamivudine is the best tolerated NRTI. Its most common adverse effects include headache, malaise, fatigue and insomnia. Pancreatitis is rare. Gastrointestinal complaints are common with lamivudine zidovudine therapy but are probably mainly due to the zidovudine component. Lamivudine resistance sometimes occurs early in treatment. Cross resistance to zalcitabine, didanosine and abacavir can occur simultaneously. Withdrawal of lamivudine in patients infected with both hepatitis B virus and HIV can cause a flareup of hepatitis symptoms.

Lamivudine is associated with an increased risk of pancreatitis in children and should be used with great caution in children who have had pancreatitis or are at high risk for it. Dosage adjustment is necessary in patients with renal impairment. Lamivudine should not be used in combination with zalcitabine, because they inhibit each other's activation by phosphorylation. Trimethoprim inhibits the renal elimination of lamivudine.

Abacavir

Abacavir (*Ziagen*) is a guanosine nucleoside analogue indicated for the therapy of HIV-1 infection in adults and children. It is used as part of a multidrug regimen and is available in a fixed dose combination with zidovudine and lamivudine (*Trizivir*). It is also used for postexposure HIV infection prophylaxis.

Abacavir is associated with side effects such as anorexia, nausea, vomiting, malaise, headache and insomnia. *A potentially fatal hypersensitivity reaction develops in approximately 5% of patients, usually early in the course of treatment.* Fever and rash are the most common symptoms of this reaction; malaise, respiratory symptoms and gastrointestinal complaints may also occur.

Resistance to abacavir may be associated with resistance to zidovudine, didanosine and lamivudine.

Abacavir undergoes extensive hepatic metabolism; therefore, patients with liver disease should be monitored closely if this drug is given. Ethanol inhibits the metabolism of abacavir because it competes for metabolism by alcohol dehydrogenase. Abacavir is not known to inhibit or induce cytochrome P450 isozymes.

Zalcitabine

Zalcitabine (ddC, *Hivid*) is a cytidine analogue active against HIV-1, HIV-2, and hepatitis B virus. It is used for the treatment of HIV infection in adults and asymptomatic children as part of a multidrug regimen. It may be less effective than the other nucleoside inhibitors and is used less frequently.

Peripheral neuropathy occurs in up to 50% of patients taking zalcitabine. Stomatitis, esophageal ulceration, hepatotoxicity, rash and pancreatitis may occur. Zalcitabine should be used with caution in individuals with a history of pancreatitis, liver disease, or alcohol abuse. Dosage adjustment is necessary for individuals with renal impairment. Zalcitabine should not be used in combination with didanosine, lamivudine or stavudine.

HIV Protease Inhibitors

These drugs inhibit the activity of HIV protease. This enzyme, which is required for the production of a mature infectious virus, cleaves the gag pol polyprotein into structural proteins and active enzymes.

The protease inhibitors are used in the multidrug therapy of HIV infection. Resistance to the HIV protease inhibitors results from mutations in the protease gene and perhaps the cleavage sites of gag-pol. Although different protease mutations tend to be associated with resistance to individual drugs, resistance to one protease inhibitor is often associated with a less than optimal response to other agents of this class. Indinavir, ritonavir and lopinavir require more mutations to lose their effectiveness than do the other protease inhibitors.

All protease inhibitors can produce nausea, vomiting, diarrhea and paresthesia. Drug induced hyperglycemia and insulin resistance may precipitate the onset of diabetes mellitus or worsen existing cases. Protease inhibitors may also cause hypercholesterolemia and hypertriglyceridemia. Liver enzymes may be increased and hepatic toxicity may occur at high doses. Fat redistribution is common and can manifest as central fat accumulation, peripheral wasting, buffalo hump at the base of the neck, breast enlargement and/or lipomas.

Protease inhibitors may increase the risk of bleeding in hemophiliacs. These drugs should be used with caution in patients with diabetes, lipid disorders and hepatic disease. Dosage adjustment may be necessary.

Protease inhibitors interact with a large number of drugs because they are metabolized by and inhibit CYP3A4. Ritonavir is the most potent inhibitor of CYP3A4, with indinavir, amprenavir and nelfinavir being much less potent and saquinavir the least potent. When given as part of a combination therapy, the protease inhibitors affect plasma levels of NNRTIs as well as each other . Many drugs interact with protease inhibitors by inhibiting or inducing their metabolism; similarly, protease inhibitors inhibit or induce the metabolism of numerous drugs .

Saquinavir

Saquinavir is a potent inhibitor of HIV-1 and HIV-2 protease. *Fortovase,* a soft gel preparation of saquinavir, has largely replaced saquinavir mesylate capsules (*Invirase*) because it has improved bioavailability. Saquinavir is usually well tolerated and most frequently produces mild gastrointestinal side effects.

Ritonavir

Although ritonavir (*Norvir*) is a potent inhibitor of HIV-1 and HIV-2 protease, it is not well tolerated in higher doses. It is mainly used in low doses to increase blood levels of other protease inhibitors and to extend their dosing interval. Ritonavir is more commonly associated with gastrointestinal side effects, altered tastesensation, paresthesias and hypertriglyceridemia than are other protease inhibitors. Pancreatitis may occur in the presence or absence of hypertriglyceridemia.

Of all the protease inhibitors, ritonavir is the most potent inhibitor of CYP3A4; therefore, it tends to produce more frequent and severe interactions with other drugs. It inhibits an additional cytochrome P450 isozyme, CYP2D6 and can increase plasma concentrations of drugs that are metabolized by it (e.g., most antidepressants, some antiarrhythmics, some opioid analgesics, some neuroleptics). For example, ritonavir should not be used in conjunction with amiodarone, bepridil, flecainide, propafenone, quinidine, or pimozide. In addition to CYP3A4, ritonavir induces CYP1A2 and possibly CYP2C9 and may inhibit the breakdown of drugs metabolized by these enzymes.

Indinavir

Indinavir (*Crixivan*) is a potent inhibitor of HIV reverse transcriptase. It produces the side effects common to all protease inhibitors and also may produce nephrolithiasis, urolithiasis and possibly renal insufficiency or renal failure. *This problem occurs more frequently in children (approximately 30%) than adults (approximately 10%) and can be minimized by drinking at least 1.5 L of water daily.* Additional side effects include asymptomatic hyperbilirubinemia, alopecia, ingrown toenails and paronychia. Hemolytic anemia rarely occurs. Rifampin should not be given with indinavir.

Nelfinavir

Nelfinavir (*Viracept*) is probably the most commonly used protease inhibitor because of its low incidence of serious adverse effects. Its most common side effects are diarrhea and flatulence; these may resolve with continued use. In addition to the drugs contraindicated for use with all protease inhibitors, amiodarone, rifampin and quinidine are contraindicated in patients taking nelfinavir.

Amprenavir

Amprenavir (*Agenerase*) is administered twice daily, providing the patient with an advantage over other protease inhibitors that must be taken more frequently (e.g., indinavir, saquinavir). Common side effects of amprenavir include nausea, vomiting, diarrhea and perioral paraesthesias. Rash occurs in approximately 20 to 30% of patients and can be mild or severe (Stevens Johnson syndrome).

Amprenavir oral solution contains large amounts of the excipient propylene glycol and should not be given to children under age 4 because it can produce hyperosmolality, lactic acidosis, seizures, and/or respiratory depression. Pregnant women should not take amprenavir oral solution, as fetal toxicity may result. Amprenavir is a sulfonamide and should be used with caution in patients with sulfonamide allergy. Amprenavir oral solution and capsules contain high levels of vitamin E; therefore, patients are advised not to take supplemental vitamin E. In addition to the drugs contraindicated for use with all protease inhibitors, amprenavir should not be given with pimozide or rifampin.

Lopinavir–Ritonavir

Lopinavir is available in the United States only as a fixed dose combination with ritonavir (*Kaletra*). *In this regimen, a low dose of ritonavir is used to inhibit the rapid inactivation of lopinavir by CYP3A4.*

Side effects, which are generally mild, include diarrhea, nausea, asthenia, and headache. Pancreatitis occurs rarely. Ritonavir is a potent inhibitor of CYP3A4 and also inhibits CYP2D6. In addition to the drugs contraindicated for all protease inhibitors, flecainide, propafenone, pimozide and rifampin should not be given with lopinavir–ritonavir combination therapy.

Entry Inhibitors

Efuvirtide (T-20)

Enfuvirtide is a synthetic peptide of 36 amino acids that mimics an HR2 fragment of gp41. Its binding to the HR1 region blocks the formation of the six helix bundle structure, which is critical for the fusion process.

Resistance can occur but there is no cross resistance. Drug administration subcutaneously in combination with other antiretroviral drugs

Side effects: Local injection site reaction, hypersensitivity reaction, Eosinophilia.

Interferon's

Chemistry

Interferons are inducible endogenous cytokines (glycoproteins)

Three major classes of human interferons (IFN) are:

IFN-alpha (human leukocyte IFN), induced by viruses

IFN-beta (human fibroblast IFN), induced by viruses

IFN-gamma (human immune IFN), induced by antigens

Mechanism of antiviral action

Binding to specific receptors of the host cells

Induction of the following main enzymes

A protein kinase which inhibits protein synthesis

An oligoadenylate synthase which leads to degradation of viral mRNA

A phosphodiesterase which can inhibit tRNA

The action of these enzymes leads to an inhibition of translation (late viral RNA and protein synthesis)

Antiviral spectrum

Antiviral spectrum includes HBV, HCV, HDV, HSV, VZV, CMV and human papillomavirus (HPV).

Other effect Interferon's possess immunomodulating and antiproliferative actions and may inhibit the growth of certain cancer cells.

Pharmacokinetics

F(oral): < 1% ;

F(IM, SC): IFN-alpha > 80% ; IFN-beta » 40%

Distribution in all body tissues, except CNS and eye.

Half lives: 1-4 hours

Adverse effects

Acute flu-like syndrome (fever, headache, myalgia, arthralgia, nausea and vomiting)

Bone marrow suppression (Granulocytopenia, thrombocytopenia)

Neurotoxicity (fatigue, sleepiness, confusion, seizures) (after high doses)

Cardiotoxicity (cardiac failure) (after high doses)

Hepatotoxicity (after high doses)

Interstitial nephritis (after high doses)

Hypersensitivity reactions (rare)

Impairment of fertility

Therapeutic uses

Chronic hepatitis B and C (improvement in 25-50% of patients. Administration usually last 4-6 months. Remission may be sustained, but complete disappearance is seen only in 30% of cases)

HZV infection in cancer patients (to prevent the dissemination of the infection)

CMV infections in renal transplant patients

Refractory condylomata acuminata (given by intralesional injection. Complete clearance is seen in 36-62% of patients)

Hairy cell leukemia (in combination with zidovudine)

AIDS related Kaposi's sarcoma

References

Asmuth DM, Nguyen HH, Melcher GP et al (2004). Treatments for hepatitis B. *Clinical Infect Dis* **39:** 1353.

Drugs for non-HIV viral infections (2005). *Med Lett Drugs Ther* 23.

Gnann JW and Whitley RJ (2002). Herpes zoster. *N Engl J Med* **347:** 340.

Hammer SM et al (2006). Treatment for Adult HIV Infection, 2006. Recommendations of the International AIDS Society USA Panel. *JAMA* **296:** 827.

Kimberlin DW and Rouse DJ (2004). Genital herpes. *N Engl J Med* **350:** 1970.

Moscona A (2005). Neuraminidase inhibitors for influenza. *N Engl J Med* **353:** 1363.

Panel on Clinical Practices for Treatment of HIV Infection convened by the Department of Health and Human Services (DHHS). Guidelines for the Use of Antiretroviral Agents in HIV-1-Infected Adults and Adolescents. April 7, 2005.

Piscitelli SC, Gallicano KD: Interactions among drugs for HIV and opportunistic infections. N Engl J Med 2001; 344-984.

CHAPTER

Anticancer Drugs 22

Introduction

Malignant disease accounts for a high proportion of deaths in industrialized countries.

The treatment of anticancer drug is to give palliation, induce remission and, if possible, cure.

Cancer occurs after normal cells have been transformed into neoplastic cells through alteration of their genetic material and the abnormal expression of certain genes. Neoplastic cells usually exhibit chromosomal abnormalities and the loss of their differentiated properties. These changes lead to uncontrolled cell division and many result in the invasion of previously unaffected organs, a process called metastasis.

The cycle of cell replication includes (Fig 22-1):
M (Mitosis) phase
G1 (Gap1), period before S phase
S (DNA synthesis) phase
G2 (Gap2), period after S phase

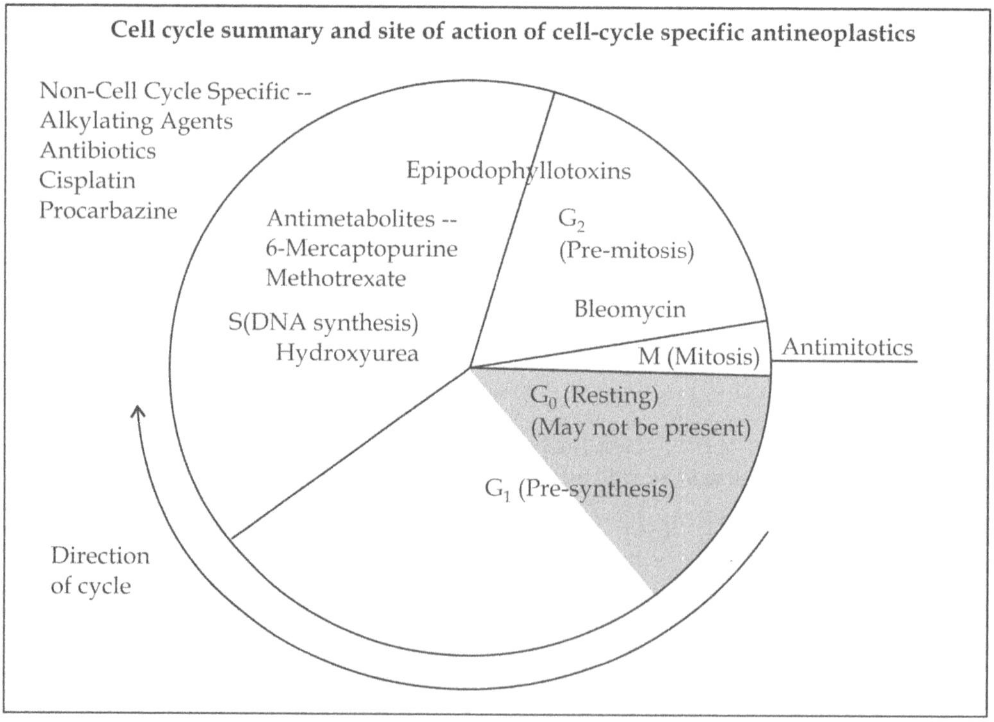

Fig 22-1: Cell cycle summary and site of action of cell cycle specific antineoplastics.

Cell Cycle Specific Agents and Cell Cycle Non Specific Agents

Cell Cycle Nonspecific Agents (CCNSA): Drugs that are active throughout the cell cycle

Alkylating Agents

Platinum Compounds

Antibiotics

Cell Cycle Specific Agents (CCSA): Drugs that act during a specific phase of the cell cycle

S Phase Specific Drug:

Antimetabolites, Topoisomerase Inhibitors

M Phase Specific Drug:

Vinca Alkaloids, Taxanes

G2 Phase Specific Drug:

Bleomycin

Mechanism of Anticancer Drugs

The sites of action of Anticancer drugs are shown in Fig 22-2.

Block nucleic acid (DNA, RNA) biosynthesis

Directly destroy DNA and inhibit DNA reproduction

Interfere transcription and block RNA synthesis

Interfere protein synthesis and function

Influence hormone homeostasis

Classification of Anticancer Drugs

The classification of anticancer drugs is illustrated below

Classification of Anticancer Drugs

I. Alkylating agents

A. Nitrogen mustards
   1. Mechlorethamine hydrochloride
   2. Cyclophosphamide
   3. Chlorambucil
   4. Melphalan
   5. Ifosfamide

B. Alkyl sulfonates
   1. Busulfan

C. Nitrosoureas
   1. Carmustine
   2. Lomustine
   3. Semustine
   4. Streptozocin

D. Ethylenimines
   1. Thiotepa

E. Triazenes
   1. Dacarbazine

II. Antimetabolites

A. Folate antagonist
   1. Methotrexate

B. Purine analogues
   1. Thioguanine
   2. Mercaptopurine
   3. Fludarabine
   4. Pentostatin
   5. Cladribine

C. Pyrimidine analogues
   1. Cytarabine
   2. Fluorouracil

III. Antibiotics

A. Anthracyclines
   1. Doxorubicin hydrochloride
   2. Daunorubicin
   3. Idarubicin

B. Bleomycins
   1. Bleomycin sulfate

C. Mitomycin

D. Dactinomycin

E. Plicamycin

IV. Plant-derived products

A. Vinca alkaloids
   1. Vincristine
   2. Vinblastine

B. Epipodophyllotoxins
   1. Etoposide
   2. Teniposide

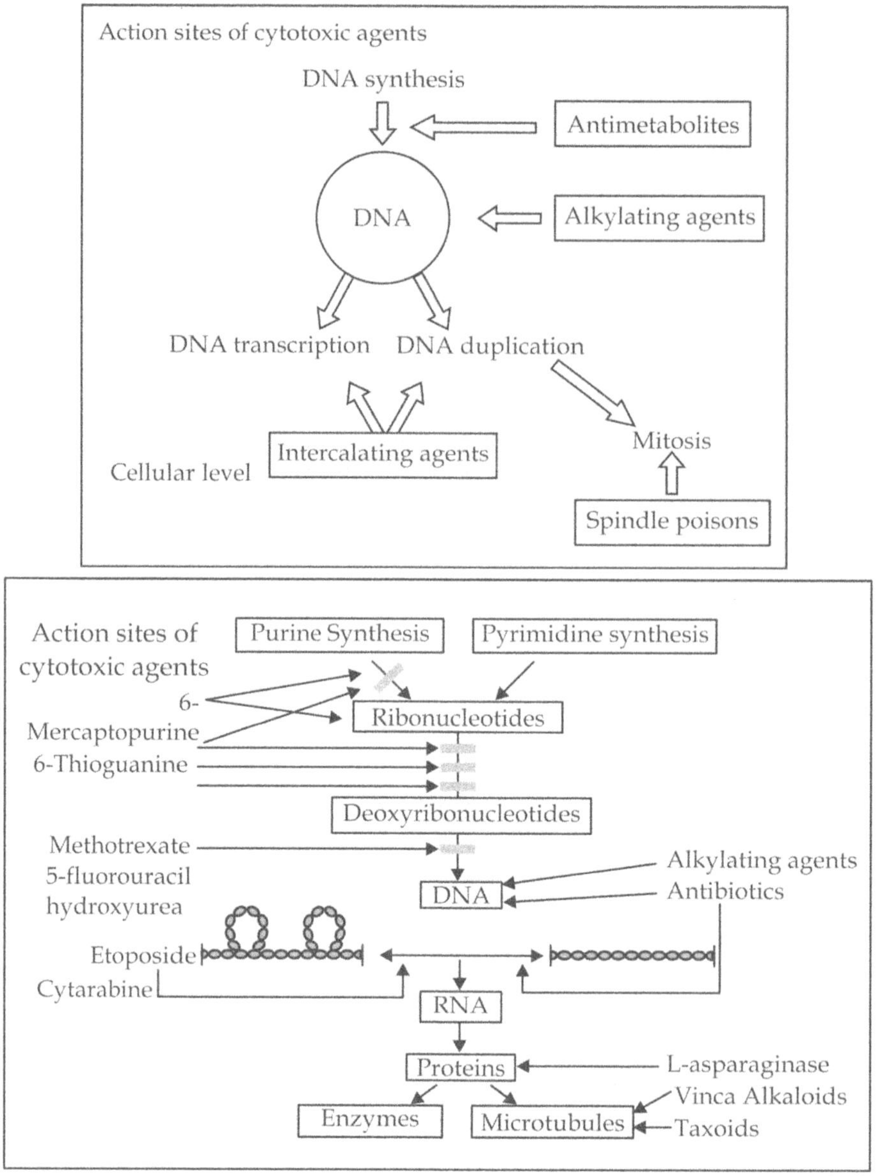

Fig 22-2: Sites of action of antineoplastics.

C. Taxanes: paclitaxel

V. Enzymes

A. L-Asparaginase

VI. Hormonal agents

A. Glucocorticoids

B. Estrogens, antiestrogens

1. Tamoxifen citrate
2. Estramustine phosphate sodium

C. Androgens, antiandrogens

1. Flutamide

D. Progestins

E. Luteinizing hormone-releasing hormone (LH-RH) antagonists

1. Buserelin
2. Leuprolide

F. Octreotide acetate

VII. Miscellaneous agents

1. Hydroxyurea
2. Procarbazine
3. Mitotane
4. Hexamethylmelamine (HMM)
5. Cisplatin
6. Carboplatin
7. Mitoxantrone

VIII. Monoclonal antibodies

IX. Immunomodulating agents

A. Levamisole

B. Interferons

1. Interferon alfa-2a
2. Interferon alfa-2b

C. Interleukins: aldesleukin

X. Cellular growth factors

A. Filgrastim

B. Sargramostim

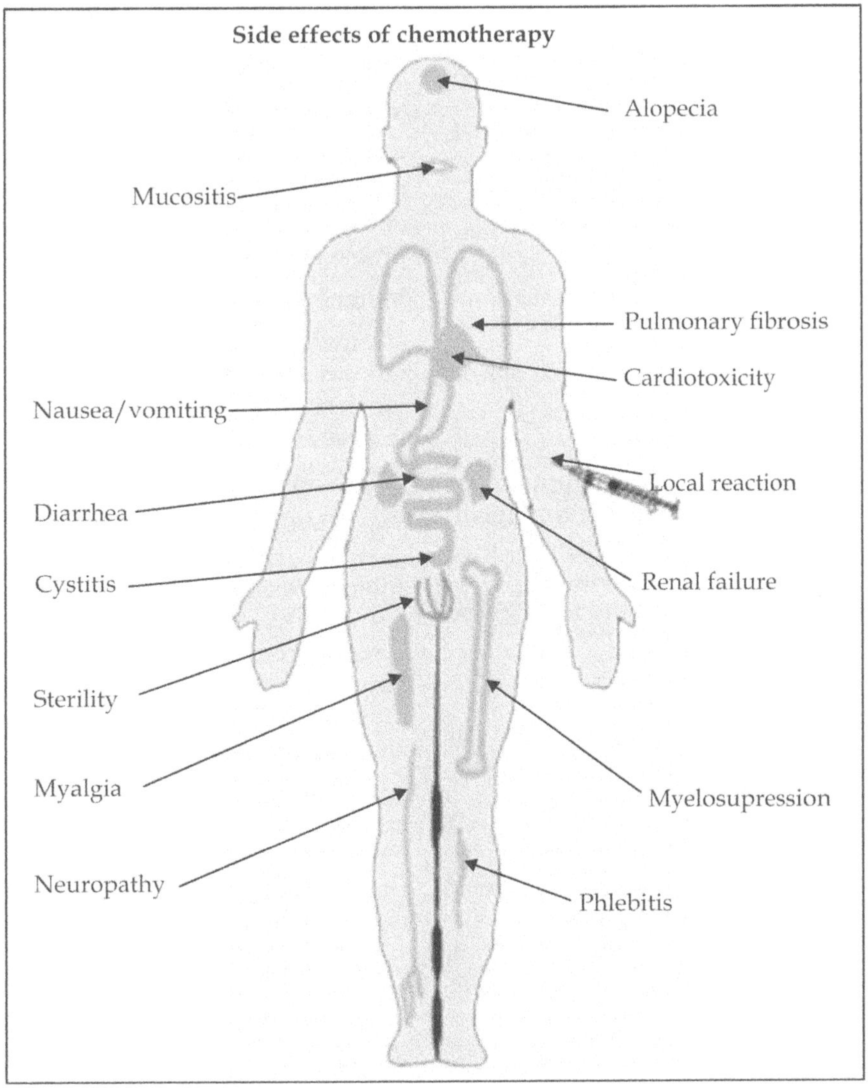

Fig 22-3 : Side effects of anticancer drugs.

Side effects of anticancer drugs

Side effects from chemotherapy (Fig 22-3) depend on the drug or combination of drugs used. Side effects vary from person to person. Some of the most common side effects are described below.

Nausea and vomiting

Drugs called antiemetics can help reduce or prevent nausea and vomiting that can occur during chemotherapy. Eating several small meals throughout the day may also help.

Hair loss (alopecia)

During treatment, your hair may get thinner or may fall out entirely, depending on which chemotherapy drugs the patients are given. Patients may also have hair loss from eyebrows, eyelashes and body. Patients hair will grow back after treatment ends, but it may be a different color or texture. Using mild shampoos, soft hair brushes and low heat when drying hair may help reduce hair loss. Some women may choose to cut their hair short before hand to gain some control.

Early menopause (when your menstrual period stops)

Some women may have menopausal symptoms such as their menstrual periods stopping, hot flashes and vaginal dryness during treatment. For women who are closer to the age of menopause (45 years or older), these symptoms may be permanent. For younger women, these symptoms may be temporary.

Fatigue

This is a common side effect. Try to get plenty of rest and ask family and friends to help. Exercise and a well-balanced diet may also help.

Infections

Because chemotherapy reduces the white blood cell count, infections are more likely to occur. Infections can be prevented by washing hands often and staying away from others who are ill. If the patient get a cut or nick, clean it right away. Monitoring of blood cell count before each treatment to make sure it is high enough to safely give chemotherapy.

Mouth and throat sores

Because the cells in the mouth and throat are fast growing, some chemotherapy drugs affect these areas causing sores or dryness. Get a dental check up before starting chemotherapy. During treatment, brush your teeth and gums after each meal and at bedtime using a soft toothbrush. Using a toothpaste with baking soda and peroxide can also help. Avoid mouthwashes that contain large amounts of alcohol.

Weight gain

Although the reasons are unclear, some women gain weight during chemotherapy. Eating nutritious food and exercising can help to maintain normal weight.

Nail weakness

Some treatments can cause damage to the fingernails and toenails. The nails become brittle and sore and may fall off. Like hair loss, nail problems are temporary.

Memory problems (chemo brain)

Chemotherapy may lead to a general sense of mental fuzziness and short term memory problems. Most women say that these symptoms improve with time.

Alkylating Agents

The Alkylating agents (Fig 22-4) are the largest class of anticancer agents, comprising five subgroups: nitrogen mustards, alkyl sulfonates, Nitrosoureas, Ethylenimines and thiazines. Several other agents, including procarbazine, Hexamethylmelamine, dacarbazine, Estra-mustine and mitomycin C, are thought to act at least inpart by alkylation.

Alkylating agents are compounds that are capable of introducing alkyl groups into nucleophilic sites on other molecules through the formation of covalent bonds. These nucleophilic targets for alkylation include the sulfhydryl, amino, phosphate, hydroxyl, carboxyl and imidazole groups that are present in macromolecules and low molecular weight compound within cells.

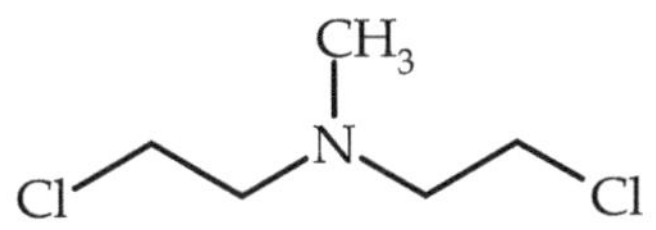

Chlormethine

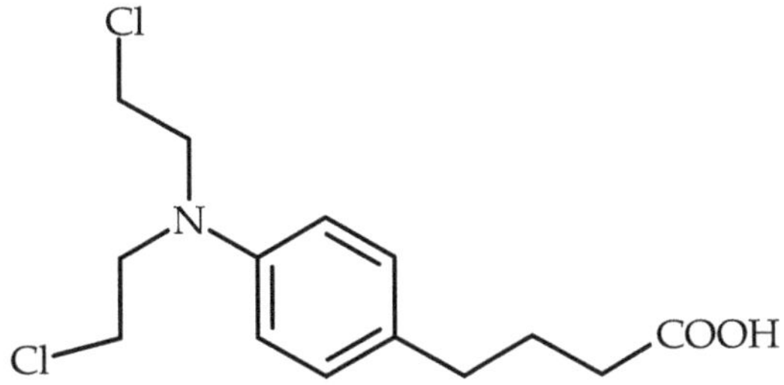

Chlorambucil

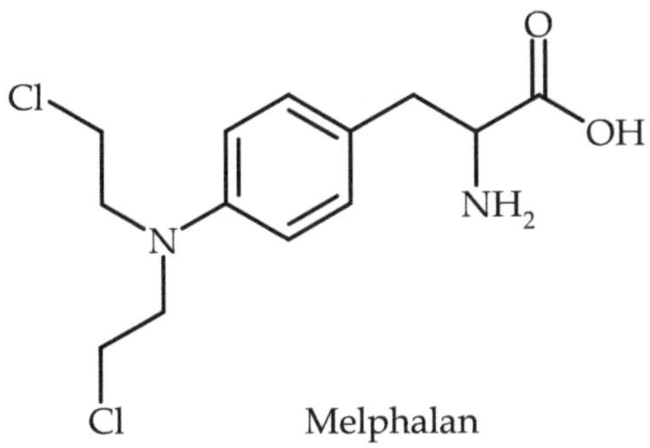

Melphalan

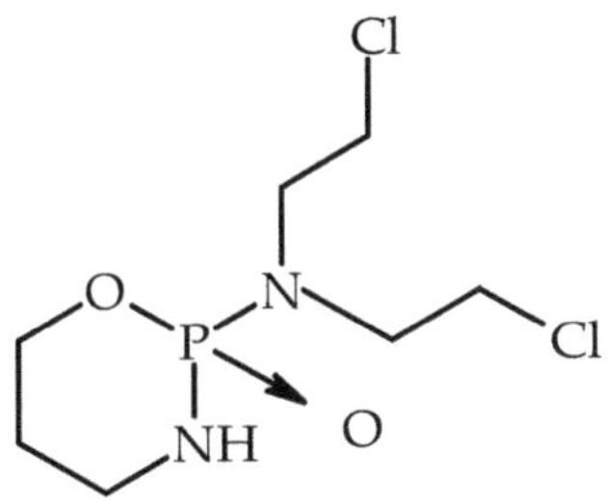

Cyclophosphamide

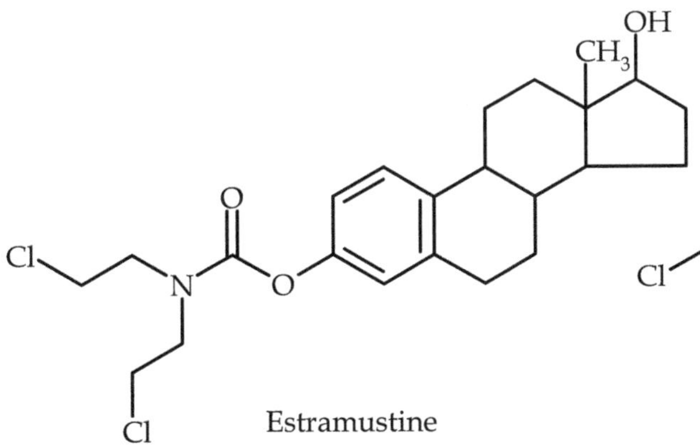

Estramustine

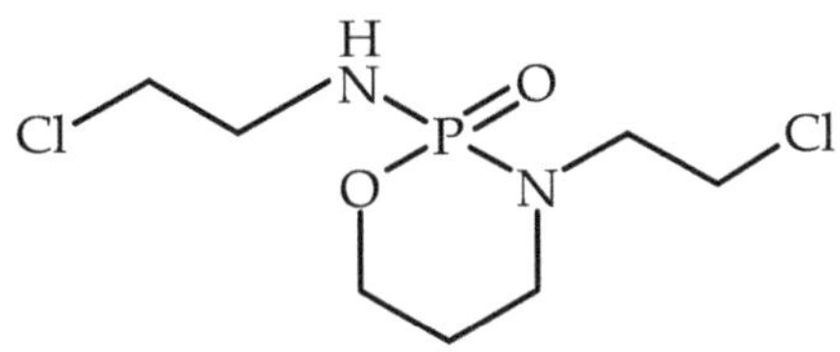

Ifosfamide

Fig 22-4: Alkylating agents.

Mechanism of Action

The macromolecular sites of alkylation damage include DNA, RNA and various enzymes. The inhibition of DNA synthesis occurs at drug concentrations that are lower than those required to inhibit RNA and protein synthesis, and the degree of DNA alkylation correlates especially well with the cytotoxicity of these drugs. This interaction also accounts for the mutagenic and carcinogenic properties of the alkylating agents. The reactions of various alkylating agents with DNA have been studied in detail and the 7-nitrogen (N_7) and 6-oxygen (O_6) of guanine have been shown to be particularly susceptible to attack by electrophilic compounds. There are several possible consequences of N_7 guanine alkylation.

Cross linkage

Bifunctional alkylating agents, such as the nitrogen mustards, may form covalent bonds with each of two adjacent guanine residues. Such interstrand cross linkages will inhibit DNA replication and transcription. Mispairing of bases. Alkylating at N_7 changes the O_6 of guanine to its enol tautomer, which can then form base pairs with thymine. This may lead to gene miscoding, with adenine–thymine pairs replacing guanine–cytosine. The result is the production of defective proteins.

Depurination

N_7 alkylation may cause cleavage of the imidazole ring and excision of the guanine residue, leading to DNA strand breakage.

Nitrogen Mustards

Mechlorethamine

Mechlorethamine (nitrogen mustard; Mustargen), a derivative of the war gas sulfur mustard, is considered to be the first modern anticancer drug. In the early 1940s it was discovered to be effective in the treatment of human lymphomas.

Mechanism of Action

Mechlorethamine in aqueous solution loses a chloride atom and forms a cyclic ethylenimmonium ion. This carbonium ion interacts with nucleophilic groups, such as the N_7 and O_6 of guanine and leads to an interstrand cross-linking of DNA. Although there is great variation among normal and tumor tissues in their sensitivity to mechlorethamine, the drug is generally more toxic to proliferating cells than to resting or plateau cells.

Pharmacokinetics

Mechlorethamine has a chemical and biological half-life in plasma of less than 10 minutes after intravenous injection. Little or no intact drug is excreted in urine.

Indications

The major indication for mechlorethamine is the treatment of non- Hodgkin's lymphomas, leukaemia's and various solid tumors.

Adverse effects

The dose-limiting toxicity of mechlorethamine is myelosuppression; maximal leukopenia and thrombocytopenia occur 10 to 14 days after drug administration and recovery is generally complete at 21 to 28 days. Lymphopenia and immunosuppression may lead to activation of latent herpes zoster infections, especially in patients with lymphomas. Mechlorethamine will affect rapidly proliferating normal tissues and cause alopecia, diarrhea, and oral ulcerations. Nausea and vomiting may occur 1 to 2 hours after injection and can last up to 24 hours. Reproductive toxicity includes amenorrhea and inhibition of oogenesis and spermatogenesis. About half of premenopausal women and almost all men treated for 6 months with MOPP chemotherapy become permanently infertile. The drug is teratogenic and carcinogenic in experimental animals.

Cyclophosphamide

Cyclophosphamide (Cytoxan) is the most versatile and useful of the nitrogen mustards.

Mechanism of Action

As with the other nitrogen mustards, Cyclophosphamide administration results in the formation of cross links within DNA due to a reaction of the two chloroethyl moieties of Cyclophosphamide with adjacent nucleotide bases. Cyclophosphamide must be activated metabolically by microsomal enzymes of the cytochrome P450 system before ionization of the chloride atoms and formation of the cyclic ethylenimmonium ion can occur. The metabolites phosphoramide mustard and acrolein are thought to be the ultimate active cytotoxic moiety derived from Cyclophosphamide.

Pharmacokinetics

Cyclophosphamide can be given orally, intramuscularly or intravenously. The plasma half-life of intact cyclophosphamide is 6.5 hours. Only 10 to 15% of the circulating parent drug is protein bound, whereas 50% of the alkylating metabolites are bound to plasma proteins. Since cyclophosphamide and its metabolites are eliminated primarily by the kidneys, renal failure will greatly prolong their retention.

Indications

Cyclophosphamide has a wide spectrum of antitumor activity. In lymphomas, it is frequently used in combination with vincristine and prednisone (CVP [or COP] regimen) or as a substitute for mechlorethamine the MOPP regimen (C-MOPP).

High dosages of intravenously administered Cyclophosphamide are often curative in Burkitt's lymphoma, a childhood malignancy with a very fast growth rate. Oral daily dosages are useful for less aggressive tumours, such as nodular lymphomas, myeloma, and chronic leukaemia's.

Cyclophosphamide is a component of CMF (cyclophosphamide, methotrexate, 5-fluorouracil) and other drug combinations used in the treatment of breast cancer.

Cyclophosphamide also can be employed as an alternative to azathioprine in suppressing immunological rejection of transplant organs.

Adverse Effects

Bone marrow suppression

Cyclophosphamide reduces the number of circulating lymphocytes and impairs the function of both humoral and cellular (i.e., B and T cell) aspects of the immune system. Nausea may occur a few hours after administration.

Alopecia is more common than with other mustards.

A toxicity that is unique to cyclophosphamide and ifosfamide is cystitis. Dysuria and decreased urinary frequency are the most common symptoms.

Rarely, fibrosis and a permanently decreased bladder capacity may ensue. The risk of development of carcinoma of the bladder also is increased. Large intravenous doses have resulted in impairment of renal water excretion, hyponatremia and increased urine osmolarity and have been associated with hemorrhagic subendocardial necrosis, arrhythmias and congestive heart failure.

Other effects of chronic drug treatment include infertility, amenorrhea, and possible mutagenesis and carcinogenesis.

Ifosfamide

Ifosfamide (Ifex) is an analogue of Cyclophosphamide that requires metabolic activation to form 4-hydroxy ifosfamide. In general, the metabolism, serum half-life, and excretion of ifosfamide are similar to those of cyclophosphamide.

Indications

Ifosfamide is active against a broad spectrum of tumors, including germ cell cancers of the testis, lymphomas, sarcomas and carcinomas of the lung, breast and ovary. It is thought to be more active than cyclophosphamide in germ cell cancers and sarcomas.

Adverse Effects

May produce alopecia, nausea, vomiting, infertility and second tumors, particularly acute leukaemias. Neurological symptoms including confusion, somnolence and hallucinations have also been reported.

Melphalan

Melphalan (Alkeran) is an amino acid derivative of Mechlorethamine that possesses the same general spectrum of antitumor activity as do the other nitrogen mustards.

Indications

The major indications for Melphalan are in the palliative therapy of multiple myeloma and cancers of the breast or ovary. Because it does not produce alopecia, Melphalan is occasionally substituted for Cyclophosphamide in the CMF regimen for breast cancer.

Adverse Effects

Melphalan produces less nausea and vomiting than does Cyclophosphamide; however, its bone marrow suppression tends to be more prolonged and affects both white cells and platelets.

Chlorambucil

Chlorambucil is aromatic nitrogen mustard that is intermediate in chemical reactivity between mechlorethamine and Melphalan. Its mechanisms of action and range of antitumor activity are similar to others. It is well absorbed orally, but detailed information concerning its metabolic fate in humans is lacking.

Indications

Chlorambucil is used primarily as daily palliative therapy for chronic lymphocytic leukemia, Walden strö̈om's macroglobulinemia, myeloma and other lymphomas.

Adverse Effects

Bone marrow toxicity is the major side effect of chlorambucil. Nausea is uncommon or mild and hair loss does not occur. Chlorambucil shares the immunosuppressive, teratogenic and carcinogenic properties of the nitrogen mustards.

Nitrosoureas

Carmustine, Lomustine and Semustine

The nitrosoureas are alkylating agents that are highly lipid soluble and share similar pharmacological and clinical properties. Carmustine (BCNU), lomustine (CCNU), and semustine (methyl-CCNU) are chemically unstable, forming highly reactive decomposition products. The chemical half-life of these drugs in plasma is only 5 to 15 minutes. Their marked lipid solubility facilitates distribution into the brain and cerebrospinal fluid (CSF).

Mechanism of Action

The chloroethyl moiety of these nitrosoureas is capable of alkylating nucleic acids and proteins and producing single-strand breaks and interstrand cross-linkage of DNA. Both alkylation and carbamoylation contribute to the therapeutic and toxic effects of the nitrosoureas. These agents can kill cells in all phases of the cell cycle.

Pharmacokinetics

Oral absorption of lomustine and semustine is complete, but degradation and metabolism are so rapid that the parent drug cannot be detected after oral administration. Although the plasma half lives of the parent drugs are only a few minutes, degradation products with antitumor activity may persist for longer periods.

Indications

Carmustine and lomustine can produce remissions that last from 3 to 6 months in 40 to 50% of patients with primary brain tumors. Both drugs also are used as secondary treatment of Hodgkin's disease and in experimental combination chemotherapy for various types of lung cancer. Other tumors in which remission rates of 10 to 30% have been obtained are non Hodgkin's lymphomas, multiple myeloma, melanoma, renal cell carcinoma and colorectal cancer.

Adverse Effects

The Nitrosoureas produce severe nausea and vomiting in most patients 4 to 6 hours after administration. The major site of dose limiting toxicity is the bone marrow; leucopoenia and thrombocytopenia occur after 4 to 5 weeks. Less frequent side effects include alopecia, stomatitis and mild abnormalities of liver function. Pulmonary toxicity, manifested by cough, dyspnea and interstitial fibrosis, is becoming increasingly recognized as a complication of longterm nitrosourea treatment. As Alkylating agents, these drugs are potentially mutagenic, teratogenic, and carcinogenic.

Streptozocin

Mechanism of Action

Streptozocin (Zanosar), a watersoluble nitrosourea produced by the fungus Streptomyces achromogenes, acts through methylation of nucleic acids and proteins. In addition, it produces rapid and severe depletion of the pyridine nucleotides nicotinamide adenine dinucleotide (NAD) and its reduced form (NADH) in liver and pancreatic islets.

Pharmacokinetics

Streptozocin is not well absorbed from the gastrointestinal tract and must be administered intravenously or intraarterially. In preclinical studies, the plasma half life was 5 to 10 minutes.

Indications

Streptozocin produces remission in 50 to 60% of patients with islet cell carcinomas of the pancreas. It is also useful in malignant carcinoid tumors.

Adverse Effects

Almost all patients have nausea and vomiting. The major toxicity is renal tubular damage, which may be severe in 5 to 10% of patients taking streptozocin.

Treatment of metastatic insulinomas may result in the release of insulin from the tumor and subsequent hypoglycemic coma. Less severe toxicities include diarrhea, anemia and mild alterations in glucose tolerance or liver function tests.

Alkyl Sulfonates

Busulfan

Mechanism of Action

Busulfan is a bifunctional methanesulfonic ester that forms intrastrand cross-linkages with DNA.

Pharmacokinetics

The drug is well absorbed after oral administration and has a plasma half life of less than 5 minutes. Metabolites and degradation products are excreted primarily in the urine.

Indications

Busulfan is used in the palliative treatment of chronic granulocytic leukemia. Daily oral therapy results in decreased peripheral white blood cells and improved symptoms in almost all patients during the chronic phase of the disease. Excessive uric acid production from rapid tumor cell lysis should be prevented by co administration of allopurinol.

Adverse Effects

At usual therapeutic dosages, Busulfan is selectively toxic to granulocyte precursors rather than lymphocytes. Thrombocytopenia and anemia and less commonly, nausea, alopecia, mucositis and sterility also may occur. Unusual side effects of Busulfan include gynecomastia, a general increase in skin pigmentation and interstitial pulmonary fibrosis.

Ethylenimines

Thiotepa

Mechanism of Action

Although thiotepa is chemically less reactive than the nitrogen mustards, it is thought to act by similar mechanisms.

Pharmacokinetics

Its oral absorption is erratic. After intravenous injection, the plasma half life is less than 2 hours. Urinary excretion accounts for 60 to 80% of eliminated drug.

Indications

Thiotepa has antitumor activity against ovarian and breast cancers and lymphomas. However, it has been largely supplanted by cyclophosphamide and other nitrogen mustards for treatment of these diseases. It is used by direct instillation into the bladder for multifocal local bladder carcinoma.

Adverse Effects

Nausea and myelosuppression are the major toxicities of thiotepa. It is not a local vesicant and has been safely injected intramuscularly and even intrathecally.

Triazenes

Dacarbazine

Mechanism of Action

Dacarbazine (DTIC-Dome) is activated by photode composition and by enzymatic

N-demethylation. Eventual formation of a methyl carbonium ion results in Methylation of DNA and RNA and inhibition of nucleic acid and protein synthesis. As with other Alkylating agents, cells in all phases of the cell cycle are susceptible to dacarbazine.

Pharmacokinetics

The plasma half-life of dacarbazine is biphasic, with a distribution phase of 19 minutes and an elimination phase of 5 hours. The drug is not appreciably protein bound and it does not enter the central nervous system (CNS). Urinary excretion of unchanged drug is by renal tubular secretion. Dacarbazine metabolism and decomposition is complex.

Indications

Dacarbazine is the most active agent used in metastatic melanoma, producing a 20% remission rate. It is also combined with doxorubicin and other agents in the treat ment of various sarcomas and Hodgkin's disease.

Adverse Effects

Dacarbazine may cause severe nausea and vomiting. Leukopenia and thrombocytopenia occur 2 weeks after treatment, with recovery by 3 to 4 weeks. Less common is a flu-like syndrome of fever, myalgias and malaise. Alopecia and transient abnormalities in renal and hepatic function also have been reported.

Antimetabolites

Folate Antagonists

Mechanism of Action

In general, antimetabolites (Fig 22-5) used in cancer chemotherapy are drugs that are structurally related to naturally occurring compounds, such as vitamins, amino acids and nucleotides. These drugs can compete for binding sites on enzymes or can themselves become incorporated into DNA or RNA and thus interfere with cell growth and proliferation. The antimetabolites in clinical use include the folic acid analogue methotrexate, the pyrimidines (fluorouracil and cytarabine) and the purines (thioguanine, mercaptopurine, fludarabine, pentostatin and cladribine).

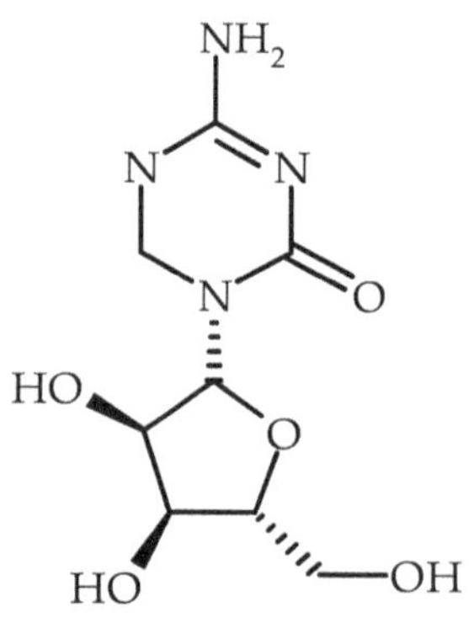

Azacitidine

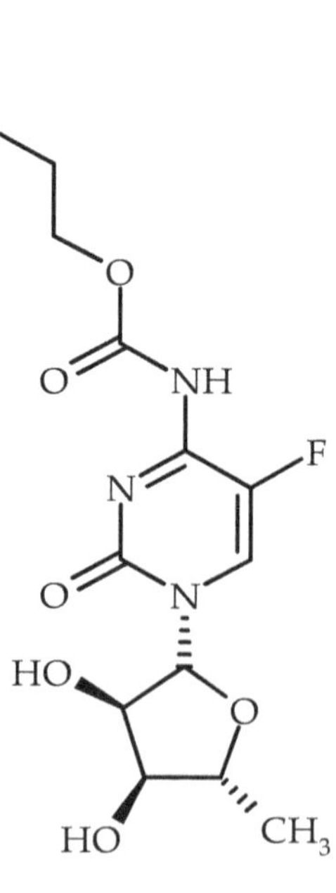

Cepecitabine

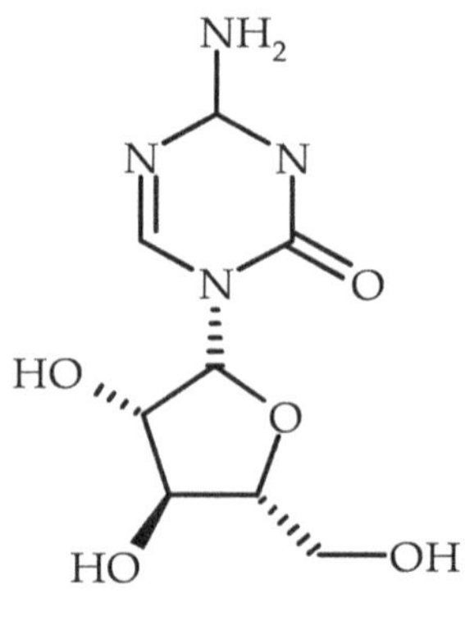

Cytarabine

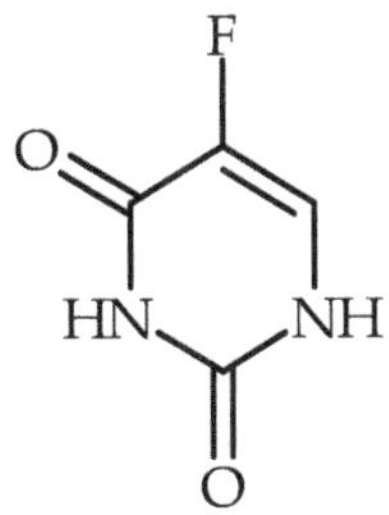

5-fluorouracil

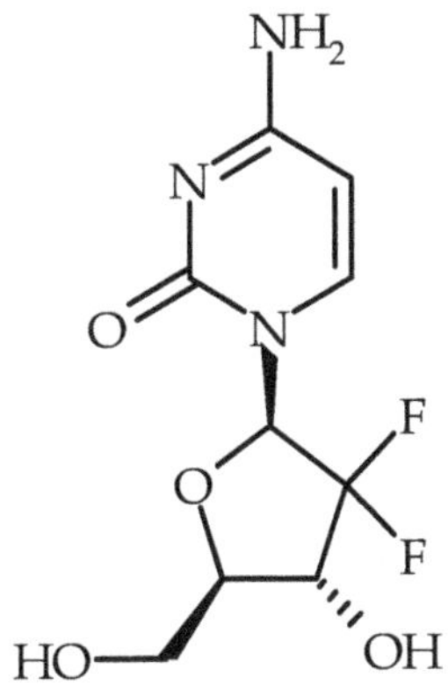

Gemcitabine

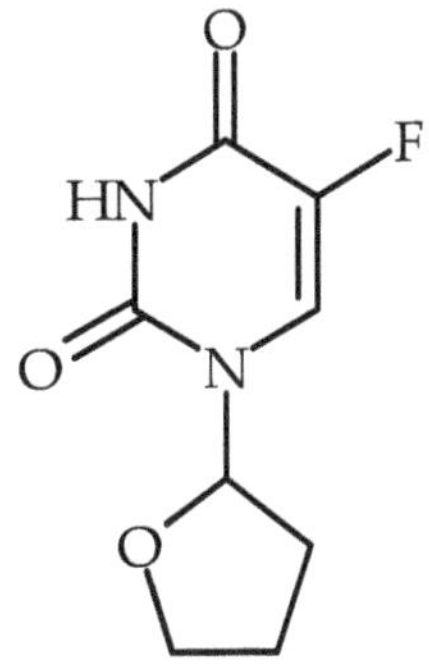

tegafur

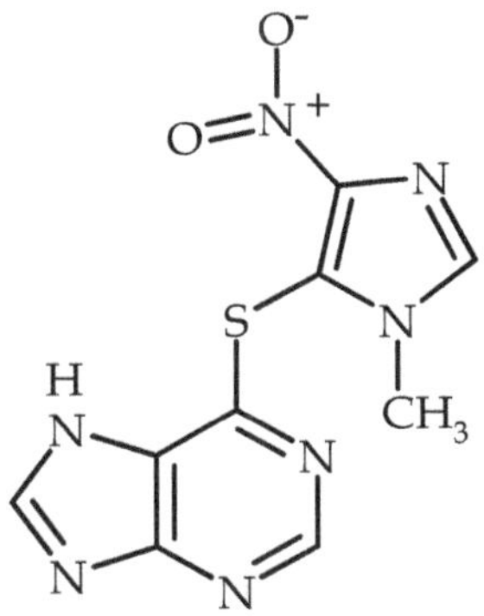

Azathioprine

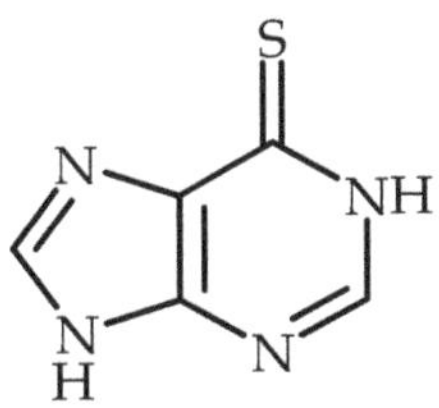

mercaptopurine

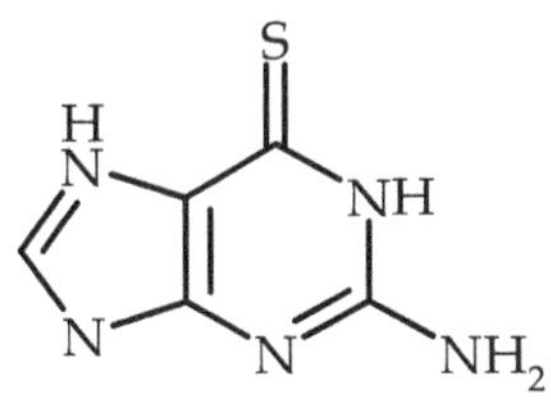

Thioguanine

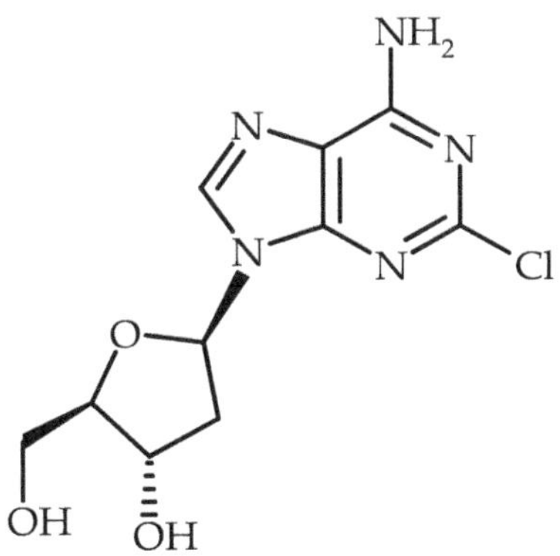

Cladribine

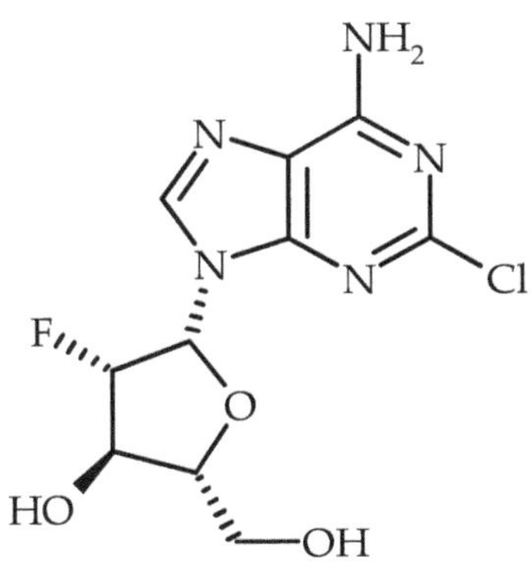

Clofarabine

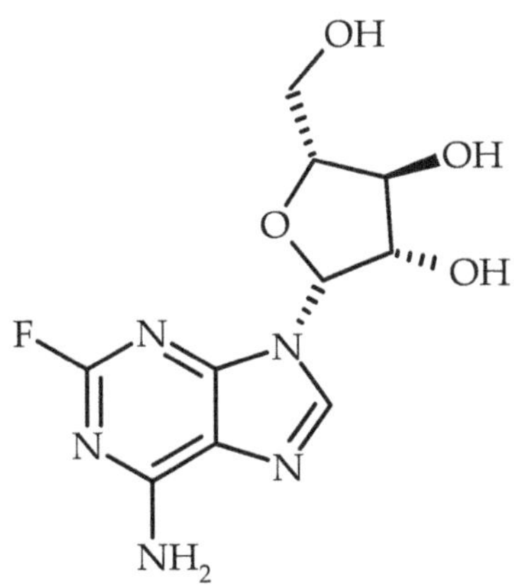

fludarabine

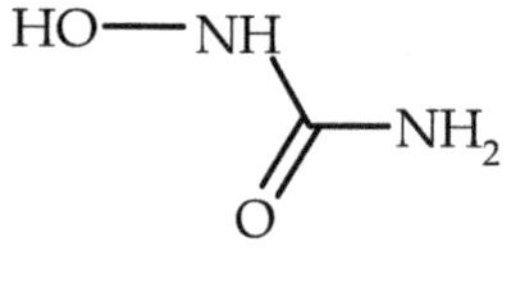

Hydroxycarbamide

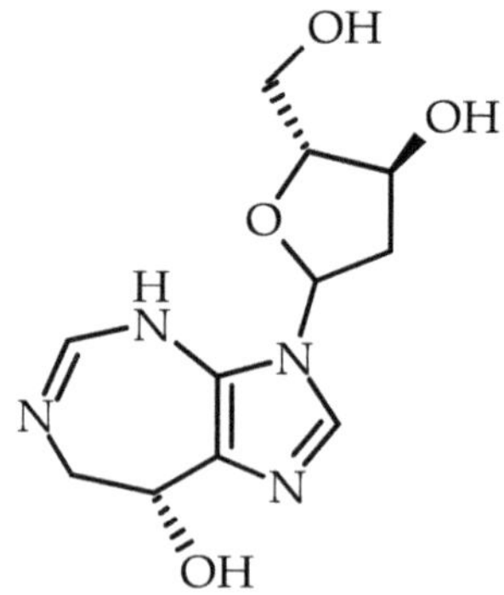

Pentostatin

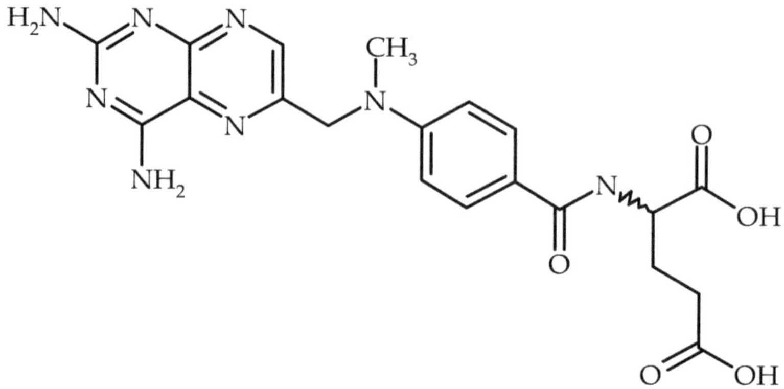

Methotrexate

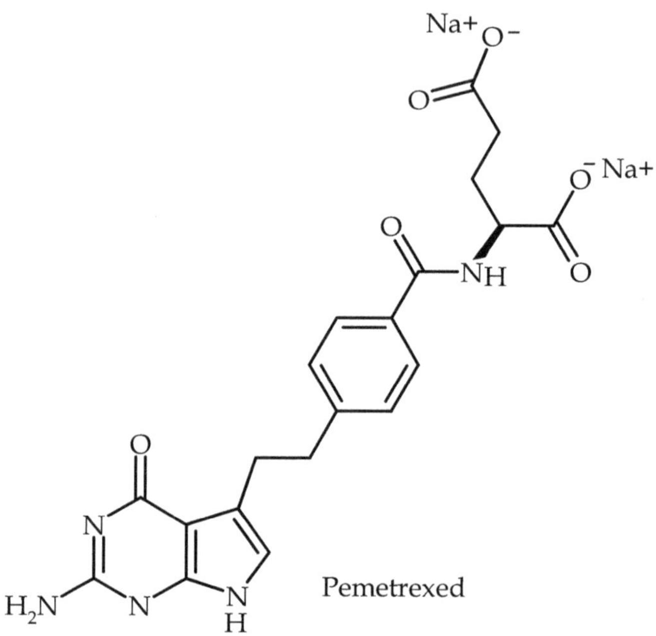

Pemetrexed

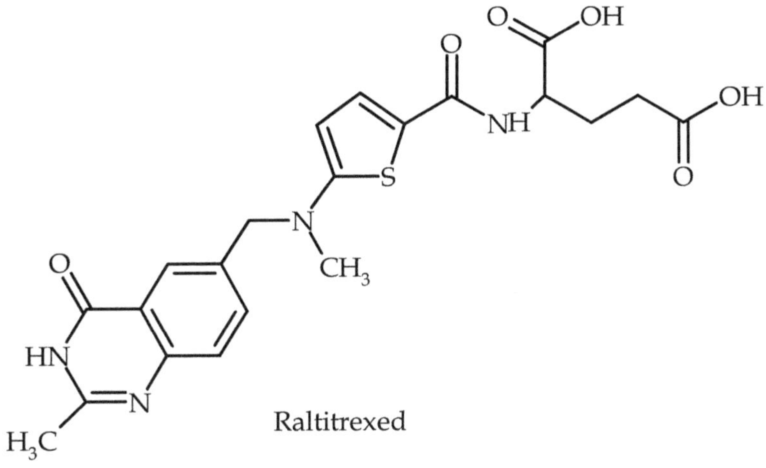

Raltitrexed

Fig 22-5: Antimetabolites

Methotrexate

Mechanism of Action

Methotrexate competitively inhibits the binding of folic acid to the enzyme dihydrofolate reductase. This enzyme catalyzes the formation of tetrahydrofolate. Tetrahydrofolate is in turn converted to N5, N10 methylenetetrahydrofolate, which is an essential cofactor for the synthesis of thymidylate, purines, methionine and glycine. The major mechanism by which Methotrexate brings about cell death appears to be inhibition of DNA synthesis through a blockage of the biosynthesis of thymidylate and purines. Cells in S-phase are most sensitive to the cytotoxic effects of methotrexate. RNA and protein synthesis also may be inhibited to some extent and may delay progression through the cell cycle, particularly from G_1 to S.

Resistance

Mammalian cells have several mechanisms of resistance to methotrexate. These include an increase in intracellular dihydrofolate reductase levels, appearance of altered forms of dihydrofolate reductase with decreased affinity for methotrexate and a decrease in methotrexate transport into cells. The relative importance of each of these mechanisms of resistance in various human tumors is not known.

Cellular uptake of the drug is by carrier mediated active transport. Drug resistance due to decreased transport can be overcome by greatly increasing extracellular methotrexate concentration, which provides a rationale for high dose methotrexate therapy. Since bone marrow and gastrointestinal cells do not have impaired folate methotrexate transport, these normal cells can be selectively rescued with reduced folate, bypassing the block of dihydrofolate reductase. Leucovorin(citrovorum factor, folinic acid, 5-formyltetrahydrofolate) is the agent commonly used for rescue.

Pharmacokinetics

Methotrexate is well absorbed orally and at usual dosages is 50% bound to plasma proteins. The plasma decay that follows an intravenous injection is triphasic, with a distribution phase, an initial elimination phase, and a prolonged elimination phase. The last phase is thought to reflect slow release of methotrexate from tissues. The major routes of drug excretion are glomerular filtration and active renal tubular secretion.

The formation of polyglutamic acid conjugates of methotrexate has been observed in tumor cells and in the liver and may be an important determinant of cytotoxicity. These methotrexate polyglutamates are retained in the cell and are also potent inhibitors of dihydrofolate reductase.

Clinical uses

High-dose methotrexate administration with leucovorin rescue has produced remissions in 30% of patients with metastatic osteogenic sarcoma. Methotrexate is one of the few anticancer drugs that can be safely administered intrathecally for the treatment of meningeal metastases. Its routine use as prophylactic intrathecal chemotherapy in acute lymphoblastic leukemia has greatly reduced the incidence of recurrences in the CNS and has contributed to the cure rate in this disease. Daily oral doses of methotrexate are used for severe cases of the nonneoplastic skin disease psoriasis and methotrexate has been used as an immunosuppressive agent in severe rheumatoid arthritis.

Adverse Effects

Myelosuppression is the major dose limiting toxicity associated with methotrexate therapy. Gastrointestinal toxicity may appear in the form of ulcerative mucositis and diarrhea. Nausea, alopecia and dermatitis are common with high-dose methotrexate. The greatest danger of high dose therapy is renal toxicity due to precipitation of the drug in the renal tubules and the drug should not be used in patients with renal impairment. Intrathecal administration may produce neurological toxicity ranging from mild arachnoiditis to severe and progressive myelopathy or encephalopathy. Chronic low dose methotrexate therapy, as used for psoriasis, may result in cirrhosis of the liver. Occasionally methotrexate produces an acute, potentially lethal lung toxicity that is thought to be allergic or hypersensitivity pneumonitis. Additionally, methotrexate is a potent teratogen and abortifacient.

Drug Interactions

Salicylates, probenecid and sulfonamides inhibit the renal tubular secretion of methotrexate and may displace it from plasma proteins. Asparaginase inhibits protein synthesis and may protect cells from methotrexate cytotoxicity by delaying progression from G_1-phase to S-phase. Methotrexate may either enhance or inhibit the action of fluorouracil, depending on its sequence of administration.

Gemcitabine

Mechanism of Action

Gemcitabine (Gemzar), an antimetabolite, undergoes metabolic activation to difluorodeoxycytidine triphosphate, which interferes with DNA synthesis and repair. It is the single most active agent for the treatment of metastatic pancreatic cancer, and it is used as a first line treatment for both pancreatic and small cell lung cancer. It is administered by intravenous infusion. The dose-limiting toxicity is bone marrow suppression.

Purine Analogues

Thioguanine (6-Thioguanine)

Mechanism of Action

Thioguanine is an analogue of the natural purine guanine in which a hydroxyl group has been replaced by a sulfhydryl group in the 6-position. Two major mechanisms of cytotoxicity have been proposed for 6-thioguanine:

1. incorporation of the thio nucleotide analogue into DNA or RNA and
2. feedback inhibition of purine nucleotide synthesis.

Both of these actions require initial activation of the drug by the enzyme hypoxanthine guanine-phosphor ribosyl transferase (HGPRTase). The product of this reaction, 6-TGMP, can eventually be converted to deoxy-6-thioguanosine-triphosphate (dTGTP), which has been shown to be incorporated into DNA.

Resistance

Resistance of human leukemia cells to thioguanine has been correlated with decreased activity of HGPRTase and to increased inactivation of the thio nucleotides by alkaline phosphatase.

Pharmacokinetics

Thioguanine is slowly absorbed after oral administration; parent drug levels are barely detectable and peak levels of metabolites occur only after 6 to 8 hours. Total urinary excretion of metabolites in the first 24 hours is 24 to 46% of the administered dose.

Indications

Thioguanine is used primarily as part of a combined induction of chemotherapy in acute myelogenous leukemia.

Adverse Effects

Myelosuppression, with leucopoenia and thrombocytopenia appearing 7 to 10 days after treatment and mild nausea are the most common adverse effects. Liver toxicity with jaundice has been reported in some patients but appears to be less common than with mercaptopurine.

Mercaptopurine (6-Mercaptopurine)

Mechanism of Action

Mercaptopurine (Purinethol) is an analogue of hypoxanthine and was one of the first agents shown to be active against acute leukemias. It is now used as part of maintenance therapy in acute lymphoblastic leukemia. Mercaptopurine must be activated to a nucleotide by the enzyme HGPRTase. This metabolite is capable of inhibiting the synthesis of the normal purines adenine and guanine at the initial aminotransferase step and inhibiting the conversion of inosinic acid to the nucleotides adenylate and guanylate at several steps. Some mercaptopurine is also incorporated into DNA in the form of thioguanine.

Resistance

Resistance to mercaptopurine may be a result of decreased drug activation by HGPRTase or increased inactivation by alkaline phosphatase.

Pharmacokinetics

The plasma half-life of an intravenous bolus injection of mercaptopurine is 21 minutes in children and 47 minutes in adults. After oral administration, peak plasma levels are attained within 2 hours. The drug is 20% bound to plasma proteins and does not enter the CSF. Xanthine oxidase is the primary enzyme involved in the metabolic inactivation of mercaptopurine.

Indications

Mercaptopurine is used in the maintenance therapy of acute lymphoblastic leukemia. It also displays activity against acute and chronic myelogenous leukemias.

Adverse Effects

The major toxicities of mercaptopurine are Myelosuppression, nausea, vomiting, and hepatic toxicity.

Fludarabine

Mechanism of Action

Fludarabine (Fludara) is a fluorinated purine analogue of the antiviral agent vidarabine. The active metabolite,2-fluoro-ara-adenosine triphosphate, inhibits various enzymes involved in DNA synthesis, including DNA polymerase, ribonucleotide reductase, and DNA primase. Unlike most antimetabolites, it is toxic to nonproliferating as well as dividing cells, primarily lymphocytes and lymphoid cancer cells.

Indications

The drug is highly active in the treatment of chronic lymphocytic leukemia, with approximately 40% of patients achieving remissions after previous therapy with alkylating agents has failed. Activity is also seen in the low-grade lymphomas.

Adverse Effects

The major side effect is myelosuppression, which contributes to fevers and infections in as many as half of treated patients. Nausea and vomiting are mild.

Occasional neurotoxicity has been noted at higher doses, with agitation, confusion, and visual disturbances.

Pentostatin

Mechanism of Action

Pentostatin is a purine isolated from fermentation cultures of the microbe Streptomyces antibiotics. Its mechanism of action involves inhibition of the enzyme adenosine deaminase, which plays an important role in purine salvage pathways and DNA synthesis. The resulting accumulation of deoxyadenosine triphosphate (dATP) is highly toxic to lymphocytes.

Indications

Pentostatin is effective in the therapy of hairy cell leukemia, producing remissions in 80 to 90% of patients and complete remissions in more than 50%.

Adverse Effects

The major toxic effects of the drug include myelosuppression, nausea, and skin rashes.

Cladribine

Mechanism of Action

Cladribine (Leustatin) is a synthetic purine nucleoside that is converted to an active cytotoxic metabolite by the enzyme deoxycytidine kinase. Like the other purine antimetabolites, it is relatively selective for both normal and malignant lymphoid cells and kills resting as well as dividing cells.

The drug is highly active against hairy cell leukemia, producing complete remissions in more than 60% of patients treated with a single 7-day course.

Pyrimidine Analogues

Cytarabine

Mechanism of Action

Cytarabine (cytosine arabinoside, ara-C, Cytosar-U) is an analogue of the pyrimidine nucleosides cytidine and deoxycytidine. It is one of the most active agents available for the treatment of acute myelogenous leukemia. Cytarabine kills cells in the S-phase of the cycle by competitively inhibiting DNA polymerase. The drug must first be activated by pyrimidine nucleoside kinases to the triphosphate nucleotide ara-cytosine triphosphate (ara-CTP). The susceptibility of tumor cells to cytarabine is thought to be a reflection of their ability to activate the drug more rapidly (by kinases) than to inactivate it (by deaminases).

Pharmacokinetics

Cytarabine is rapidly metabolized in the liver, kidney, intestinal mucosa and red blood cells and has a half life in plasma of only 10 minutes after intravenous bolus injection. The major metabolite, uracil arabinoside (ara-U), can be detected in the blood shortly after cytarabine administration. About 80% of a given dose is excreted in the urine within 24 hours, with less than 10% appearing as cytarabine; the remainder is ara-U. When the drug is given by continuous infusion, cytarabine levels in CSF approach 40% of those in plasma.

Indications

Cytarabine is used in the chemotherapy of acute myelogenous leukemia, usually in combination with an anthracycline agent, thioguanine or both. It is less useful in acute lymphoblastic leukemia and the lymphomas and has no known activity against other tumors. It has been used intrathecally in the treatment of Meningeal leukemias and lymphomas as an alternative to methotrexate.

Adverse Effects

Myelosuppression is a major toxicity, as is severe bone marrow hypoplasia. Nausea and mucositis also may occur. Intrathecal administration occasionally produces arachnoiditis or more severe neurological toxicity.

Fluorouracil

Mechanism of Action

Fluorouracil (5-fluorouracil, Efudex, Adrucil) is a halogenated pyrimidine analogue that must be activated metabolically. The active metabolite that inhibits DNA synthesis is the deoxyribonucleotide 5- fluoro 2- deoxyuridine-S-phosphate(FdUMP).5-Fluorouracil is selectively toxic to proliferating rather than non-proliferating cells and is active in both the Gand S-phases. The target enzyme inhibited by 5-fluorouracil is thymidylate synthetase, which catalyzes the reaction.The carbon-donating cofactor for this reaction is N5,N10methylenetetrahydrofolate, which is converted to dihydrofolate. The reduced folate cofactor occupies an allosteric site on thymidylate synthetase, which allows for the covalent binding of 5-FdUMP to the active site of the enzyme.

Another action proposed for 5-fluorouracil may involve the incorporation of the nucleotide 5-fluorouridine triphosphate (5-FUTP) into RNA. The cytotoxic role of these "fraudulent" 5-fluorouracil containing RNAs is not well understood.

Several possible mechanisms of resistance to 5-fluorouracil have been identified, including increased synthesis of the target enzyme, altered affinity of thymidylate synthetase for FdUMP, depletion of enzymes (especially uridine kinase) that activate 5-fluorouracil to nucleotides, an increase in the pool of the normal metabolite deoxyuridylic acid (dUMP), and an increase in the rate of catabolism of 5-fluorouracil.

Pharmacokinetics

The drug has been administered orally, but absorption by this route is erratic. The plasma half-life of 5-fluorouracil after intravenous injection is 10 to 20 minutes. It readily enters CSF. Less than 20% of the parent compound is excreted into the urine, the rest being largely metabolized in the liver.

Indications

5-Fluorouracil is used in several combination regimens in the treatment of breast cancer. It also has palliative activity in gastrointestinal adenocarcinomas, including those originating in the stomach, pancreas, liver, colon and rectum. Other tumors in which some antitumor effects have been reported include carcinomas of the ovary, cervix, oropharynx, bladder and prostate. Topical 5-fluorouracil cream has been useful in the treatment of premalignant keratoses of the skin and superficial basal cell carcinomas, but it should not be used in invasive skin cancer.

Adverse Effects

Nausea is usually mild if it occurs at all Myelosuppression is most severe after intravenous bolus administration, with leukopenia and thrombocytopenia appearing 7 to 14 days after an injection. Daily injection or continuous infusion is most likely to produce oral mucositis, pharyngitis, diarrhea and alopecia. Skin rashes and nail discoloration have been reported as have photosensitivity and increased skin pigmentation on sun exposure. Neurological toxicity is manifested as acute cerebellar ataxia that may occur within a few days of beginning treatment.

Antibiotics

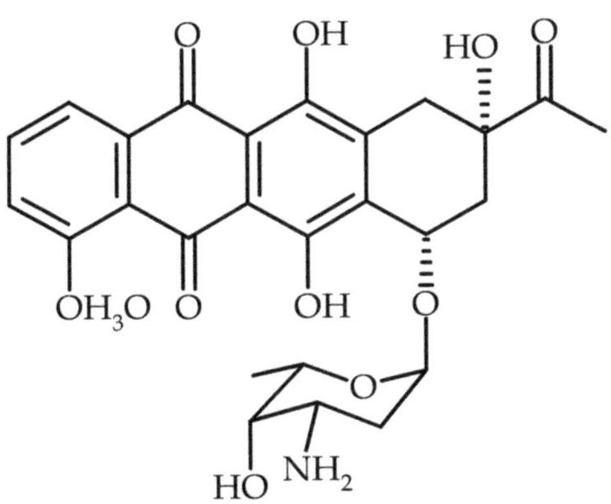

Daunarubicin

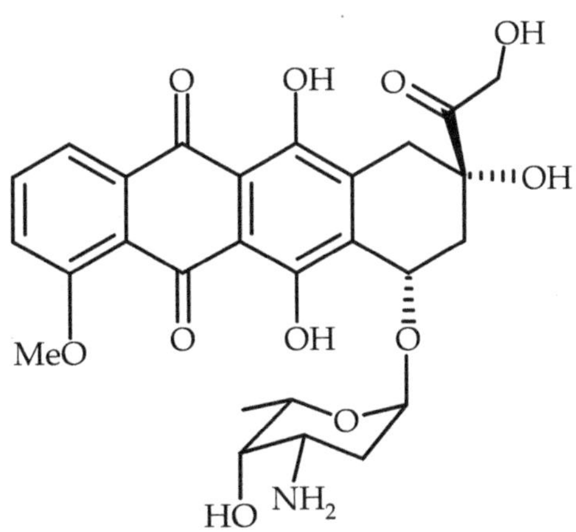

Doxorubicin

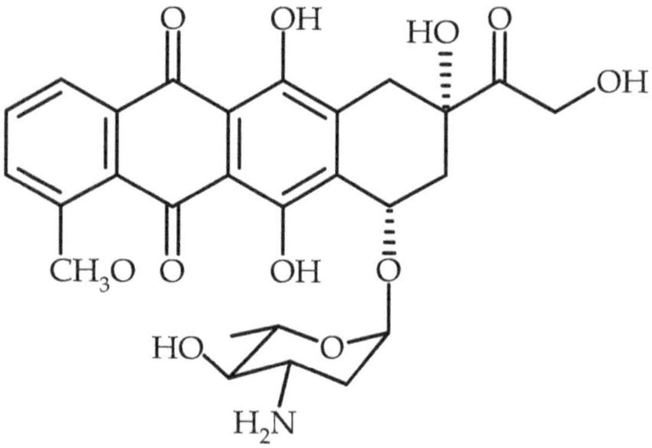

Epirubicin

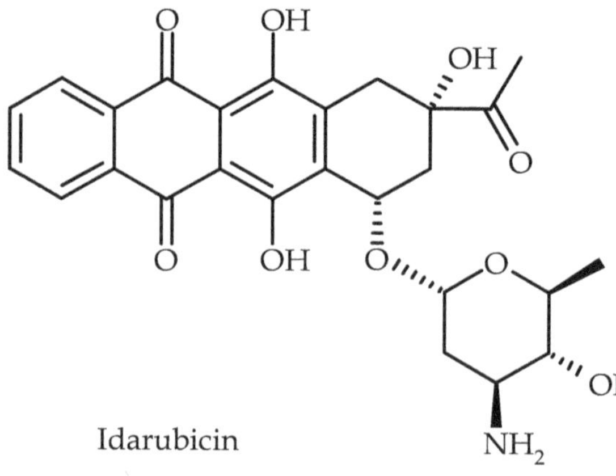

Idarubicin

Fig 22-6: Antibiotics

Doxorubicin and Daunorubicin

The anthracycline antibiotics are fermentation products of Streptomyces peucetius.

Daunorubicin (Cerubidine) is used to treat acute leukemias, while its structural analogue, doxorubicin (Adriamycin) is extensively employed against a broad spectrum of cancers (Fig 22-6).

Mechanism of Action

Doxorubicin binds tightly to DNA by its ability to intercalate between base pairs and therefore is preferentially concentrated in nuclear structures. Intercalation results in steric hindrance, hence production of single strand breaks in DNA and inhibition of DNA synthesis and DNA dependent RNA synthesis. The enzyme topoisomerase II is thought to be involved in the generation of DNA strand breaks by the anthracyclines. Cells in S phase are most sensitive to doxorubicin, although cytotoxicity also occurs in other phases of the cell cycle.

In addition to the intercalation mechanism described, the anthracycline ring of doxorubicin can undergo one electron reduction to form free radicals and participate in further electron transfer. These highly active substances can then react with tissue macromolecules. This type of interaction suggests an alternative mechanism of cytotoxicity for the anthracyclines. In particular, the cardiac toxicity of anthracyclines may result from the generation of free radicals of oxygen.

Resistance

Resistance to the anthracyclines usually involves decreased drug accumulation due to enhanced active efflux of drug. This form of drug resistance is common among the large, heterocyclic naturally derived anticancer agents. It is termed multidrug resistance because of the high degree of cross resistance among the anthracyclines, vinca alkaloids, dactinomycin and podophyllotoxins .

Pharmacokinetics

Doxorubicin is not absorbed orally and because of its ability to cause tissue necrosis must not be injected intramuscularly or subcutaneously. Distribution studies indicate rapid uptake in all tissues except the CNS. Extensive tissue binding, primarily intranuclear, accounts for the prolonged elimination half-life. The drug is extensively metabolized in the liver to hydroxylated and conjugated metabolites and to aglycones that are primarily excreted in the bile.

Indications

Doxorubicin is one of the most effective agents used in the treatment of carcinomas of the breast, ovary, endometrium, bladder and thyroid and in oat cell cancer of the lung. It is included in several combination regimens for diffuse lymphomas and Hodgkin's disease. Doxorubicin can be used as an alternative to daunorubicin in acute leukemias and is useful in Ewing's sarcoma, osteogenic sarcoma, soft-tissue sarcomas, and neuroblastoma.

Adverse Effects

The most important toxicities caused by doxorubicin involve the heart and bone marrow. Acutely, doxorubicin may cause transient cardiac arrhythmias and depression of myocardial function. Doxorubicin may cause radiation recall reactions, with flare ups of dermatitis, stomatitis, or esophagitis that had been produced previously by radiation therapy. Less severe toxicities include phlebitis and sclerosis of veins used for injection, hyperpigmentation of nail beds and skin creases and conjunctivitis. Because of its intense red color, doxorubicin will impart a reddish color to the urine for 1 or 2 days after administration.

Idarubicin

Idarubicin (Idamycin) differs from its parent compound, daunorubicin, by the absence of the methoxy group in the anthracycline ring structure. Its mechanisms of action and resistance are similar to those of doxorubicin and daunorubicin; however, it is more lipophilic and more potent than these other anthracyclines. Idarubicin undergoes extensive hepatic metabolism and biliary excretion.

Bleomycin

The Bleomycin are a group of glycopeptides that are isolated from *Streptomyces verticillus*. The clinical preparation, bleomycin sulfate (Blenoxane), is a mixture of several components.

Mechanism of Action

Bleomycin binds to DNA, in part through an intercalation mechanism, without markedly altering the secondary structure of the nucleic acid. The drug produces both single- and double-strand scission and fragmentation of DNA. It is thought that the bleomycins, which are avid metal-chelating agents, form a bleomycin–Fe complex that can donate electrons to molecular oxygen, thus forming the superoxide and hydroxyl free radicals. It is these highly reactive intermediates that attack DNA and produce DNA strand breakage and maximum cytotoxicity in the late G_2 and early M-phases of the cell cycle.

Pharmacokinetics

Bleomycin is poorly absorbed orally, but it can be given by various parenteral routes. Its plasma half life is not affected by renal dysfunction as long as creatinine clearance is greater than 35 mL/minute. Bleomycin hydrolase, which inactivates bleomycin, is an enzyme that is abundant in liver and kidney but virtually absent in lungs and skin; the latter two organs are the major targets of bleomycin toxicity. It is thought that bleomycin induced dermal and pulmonary toxicities are related to the persistence of relatively high local concentrations of active drug.

Indications

Bleomycin, in combination with cisplatin or etoposide, is important as part of the potentially curative combination chemotherapy of advanced testicular carcinomas. Bleomycin is used in some standard regimens for the treatment of Hodgkin's and non-Hodgkin's lymphomas, and it is useful against squamous cell carcinomas of the head and neck, cervix and skin.

Adverse Effects

Rarely, Bleomycin also may cause allergic pneumonitis. Bleomycin skin toxicity is manifested by hyperpigmentation, erythematosus rashes, and thickening of the skin over the dorsum of the hands and at dermal pressure points, such as the elbows. Many patients develop a low grade transient fever within 24 hours of receiving bleomycin. Less common adverse effects include mucositis, alopecia, headache, nausea and arteritis of the distal extremities.

Mitomycin

Mechanism of Action

Mitomycin (mitomycin C, Mitocin-C, Mutamycin) is an antibiotic that is derived from a species of Streptomyces. It is sometimes classified as an alkylating agent because it can covalently bind to and cross-link DNA. Mitomycin is thought to inhibit DNA synthesis through its ability to alkylate double strand DNA and bring about interstrand cross linking. There is evidence that enzymatic reduction by a reduced nicotinamide-adenine dinucleotide phosphate (NADPH) dependent reductase is necessary to activate the drug.

The drug is rapidly cleared from serum after intravenous injection but is not distributed to the brain.

Adverse Effects

The major toxicity associated with mitomycin therapy is unpredictably long and cumulative myelosuppression that affects both white blood cells and platelets. A syndrome of microangiopathic hemolytic anemia, thrombocytopenia and renal failure also has been described. Renal, hepatic and pulmonary toxicity may occur.

Dactinomycin

Mechanism of Action

Dactinomycin (actinomycin D, Cosmegen) is one of a family of chromopeptides produced by Streptomyces. It is known to bind noncovalently to double strand DNA by partial intercalation, inhibiting DNA-directed RNA synthesis. The drug is most toxic to proliferating cells, but it is not specific for any one phase of the cell cycle.

Resistance

Resistance to dactinomycin is caused by decreased ability of tumor cells to take up and retain the drug, and it is associated with cross resistance to vinca alkaloids, the anthracyclines, and certain other agents (multidrug resistance).

Pharmacokinetics

Dactinomycin is cleared rapidly from plasma, does not enter the brain, is not appreciably metabolized or protein bound, and is gradually excreted in both bile and urine. Virtually no drug is detected in CSF.

Indications

Dactinomycin is used in curative combined treatment of Wilms' tumor, Ewing's sarcoma, rhabdomyosarcoma and gestational choriocarcinoma. It is active in testicular tumors, lymphomas, melanomas and sarcomas, although its use in most of these malignancies has been supplanted by other agents.

Adverse Effects

The major side effects of dactinomycin are severe nausea, vomiting and myelosuppression. Mucositis, diarrhea, alopecia and radiation recall reactions may occur. The drug is immunosuppressive and carcinogenic.

Plicamycin

Mechanism of Action

Plicamycin (mithramycin, Mithracin) is one of the chromomycin group of antibiotics produced by Streptomyces tanashiensis. Plicamycin binds to DNA and inhibits transcription. It also inhibits resorption of bone by osteoblasts, thus lowering serum calcium levels.

Indications

The major indication for plicamycin therapy is in the treatment of life-threatening hypercalcemia associated with malignancy. Plicamycin also can be used in the palliative therapy of metastatic testicular carcinoma when all other known active drugs have failed.

Plant-Derived Products

Three classes of plant-derived drugs (Fig 22-7), the vinca alkaloids (vincristine, vinblastine, and vinorelbine), the epipodophyllotoxins (etoposide and teniposide) and the taxanes (paclitaxel and taxotere), are used in cancer chemotherapy. These classes differ in their structures and mechanisms of action but share the multidrug resistance mechanism, since they are all substrates for the multidrug transporter P-glycoprotein.

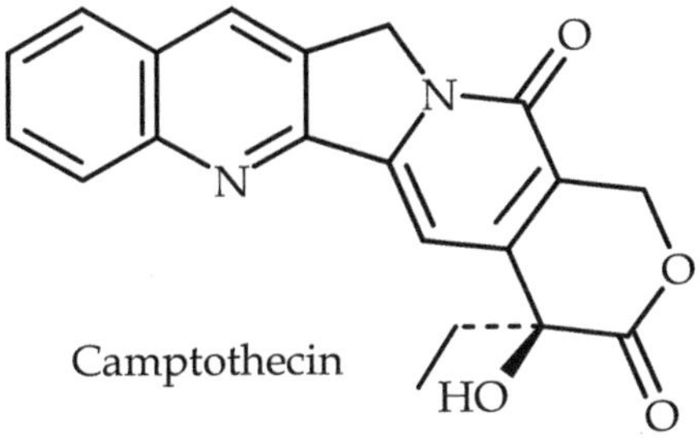

Camptothecin

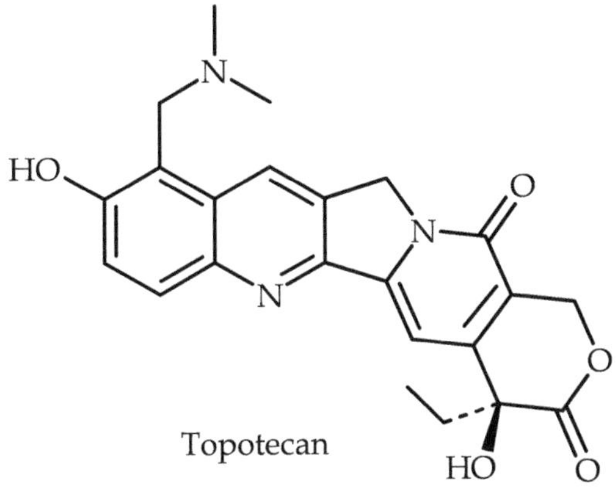

Topotecan

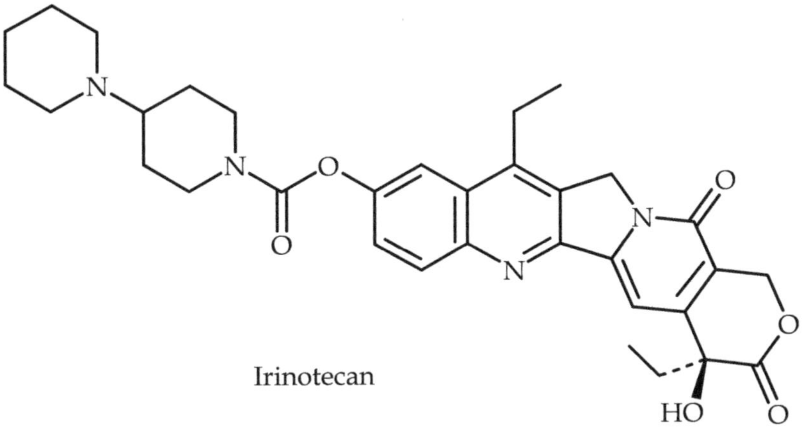

Irinotecan

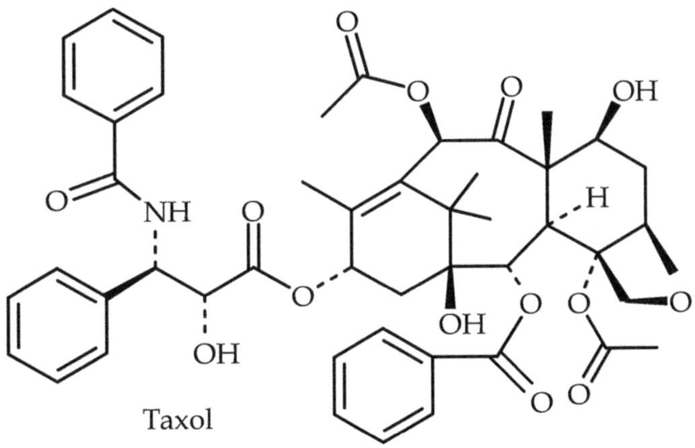

Taxol

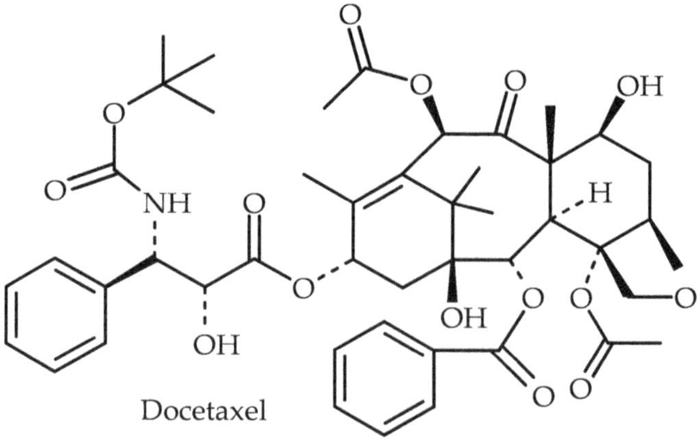

Docetaxel

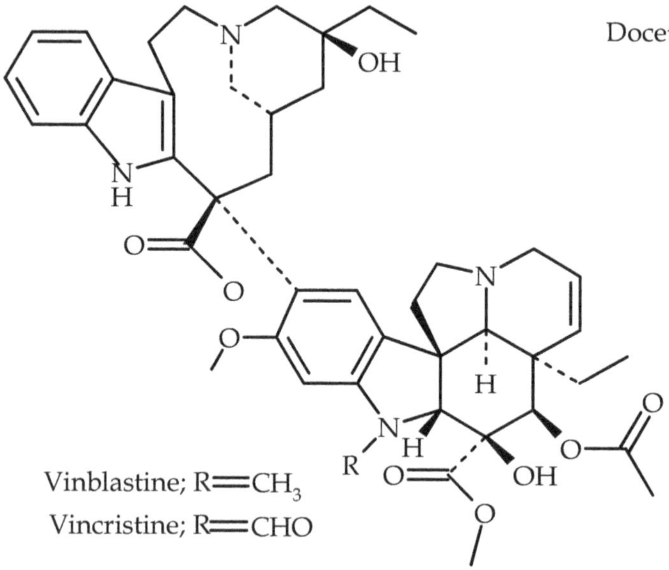

Vinblastine; R=CH_3
Vincristine; R=CHO

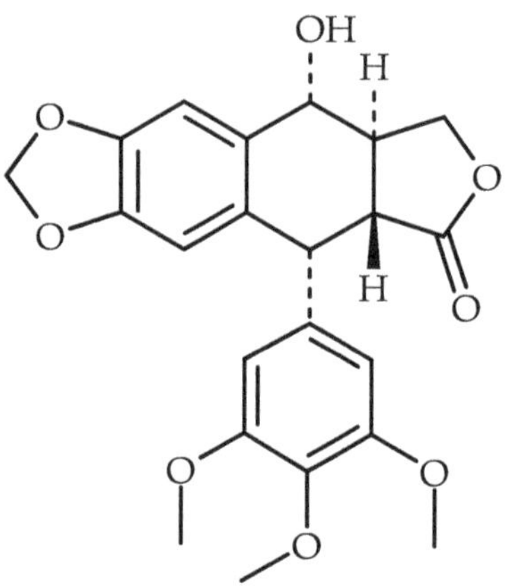

Podophyllotoxin

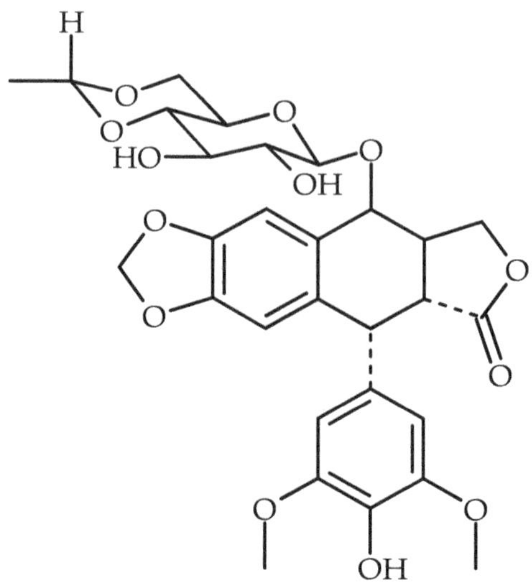

Etoposide

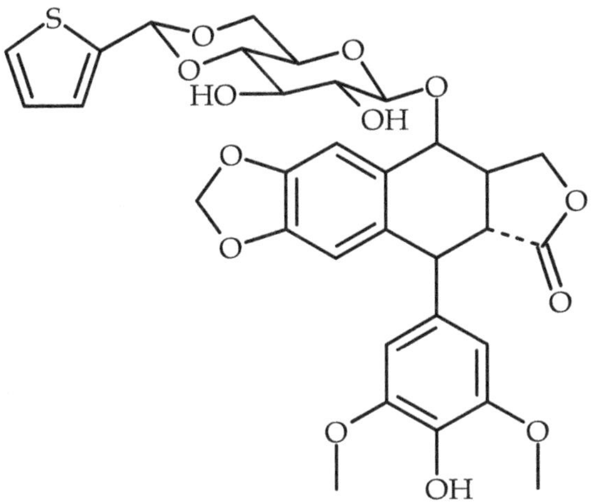

Teniposide

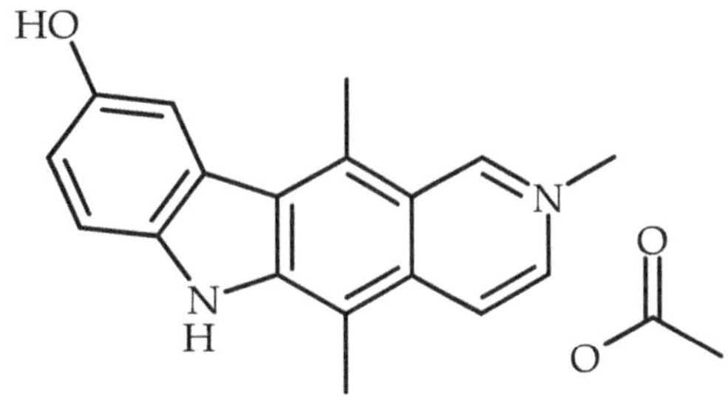

Eliptinum

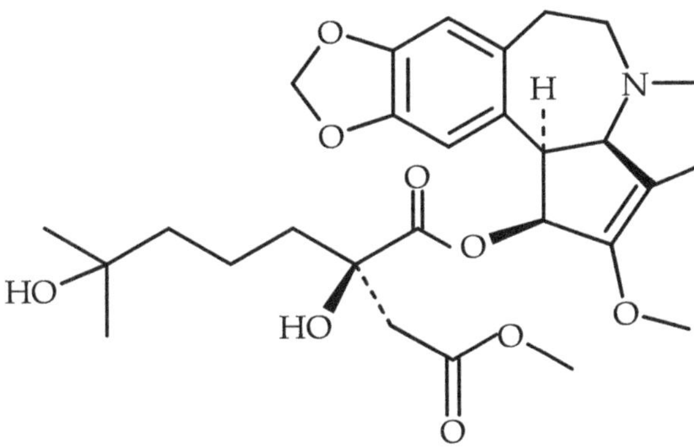

Homoharringtonine

Fig 22-7: Plant derived products.

Vinca Alkaloids

Vincristine, Vinblastine and Vinorelbine. Vincristine (Oncovin) and vinblastine (Velban) are both produced by the leaves of the periwinkle plant. Despite their structural similarity, there are significant differences between them in regard to clinical usefulness and toxicity.

Mechanism of Action

The vinca alkaloids bind avidly to tubulin, a class of proteins that form the mitotic spindle during cell division. The drugs cause cellular arrest in metaphase during mitosis, and cell division cannot be completed. Although the vinca alkaloids usually have been regarded as phase specific in the cell cycle, some mammalian cells are most vulnerable in the late S-phase.

Resistance

Resistance to vinca alkaloids has been correlated with a decreased rate of drug uptake or an increased drug efflux from these tumor cells. Cross-resistance usually occurs with anthracyclines, dactinomycin, and podophyllotoxins.

Pharmacokinetics

Both vincristine and vinblastine are extensively bound to tissues and only small amounts of the drug are distributed to the brain or CSF. The plasma disappearance of vinblastine and vinorelbine is triphasic. Similar clinical pharmacokinetics have been noted with vincristine and vinorelbine. Biliary excretion is the major route of drug excretion.

Indications

Vincristine is an important component of the curative combination chemotherapy for acute lymphoblastic leukemia, Hodgkin's disease (the MOPP regimen), and non-Hodgkin's lymphomas. It is also used in several regimens for pediatric solid tumors, including Wilms' tumor, Ewing's sarcoma, rhabdomyosarcoma, and neuroblastoma; in adult tumors of the breast, lung, and cervix; and in sarcomas.

Adverse Effects

Neurological toxicity is the major dose limiting toxicity of vincristine, whereas bone marrow toxicity is limiting for vinblastine. Severe neutropenia occurs in approximately half of the patients receiving vinorelbine. Severe leukopenia is the major side effect of vinblastine.

Epipodophyllotoxins

Etoposide

Mechanism of Action

Etoposide (VePesid) is a semisynthetic derivative of podophyllotoxin that is produced in the roots of the American mandrake, or May apple. Unlike podophyllotoxin and vinca alkaloids, etoposide does not bind to microtubules. It forms a complex with the enzyme topoisomerase II, which results in a single-strand breakage of DNA. It is most lethal to cells in the S- and G_2-phases of the cell cycle. Drug resistance to etoposide is thought to be caused by decreased cellular drug accumulation.

Indications

Etoposide is most useful against testicular and ovarian germ cell cancers, lymphomas, small cell lung cancers and acute myelogenous and lymphoblastic leukemia.

Adverse Effects

Toxicities include mild nausea, alopecia, allergic reaction, phlebitis at the injection site and bone marrow toxicity.

Teniposide

Teniposide (VM-26, Vumon) is closely related to etoposide in structure, mechanisms of action and resistance and adverse effects. It is more lipophilic and approximately threefold more potent than etoposide. Its major uses have been in pediatric cancers, particularly in acute lymphoblastic leukemias.

Taxanes

Paclitaxel

Mechanism of Action

Paclitaxel (Taxol) is a highly complex, organic compound isolated from the bark of the Pacific yew tree. It binds to tubulin dimers and microtubulin filaments, promoting the assembly of filaments and preventing their depolymerization. This increase in the stability of microfilaments results in disruption of mitosis and cytotoxicity and disrupts other normal microtubular functions, such as axonal transport in nerve fibers.

Resistance

The major mechanism of resistance that has been identified for paclitaxel is transport out of tumor cells, which leads to decreased intracellular drug accumulation. This form of resistance is mediated by the multidrug transporter P-glycoprotein.

Pharmacokinetics

Paclitaxel's large volume of distribution indicates significant tissue binding. The drug is extensively metabolized by the liver, and doses must be reduced in patients with abnormal liver function or with extensive liver metastases. Very little of the drug is excreted in the urine.

Indications

Paclitaxel is among the most active of all anticancer drugs, with significant efficacy against carcinomas of the breast, ovary, lung, head, and neck. It is combined with cisplatin in the therapy of ovarian and lung carcinomas and with doxorubicin in treating breast cancer.

Adverse Effects

Myelosuppression is the major side effect of paclitaxel. Alopecia is common, as is reversible dose-related peripheral neuropathy. Most patients have mild numbness and tingling of the fingers and toes beginning a few days after treatment. Mild muscle and joint aching also may begin 2 or 3 days after initiation of therapy. Nausea is usually mild or absent. Severe hypersensitivity reactions may occur. Cardiovascular side effects, consisting of mild hypotension and bradycardia, have been noted in up to 25% of patients.

Enzymes

L-Asparaginase

Mechanism of Action

The enzyme L-asparaginase (Elspar) is derived from the bacteria Escherichia coli and Erwinia carotovora. It catalyzes the hydrolysis of L-asparagine to aspartic acid and ammonia. L-Glutamine also can undergo hydrolysis by this enzyme, and during therapy, the plasma levels of both amino acid substrates fall to zero. Tumor cells sensitive to L-asparaginase are deficient in the enzyme asparagine synthetase and therefore cannot synthesize asparagine. Depletion of exogenous asparagine and glutamine inhibits protein synthesis in cells lacking asparagine synthetase, which leads to inhibition of nucleic acid synthesis and cell death.

Pharmacokinetics

The half-life of L-asparaginase in human plasma is 6 to 30 hours. The drug remains primarily in the intravascular space, so its volume of distribution is only slightly greater than that of the plasma. Metabolism and disposition are thought to occur through serum proteases, the reticuloendothelial system, and especially in patients with prior exposure to the drug, binding by antibodies. The drug is not excreted in urine, and very little appears in the CSF.

Indications

The major indication for L-asparaginase is in the treatment of acute lymphoblastic leukemia; complete remission rates of 50 to 60% are possible. Lack of cross resistance and bone marrow toxicity make the enzyme particularly useful in combination chemotherapy.L-Asparaginase also can be used in the treatment of certain types of lymphoma. It has no role in the treatment of nonlymphocytic leukemias or other types of cancer.

Adverse effects

Since it is a foreign protein, L-asparaginase may produce hypersensitivity reactions, including urticarial skin rashes and severe anaphylactic reactions. One third of patients have nausea, anorexia, weight loss, and mild fever. Severe hepatic toxicity occurs in fewer than 5% of cases. Patients receiving L-asparaginase may develop symptoms of CNS toxicity, including drowsiness, confusion, impaired mentation, and even coma. Pancreatitis occurs in 5 to 10% of cases. Hyperglycemia, possibly due to inhibition of insulin synthesis, also may occur. L-Asparaginase differs from most cytotoxic drugs in its lack of toxicity to bone marrow, gastrointestinal tract, and hair follicles.

Hormone Derivatives

Tamoxifen

The structure of Tamoxifen is shown in Fig 60-8.

Tamoxifen (Nolvadex) is a synthetic antiestrogen used in the treatment of breast cancer.

Mechanism of Action

Normally, estrogens act by binding to a cytoplasmic protein receptor, and the resulting hormone–receptor complex is then translocated into the nucleus, where it induces the synthesis of ribosomal RNA (rRNA) and messenger RNA

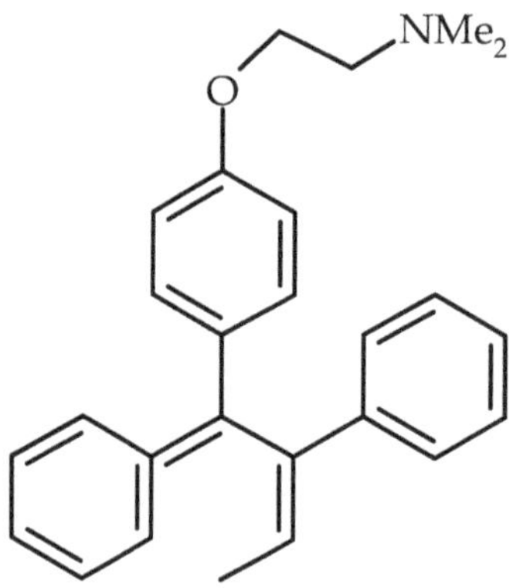

Tamoxifen

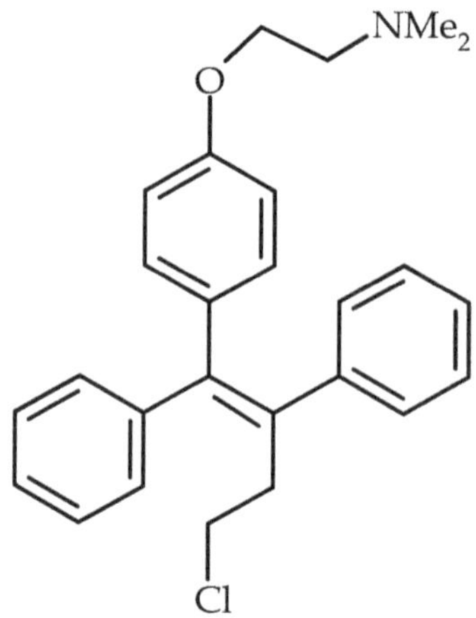

Tamoxifen

Fig 22-8: Hormone derivatives.

(mRNA) at specific sites on the DNA of the target cell. Tamoxifen also avidly binds to estrogen receptors and competes with endogenous estrogens for these critical sites. The drug–receptor complex has little or no estrogen agonist activity. Tamoxifen directly inhibits growth of human breast cancer cells that contain estrogen receptors but has little effect on cells without such receptors.

Pharmacokinetics

Tamoxifen is slowly absorbed, and maximum serum levels are achieved 4 to 7 hours after oral administration. The drug is concentrated in estrogen target tissues, such as the ovaries, uterus, vaginal epithelium, and breasts. Hydroxylation and glucuronidation of the aromatic rings are the major pathways of metabolism; excretion occurs primarily in the feces.

Adverse effects

Tamoxifen administration is associated with few toxic side effects, most frequently hot flashes (in 10–20% of patients) and occasionally vaginal dryness or discharge. Mild nausea, exacerbation of bone pain, and hypercalcemia may occur.

Estramustine

Estramustine phosphate sodium (Emcyt) is a hybrid structure combining estradiol and a nitrogen mustard in a single molecule. The drug has been approved for use in prostatic carcinomas and will produce clinical remissions in one third of patients who have failed to respond to previous estrogen therapy.

Mechanism of action

The mechanism of action of estramustine is not well defined, but it does not appear to require either alkylation of DNA or the presence of estrogen receptors in tumor cells.

Adverse effects

The toxicities of the drug are similar to those of estrogen therapy: breast tenderness and enlargement (gynecomastia), fluid retention, mild nausea and an increased risk of thrombophlebitis and pulmonary embolism. The drug is not myelosuppressive.

Flutamide

Flutamide (Eulexin) is a nonsteroidal antiandrogen compound that competes with testosterone for binding to androgen receptors. The drug is well absorbed on oral administration. It is an active agent in the hormonal therapy of cancer of the prostate and has been shown to complement the pharmacological castration produced by the gonadotropin-releasing hormone (GnRH) agonist leuprolide. Flutamide prevents the stimulation of tumor growth that may occur as a result of the transient increase in testosterone secretion after the initiation of leuprolide therapy.

Adverse Effects

The most common side effects of flutamide are those expected with androgen blockade: hot flashes, loss of libido, and impotence. Mild nausea and diarrhoea occur in about 10% of patients.

Buserelin and Leuprolide

Buserelin (Suprefact) and leuprolide (Lupron) are peptide analogues of the hypothalamic hormone LH-RH (luteinizing hormone-releasing hormone). Chronic exposure of the pituitary to these agents abolishes gonadotropin release and results in markedly decreased estrogen and testosterone production by the gonads.

Indications

Their major clinical use is in the palliative hormonal therapy of cancer of the prostate.

Somatostatin Analogue

Octreotide acetate (Sandostatin) is a synthetic peptide analogue of the hormone somatostatin. Its actions include inhibition of the pituitary secretion of growth hormone and an inhibition of pancreatic islet cell secretion of insulin and glucagon.

Pharmacokinetics

Unlike somatostatin, which has a plasma half-life of a few minutes, octreotide has a plasma elimination half-life of 1 to 2 hours. Excretion of the drug is primarily renal.

Indications

Octreotide is useful in inhibiting the secretion of various autacoids and peptide hormones by metastatic carcinoid tumors (serotonin) and islet cell carcinomas of the pancreas (gastrin, glucagon, insulin, vasoactive intestinal peptide). The diarrhea and flushing associated with the carcinoid syndrome are improved in 70 to 80% of the patients treated with octreotide.

Adverse effects

Its side effects, which are usually mild, include nausea and pain at the injection site. Mild transient hypoglycemia or hyperglycemia may result from alterations in insulin, glucagon, or growth hormone secretion.

Miscellaneous Agents

Hydroxyurea

Hydroxyurea (Hydrea) inhibits the enzyme ribonucleotide reductase and thus depletes intracellular pools of deoxy ribonucleotides, resulting in a specific impairment of DNA synthesis. The drug therefore is an S-phase specific agent whose action results in an accumulation of cells in the late G_1- and early S-phases of the cell cycle.

Pharmacokinetics

Hydroxyurea is rapidly absorbed after oral administration, with peak plasma levels achieved approximately 1 to 2 hours after drug administration; its elimination half-life is 2 to 3 hours. The primary route of excretion is renal, with 30 to 40% of a dose excreted unchanged.

Indications

Hydroxyurea is used for the rapid lowering of blood granulocyte counts in patients with chronic granulocytic leukemia. The drug also can be used as maintenance therapy for patients with the disease who have become resistant to busulfan. Only a small percentage of patients with other malignancies have had even brief remissions induced by hydroxyurea administration.

Adverse Effects

Hematological toxicity, with white blood cells affected more than platelets, may occur. Megaloblastosis of the bone marrow also may be observed. Recovery is rapid, generally within 10 to 14 days after discontinuation of the drug. Some skin reactions, including hyperpigmentation and hyperkeratosis, have been reported with chronic treatment.

Procarbazine

Procarbazine (Matulane) may autooxidize spontaneously, and during this reaction hydrogen peroxide and hydroxyl free radicals are generated. These highly reactive products may degrade DNA and serve as one mechanism of procarbazine induced cytotoxicity. Cell toxicity also may be the result of a transmethylation reaction that can occur between the N-methyl group of procarbazine and the N_7 position of guanine.

Pharmacokinetics

Procarbazine is rapidly absorbed after oral administration and has a plasma half life of only 10 minutes. The drug crosses the blood brain barrier, reaching levels in CSF equal to those obtained in plasma. Metabolism is extensive and complex. Urinary excretion accounts for 70% of the procarbazine and its metabolites lost during the first 24 hours after drug administration.

Indications

Procarbazine is also used in various combination chemotherapy protocols for non-Hodgkin's lymphomas and small cell anaplastic (oat cell) carcinoma of the lung. Limited antitumor effects have been observed against multiple myeloma, melanoma, and non oat cell lung cancers.

Adverse Effects

The major side effects associated with procarbazine therapy are nausea and vomiting, leukopenia, and thrombocytopenia. Skin rashes have been reported, as have rare cases of allergic interstitial pneumonia. Procarbazine administration produces a high degree of chromosomal breakage, and the compound is mutagenic, teratogenic, and carcinogenic in experimental systems. Procarbazine may potentiate the effects of tranquilizers and hypnotics. Hypertensive episodes can result if procarbazine is administered simultaneously with adrenomimetic drugs or with tyramine containing foods. Rarely, a reaction to alcohol similar to that provoked by disulfiram may occur.

Mitotane

The observation that mitotane (Lysodren) could produce adrenocortical necrosis in animals led to its use in the palliation of inoperable adrenocortical adenocarcinomas. A reduction in both tumor size and adrenocortical hormone secretion can be achieved in about half of the patients taking the drug. Because normal adrenocortical cells also are affected, endogenous glucocorticoid production should be monitored and replacement therapy administered when appropriate.

Pharmacokinetics

Mitotane is incompletely absorbed from the gastrointestinal tract after oral administration. However, once absorbed, it tends to accumulate in adipose tissue. Mitotane is slowly excreted and will appear in the urine for several years.

Adverse Effects

The major toxicities associated with its use are anorexia, nausea, diarrhoea, lethargy, somnolence, dizziness, and dermatitis.

Hexamethylmelamine

Although both DNA and RNA synthesis are inhibited in cells exposed to Hexamethylmelamine (Hexalen), the molecular mechanisms of these effects are not known.

Pharmacokinetics

Hexamethylmelamine is readily absorbed after oral administration, with peak plasma levels achieved after 1 hour. The drug is readily metabolized to form a number of demethylated metabolites. Urinary elimination is the primary route of drug excretion.

Indications

Hexamethylmelamine is useful for the treatment of ovarian adenocarcinoma and is frequently combined with cyclophosphamide, cisplatin, and doxorubicin in the treatment of this tumor. It also has some activity against small cell lung cancer.

Adverse Effects

Nausea and vomiting are the major toxicities associated with Hexamethylmelamine administration. Myelosuppression and a peripheral neuropathy also may occur.

Cisplatin

Cisplatin (Platinol) is an inorganic coordination complex with a broad range of antitumor activity. It is especially useful in the treatment of testicular and ovarian cancer. It binds to DNA at nucleophilic sites, such as the N_7 and O_6 of guanine, producing alterations in DNA structure and inhibition of DNA synthesis. Adjacent guanine residues on the same DNA strand are preferentially cross linked. This platinating activity is analogous to the mode of action of Alkylating agents. Cisplatin also binds extensively to proteins. It does not appear to be phase specific in the cell cycle.

Pharmacokinetics

Cisplatin shows biphasic plasma decay with a distribution phase half-life of 25 to 49 minutes and an elimination half-life of 2 to 4 days. More than 90% of the drug is bound to plasma proteins, and binding may approach 100% during prolonged infusion. Cisplatin does not cross the blood-brain barrier. Excretion is predominantly renal and is incomplete.

Adverse Effects

Renal toxicity is the major potential toxicity of cisplatin. Severe nausea and vomiting that often accompany cisplatin administration may necessitate hospitalization. Cisplatin has mild bone marrow toxicity, yielding both leucopoenia and thrombocytopenia. Anemia is common and may require transfusions of red blood cells. Other reported toxicities include peripheral neuropathies with paresthesias, leg weakness, and tremors. Excessive urinary excretion of magnesium also may occur.

Carboplatin

Carboplatin (Paraplatin) is an analogue of cisplatin.

Pharmacokinetics

Its plasma half-life is 3 to 5 hours, and it has no significant protein binding. Renal excretion is the major route of drug elimination.

Indications

Despite its lower chemical reactivity, carboplatin has antitumor activity that is similar to that of cisplatin against ovarian carcinomas, small cell lung cancers, and germ cell cancers of the testis. Most tumors that are resistant to cisplatin are cross resistant to carboplatin.

The major advantage of carboplatin over cisplatin is a markedly reduced risk of toxicity to the kidneys, peripheral nerves and hearing; additionally, it produces less nausea and vomiting.

Adverse Effects

It is, however, more myelosuppressive than cisplatin. Other adverse effects include anemia, abnormal liver function tests, and occasional allergic reactions.

Mitoxantrone

Mitoxantrone (Novantrone) is a synthetic Anthraquinone that is structurally and mechanistically related to the anthracyclines. It intercalates with DNA and produces single strand DNA breakage. It is cross resistant with doxorubicin in multidrug resistant cells and in patients who have failed to respond to doxorubicin therapy.

Indications

Mitoxantrone is active against breast carcinomas, leukemias and lymphomas. Its antitumor efficacy in patients with breast cancer is slightly lower than that of doxorubicin.

Adverse Effects

Its major toxicity is myelosuppression; mucositis and diarrhoea also may occur. Mitoxantrone produces less nausea, alopecia, and cardiac toxicity than does doxorubicin.

Immunomodulating Agents

Levamisole

Levamisole (Ergamisol) is an antiparasitic drug that has been found to enhance T-cell function and cellular immunity. The drug improves survival of patients with resected colorectal cancers when combined with 5-fluorouracil; the mechanism of this interaction is not known. Levamisole does not have antitumor activity against established or metastatic cancer and has not been found useful in the adjuvant therapy of cancers other than colorectal cancer.

Adverse Effects

The major adverse effects of levamisole are nausea and anorexia. Skin rashes, itching, flu-like symptoms and fevers also have been observed.

Interferon Alfa-2b

Interferon alfa-2b (Intron A) is a recombinant DNA product derived from the interferon alfa-2b gene of human white blood cells. Its mechanism of antitumor action involves binding to a plasma membrane receptor but is otherwise poorly understood. Its serum half-life is 2 to 3 hours after parenteral administration.

Indications

Interferon alfa-2b is useful in the treatment of a rare form of chronic leukemia, hairy cell leukemia, in which it produces remissions in 60 to 80% of patients. However, it has minimal antitumor activity in most human cancers. Remissions lasting a few months have been observed in 10 to 20% of patients with lymphomas, multiple myeloma, melanoma, renal cell carcinoma, and ovarian carcinoma.

Adverse Effects

The adverse effects of interferon alfa-2b include fever and a flu-like syndrome of muscle ache, fatigue, headache, anorexia, and nausea. Other less common side effects include leukopenia, diarrhoea, dizziness, and skin rash.

Interleukins

Aldesleukin

Aldesleukin (IL-2, Proleukin) is a human recombinant interleukin-2 protein. Its antitumor action is thought to include multiple effects on the immune system, such as enhancement of T-lymphocyte cytotoxicity, induction of natural killer cell activity, and induction of interferon production.

Indications

Aldesleukin has been used alone and in combination with lymphokine activated killer (LAK) cells or tumor-infiltrating lymphocytes (TIL).

Adverse Effects

Several serious toxicities have been observed, with a fatality rate of 5% in the initial studies. The major adverse effect is severe hypotension in as many as 85% of patients, which may lead to myocardial infarctions, pulmonary edema, and strokes. This hypotension is thought to be due to a capillary leak syndrome resulting from extravasation of plasma proteins and fluid into extravascular space and a loss of vascular tone. Patients with significant cardiac, pulmonary, renal, hepatic, or CNS conditions should not receive therapy with aldesleukin. Other adverse reactions include nausea and vomiting, diarrhoea, stomatitis, anorexia, altered mental status, fevers, and fatigue.

Cellular Growth Factors

Filgrastim

Filgrastim (Neupogen) is a human recombinant granulocyte colony–stimulating factor (rG-CSF) produced using recombinant DNA technology. It acts on precursor hematopoietic cells in the bone marrow by binding to specific receptors that stimulate cellular proliferation and differentiation into neutrophils. It also enhances some neutrophil functions, including phagocytosis and antibody-dependent killing.

Indications

Filgrastim is used to accelerate recovery of neutrophils after chemotherapy, both to prevent infections and to shorten the duration of neutropenia in patients in whom infections have developed.

Adverse Effects

The drug is generally well tolerated, with the major adverse reaction being mild to moderate bone pain secondary to stimulation of bone marrow proliferation.

Sargramostim

Sargramostim (GM-CSF, Leukine, Prokine) is a human recombinant granulocyte and macrophage colony stimulating factor that stimulates the production and potentiates the function of both granulocytes and macrophages from hematopoietic progenitor cells. It is used to accelerate bone marrow repopulation after high-dose chemotherapy, radiation therapy, and bone marrow transplantation.

Adverse Effects

Adverse effects associated with sargramostim use include bone pain (similar to that of filgrastim), fatigue, fevers, skin rash, malaise, and fluid retention.

New Drug Therapies for Cancer

Imantinib

Imantinib mesylate (Gleevec) is a rationally designed inhibitor of the tumor-specific bcr-abl kinase. The Philadelphia chromosome, present in nearly all patients with chronic myelogenous leukemia (CML), is produced by a chromosomal rearrangement linking the bcr and the abl genes. The bcr-able kinase is therefore a unique drug target in leukemic cells, and imantinib selectively and potently inhibits this kinase. Remissions in CML patients are achieved with high frequency and very low toxicity, and this compound may become a front-line agent for treating this cancer. Unfortunately, drug resistance has already been observed in the clinic as a result of mutations in the bcr-abl kinase, and this magic bullet does not appear to be curative for CML patients. Extension of the use of imantinib to other tumor types with overexpression of c-kit kinase or platelet-derived growth factor kinase is undergoing development because of its observed activity against these kinases.

Herceptin

The introduction of herceptin (Trastuzumab) into clinical practice for the treatment of breast cancer marks a major advance in the use of monoclonal antibody cancer therapy. Herceptin is a humanized antibody directed against the HER-2 antigen that is over expressed on the tumor cell surface in approximately 25% of breast cancer patients. HER-2/neu/erbB2 over expression marks an aggressive estrogen receptor–negative form of breast cancer. Therefore, a therapeutic agent selective for this target is particularly valuable. Herceptin is administered by intravenous infusion and in conjunction with paclitaxel can extend survival in patients with HER-2/neu/erbB2 over expressing metastatic breast cancer. Herceptin use is associated with infusion related hypotension, flushing and bronchoconstriction, and skin rash but no bone marrow toxicity. Herceptin appears to sensitize patients to cardiotoxicity, an important concern in patients also receiving doxorubicin.

Iressa

Iressa (ZD1839) is an orally active tyrosine kinase inhibitor selective for the epidermal growth factor (EGF) receptor tyrosine kinase. Iressa is undergoing clinical trials in the treatment of various solid tumours, including head and neck cancer, breast cancer and non-small cell lung cancer. Its antitumor activity is derived from the fact that the EGF receptor and EGF signalling are frequently over activated in sensitive tumours. The major side effects include diarrhoea and skin rash. Bone marrow toxicity has not been a dose-limiting problem.

References

DeVita VT, Hellman S, and Rosenberg SA (eds.) (1993). Cancer: Principles and Practice of Oncology (4thed.). *Philadelphia: Lippincott.*

Faroni RE and DeCupis A (2000). The role of polypeptide growth factors in human carcinomas: New targets for a novel pharmacological approach. *Pharmacol Rev* **52:** 179–206.

Foye WO (ed.) (1995). Cancer Chemotherapeutic Agents. *NewYork: American Chemical Society.*

George DJ (2002). Receptor tyrosine kinases as rational targets for prostate cancer treatment: Platelet-derived growth factor receptor and imantinib mesylate. *Urology* **60:** 115–121.

Habib NA (2000). Cancer Gene Therapy: Past Achievements and Future Challenges. *New York: Kluwer/Plenum.*

Kirby RS, Christmas TJ and Brawer MK (2001). Prostate Cancer (2nd ed.). *New York: Mosby.*

Suffness M (1995). Taxol: Science and Applications. *Boca Raton, FL: CRC.*

Vinorelbine for treatment of advanced non-small cell lung cancer (1995). *Med Lett Drugs Ther* **37:** 72–73.

CHAPTER

Chemotherapy of Sexually Transmitted Diseases 23

Infections known as sexually transmitted diseases (STDs) are typically spread through sexual contact with an infected person. Spirochetes, viruses, parasites, and bacteria are the causative agents of STDs. Most STDs affect both sexes, although, for many, women may experience more severe health issues as a consequence. An STD in a pregnant woman might have a major health impact on her unborn child. If bacteria or parasites cause STDs, antibiotics or other medications can be used to treat an infection. There is no treatment for STDs that are caused by viruses.

BACTERIAL STDs

- Chlamydia
- Gonorrhea
- Vaginitis
- Pelvic Inflammatory Disease

PARASITIC STDs

- Crabs
- Vaginitis

VIRAL STDs

- HIV/ AIDS
- Hepatitis A, B, C
- Herpes

PROTOZOANS

- Trichomoniasis
- Vaginitis

Chlamydia

A common sexually transmitted illness called Chlamydia is brought on by the bacteria Chlamydia trachomatis.

Symptoms & Signs:

Women's Chlamydia Symptoms:

- Bleeding between menstrual cycles
- discomfort during sex; bleeding after sex.
- an abnormal vaginal discharge.
- pain or a burning sensation while urination.
- Lower abdomen ache occasionally accompanied by nausea.

Symptoms in men include

- Testicular soreness and/or swelling.
- White/cloudy, watery unusual penile secretion.
- During urination, there may be discomfort or burning.

Diagnosis

1. Urine test

2. Swab test

Chemotherapy

- Azithromycin - 1gm p.o. single dose.
- Doxycycline 100mg B.I.D 7 days.

Pregnancy

Doxycycline is more affordable, But Doxycycline and Ofloxacin are contraindicated during pregnancy; repeat testing should be done three weeks following the end of the course of medication.

- 500mg QID X 7 days of erythromycin base.
- Azithromycin is recommended when compliance is a problem.
- Erythromycin frequently causes more GI adverse effects; compliance testing should be done three weeks following the conclusion of treatment.

Epididymitis

It is an inflammation of the epididymis, a tube at the rear of the testicles that stores and transports sperm. An infection, either a bacterial or a sexually transmitted infection, is what causes epididymitis.

Escherichia coli and Pseudomonas species are the causative organisms. The incubation period is days to weeks (depends upon organism).

Transmission Factors: In children, urinary tract infections are most frequently linked to it. In adolescent, sexually active males are prone to it. It is frequently brought on in older men by an enlarged prostate gland.

Signs and symptoms

These include

- low-grade fever and chills.
- Ache and discomfort in the groin area and the testicles.
- Painful, itchy, and enlarged scrotum, and enlarged lymph nodes in the crotch.

Diagnosis

- The complete blood count (CBC) and Doppler ultrasound are used to diagnose the condition. Nuclear medicine testicular scan, urine analysis, and culture.

Chemotherapy

- Ceftriaxone 250 mg IM And Doxycycline 100mg BID X 10 days (or).
- Ofloxacin 300 mg p.o. BID X 10 days (or).
- Levofloxacin 500 mg p.o. q day X 10 days.
- Should see improvement 3 days after treatment initiated
- Use Ofloxacin if Levofloxacin is not likely STD related or allergic to Cephalosporin's or Tetracycline.

Gonorrhea

Gonorrhea is a bacterial infection that is spread by sexual contact and is described as the "clap" at times. Causative Organism bacteria isNeisseria gonorrhea.

Most often, STDs are caused by Chlamydia trachomatis (CT) and Neisseria gonorrhea (GC)

Incubation Time: 2 to 14 Days.

Transmission factors

- When engaged vaginally, orally, or anally with an infected people.
- It can be transferred to a newborn during birthing by a pregnant woman.

Signs & Symptoms

Symptoms in Women

- Strong-smelling vaginal discharge that may be thin and watery or thick and yellow-green.
- Anus irritation or discharge.
- Abnormal vaginal bleeding.
- Possibility of low abdominal or pelvic tenderness.
- Pain or a burning sensation when passing urine.
- Low abdominal pain, occasionally accompanied by nausea.

Symptoms in men

- White, yellow, or green thick discharge from the tip of the penis.
- Testicular & prostate gland inflammation.
- Irritation or discharge from the penis.
- Urethral itch & pain.

Diagnosis

- Urine test
- Swab test
- Urethral microscopic analysis.

HIV/AIDS

AIDS, HIV, and human immunodeficiency virus are further names for acquired immunodeficiency syndrome. Human immunodeficiency virus is referred to as HIV in which the immune system cells in the body are killed or damaged. Acquired immunodeficiency syndrome is referred to as AIDS. It is the most severe stage of HIV infection.

The responsible organism - HIV (human immunodeficiency virus)

Transmission Factors

- Sharing drug needles or coming into contact with an infected person's blood are other ways to contract the disease.
- Women may give it to their unborn children during pregnancy or childbirth.

  Incubation Period: 2 weeks to 6 months.

  Signs and symptoms include swollen glands and flu-like symptoms, fever (the most frequent symptom), swollen glands, sore throat, rash, fatigue, aches and pains in the muscles and joints, and headache.

Diagnosis

- ELISA (enzyme-linked immunosorbent assay).
- Point-of-care tests
- CD4 cell analysis
- Western blot assay.

Chemotherapy

- Abacavir-300 mg twice daily or 600 mg once daily (or),
- Emtricitabine-200 mg once daily (or),
- Lamivudine-150 mg twice daily or 300 mg once daily (or),
- Zidovudine-250–300 mg twice daily and,
- Dolutegravir-50 mg once daily(or)Raltegravir-400 mg twice daily,

SYPHILIS

Spirochetes are the source of the sexually transmitted infection known as syphilis. The causative organism is the spirochete Treponemapallidum.

Transmission factors: Syphilis is spread through direct contact with a syphilis sore during vaginal, anal, or oral sex. Additionally, an infected mother might pass the infection to her unborn child.

Signs and symptoms

1. Primary: A tiny sore known as a chancre is the initial symptom of syphilis. The sore appears at the spot which is usually painless.
2. Secondary: Weight loss, fever, swollen lymph nodes, moist warts in the groin, and white patches on the inside of the mouth.
3. Tertiary – The brain, nerves, eyes, heart, blood vessels, liver, bones, and joints can all be damaged by disease. Severe heart, brain, and nerve issues that can cause death, blindness, dementia, deaf, impotency are common symptoms.

Diagnosis

- Treponamapallidum particle agglutination test (TPPA).
- Microhemagglutination assay (MHA-TP).

Chemotherapy

- Three doses of long-acting Benzathine penicillin G at weekly intervals at tertiary stage.
- Single dose injection of Benzathine penicillin G at early stage.
- Doxycycline 100mg p.o. BID X 14 days or Tetracyckube 500mg p.o. QID X 14 days.
- Serologic f/u upto 12 months after treatment.

PART - IV

IMMUNOPHARMACOLOGY

CHAPTER

Immunosuppressants and Immunostimulants 24

Introduction

Immune system

- Is designed to protect the host from harmful foreign molecules.
- This system can result into serious problem.
- Allograft introduction can elicit a damaging immune response.

Immune system include two main arms

1. Cell-mediated immunity. (Fig 24-1)
2. Humoral (antibody-mediated immunity). (Fig 24-2)

Cell-mediated Immunity

- TH1 produce more IL-2, TNF-β and IFN-γ.

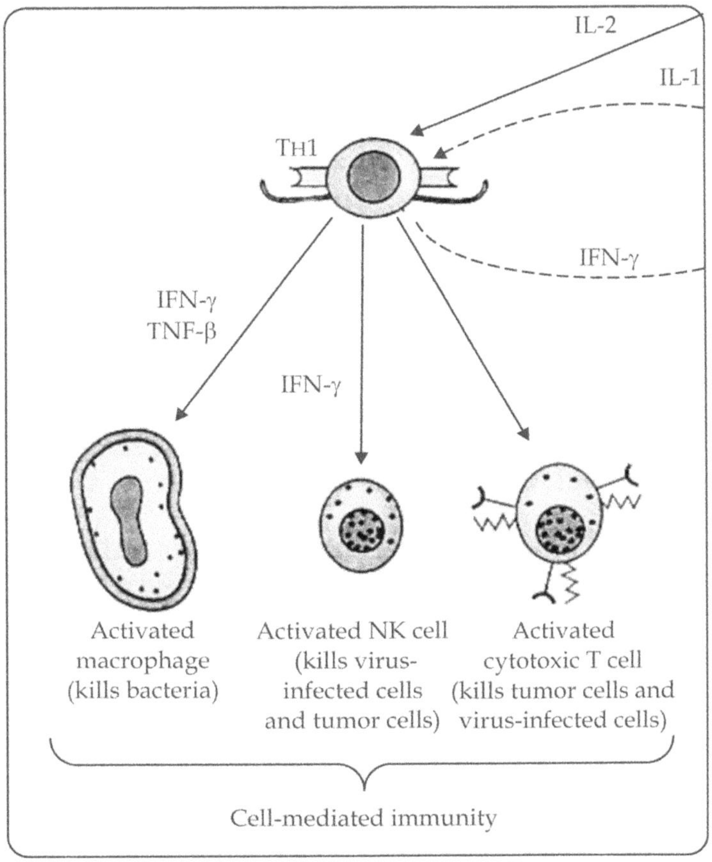

Fig 24-1: Cell mediated immunity.

- Activate
  - o NK cells (kill tumor & virus infected cells).
  - o Cytotoxic T cells (kill tumor & virus infected cells).
  - o Macrophages (kill bacteria).

Humoral Immunity

B-lymphocytes TH2 produces (interleukins) IL-4 and IL-5 which in turn causes:

B cells proliferation & differentiation into

- Memory B cells
- Antibody secreting plasma cells

Immunosuppressant Drugs

I. Inhibitors of cytokine (IL-2) production or action:

1. Calcineurin inhibitors
   - Cyclosporine
   - Tacrolimus (FK506)
2. Sirolimus (Rapamycin).

II. Inhibitors of cytokine gene expression

- Corticosteroids

III. Cytotoxic drugs

1. Inhibitors of purine or pyrimidine synthesis (Antimetabolites):

- Azathioprine
- Mycophenolate Mofetil
- Leflunomide
- Methotrexate
- Alkylating agents
- Cyclophosphamide

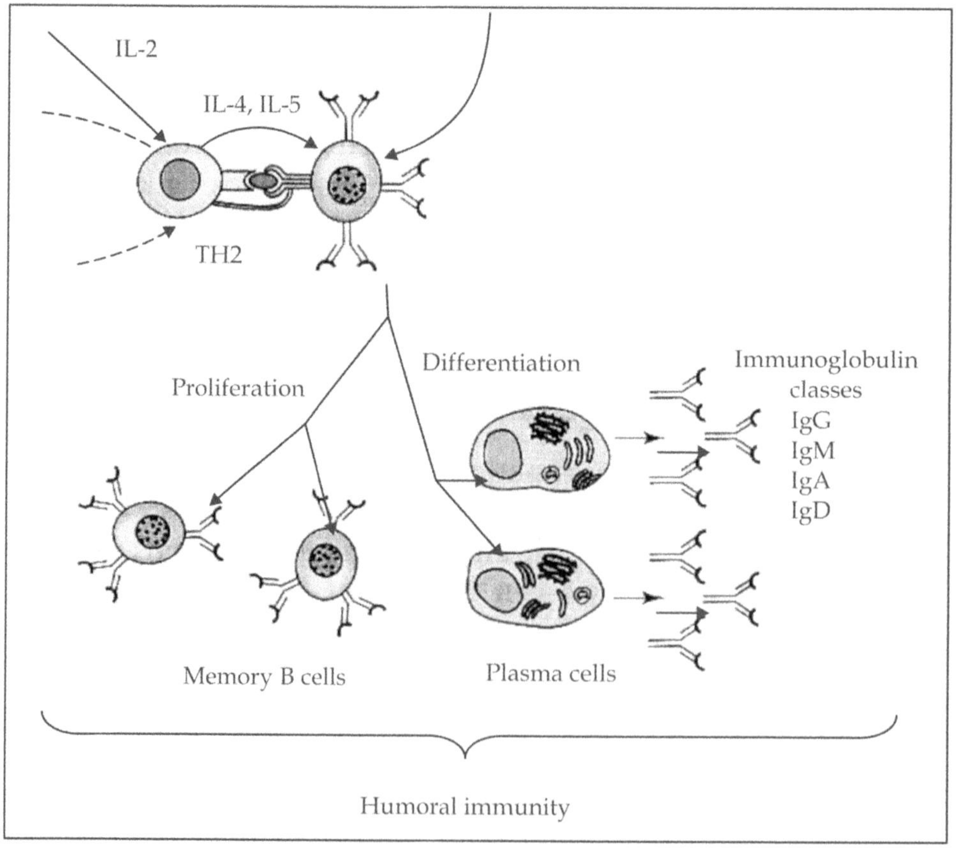

Fig 24-2: Humoral immunity.

IV. Immunosuppressive antibodies

Those block T cell surface molecules involved in signaling immunoglobulins

- Antilymphocyte globulins (ALG).
- Antithymocyte globulins (ATG).
- Rho (D) immunoglobulin.
- Basiliximab
- Daclizumab
- Muromonab-CD3

V. Interferon

VI. Thalidomide

Cyclosporine

Chemistry: Cyclosporine (Fig 24-3) is a fungal polypeptide composed of 11 amino acids.

Mechanism of Action: (Fig 24-4)

Acts by blocking activation of T cells by inhibiting interleukin-2 production (IL-2). Decreases proliferation and differentiation of T cells. Cyclosporine binds to cyclophilin (immunophilin) intracellular protein receptors. Cyclosporine- immunophilin complex inhibits calcineurin, a phosphatase necessary for dephosphorylation of transcription factor (NFATc) required for interleukins synthesis (IL-2). NFATc (Nuclear Factor of Activated Tells). Suppresses cell-mediated immunity.

Pharmacokinetics

Can be given orally or i.v. infusion. Orally (25 or 100 mg) soft gelatin capsules, microemulsion. Orally, it is slowly and incompletely absorbed. Peak levels is reached after 1-4 hours, elimination half life 24 hr. Oral absorption is delayed by fatty meal (gelatin capsule formulation). Micro emulsion (has higher bioavailability is not affected by food). 50 - 60% of cyclosporine accumulates in blood (erythrocytes–lymphocytes). Metabolized by CYT-P450 system (CYP3A4). Excreted mainly through bile into faeces, about 6% is excreted in urine.

Therapeutic Uses

Organ transplantation (kidney, liver, heart) either alone or with other immunosuppressive agents (Corticosteroids).

Autoimmune disorders (low dose 7.5 mg/Kg/d). E.g., endogenous uveitis, rheumatoid arthritis, active Crohn's disease, psoriasis, nephrotic syndrome, severe corticosteroid dependent asthma, early type I diabetes.

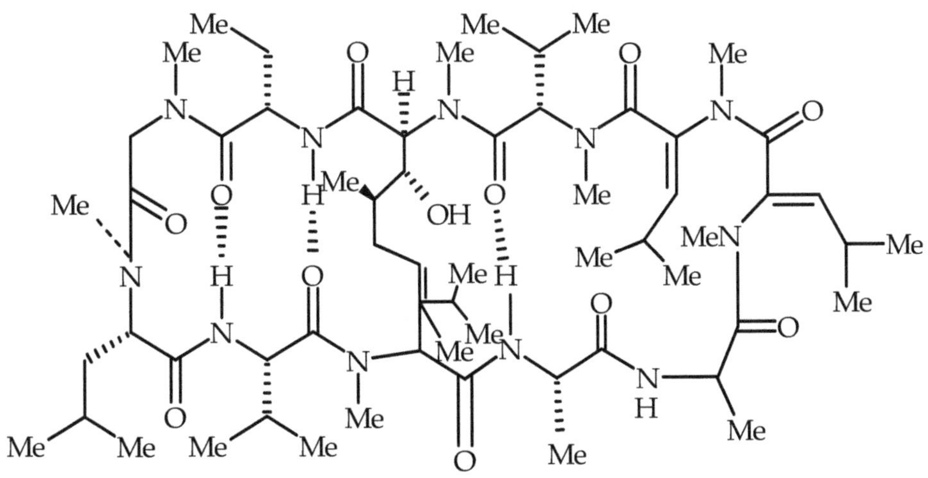

Fig 24-3: Structure of cyclosporine.

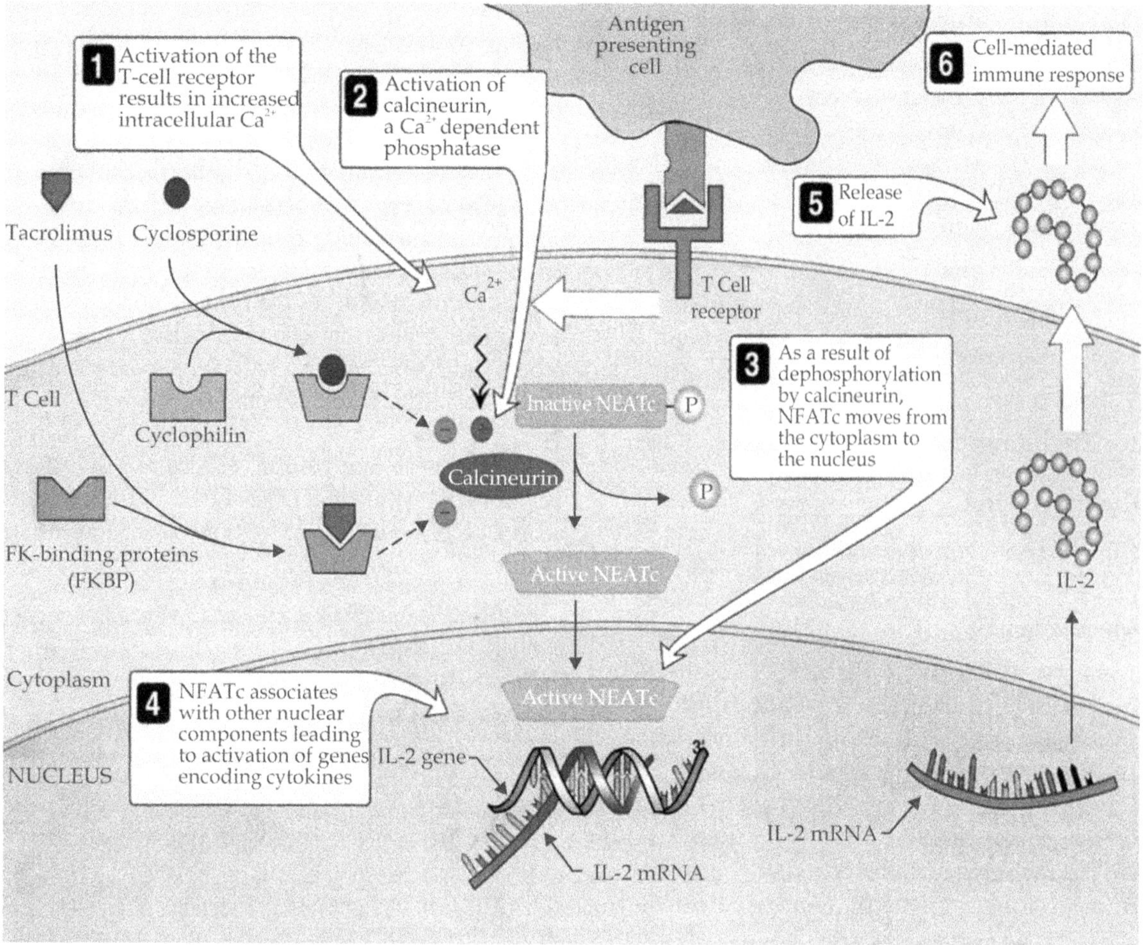

Fig 24-4: Cyclosporine mechanism of action.

Graft versus host disease after stem cell transplants.

Adverse Effects (Dose dependent)

Nephrotoxicity (increased by NSAIDs and Aminoglycosides), Liver dysfunction, Hypertension, hyperkalemia. (K^+-sparing diuretics should not be used), Hyperglycemia, Viral infections (Herpes cytomegalovirus), Lymphoma (Predispose recipients to cancer), Hirsutism, Neurotoxicity (tremor), Gum hyperplasia, Anaphylaxis after i.v.

Drug Interactions

- Clearance of cyclosporine is enhanced by co administration of CYT p450 inducers (Phenobarbitone, Phenytoin & Rifampin)® rejection of transplant.
- Clearance of cyclosporine is decreased when it is co administered with erythromycin or Ketoconazole, Grapefruit juice® cyclosporine toxicity.

Tacrolimus (Fk506)

- A fungal Macrolides antibiotic. (Fig 24-5, Fig 24-6)
- Chemically not related to cyclosporine
- Both drugs have similar mechanism of action.
- The internal receptor for tacrolimus is immunophilin (FK-binding protein, FK-BP).

- Tacrolimus-FKBP complex inhibits calcineurin.

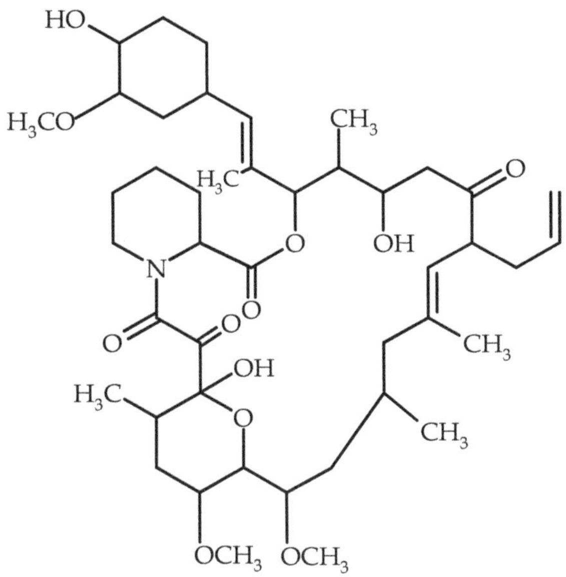

Tacrolimus

Fig 24-5: Structure of tacrolimus.

Kinetics

Given orally or i.v or topically (ointment). Oral absorption is variable and incomplete, reduced by fat and carbohydrate meals. Half-life after i.v. form is 9-12 hours. Highly bound with serum proteins and concentrated in erythrocytes. Metabolized by P450 in liver and excreted mainly in bile and minimally in urine.

Uses

- Organ and stem cell transplantation
- Prevention of rejection of liver and kidney transplants (with glucocorticoids).
- Atopic dermatitis and psoriasis (topically).

Side Effects

- Nephrotoxicity (more than CsA), Neurotoxicity (more than CsA), Hyperglycemia (require insulin), GIT disturbances, Hyperkalemia, Hypertension, Anaphylaxis
- Drug interactions as cyclosporine.

Differences between CsA and TAC

TAC is more favorable than CsA due to:

- TAC is 10–100 times more potent than CsA in inhibiting immune responses.
- TAC has decreased episodes of rejection.
- TAC is combined with lower doses of glucocorticoids.

But

- TAC is more nephrotoxic and neurotoxic. SRL blocks the progression of activated T cells from G1 to S phase of cell cycle (Antiproliferative action).
- It does not block the IL-2 production but blocks T cell response to cytokines.
- Inhibits B cell proliferation & immunoglobulin production.

Pharmacokinetics

Given orally and topically, reduced by fat meal, extensively bound to plasma proteins, Metabolized by CYP3A4 in liver, Excreted in feces.

Uses

Solid organ allograft, Renal transplantation alone or combined with (CsA, tacrolimus, steroids, Mycophenolate), Heart allograft, in halting graft vascular disease, Hematopoietic stem cell transplant recipients, topically with cyclosporine in uveoretinitis.

Side effects

Hyperlipidemia (cholesterol, triglycerides), Thrombocytopenia, Leucopenia, Hepatotoxicity, Hypertension, GIT dysfunction

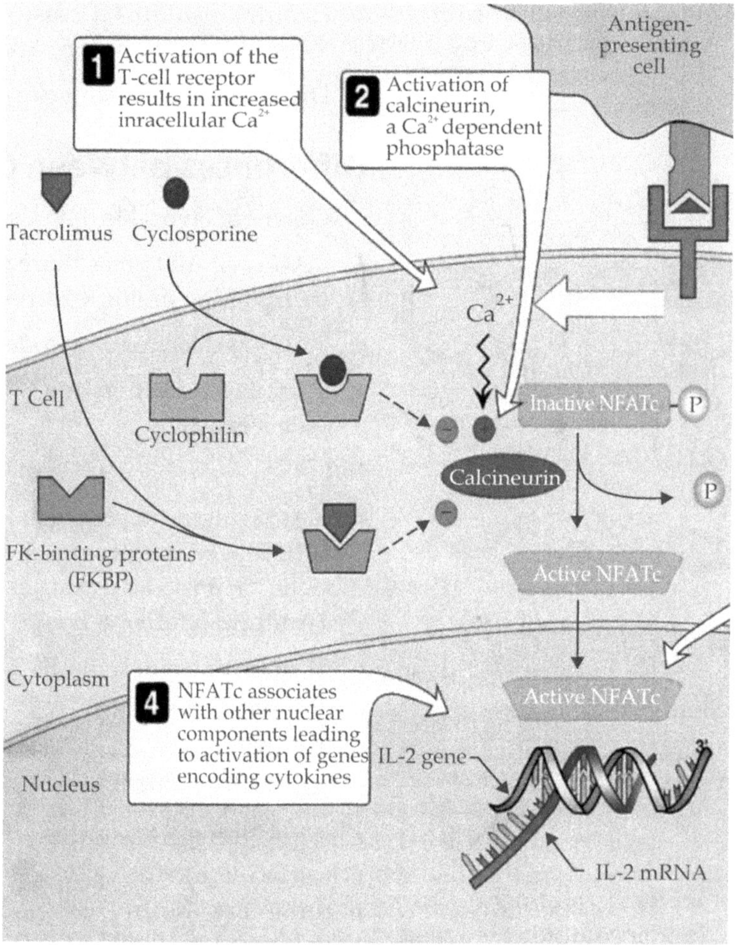

Fig 24-6: Tacrolimus mechanism of action.

Corticosteroids

Prednisone, Prednisolone, Methylprednisolone, Dexamethasone (Fig 24-8)

They have both anti inflammatory action and immunosuppressant effects.

Mechanism of Action

Bind to Glucocorticoid receptors and the complex interacts with DNA to inhibit gene transcription of inflammatory genes. Decrease production of inflammatory mediators as prostaglandins, leukotrienes, histamine, PAF, bradykinin. Decrease production of cytokines IL-1, IL-2, interferon, TNF. Stabilize lysosomal membranes. Decrease generation of IgG, nitric oxide and histamine. Inhibit antigen processing by macrophages. Suppress T-cell helper function. Decrease T lymphocyte proliferation.

Pharmacokinetics

Can be given orally or parenterally.

Indications

- Are first line therapies for solid organ allograft & haematopoietic stem cell transplantation.
- Autoimmune diseases as refractory rheumatoid arthritis, systemic lupus erythematosus, asthma
- Acute or chronic rejection of solid organ allografts.

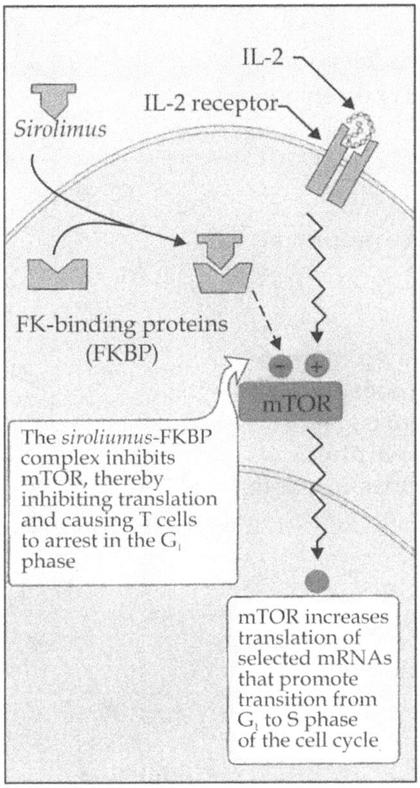

Fig 24-7: Sirolimus mechanism of action.

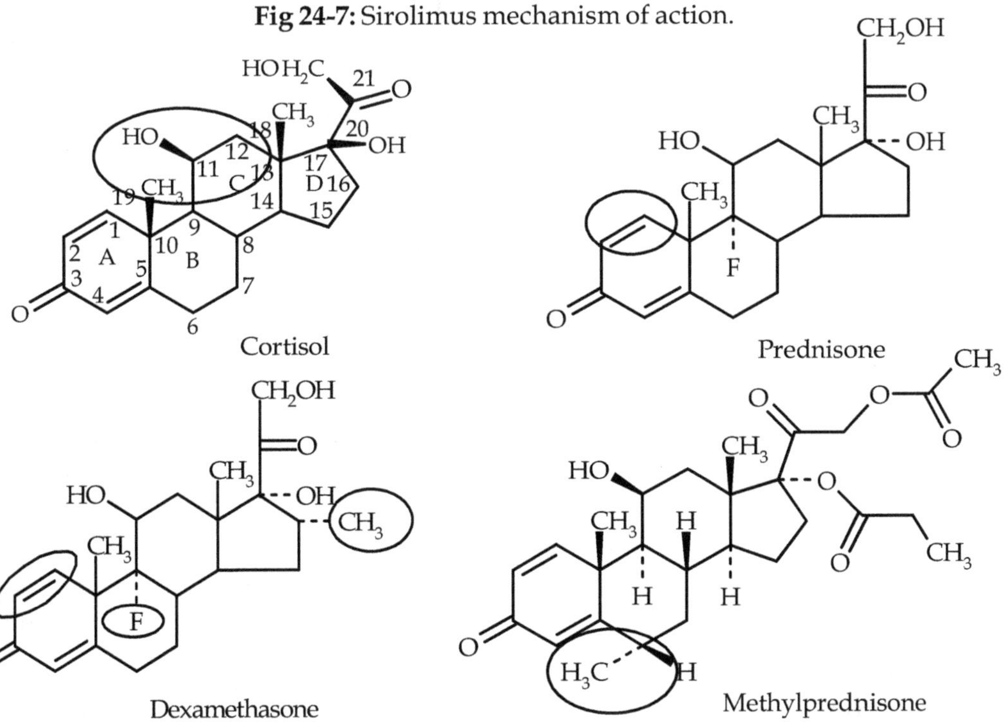

Fig 24-8: Structure of corticosteroids.

Adverse Effects

Adrenal suppression, Osteoporosis, Hypercholesterolemia, Hyperglycemia Hypertension, Cataract, Infection.

Azathioprine

Chemistry: Derivative of mercaptopurine. (Fig 6-10)

Mechanism of Action

Cleaved to 6-mercaptopurine then to 6-mercaptopurine nucl eotide, thioinosinic acid (nucleotide analog). Inhibits de novo synthesis of purines required for lymphocytes proliferation. Prevents clonal expansion of both B and T lymphocytes.

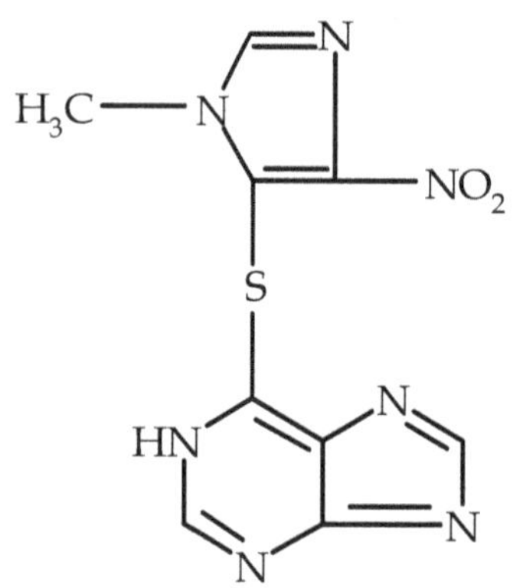

Fig 24-9: Structure of azathioprine.

Pharmacokinetics

Orally or intravenously. Widely distributed but does not cross Blood brain barrier . Metabolized in the liver to 6-mercaptopurine or to thiouric acid (inactive metabolite) by xanthine oxidase. Excreted primarily in urine.

Drug Interactions

- Co administration of allopurinol with azathioprine may lead to toxicity due to inhibition of xanthine oxidase by allopurinol.

Uses

- Acute glomerulonephritis
- Systemic lupus erythematosus
- Rheumatoid arthritis
- Crohn's disease.

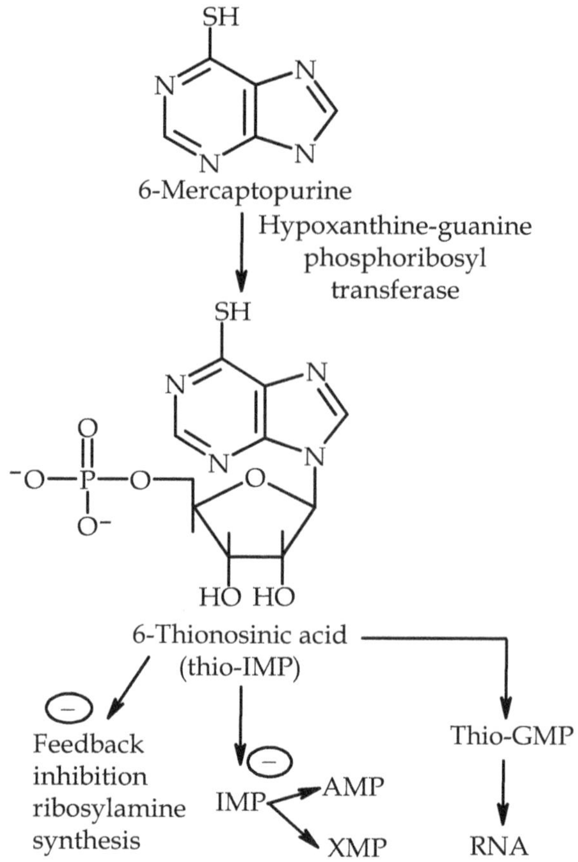

Fig 24-10: Azathioprine mechanism of action.

Adverse Effects

Bone marrow depression: leucopenia, thrombocytopenia, Gastrointestinal toxicity, Hepatotoxicity, Increased risk of infections.

Mycophenolate Mofetil

Is a semi synthetic derivative of mycophenolic acid from fungus source. Prodrug; is hydrolyzed to mycophenolic acid. The structure of Mycophenolete Moletilis shown in Fig 24-11.

Mechanism of Action (Fig 24-12)

Inhibits de novo synthesis of purines. Mycophenolic acid is a potent inhibitor of inosine monophosphate dehydrogenase (IMP), crucial for purine synthesis® deprivation of proliferating T and B cells of nucleic acids.

Pharmacokinetics

Given orally, i.v. or i.m. rapidly and completely absorbed after oral administration. It undergoes first pass metabolism to give the active moiety, mycophenolic acid (MPA). MPA is extensively bound to plasma protein. Metabolized in the liver by Glucuronidation. Excreted in urine as Glucuronide conjugate. Dose: 2-3 g/d

Clinical Use

Solid organ transplants for refractory rejection.

Steroid refractory hematopoietic stem cell transplant patients.

Combined with prednisone as alternative to CSA or tacrolimus.

Rheumatoid arthritis & dermatologic disorders.

Side Effects

GIT toxicity: Nausea, Vomiting, diarrhea, abdominal pain, Leucopenia, Neutropenia, Lymphoma.

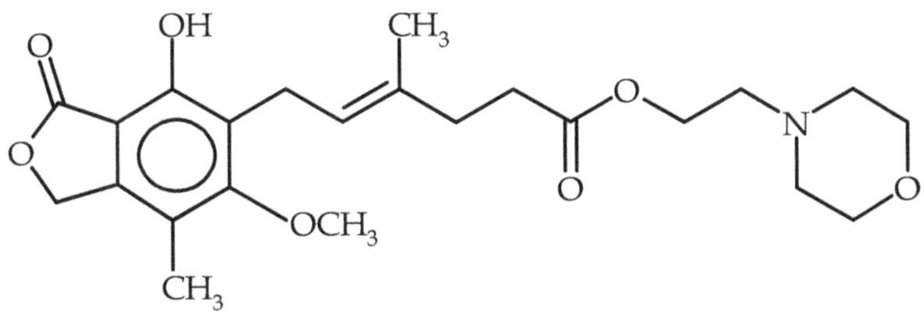

Fig 24-11: Structure of mycophenolate mofetil.

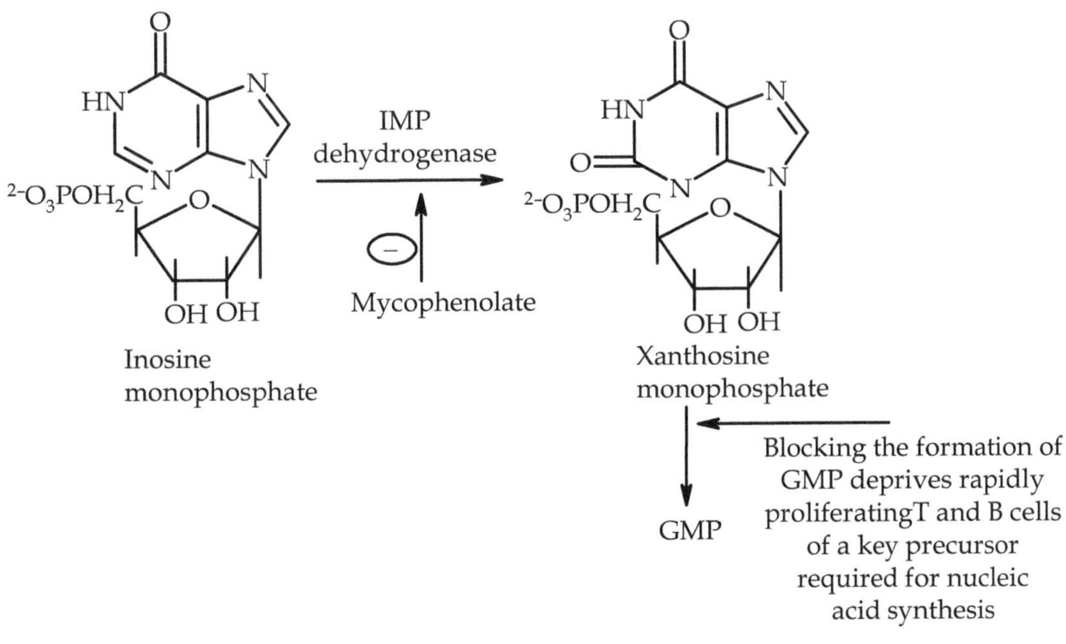

Fig 24-12: Mycophenolate mofetil mechanism of action.

Leflunomide

It is a prodrug. Active metabolite undergoes enterohepatic circulation. Has long duration of action, can be given orally. Antimetabolite immunosuppressant. Pyrimidine synthesis inhibitor. Approved only for rheumatoid arthritis. The structure of Leflunomide is shown in Fig 24-13.

Side Effects

1. Elevation of liver enzymes
2. Renal impairment
3. Teratogenicity
4. Cardiovascular effects (tachycardia).

Methotrexate

A folic acid antagonist. Orally, parentrally (i.v., i.m). Excreted in urine. Inhibits dihydrofolate reductase required for folic acid activation (tetrahydrofolic). Inhibition of DNA, RNA and protein synthesis.Interferes with T cell replication. The structure of Methotrexate is shown in Fig 24-14, 24-15.

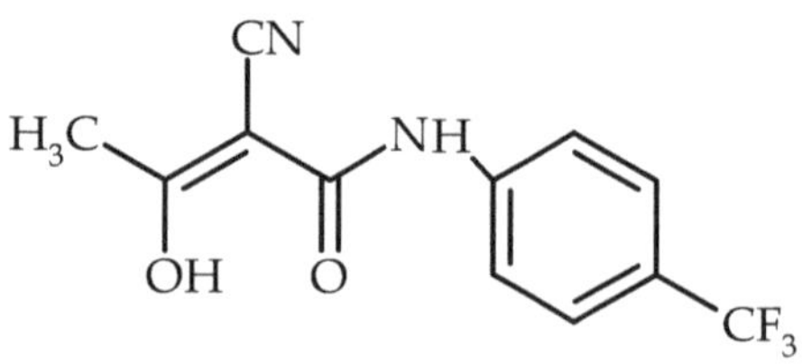

Fig 24-13: Structure of leflunomide.

Clinical Use

- Rheumatoid arthritis and psoriasis and Crohn's disease.
- Graft versus host disease.

Side Effects

Nausea, vomiting, diarrhea, Alopecia, Bone marrow depression, Pulmonary fibrosis, Renal and hepatic disorders.

Antilymphocyte Globulins (ALG) and Antithymocyte Globulins (ATG)

Polyclonal antibodies obtained from plasma or serum of horses hyper-immunized with human lymphocytes. Binds to the surface of circulating T lymphocytes, which are phagocytosed in the liver and spleen giving lymphopenia and impaired T-cell responses & cellular immunity.

Kinetics

Given i.m. or slowly infused intravenously. Half life extends from 3-9 days.

Uses

- Combined with cyclosporine for bone marrow transplantation.
- To treat acute allograft rejection.
- Steroid resistant rejection.

Side Effects

Antigenicity, Leucopenia, thrombocytopenia, Risk of viral infection, Anaphylactic and serum sickness reactions (Fever, Chills, Flu-like syndrome).

Muromonab-CD3

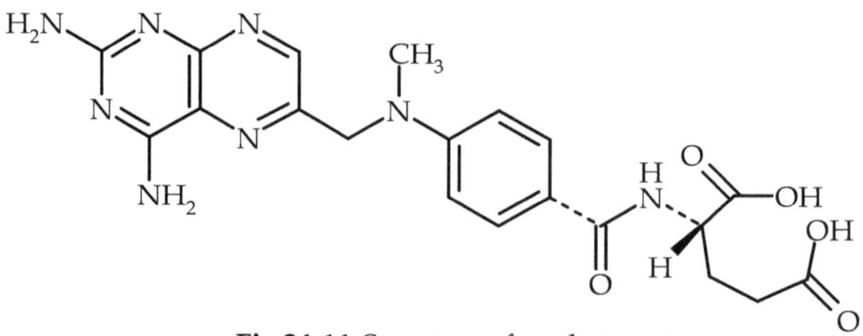

Fig 24-14: Structure of methotrexate.

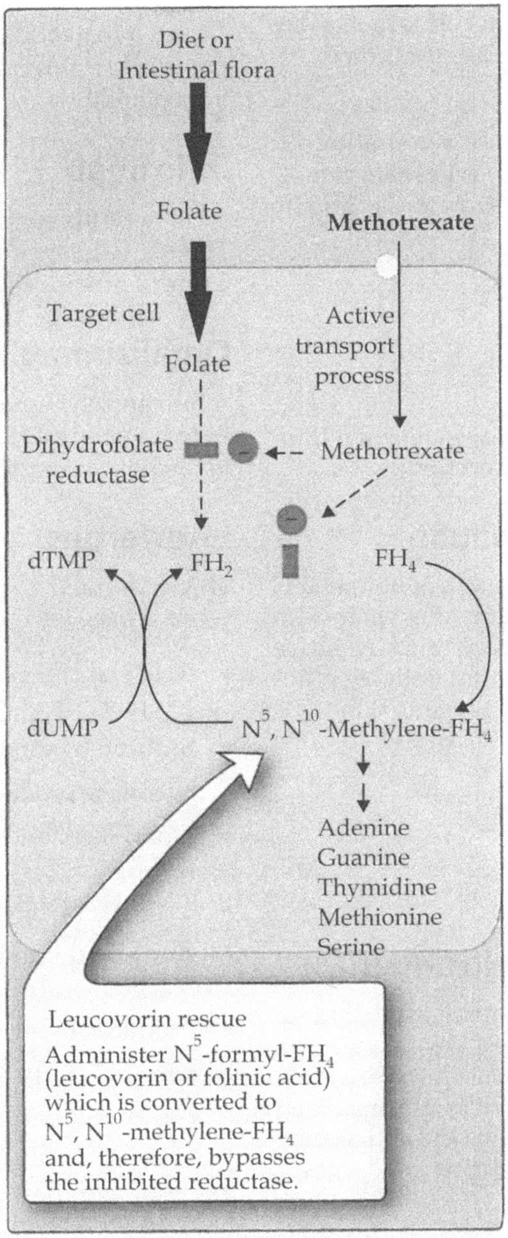

Fig 24-15: Methotrexate mechanism of action.

It is a murine monoclonal antibody. Prepared by hybridoma technology. Directed against glycoprotein CD3 antigen of human T cells. Given i.v. Metabolized and excreted in the bile.

Mechanism of Action

The drug binds to CD3 proteins on T lymphocytes (antigen recognition site) leading to transient activation and cytokine release followed by disruption of T-lymphocyte function, their depletion and decreased immune response. Prednisolone, Diphenhydramine are given to reduce cytokine release syndrome.

Clinical Uses

Used for treatment of acute renal allograft rejection and steroid resistant acute allograft. To deplete T cells from bone marrow donor prior to transplantation.

Side Effects

- Anaphylactic reactions.
- Fever
- CNS effects (seizures)
- Infection, Cytokine release syndrome (Flu-like illness to shock like reaction).

Rh_o (D) immune Globulin

Rh_o (D) is a concentrated solution of human IgG containing higher titer of antibodies against Rh (D) antigen of red cells. Given to Rh-negative mother within 24-72 hours after delivery of Rh positive baby (2 ml, i.m.) to prevent hemolytic disease of the next Rh positive babies (erythroblastosis fetalis).

Side Effects

- Local pain
- Fever

Basiliximab and Daclizumab

Obtained by replacing murine amino acid sequences with human ones. Basiliximab is a chimeric human mouse IgG (25% murine, 75% human protein). Daclizumab is a humanized IgG (90% human protein). Have less antigenicity and longer half lives than murine antibodies.

Mechanism of Action

IL-2 receptor antagonists, Are Anti-CD25. Bind to CD25 (α-subunit chain of IL-2 receptor on activated lymphocytes). Block IL-2 stimulated T cells replication and T-cell response system.

Kinetics

Basiliximab is more potent than Daclizumab. Given i.v. Half life Basiliximab (7 days). Daclizumab (20 days).

Clinical Uses

Given with CsA and corticosteroids for Prophylaxis of acute rejection in renal transplantation.

Infliximab

A chimeric human mouse IgG . Directed against TNF-α. It is approved for ulcerative colitis, Crohn's disease and rheumatoid arthritis

Omalizumab

A humanized monoclonal IgE . Directed against Fc receptor on mast and basophils. It is approved for asthma in steroid refractory patient.

Interferons

Three families:

- Type I IFNs (IFN-α, β):
- Acid stable proteins; act on same target cell receptor
- Induced by viral infections
- leukocyte produces IFN-α
- Fibroblasts and endothelial cells produce IFN-β
- Type II IFN (IFN-γ):
- Acid-labile; acts on separate target cell receptors
- Produced by Activated T lymphocytes.

Interferon Effects

IFN- γ: Immune Enhancing

Increased antigen presentations with macrophage, natural killer cell, cytotoxic T lymphocyte activation

IFN- α, β: Effective in inhibiting cellular proliferation (more effective than IFN- ã in this regard)

Clinical Uses

Treatment of certain infections e.g., Hepatitis C (IFN- α).

Autoimmune diseases e.g., rheumatoid arthritis.

Certain forms of cancer e.g. melanoma, renal cell carcinoma.

Multiple sclerosis (IFN- β): reduced rate of exacerbation.

Fever, chills, Myelosuppression.

Thalidomide

A sedative drug.

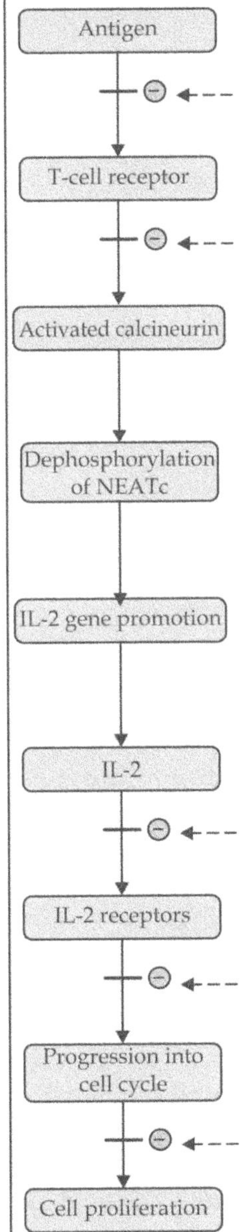

DRUG	ACTION	ADVERSE EFFECTS
Antithymocyte globulins	Destruction of T lymphocytes	Profound immunosuppression
Muromonab-CD3	Destruction of T lymphocytes	Cytokine release syndrome
Cyclosporine	Blocks calcineurin and inhibits IL-2 synthesis	Nephrotoxicity, neurotoxicity, hepatotoxicity
Tacrolimus (FK506)	Blocks calcineurin and inhibits IL-2 synthesis	Nephrotoxicity, neurotoxicity, diabetes
Basiliximab	Blocks the IL-2 receptor	Gastrointestinal disorders
Daclizumab	Blocks the IL-2 receptor	Gastrointestinal disorders
Sirolimus	Blocks cytokine-stimulated cell proliferation	Hyperlipidemia, thrombocytopenia, leukopenia, headache, nausea
Azathioprine	Inhibits purine synthesis	Bone marrow suppression, hepatotoxicity, thrombocytopenia, anemia, neoplasia
Mycophenolate mofetil	Inhibits purine synthesis	GI upset, nausea, diarrhea, leukopenia, tumors, increases susceptibility to infection

Fig 24-16: Mechanism of action and adverse effects of immunosuppressant's

Table 24-1: Clinical uses of immunosuppressive agents.

Disease	Agent Used
Autoimmune Disease:	
Acute glomerulonephritis	Prednisone*, mercaptopurine. Cyclophosphamide.
Autoimmune hemolytic anemia.	Prednisone*, Cyclophosphamide, mercaptopurine, azathioprine, high dose β-globulin.
Organ transplant:	
• Renal	Cyclosporine, Azathioprine, Prednisone, ALG,
• Heart	Tacrolimus.
• Liver	Cyclosporine, Prednisone, Azathioprine, Tacrolimus.
• Bone marrow	Cyclosporine, Cyclophosphamide, Prednisone, Methotrexate, ALG, total body radiation.

Teratogenic (Class-X).

Can be given orally.

Has immunomodulatory actions.

Inhibits TNF-α

Reduces phagocytosis by neutrophils

Increases IL-10 production

Clinical Uses

Myeloma.

Rheumatoid arthritis.

Graft versus host disease.

Leprosy reactions.

Treatment of skin manifestations of lupus erythematosus.

Immunostimulants

A number of disorders can be treated with immunostimulating agents (also known as biological response modifiers or immunomodulating agents); these drugs enhance the body's immune response. These conditions include immunodeficiency diseases, cancer, some types of viral and fungal infections, and certain autoimmune disorders. The drugs may work on cellular or humoral immune systems or both.

Immunostimulating agents are nonspecific; they cause general stimulation of the immune system. Among the agents capable of general potentiation of the immune system are extracts and derivatives from bacteria, yeast, and fungi. They also include a variety of peptides, cytokines, and synthetic compounds. In most cases, the pharmacology of these agents has not been well described.

The most commonly used agents are

Bacillus Calmette-Guérin

Levamisole

Immune Globulin

Bacillus Calmette-Guérin

Bacillus Calmette Guérin (BCG) is a viable attenuated strain of Mycobacterium bovis. Nonviable strains of the bacterium also have been shown to augment the immune response. The smallest active compound derived from BCG thus far has been identified as muramyl dipeptide. The T cell is a principal target for BCG. It also appears to stimulate natural killer cells, which in turn can kill malignant cells. It has been suggested that BCG cross-reacts immunologically with tumor cell antigens. BCG immunotherapy has been most successful in the treatment of bladder cancers. It is instilled directly into the bladder, where it is held for 2 hours before urination.

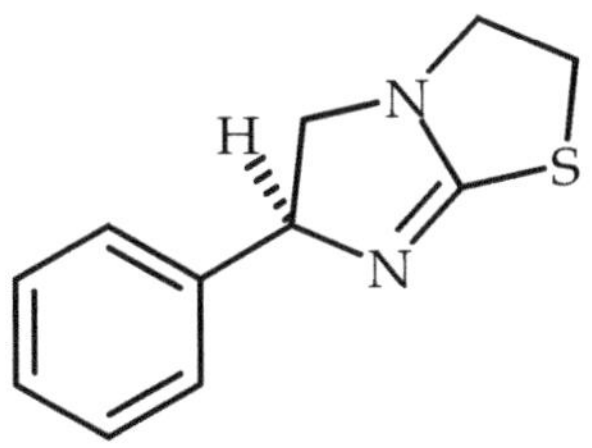

Fig 24-17: Structure of levamisole.

The most dangerous complications of BCG therapy are severe hypersensitivity and shock. Chills, fever, malaise, immune complex and renal disease are among the other side effects. The route of administration influences the nature of the side effects.

Levamisole

Levamisole (Ergamisol) (Fig 24-17) was originally developed as an antihelminthic drug . It potentiates the stimulatory effects of antigens, mitogens, lymphokines, and chemotactic factors on lymphocytes, granulocytes and macrophages. It has been shown to increase T cell-mediated immunity. Levamisole has been used successfully in treating chronic infections. It also has been approved for use in combination with fluorouracil in the treatment of colorectal cancer.

Immune Globulin

Immune globulin is isolated from pooled human plasma either from donors in the general population or from hyperimmunized donors. It is used principally in the treatment of certain immune deficiencies. Standard immune globulin solutions contain a distribution of all subclasses, with antibody titers for most major bacterial, viral, and fungal pathogens. Immune globulin, given intramuscularly or intravenously, is recommended in the treatment of primary humoral immunodeficiency, congenital agammaglobulinemias, common variable immunodeficiency, severe combined immunodeficiency, idiopathic thrombocytopenic purpura, and autoimmune hemolytic anemia. There are six licensed preparations of immune globulin. The principal side effects are possible anaphylactoid reactions and severe hypotension.

Thymic Factors

Thymic factors are naturally occurring substances that promote T-lymphocyte differentiation and differentiation of early stem cells into prothymocytes. Each of the available preparations (e.g., thymic humoral factor, thymosin fraction 5, and thymodulin) are mixtures of several polypeptides isolated from a calf thymus extract. By promoting the formation of T lymphocytes, thymic factors are used to enhance T-lymphocytic functions. Thymic factors have been used with some success in clinical trials in patients with severe combined immunodeficiency, DiGeorge's or Nezelof's syndrome and viral disorders. Studies with thymodulin show promise in treating symptoms in asthmatics and patients with allergic rhinitis. The primary consideration in the use of thymic factors for immunodeficiency states is the presence of T-lymphocyte precursors. Few major side effects have been reported, especially with purer forms produced by genetic engineering. Crude thymic preparations have produced allergic side effects in some patients.

Cytokines

An exciting application of immunomodulating therapy is in the use of cytokines (lymphokines, monokines). As mentioned earlier in this chapter, immune cell function is regulated by cytokines produced by leukocytes or other supporting cells. With the advent of genetic engineering, cytokines can be produced in pure form and in large quantities.

Interleukin-2

IL-2 (Proleukin) is a cytokine that promotes the proliferation, differentiation and recruitment of T and B lymphocytes, natural killer cells, and thymocytes. Human recombinant IL-2 is designated as rIL-2. rIL-2 binds to IL-2 receptors on responsive cells and induces proliferation and differentiation of T helper cells and T cytotoxic cells. It also can induce B-lymphocyte proliferation, activate macrophage activity, and augment the cytotoxicity of natural killer cells. rIL-2 is administered systemically as an immunostimulating agent in patients with AIDS and to augment specific antitumor immunity. Patients with renal cell carcinoma or melanoma have been effectively treated with rIL-2 in combination with adoptive transfer immunotherapy. The latter refers to the injection of the patient's own cytokine activated killer cells or tumor infiltrating lymphocytes after they reside in tissue culture for several weeks in the presence of rIL-2. Systemic administration of rIL-2 causes fever, nausea, vomiting, fatigue, and malaise. Other adverse affects include flushing, diarrhea, chills, rash, edema, symptomatic hypotension, and certain renal abnormalities. These tend to occur at increased dosage levels and are attenuated by reducing the dosage.

Myeloid Colony–Stimulating Factors

Recombinant granulocyte macrophage colony–stimulating factor (GM-CSF) (Sargramostim) and granulocyte stimulating factor (G-CSF) (Filgrastim) are cytokines or growth factors, that support the survival, clonal expansion, and differentiation of hematopoietic cells. These factors are normally produced in the body by monocytes, fibroblasts, and endothelial cells. GMCSF induces bone marrow progenitor cells belonging to the granulocyte or macrophage lineage to divide and differentiate into mature cells.

G-CSF induces the maturation of granulocyte progenitor cells. In general these recombinant cytokines are indicated for acceleration of the recovery of circulating white blood cells in patients who have depressed hematopoiesis, as a result of either chemotherapy or congential disorders of hematopoiesis.

Adverse effects are those commonly observed following the administration of molecules produced by biotechnological means. They include diarrhea, asthenia, rash, malaise, fever, headache, bone pain, chills, and myalgia. Many of these effects can be ameliorated by the administration of analgesics and antipyretics.

Other Cytokines

Human recombinant interferon α(rIFN-α) and rIL-1 also show promise as immuno stimulators, principally as adjuvants in the treatment of viral and malignant disorders.

rIFN-α is produced by leukocytes and inhibits viral DNA and RNA replication. At lower doses, it can stimulate macrophages, T lymphocytes, and natural killer cell activity.

rIL-1 is produced by macrophages in the host and is necessary for activation and development of immune cells. Intravenous administration of rIL-1 is associated with the general augmentation of immune responses.

rIL-6 is a protein that stimulates lymphocyte and megakaryocyte proliferation. It is in clinical trials in patients with refractory cancer and myelodysplastic syndrome.

References

Ahmet Demirkiran et. al (2009). Conversion from calcineurin inhibitor to Mycophenolate Mofetil-based immunosuppression changes the frequency and phenotype of CD4+FoxP3+ regulatory t cells, Transplantation, April 2009.

Nicola NA (ed.) (1995). Guidebook to Cytokines and Their Receptors. New York: Oxford University Press.

Naesens M, Kuypers DR and Sarwal M (2009). "Calcineurin inhibitor nephrotoxicity". *Clin. J. Am. Soc. Nephrol.* **4(2):** 481–509.

N A Gillett and C Chan (2000). "Applications of immunohistochemistry in the evaluation of immunosuppressive agents". *Human & Experimental Toxicology* **19(4)**: 251–254.

Nakamura T and Matsumoto K (1994). Growth Factors: Cell Growth, Morphogenesis, and Transformation. *Boca Raton*, FL: CRC.

S Roy and HH Loh (1996). "Effects of opioids on the immune system". *Neurochem Res.* **21(11):** 1375–1386.

CHAPTER

Protein Drugs, Monoclonal Antibodies and Biosimilars

25

A medication that is extremely similar to a biologic medication in terms of structure and function is known as a biosimilar or biosimilar drug.

A Biologic drug is a living system, such as yeast, bacteria, or animal cells.

Features of Biosimilar Medicine

Similarity to the Reference Drug

The reference medicine's physical, chemical, and biological features are strikingly similar to those of the biosimilar. There may be modest changes in safety or efficacy from the reference drug.

There are no clinically significant variations as compared to the reference medication.

Clinical performance shouldn't differ in any way. Any variations will not affect safety and efficacy, according to clinical trials supporting the approval of a biosimilar.

Biosimilar variation is kept to a minimum.

Minor variation is only permitted if research demonstrates that it has no impact on the biosimilar's safety and effectiveness. The permitted range of variation for a biosimilar is the same as the permitted range of variation between batches of the reference drug.

Similar strict standards of quality, safety and efficacy

Similar stringent quality, safety, and efficacy requirements that are used to approve any other medication also apply to biosimilars.

Comparison of development and characteristics between generics and biosimilar

Generic medicine	Biosimilar medicine
Obtained by chemical synthesis	Obtained from biological source
it is usually possible to get the exact identical molecule	Due to novel biomanufacturing techniques and natural biological processes, it is possible to replicate the molecule with a high degree of resemblance.
Most molecules are smaller and are easier to characterize.	Larger, structurally more complex molecules in general need for a variety of approaches to characterise them
complete pharmaceutical quality data is required	criteria for complete pharmaceutical quality data and extra quality tests contrasting the biosimilar's biological activity and structure using the reference drug

Contd...

Generic medicine	Biosimilar medicine
standards for comprehensive pharmaceutical quality data and additional quality tests comparing the biological activity and composition of the reference medicine with the biosimilar is required	Utilizing comparability studies to show biosimilarity during development (a thorough head-to-head comparison of the biosimilar to the reference drug to demonstrate high degree of biological and chemical similarities function, effectiveness, security, and immunogenicity)
Pharmacokinetic bioequivalence studies are mostly required for clinical data.	Safety and efficacy data may be necessary in addition to comparative pharmacokinetic and pharmacodynamic investigations, particularly for more complicated biological drugs
Based on established bioequivalence, all permitted uses for the reference drug can be given without additional testing.	Each indication requires justification of efficacy and safety. Confirmatory clinical trials using the biosimilar, however, are typically not required in each indication that has been given for reference standard.

Data requirements for approval of a Biosimilars

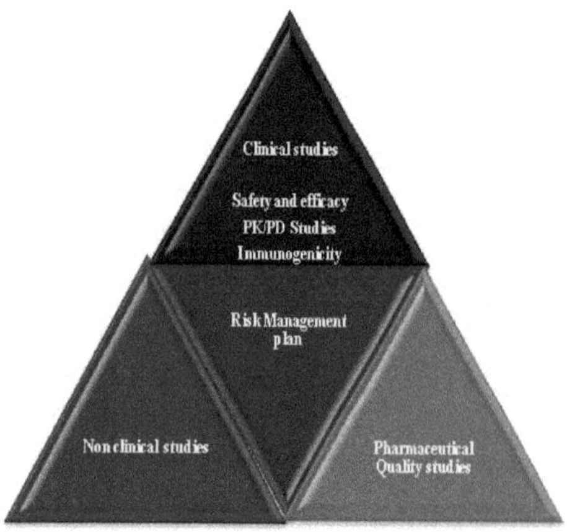

Overview of biosimilar development compared with a reference medicine:

Biological medicine with new active substance (e.g. reference medicine)	**Biosimilar medicine**
Earlier knowledge of safety and efficacy not known	It depends on knowledge of safety and efficacy from years of clinical use with the reference medicine
Direct patient testing of safety and effectiveness is the goal of development.	By achieving biosimilarity, development tries to show comparable safety and efficacy.
Only manufacturing changes made during development, such as creating larger batches for clinical trials, are subject to comparability tests.	Thorough analyses of comparability with the reference drug
non-clinical data (pharmacology and toxicology) is required	non-clinical data requirement is determined by the quality studies outcome
Standard clinical trials to prove safety and efficacy for all alleged therapeutic indications are required	Comparative clinical trials to rule out differences with clinical significance
trials that primarily evaluate a treatment with a placebo or the industry standard of care using "hard" endpoints (such as long-term outcome, mortality, a pertinent patient, structural damage) population to exhibit that it is beneficial	Trials with sensitive endpoints in a population where product-related adverse events are common, primarily intended to demonstrate clinical parity with the reference drug.
Studies on safety and effectiveness in the target group form the basic foundation for the positive benefit-risk relationship.	Based on proving biosimilarity, there is a favourable benefit-risk ratio (using comparability studies)

The development of biosimilars heavily relies on "comparability studies" to prove their biosimilarity to the reference drug. This calls for a thorough side-by-side comparison of the reference drug and the biosimilar. Comparability is intended to be a sequential process. It is tailored specifically for each product.

Biosimilar development is comparative and progresses in a step-wise manner

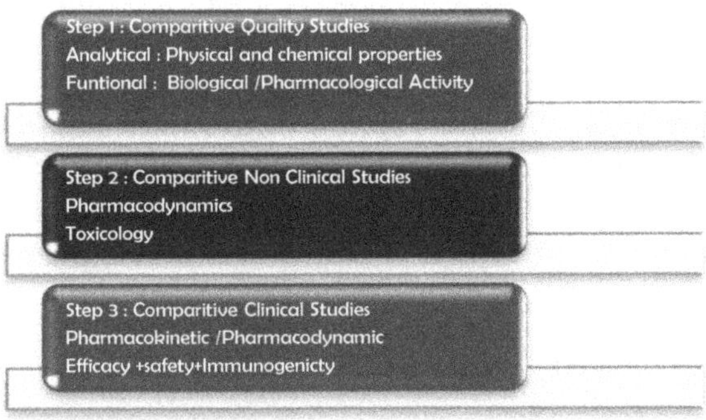

Some Biosimilars approved:

Polysaccharides

Low-molecular weight heparins

- Enoxaparin sodium

Proteins

Growth factors

- Epoetin
- Filgrastim
- Pegfilgrastim

Hormones

- Follitropin alfa
- Insulin glargine
- Somatropin (growth hormone)
- Teriparatide
- Insulin lispro

Fusion proteins

- Etanercept

Monoclonal antibodies

- Adalimumab
- Infliximab
- Rituximab
- Bevacizumab
- Trastuzumab

Benefits of Biosimilars

Cost-cutting through competition

The cost of biologic medications can be very high. For instance, a biologic cancer treatment may cost each patient hundreds or even thousands of dollars per year. The reference drug monopoly will be broken and prices will be reduced if there are several biosimilars available.

Improved accessibility for patients

More biosimilars being used means that more people can access these therapeutic alternatives globally.

Encouragement for innovation

Before the patent on the reference drug expires, biosimilars cannot be sold. In the wake of expired patents, having novel, patentable new biologic products may be crucial to sustain a significant market share hold. In order to promote innovation, pharmaceutical companies will be urged to invest more in cutting-edge R&D fields.

Disadvantages

Extrapolating from indications

Without conducting a proper clinical trail they are prescribed to the patients and that may lead to development of many adverse effects.

Safety and efficacy

Although clinical testing was carried, they are not having the same safety and efficacy, making them incompatible.

Monoclonal Antibodies

Monoclonal antibodies (mAbs) are a kind of antibodies made by identical B cell clones in response to a specific antigen. The protein sequence, antigen-binding site area, binding affinity for their targets, and identical downstream functional effects are only a few of the characteristics that monoclonal antibodies share.

These features of mAbs emphasise how they differ from polyclonal antibodies, which have variable activity and identify various antigen epitopes. mAbs are a crucial class of therapeutic molecules that are currently being tested in clinical trials to treat a variety of conditions.

The first generation of monoclonal antibodies created using hybridoma technique were murine mAbs. They are structurally devoid of human elements and may cause the production of human anti-mouse antibodies (HAMAs). The HAMA response led to hypersensitivity events in the recipients, such as anaphylaxis and serum sickness, which sped up the clearance of antibodies or diminished their effectiveness. To get around these issues, transgenic animals and genetic engineering techniques were developed. This allowed a changed cell line to produce an altered antibody that was more structurally similar to human antibodies. Because the variable section of these modified antibodies is murine and the constant region is human, they are referred to as chimeric mAbs.

Structure

An antibody molecule is made up of four polypeptide chains, comprising two identical heavy (H) and two light (L) chains, and has a Y-shaped structure with a total molecular weight of about 150 kDa. The stability of heavy and light chains close to one another is provided by covalent connections, particularly disulfide interactions. Both constant (CH and CL, respectively) and variable (VH and VL, respectively) domains make up each heavy and light chain. Known as "antigen binding fragments" or Fabs, the two identical arms that make up each antibody serve as antigen-binding sites. Each Fab has a constant area and a variable region called Fv (made by the VH and VL domains) (formed by the CH and CL domains).

The highly variable region known as Fv is in charge of the antibody's precise binding to the antigen, which contributes to the antibody's direct effects like blocking or neutralising the antigen. Complementarity determining regions, also known as CDR1, CDR2, and CDR3, are three hypervariable areas found in the variable regions of light and heavy chains that enable the recognition of a variety of antigenic specificities.

Immunoglobulin G (IgG), IgM, IgD, IgE, and IgA are among the five classes of antibodies, each of which has a unique effector mechanism for recognising and removing the antigens. Additionally, the Fc region can interact with a number of receptors, including complement system subunits and Fc receptors, which are found on immune cells (such as C1q). The effector activities of antibodies, including as antibody-dependent cell cytotoxicity (ADCC), antibody-dependent cellular phagocytosis (ADCP), and complement-dependent cytotoxicity (CDC), are launched as a result of Fc recognition by immune system components.

The production process of monoclonal antibodies

Hybridoma technique

The same antigen's epitope is recognised by monoclonal antibodies, which are produced from a single B cell clone. Milstein and Köhler produced mAbs using the hybridoma method for the first time in 1975. This process entails several steps. Mice are first inoculated with particular antigens that have been properly emulsified with an adjuvant. Once enough antibody has been produced, the animal is usually slaughtered two weeks following the booster dose. Blood is collected to test the adequate level of antibody production using methods like ELISA and flow cytometry. Following sacrifice, the spleen is separated, and tissue digestion using an enzymatic or mechanical process may be used to release B cells.

Making a fusion between B lymphocytes and myeloma cells is the subsequent phase (that are immortal like cancer cells). Myeloma cells need to be pre-pared before fusing by being cultured with 8-azaguanine, which makes them sensitive to hypoxanthine aminopterin-thymidin (HAT) media. Polyethylene glycol (PEG) is used to carry out the fusion process, which causes the cell membrane to fuse. A variety of cells, including fused B cells with myeloma cells, unfused B cells, unfused myeloma cells, B cells fused to B cells, and myeloma cells fused to myeloma cells, will exist after the fusing process. Therefore, only B cells merged with myeloma cells should be chosen using a selective media called hypoxanthine, aminopterin, and thymidine (HAT) medium.

The metabolites of the salvage pathway of nucleoside synthesis are hypoxanthine and thymidine, two elements of this medium. Only cells that possess hypoxanthine-guanine-phosphoribosyl transferase (HGPRT), a crucial enzyme for the salvage synthesis of nucleic acids, would therefore be able to survive. Because unfused myeloma cells lack HGPRT, they are unable to replicate their nucleic acids and cannot develop in HAT media. Unfused B cells, on the other hand, have a short lifespan and are unable to develop normally. Only "hybridomas," or fusing B cell and myeloma cells, may therefore develop in the medium. It should be emphasised that the presence of ami nopterin also inhibits the "de novo" pathway, a different route for the synthesis of nucleic acids

Problems with using this technique.

The hybridoma technique has a fairly drawn-out development phase because it takes roughly 6 to 8 months to produce enough mAbs. The antibodies' murine origin, on the other hand, means that upon repeated administration, they may provoke the HAMA response in the host, which could hasten mAb clearance and result in unfavourable allergic reactions. Antibody engineering techniques were developed to produce fewer immunologic chimeric or humanised antibodies, which solved this problem.

Phage display technique

A different approach to the conventional hybridoma technology for producing monoclonal antibodies is phage display. By introducing the DNA fragment into the coat protein gene of the phage, George P. Smith demonstrated in 1985 how a peptide of interest might be exhibited on the surface of filamentous phages. Then, Parmley and Smith discuss the "panning" or "biopanning" procedure, which involves selection and affinity enrichment in order to isolate peptide-phage fusions based on their unique binding affinities. McCafferty and Winter created combinatorial antibody libraries on filamentous phages to generate antigen-specific mAbs using phage display technology for the first time.In this technique, a gene sequence encoding for a specific antibody is incorporated into the DNA sequence of a filamentous bacteriophage, causing the production of an interest protein on the bacteriophage capsid surface. These phage libraries could be created from healthy donors (producing naive libraries), people who have a specific condition, like metastatic cancer or a specific infection, or people who have received immunisation against a specific antigen (creating immunised libraries). M13 is a filamentous bacteriophage that is frequently employed in phage display to produce antibodies. Escherichia coli (E. coli) strains are infected by this phage.

Problems

Most expensive and difficult technique.

Applications of monoclonal antibodies

Therapeutic applications of mAbs in cancer therapy:

It is possible to create monoclonal antibodies that are particularly targeted at a target antigen present on cancer cells. Following the identification of proto-oncogenes and certain tumour antigens, a number of therapeutic mAbs have been approved against various cancer types. An antibody called MAB 17-1A that targets the epithelial cell surface antigen was authorised in 1994 for the purpose of identifying adenocarcinomas. It was effective in lowering colorectal cancer death and incidence rates. Rituximab, a chimeric anti-CD20 antibody, was authorised for the treatment of non-Hodgkin B cell lymphoma in 1997. Rituximab interacts with the CD20 antigen that is expressed on B cell malignancies, and subsequently the immune system effectively destroys the cancerous cells as a result. The other mAbs against CD20 antigen are Ibritumab (Zevalin®), Obinutuzumab (Gazyva®), and Ofatumumab (Arzera®).

Therapeutic applications of mAbs in the treatment of autoimmune diseases mAbs may be able to reduce immune system activation in autoimmune disorders or organ transplantation. 9290.

Therapeutic applications of mAbs in the treatment of graft-versus-host disease

To lessen allograft rejection, two monoclonal antibodies have been licenced, including OKT3 (a murine IgG2a antibody against human CD3) and antibodies against IL-2 receptor (CD25). Patients who undergo bone marrow transplantation may develop graft-versus-host disease (GVHD), which can be fatal. Major histocompatibility (MHC) molecules in the host interact with alloreactive donor T cells to cause immune system activation and increased cytokine release, which is what causes GVHD [60]. GVHD may be prevented by focusing on T cells before they become activated. The expression of CD25 on T cells is thought to be a crucial step in the activation of these cells' alloreactive responses. As a result, anti-CD25 monoclonal antibody therapy may suppress T cells and be a useful therapeutic agent.

Therapeutic applications of mAbs in the treatment of asthma

The pathophysiology of allergic asthma, which results in bronchial hyperresponsiveness, is significantly influenced by high blood immunoglobulin E (IgE) levels. Recombinant humanised anti-IgE antibody administration has been found to reduce blood IgE levels and asthma symptoms in patients with mild to severe allergic asthma. These antibodies can function by combining with free IgE to block IgE's interaction with the receptor that is expressed on mast cells and basophils. Omalizumab (Xolair®), a humanised monoclonal antibody, effectively blocks IgE binding to its FcR1 receptor in individuals with severe asthma.

Other therapeutic applications: using mAbs in the treatment of sepsis and viral infections

Sepsis is seen as an inflammatory immunological condition that develops in response to an infection and may be life-threatening. Sepsis is primarily brought on by bacterial infections, although it can also be brought on by viral, fungal, or protozoan infections. It may be effective to combat inflammatory response by targeting inflammatory mediators like TNF- or its receptor. However, it may be more beneficial to treat septic shock by blocking bacterial toxin or significant bacterial components like endotoxin or lipid-A (a component of gram-negative bacteria). In patients with sepsis, the effectiveness of two different types of mAbs, including HA-1A (Centoxin), a human IgM, and E5 (XoMA, Berkeley, CA), a murine IgM mAb, has been demonstrated.

Monoclonal antibodies in the diagnostic assays

Monoclonal antibodies are useful biological reagents in immunodiagnostic assays due to their high specificity and high affinity binding capabilities. They can be employed in serological analyses to find antibodies against a certain antigen or for the diagnosis of infectious disorders and the detection of specific antigens. Numerous immunodiagnostic assays, such as immunohistochemistry (IHC) or immunocytochemistry (ICC), enzyme-linked immunosorbent assay (ELISA), western blot, immunodot blot, radio immuno assay (RIA), immunofluorescence (IF), flow cytometry, and microscopy (electron, fluorescence, confocal), frequently use monoclonal antibodies.

Therapeutic Protein

Therapeutic protein pharmaceuticals are a significant class of medications that benefit patients who most require cutting-edge treatments.

Therapeutic proteins are defined as proteins created in laboratories specifically for use in medicinal products. Proteins that people lack or have low levels of with a disease like Cancer or an infectious disease Hemophilia, anaemia, and multiple sclerosis, Hepatitis B/C, and other diseases are synthesised on a vast scale using genetic engineering supplied modified host cells.

Protein therapies refers to this medicinal strategy for treating diseases with proteins and peptides. Protein therapy is comparable to gene therapy but different from protein is given to the patient during gene and protein therapies. Developed in the 1920s, human insulin is thought to a first-generation therapeutic protein.

Proteins are considered for the following facts:

- Lower side effects: because of the great selectivity, proteins have less chance of interfering with regular biological processes. Examples of diverse functional groups include free thiols (on cysteine residues) and amines (on the N-terminus or on lysine residues).
- Less likely to cause immunological reactions because the body manufactures many of the proteins on its own.
- Compared to small molecule medications, clinical development and FDA clearance times are quicker.

Scope of Protein Therapeutics

- It is hoped that the protein, which is not present in sufficient amounts, will work as it is intended to.
- Use of certain proteins to address, for instance Some people have been assessed for cardiovascular disease studies. especially when arteries or veins enlarge the proper kinds of proteins could aid in this situation by creating new blood flow channels.
- Some medical professionals advise this kind of protein therapy.
- Eventually, it might be so successful that it eliminates 4the necessity of intricate procedures like bypass surgery.

Classification

Based on pharmacological effect, the following classification applies:

Group I: Protein therapies with enzymatic or regulatory activity

a: Substituting a protein that is inadequate or abnormal Exubera, Increlex, etc.

b: Improvement of an already-existing route, such as Ovidrel, Neupogen.

c: Offers a brand-new feature or activity, like Myoblock.

Group II: Protein therapies with unique targeting activity.

Avastin is an example of a substance that interferes with a molecule or organism. B: Delivers additional compounds or proteins (such as radionuclides, cytotoxic substance or effector protein), for instance, Ontak.

Group III: Vaccines against proteins

a: Guarding against a harmful foreign agent, such as Engerix.

b: Managing an autoimmune condition, such as with Rophylac.

Group IV: Diagnostics of proteins, such as Geref.

Classification based on molecular types

Drugs based on antibodies, Fc fusion proteins, anticoagulants, blood factors, growth factors, hormones, interferon, bone, thrombolytic, interleukin, and morphogenetic proteins are grouped according to molecular categories.

Molecular mechanism-based classification:

- Non-covalent target binding, such as with – mAbs.
- Affecting covalent bonds, such as those in enzymes.
- Exerting without interacting with anything specifically, like serum albumin.

Methods Used to Produce Recombinant Proteins

- Recombinant protein synthesis in microbial bioreactors.
- Ex: *E. coli* expression system and the yeast *Saccharomyces cerevisiae.*
- Bioreactors made from mammalian cells.

For instance, bioreactors for Chinese Hamster Ovary Cells (CHO).

- "Pharming" with animal bioreactors

Production of Recombinant Therapeutic Proteins in the Milk of Transgenic Animals.

Eg, Cows, sheep, pigs etc.

1. Microbial bioreactors

Escherichia coli (a bacterium) and *Saccharomyces cerevisiae* & *Pichia pastoris* (yeasts) were revealed to be the first microbial bioreactors. The creation of basic polypeptides like insulin and growth hormone for humans. However, it was discovered that microbial bioreactors were inappropriate for proteins that have extensive folding or significant posttranslational modifications such as the coagulation factors, or specialized antibodies. As a result, large-scale mammalian cell culture was developed, using Chinese Hamster Ovary (CHO) cell culture as an example.

Human Insulin Production

- Creating the DNA with the nucleotide sequences for insulin's A and B polypeptide chains.
- Insulin gene insertion into a plasmid and restriction enzyme plasmid (circular DNA)
- Plasmodidic DNA is cleaved by restriction enzymes.
- DNA ligase agglutinates the plasmidic DNA and insulin gene i. e Plasmid + gene for insulin.
- E. coli bacteria were given recombinant plasmids.

- E. coli is a factory that produces insulin.
- Using mutant E. coli to prevent insulin breakdown.
- When a bacterium reproduces, the insulin gene also does.
- Plodiad E Coli.
- A byproduct of insulin, such as the A or B chain, formed some of the protein.
- A and B chain extraction and purification.
- A- and B-chain connections created by a process that produces disulfide traverse bridges.
- Results in Pure synthetic human insulin.

2. Cell culture bioreactors

These methods enabled the production of many cytokines, monoclonal antibodies, and other intricate bioactive compounds. But there are proteins that, because of a combination of intricate design and size. Therapeutic dosage has so far evaded (failed to be) researchers.

For instance, commercial recombinant manufacturing of intricate compounds like antithrombin and alpha1-antitrypsin has not yet been accomplished in microorganisms or plants.

Cell culture systems have a significant initial investment cost, a lack of scale-up (or scale-down) flexibility, and utilise a lot of cultural media

This resulted in the creation of transgenics technology, such as production of Therapeutic Recombinant Proteins in the Milk of Genetically Modified Animals.

1. **Production of Recombinant Therapeutic Proteins in the Milk of Transgenic Animals**

An animal that has undergone genetic modification to acquire particular traits (genes) that it would not otherwise possess is referred to as transgenic. Various kinds of transgenic animals have been created. Created to address particular societal demands. Transgenic disease models and transgenic animals are included.

Applications

- Recombinant proteins are made from recombinant DNA and are employed in a variety of medical procedures.
- Hematogenous growth factor.
- The Interferon.
- The hormones.
- Vaccines using recombinant proteins.
- Clotting and tissue/bone growth factors.
- Modifiers of biological reaction.
- Therapeutic, diagnostic, and monoclonal antibodies.
- The use of recombinant proteins in biotechnology, medicine, and research is widespread.

References

Weise M, Bielsky MC, De Smet K, et al. Biosimilars: what clinicians should know. Blood 2012; 120(26):5111-7.

Weise M, Kurki P, Wolff-Holz E, et al. Biosimilars: the science of extrapolation. Blood 2014; 124(22):3191-6.

Padda IS, Bhatt R, Rehman O, et al. Biosimilars Use In Medicine For Inflammatory Diseases. [Updated 2022 Jan 6]. In: StatPearls [Internet]. Treasure Island (FL): StatPearls Publishing; 2022 Jan-.

Sadeghalvad, Mona & Rezaei, Nima. (2021). Introduction on Monoclonal Antibodies. 10.5772/intechopen.98378.

Chiu ML, Goulet DR, Teplyakov A, Gilliland GL. Antibody Structure and Function: The Basis for Engineering Therapeutics. Antibodies (Basel). 2019; 8(4):55.

Parray HA, Shukla S, Samal S, et al. Hybridoma technology a versatile method for isolation of monoclonal antibodies, its applicability across species, limitations, advancement and future perspectives. Int Immunopharmacol. 2020; 85:106639.

Holzlöhner P, Hanack K. Generation of Murine Monoclonal Antibodies by Hybridoma Technology. J Vis Exp. 2017 Jan 2; (119):54832.

Vanhove B. Anticorps monoclonaux en transplantation [Monoclonal 19 antibodies in organ transplantation]. Med Sci (Paris). 2009; 25(12):1121-1125.

Matucci A, Vultaggio A, Maggi E, Kasujee I. Is IgE or eosinophils the key player in allergic asthma pathogenesis? Are we asking the right question? Respir Res. 2018; 19(1):113.

Hu J, Chen J, Ye L, Cai Z, Sun J, Ji K. Anti-IgE therapy for IgE-mediated allergic diseases: from neutralizing IgE antibodies to eliminating IgE+ B cells. Clin Transl Allergy. 2018; 8:27.

Loureiro CC, Amaral L, Ferreira JA, et al. Omalizumab for Severe Asthma: Beyond Allergic Asthma. Biomed Res Int. 2018; 2018:3254094.

PART – V

PRINCIPLES OF TOXICOLOGY

CHAPTER

General Toxicity Testing 26

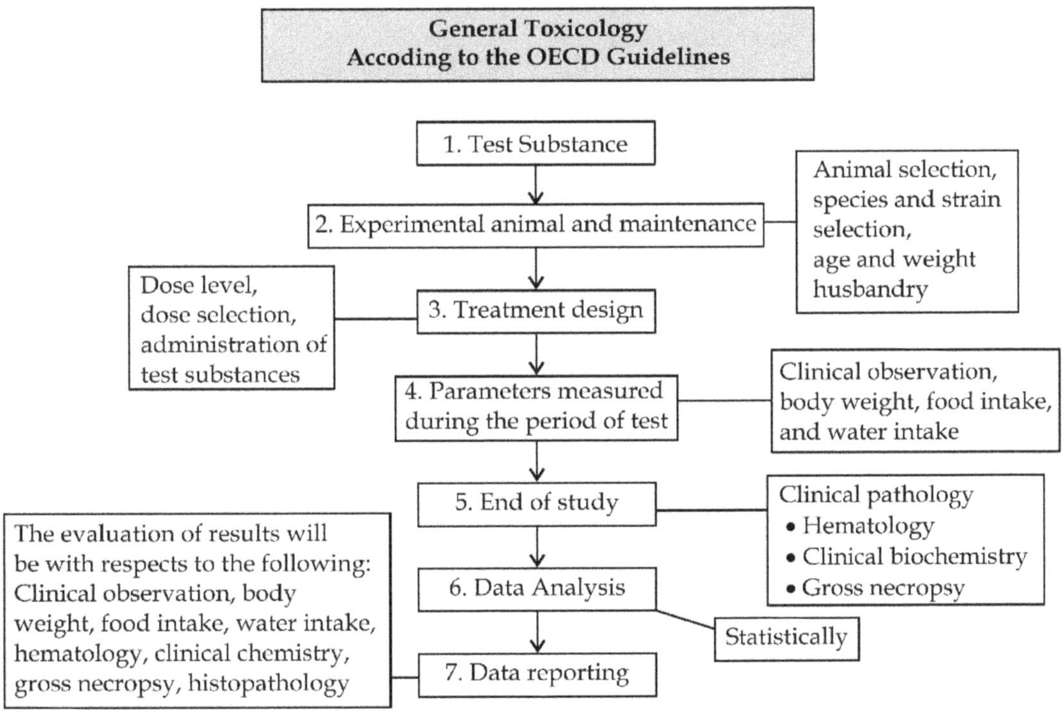

General Toxicity Testing (GTT) was the term used to describe a number of toxicity tests necessary by international standards for conformance to Good Laboratory Practices (GLP) for demonstration of safety in experimental animals before human testing. Acute and sub-acute chronic toxicity are included. These studies are carried out in accordance with "OECD criteria for chemical testing." Both rodents and non-rodents are used in their execution.

Preclinical research is a requirement for all new pharmaceutical medications under international standards pertaining to human health. Toxicology studies are one of the Preclinical inquiry phases, and they are carried out in accordance with the relevant standards and quality system (OECD GLP).

Preclinical Studies

Includes

- Phytochemistry, Development of the products.
- Formulation
- Complete pharmacologic and pharmacokinetic profile
- Safety study - Toxicology
- Efficacy study.

Acute Toxicity

The goal of acute toxicity studies is to identify the immediate effects of chemicals on experimental animals following the administration of a single dosage (or several doses) within a time frame of no more than 24 hours. According to the guidelines, the dose can range between 2000 and 5000 mg/kg BW.

Studies on acute toxicity's goal

According to regulatory rules and information, the guide on dosages for the subacute test identifies a dose that causes serious side effects and provides an estimate of the lowest amount that causes death.

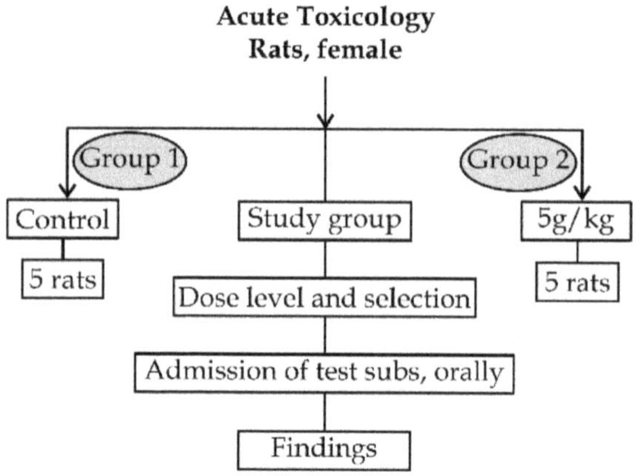

Principle: in the main study only moderately toxic doses are used, and the administration of doses that are expected to be lethal should be avoided.

Sighting study: Groups of animals of a single sex (normally females) are dosed in a stepwise procedure using the fixed doses of 5, 50, 300 and 2000 mg/kg (exceptionally 5000 mg/kg). If dose causes acute effect, stop at that dose, if not cont until the highest dose.

Main study

Two groups of 5 rats each, one control and one test

Acute Oral Toxicity: Up-and-Down Procedure

Sighting study: step wise Main study: Two groups of 5 rats each, one control and one test.

Acute Toxicity (OECD Guideline 420, 425) Parameters

Mortality, Clinical pathology, Gross necropsy, Weight change, Clinical observations Points to consider: Dose selection for repeat dose studies

Objective: To determine Maximum Tolerated Dose (MTD) No Observable Effect Level (NOEL).

Duration: 14 days after single dose Animals Required: (rodent).

Subacute Toxicity

The effect of exposure from 1 day to 30 days

Repeated Dose 28-day Oral Toxicity Study in Rodents

Principle: gives details on the potential health risks associated with daily oral exposure to the test chemical. The technique is based on repeatedly giving the material of interest orally over a short period of time (one dose level daily during 28 days). This recommendation is mostly for usage with rodents (rat preferably). For each dose level, a minimum of 10 animals—5 male and 5female—should be used. It is recommended to use three test groups. The test substance is given orally, through the meal, or through drinking water.

If no effects would be anticipated at a dose of 1000 mg/kg bw/d, a limit test may be carried out.

Duration: 28 days daily dosing, observe daily Animals Required: 2 species (rodent).

Parameters: Mortality, sign of toxicity, Clinical pathology, Histology, Weight change, Clinical observation.

Chronic Toxicity

Daily exposure for 3 months or more

These studies on chronic toxicity aim to describe the profile of a chemical in a mammalian species after prolonged and repetitive exposure (mainly rodents). The Test Guideline concentrates on oral administration and rodents. It is best to use both genders. For rodents, a minimum of 20 animals per sex in each group should typically be employed at each dose level, while a minimum of 4 animals per sex in each group is advised for non-rodents. The concurrent control group should be utilised in addition to at least three dosing levels. Daily exposure is the norm, but it can change depending on the route taken (oral, dermal, or inhalation), and it should be modified in accordance with the toxicokinetic profile of the test substance.

Objective: To characterize dose-response relationships following repeated doses To identify and characterize specific organs affected after repeated administration

Duration: Rodents - 6 to 24 months; non-rodents (monkey) - 12 months or longer or up to 10% of species' lifespan. Length depends on intended period of human exposure.

Animals Required:

2 species (rodent and non-rodent)

Parameters: Mortality, Clinical pathology, Clinical observation, Behavioral Assessment, Histology, Weight change

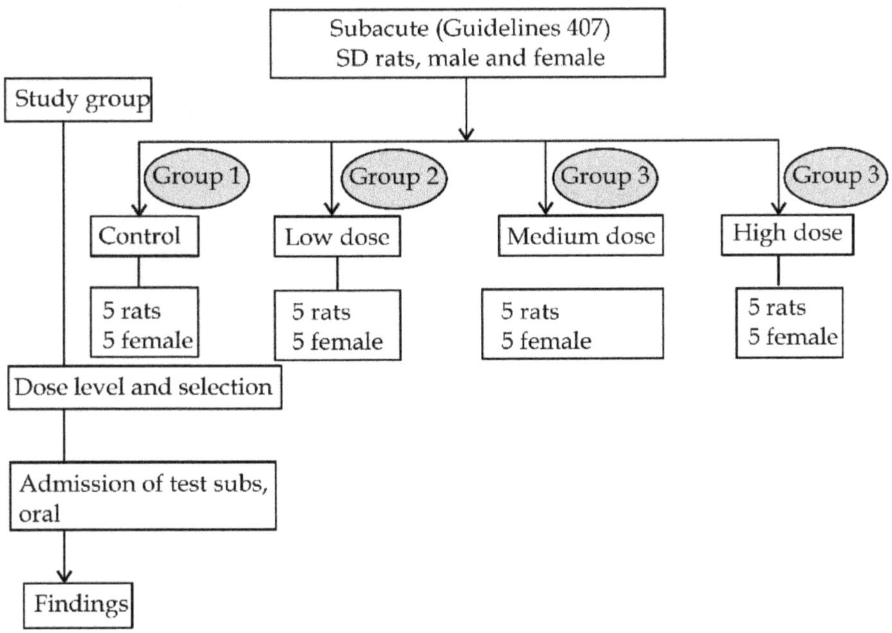

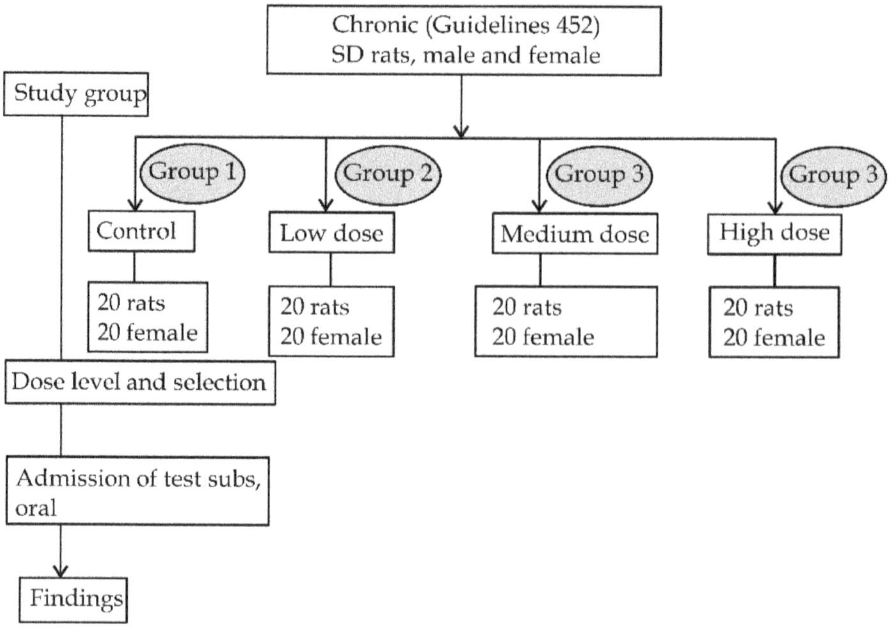

Non Rodent Animal Species

- Dogs, Pigs and Monkeys are the most commonly used animals in preclinical studies.
- Ideally, the species of choice should have the same pharmacokinetic profile as in humans, however, this information is either incomplete or missing,
- Under such circumstance, select the most sensitive species for evaluating the safety of the substance.

Clinical Chemistry

- The hepatic leakage enzymes ALT, AST, SDH, and LDH.
- AP and GGT, cholestatic enzymes.
- Tests of liver function: - Bile acids, ammonia, total bilirubin, direct bilirubin, and indirect bilirubin.
- Amylase and lipase are two pancreatic markers.
- Triglycerides and cholesterol are lipid parameters.
- Creatine kinase (CK), AST, ALT, and LDH are muscle parameters.
- Calcium and potassium: Renal parameters should be assessed concurrently because kidney function frequently affects these values.
- Urea nitrogen and creatinine are two kidney parameters that should be assessed along with renal function. - Proteins, minerals, electrolytes, acid-base balance, and haematological factors are all impacted by kidney function.

Hematology

- RBC,
- WBC,
- PLT,
- HB,
- Neutrophil %
- MCHC,
- HCT
- MCHC
- MCV

CHAPTER

Genotoxicity

27

Genotoxicity is described as an adverse impact on the integrity of genetic makeup i.e., DNA, RNA

Mechanisms of genotoxicity: Genotoxic substances interact at particular places in DNA causing deletion, inversion, translocation, duplication and nondisjunction and lesions.

Deletion occurs due to strand breakage, leading to loss of chromosome. Inversion occurs when a strand segment breaks off and reattaches. If reattachments lead to mismatch, then it cause translocation. When gene sequence is repeated, it cause duplication. Nondisjunction is a mechanism of genotoxicity where chromosomes fail to separate during meiosis.

Lesions are caused due to free radicals which adversely affect the structure of cells, proteins and also DNA.

Example

BRCA1 and BRCA2 are the 2 BRCA gene mutations that are known to cause cancer. The likelihood that a woman may develop ovarian and breast cancer is increased by certain gene abnormalities. Male breast cancer and prostate cancer risk are both increased by BRCA2 gene mutations.

Genotoxicity Assays

Somatic cells are the cells that comprise of 2 sets of chromosomes, inherited from parents, one set from each parent. Germ cells can reproduce on their own.

Somatic Cell Assays:

1. PIG-A assay in humans

2.Transgenic rodent assay

Germ Cell Assay:

1. Mouse specific locus test

2. Dominant lethal assay

Invitro Assays:

1. Chromosomal aberration assay

2. Micronucleus assay

1. PIG-A assay:

Phosphatidylinositol glycan A, a reporter gene for mutation. Detection of mutant pig-a gene is limited to mature and immature RBCs from peripheral blood samples drawn from the affected tissues.

2. Transgenic rodent assay:

By correlating the gene range of mutants with ones of those certain recognised mutagens, Genome sequencing of mutant strains could also be used to investigate chemical MOA and classify duplicate mutants produced by proliferative expansion of single mutants.

3. Lethal assay:

It looks into whether a substance causes mutations linked to foetal or embryonic demise. Most of the mutations are caused by chromosomal abnormalities in germ cells (OECD TG 478). Despite the assay's benefits, such as in vivo metabolism, pharmacokinetic properties, and Genetic repairing processes that impact the outcome, a lot of animals are needed to complete it. This assay can be combined with other bioassays, such as developmental, reproductive, or somatic cell genotoxicity investigations, to conserve animals.

4. In vitro chromosomal aberration assay (OECD TG 473):

It evaluates chemically induced structural genomic damage in cultured mammalian cells (such as CHO cells and human lymphocytes), but it takes a lot of time, calls for skilled and knowledgeable scorers, and does not accurately measure aneuploidy (i.e., changes in chromosome number). Excessive cytotoxicity that affected data interpretation in the early years of this assay's use was a significant confounding problem in many laboratories. As a result, updated standards indicating tolerable cytotoxicity levels have been published (OECD, 2016a), which has increased the test's dependability.

References

https://www.ncbi.nlm.nih.gov/books/NBK560519/

U. Satyanarayana, Biochemistry 3rd edition.

Ashutosh kumar, Methods in toxicology and pharmacology.

Rang & Dale's Pharmacology Book.

Lippincott Illustrated Review: Pharmacology Book.

CHAPTER

28

Carcinogenicity

CLASSIFICATIN OF CHEMICAL CARCINOGENS

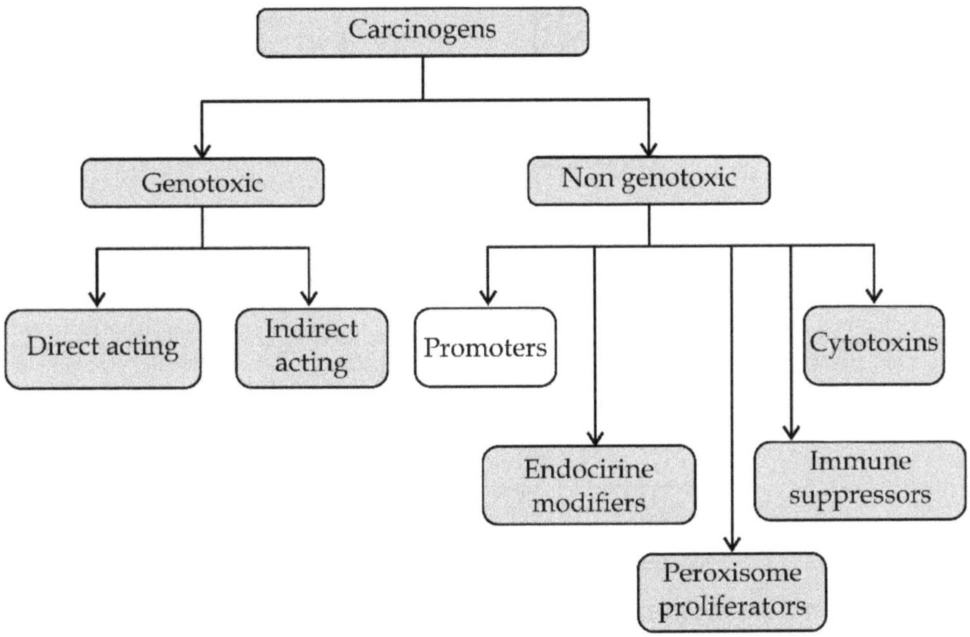

The process by which a healthy cell is changed into a cancerous cell and divides frequently to develop into cancer is known as carcinogenesis.

Chemical carcinogens are substances that start this process.

Co-carcinogens are substances that make carcinogens more effective.

Role of Proto-Oncogenes and Tumor Suppressor Genes

Two classes of genes are mainly involved in carcinogenesis

1. Proto oncogenes

- Involved in growth and differentiation
- Activated in cancers

MECHANISM OF ACTION

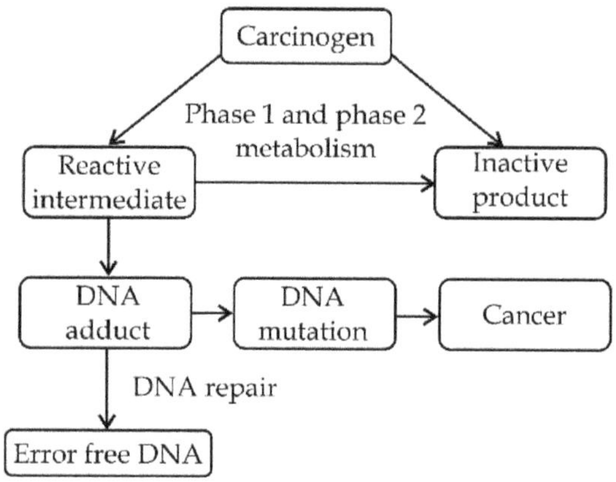

2. Tumor suppressor genes
- Negative regulators of growth
- Inactivated in cancers

Activation of Proto Oncogenes

- Point mutation.
- Chromosome translocation.
- Gene amplification.
- Ras oncogene - first activated proto-oncogene detected in a human tumor.
- Permanent activation/over expression lead to neoplastic transformation.

INACTIVATION OF TUMOR SUPPRESSOR GENE

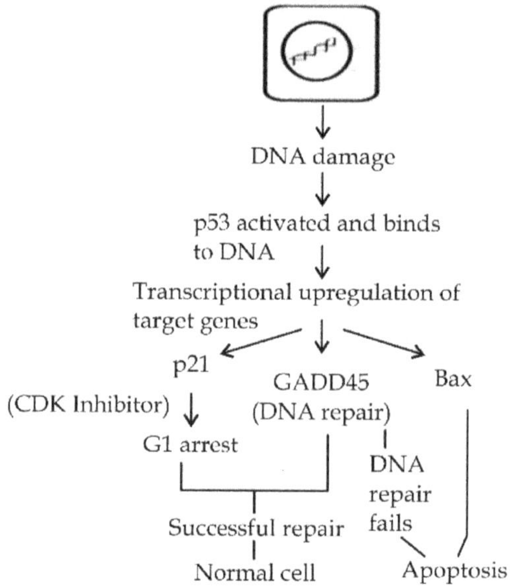

Oxidative Stress in Carcinogenesis

- Both endogenous and external factors can cause ROS.
- Attack the deoxyribose backbone as well as the purine and pyrimidine bases.
- Causes DNA damage such as single- or double-strand breaks, deoxyribose alteration, and DNA cross-linking.
- If DNA damage is not repaired adequately, it may cause a mutation that causes cancer.

STAGES OF CARCINOGENSIS

MULTISTEP PROCESS

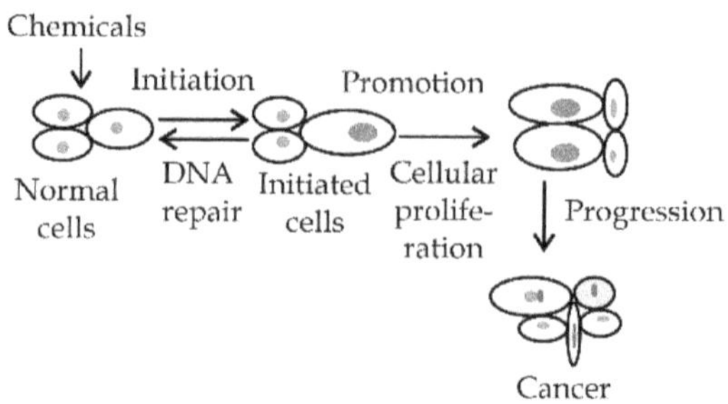

Current Perspectives

I. Impact of Technologies

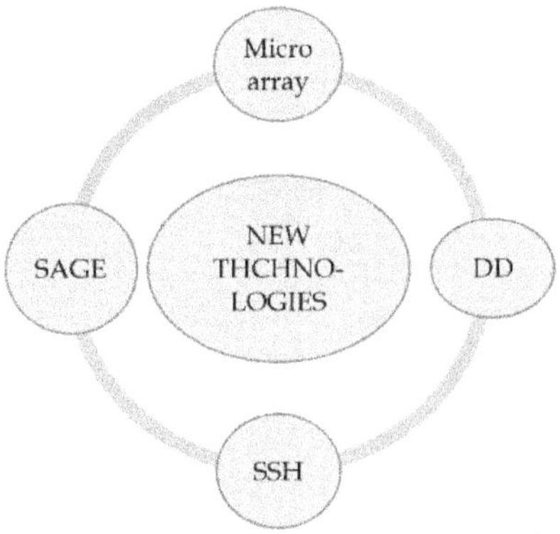

II. Biomarkers

- Carcinoembryonic antigen (CEA) - breast cancer.
- Neuron specific enolase (NSE) - lung cancer.
- α-fetoprotein (AFP) - liver cancer.
- Prostate specific antigen (PSA) - prostate cancer.

III. Biosensors

- Improve the sensitivity and specificity of the biomarker with a device that has two primary components: a sensing receptor and a detector.
- Effective early detection without discomfort using a noninvasive method.

Future Directions

- Development of new preclinical models for carcinogenesis.
- Future challenge is to develop and validate biomarkers for non.
- Genotoxic chemical carcinogens.
- Understanding chemical carcinogenesis with.
- Inter-individual variation.
- Alteration in gene expression.

References

S. M. Cohen, L. L. Arnold, Chemical carcinogenesis, Toxicol Sci 120 Suppl 1. (2011) S76-92.

L. A. Loeb, Harris C C, Advances in chemical carcinogenesis: a historical review and prospective, Cancer Res. 68(17) (2008) 6863-6872.

P. Joseph, Chemical Carcinogenesis; Recent Advances and the Future Directions, Aust-Asian J Cancer. 4(4) (2005) 7.

CHAPTER

Drug Therapy in Pregnancy

29

Pharmacokinetics

Most drugs taken by pregnant women can cross the placenta and expose the developing embryo and fetus to their pharmacological and teratogenic effects. Critical factors affecting placental drug transfer and drug effects on the fetus include the following:

1. The physicochemical properties of the drug;
2. The rate at which the drug crosses the placenta and the amount of drug reaching the fetus;
3. The duration of exposure to the drug;
4. Distribution characteristics in different fetal tissues;
5. The stage of placental and fetal development at the time of exposure to the drug; and
6. The effects of drugs used in combination.

Lipid Solubility

As is true also of other biologic membranes, drug passage across the placenta is dependent on lipid solubility and the degree of drug ionization. Lipophilic drugs tend to diffuse readily across the placenta and enter the fetal circulation. For example, thiopental, a drug commonly used for cesarean sections, crosses the placenta almost immediately and can produce sedation or apnea in the newborn infant. Highly ionized drugs such as succinylcholine and tubocurarine, also used for cesarean sections, cross the placenta slowly and achieve very low concentrations in the fetus. Impermeability of the placenta to polar compounds is relative rather than absolute. If high enough maternal fetal concentration gradients are achieved, polar compounds cross the placenta in measurable amounts. Salicylate, which is almost completely ionized at physiologic pH, crosses the placenta rapidly. This occurs because the small amount of salicylate that is not ionized is highly lipid soluble.

Molecular Size

The molecular weight of the drug also influences the rate of transfer and the amount of drug transferred across the placenta. Drugs with molecular weights of 250–500 can cross the placenta easily, depending upon their lipid solubility and degree of ionization; those with molecular weights of 500–1000 cross the placenta with more difficulty; and those with molecular weights greater than 1000 cross very poorly. An important clinical application of this property is the choice of heparin as an anticoagulant in pregnant women. Because it is a very large (and polar) molecule, heparin is unable to cross the placenta. Unlike warfarin, which is teratogenic and should be avoided during the first trimester and even beyond (as the brain continues to develop), heparin may be safely given to pregnant women who need anticoagulation. Yet the placenta contains drug transporters, which can carry larger molecules to the fetus. For example, a variety of maternal antibodies cross the placenta and may cause fetal morbidity, as in Rh incompatibility.

Placental Transporters

During the last decade, many drug transporters have been identified in the placenta, with increasing recognition of their effects on drug transfer to the fetus. For example, the P-glycoprotein transporter encoded by the *MDR1* gene pumps back into the maternal circulation a variety of drugs, including cancer drugs (e.g., vinblastine, doxorubicin) and other agents. Similarly, viral protease inhibitors, which are substrates to P-glycoprotein, achieve only low fetal concentrations—an effect that may increase the risk of vertical HIV infection from the mother to the fetus. The hypoglycemic drug glyburide cannot be measured in umbilical blood despite therapeutic maternal concentrations. Recent work has documented that this agent is effluxed from the fetal circulation by the BCRP transporter as well as by the MRP3 transporter located in the placental brush border membrane.

Protein Binding

The degree to which a drug is bound to plasma proteins (particularly albumin) may also affect the rate of transfer and the amount transferred. However, if a compound is very lipid-soluble (e.g., some anesthetic gases), it will not be affected greatly by protein binding. Transfer of these more lipid soluble drugs and their overall rates of equilibration are more dependent on (and proportionate to) placental blood flow. This is because very lipid-soluble drugs diffuse across placental membranes so rapidly that their overall rates of equilibration do not depend on the free drug concentrations becoming equal on both sides. If a drug is poorly lipid soluble and is ionized, its transfer is slow and will probably be impeded by its binding to maternal plasma proteins. Differential protein binding is also important since some drugs exhibit greater protein binding in maternal plasma than in fetal plasma because of a lower binding affinity of fetal proteins. This has been shown for sulfonamides, barbiturates, phenytoin and local anesthetic agents.

Placental and Fetal Drug Metabolism

Two mechanisms help protect the fetus from drugs in the maternal circulation:

1. The placenta itself plays a role both as a semi permeable barrier and as a site of metabolism of some drugs passing through it. Several different types of aromatic oxidation reactions (e.g., hydroxylation, *N*-dealkylation, demethylation) have been shown to occur in placental tissue. Pentobarbital is oxidized in this way. Conversely, it is possible that the metabolic capacity of the placenta may lead to creation of toxic metabolites, and the placenta may therefore augment toxicity (e.g., ethanol, benzpyrenes).
2. Drugs that have crossed the placenta enter the fetal circulation via the umbilical vein. About 40–60% of umbilical venous blood flow enters the fetal liver; the remainder bypasses the liver and enters the general fetal circulation. A drug that enters the liver may be partially metabolized there before it enters the fetal circulation. In addition, a large proportion of drug present in the umbilical artery (returning to the placenta) may be shunted through the placenta back to the umbilical vein and into the liver again. It should be noted that metabolites of some drugs may be more active than the parent compound and may affect the fetus adversely.

Pharmacodynamics

Maternal Drug Actions

The effects of drugs on the reproductive tissues (breast, uterus, etc.,) of the pregnant woman are sometimes altered by the endocrine environment appropriate for the stage of pregnancy. Drug effects on other maternal tissues (heart, lungs, kidneys, central nervous system, etc) are not changed significantly by pregnancy, although the physiologic context (cardiac output, renal blood flow, etc) may be altered, requiring the use of drugs that are not needed by the same woman when she is not pregnant. For example, cardiac glycosides and diuretics may be needed for heart failure precipitated by the increased cardiac workload of pregnancy or insulin may be required for control of blood glucose in pregnancy induced diabetes.

Therapeutic Drug Actions in the Fetus

Fetal therapeutics is an emerging area in perinatal pharmacology. This involves drug administration to the pregnant woman with the fetus as the target of the drug. At present, corticosteroids are used to stimulate fetal lung maturation when preterm birth is expected. Phenobarbital, when given to pregnant women near term, can induce fetal hepatic enzymes responsible for the glucuronidation of bilirubin, and the incidence of jaundice is lower in newborns when mothers are given Phenobarbital than when Phenobarbital is not used. Before phototherapy became the preferred mode of therapy for neonatal indirect hyperbilirubinemia, Phenobarbital was used for this indication. Administration of Phenobarbital to the mother was suggested recently as a means of decreasing the risk of intracranial bleeding in preterm infants. However, large randomized studies failed to confirm this effect. Antiarrhythmic drugs have also been given to mothers for treatment of fetal cardiac arrhythmias. Although their efficacy has not yet been established by controlled studies, digoxin, flecainide, procainamide, verapamil, and other antiarrhythmic agents have been shown to be effective in case series. During the last decade it has been shown that maternal use of zidovudine decreases by two thirds transmission of HIV from the mother to the fetus and use of combinations of three antiretroviral agents can eliminate fetal infection almost entirely.

Predictable Toxic Drug Actions in the Fetus

Chronic use of opioid by the mother may produce dependence in the fetus and newborn. This dependence may be manifested after delivery as a neonatal withdrawal syndrome. A less well understood fetal drug toxicity is caused by the use of angiotensin converting enzyme inhibitors during pregnancy. These drugs can result in significant and irreversible renal damage in the fetus and are therefore contraindicated in pregnant women. Adverse effects may also be delayed, as in the case of female fetuses exposed to diethylstilbestrol, who may be at increased risk for adenocarcinoma of the vagina after puberty.

Teratogenic Drug Actions

A single intrauterine exposure to a drug can affect the fetal structures undergoing rapid development at the time of exposure. Thalidomide is an example of a drug that may profoundly affect the development of the limbs after only brief exposure. This exposure, however, must be at a critical time in the development of the limbs. The thalidomide phocomelia risk occurs during the fourth through the seventh week of gestation because it is during this time that the arms and legs develop. Listed in Following Fig 29-1.

Teratogenic Mechanisms

The mechanisms by which different drugs produce teratogenic effects are poorly understood and are probably multifactorial. For example, drugs may have a direct effect on maternal tissues with secondary or indirect effects on fetal tissues. Drugs may interfere with the passage of oxygen or nutrients through the placenta and therefore have effects on the most rapidly metabolizing tissues of the fetus. Finally, drugs may have important direct actions on the processes of differentiation in developing tissues. For example, vitamin A (retinol) has been shown to have important differentiation-directing actions in normal tissues. Several vitamin A analogs (isotretinoin, etretinate) are powerful teratogen, suggesting that they alter the normal processes of differentiation. Finally, deficiency of a critical substance appears to play a role in some types of abnormalities. For example, folic acid supplementation during pregnancy appears to reduce the incidence of neural tube defects (e.g., spina bifida).

Continued exposure to a teratogen may produce cumulative effects or may affect several organs going through varying stages of development. Chronic consumption of highdoses of ethanol during pregnancy, particularly during the first and second trimesters, may result in the fetal alcohol syndrome. In this syndrome, the central nervous system, growth, and facial development may be affected.

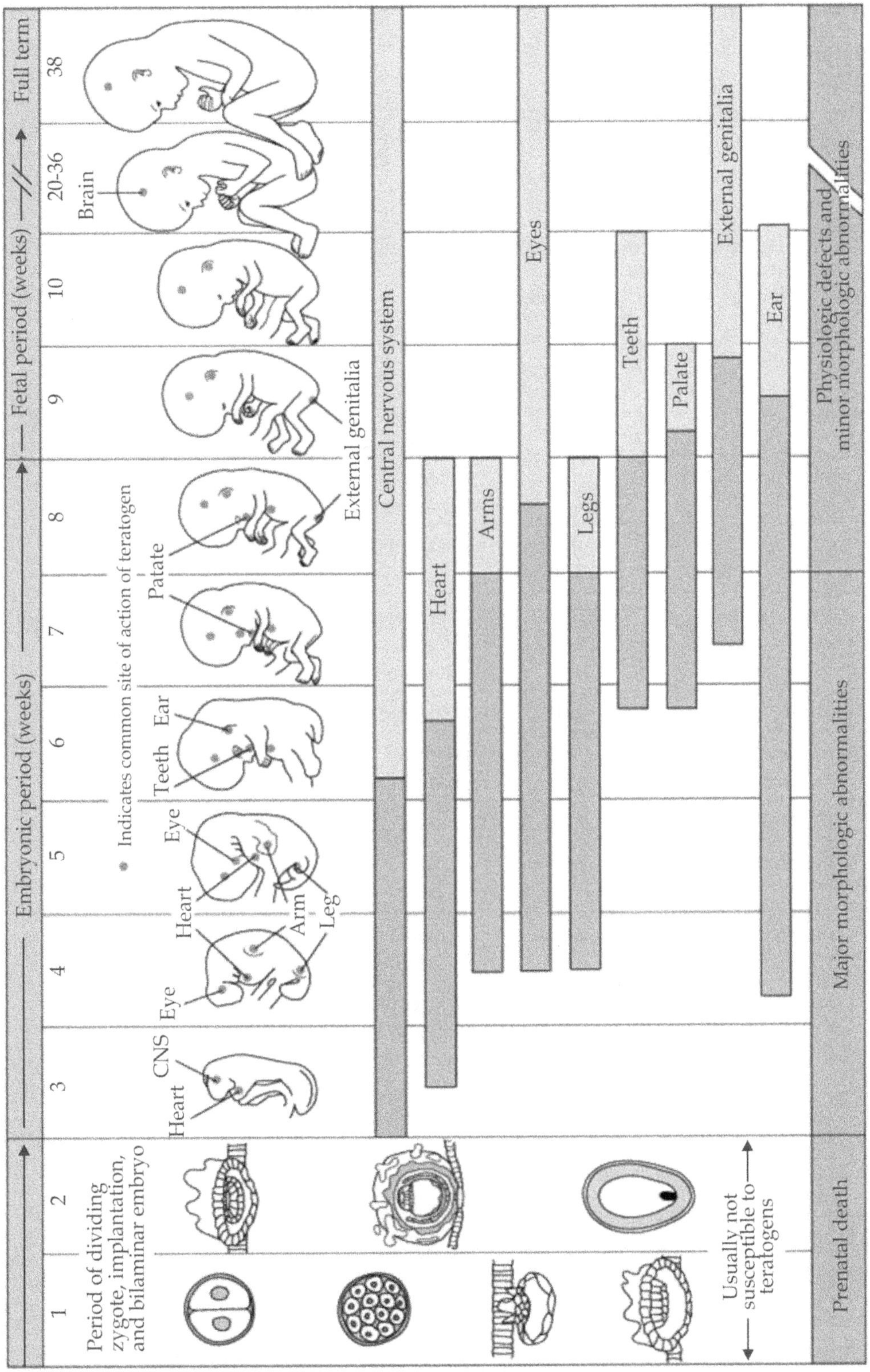

Fig 29-1: Schematic diagram of critical periods of human development.

Defining a Teratogen

To be considered teratogenic, a candidate substance or process should

1. result in a characteristic set of malformations, indicating selectivity for certain target organs;
2. exert its effects at a particular stage of fetal development, i.e., during the limited time period of organogenesis of the target organs and
3. show a dose dependent incidence. Some drugs with known teratogenic or other adverse effects in pregnancy are listed in Following Table 29.1.

Table 29-1: Drugs with known teratogenic or other adverse effects.

Drug	Trimester	Effect
ACE inhibitors	All, especially second and third	Renal damage
Aminopterin	First	Multiple gross anomalies
Amphetamines	All	Suspected abnormal developmental patterns, decreased school performance
Androgens	Second and third	Masculinization of female fetus
Antidepressants, tricyclic	Third	Neonatal withdrawal symptoms have been reported in a few cases with clomipramine, desipramine and imipramine
Barbiturates	All	Chronic use can lead to neonatal dependence.
Busulfan	All	Various congenital malformations; low birth weight
Carbamazepine	First	Neural tube defects
Chlorpropamide	All	Prolonged symptomatic neonatal hypoglycemia
Clomipramine	Third	Neonatal lethargy, hypotonia, cyanosis, hypothermia
Cocaine	All	Increased risk of spontaneous abortion, abruption placenta and premature labor; neonatal cerebral infarction, abnormal development, and decreased school performance
Cyclophosphamide	First	Various congenital malformations
Cytarabine	First, second	Various congenital malformations
Diazepam	All	Chronic use may lead to neonatal dependence
Diethylstilbestrol	All	Vaginal adenosis, clear cell vaginal adenocarcinoma
Ethanol	All	Risk of fetal alcohol syndrome and alcohol-related neurodevelopment defects

Table 29.1 Contd...

Drug	Trimester	Effect
Etretinate	All	High risk of multiple congenital malformations
Heroin	All	Chronic use leads to neonatal dependence
Iodide	All	Congenital goiter, hypothyroidism
Isotretinoin	All	Extremely high risk of CNS, face, ear and other malformations
Lithium	First	Ebstein's anomaly
Methadone	All	Chronic use leads to neonatal dependence
Methotrexate	First	Multiple congenital malformations
Methylthiouracil	All	Hypothyroidism
Metronidazole	First	May be mutagenic (from animal studies; there is no evidence for mutagenic or teratogenic effects in humans)
Organic solvents	First	Multiple malformations
Misoprostol	First	Möbius sequence
Penicillamine	First	Cutis laxa, other congenital malformations
Phencyclidine	All	Abnormal neurologic examination, poor suck reflex and feeding
Phenytoin	All	Fetal hydantoin syndrome
Propylthiouracil	All	Congenital goiter
Streptomycin	All	Eighth nerve toxicity
Smoking (constituents of tobacco smoke)	All	Intrauterine growth retardation; prematurity; sudden infant death syndrome; perinatal complications
Tamoxifen	All	Increased risk of spontaneous abortion or fetal damage
Tetracycline	All	Discoloration and defects of teeth and altered bone growth
Thalidomide	First	Phocomelia (shortened or absent long bones of the limbs) and many internal malformations
Trimethadione	All	Multiple congenital anomalies
Valproic acid	All	Neural tube defects, cardiac and limb malformations
Warfarin	First	Hypoplastic nasal bridge, chondrodysplasia
	Second	CNS malformations
	Third	Risk of bleeding. Discontinue use 1 month before delivery.

FDA Pregnancy Categories

A – Studies in pregnant woman, no risk.

B – Animal studies no risk, but human not adequate or animal toxicity but human studies no risk.

C – Animal studies show toxicity, human studies inadequate but benefit of use may exceed risk.

D – Evidence of human risk, but benefit may outweigh.

X – Fetal abnormalities in humans, risk > benefit: contraindicate in pregnant women.

Table 29-2: Effect of drugs during pregnancy analgesics and anti-inflammatory drugs.

Drugs	FDA Pregnancy Categories	Nature of Effect
Acetaminophen	B	Acetaminophen is analgesic-antipyretic of choice for use near term.
Aspirin	C (D if full-dose aspirin in 3rd trimester)	Maternal - aspirin use late in gestation can cause increased bleeding at delivery and delay the onset of labor. Neonatal - prolong constriction of ductus arteriosus, pulmonary hypertension, platelet function, and bleeding, intracranial hemorrhage.
Indomethacin	B (D if use long term than 48 hr or after 34-week gestation)	Premature closure of ductus arteriosus, neonatal pulmonary hypertension.
Ibuprofen	B (D if use in the 3rd trimester)	Similar to aspirin and indomethacin.
Diclofenac	B_M (D if use in the 3rd trimester)*	Inhibition of labor, prolongation of pregnancy and suppression of fetal renal function. If use in the 3rd trimester close to delivery, persistant pulmonary hypertension of the newborn may occur.
Piroxicam	B (D if use in the 3rd trimester)	Inhibition of labor, prolongation of pregnancy. If use in the 3rd trimester close to delivery, persistent pulmonary hypertension of the newborn may occur.

*Category with a subscript M (e.g., CM) refers to the risk factor that the manufacturer rated its product in its professional literature.

Anticoagulants

Drugs	FDA Pregnancy Categories	Nature of Effect
Heparin	C	Heparin is usually the drug of choice for anticoagulation during
Warfarin	D	Warfarin may produce the "Fetal Warfarin Syndrome" or "Warfarin Embryopathy" include nasal hypoplasia, neonatal respiratory distress, axial skeleton and proximal femur are affected, spontaneous abortion, stillbirths, CNS defects.

Anticonvulsants

Drugs	FDA Pregnancy Categories	Nature of Effect
Phenytoin	D	Mild to moderate growth deficiency , wide anterior fontanelle,hypertelorism, depressed nasal bridge, short nose with bowed upper lip, cleft lip and palate, hypoplasia of distal phalanges .
Sodium valproate	D	High forehead, epicanthal folds, broad nasal bridge, long philtrum, small mouth, cleft lip, neural tube defect, hypospadias.
Carbamazepine	C	Craniofacial defect, neural tube defects.
Phenobarbital	D	Cleft lip and palate, cardiac defects.

Antimicrobial Drugs

Drugs	FDA Pregnancy Categories	Nature of Effect
Penicillins	B	Penicillins are without teratogenic risk.
Cephalosporins	B	Cephalosporins are thought to be without teratogenic risk.
Erythromycin	B	Pregnant women are at increased risk for hepatotoxicity caused
Aminoglycosides	C	Congenital hearing loss, deafness.
Chloramphenicol	C	Risk for development of blood dyscrasias and aplastic anemia. Particular caution should be exercised near term because the "Gray Baby" syndrome is resulted.
Tetracycline's	D; B (topical)	Tetracycline's have been reported to cause congenital Abnormalities, particularly staining of the teeth and retardation of the developing skeletal system.
Fluoroquinolones (e.g., Ciprofloxacin, Norfloxacin, Ofloxacin)	C	Fluoroquinolones were shown to cause erosion of the cartilage and other arthropathies in fetuses. These drugs should not be used in pregnancy.
Sulfonamides (e.g., Sulfadiazine)	B (D at term)	Evidence associating sulfonamide use near term with hyperbilirubinemia, hemolytic anemia (in G-6-PD deficiency), competition of albumin site-neonatal kernicterus.
Co-Trimoxazole	C	Do not use at term to avoid kernicterus in the new born and use during pregnancy only if risk outweigh the benefits since folic acid metabolism may be effected.
Metronidazole	B_M*	The manufacturer and the Centers for Disease Control (CDC) consider Metronidazole to be contraindicated during 1st trimester in patients with trichomoniasis. Use for trichomoniasis during the 2nd and 3rd trimester may be acceptable if alternate therapies have failed.

Cardiovascular Drugs

Drugs	FDA Pregnancy Categories	Nature of Effect
Antiarrhythmics Amiodarone	D	Neonatal hypothyroidism with or without goiter, as well as hyperthyroidism.
-Digoxin	C	Digoxin is not a teratogen. It may be given to pregnant women to treat fetal CHF and supraventricular tachycardia. Maternal digitalis toxicity has been associated with fetal toxicity.
ß-Adrenergic blocking agents -Atenolol -Pindolol -Metoprolol -Propranolol	 C B B C	These agents are thought to be generally safe in pregnancy but these have also been associated with intrauterine growth. Retardation and neonatal hypoglycemia and hypotension.
Angiotensin-converting enzyme (ACE) inhibitors (e.g., Captopril, enalapril, lisinopril, fosinopril)	C	Fetal abnormalities, including death can be caused and these drugs should not be used in pregnancy.
Calcium - channel blocking agents (e.g., Nifedipine, Diltiazem, verapamil)	C	A small, transient decrease in uterine activity occurred with all doses.
Diuretics Hydrochlorothiazide (HCTZ) -Furosemide -Amiloride 5 mg.+ HCTZ 50 mg. (Moduretic®)	 B C B_M*	 Neonatal hypoglycemia, hyponatremia, hypokalemia and thrombocytopenia. Crosses the placenta. Increases fetal urine production, electrolyte disturbances reported. Animal studies using amiloride alone had not shown adverse effects in the fetus but in human studies some newborns had hypospadias, renovascular hypertension.
Isosorbide dinitrate	C_M*	No reports on the use in human pregnancy. It produces embryo toxicity in rabbits.
Hydralazine	B (oral); C (IV)	Hydralazine is the Parentral drug of choice used in pregnancy.
Methyldopa	C	Antihypertensive of choice used in pregnancy.
Reserpine	C	Produces edema of the nasal mucosa in the neonate, hypothermia and bradycardia.

Gastrointestinal Drugs

Drugs	FDA Pregnancy Categories	Nature of Effect
Antacid -Magnesium hydroxide -Aluminum hydroxide -Sucralfate	B C B	The safety of antacid use during the 1st trimester of pregnancy has not been established. 2nd and 3rd trimester use appears to be without adverse effects. Sucralfate is poorly absorbed and no adverse effects to the fetus have been reported.
-Antiulcer **H2-blocker** -Cimetidine -Famotidine -Ranitidine -Nizatidine Proton-Pump Inhibitor -Omeprazole	B B B C C_M*	Crosses the placenta. Available evidence suggests safe use during pregnancy and breast-feeding. Severe congenital anomalies; anencephaly, severe talipes inhuman. Long term high dose consumption was carcinogenic in rats, producing gastrointestinal tumors.
Laxative -Bulk laxatives (Psyllium) - Mineral oil - Castor oil	B C X	These are agent of choice. Mineral oil should be avoided. Castor oil may cause pelvic congestion.
Metoclopramide	B	Crosses the placenta. Available evidence suggests safe use during pregnancy and breast-feeding.

Sedative and Hypnotics

Drugs	FDA Pregnancy Categories	Nature of Effect
Benzodiazepines (e.g., Clorazepate, Diazepam, Lorazepam)	D	Neonatal depression, apnoeic spells, "floppy baby syndrome" (muscular relaxation, poor sucking, disturbances in thermoregulation and regurgitation), withdrawal symptom.
Phenobarbital	D	Neonatal depression, neonatal feeding difficulties, neonatal bleeding, withdrawal symptom.

Antidiabetic Agents

Drugs	FDA Pregnancy Categories	Nature of Effect
Sulfonylurea's (e.g., Chlorpropamide, glyburide, glipizide)	C	May cause prolonged hypoglycemia or hyperinsulinism in the newborn.
Biguanides (e.g., Metformin)	B	
Insulin	B	Does not cross the placenta. Insulin is the drug of choice for the control of diabetes mellitus during pregnancy.

Sex Hormone

Drugs	FDA Pregnancy Categories	Nature of Effect
Diethyl Stilbestrol (DES)	X	DES causes a number of reproductive tract abnormalities in both female and male offspring exposed in utero.
Estradiol	X	Vaginal adenosis Feminization of male fetus hypotrophic testis, abnormal spermatogenesis, epididymal cyst.
Progesterone	X ; B (oral capsules per manufacturer)	It may produces the "VACTERL syndrome" (vertebral, anal, cardiovascular, tracheal, esophageal, renal and limb defects)

Respiratory Drugs

Drugs	FDA Pregnancy Categories	Nature of Effect
Antitussives		
-Codeine	C (D if used for prolonged periods or in high dose at term)	Typical symptoms of narcotic withdrawal were noted in the infants shortly after birth but not in the mother.
-Dextromethorphan	C	Toxicity in the fetus and newborn after the use of dextromethorphan.
Bronchodilators		
-Aminophylline	C	Theophylline is the bronchodilator of choice for asthma and COPD in the pregnant patient but should have theophylline concentration monitored frequently for dosage adjustments.
-Theophylline	C	
-Terbutaline	B_M*	Only rare reports of serious toxicity in the fetus or newborn have appeared.

Antihistamines and Nasal Decongestants

Drugs	FDA Pregnancy Categories	Nature of Effect
Chlorpheniramine Cetirizine Loratadine Diphenhydramine Dimenhydrinate	B B B B B	These agents use during pregnancy has not been associated with an increase risk of fetal malformation.
Pseudoephedrine	C	Some study shown about six major birth defect categories: cardiovascular defects, oral clefts, spina bifida, polydactyly, limb reduction defects and hypospadias.
Tripolidine	C_M*	Cardiovascular, spina bifida, polydactyly and limb reduction defects.

Miscellaneous

Drugs	FDA Pregnancy Categories	Nature of Effect
Smoking	X	Increased Perinatal Risk: Spontaneous abortion, Preterm birth, Intrauterine growth restriction/small for gestation age -100 to 320 g. reduction in expected birthweight. Increased Postnatal Risk: Small head circumference; decreased Auditory, language and cognitive performance; low IQ; increased incidence of asthma, bronchitis, pneumonia; increased risk of sudden infant death syndrome.
Caffeine	Should be avoided	High dose (>7 cups/day); low birth weight (<2500 g.) neurological impairment, growth retardation.
Alcohol	X	Fetal Alcohol Syndrome includes Intrauterine Growth Retardation (IUGR), microcephaly, postnatal growth deficiency, developmental delay, mental retardation and craniofacial anomalies.
Isotretinoin	X	Isotretionin is potent teratogen (e.g., CNS, cardiac anomalies, facial abnormalities, deafness and blindness)
Lithium	D	Neonatal hypotonia, poor sucking power, diminished reflexes for days.
Corticosteroids	C	When appropriate, corticosteroids can be administered by aerosol inhalation or intrasynovial injection to minimize systemic availability. Corticosteroids use during pregnancy may cause an increased risk for maternal gestation diabetes, hypertension, and excessive weight gain.

References

Barbara GW, Joseph TD, Terry LS and Cynthia WH (2000). Pharmacotherapy Handbook. 2nd ed. *Stamford (CT): Appleton & Lange.*

Charles FL, Lora LA, Morton PG and Leonard LL (2000-2001). Drug Information Handbook. 8th ed. *Hudson (OH):Lexi-Comp.*

Gerald GB, Roger KF and Sumner JY (1998). Drugs in Pregnancy and Lactation. 5th ed. *Baltimore (MD): Lippincott Williams & Wilkins.*

Koren G and Pastuszak A (1990). Prevention of unnecessary pregnancy terminations by counseling women on drug, chemical, and radiation exposure during the first trimester. *Teratology* **41:** 657.

Nottarianni LJ (1990). Plasma protein binding of drugs in pregnancy and in neonates. *Clin Pharmacokinet* **18:** 20.

Philip OA and James EK (1997-1998). Handbook of Clinical Drug Data. 8th ed. *Stamford (CT): Appleton & Lange.*

Robert JB (2002). Effects of Certain Prenatal Drugs on the Fetus and Newborn. *Pediatrics* **23(1):** 17-23.

van Lingen RA et al (2002). The effects of analgesia in the vulnerable infant during the perinatal period. *Clin Perinatol* **29:** 511.

CHAPTER

30

Mutagencity

It refers to the formation of long-lasting alterations in the genetic material's informational content.

Types of Mutations

1. **Spontaneous mutations:**

   The sum of everything that might go wrong with DNA during an organism's life cycle is what causes spontaneous mutations, according to science (Glickman et al., 1986). Therefore, all mutagenic and antimutagenic biological mechanisms combine to produce the types and quantities of spontaneous mutations. They are primarily brought on by erroneous nucleotides being incorporated into the developing DNA chain or during DNA replication. The DNA sequence is altered to cause them.

   Example: Sickle cell disease. Because it is easy to possess the sickle cell anaemia gene in regions with a significant prevalence of malaria, it occurs spontaneously and has persisted for new generations.

2. **Induced mutations:**

   These occur as a result of natural processes going wrong, brought on by mutagens, i.e. Through the use of chemical or physical agents and caused by replication mistakes, tautomer shifts, extra - chromosomal predisposing factors, uneven cross-overs, etc.

   Physical mutagens: Radiation, X-rays, Thermal neutrons etc.

   Chemical mutagens: Bromouracil, Nitrous acids and other alkylating agents.

   Example of induced mutation: A mutation in the sex cell genetics. The sex cell genes become mutated when the gonads are exposed to mutagens like radiation.

3. **Point mutation:**

   The entire DNA sequence can be altered by a particular point mutation. The amino acid which the nucleotides encode for can mutate if one of the purines or pyrimidine's is altered. It takes place during replication.

   Example: Hereditary spherocytosis caused by defect in genes essential for proteins in RBC membrane.

4. **Frameshift mutation:**

   The addition or removal of nucleotide bases in amounts which were n't really multiples of 3 is referred to as a frameshift mutation in a gene. Because a gene code consists of triplet codons which code for 20 amino acids to form a protein. If there is a deletion or insertion in a codon, which lead to mismatch of whole gene sequence.

   Example: Cohn's disease- Insertion of cytosine in NOD2 gene which may change the gut bacteria leading to inflammation in the intestine.

Mutagenicity Testing Methods

1. **Ames test:** It is a screening test to determine the level of mutagenicity of particular substance that cause change in structure of DNA. Bacteria like salmonella and E. coli which lack histidine are used to test mutation. Colony formation is the measurement parameter.

2. **Comet assay:** The mass of the big molecule is reduced when the helical structure duplex DNA undergoes strand breakdown, and those strands can be expanded out by electrophoresis. DNA migration is affected by the size and number of DNA's cut ends. While increasing with damage, tail length eventually attains a peak which is determined by the electrophoretic conditions rather than the size of the fragments.

References

https://www.ncbi.nlm.nih.gov/books/NBK560519/

U. Satyanarayana, Biochemistry 3rd edition

Ashutosh kumar, Methods in toxicology and pharmacology

Rang & Dale's Pharmacology Book

Lippincott Illustrated Review: Pharmacology Book.

CHAPTER

Introduction to Toxicology 31

The discipline of toxicology consider the adverse effects of chemicals, including drugs, and other agents, such as biological toxins and radiation, on biological systems. Toxicity associated with drug action can generally be characterized as either an extension of the therapeutic effect, such as the fatal central nervous system (CNS) depression that may follow a barbiturate overdose, or as an effect that is unrelated to the therapeutic effect, such as the liver damage that may result from an acetaminophen overdose. The target organ for the expression of xenobiotic toxicity is not necessarily the tissue or organ in which the drug produces its therapeutic effect, nor is it necessarily the tissue that has the highest concentration of the agent. For example, lead accumulates in bone but produces no toxicity there; certain chlorinated pesticides accumulate in adipose tissue but produce no local adverse effects. Drugs such as acetaminophen cause necrosis in the centrilobular portion of the liver at a site of the monooxygenase enzymes that bioactivate the analgesic. It is necessary to distinguish between the intrinsic toxicity of a chemical and the hazard it poses. While a chemical may have high intrinsic toxicity, it may pose little or no hazard if exposure is low. In contrast, a relatively nontoxic chemical may be quite hazardous if exposure is large or the route of exposure is not physiological.

Manifestations of Toxicity

Organ Toxicity

The events that initiate cell death are not completely understood. The common final stages of necrotic cell death are disruption of normal metabolic processes and ensuing inability to maintain intracellular electrolyte homeostasis. If it is severe or prolonged enough, the cell will not regain normal function. At the same time, other cells show apoptotic cell death, characterized by cell shrinkage, cleavage of DNA between nucleosomes and formation of apoptotic bodies. Some chemicals are metabolized to reactive products that bind to cellular macromolecules. If such binding impairs the function of crucial macromolecules, cell viability is lost. How severely organ function will be impaired depends on the reserve capacity of that organ. The ultimate outcome will depend on the affected organ's regenerative capacity and response to damage. The organ Toxicity is shown in Fig 31-1.

Pulmonary Toxicity

Inhaled gases, solid particles, or liquid aerosols may deposit throughout the respiratory system, depending on their chemical and physical properties. The large surface area of the respiratory passages and alveolar region and the large volume of air delivered to that area (approximately 6–7 L/minute in a young man) provide great opportunity for interaction between inhaled materials and lung damage and those that have entered the body by ingestion, injection, or dermal absorption. Exposure of the lungs to xenobiotics may result in a number of disease conditions including bronchitis, emphysema, asthma, hypersensitivity pneumonitis, pneumoconiosis and cancer. During repair, damaged lung alveolar epithelium may be replaced by fibrous tissue that does not allow for gas exchange, which intensities the damage caused by the initial lesion.

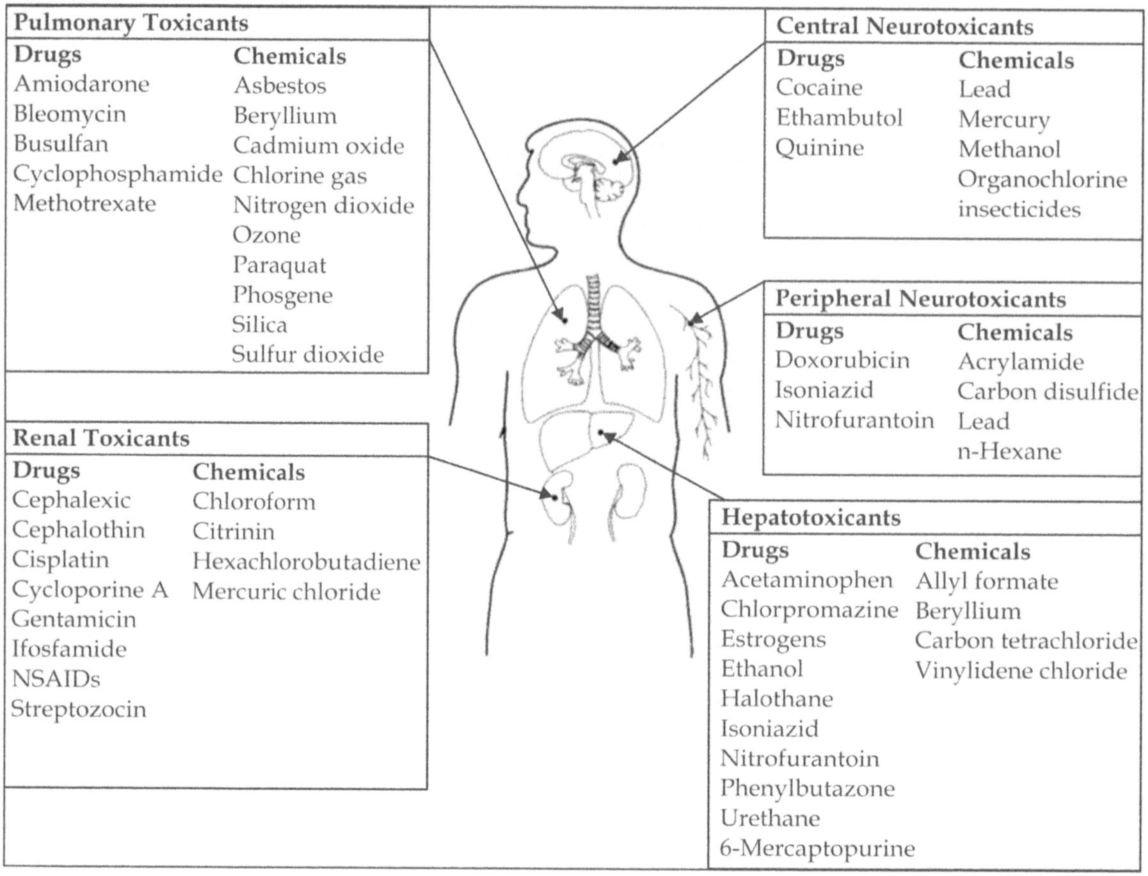

Fig 31-1: Organ toxicity of selected chemicals.

Hepatotoxicity

The blood draining the stomach and small intestine is delivered directly to the liver via the hepatic portal vein, thus exposing the liver to relatively large concentrations of ingested drugs or toxicants. Hepatic exposure to agents that undergo bioactivation to toxic species can be significant. Hepatic necrosis can be classified by the zone of the liver tissue affected. Xenobiotics, such as acetaminophen or chloroform, that undergo bioactivation to toxic intermediates cause necrosis of the cells surrounding the central veins (centrilobular) because the components of the cytochrome P450 system are found in those cells in abundance. At higher doses or in the presence of agents that increase the synthesis of cytochrome P450 (inducers), the area of necrosis may incorporate the tissue. Examples of inhaled xenobiotics that cause midzonal area (midway between the portal triad and central vein). Cells around the portal triad are exposed to the highest concentrations; necrosis occurs with direct-acting agents. A single large dose of a hepatotoxin may cause liver necrosis yet resolve with little or no tissue scarring. Continued exposure to the toxic agent, however, can result in hepatic cirrhosis and permanent scarring. Allergic reactions to drugs produce foci of necrosis that are scattered throughout the liver. Other agents cause severe (chlorpromazine) or mild (estrogens) cholestatic liver damage, including cholestasis and infiammation of the portal triad and hepatocellular necrosis.

Nephrotoxicity

The kidneys are susceptible to toxicity from xenobiotics because they too have a high blood flow. Cells of the tubular nephron face double-sided exposure, to agents in the blood on the basolateral side and in the filtered urine on the luminal side. Proximal tubule cells are generally the site of nephrotoxicity, since these cells have an abundance of cytochrome P450 and can transport organic anions and cations from the blood into the cells, thereby concentrating these chemicals many fold. Chemically induced kidney damage is typically seen as acute tubular necrosis (ATN). The cells in the proximal tubule are affected. Reabsorption of water, electrolytes, glucose and amino acids is impaired. Feedback mechanisms decrease glomerular filtration and thus prevent delivery of large volumes of water to nephrons segments. Urine output may be increased, decreased, or unchanged. Markers of glomerular filtration, blood urea nitrogen (BUN) and creatinine are increased only if filtration falls by 80%. The urine may contain glucose and protein, including proteinaceous casts formed in the nephron of tubular debris.

Neurotoxicity

Although the CNS is protected from a number of xenobiotics by the blood-brain barrier, the barrier is not effective against lipophilic compounds, such as solvents or insecticides. Similarly, the peripheral nervous system is protected by a blood-neural barrier. The barriers are less well developed in the immature nervous system, rendering the fetus and neonate even more susceptible to neurotoxicants. Neural tissue susceptibility is due in large part to its high metabolic rate, high lipid content, and for the CNS, high rate of blood flow. Since damaged neural tissue cannot easily replicate, glial and other nonconducting cells may proliferate and occupy the space of the dead neurons and the damage may be expressed as deficits of sensory and motor functions and behavior. Alternatively, other neurons may take on the functions of the damaged neurons such that there is little or no perceptible damage.

Immunotoxicity

A number of drugs and environmentally and occupationally important chemicals can impair the activity of one or more components of the immune system. Immunodeficiency may result in increased susceptibility to infection, decreased surveillance against precancerous or cancerous cells, or tissue-damaging reactions. Allergic and autoimmune reactions are examples of this form of toxicity. Clinical expressions of cutaneous allergic reactions include eczematous, indurate-infiammatory, and urticarial eruptions. Irritant responses causing direct damage to the skin may be confused with allergic responses involving immune mechanisms. An important difference is that allergic reactions require an initial exposure to sensitize the individual; dermatitis is then elicited by minimal subsequent exposure to the agent.

Toxic Effects on Genetic Material and Cell Replication

Mutagenesis, teratogenesis and carcinogenesis are different manifestations of damage to genetic material (genotoxicity). Chemically induced genotoxicity occurs in several steps and at each step there is opportunity for repair. Generally, xenobiotics are not themselves mutagenic, but rather they must be bioactivated to metabolites that are sufficiently reactive to bind to DNA and disrupt its coding. The reactive intermediates must be formed close enough to the DNA to interact with it before interacting with other less important macromolecules or before being further metabolized to inactive forms. Nongenotoxic carcinogens act by altering cell replication control.

Reproductive Toxicity

Most drugs and chemicals pose a threat to the developing fetus. An estimated 4 to 5% of developmental defects in humans result from prenatal exposure to drugs or environmental chemicals. This is particularly important, since women with irregular menstrual cycles may be exposed to teratogens and enter the sensitive period of organogenesis before pregnancy is suspected. Gestation is generally considered to consist of three periods of development, each with differing sensitivities to chemicals. During the preimplantation or predifferentiation phase, expression of toxicity is an all-or-none phenomenon; damage to the embryo results in either death or no effect. Organogenesis occurs during the embryonic period (the first 3 months of pregnancy) and therefore, susceptibility to teratogenesis is high; the embryo is particularly vulnerable to teratogens on days 25 through 40. The fetal period consists of the last 6 months of gestation and is a time of reduced susceptibility to teratogenic alterations. Certain organs, such as the genitals and the nervous system, however, are still undergoing differentiation during this period. Functional impairment in tissues without marked structural damage and growth retardation is the most common effect of chemical exposure during the fetal period. Chemicals such as 1,2-dibromo-3-chloropropane can disrupt spermatogenesis, leading to impaired reproductive function, including sterility. Men and women undergoing cancer chemotherapy with alkylating drugs are at increased risk for sterility.

Exposure to Nontherapeutic Toxicants

Worldwide production of chemicals has increased dramatically in recent decades, resulting in increased human exposure. This applies not only to workers who manufacture the chemicals and final products but also to those who use the products or are exposed through contamination of surface and ground water and air.

Air Pollution

Industrial activity has polluted the outdoor air with a number of chemicals known to be hazardous to human health. These include a variety of gases, such as carbon monoxide, ozone, and the oxides of sulfur and nitrogen. Unacceptable levels of air pollutants can occur indoors as well. While some of these pollutants may be the same as for the outdoor air, they also include biological agents (e.g., fungal spores, viruses, bacteria, actinomycetes), volatile organic compounds, carbon dioxide and formaldehyde.

Gases

Carbon monoxide arises from the incomplete combustion of organic material. Of principal concern is its generation by the internal combustion engine and by home heating units, particularly in poorly ventilated areas. Carbon monoxide emission by automobiles in closed garages and by unvented space heaters results in numerous deaths each year. Following inhalation, carbon monoxide binds to hemoglobin, displacing oxygen and forming carboxyhemoglobin. This decreases the oxygen-carrying capacity of the blood and impairs the blood cells' ability to release bound oxygen. The resulting hypoxia is the principal mechanism of carbon monoxide toxicity.

Nitrogen oxides, principally nitrogen dioxide, and ozone are classified as oxidizing pollutants. The major source of nitrogen dioxide is the internal combustion engine. Photolysis of nitrogen dioxide by ultraviolet radiation liberates oxygen atoms, which can then combine with molecular oxygen to form ozone. Both gases cause irritation of the deep lung and can result in increased susceptibility to respiratory infection, pulmonary edema and impaired lung function.

Oxides of sulfur (principally sulfur dioxide) are generated during the burning of fossil fuels, most notably coal, and are classified as reducing pollutants because of the types of reactions they undergo. Particulate matter associated with most emissions promotes the conversion of sulfur dioxide to the more toxic sulfuric acid and facilitates deposition in the deep lungs. The acid can cause Bronchospasm and lung damage, including alveolitis. Asthmatic episodes can be exacerbated by sulfur dioxide and sulfuric acid.

Particulates

Industrial processes, such as milling and mining, construction work and the burning of wood or fossil fuel, generate particulates that can be directly toxic or can serve as vectors for the transfer of bound material, such as sulfuric acid, metals and hydrocarbons, into the lungs. Natural products such as pollen, anthrax spores, and animal dander can elicit toxic reactions on inhalation or skin contact. The inhalation of asbestos, silica or coal dust can cause pneumoconiosis, which may develop into serious lung disease. The size of the particle, ventilator rate and depth of breathing will determine the extent of pulmonary deposition.

Food Additives and Contaminants

Thousands of substances are added to foods to enhance their marketability (appearance, taste, texture, etc.), storage properties, or nutritive value, any of which may cause toxicity in susceptible individuals. Microbial or fungal contamination of food, either during processing or storage, can introduce potent toxins into food.

Solvents

Solvents are generally classified as aliphatic or aromatic and either type may be halogenated, most commonly with chlorine.

The toxicity of representative solvents is summarized **in Table 31-1.** Occupational exposure to solvents occurs in cleaning, degreasing, painting and gluing. Exposure to solvents is generally through inhalation of vapors, although direct skin contact also occurs. The concentration of solvent in air is determined by the vapor pressure of the solvent, the ambient temperature and the effectiveness of ventilation systems.

These factors and the rate of pulmonary air exchange will affect the extent of exposure. Sniffing glue fumes is one form of substance abuse. Solvents are generally lipid-soluble and therefore they are readily absorbed across the skin. Once absorbed, they tend to concentrate in the brain and CNS dysfunction is common at high exposures. Symptoms can range from confusion to unconsciousness. Solvents often undergo bioactivation and may cause systemic toxicity as a result of the formation of reactive intermediates.

Table 31-1: Toxicity of selected solvents.

Solvent	Uses	Effect and Mechanism
Aliphatic solvents		
Chloroform	Drug purification	Hepatic centrilobular necrosis, likely from reactive metabolites
Trichloroethylene	Degreasing, dry cleaning	Sensitizes the myocardium to epinephrine, interferes with alcohol metabolism
Methylene chloride	Degreasing, paint stripping, aerosol propellant	Metabolized to CO, resulting in formation of carboxyhemoglobin
Hexane, methyl n-butyl ketone	Wood glue, plastics manufacturing	Polyneuropathy from their metabolite, 2,5-hexanedione
Aromatic solvents		
Benzene	Petroleum product, adhesives and coatings	Leukemia, aplastic anemia, likely from reactive intermediates
Toluene	Adhesives	Cerebellar degeneration with repeated high-dose exposure (glue sniffing)

Insecticides

The prototypical organochlorine insecticide is DDT. It was first used in World War II for vector control of malaria. The organochlorine insecticides are very stable in the environment. This persistence allows toxic concentrations to build up in nontarget organisms. Organophosphate insecticides (e.g., malathion, parathion, diazinon) undergo metabolic activation to yield an oxygenated metabolite that will react with the active site of acetylcholinesterase (AChE), resulting in irreversible enzyme inhibition. Symptoms of poisoning are due to excessive stimulation of cholinergic receptors. In cases of lethal poisoning in humans, death is from respiratory failure. Distal neuropathy of the lower limbs also has been seen. The carbamate insecticides also inhibit AChE. The mechanism of inhibition is similar, but the reaction is reversible.

Herbicides and Rodenticides

Pesticides

Pesticides are chemicals used to eliminate unwanted organisms. Common targets for pesticides include insects, weeds (herbicides), fungi and rodents. Poisoning from pesticides often affects professional exterminators, agricultural workers and consumers

Table 31-2: Toxicity of selected pesticides.

Class and Examples	Effect and Mechanism
Organochlorine insecticides DDT, chlordane, aldrin, heptachlor	Neuronal hyperactivity; convulsions; impaired vision, concentration and memory Altered membrane permeability to Na^+,K^+ Block repolarization by inhibiting Na^+,K^+ -ATPase Block GABA-stimulated chloride uptake
Organophosphate insecticides Bromophos, chlorpyrifos, parathion, malathion, diazinon	Bronchoconstriction and secretion, muscular weakness or paralysis, CNS depression, including respiratory centers Inhibition of acetylcholinesterase (reversible or irreversible)
Carbamate insecticides Carbaryl	Same as organophosphate insecticides Inhibition of acetylcholinesterase (reversible)
Pyrethrin and pyrethroid insecticides Pyrethrin I, II; fenvalerate, permethrin	Neuronal hyperactivity, incoordination, tremors with hyperthermia,seizures Delayed inactivation of channels in excitable tissues, causing repetitive firing and at high doses, depolarization Block GABA-stimulated chloride uptake
Chlorophenoxy herbicides 2,4-D; 2,4,5-T	Muscle weakness, aching and tenderness; hypotonia
Bipyridyl herbicides Paraquat, diquat	Delayed respiratory distress, fibrosis and atelectasis Gastrointestinal, liver and kidney toxicity Formation of reactive oxygen species
Rodenticides Compound 1080, warfarin, strychnine	Block tricarboxylic acid cycle (fluoroacetates) Prevent blood clotting Induce seizures

ATPase, adenosine triphosphatase; GABA, _-aminobutyric acid; 2,4-D, 2,4-dichlorophenoxyacetic acid; 2,4,5-T, 2,4,5-trichlorophenoxyacetic acid.

(Table 31-2). More than half of the poisonings due to agricultural pesticides affect children.

Herbicidal activity generally consists of interference with plant-specific biochemical reactions. Thus, mammalian toxicity is generally low and not predictable from the mechanism of herbicidal action. In contrast, rodenticide target selectivity is not based on differences in biochemistry between humans and rodents but rather on differences in physiology or behavior, especially feeding behavior. For example, an emetic may be included in a rodenticide formulation to promote vomiting in humans who accidentally consume the product; rodents do not have a vomit reflex.

The chlorophenoxy herbicides, 2,4-dichlorophenoxyacetic acid (2,4-D) and 2,4,5-trichlorophenoxyacetic acid (2,4,5-T), were used in defoliating operations in Vietnam and the adverse health effects of the contaminant 2,3,7,8-tetrachlorodibenzodioxin (dioxin) continue to be controversial. The bipyridyl herbicides paraquat and diquat are broad-spectrum herbicides. As little as 10 mL of paraquat concentrate is lethal in adults. Paraquat damages the lungs and may result in the appearance of a respiratory distress syndrome appearing 1 or 2 weeks after poisoning. In contrast, diquat causes minimal lung damage because it does not selectively accumulate in the lung. Acute renal failure, liver toxicity and gastrointestinal damage are sequelae to diquat poisoning. Warfarin, a coumarin anticoagulant, is incorporated into cornmeal for use as a rat poison. Repeated exposure results in sufficient inhibition of prothrombin synthesis to cause fatal internal hemorrhage.

References

Ellenhorn MJ (1997). Ellenhorn's Medical Toxicology: Diagnosis and Treatment of Human Poisoning (2nd ed.). *Baltimore: Williams & Wilkins.*

Gosselin RE, Smith RP and Hodge HC (1984). Clinical Toxicology of Commercial Products (5th ed.). *Baltimore: Williams & Wilkins.*

Haddad LM, Shannon MW and Winchester JF (1998). Clinical Management of Poisoning and Drug Overdose (3rd ed.). *Philadelphia: Saunders.*

Hayes AW (ed.) (2001). Principles and Methods of Toxicology (4th ed.). *Philadelphia: Taylor & Francis.*

Klaassen CD (ed.) (2001). Casarett and Doull's Toxicology, the Basic Science of Poisons (6th ed.). *New York:McGraw Professional.*

CHAPTER

Heavy Metal Intoxication and Chelators

32

Some metals such as iron are essential for life, while others such as lead are present in all organisms but serve no useful biologic purpose. Some of the oldest diseases of humans can be traced to heavy metal poisoning associated with metal mining, refining, and use. Even with the present recognition of the hazards of heavy metals, the incidence of intoxication remains significant and the need for preventive strategies and effective therapy remains high. When intoxication occurs, chelator molecules (from *chela* "claw"), or their *in vivo* biotransformation products, may be used to bind the metal and facilitate its excretion from the body.

Definitions

Metals' originally included only gold, silver, copper, iron, lead, and tin. Metals are dense, malleable, lustrous, conduct heat and electricity, these are cations.

'Metalloids' are elements with features intermediate between metals and non-metals. Example: arsenic

Heavy Metal

A metal having an atomic weight greater than sodium, a density greater than 5 g/cm^3 usually includes lead, cadmium, arsenic and mercury many others may variably be added to list.

Lead

Lead paint

The use of lead in residential paint was banned in 1977. Lead-containing pigments still are used for outdoor paint products because of their bright colors and weather resistant properties. Tetraethyl and tetramethyl lead are still used as additives in gasoline in several countries

Sources of Exposure

Soil and dust

Paint chips

Contaminated water

Parents lead related occupation

Folk remedies

Congenital exposure

Toxicokinetics

Absorption: In Lungs it depends on size of the particles. In GI absoroption in Adults is about 20-30% and in Children as much as 50% of dietary lead. Inadequate intake of iron, calcium and total calories are associated with higher lead levels. In case of Skin Inorganic lead is not absorbed, where as Organic lead is well absorbed.

Distribution: Lead is distributed extensively throughout tissues: bone, teeth, liver, lung, kidney, brain and spleen. It is carried by binding to the RBC. In body lead storage in bones can constitute a source of remobilization and continue toxicity after the exposure to it has ceased. Lead crosses the BBB and concentrates in the gray matter and even it crosses the placenta.

Excretion: Lead is mainly excreted through Kidneys. The excretion increases with increasing body stores (30 mg, 200 mg/day) and it is also excreted in Feces.

Clinical Manifestation

Acute toxicity results in acute encephalopathy, renal failure and severe GI symptoms.

Chronic and Long Term Toxicity: Pathophysiology in chronic toxicity includes that, its affinity for SH groups and is toxic to zinc dependent enzyme systems and inhibits Heme synthesis: hemoglobin, cytochromes, Steroid metabolism and membrane integrity and interference in vitamin D synthesis in renal tubular cells (conversion of 1-hydroxyvitamin D to 1, 25-hydroxy vitamin D)

General Signs and Symptoms of Lead Toxicity

Fatigue, Irritability, Lethargy, Paresthesis, Myalgias, Abdominal pain, Tremor, Headache, Vomiting, Weight loss, Constipation, Loss of libido, Motor neuropathy, Encephalopathy, Cerebral edema, Seizures, Coma, Severe abdominal cramping, Epiphyseal lead lines in children (growth arrest), Renal failure. Table 32-1 shows the signs and symptoms of lead toxocity.

Table 32-1: Range of lead induced health effects in adults and children.

Blood lead levels	Adults	Children
10 µg/dL	Hypertension may occur	Crosses placenta Impairment IQ, growth Partial inhibition of heme synthesis
20 µg/dL	Inhibition of heme synthesis Increased erythrocyte protoporphyrin	Beginning impairment of nerve conduction velocity
30 µg/dL	Systolic hypertension Impaired hearing(↓)	Impaired vitamin D metabolism
40 µg/dL	Infertility in males Renal effects Neuropathy Fatigue, headache, abd pain	Hemoglobin synthesis inhibition
50 µg/dL	Anemia, headache, tremor	Colicky abdomen pain, neuropathy
100 µg/dL	Lethargy, seizures, encephalopathy	Encephalopathy, anemia, nephropathy, seizures

Table 32-2: Class of child based on lead concentration.

Class	Blood Lead Concentrated (µg/dL)	Comment
I	≤ 9	A child in class 1 is not considered to be lead poisoned.
II A	10-14	Many children (or a large proportion of children) with blood lead levels in this range should trigger communitywide childhood lead poisoning prevention activities. Children in this range may need to be rescreened more frequently.
II B	15-19	A child in class IIB should receive nutritional and educational interventions and more frequent screening. If the blood lead level persists in this range, environmental investigation and intervention should be done.
III	20-44	A child in class III should receive environmental evaluation and remediation and a medical evaluation. Such a child may need pharmacologic treatment of lead poisoning.
IV	45-69	A child in class IV needs both medical and environmental interventions, including chelation therapy.
V	≥70	A child with class V lead poisoning poses a medical emergency. Medical and environmental management must begin immediately.

Childhood Lead Poisoning

Childhood lead poisoning (Table 32-2) is now defined as a blood lead level of 10 mg/dl.

The average lead level of American children is 2 mg/dl and 8.9% of American children have lead poisoning. Lead intoxication is more prevalent in minority groups and among those living in the northeast.

Neurotoxicity of Lead in Childhood

Severe lead intoxication causes mental retardation and decreases 5 points in IQ for every 10 mg/dl increase in blood lead level population.

Other adverse developmental outcomes are: Aggression, Hyperactivity, Antisocial behaviors, Learning disability, impairment in memory, auditory processing and visual motor integration. These effects has been demonstrated with blood lead levels as **low as 6 mg/dl**

Diagnosis

Evaluation of clinical symptoms and signs

CBC

Serum iron levels, TIBC, ferritin

Abdominal radiographs (for recent ingestion of lead-containing material)

Whole blood lead level

X-ray fluorescence (XRF) to asses body burden.

Treatment

Environmental inspection/hazard reduction

Nutritional supplementation

Chelation therapy

Nutritional Supplementation

Iron supplementation

Calcium supplementation - calcium rich foods

Phosphorus supplementation

Frequent food consumption regular meals + snacks

Chelation Therapy

BLL > 70 mg/dl or encephalopathy

Hospital admission

Administration of a parenteral chelator

BLL > 45 mg/dl oral chelator

BLL 25-45 mg/dl if these levels persist despite environmental intervention

Arsenic

Sources

Groundwater, Arsenic containing mineral ores, Industrial processes Semiconductor manufacturing (gallium arsenide), Fossil fuels, Wood treated with arsenic preservatives, Metallurgy, Smelting (copper, zinc, lead) and refining of metals and ores, Glass manufacturing.

Commercial products: Wood preservatives, Pesticides, Herbicides, Fungicides

Food: Seafood and fish

Others: Antiparasitic drugs, Folk remedies

Toxicokinetics

$T_{1/2}$ of inorganic arsenic in the blood is 10 hr and of organic arsenic is around 30 hours. 24 weeks after the exposure ceases, most of the remaining arsenic in the body is found in keratin rich tissues (nails, hair, skin). Inorganic arsenic is converted to organic arsenic (biomethylation to monomethyl arsonic- MMA or DMA) in the liver. This may represent a process of detoxification. Renally excreted (30-50% of inorganic arsenic is excreted in about 3 days). Both forms are excreted depend on the acuteness of the exposure and dose. Toxicokinetics are shown in Table 32-3.

Pathophysiology

Trivalent forms bind to Sulfhydryl groups leading to inhibition of enzymatic systems which inhibits the Krebs cycle and oxidative phosphorylation. These lead to inhibition of ATP production. The pentavalent forms can replace the stable phosphate ester bond in ATP and produce an arsenic ester stable bond which is not a high energy bond. This leads to endothelial damage, loss of capillary integrity, capillary leakage, volume loss, shock.

Table 32-3: Manifestations of acute arsenic poisoning.

Bodily system affected	Symptoms or signs	Time of onset
Systemic	Thirst Hypovolemia, Hypotension	Minutes Minutes to hours
Gastrointestinal	Garlic or metallic taste Burning mucosa Nausea and vomiting Diarrhea Abdominal pain Hematemesis Hematochezia, melena Rice water stools	Immediate Immediate Minutes Minutes to hours Minutes to hours Minutes to hours Hours Hours
Hematopoietic system	Hemolysis Hematuria Lymphopenia Pancytopenia	Minutes to hours Minutes to hours Several weeks Several weeks
Pulmonary (primarily in inhalational exposures)	Cough Dyspnea Chest Pain Pulmonary edema	Immediate Minutes to hours Minutes to hours Minutes to hours
Liver	Jaundice Fatty degeneration Central necrosis	Days Days Days
Kidneys	Proteinuria Hematuria Acute renal failure	Hours to days Hours to days Hours to days

Biological Monitoring

Urinary arsenic measurement

Spot sample (mcg/L)

Timed urine collection (mcg/24 hours)

Normal values

Spot urine= ~10 mcg/L (10-150 mcg/L)

24 hours urine collection=<25 mcg/24 hours

Whole blood= <1mcg/L (usually is elevated in acute intoxication)

Ingestion of seafood may elevate urinary arsenic levels if urinary arsenic levels are high ask the patient whether the ingested seafood in the last 72 hours. Speciation can be performed in several laboratories by determining methylated derivatives in the urine. These levels are not influenced by the presence of organic arsenic from marine origin.

Treatment of acute poisoning

Gastric lavage

Activated charcoal does not bind well to inorganic arsenic

Whole bowel irrigation with polyethylene glycol

Skin decontamination in dermal exposure

Supportive care

Chelation therapy should be instituted promptly (minutes to hours) with BAL (British anti-Lewisite)- IM, Succimer (DMSA)- PO, DMPS - PO, IV, D-Penicillamine is less effective

Cadmium

A metal most often encountered in earth's crust combined with chlorine (cadmium chloride), oxygen (cadmium oxide), or sulfur (cadmium sulfide). It exists as small particles in air, result of smelting, soldering or other high temp industrial processes. It is obtained as byproduct by smelting of zinc, lead, copper ores. Used mainly in metal plating, producing pigments, batteries, plastics and as a neutron absorbent in nuclear reactors. Cadmium is a byproduct of smelters.

Exposure Sources – Tobacco

Tobacco smoke (a one pack a day smoker absorbs roughly 5 to 10 times the amount absorbed from the average daily diet). Through Food (only a small amount is absorbed). Itai Itai disease (cadmium contamination + diet low in calcium & vitamin D). Cadmium a component of chuifong tokwan, sold illegally as a miracle herb.

Biologic Fate

Cadmium has no known beneficial function in the human body. It is transported in the blood by binding to metallothionein. Greatest concentrations found in kidneys & liver. Urinary excretion is slow. Biologic half-life may be up to 30 yr.

Cadmium a Health Hazard

Mainly affects lungs and kidneys, secondary effects are shown on skeletal system. It binds to Sulfhydryl groups, displacing other metals from metalloenzymes, by disrupting those enzymes competes with calcium for binding sites on regulatory proteins.

Lipid peroxidation has been demonstrated.

Respiratory Effects

Acute inhalation may mimic metal fume fever, Fever, chills & decreases in FVC and FEV1. Initial symptoms: flu like symptoms, later: chest pain, cough, dyspnea. Bronchospasm and hemoptysis may occur rarely. Chronic inhalation may result in impairment of pulmonary function with reduction in ventilatory capacity.

Renal Effects

May cause tubular and glomerular damage with resultant proteinuria

May follow chronic inhalation or ingestion

Latency period is of ~10 yr

Nephropathy is progressive & irreversible.

Chronic exposure causes progressive renal tubular dysfunction. Toxic effects are dose related.

Critical renal concentration decrease GFR, causes chronic renal failure and kidney stones are more common.

Skeletal Effects

Bone lesions occur late in severe chronic poisoning, Pseudo fractures may also occur. Other effects like Osteomalacia and osteoporosis may appear to be secondary to increased urinary calcium and phosphorus losses.

Signs and Symptoms

Acute toxicity

Food poisoning (ingestion)

Bronchitis (inhalation)

Interstitial pneumonitis (inhalation)

Pulmonary edema (inhalation)

A condition that mimics metal fume fever

Chronic toxicity

Chronic exposure may result in renal dysfunction and bone disease.

Mild anemia, anosmia and yellow discoloration of the teeth may occur.

Evaluation

Inhalation

Chest radiograph

Chronic exposure

Renal tests

Serum electrolytes, BUN, serum and urinary creatinine, serum creatinine, cadmium in blood and urine and urinary protein are estimated.

Direct Biologic Indicators

24 hour urine cadmium – reflects exposure over time an total body burden

Blood cadmium

Cadmium in hair – not reliable.

Indirect Biologic Indicators

Urinary β_2-microglobulin – evaluate urine levels > 300 mg/g creatinine

Urinary RBP

Urinary metallothionein (MT)

Treatment and Management

Acute Exposure

No proven treatment. Supportive treatment includes fluid replacement, oxygen and mechanical ventilation. With ingestion, gastric decontamination by emesis or gastric lavage soon after exposure. Activated charcoal not proven effective.

Chronic - Prevent further exposure

Mercury

Occurs in three forms (elemental, inorganic salts, and organic compounds)

Contamination results from mining, smelting and industrial discharges. Mercury in water can be converted by bacteria to organic mercury (more toxic) in fish. It can also be found in thermometers, dental amalgams, fluorescent light bulbs, disc batteries, electrical switches, folk remedies, chemistry sets and vaccines.

Exposure

Elemental Mercury

It is liquid at room temperature that volatizes readily and has rapid distribution in body by vapor, poor in GI tract.

Inorganic Mercury

It is poorly absorbed in GI tract, but can be caustic and dermal exposure has resulted in toxicity.

Organic Mercury

It is lipid soluble and well absorbed via GI, lungs and skin and can cross placenta and into breast milk.

Elemental Mercury

At high concentrations, vapor inhalation produces acute necrotizing bronchitis, pneumonitis and death.

Long term exposure affects CNS.

Early: insomnia, forgetfulness, anorexia, mild tremor

Late: progressive tremor and erythrism (red palms, emotional lability and memory impairment)

Salivation, excessive sweating, renal toxicity (proteinuria, or nephrotic syndrome)

Dental amalgams do not pose a health risk.

Inorganic Mercury

Gastrointestinal ulceration or perforation and hemorrhage are rapidly produced, followed by circulatory collapse. Breakdown of mucosal barriers leads to increased absorption and distribution to kidneys (proximal tubular necrosis and anuria). Acrodynia (Pink disease) usually from dermal exposure.

Maculopapular rash, swollen and painful extremities, peripheral neuropathy, hypertension and renal tubular dysfunction are seen.

Organic Mercury

Toxicity occurs with long term exposure and effects the CNS.

Signs progress from paresthesias to ataxia, followed by generalized weakness, visual and hearing impairment, tremor and muscle spasticity, and then coma and death.

Teratogen with large chronic exposure.

Asymptomatic mothers with severely affected infants.

Infants appeared normal at birth, but psychomotor retardation, blindness, deafness, and seizures developed over time.

Diagnosis and Treatment

Diagnosis made by history and physical and lab analysis. Inorganic mercury can be measured in 24 hour urine collection; organic mercury is measured in whole blood. The most important and effective treatment is to identify the source and end the exposure. Chelating agents (DMSA) may enhance inorganic mercury elimination. Dimercaprol may increase mercury concentration in the brain.

Chelating Agents

Introduction

An ideal chelator should have high solubility in water, resistance to biotransformation, ability to reach the sites of metal storage, retain chelating ability at the pH of body fluids and the property of forming metal complexes that are less toxic than the free metal ion.

Characteristics of an Ideal Chelator

- Greater Affinity, Low toxicity
- Ability to compete with natural chelators
- Ability to penetrate cell membranes
- Rapid elimination of the toxic metal
- High water solubility
- Capacity to form non toxic complexes
- Same distribution as the metal

During Second World War, dimercaprol (also named British Anti-Lewisite or BAL), an organic dithiol compound, was developed as an experimental antidote against the arsenic-based poison gas Lewisite. After World War II, mass lead poisoning was observed in large number of navy personnel, later identified as a result of their jobs repainting the hulls of ships. This introduced the medical use of EDTA as a lead chelating agent. BAL has dominated medical prescriptions for general metal intoxication due to its high efficacy for human arsenic and mercury poisoning. In the 1960s, BAL was modified into meso 2,3-dimercaptosuccinic acid (DMSA), a related dithiol with far fewer side effects. Another dithiol, sodium 2,3-dimercaptopropane 1,sulfonate (DMPS), was introduced as a mercury chelating agent by researchers in the former Soviet Union. Chelation therapy has historically been used in attempts to reduce the body burden of toxic metals in highly symptomatic patients with elevated biological markers. Chelating agents can affect metal toxicity by mobilizing the toxic metal mainly into urine. A chelating agent forming a stable complex with a toxic metal may shield biological targets from the metal ion, thereby reducing the local toxicity. Desferrioxamine (DFOA), an iron chelator, completely covers the surface of Fe^{3+} during complex formation, thereby preventing iron catalyzed free radical reactions. However, sometimes a chelator may expose the metal to the biological environment and thus increase the toxicity of the metal. Ethylenediamine tetraacetic acid (EDTA) is not able to shield the surface of the Fe^{3+} ion, but forms an open complex (basket complex), thereby increasing the catalytic capacity of Fe^{3+} for generating oxidative stress. Preferred ligands for soft and borderline ions such as Pb^{2+}, Hg^{2+}, Cd^{2+} and As^{3+} are thiolates and amines. Consequently, known metal-binding sites in most cases contain Cys or His residues. Many of these sites consist of contiguous short stretches of amino acid sequences that overlap between neighboring peptides with binding activity which are used to tentatively determine major binding motifs. The majority of proteins and peptides that function in the uptake, distribution, storage or detoxification of essential and non-essential metal ions possess one or several metal-binding sites. The -Cys-X-X-Cys- and -Cys-Cys- motifs of various proteins are well known for their heavy metal binding properties. It has long been acknowledged that sulfhydryl-containing compounds have the ability to chelate metals. The sulfur-containing amino acids methionine and cysteine, N-acetylcysteine, an acetylated analogue of cysteine, the methionine metabolite S-adenosylmethionine, α-lipoic acid, and the tripeptide glutathione (GSH) all contribute to the chelation and excretion of metals from the human body.

Common Chelating Agents: Pharmacology and Toxicology

Calcium Disodium Ethylenediamine Tetraacetic Acid ($CaNa_2EDTA$)

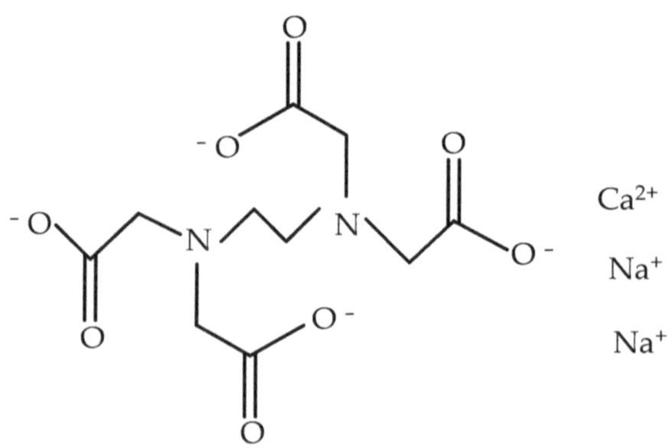

Fig 32-1: Structure of calcium disodium ethylenediamine tetraacetic acid.

Calcium disodium ethylenediamine tetraacetic acid ($CaNa_2EDTA$) Fig 32-1 is the most commonly used chelating agent. It is a derivative of ethylenediamine tetraacetic acid (EDTA); a synthetic polyamino-polycarboxylic acid and since 1950s has been one of the mainstays for the treatment of childhood lead poisoning. The drug has been claimed beneficial in vascular disease since 1955. It is believed that chelation therapy may alter plaque morphology and volume, or improve endothelial function, and suggest that it might replace coronary artery bypass draft surgery. Several theories have been proposed to support latter mainly focusing on calcium chelation. EDTA is said to work in vascular conditions either by removing calcium found in fatty plaques either directly via chelation effect or alternately by stimulating release of hormones that in turn cause calcium removal or lower cholesterol levels. Another theory suggests that EDTA therapy may reduce the oxidative stress injury and inflammation in blood vessel walls. Although a number of trials conducted indicate the utility of $CaNa_2EDTA$ in coronary heart disease, the evidence in the absence of the controlled trial is not as convincing. In view of reports where symptomatic improvements have been comparable with placebo effects and the risks associated with the therapy, it has been facing criticism. The American Heart Association has stated that "there have been no adequate, controlled, published scientific studies using currently approved scientific methodology to support this therapy for coronary heart disease. Using this form of unproven treatment for coronary heart disease may deprive patients of the well established benefits from the many other valuable methods of treating these diseases" for the program to assess alternative treatment strategies to achieve cardiac health (PATCH) investigators also concluded after a randomized control trial with 84 patients that there is no evidence to support a beneficial effect of calcium chelation therapy with EDTA in patients with ischemic heart disease, stable angina and a positive treadmill test for ischemia. Another sub-study under PATCH rejects the proposed benefits of EDTA in combination with vitamins to improve impaired endothelium-dependent brachial artery flow-mediated vasodilation in patients with coronary artery disease. But recently all randomized clinical trials have been underpowered and the NCCAM and the National Heart, Lung, and Blood Institute launched the Trial to Assess Chelation Therapy (TACT). TACT is the first largest, multicenter study to assess safety and efficacy of EDTA chelation therapy for patients with coronary artery disease. This placebo controlled, double-blind trial has started recruiting participants, aiming at 2,372 sample size, aged 50 years with prior myocardial infarction to test whether EDTA chelation therapy, high dose vitamin therapy, or both are effective in secondary prevention. The study started in 2003 and was expected to complete in 5 years.

$CaNa_2EDTA$ can be valuable for the treatment of poisoning by metals that have higher affinity for chelating agent than does Ca^{2+}. The successful use of $CaNa_2EDTA$ in the treatment of lead poisoning is due, in part, to the capacity of lead to displace calcium from the chelate. Initially EDTA was introduced as its sodium salt (NaEDTA) which when administered *in vivo* resulted in the urinary excretion of calcium leading to hypocalcaemia with the risk of tetany due to the formation of its calcium complex. To overcome this hazard, $CaNa_2EDTA$ was introduced for the treatment of lead poisoning. The Pb-EDTA complex has high stability constant thus $CaNa_2EDTA$ was found to chelate lead from the body fluids, excreting $PbNa_2EDTA$ leaving Ca behind.

Pharmacological Profile

$CaNa_2EDTA$ is poorly absorbed in the gastrointestinal tract (<5%) thus can only be administered by parenteral route. Intravenous administration of this drug results in good absorption but is very painful at the injection site. Hence intravenous injection could be given either by diluting in 5% dextrose or saline (i.v infusion). $CaNa_2EDTA$ is distributed mainly in the extracellular fluids, which limits its capacity to chelate out metals from inside the cells. The latter also contributes to one of its major drawbacks that of redistributing lead from other tissues to the brain. Reporting the same, recommended avoiding the use of $CaNa_2EDTA$ for lead mobilization tests in children. It was suggested that $CaNa_2EDTA$ when administered in animals chronically exposed to lead, mobilizes the metal deposited in hard tissue for chelation. This then allows mobilized circulating lead to redistribute in soft tissues like the brain and liver in order to achieve equilibrium. $CaNa_2EDTA$ is not significantly metabolized and is excreted rapidly by glomerular filtration, entirely unchanged in urine, 50% of which appears within one hour. The drug shows an elimination half life of 1.4 to 3 hours in adult and is entirely excreted within 24 hours. The risks associated with $CaNa_2EDTA$ therapy are substantial, including renal failures, arrhythmias, tetany, hypocalcaemia, hypotension, bone marrow depression, prolonged bleeding time, convulsions, respiratory arrest, etc. Although the nephrotoxicity by $CaNa_2EDTA$ is dose dependent and reversible after cessation of therapy yet exceeding maximal daily dose of 75 mg/kg could be fatal. However, there also are reports that highlight the efficacy of EDTA in chronic renal artery diseases. Other adverse effects may include fatigue, headache, fever, nasal congestion, lacrimation, mucocutaneous lesions, glycosuria, myalgia, hepatotoxicity, increased urinary frequency, hypotension, abnormal changes in ECG and gastrointestinal symptoms. Prolonged treatment with $CaNa_2EDTA$ results in depletion of essential metal, especially Zn, Cu and Mn. It has been reported that zinc supplementation during and after chelation is also beneficial. Although zinc depletion by $CaNa_2EDTA$ therapy is rapidly reversible by zinc supplementation, it is considered to be key mechanism for teratogenic effects of the drug, especially when administered between days 11 to 14 at doses comparable to humans. This allows the use of EDTA as a research tool to study mechanisms and role of zinc dependent molecules at critical periods of pregnancy. $CaNa_2EDTA$ has the LD_{50} value of 16.4 mmol/kg in mouse. The drug is contraindicated in pregnancy, active renal diseases or anuria, hepatitis, and hypersensitivity to edentate products.

Calcium Trisodium DTPA

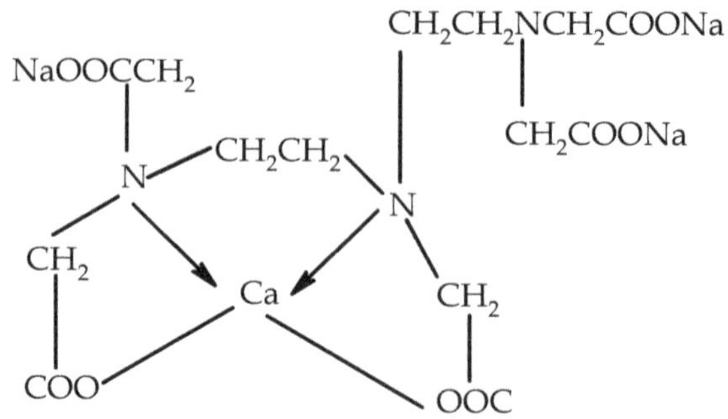

Fig 32-2: Structure of calcium trisodium DTPA.

Calcium or zinc trisodium diethylenetriamine-pentaacetate ($CaNa_3DTPA$ or $ZnNa_3DTPA$ respectively) Fig 32-2 have been used against plutonium and other transuranic elements like californium, americium and curium. The drug is effective against cobalt and zinc poisoning in experimental models. Its efficacy against acute cadmium poisoning is promising however is less effective as compare to carbodithioates .

Pharmacological Profile

Like $CaNa_2EDTA$, $CaNa_3DTPA/ZaNa_3DTPA$ is poorly absorbed in the gastrointestinal tract, and thus they are parenterally administered and are distributed extracellularly. They may be administered by intravenous or intramuscular routes or by inhalation through a nebulizer, where the former are painful. $CaNa_3DTPA$ shows an expected disadvantage of depleting Zn from the system that may be overcome by supplementation or using the zinc salt of the drug. Despite this disadvantage, although $CaNa_3DTPA$ is still preferred over the Zn form due to its higher efficacy, it is not recommended for prolonged therapy. Although $CaNa_3DTPA$ is well tolerated, some adverse effects may be observed, including nausea, vomiting, diarrhea, chills, fever and muscle cramps during the first 24 hr. $CaNa_3DTPA$ is teratogenic like $CaNa_2EDTA$ due to its Zn and Mn depletion effect that is confirmed by the teratogenic effects of $ZnNa_3DTPA$ at a dose 16 times lower than $CaNa_3DTPA$. Thus, although the drug is contraindicated during pregnancy $ZnNa_3DTPA$ may be carefully administered if unavoidable. Other contraindications include prescription to children, in patients with renal insufficiency and bone marrow depression.

D-Penicillamine

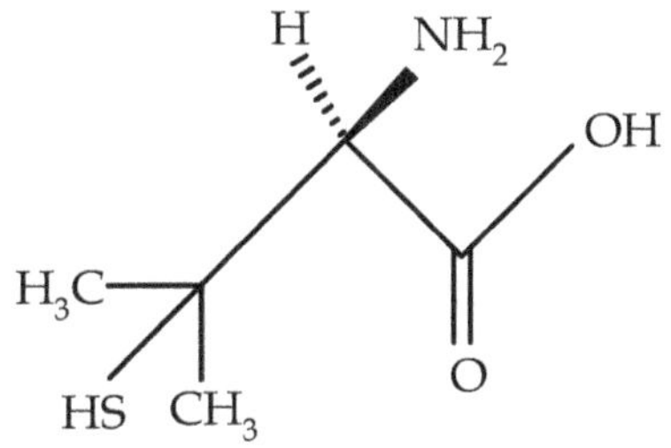

Fig 32-3: Structure of D-Penicillamine.

D-Penicillamine (DPA; β-β-dimethylcysteine or 3-mercapto-D-valine) (Fig 32-3) is a sulfhydryl containing amino acid and a degradation product of penicillin. Only the D isomer is used because the L isomer causes optic neuritis. DPA is used mainly as a chelating agent in heavy metal toxicity viz. lead, mercury and copper poisoning (Wilson's disease).

Pharmacological Profile

DPA is well absorbed via the gastrointestinal tract and can be administered orally or by i.v route. It is approximately 50% absorbed orally and mainly follows extracellular distribution. Peak plasma concentration is reached between 1 and 4 hours after oral administration. A minimal drug fraction under goes hepatic metabolism to disulfides, and most of the drug is excreted unchanged in urine. Elimination half life ranges from 1 to more than 7 hours. Although low adverse reactions have been reported, some serious ones including thrombocytopenia and leukocytopenia (incidence 5–15%), and rarely aplastic anemia may occur. Prolonged DPA treatment may lead to anorexia, nausea and vomiting. The ulcerogenic activity of DPA in rats, which may involve the stimulation of histaminergic (H_1 and H_2) receptors, has been reported. Other toxic effects of DPA include gastrointestinal disturbances (10–30%), changes/loss of taste (5–30%), hair loss (1–2%), and partly proteinuria (5–20%). Severe adverse effects are autoimmune phenomena such as pemphigus, DPA-induced lupus erythematosus, polymyositis/dermatomyositis, membranous glomerulopathy and hypersensitivity pneumonitis. DPA is a well recognized teratogen and lathyrogen that causes skeletal, cutaneous and pulmonary abnormalities. The most important contraindication is in patients allergic to penicillin and in cases of renal insufficiency. Co administration of DPA to patients receiving gold therapy, antimalarial or cytotoxic drugs, phenyl-butazone, or oxyphenbutazone must be contraindicated since it can result in more serious adverse reactions.

British Anti Lewisite (BAL)

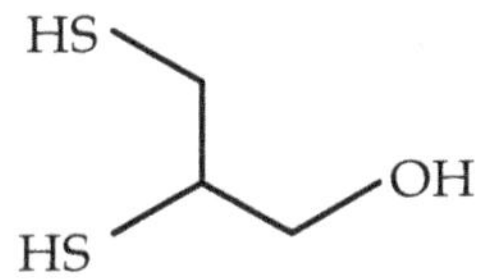

Fig 32-4: Structure of dimercaprol.

2,3-Dimercaprol (BAL) (Fig 32-4) is a traditional chelating agent developed by British biochemists at Oxford University during World War II. BAL has a 3 carbon backbone with two sulfhydryl (–SH) groups and a hydroxyl group. It has been used clinically since 1949 in arsenic, cadmium and mercury poisoning. It is an oily, clear, colorless liquid with a pungent, unpleasant typical mercaptan smell. It detoxifies lewisite by forming a five membered stable complex with arsenic. In humans and experimental models, the antidotal efficacy of BAL has been shown to be most effective when administered immediately after the exposure. Besides rapid mobilization of arsenic and mercury from the body, it causes a significant increase in brain deposition of arsenic and mercury compounds.

Pharmacological Profile

Due to its oily nature, the drug is not absorbed orally and administration of BAL requires deep intra-muscular injection that is extremely painful and allergenic. It was found to mobilize and relocate lead to the brain, increasing its neurotoxic effects. Although treatment with dimercaprol increases the excretion of cadmium, there is a concomitant increase in renal cadmium concentration, so its use should be avoided in cases of cadmium toxicity. The drug has a short half life. Thus, the major drawbacks of BAL include:

1. Low therapeutic index (small margin of safety)
2. Tendency to redistribute arsenic to brain and testes
3. Need for (painful) intramuscular injection
4. Unpleasant odor (rotten eggs)

Other common adverse effects include fever, conjunctivitis (eye inflammation), lacrimation (tearing), constricted feeling (chest, limbs, jaw, abdomen), headache, paresthesias (tingling sensation), tremor, nausea and pain at the injection site. More serious complications may be infections (abscesses) at the injection site, liver damage, elevated blood pressure and heart rate, and hemolysis (destruction of red blood cells) in patients with glucose-6-phophate deficiency (G6PD)

Meso-2,3-Dimercaptosuccinic Acid (DMSA)

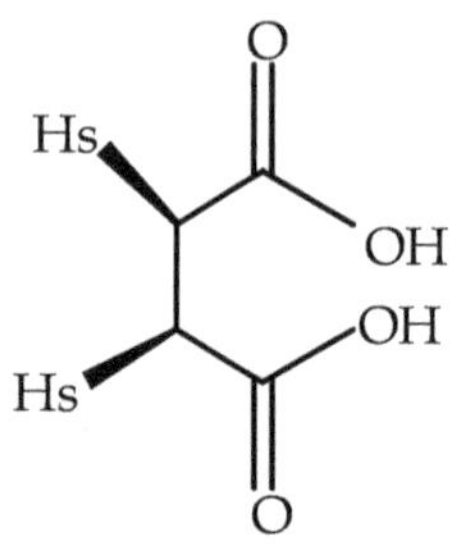

Fig 32-5: Structure of meso-2,3-dimercaptosuccinic acid.

A chemical derivative of dimercaprol which has gained more and more attention, is meso-2,3-dimercaptosuccinic acid (DMSA) (Fig 32-5). DMSA is a dithiol compound (containing two sulfhydryl, or –SH, groups) and an analogue of dimercaprol (BAL). It was 40 years ago when initial studies identified DMSA as an effective antidote to heavy metal poisoning. Subsequently DMSA was studied for more than twenty years in the People's Republic of China, Japan and Russia before scientists in Europe and the United States "discovered" the substance and its potential usefulness in the mid-1970s.

Pharmacological Profile

The hydrophilic nature of DMSA causes considerable absorption in gastro intestinal tract thus possible oral route of administration creates its distinct advantage over BAL. The drug is 95% plasma protein bound, most likely by virtue of binding on one of its sulfhydryl groups to a cysteine residue on albumin, leaving the other –SH available to chelate metals. DMSA has a large therapeutic window and is the least toxic amongst the dithiol compounds. No significant loss of essential metals like zinc, iron, calcium and magnesium are observed. However, metabolism of copper may be altered in humans after administration of DMSA. A major drawback associated with DMSA is its extracellular distribution, since it is unable to cross the cell membrane. Adverse reaction of DMSA includes gastrointestinal discomfort, skin reaction, mild neutropenia and elevated liver enzymes. The LD_{50} value of sodium salt of DMSA is about 3% greater than that of DMPS, in mice it is: 2.4 for i.v., 3.8 for i.m., 4.4 for i.p., and 8.5 gm/kg for oral route.

Numerous animal and human studies have shown that DMSA administration increases urinary mercury excretion and reduces blood and tissue mercury concentration. Chelation therapy with DMSA must be initiated shortly after exposure to prevent accumulation and avoid toxicity. Studies in animal models have shown that neither DMSA nor any other chelating or mobilizing agents were able to ameliorate the brain burden of mercury. The treatment with DMSA after exposure to inorganic mercury caused an increased elevation of mercury into motor axons presumably owing to redistribution of mercury, which was mobilized from non neural tissues (e.g., kidneys and liver).

Sodium 2,3 Dimercaptopropane-l-Sulphonate (DMPS)

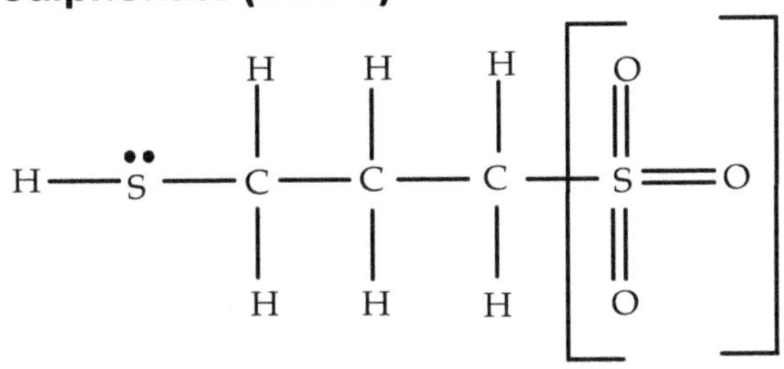

Fig 32-6: Structure of sodium 2,3 dimercaptopropane-l-sulphonate.

Sodium 2,3-dimercaptopropane sulfonate (DMPS) (Fig 32-6) is another analogue of BAL. DMPS is not considered as an appropriate drug against lead toxicity. A pilot study of DMPS in lead poisoned children by Gersl and co-workers indicates less efficiency than $CaNa_2EDTA$ and DMSA. DMPS, although known for its antidotal efficacy against mercury, it has also been reported to have limited efficacy for treating lead and arsenic poisoning. The drug is registered in Germany for treatment of mercury intoxication, but it is not approved in the United States, so unless special permission is given by the U.S. Food and Drug Administration, it is unlawful for physicians to use it in the United States, nor is it lawful for pharmacies to compound it. Still, DMPS is being illegally used by members of the alternative health industry to treat people allegedly suffering from mercury intoxication, most often claimed to be due to amalgam dental fillings.

Pharmacological Profile

DMPS, being hydrophilic in nature, is mainly distributed in the extracellular space but may enter cells by specific transport mechanisms. Thus, DMPS is known to be distributed both in the extracellular and to small extent in intracellular spaces. DMPS appears to be bio transformed in humans to acyclic and cyclic disulphides. The drug and its metabolites are rapidly eliminated from the body through the kidneys. It is important to note that this drug does not redistribute arsenic, lead, or inorganic mercury to the brain. No major adverse effects following DMPS administration in humans or animals have been reported. Adverse reactions during treatment with DMPS include gastrointestinal discomfort, skin reactions, mild neutropenia and elevated liver enzymes. Some patients, especially those with allergic asthma symptoms, may develop hypersensitivity to DMPS. Further, oral administration of DMPS did not adversely affects late gestation, parturition or lactation in mature mice and fetal and neonatal development do not appear to be adversely affected.

New DMSA Analogues

The known chelating agent DMSA has been found to have fewer side effects with greater efficacy. The heavy metal chelating property of DMSA is due to the presence of vicinal dithiol groups that may also act as an oxygen radical scavenger and thus inhibit lipid peroxidation, giving an added advantage of fighting heavy metal induced oxidative stress. However, its hydrophilic properties do not allow it to cross the cell membrane. It was recently observed that esters of DMSA might be more effective antidotes for heavy metal toxicity. A large number of esters of DMSA have been synthesized aiming to for achieve optimal chelation and transport effects, compared to DMSA. These esters are mainly the mono and diesters of DMSA that have been studied experimentally with the aim of enhancing tissue uptake of chelating agents. In order to make the compounds more lipophilic, the carbon chain length of the parent DMSA was increased by controlled esterification with the corresponding alcohol (methyl, ethyl, propyl, isopropyl, butyl, isobutyl, pentyl, isopentyl and hexyl). It has also been reported that these mono and diesters have a better potential in mobilizing heavy metal from the tissues in mice. The effects of seven different monoalkyl esters of DMSA on the mobilization of lead in mice and observed that after a single parenteral dose of the chelator DMSA there was a 52% reduction in the lead concentrations while with the monoesters the reduction varied from 54% to 75%. In most of these published reports, it has been observed that the analogues of DMSA were capable of crossing the biomembranes and were more effective in reducing arsenic burden in acute and sub chronic intoxication. These studies have also suggested that the monoesters may be preferred over DMSA diesters owing to their higher efficacy against arsenic intoxication and lower toxicity.

Monoisoamyl DMSA (MiADMSA)

Monoisoamyl DMSA was synthesized by controlled esterification of DMSA with isoamyl alcohol. Controlled esterification made MiADMSA, a C5 branched chain alkyl monoester of DMSA which was lipophilic in nature as compared to the parent DMSA. Chelation studies with MiADMSA found it to be highly effective in reducing heavy metal burden from various organs in heavy metal exposed animals.

Pharmacological Profile

MiADMSA is a potential drug candidate that is still in its developmental phase thus, its entire pharmacological profile has not been established yet. However, studies to date highlight the efficacy and safety of the new molecule in lead and arsenic acute and chronic toxicity in experimental animals. Results suggest that MiADMSA administration increases the activity of ALAD, a specific lead toxicity biomarker in all the age groups and increased blood GSH levels in young rats. MiADMSA was also found to potentiate the synthesis of MT in liver and kidneys and GSH levels in liver and brain, along with significantly reducing the GSSG levels in tissues. MiADMSA is capable of mobilizing intracellularly bound cadmium and is seen to provide antioxidant functions by removing cadmium from the site of deleterious oxidation reactions. The reduced sulfhydryl groups in this compound may also participate in antioxidant reactions and possibly retard propagation of oxidative damage induced by cadmium. Recently Flora and Mehta suggested reversal of arsenic induced dysfunctioning with concomitant treatment of MiADMSA *in vitro* and *in vivo*. Employing IR spectroscopy they suggested that MiADMSA binds to arsenic to form an adduct which prevents arsenic from exerting its toxic effect in both models. Mehta and Flora, reported for the first time the comparison of the role in metal redistribution of different chelating agents (three amino and four thiol chelators) on hepatotoxicity and oxidative stress in chelating agent-induced metallothionein in rats. The interaction of MiADMSA and DMSA with essential metals is same. MiADMSA was found to be safe in adult rats followed by young and old rats. Our group reported for the first time the toxicological data of MiADMSA, when administered in male and female rats through the oral as well as the intraperitoneal (i.p.) route (25, 50 and 100 mg/kg for three weeks). The oral route of administration was found better when compared to the i.p. route based on the histopathological studies of the liver and kidney tissues. MiADMSA was seen to be slightly more toxic in terms of copper loss and some biochemical variable in the hepatic tissue in females as compared to male rats. The studies concluded that the administration of MiADMSA in female rats is confounded with side effects and may require caution during its use. No observed adverse effect levels (NOAELs) for maternal and developmental toxicity of MiADMSA were 47.5 mg/kg and 95 mg/kg/day, respectively, indicating that MiADMSA would not produce developmental toxicity in mice in the absence of maternal toxicity. Mehta et al. have suggested that MiADMSA had no effect on length of gestation, litter-size, sex ratio, viability and lactation. Taubeneck et al. showed that the developmental toxicity of DMSA is mediated mainly through disturbed copper metabolism and this may also be true for MiADMSA. It is reported that the toxicity of DMSA with LD_{50} of 16 mmol/kg is much lower than the toxicity of MiADMSA with LD_{50} of 3 mmol/kg, but lesser than BAL (1.1 mmol/kg).

Monomethyl DMSA (MmDMSA) and Monocyclohexyl DMSA (MchDMSA)

MmDMSA has a straight and branched chain methyl group, while MchDMSA has a cyclic carbon chain. Thus, they both have better lipophilic characteristics and might penetrate cells more readily that extracellularly acting chelating agent like DMSA. Both these chelating agents are orally active. Jones et al. in their *in vivo* study on male albino mice exposed to cadmium for seven days, observed that administration of MmDMSA and MchDMSA produced significant reductions in whole body cadmium levels. Further, no redistribution of cadmium in brain was observed. The *in vivo* evaluation of these monoesters derived from higher alcohols (C_3-C_6 monoesters) proved to have better efficacy as compared to the monoesters derived from lower ones (C_1-C_2 monoesters). Their ability to be administered orally suggests that they may possess considerable advantages in the clinical treatment of lead toxicity however; extensive studies are further required to reach a final conclusion.

Deferoxamine (DFO)

Deferoxamine (Fig 32-7) is a trihydroxamic acid, siderphore secreted by Streptomyces pilosus, a fungus. This chelating agent is known for its strong binding affinity for trivalent iron and less affinity for other metals making it a specific chelating agent for iron related diseases such as thalassaemia major as well as aluminium poisoning associated with chronic renal dialysis.

Pharmacological Profile

The absorption of DFO in the gastrointestinal tract is low and thus it is administered mainly through intravenous injection or infusion. It is mainly distributed extracellularly and the protein binding in plasma is low (<10%). It complexes with iron and is excreted rapidly as ferrioxamine, mainly through kidney and one third into bile through faces. Thus, its efficacy also is determined by adequate urine output and may be facilitated by dialysis in case of dysfunctioning. This drug is generally well tolerated with few cases where side effects include opthalamic and auditory toxicity, bacterial and fungal infections, alterations in blood histology, allergic and skin reaction besides few reported adverse effect on lungs, kidney and nervous system. The total intravenous dose of deferoxamine should generally not exceed 80 mg/kg/24 hours. The intramuscular route of administration is not recommended in circulatory shock states.

Deferiprone (L1)

Deferiprone (L1; CP20; 1,2-dimethyl-3-hydroxypyrid-4-one) (Fig 32-8) is an iron chelator and is considered a suitable alternative to deferoxamine in the trasfusional iron overload. It is comparatively less expensive than deferoxamine. Clinical studies suggest that combined administration of deferoxamine and deferiprone for three days per week is very effective in depleting iron overload accompanied by improvement in the cardiac function in transfusion dependent thalassemia patients. It may be noted that deferoxamine is known for reversal of cardiac dysfunction and deferiprone has also shown cardio-protective effects. These may be attributed to reduction in

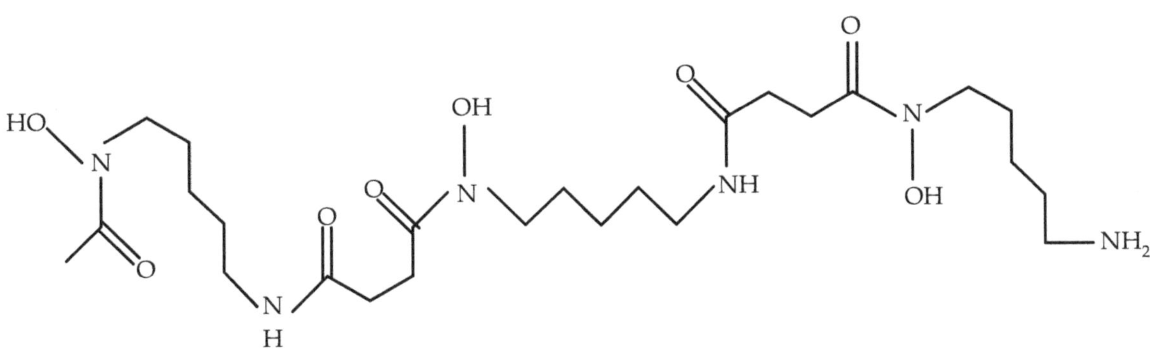

Fig 32-7: Structure of deferoxamine.

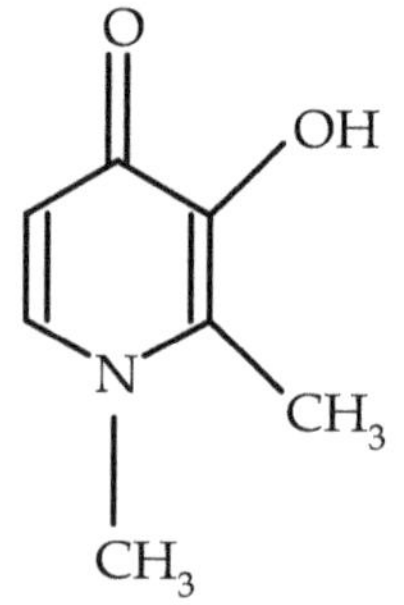

Fig 32-8: Structure of deferiprone.

iron overload however, the specific mechanism is not clear. Besides, due to higher incidences of agranulocyrosis, treatment must be closely monitored.

Pharmacological Profile

The major advantages include oral administration and rapid absorption through gastrointestinal tract. L1 is mainly excreted via renal route and has a half life of 47–134 minutes. Dosages of 75–100 mg/kg body weight/day of L1 have been considered effective to maintain stable iron balance and to reduce serum ferritin levels within one year of treatment in iron overloaded thalassemic patients. L1 is rapidly absorbed mainly from the stomach and reaches the circulation quickly. However, there might be the possibility of food-drug interaction or other gastric factors that delays the appearance of the drug in blood following oral administration. L1 is mainly metabolized as glucoronide conjugates and excreted from urine. Wide variation in the metabolism and clearance of L1 amongst patients have been observed, which mainly depend on iron overload and availability of chelatable iron. The main reported side effects during a deferiprone therapy are arthropathy, gastrointestinal symptoms, headache, and moderate zinc deficiency. These adverse reactions are usually reversed on reducing the dose or discontinuing the drug. Except for severe joint symptoms in few patients, most of the subjects in different clinical trials have been able to continue with L1 therapy for a long term. The most severe, but rare complication following administration of deferiprone is agranulocytosis or neutropenia.

TETA

Tetraethylenetetraamine or trientine (Fig 32-9) is a drug of choice for acute copper intoxication. Although nowadays there is less use of copper utensils, in ancient times the use of copper utensils could lead to extensive exposure to copper. Increased urinary copper excretion has been reported after administration of TETA.

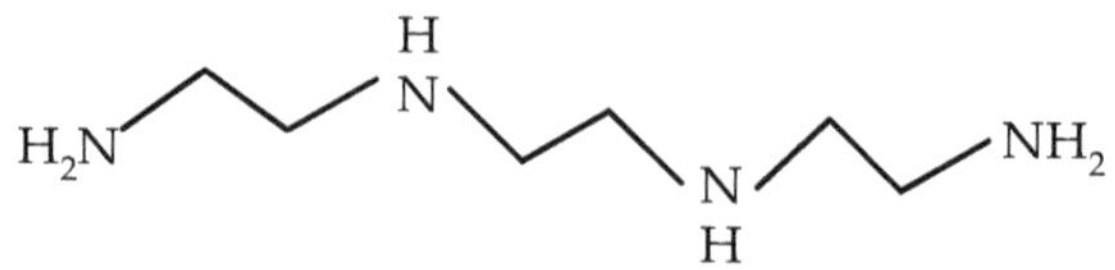

Fig 32-9: Structure of TETA.

Pharmacological Profile

Normally TETA is administered through the oral route but its absorption is relatively poor, evident from the recovery observed in urine and caracass after administration of an oral dose of C^{14}-labeled TETA. Two major metabolites of TETA have been identified, i.e., N1-acetyltriethylenetetramine (MAT) and N1,N10-diacetyltriethylene-tetramine (DAT). The former plays a significant role in the molecular mechanism by which TETA extracts copper from the system. The 5–18% of TETA that is systemically absorbed is said to be extensively metabolized, with the majority being excreted in urine as metabolite(s). Wilson's disease is characterized by disturbance in copper homeostasis which is inherited and leads to progressive increase in accumulation of copper and may even be fatal if not cured. Wilson's disease was originally treated with DPA but TETA was a better chelator and found to be potentially free of side effects like those of DPA. The recommended dosage to treat Wilson's disease patients is 0.75–2 g/day. The oral LD_{50} for rats for TETA is 2.5 g/kg body weight and is very close to the recommended dose for treatment of Wilson's disease.

Nitrilotriacetic Acid (NTA)

Nitrilotriacetic acid (NTA, $C_6H_9NO_6$), (Fig 32-10) is a polyamino carboxylic acid and is also used

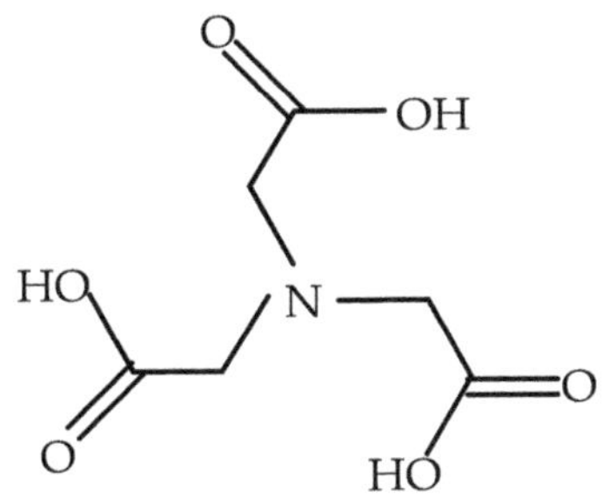

Fig 32-10: Structure of nitrilotriacetic acid.

as a chelating agent which forms coordination compounds (chelates) with metal ions such as Ca^{2+}, Cu^{2+} or Fe^{3+}. The uses of NTA are quite similar to EDTA. However, in contrast to EDTA, NTA is easily biodegradable. NTA is available in two forms, one that is a sodium derivative (Na_3NTA) and the other iron (FeNTA). Both of these forms have been used as chelating agents. NTA has been used shown to possess the ability to mobilize nickel from brain, heart, kidney and liver of nickel poisoned rats. In a comparative study with six metal binding agents, NTA was highly effective in dialyzing out nickel from the subcellular fractions of liver, kidney and blood corpuscles in rats that were exposed to nickel sulphate. Apart from nickel mobilization, a single dose of NTA has been tried in the removal of manganese from various organs and plasma in rats. Results from these studies have indicated that NTA binds rapidly to Mn and forms stable and diffusible complexes that result in faster excretion of Mn from the rats. Since NTA is considered to be non-mutagenic *in vitro* an epigenetic mechanism is assumed, based on the fact that there is sustained cytotoxicity of zinc ions transfer to the urinary tract. Vacuolated cells of the proximal tubules represent the earliest lesions, followed by sloughing, necrosis/apoptosis and proliferation. With chronic application of a high dose level, these alterations lead as a continuum to hyperplastic foci, adenomas, and adenocarcinomas. This ability of both NTA to form tumors cannot be ruled out. Studies however have indicated that tumor formation ability of both NTA is highly route and dose dependented. While FeNTA causes an iron overload and lipid peroxidation in cells and is genotoxic, Na_3NTA predominantly binds to zinc and calcium, thereby exerting its toxic effects.

References

Andersen, O (1999). Principles and recent developments in chelation treatment of metal intoxication. *Chem. Rev.*, **99**: 2683-2710.

Baum, C.R (1999). Treatment of mercury intoxication. *Curr. Opin. Pediatr.*, **11:** 265-268.

Borja-Aburto VH et al (1999). Blood lead levels measured prospectively and risk of spontaneous abortion. *Am J Epidemiol* **150:** 590.

Canfield RL et al (2003). Intellectual impairment in children with blood lead concentrations below 10 g per deciliter. *N Engl J Med* **348:** 1517.

Cheng Y et al (2001). Bone lead and blood lead levels in relation to baseline blood pressure and the prospective development of hypertension. *Am J Epidemiol* **153:** 165.

Clarkson TW (2002). The three modern faces of mercury. *Environ Health Perspect* **110 (Suppl 1):** 11.

Cremin JD et al (2001). Oral succimer decreases the gastrointestinal absorption of lead in juvenile monkeys. *Environ Health Perspect* **109:** 613.

Dargan PI et al (2003). Case report: Severe mercuric sulphate poisoning treated with 2,3-dimercaptopropane-1-sulphonate and haemodiafiltration. *Crit Care* **7:** R1.

Guldager, B.; Jorgensen, P.J. and Grandjean, P (1996). Metal excretion and magnesium retention in patients with intermittent claudication treated with intravenous disodium EDTA. *Clin. Chem.*, **42:** 1938-1942.

Jones, M.M (1994). Design of new chelating agents for removal of intracellular toxic metals. In Coordination Chemistry: A Century of Progress; Kauffman, G.B., Ed.; *The American Chemical Society*: Washington, DC, USA, 427-438.

LSRO [Life Sciences Research Office] (2004). *Review and Analysis of the Literature on the Potential Adverse Health Effects of Dental Amalgam.* LSRO: Bethesda.

National Research Council. *Arsenic in Drinking Water: 2001 Update.* National Academy Press, 2001. [http://search.nap.edu/books/0309076293/html/]

CHAPTER 33

Management of Barbiturates, Morphine, Organophosphorous Compound Poisoning

Opioid analgesic overdose is a potentially fatal illness that can be avoided by using proper prescribing techniques, educating patients about the dangers of medication addiction, administering medications incorrectly, and abusing medications. Understanding the harmful effects of opioid analgesics depends on three characteristics. First, an overdose of opioid analgesics can have potentially fatal toxic consequences on several organ systems. Second, an overdose frequently causes typical pharmacokinetic characteristics to be disturbed, which can significantly prolong intoxication. Third, different opioid formulations have different lengths of action, and failing to identify these differences might result in treatment choices that are occasionally fatal.

Clinical Symptoms of Morphine Poisoning

It is possible to diagnose opioid toxicity even though the characteristic toxidrome of apnea, stupor, and miosis does not always occur. Respiratory depression is the predominant sign of opioid intoxication. When therapeutic doses of opioids are provided to individuals who have not developed an opioid tolerance, all respiratory activity phases noticeably diminish, with the degree of the decline depending on the dose administered. However, the most readily apparent anomaly in cases of opioid overdose at the bedside is a decrease in breathing rate that results in apnea. When a patient is awake but not in physiologic sleep, a respiratory rate of 12 breaths per minute or less strongly supports acute opioid intoxication, especially if miosis or stupor are present.

Miosis by itself cannot be used to diagnose opioid intoxication. Poisoning from meperidine, propoxyphene, or tramadol can also cause pupils to become typically reactive or mydriatic. Contrarily, overdosing on antipsychotic medications, anticonvulsants, alcohol, and other sedative hypnotic substances can result in miosis and coma, but typically lack the respiratory depression that characterises opioid toxicity.

Hypothermia may result from an unconscious state that persists in a cool environment or through erroneous attempts by onlookers to treat an opioid overdose by submerging a patient in cold water. In addition, rhabdomyolysis, myoglobinuric renal failure, and the compartment syndrome may affect those who have remained immobile while in an opioid-induced coma. Elevated serum aminotransferase concentrations in connection with acetaminophen- or hypoxemia-induced liver damage are among other test findings. Tramadol, propoxyphene, and meperidine overdose have all been linked to seizure occurrence.

Diagnosis of Morphine Poisoning

The physician should evaluate the diagnosis of opioid analgesic overdose if the patient exhibits hypopnea or apnea, miosis, or stupor. This diagnosis can be deduced from the patient's vital signs, medical history, and physical examination. Restoration of breathing and oxygenation takes precedence over learning the history of the current illness, doing a physical exam, or ordering diagnostic tests in patients with severe respiratory depression.

The clinician should find out about the patient's use of all opioid analgesics, acetaminophen (including products co-formulated with acetaminophen), and illicit drugs after the patient's condition has stabilised. They should also find out if the patient has come into contact with anyone who is receiving pharmacologic treatment for chronic pain or opioid dependence. The clinician should assess the respiratory effort level, the size and responsiveness of the pupils, and any auscultatory signs that could be indicative of pulmonary edoema while doing the physical examination. To enable a comprehensive search for fentanyl patches, the patient should be completely undressed. The doctor should also palpate muscle groups because the hardness, edoema, and discomfort associated with compartment syndrome (which happens when unconscious individuals lie on a muscle compartment for an extended period of time) need immediate attention.

For a number of reasons, qualitative tests of urine for drugs of abuse (also known as toxicology screens) rarely have an impact on decisions regarding patient care and play a little role in the early assessment and treatment of opioid intoxication. First, naloxone should never be withheld from an apnea patient since it is impossible to obtain the findings of qualitative tests. Second, regardless of the cause, there are little differences in the treatment of opioid overdose. Finally, traditional toxic screenings rarely detect methadone, fentanyl, hydromorphone, and other substances, therefore they don't offer any clinically relevant information. Greater analytical precision, however, does not alter the fact that patients who have deviated from prescribed treatment plans can be identified by clinicians with expertise in pain management, mental health, or other areas of medicine using newer qualitative screens that detect a wider range of opioid analgesics.

Management of Morphine Poisoning

Patients with apnea require a mechanical or pharmaceutical stimulus to breathe. A bag-valve mask should be used to ventilate patients with stupor whose respiration rates are 12 breaths per minute or fewer, and chin-lift and jaw-thrust procedures should be used to ensure that anatomical placement aids to reduce hypercarbia. Although the connection between the partial pressure of carbon dioxide and acute lung injury is unknown, restoring oxygenation and preventing the supposed sympathetic surge that leads to pulmonary edema following the reversal of apnea can be achieved with little risk by providing appropriate ventilation.

The opioid overdose remedy naloxone is a competitive mu opioid-receptor antagonist that eliminates all symptoms of intoxication caused by opioids. It is effective when administered by parenteral, intranasal, or pulmonary routes, however oral administration results in low bioavailability due to substantial first-pass metabolism. Naloxone plasma levels are initially lower, the volume of distribution is larger, and the elimination half-life is longer in individuals with opioid dependency than in patients without dependence. When naloxone for adults is taken intravenously, the beginning of effect is less than 2 minutes, and its apparent duration of action is 20 to 90 minutes, a much shorter period than that of many opioids.

To establish the naloxone dosage that is most effective, empirical trials are required.

Patients who don't respond to the first dose of naloxone should keep taking it in increasing amounts until their breathing starts to come back. Naloxone has essentially no side effects and is routinely prescribed as an injectable solution in doses of 0.4 mg and 1 mg per millilitre for adults. Children under the age of five or with a body weight of up to 20 kg are referred to as paediatric patients. Because the dose of naloxone required to counteract the effects of an overdose is substantially higher per kilogramme of body weight in paediatric patients with opioid intoxication than in adult patients, bigger doses of the drug are typically needed.

Orotracheal intubation, a process that safely assures oxygenation and ventilation while giving protection against aspiration, provides an alternative to the administration of naloxone. Activated charcoal should only be used for gastrointestinal cleansing in patients who present within an hour of intake; outside of this window, charcoal has little benefit and makes it more difficult to see the airway anatomy during orotracheal intubation. If a patient needs a naloxone infusion or an orotracheal intubation, has persistent respiratory depression, or is intoxicated by long-acting or extended-release opioid formulations, they should be admitted to an intensive care unit.

Even when fentanyl usage is not suspected, the physician should check the patient for fentanyl patches once the patient's condition has stabilised. The delayed toxicity of fentanyl patches has been linked to superficial physical examination. Particular attention should be paid to the axillae, perineum, scrotum, and oropharynx. Any patches should be removed, and the skin should be cleaned with soap and cool water. Polyethylene glycol whole-bowel irrigation may be helpful for a patient who has consumed a fentanyl patch to hasten the patch's removal.

Clinical Symptoms and Management of Barbiturates Poisoning

A group of sedative-hypnotic medications called barbiturates. They are frequently utilised as antiepileptics (Phenobarbital) and to induce general anaesthesia (thiopental). Some states utilise barbiturates for both lethal injection executions and physician-assisted suicide/euthanasia. Due to the lower risk of overdose and the availability of an antidote to reverse poisoning, benzodiazepines like alprazolam, diazepam, and lorazepam have essentially replaced them in therapeutic practise.

Clinical Symptoms of Barbiturates Poisoning

Barbiturates can cause a variety of symptoms, but the most typical ones are difficulties thinking, a reduced level of consciousness, bradycardia, or a rapid and weak pulse, poor coordination, vertigo, nausea, muscle weakness, thirst, and oliguria. Coma, hypotension (low blood pressure), and respiratory depression, which are demonstrated by cyanosis and hypotension, are characteristics of fatal cases. Another side effect of barbiturate overdose that causes respiratory depression and mortality is pulmonary edoema. It's crucial to find out if the person has consumed any additional drugs, such as alcohol, benzodiazepines, or opiates, that could have cumulative effects.

Chronic drug users may experience significant withdrawal symptoms 8 to 15 hours after quitting. Anxiety, sleeplessness, tremors, heat, sweating, convulsions, circulatory failure, and maybe death are among the symptoms.

The physical examination should include periodic checks of the patient's vital signs, neurologic condition, and mental status. Barbiturates have also been linked to pulmonary eosinophilia and thrombocytopenia (with febarbamate).

Diagnosis

Evaluation sometimes includes a qualitative evaluation of the amount of drug taken with a plasma or urine screening test, as with the majority of drug- and medication-related toxicities. The two most significant correlates of toxicity have been identified as plasma barbiturate concentration and swallowed dose. Barbiturates and other compounds in the body can be found using immunoassays (EIA), which can be both affordable and sensitive. Gas chromatography/mass spectrometry (GC/MS), another frequently used technique, can further identify and confirm the presence of a specific barbiturate.

Management of Barbiturates Poisoning

Since there is no specific treatment for overdose, supportive care is nevertheless used to treat barbiturate toxicity. As with any overdose, the initial step in therapy is to evaluate the patient's airway, breathing, and circulation. Intubation and mechanical ventilation may be required in cases of severe sedation and respiratory depression. A nasogastric tube can be used to administer activated charcoal treatment early on, which may be beneficial. Most patients will require observation or admission. The patient should get counselling regarding the risks of abusing barbiturates while they are recovering. Barbiturates can lead to physical reliance and tolerance over time. Therefore, abrupt termination can result in withdrawal symptoms.

Forcible alkaline diuresis and, in more severe cases, hemodialysis are additional alternatives for treating barbiturate toxicity. Megimide, also known as bemegride, is a central nervous system stimulant that raises respiration and can be used to counteract the harmful effects of depressants. However, it is an emetic that causes emesis and aspiration to be of concern.

Restoring the inhibitory tone of the central nervous system (CNS) is a necessary part of managing long-term use. Barbiturates should be stopped gradually with drugs that show cross-tolerance, with benzodiazepines being the preferred choice because abrupt withdrawal might cause severe symptoms.

Clinical Symptoms and Management of Organophosphosphorus Compound Poisoning

In most people who are exposed to organophosphates, pesticides are involved. The first organophosphate insecticide was developed in the middle of the 1800s, but it wasn't until World War II that it was widely utilised. Organophosphates are substances that are employed as drugs, pesticides, and weaponsized nerve agents. Small pupils, sweating, muscle tremors, confusion, increased saliva and tear production, diarrhoea, nausea, and vomiting are a few symptoms. It can take hours for symptoms to go away once they first arise.

Clinical Symptoms of Organophosphosphorus Compound Poisoning

Both the sympathetic and parasympathetic nervous systems are stimulated by organophosphates. Symptoms of excessive parasympathetic stimulation are a common clinical situation. Children are an exception since their symptoms are frequently mediated by nicotinic receptors.

There are a few mnemonic devices that can help you recall the signs of organophosphate poisonings and the relevant receptor.

For nicotinic signs of acetylcholinesterase inhibitor toxicity, think of the days of the week:

- Monday = Mydriasis
- Tuesday = Tachycardia
- Wednesday = Weakness
- Thursday = Hypertension
- Friday = Fasciculations.

The more common mnemonic that captures the muscarinic effects of organophosphate poisonings is DUMBELS:

- D = Defecation/diaphoresis
- U = Urination
- M = Miosis
- B = Bronchospasm/bronchorrhea
- E = Emesis
- L = Lacrimation
- S = Salivation.

Anxiety, disorientation, drowsiness, emotional instability, seizures, hallucinations, migraines, sleeplessness, memory loss, and circulatory or respiratory depression might also be additional symptoms. When someone passes away, respiratory failure from bronchoconstriction, bronchorrhea, central respiratory depression, or weakness/paralysis of the respiratory muscles is the most frequent cause. There are further long-term consequences if the patient recovers from the acute poisoning.

It usually takes 24 to 96 hours for intermediate neurologic symptoms to appear following exposure. Neck flexions, weakness, diminished deep tendon reflexes, cranial nerve anomalies, respiratory insufficiency, and weakness of the proximal muscles are other symptoms. These patients can fully recover their normal neurologic function in 2 to 3 weeks with supportive care. Neuropathy is another later consequence. This has something to do with particularly particular chlorpyrifos-containing organophosphate compounds. The most typical first symptom is stocking-glove paresthesia, which progresses to symmetric polyneuropathy and flaccid paralysis that begins in the lower extremities and spreads to the upper extremities.

Additionally, the following mental deficiencies could manifest in survivors:

- Confusion
- Deficit in memory
- Lethargy
- Psychosis
- Irritability
- Parkinson-like signs

Diagnosis

Organophosphate toxicity can be diagnosed either acutely or chronically, and only clinically. When there is no known history of exposure to or consumption of organophosphates, you must have a strong clinical suspicion that you are poisoned. A distinctive garlic or petroleum smell that some organophosphates have may aid in diagnosis. A trial of atropine may be used if organophosphate toxicity is suspected but not confirmed. If symptoms go away after taking atropine, acetylcholinesterase inhibitor poisoning is more likely to have occurred. Red blood cell acetylcholinesterase activity can be directly measured by some labs, however they are frequently transported to labs that are not accessible in time to inform therapy.

AChE in red blood cells may now be quickly measured using a portable device. Prior to administering pralidoxime, blood must be taken. To gauge a patient's reaction to treatment, red cell AChE can be employed because it corresponds with neuronal AChE.

As a liver acute-phase protein that circulates in the blood and has no link to symptoms, plasma AChE is not used. AChE levels in plasma can also change as a result of infections, pregnancies, and illnesses.

The CBC, glucose levels, troponin, liver and kidney function, and arterial blood gas are other blood tests that ought to be requested.

Sinus bradycardia due to parasympathetic activity will be seen on the ECG.

Management of Organophosphosphorus Compound Poisoning

Wearing personal protective equipment is the initial step in treating organophosphate poisoning victims. You must take precautions to avoid getting exposed as these patients might still have the substance on them. The patient needs to be decontaminated next. This entails taking off and discarding all clothing because it can still be contaminated after being washed. Water needs to be flushed over the patient's skin. To clean the skin, dry substances like flour, sand, or bentonite can also be utilised. Vomiting and diarrhoea after intake might reduce the amount of drug absorbed, but they should never be forced. If the patient arrives within an hour of intake, activated charcoal can be administered, but studies have not demonstrated a benefit.

Airway management is essential. Intubation may be necessary in some individuals due to bronchospasm, convulsions, or bronchorrhea. Succinylcholine must be avoided during intubation as it can prolong the paralysis. The cause is that acetylcholine esterase also breaks down succinylcholine.

Standard treatment includes cardiac monitoring, pulse oximetry, and good intravenous access.

Atropine, which competes with acetylcholine for the same muscarinic receptors as acetylcholine, is the only effective treatment for organophosphate poisoning. Up until the adult dose, the initial dose for adults is 2 to 5 mg IV or 0.05 mg/kg IV for children. If the patient is not responding to the medication, increase the dosage by two every three to five minutes until there is no longer any bronchoconstriction and the respiratory secretions have cleared. Before a severe poisoning patient starts to recover, hundreds of milligrammes of atropine administered as a bolus or continuous infusion over several days may be necessary.

As atropine only affects muscarinic receptors, pralidoxime (2-PAM) should also be used to affect nicotinic receptors. By attaching to the organophosphate, pralidoxime causes the phosphorylated AChE to be reactivated. But it must be administered within 48 hours of the poisoning for it to be effective. The substance can be used with atropine and does not depress the respiratory centre. It is challenging to evaluate the conflicting evidence about the use of oximes to treat organophosphate toxicity. All individuals who have been harmed by organophosphorus chemicals should be treated with an oxime until this is better understood and other therapies are made available.

To prevent symptoms caused by muscarinic receptors worsening, atropine must be administered prior to 2-PAM. For adults, a bolus of at least 30 mg/kg, or 20 to 50 mg/kg for kids, should be administered gradually over 30 minutes. Cardiac arrest may result from fast administration. A continuous infusion of at least 8 mg/kg/hr for adults and 10 to 20 mg/kg/hr for kids should begin after the bolus and may be required for many days.

References

Mendes PA, Pereira TC, Pina R, Santos R. Chlorpyrifos-Induced Delayed Neurotoxicity with A Rare Presentation of Flaccid Quadriplegia: A Diagnostic Challenge. Eur J Case Rep Intern Med. 2018; 5(1): 000751.

Chen KX, Zhou XH, Sun CA, Yan PX. Manifestations of and risk factors for acute myocardial injury after acute organophosphorus pesticide poisoning. Medicine (Baltimore). 2019 Feb; 98(6): e14371.

Sikary AK. Homicidal poisoning in India: A short review. J Forensic Leg Med. 2019 Feb; 61:13-16.

Dardiotis E, Aloizou AM, Siokas V, Tsouris Z, Rikos D, Marogianni C, Aschner M, Kovatsi L, Bogdanos DP, Tsatsakis A. Paraoxonase-1 genetic polymorphisms in organophosphate. metabolism. Toxicology. 2019 Jan 01; 411:24-31.

Jokanović M. Neurotoxic effects of organophosphorus pesticides and possible association with neurodegenerative diseases in man: A review. Toxicology. 2018 Dec 01; 410:125-131.

Boyer EW. Management of opioid analgesic overdose. N Engl J Med. 2012 Jul 12;367(2): 146-55.

Drugs and Lactation Database (LactMed) [Internet]. National Library of Medicine (US); Bethesda (MD): 2006. Phenobarbital.

Roberts DM, Buckley NA. Enhanced elimination in acute barbiturate poisoning - a systematic review. Clin Toxicol (Phila). 2011 Jan; 49(1): 2-12.

CHAPTER

Management of the Poisoned Patient

34

Poisoning is common and results in significant morbidity and mortality. The emergency physician should approach the evaluation and management of the poisoned patient with an unknown exposure in a stepwise fashion. Clues from the history, physical exam and laboratory studies can often lead the emergency physician to the correct diagnosis. Gastrointestinal decontamination should not be performed routinely and its use should be individualized in each patient. Poison centers and toxicologists can serve as a valuable resource in the management of the poisoned patient.

Introduction

Poisoning and intoxication are common and result in a significant number of emergency department visits yearly. More than 50% of these exposures involved children. A majority of paediatric exposures are exploratory ingestions involving small quantities of non-toxic substances. On the other hand, adults are more likely. In a majority of cases the emergency physician (EP) will have an exposure history on which to develop a management plan. There are situations, such as with an altered level of consciousness or seizure, in which the poisoned patient presents to the emergency department (ED) and there is no history of drug or chemical exposure. These situations require the EP to develop a systematic approach to evaluating and managing the patient so that potential morbidity and mortality can be prevented.

Clinical Evaluation

The patient interviewer should determine the substance(s) to which the patient was exposed. Additionally, how and when the patient was exposed, was the route of exposure through ingestion, inhalation, dermal, or parenteral. The route and timing of exposure influence the pharmacokinetics and are helpful in determining the onset and duration of symptoms. Did the patient ingest a sustained release preparation? Many medications are available as extended release forms to facilitate once daily dosing.

Delayed absorption of these products can result in delayed onset of clinical effects and thus prolong the duration of effects. It is important to inquire as to why the exposure occurred. Was it an accidental ingestion, suicide attempt, or therapeutic misadventure? Often suicidal patients will divulge the substance ingested, however it is important for the EP to remain skeptical about the validity of the history. Suicidal patients may attempt to deceive the EP by providing a fictitious history. Alternate sources of information should be sought, especially in patients with an altered mental status. Friends and family that accompany the patient to the ED should be questioned. Emergency medical service personnel can provide valuable information regarding pill bottles, chemical containers, or drug paraphernalia.

In some cases, it is important to obtain an occupational history and inquire about hobbies as these can result in chemical exposures. In situations involving an occupational exposure it is helpful to inquire about material safety data sheets. These forms are federally required of employers and help to identify the chemical constituents of products in the workplace.

These can be useful as many products have similar names, but contain different chemical compounds.

Further history including underlying medical illnesses and medication use are also important. Adverse drug events and drug interactions are common and easily overlooked.

Additionally, the EP should specifically ask the patient about the use of over the counter medications and herbal products.

Both patients and physicians may overlook potential interactions between herbal products and prescription medications.

The physical examination of the poisoned patient should be focussed on identifying signs or complications of the drug/chemical to which the patient has been exposed.

In situations where the exposure agent is not known it is important for the EP to conduct a thorough physical exam. The key elements of the physical exam of the poisoned patient are the vitals signs, neurologic examinations and skin findings. Alteration of vital signs can be extremely helpful in narrowing down potential etiologies and combined with other exam findings can establish a toxic syndrome, or toxidrome (Tables 34-1 and 34- 2). Examination of the poisoned patient should not illicit any focal neurologic findings (except those that could result from hypoglycemia).

The neurologic examination should identify changes in level of consciousness, document pupil size and abnormal eye movements and assess for any abnormal neuromuscular findings Pupil sizes are helpful in narrowing down a differential diagnosis. Mydriasis can be seen with sympathomimetic or anticholinergic agents, as well as ethanol/sedative-hypnotic withdrawal. Opioids, cholinergic agents and alpha 2 agonists can produce miosis. However, in cases where there has been a hypoxic insult or co ingestion the pupil size may be misleading. Nystagmus may be seen in phencyclidine, phenytoin, carbamazepine, ethanol, or sedative hypnotic intoxications.

Abnormal neuromuscular findings include hyperreflexia, clonus and increased muscle tone or rigidity. Patients that ingest drugs with anti-cholinergic effects, such as tricyclic antidepressants or diphenhydramine, often demonstrate hypertonia or myoclonus. Serotonin syndrome and neuroleptic malignant syndrome can both present with an increase in muscle tone. Seizures should remain in the differential for patients that present with an increase in muscle tone accompanied by a change in level of consciousness. If a focal finding is discovered it should be presumed that a central nervous system lesion (e.g., ischemic or hemorrhage cerebrovascular accident, etc.,) is present.

Skin findings may also help determine aetiology for a patient's presentation. A diaphoretic patient suggests exposure to sympathomimetic or cholinergic agents, Salicylates, or drug induced hypoglycaemia. Dry flushed skin is indicative of anti cholinergic toxicity. Bruising may be found in patients that have developed a coagulopathy from long acting anticoagulant rodenticides.

Numerous drugs and chemicals are hepatotoxic and could result in jaundice from liver failure. Needle track marks would suggest that the patient is an intravenous drug user. Lastly, blisters or bullae may be noted on dependent body surfaces of subjects who have been immobile for a prolonged period of time. These lesions were previously considered to be pathognomonic for barbiturate poisoning, however they have subsequently been reported with exposure to multiple agents including: diazepam, carbon monoxide and amitriptyline.

Although some believe direct toxicity is the etiology it is more likely that pressure from an extended period of immobility results in skin blistering. Any patient presenting with coma and skin blisters should alert the EP to monitor

Table 34-1: Toxindromes

Sympathometic	OPIOID
Hyperthermia	Coma
Hypertension	Miosis
Tachycardia	Respiratory Depression
Delirium	Hypotension Seizures (Hypoxia, Meperidine, Propoxyphene, Tramadol)
Agitation	
Seizures	
Anticholinergic	**Cholinergic**
Delerium	D-diarrhea
Hallucinations	U-urination
Hyperthermia	M-miosis
Mydriasis	B-bradycardia, bronchorrhea, bronchospasm
Tachycardia	E-emesis
Dry. Flushed skin	L-lacrimation
Urinary retention	S-salivation
	M-mydriasis
	T-tachycardia
	W-weakness
	(t) (H) – Hypertension
	F-fasiculations
Sedative Hypnotic	
CNS Depression	
Respiratory Depression	
Hypotension (mild)	
Bradycardia (mild)	

for possible complications of prolonged immobility including rhabdomyolyisis, compartment syndrome and compression neuropathies.

General Management

The general management of the poisoned patient should ensure that the patient is maintaining their airway and is adequately oxygenating and ventilating. Endotracheal intubation may be required if there is concern for aspiration or inadequate oxygenation/ventilation. If intubation is required all induction and neuromuscular blocking agents may be used with one exception; succinylcholine should be avoided in cases of organophosphate poisoning as these agents inhibit the enzyme pseudocholinesterase that is responsible for succinylcholine metabolism.

When used in this situation it could result in prolonged paralysis. Intravenous access should be obtained and a second i.v or central venous catheter placed if the patient is hypotensive. Initially, a bolus of crystalloid fluids should be given for hypotension. Persistent hypotension should be treated with a direct acting vasopressor such as norepinephrine.

Additional pharmacological therapy should be focused at the underlying cause of the hypotension (e.g., sodium bicarbonate for tricyclic antidepressants, glucagon for beta blockers, etc). Patients should have continuous cardiac monitoring and frequent blood pressure assessments.

In evaluating cases of altered mental status it is helpful to remember the mnemonic DON'T: dextrose, oxygen, naloxone, and thiamine. A rapid bedside glucose should be obtained on all patients with an altered mental status. An oxygen saturation with continuous monitoring should be obtained and high-flow oxygen provided. Naloxone may be administered in cases of suspected opioid toxicity.

It should be remembered that not all opiates cause miosis (e.g., meperidine, propoxyphene), and judicious use of naloxone might prove diagnostic in cases that are unclear. Naloxone should be dosed and titrated to ensure the patient is protecting their airway and is adequately oxygenating and ventilating. In adult patients it is generally recommended to start with a low dose (0.2 0.4 mg) in order to prevent precipitating acute opioid withdrawal. Synthetic opioids, such as fentanyl, may require larger amounts (up to 10 mg) of naloxone.

Almost all available opioids have a half life longer than naloxone. Thus, the patient should be monitored for recurrent respiratory depression. If needed a naloxone infusion may be started at an hourly rate equal to two-thirds the total amount of naloxone initially required to achieve adequate respirations.

This rate may then be titrated to clinical effect. Naloxone has a good safety profile; however, cases of pulmonary edema have been reported after administration to patients with profound respiratory depression. The etiology of this is not clear but might be related to a catecholamine surge caused by precipitating opioid withdrawal.

This could produce an increase in pulmonary capillary hydrostatic pressure with resultant pulmonary edema. A second theory is that with profound CNS and respiratory depression attempts are made to inhale against a closed glottis generating a negative intrathoracic pressure that pulls fluid into the alveoli.

Lastly, intravenous thiamine should be administered to those patients who are alcoholic or malnourished. It is commonly thought that glucose should not be administered without thiamine for fear of precipitating Wernicke's encephalopathy. There is no literature to support this practice and hypoglycemic patients should be given intravenous dextrose immediately.

Thiamine can be provided concurrently or soon thereafter without concerns of causing or worsening potential Wernicke's encephalopathy. An indepth discussion of antidotes is beyond the scope of this article, but antidote administration is important and can be life saving in certain cases. Provision of aggressive and timely supportive care is critical in the management of the poisoned patient to decrease morbidity and mortality.

Diagnostic Adjuncts

An EKG should be obtained in most poisoned patients. Bradycardia and tachycardia can suggest potential toxicologic etiologies. Identification of conduction delays is extremely important in the poisoned patient. A QRS duration greater than 100 msec suggests an agent such as a tricyclic antidepressant (TCA), diphenhydramine, cocaine, propoxyphene, hydroxychlorquine, or any Class IA or IC antiarrhythmic. Other findings that suggest TCA or possibly other sodium channel blocker toxicity include an R wave in lead aVR greater than 3 mm or an R/S ratio in that lead greater than 0.7.

A prolonged QRS duration can serve as a prognostic tool. In one case series of patients with TCA toxicity a QRS duration greater than 100 msec was associated with a 33% incidence of seizures and 14% incidence of ventricular arrhythmias. This risk of arrhythmias increased to 50% with a QRS duration greater than 160 msec.

A prolonged QT interval should also be identified. The list of drugs that result in prolongation of the QT interval is extensive. The common feature of these agents is blockade of the delayed rectifier potassium channels. This results in a delay in repolarization translating to QT prolongation. Agents causing a prolonged QT interval place the patient at increased risk for torsades de pointes. Any patient displaying evidence of a prolonged QRS or QT interval deserves admission for cardiac monitoring. Although laboratory testing has advanced significantly it is important to remember the most helpful laboratory tests are those commonly available such as serum chemistries, ABG's, etc. These tests can be rapidly obtained and while they may not be diagnostic they can provide clues regarding potential exposures.

They also serve to rule out other comorbidities or complications of poisoning such as electrolyte abnormalities or rhabdomyolysis. Methanol, metformin, iron, isoniazid, ethylene glycol, salicylates, cyanide, and carbon monoxide can all result in an anion gap metabolic acidosis. Other causes including uremia, diabetic/alcoholic ketoacidosis and lactic acidosis should be excluded. Since acetaminophen is ubiquitous in over-the-counter and prescription pain medicines an acetaminophen level should be obtained on all patients with an intentional ingestion or those cases in which a history cannot be obtained.

Radiologic studies should be ordered as needed to evaluate for complications related to the exposure. Poisonings associated with a decreased level of consciousness can result in aspiration. Some drugs, including opioids and salicylates, can cause non cardiogenic pulmonary edema. A chest x ray is warranted in those with respiratory complaints or compromise. A CT scan of the head is indicated in patients with focal neurologic findings or in cases where the mental status fails to improve following a period of observation. The utility of abdominal radiographs in the poisoned patient is limited. Most compounds are unable to be visualized on an x ray, however several drugs and chemicals are known to be radio-opaque. These can be remembered by the mnemonic.

CHIPES: chloral hydrate, heavy metals, iron, phenothiazines, (body) packers, enteric coated drugs and salicylates. It should be noted that even in these cases a negative radiograph does not exclude their presence.

Gastrointestinal Decontamination

Gastrointestinal decontamination is a source of great controversy in medical toxicology and recently there has been a shift toward less aggressive GI decontamination. Intuitively, if one is able to remove or bind a toxic substance that the risk of toxicity would be decreased.

However, this has not been demonstrated in clinical practice. Gastric emptying used to be commonplace; however, there are very few situations in which gastric emptying should be considered. Ipecac has no place in the emergency department management of the poisoned patient.

It has been shown to be most effective if given within 30 minutes of ingestion. Given that most patients present to the ED well beyond 30 minutes ipecac is not likely to be helpful. Persistent vomiting could also delay administration of activated charcoal or other therapies. Likewise, the use of gastric lavage has decreased significantly in the last decade.

However, if any benefit exists it is most likely in those who are lavaged within one hour of ingestion. There are risks to lavage including GI tract perforation, aspiration and fluid/electrolyte abnormalities.

Administration of activated charcoal is the most popular approach to GI decontamination. The true efficacy and clinical benefit of activated charcoal remains to be seen.

Activated charcoal decreases absorption and that the greatest effect occurs if given within one hour of ingestion. Activated charcoal is contraindicated in those with an un-protected airway. Multiple dose activated charcoal (MDAC) should only be considered in situations involving ingestions of theophylline, dapsone, carbamazepine, phenobarbital and quinine. If MDAC is utilized, it should be ensured that activated charcoal without sorbitol is administered.

Use of cathartics such as sorbitol or magnesium citrate is discouraged. These agents act by producing an osmotic gradient and pull fluid into the GI tract to facilitate catharsis. A single dose of sorbitol with the first dose of activated charcoal is acceptable; whole bowel irrigation (WBI) involves the administration of a large volume of an osmotically balanced solution, such as polyethene glycol (GoLytely), to facilitate evacuation of the GI tract. Given the large volumes that must be administered a nasogastric tube is often required. Its use could be considered in situations in which an enteric coated or sustained release preparation of a drug has been ingestion.

Such formulations have prolonged absorptions kinetics and in theory WBI might promote evacuation and decrease absorption. Certain compounds, such as lithium, iron and other heavy metals do not adsorb to activated charcoal and WBI potentially decreases systemic absorption.

Again, no definitive clinical evidence demonstrates improved outcomes. WBI is contraindicated in those with an unprotected airway, significant GI bleeding, bowel obstruction, or nonintact GI tract.

The ability to enhance elimination of drugs or chemicals from the body is limited. Urinary alkalinization can only be routinely recommended for the treatment of moderate severe salicylate toxicity.

The goal is to increase the urine pH to greater than 7.5 with IV sodium bicarbonate. The alkaline pH results in ionization of the salicylate and traps it in the renal tubule thus preventing reabsorption and promoting excretion. Fluid and electrolyte status must be monitored closely as hypokalemia or fluid overload may result.

Other agents (phenobarbital, methotrexate, chlorpropamide) have increased excretion with alkalinization, however a clinical benefit has not been proven. Hemodialyisis should be considered in cases of salicylate, theophylline, lithium, ethylene glycol and methanol poisonings.

Disposition

Proper disposition of the poisoned patient is paramount. Patients that are demonstrating signs of toxicity require admission to the hospital for further evaluation and management. The decision making is more complicated for asymptomatic patients.

As a general rule, if a patient ingested an immediate release formulation of a drug, has been observed for six hours, and remains asymptomatic with normal vital signs, and normal laboratory studies/EKG the patient can be dispositioned to psychiatry or discharged.

Patients who have ingested an enteric coated or sustained release preparation require an extended period of observation that often necessitates admission. Clinicians should be aware many pharmaceutical preparations (that although not specifically marketed as extended release preparations) have prolonged absorption kinetics and/or half lives. These agents, such as sulfonylureas and amlodipine, should be treated with prolonged observation in a similar fashion to extended release preparations.

The diagnosis and management of the poisoned patient with an unknown exposure can be challenging for the EP. It is important that the EP approach the patient in a logical fashion. The history, physical exam, and appropriate laboratory studies can often help guide the EP toward a diagnosis. Initiation of aggressive supportive care is the most important aspect of management in the care of poisoned patients. Early consultation with a poison center or toxicologist can help facilitate the evaluation, management, and disposition of the poisoned patient.

Table 34-2: Some specific antidotes for toxic drugs and chemicals

Agent	Antidote	Mechanism of Action
Drugs		Ionically neutralizes heparin
Heparin	Protamine	Inactivates toxic metabolite
Acetaminophen	*N*-acetylcysteine	Displaces drugs from receptors
Narcotics and opioids	Naloxone	Reverses glucose depletion
Insulin, oral hypoglycemics	Glucose	
Chemicals		
Methanol		
Ethylene glycol	Ethanol	Blocks metabolism to toxic metabolite
Botulinum toxin	Ethanol	Blocks metabolism to toxic metabolite
Cyanide	Antiserum	Immunologically neutralizes toxicant
	Sodium nitrate	Forms methemoglobin, which binds cyanide, thus removing it from active pool
	Sodium thiosulfate	Provides a source of sulfur to detoxify cyanide
Organophosphates		Displaces acetylcholine from its receptor
	Atropine	
		Reactivates acetylcholinesterase
Carbon monoxide	Pralidoxime	Displaces toxicant from hemoglobin
Nitrites	Oxygen	Reduces methemoglobin to hemoglobin
Arsenic	Methylene blue	Forms inactive complex with metal
Iron	Dimercaprol	Forms inactive complex with metal
Lead	Deferoxamine	Forms inactive complete with metal
Warfarin	Calcium disodium edetate	Stimulates coagulation factor synthesis
	Vitamin K	

A General Approach to the Treatment of Acute Poisoning

Provide emergency management

Perform cardiopulmonary resuscitation if necessary.

If victim is in a coma, administer naloxone hydrochloride (in narcotic or opioid overdose) and 50% glucose (in case of insulin shock)

Evaluation

Identify the toxic agent and dose if possible

Assess vital signs and level of consciousness

Conduct laboratory tests

Reduce absorption and enhance removal of poison

Irrigate eyes and skin if involved Induce emesis with syrup of ipecac if victim is conscious and has not ingested acids, alkali, hydrocarbons, or petroleum distillates

Perform gastric lavage if victim is unconscious or in some instances when conscious

Administer activated charcoal to bind poison

Administer milk or water if alkali, acid, hydrocarbon, or petroleum distillates have been ingested

Administer antidote, if one exists, that is specific for the poison

Consider forced diuresis, urine acidification, or alkalinization if specific antidotes are not available

Hemodialysis or charcoal hemoperfusion may be appropriate for rapid elimination if antidotes are not available

References

Lai MW, Klein-Schwartz W, Rodgers GC, et al. (2005). Annual Report of the American Association of Poison Control Centers' National Poisoning and Exposure Database. *Clin Toxicol.* **44:** 803-932.

Sporer KA and Khayam-Bashi H (1996). Acetaminophen and Salicylate Levels in Patients with Suicidal Ingestion or Altered Mental Status. *Am J Emerg Med.*; **14:** 443-6.

Greenberg MI, Cone DC and Roberts JR (1996). Material Safety Data Sheet: A Useful Resource for the Emergency Physician. *Ann Emerg Med.* **27:** 347-352.

Budnitz DS, Pollock DA, Weidenbach KN, et al (2006). National Surveillance of Emergency Department Visits for Outpatient Adverse Drug Events. *JAMA.* **296:** 1858-1866.

Juurlink DN, Marndani M, Kopp A, et al (2003). Drug-Drug Interactions Among Elderly Patients Hospitalized for Drug Toxicity. *JAMA.* **289:** 1662-8.

Kennedy J (2005). Herb and Supplement Use in the US Population. *Clin Ther.* **27:** 1847-58.

CHAPTER

Chronopharmacology 35

Introduction

Chronopharmacology is a branch of medicine that focuses on maximizing the effects of drugs and minimising their adverse effects by timing their administration in relation to an organism's circadian cycle. The objective is to improve our knowledge of predictable and periodic events.

The field of study known as chronobiology deals with the phenomenon of rhythmicity in living organisms. Its roots are chronos (time), bios (life), and logos (examine of). It serves as an objective representation of organic time formations and has an important role in science. Circadian rhythms alter behavior, body composition, and characteristic of living things at many biochemical levels. Chronobiology's goal is optimizing pharmaceutical treatments while taking rhythm dependencies into account. Medication kinetics and dynamics exhibit predictable time-varying disease manifestation and severity.

A 24-hour periodic oscillation of an organism's internal biological, physiological, and behavioural features is referred to as a circadian rhythm. In the field of medicine, the ideas of chronobiology and chronopharmacology have gained importance. Circadian variation in blood pressure and coronary heart disease occurs today.

Today, it is clear that blood pressure, coronary heart disease, and the prevalence of acute cardiovascular illness vary during the day (ischemia, infarction, stroke and sudden death). The episodes of nevertheless also have organic rhythms.

Circadian rhythms are thought to persist while free-jogging since they are endogenous in nature. infections such as hypertension, MI (myocardial infarction), and congestive coronary heart disease

Understanding of circadian rhythms' atomic command and Following flagging routes, a new restorative treatment has been considered. So, a sophisticated knowledge on how to do anything more effectively and makes use of modern drugs safely.

A common method for achieving balance in side effects and treating wellbeing is to regularly combine pharmacological treatments. The rhythmic alternation of both desired (effectiveness) as well as adverse (toxicity, tolerance) impacts on the organism as a whole. Throughout a 24-hour period, there are highs and lows in physiological factors that are not dispersed at random, but the biological clocks, often known as pacemakers, are in control. In chronokinetics, the absorption, distribution, and drug excretion and metabolism according to the time of day, a year or a menstrual cycle.

Chronoesthesy, which can no longer be characterised by methods of chronokinetic changes, is the rhythmic variation in susceptibility or sensitivity of a target device to a medication. In Humans' skin, bronchial tree, and stomach are potential targets.

Cause for Chronopharmacology

Auto induction: The enzymes responsible for its removal will increase with repeated administration; this process is known as vehicle mobile induction growing its clearance. Vehicle movable induction is the term used to describe this. It is based on the drug's dose and focus. It has some therapeutic effects. It affects how long it takes to reach a stable state and restricts one's ability to apply information from a single dose to multiple doses taken continuously. The distribution of carbamazepine shows a time-dependent characteristic.

Auto inhibition: It may also develop as a result of the metabolism of some pills. The drug's metabolites increase in attention and also impede the metabolism of the specific medicine.

Food effects: The primary cause of diurnal fluctuations is food. Food slows or delays gastric emptying, which frequently results in a decrease at the peak concentration and an increase at the time of occurrence after a single dose. It is a major contributing factor in patients with circadian variations who prefer to consume more at night than in the morning. The rate of entrance into the liver and the attention of medication entering the liver are slowed and prolonged when absorption is slowed by means of food, and as a result, metabolism is slowed.

Classification of Chronopharmacology

It is classified as below:

Chronopharmaceutics: A field of pharmaceutics devoted to the creation and evaluation of drug delivery systems that release a bioactive agent at a rhythm that preferably matches the organic requirement of a certain disease therapy has been described.

Chronopharmacokinetics

In addition to excretion, it alludes to periodic variations in drug absorption. Chronopharmacokinetics examines changes in drug distribution, metabolism, excretion, and absorption. Circadian changes in liver enzyme activity, gastrointestinal motility, gastrointestinal blood flow, and medication protein binding. Over the past 20 years, numerous chronopharmacokinetic studies have been conducted. The findings of those studies show that medication kinetics are affected by point of management. Studies in men have been published, especially in relation to cardiovascular active medications, non-steroidal anti-inflammatory medications (NSAIDs), local anaesthetics, anticancer medications, psychiatric medications, antibiotics, and anti-asthmatic medications.

Chronotherapeutics

Chronotherapeutics is a treatment strategy that synchronised in vivo drug availability to healthy rhythms of illness in order to maximise healing effects and reduce side effects. It is based on the finding that there may be a relationship between the peak-to-via rhythmic interest in disease symptoms and risk factors, pharmacologic sensitivity, and the pharmacokinetics of many drugs. It also considers predictable management time dependent variant with within the pharmacokinetics of drugs as well as the susceptibility because of temporal organisation of physiochemical system and function of frame as circadian. The administration of medication when it is easiest and best tolerated is one method for improving the efficacy of pharmacotherapy. This basically refers to the observation that every metabolic event experiences rhythmic changes in time. It is essentially based on the observation that the peak-to-trough rhythmic interest in disease symptoms and risk indicators, pharmacologic sensitivity, and the pharmacokinetics of many medications may be interdependently correlated. It is increasingly becoming more obvious that patients should take their medications at a distinct time that is even more unique than was previously thought as more is learned about chronobiology and chronotherapeutics.

Advantages of Chronotherapeutics

1. It prevents drug overdoses.
2. It increases the appropriateness of the drug's use.
3. It lessens the unwanted side effects of a drug and makes it easier to worry about the treatment for a little period of time.

Need of Chronotherapeutics

In cases when patients already have renal, cardiac, and hepatic abnormalities of the body, it is necessary to evaluate treatment to shorten the period of treatment. Medication buildup in certain organs causes increased toxicity, which may also cause the organ's function to decline. Thus, chronotherapeutics will play a crucial role in the treatment of disorders, especially those that affect the centre of the frame.

Chronopharmacotherapy

It is a setting where the administration of medications is coordinated with biological rhythms to maximise therapeutic efficacy. It covers both the analysis of drug repercussions on rhythmic qualities as well as the study of drug effects as a feature of biologic timing. Histamine, sodium salicylate, acetylcholine, halothane, prostaglandin F2alpha, reserpine, Cyproheptadine, ethanol, insulin, chlorothiazide, oxymetholone, orcinprenaline, and SCH 1000, as well as Indomethacin, lignocaine, ACTH, cortisol, and several synthetic corticosteroids.

Advantage of Chronopharmacotherapy

1. It stops any kind of substance from becoming overdosed.
2. As a result, the cost of a drug goes up since it makes the use of the drug more necessary.
3. It helps in worrying out the treatment for only a specific or constrained period of time and decreases the vain side effects of a drug.

Disadvantage of Chronopharmacotherapy

1. A person might occasionally be denied a moment of relaxation.
2. The individual appears to be hardly helpful throughout chronotherapy.
3. The person wants to stay awake till the next relaxation plan, thus he wants to get himself involved in order to keep himself awake until the subsequent agenda.
4. The patient wants to recommend the expert automatically to avoid reactions from you.

Ideal Characteristics of Chronopharmacotherapy

1. Its internal cut-off parameters for use are non-poisonous.
2. It must have a real-time clock and a specific biomarker that is active for a given illness state.
3. It wishes to have a framework for grievance management.
4. It is biodegradable and biocompatible, especially for parenteral organisations.
5. It is easy to make at a reasonable cost.
6. It is easy to control into patients so you can increase consistency to dimension routine.

Two interlocked feedback loops of repressors and activators, such as those necessary for xenobiotic metabolism, control the expression of output genes. These loops' components heavily rely on auxiliary substances like kinases, the proteasome machinery, DHBS family RNA binding proteins (beige), histone methyl transferases (HMTs), and histone deacetylases (HDACs) (grey). Important output gene involved in detoxification metabolism transcriptional control (blue). Red is used to highlight all rhythmic factors that affect medication transport and metabolism. In their respective organs, the circadian clock's distinctive effects on these processes are indicated.

References

Amol A. Patil1*, Manohar D. Kengar1, Suhas A. Mane2, Sujit A. Wagmare1, Dnyaneshwar M. Nirmale1, ISSN: 2455- 2631, February 2020 IJSDR | Volume 5, Issue 2.

Lemmer B. Circardian rhythams and drugdelivery. Int J Controlled Release 1991; 16:63-74. AhmedElsharkawy1*, Ahmed Ramadan1, Ma

Lemmer, BjÖRn and Labrecque, Gaston (1987)'Chronopharmacology and Chronotherapeutics: Definitions and Concepts',Chronobiology International,4:3,319-329.

Index

M

N

U

V

W

X

Y

Z

www.ingramcontent.com/pod-product-compliance
Lightning Source LLC
Chambersburg PA
CBHW080935240926
51849CB00004BA/463
* 9 7 8 9 3 4 8 7 3 4 1 5 0 *